토익마법

2주의 기적

이교희 지음

실전편1 **RC**

BM (주)도서출판 성안당

머리말

독자 여러분께

'토익 마법 – 2주의 기적'과 '토익 마법 – 2주의 기적 990'에 이어 **'토익 마법 – 2주의 기적 실전편'**을 새롭게 선보입니다. 본 교재를 통해 많은 문제를 풀어 보면서 시험에 완벽히 대비하시기 바랍니다.

실전 문제집을 만들면서 가장 신경 쓴 부분은 수험생들이 최대한 다양한 문제를 경험할 수 있도록 하는 것이었습니다. 시중의 다른 실전 문제집들과 달리 '토익 마법 – 2주의 기적 실전편'에 들어 있는 문제를 풀면 실제 시험에서 마주할 수 있는 거의 모든 유형의 문제를 접하게 될 것입니다. 또한 모든 어휘와 표현, 문제 유형을 실제 토익에 출제된 적이 있는 것들만으로 구성하였으며, 고난도 문제의 비중을 실제 시험보다 다소 높게, 반복적으로 다룸으로써 수험생들이 자신감을 갖고 시험에 임할 수 있도록 설계했습니다.

문제를 풀기 전에 반드시 '필독 서론'을 읽고 숙지해서 더 효율적으로 학습하시기 바랍니다. 시간을 재면서 문제를 풀고, 정답을 맞힌 문제라도 해설을 다 읽어 볼 것을 권장합니다. 몰랐던 단어는 따로 정리해서 암기하고, 틀린 문제에 사용된 문법은 기본서를 통해 꼼꼼하게 복습하시기 바랍니다. 또한 각 문장의 주요 성분과 수식어구가 어느 부분인지, 각 요소들이 어떤 문법으로 연결되어 있는지도 잘 살펴보시기 바랍니다.

한 세트를 이틀에 걸쳐 공부하면 2주의 기적을 맛볼 수 있습니다. 예를 들어 첫째 날에는 문제 풀이와 어휘 정리에 집중하고, 다음날에는 문법 복습과 문장 분석에 할애하는 방식으로 공부할 수 있습니다.

이 교재와 함께 준비하신 모든 분들이 목표한 점수를 반드시 달성하시기를 진심으로 바랍니다. 인류의 소망이신 예수 그리스도의 이름으로 모든 독자 여러분을 축복합니다.

저자 이교희 올림

추신 이번에도 책을 출간해 주신 성안당, 가장 든든한 파트너 이재명 부장님과 김은주 부장님, 제작 과정에 참여해 주신 모든 분들, 안산 이지어학원 김창로 원장님, 저를 위해 기도해 주시는 아름빛 교회 형제들, 그리고 날이 갈수록 더욱 사랑스러운 나의 가족, 고맙습니다.

목차

 **저자 선생님과 함께 공부하기**

- 우측 QR코드로 접속해서 저자 선생님이 올려 주신 부가학습 자료와 질문 코너를 이용해 보세요.
- 단어 시험지, 추가 어휘 문제를 다운받거나 고난도 문제에 대한 강의를 볼 수 있습니다.
- 저자에게 질문하는 코너를 통해 교재에서 궁금했던 내용을 바로 질문하고 답변 받을 수 있습니다.

저자 질문 코너

고난도 문제
무료 동영상 강의

단어 시험지

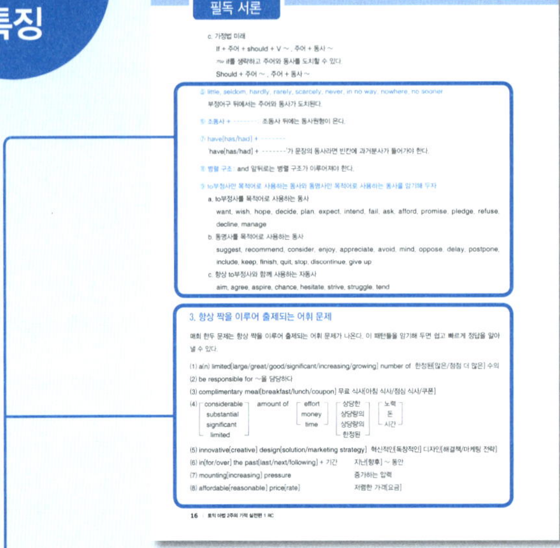

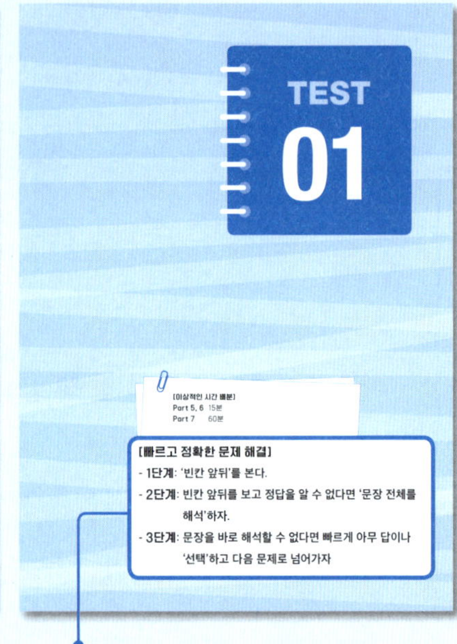

1 만점을 향한 필수 전략

실전 문제에 들어가기 전 학습 효과를 극대화하기 위해
각 유형의 공략법을 제시합니다.

2 시간의 부족을 해결하는 실전 가이드

문제 풀이의 3단계를 알려줌으로써 실전에서
시간을 단축하고 정답률을 극대화합니다.

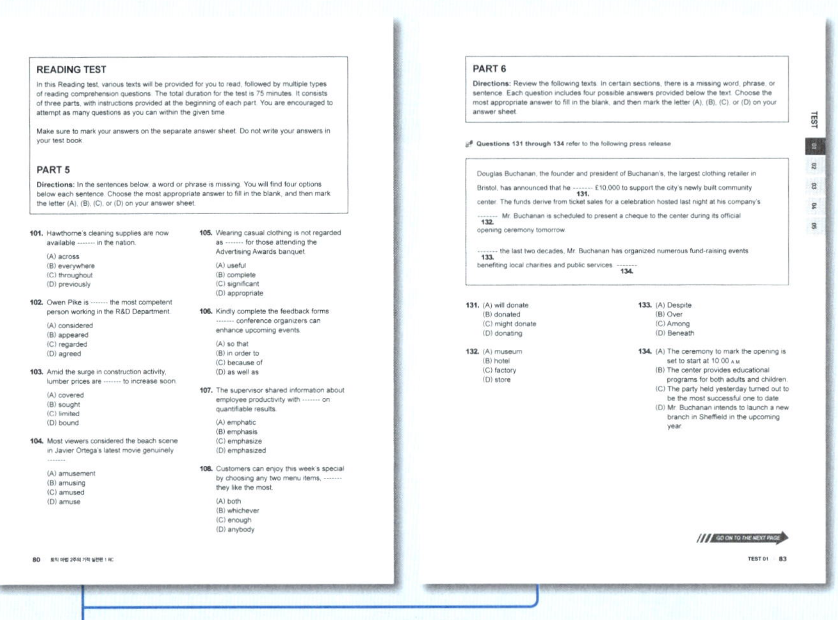

3 완성도 높은 실전 문제

토익에 나온 모든 유형의 문제를 수록하여 실전에 완벽하게 대비할 수 있게 했습니다.

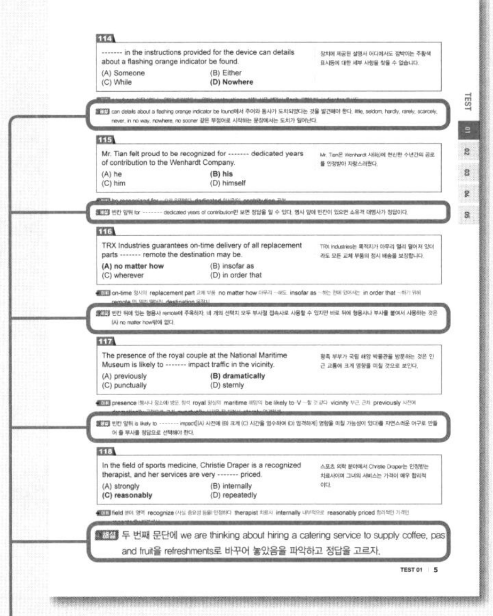

5 한눈에 보이는 정답

지문 속에 정답의 근거를 표시하여, 각 문제에
대한 핵심 문장을 보고 정답을 이해하게 됩니다.

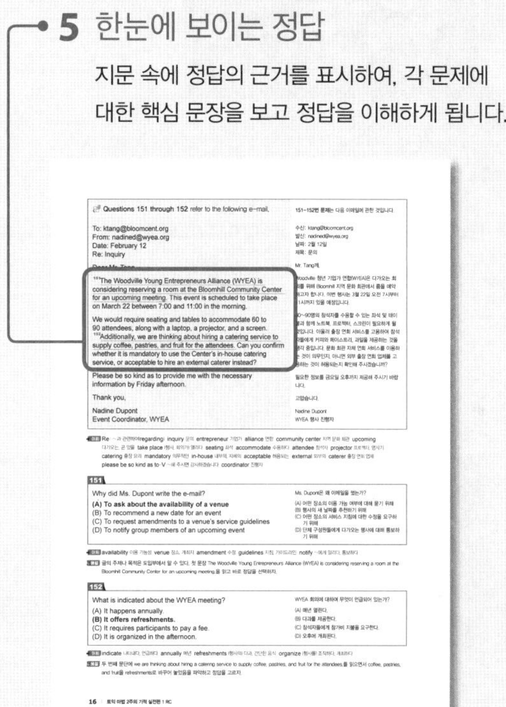

4 고득점을 위한 저자의 비법

모든 문제에 정답과 오답을 자세하게 설명합니다.
토익 10회 만점 저자의 오랜 경험과 연구를 통한
노하우가 담긴 실전 팁도 함께 제공됩니다.

7 저자와의 직접 소통

블로그와 유튜브를 통해 저자와 소통이
가능하며, 토익을 학습하며 부딪히는 다양한
문제들을 바로 해결할 수 있습니다.

토익 마법 블로그: blog.naver.com/toeicmagic

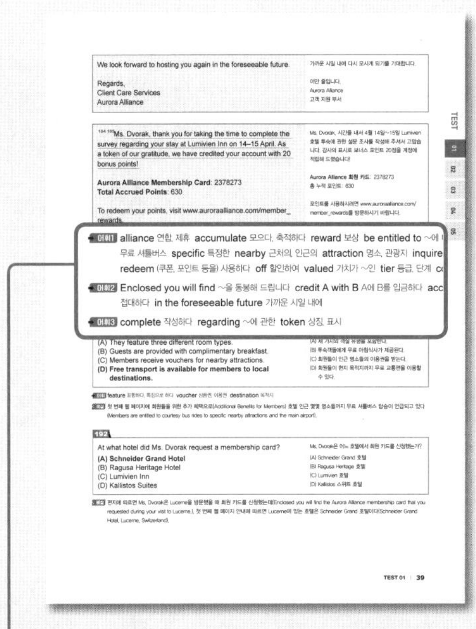

6 지문 이해를 돕는 필수 어휘

점수 상승의 필수 요소인 어휘를 지문에서 실제
쓰이는 뜻으로 제시하여 독해 실력을 향상시킵니다.

TOEIC이란?

▶ TOEIC

Test Of English for International Communication(국제적 의사소통을 위한 영어 시험)의 약자로, 영어가 모국어가 아닌 사람들이 비즈니스 현장 또는 일상생활에서 원활한 의사소통에 필요한 실용영어 능력을 갖추었는가를 평가하는 시험이다.

▶ TOEIC 시험 구성

구성	PART	유형		문항 수	지문	번호	시간	배점
L/C	1	사진 묘사		6		1~6	45분	495점
	2	질의 응답		25		7~31		
	3	짧은 대화		39	지문 13 x 3	32~70		
	4	짧은 담화		30	지문 10 x 3	71~100		
R/C	5	단문 빈칸 채우기 (문법/어휘)		30		101~130	75분	495점
	6	장문 빈칸 채우기 (문법/어휘/문장 고르기)		16	지문 4 x 4	131~146		
	7	지문 독해	단일 지문	29	지문 10	147~175		
			이중 지문	10	이중 지문 2 x 5	176~185		
			삼중 지문	15	삼중 지문 3 x 5	186~200		
Total	**7 PARTS**			**200 문항**			**120분**	**990점**

▶ TOEIC 평가 항목

Listening Comprehension	Reading Comprehension
단문을 듣고 이해하는 능력	읽은 글을 통해 추론해 생각할 수 있는 능력
짧은 대화문을 듣고 이해하는 능력	장문에서 특정한 정보를 찾을 수 있는 능력
비교적 긴 대화문에서 주고받은 내용을 파악할 수 있는 능력	글의 목적, 주제, 의도 등을 파악하는 능력
장문에서 핵심이 되는 정보를 파악할 수 있는 능력	뜻이 유사한 단어들의 정확한 용례를 파악하는 능력
구나 문장에서 화자의 목적이나 함축된 의미를 이해하는 능력	문장 구조를 제대로 파악하는지, 문장에서 필요한 품사, 어구 등을 찾는 능력

TOEIC 수험 정보

▶ TOEIC 접수 방법

1. 한국 토익 위원회 사이트(www.toeic.co.kr)에서 시험일 약 2개월 전부터 온라인으로 24시간 언제든지 접수할 수 있다.
2. 추가 시험은 2월과 8월에 있으며 이외에도 연중 상시로 시행된다.
3. JPG 형식의 본인의 사진 파일이 필요하다.

▶ 시험장 준비물

1. 신분증: 규정 신분증(주민등록증, 운전면허증, 기간 만료 전의 여권, 공무원증, 장애인 복지 카드 등)
2. 필기구: 연필과 지우개(볼펜이나 사인펜은 사용 금지)
3. 아날로그 손목시계(전자식 시계는 불가)

▶ TOEIC 시험 진행 시간

9:20	입실 (09:50 이후 입실 불가)
09:30 ~ 09:45	답안지 작성에 관한 오리엔테이션
09:45 ~ 09:50	휴식
09:50 ~ 10:05	신분증 확인
10:05 ~ 10:10	문제지 배부 및 파본 확인
10:10 ~ 10:55	듣기 평가 (LISTENING TEST)
10:55 ~ 12:10	읽기 평가 (READING TEST)

▶ TOEIC 성적 확인

시험일로부터 약 10~12일 후 인터넷 홈페이지 및 어플리케이션을 통한 성적 확인이 가능하다. 최초 성적표는 우편이나 온라인으로 발급받을 수 있다. 우편으로는 발급받기까지 성적 발표 후 약 7~10일이 소요되며, 온라인 발급을 선택하면 즉시 발급되며, 유효기간 내에 홈페이지에서 본인이 직접 1회에 한해 무료로 출력할 수 있다. TOEIC 성적은 시험일로부터 2년간 유효하다.

▶ TOEIC 점수

TOEIC 점수는 듣기 영역(LC)과 읽기 영역(RC)을 합계한 점수로 5점 단위로 구성되며 총점은 990점이다. TOEIC 성적은 각 문제 유형의 난이도에 따른 점수 환산표에 의해 결정된다. 성적표에는 전체 수험자의 평균과 해당 수험자가 받은 성적이 백분율로 표기되어 있다.

'토익 마법 – 2주의 기적 실전편 1 RC'의 학습 효과를 극대화하기 위해 이 내용을 반드시 숙지하고 필요한 부분을 암기하자.

1. RC 문제 풀이의 기본 원칙 – 빨리 맞혀라! 빨리 맞힐 수 없다면 빨리 찍어라!

풀이 방식을 모르는 문제가 나왔다면 고민하지 말고 빨리 아무거나 찍자. 풀 수도 없는 문제를 붙잡고 생각하느라 시간을 낭비하는 것은 바보 같은 짓이다. 이후에 쉬운 문제가 있어도 시간이 모자라면 놓칠 수밖에 없기 때문이다.

빠르고 정확하게 문제를 해결하기 위해 '빈칸 앞뒤 몇 단어'만 보고 문제를 푸는 기술을 익히자. 해설집을 보면, 각 문제마다 빈칸 앞뒤 어디를 보고 정답을 알 수 있는지 나와 있다.
Part 5 문법 문제 유형의 대다수는 빈칸 앞뒤를 보면 정답을 알 수 있다. Part 5 어휘 문제도 상당수는 빈칸 앞뒤 몇 단어의 의미만 생각하면 정답이 나온다.
Part 6에서는 서너 문제 정도 문법이 나오는데, 이것들은 Part 5 문법 문제와 같은 방식으로 빈칸 앞뒤를 보며 해결하면 된다. 나머지 12~13문제는 지문을 읽으며 문맥을 통해 정답을 알아내야 한다. 문제 풀이 방식을 요약하자.

1단계 | '빈칸 앞뒤'를 본다.
2단계 | 빈칸 앞뒤를 보고 정답을 알 수 없다면 '문장 전체를 해석'하자.
3단계 | 문장이 얼른 해석되지 않으면 빨리 아무거나 '찍고' 다음 문제로 넘어가자.

이러한 방식으로 문제를 풀면 Part 5, 6를 15분 만에 끝낸다는 목표를 세울 수 있다. 기억하자. 우리의 목표는 Part 5, 6를 15분 만에 해결하는 것이다. 많은 시간을 Part 7 문제 풀이에 할애할 수 있다면 고득점의 확률이 높아질 것이다.

2. 절대 틀리면 안 되는 문제

대부분의 문제는 하나 틀리면 5점이 감점되지만, 무조건 그런 것은 아니다. Part 5, 6에 출제되는 문법 문제들은 유형을 분류한 후에 다시 출제 빈도에 따라 '거의 매회 출제되는 문제', '자주 출제되는 문제(2~4개월에 한 번 출제)', '가끔 출제되는 문제(매년 3~4회 출제)', '드물게 출제되는 문제'로 나눌 수 있다. 이중 '거의 매회 출제되는 문제'를 틀리면, 감점은 5점에 그치지 않고 최소 10점, 많게는 30점까지도 이를 수 있다. 본서에 실려 있는 문제들의 각 유형마다 출제 빈도가 얼마나 되는지 미리 알아보고, 실전 훈련을 할 때 '거의 매회 출제되는 문제'는 절대 틀리지 않도록 주의를 기울이자.

(1) 거의 매회 출제되는 문제

① [품사 문제] 형용사가 정답인 문제

(선택지에 형용사가 없을 때는 분사가, 형용사와 분사가 모두 있을 때는 대부분 형용사가 정답이다.)

   a. (관사) + ------- + 명사

   b. be[become / remain / stay / seem / appear / prove] + -------

② [품사 문제] 부사가 정답인 문제

   a. 주어 + ------- + 동사   b. 조동사 + ------- + 동사원형

   c. 1형식 자동사 + -------   d. 타동사 + 목적어 + -------

   e. be + p.p. + -------   f. be + ------- + p.p.

   g. be + ------- + V-ing   h. have + ------- + p.p.

   i. be + ------- + 형용사   j. ------- + 형용사 + 명사

   k. ------- + 준동사(동명사, to부정사, 분사)   l. ------- + 전치사 + 명사

   m. ------- + 부사   n. ------- + 한정사(관사, 소유격 (대)명사) + 명사

   o. -------, 주어 + 동사

③ [품사 문제] 명사가 정답인 문제

   a. ------- + 동사 (주어 자리)

   b. 타동사 / 전치사 + ------- (목적어 자리, 동명사가 정답으로 출제되기도 한다.)

   c. 관사 + ------- + 전치사

   d. (관사) + 형용사 + -------

   e. 소유격 (대)명사 + -------

   f. 명사 + ------- (복합명사)

   g. 명사와 동명사의 구별: 빈칸 뒤에 목적어가 있으면 동명사, 없으면 명사가 정답이다.

④ [품사 문제] 부사절 접속사 VS 전치사

빈칸 뒤에 '주어 + 동사'나 분사 구문이 보이면 접속사가 정답이다.

⑤ [대명사 문제] 인칭대명사의 격

   a. ------- + 명사: 명사 앞 빈칸에는 소유격 대명사가 정답이다.

   b. ------- + 동사: 주어 자리에는 주격 대명사와 소유대명사가 들어갈 수 있다. 앞부분을 읽어 보고 선택해야 하지만, 거의 대부분 주격 대명사가 정답이다. 소유대명사가 정답일 때는 보통 앞부분에 '소유격 + 명사'가 있다.

   c. 타동사 / 전치사 + ------- : 목적어 자리에는 목적격 대명사뿐만 아니라 소유대명사와 재귀대명사도 들어 갈 수 있다.

      • 소유대명사가 정답일 때는 보통 앞부분에 '소유격 + 명사'가 있다.

      • 행위의 주체와 대상이 동일할 때는 재귀대명사가, 그렇지 않으면 목적격 대명사가 정답이다.

   d. by + ------- : by 뒤에 빈칸이 있으면 무조건 재귀대명사가 정답이다.

   e. 부사 자리: 빈칸이 부사 자리일 때는 재귀대명사가 정답이다.

   f. a(n) + 명사 + of + ------- : 이 자리는 소유대명사나 one's own이 정답이다.

⑥ [어형 문제] 능동태 VS 수동태

빈칸 뒤에 목적어가 있으면 능동태가, 목적어가 없으면 수동태가 정답이다.

⑦ [어형 문제] 동사 VS 준동사

절 안에 동사가 보이지 않으면 동사가 정답이다. 동사가 이미 있다면 준동사가 정답이다.

⑧ 수의 일치

  a. 주어와 동사의 수의 일치

    • 혼동을 피하기 위해 주어와 동사 사이에 있는 수식어구(전치사구, 분사 구문, 관계대명사 절 등)를 제거해야 한다.

    • 주어와 동사의 수의 일치에서는 동사의 태나 시제 같은 요소를 복합적으로 생각해야 한다.

  b. one[each / either / neither] of + 복수 명사 + 단수 동사

  c. 부정 수량형용사와 명사의 수의 일치

    • each, every, another + 셀 수 있는 명사 단수형

    • many, a number of, various, a variety of, several, a few, few, fewer, both, one of + 셀 수 있는 명사 복수형

    • much, a little, little, less + 셀 수 없는 명사

    • any, some, most, all, other + 셀 수 있는 명사 복수형 / 셀 수 없는 명사

    * any 뒤에는 셀 수 있는 명사 단수형도 사용할 수 있다.

  d. most[half / some / the rest / 분수 / ~ percent] of + 셀 수 있는 명사 복수형 / 셀 수 없는 명사 + ------- : 빈칸에 넣을 동사를 선택할 때는 바로 앞에 있는 명사의 수에 일치시킨다.

  e. 선행사 + 주격 관계대명사 + 동사: 주격 관계대명사 앞뒤에 있는 선행사와 동사는 서로 수가 일치해야 한다.

⑨ [어형 문제] 현재분사 VS 과거분사

  a. ------- + 명사: 수식받는 명사와 수식하는 분사의 관계가 능동인지 수동인지 생각한다.

  b. be[become / remain / stay / seem / appear / prove] + -------
    주어와 보어 자리에 들어갈 분사의 관계가 능동인지 수동인지 생각한다.

  c. make / keep / leave / find / consider / deem + 목적어 + -------
    목적어와 목적격 보어 자리에 들어갈 분사의 관계가 능동인지 수동인지 생각한다.

  d. 부사절이 분사 구문인 경우: 주절의 주어와 빈칸에 들어갈 분사의 관계가 능동인지 수동인지 생각한다.

  e. 명사 + ------- : 빈칸으로 시작하는 분사 구문이 앞에 있는 명사를 수식하는 구조이고, 빈칸 뒤에 목적어가 있으면 현재분사가, 목적어가 없으면 과거분사가 정답이다.

  f. 자동사의 분사는 현재분사만 선택해야 한다: existing, lasting, remaining, rising, declining

  g. 항상 현재분사만 선택해야 하는 경우:
    challenging, demanding, rewarding, missing, opposing,outstanding, promising

  h. 항상 과거분사만 선택해야 하는 경우:
    accomplished, complicated, crowded, dedicated, detailed, distinguished, experienced, impressed, acclaimed, informed, involved, repeated, skilled, specialized, sophisticated, valued, varied, expired, authorized

i. as + p.p. 형태의 관용 표현을 기억하자.

as discussed / as noted / as mentioned / as stated / as stipulated / as indicated / as printed / as advertised / as projected

(2) 자주 출제되는 문제 (2~4개월에 한 번)

① 관계사

a. 기본 문장 구조

선행사 + 관계대명사 + 불완전한 절

선행사 + 관계부사 + 완성된 절

선행사 없음 + 복합 관계대명사 + 불완전한 절

선행사 없음 + 복합 관계부사 + 완성된 절

b. 선행사 + ------- + 동사: 주격 관계대명사가 정답이다.

c. 선행사 + ------- + 주어 + 타동사[전치사]: 빈칸 뒤에 목적어가 없을 때는 목적격 관계대명사가 정답이다.

d. 선행사 + 전치사 + ------- : 목적격 관계대명사가 정답이다.

e. 선행사 + all[most / half / some / one / 숫자 / none] of + ------- + 동사: 목적격 관계대명사가 정답이다.

f. 선행사 + ------- + 완성된 문장: 소유격 관계대명사(whose)나 관계부사가 정답이다.

g. 목적격 관계대명사와 '주격 관계대명사 + be동사'는 생략할 수 있다.

h. however(no matter how) 뒤에는 항상 형용사나 부사를 붙여서 사용한다.

i. 전치사 뒤나 쉼표 뒤에는 관계대명사 that을 사용할 수 없다.

j. 관계대명사 what과 관계부사 how는 반드시 선행사 없이 사용한다.

k. 관계부사의 선행사를 생략할 수 있다. (the place) where, (the time) when, (the reason) why

l. 복합 관계대명사는 명사절이나 부사절을, 복합 관계부사는 부사절을 이끌어 준다.

m. 빈칸 뒤에 *sb* think[believe / guess / suppose]가 있으면 삽입 구문이므로 제외하고 문제를 풀자.

n. 선택지에 관계사가 두 개 이상 포함되어 있다면, 십중팔구 관계사가 정답이다. 일단 관계사만 가지고 문제를 풀어 보자. 관계사가 정답이 아닌 것으로 드러나면 다른 선택지를 살펴보자.

② 비교

a. as ------- as가 보이면 원급이 정답이다. twice, three times, four times 같은 배수 표현도 원급이 정답임을 보여준다.

b. 빈칸 뒤에 than이 보이면 비교급이, 빈칸 앞에 비교급이 보이면 than이 정답이다.

c. 비교급을 강조하는 부사를 암기해야 한다.

much, still, even, far, a lot, considerably, significantly, substantially, greatly, noticeably, remarkably

d. −or형 비교급은 to와 함께 사용한다.

prior to, superior to, inferior to, senior to, junior to

e. 빈칸 앞에 관사 the가 있으면 최상급이 정답이다. (that) ~ ever, one of ~, of all, 'in + 기준 명사 (예: in the world)', '서수'가 보일 때도 최상급을 정답으로 선택해야 한다.

③ 부사절 접속사

    a. 완성된 절 + ------- + 주어 + 동사 ~

    앞에 있는 완성된 절이 주절, 빈칸 이후가 부사절이다. 빈칸에 부사절 접속사가 들어가야 한다.

    b. ------- + 주어 + 동사 ~ , 주어 + 동사 ~

    쉼표 앞이 부사절, 쉼표 뒤가 주절이다. 빈칸에 부사절 접속사가 들어가야 한다.

④ 시제

    a. 문장 안에 'since + 시점'이나 'for[over/in] the last[past] + 기간'이 있으면 현재완료 시제가 정답이다.

    b. 선택지가 접속사나 전치사로 구성되어 있을 때, 주절의 시제가 현재완료라면 since나 for가 정답이다.
      선택지에 since와 for가 모두 있는 경우, 빈칸 뒤가 '시점'이면 since를, '기간'이면 for가 정답이다.

    c. 문장 안에 last, ago, yesterday, 'in + 과거 연도[세기]', once, at one time, recently 등이 보이면 과거
      시제가 정답이다.

    d. 문장 안에 usually, often, sometimes 등이 보이면 현재 시제가 정답이다. 또한 '반복되는 동작'이나 '지속
      되거나 유지되는 상태'는 현재 시제로 나타낸다는 사실도 기억하자.

    e. 문장 안에 'next + 시간', in the future, someday, sometime, 'in + 시간', tomorrow, later today 등이
      보이면 미래 시제가 정답이다.

    f. 문장 안에 'by + 미래 시점', 'as of + 미래 시점', 'by the time + S + 현재 시제 동사' 등이 보이면 미래완료
      시제가 정답이다.

    g. 문장 안에 'by the time + S + 과거 시제 동사'가 보이면 과거완료 시제가 정답이다. 또한 과거의 어떤 사건
      보다 더 앞선 일을 말할 때 과거완료 시제를 사용한다는 규칙을 기억해야 한다.

    h. 주절과 종속절의 시제가 일치되어야 한다.
      Ms. Ahmed decided that she [will / **would**] not be attending the conference next month.

    i. 시간/조건 부사절에서는 미래에 있을 일을 미래 시제 대신 현재나 현재완료 시제로 나타낸다.

(3) 가끔 출제되는 문제(매년 3~4회)

① [품사 문제] 목적격 보어로 사용하는 형용사 문제

make / keep / leave / find / consider / deem + 목적어 + -------

② [대명사 문제] ------- + who ~ [분사 구문 / 형용사구 / 전치사구]

those(~하는 사람들)나 anyone(~하는 사람은 누구든지)이 정답이다.

③ [대명사 문제] ------- + 전치사구 (주로 of ~)

that이나 those가 정답. 선택지에 that과 those가 모두 있다면 앞부분을 읽어서 빈칸이 가리키는 명사가 단수
인지 복수인지를 보고 판단한다.

④ 명사절 접속사 – that(90%), whether, 의문사, 복합 관계대명사

    a. ------- + 주어 + 동사1 ~ + 동사2
      '------- + 주어 + 동사1 ~'가 주어 자리에 들어가 있으므로 명사절이다. 빈칸에는 명사절 접속사가 들어
      가야 한다.

b. be동사 / 타동사 / 전치사 + ------- + (주어) + 동사 ~

'------- + (주어) + 동사 ~'가 보이나 목적어 자리에 들어가 있으므로 명사절이다. 빈칸에는 명사절 접속사가 들어가야 한다.

⑤ 상관접속사 문제 – 짝을 찾아내면 된다

a. either A or B

b. neither A nor B

c. both A and B

d. between A and B

e. not only A but (also) B

f. whether A or B / whether A or not

g. would rather A than B

h. no sooner A than B

i. so + 형용사/부사 + that 절

j. such + (a/an) + (형용사) + 명사 + that 절

k. ------- + S + can[may/will] + V: 빈칸 뒤에 'S + can[may/will] + V'가 있으면 언제나 so (that)가 정답이다.

(4) 드물게 출제되는 문제

① [어형 문제] 4형식 동사 능동태 VS 수동태

give, send, award, offer, grant 같은 동사가 4형식 문장에 사용되었을 때는 빈칸 뒤에 목적어가 두 개 있으면 능동태가, 하나만 있으면 수동태가 정답이다.

② [어형 문제] 명사를 목적격 보어로 사용하는 5형식 동사 능동태 VS 수동태

name, appoint, call, make, consider 동사가 5형식 문장에 사용되었을 때 빈칸 뒤에 명사가 연달아 두 개 있으면 각각 목적어와 목적격 보어이므로 능동태가 정답이다. 빈칸 뒤에 명사가 하나만 있으면 목적격 보어이다. 목적어가 없는 것이므로 수동태가 정답이다.

③ [어형 문제] 목적격 보어에 to부정사를 사용하는 5형식 동사 능동태 VS 수동태

enable, allow, permit, encourage, persuade, advise, invite, ask, request, require, expect, cause 동사가 5형식 문장에 사용되었을 때 빈칸 뒤에 to부정사가 있으면 목적격 보어이다. 목적어가 없는 것이므로 수동태가 정답이다.

④ [가정법 문제] 모양 맞추기 게임과도 같다

a. 가정법 과거

If + 주어 + 과거 시제 동사[be동사는 were만 가능] ~ , 주어 + would[could / should / might] + V ~

≫≫ if 절의 동사가 were일 때는 if를 생략하고 주어와 동사를 도치할 수 있다.

Were + 주어 ~ , 주어 + would[could / should / might] + V

b. 가정법 과거완료

If + 주어 + had p.p. ~ , 주어 + would[could / should / might] + have p.p. ~

≫≫ if를 생략하고 주어와 동사를 도치할 수 있다.

Had + 주어 + p.p. ~ , 주어 + would[could / should / might] + have p.p. ~

c. 가정법 미래

If + 주어 + should + V ~ , 주어 + 동사 ~

>>> if를 생략하고 주어와 동사를 도치할 수 있다.

Should + 주어 ~ , 주어 + 동사 ~

⑤ little, seldom, hardly, rarely, scarcely, never, in no way, nowhere, no sooner
부정어구 뒤에서는 주어와 동사가 도치된다.

⑥ 조동사 + -------: 조동사 뒤에는 동사원형이 온다.

⑦ have[has/had] + -------

'have[has/had] + -------'가 문장의 동사라면 빈칸에 과거분사가 들어가야 한다.

⑧ 병렬 구조: and 앞뒤로는 병렬 구조가 이루어져야 한다.

⑨ to부정사만 목적어로 사용하는 동사와 동명사만 목적어로 사용하는 동사를 암기해 두자

a. to부정사를 목적어로 사용하는 동사

want, wish, hope, decide, plan, expect, intend, fail, ask, afford, promise, pledge, refuse, decline, manage

b. 동명사를 목적어로 사용하는 동사

suggest, recommend, consider, enjoy, appreciate, avoid, mind, oppose, delay, postpone, include, keep, finish, quit, stop, discontinue, give up

c. 항상 to부정사와 함께 사용하는 자동사

aim, agree, aspire, chance, hesitate, strive, struggle, tend

3. 항상 짝을 이루어 출제되는 어휘 문제

매회 한두 문제는 항상 짝을 이루어 출제되는 어휘 문제가 나온다. 이 패턴들을 암기해 두면 쉽고 빠르게 정답을 알아 낼 수 있다.

(1) a(n) limited[large/great/good/significant/increasing/growing] number of 한정된[많은/점점 더 많은] 수의

(2) be responsible for ~을 담당하다

(3) complimentary meal[breakfast/lunch/coupon] 무료 식사[아침 식사/점심 식사/쿠폰]

(4) considerable / substantial / significant / limited amount of effort / money / time 상당한 / 상당량의 / 상당량의 / 한정된 노력 / 돈 / 시간

(5) innovative[creative] design[solution/marketing strategy] 혁신적인[독창적인] 디자인[해결책/마케팅 전략]

(6) in[for/over] the past[last/next/following] + 기간   지난[향후] ~ 동안

(7) mounting[increasing] pressure   증가하는 압력

(8) affordable[reasonable] price[rate]   저렴한 가격[요금]

(9) 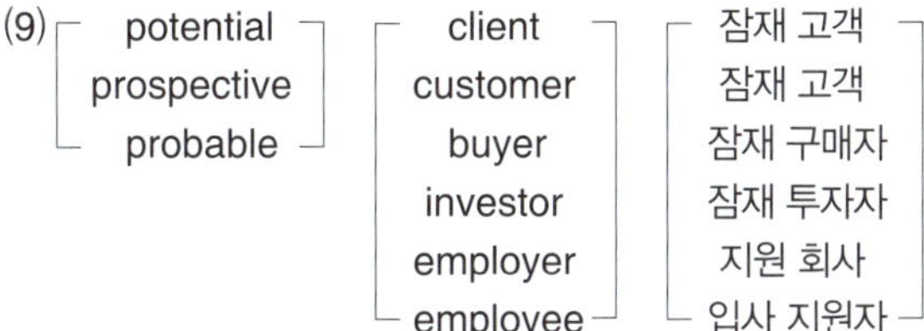

(10) qualified[successful] candidate[applicant]　자격을 갖춘 지원자, 합격자

(11) be eligible[qualified] to-V[for N]　〜할[〜의] 자격이 있다

(12) be concerned[worried/anxious] about　〜에 대해 걱정하다

　　　concerns[worries/anxiety] about　〜에 대한 걱정

(13) handle[address/deliver/answer/report] promptly　즉시 처리하다[처리하다/배달하다/대답하다/보고하다]

(14) promptly[exactly/precisely] at + 시각　정각 〜시에

(15) 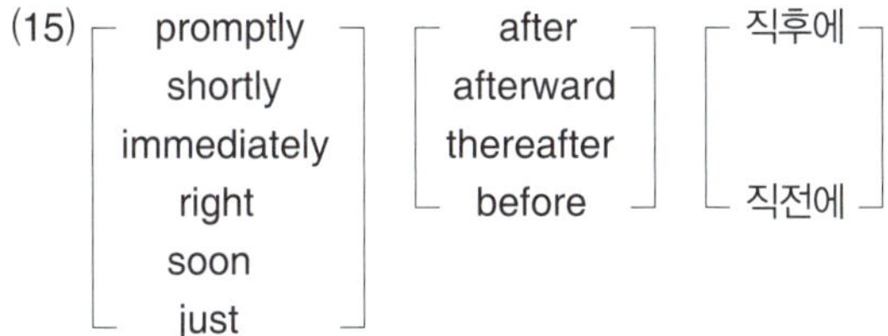

(16) conveniently[perfectly/ideally] located[situated]　편리한 곳에[딱 좋은 곳에] 위치하고 있는

(17) and also 그리고 또한 / then 그 다음에 / therefore 그래서, 따라서 / thus 그래서, 따라서 / so 그래서, 따라서

(18) have always[already/recently/finally/consistently] p.p.　항상[이미/최근에/마침내/지속적으로] 〜했다

(19) far too 너무, far beyond 〜을 훨씬 뛰어넘는

(20) be readily[easily/always/generally/usually/freely] available

　　　바로[쉽게/항상/일반적으로/대체로/무료로] 이용할[구할] 수 있는

(21) 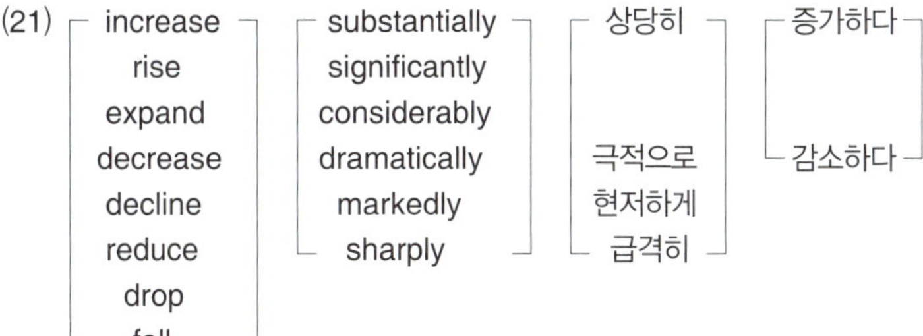

(22) nearly[almost] 숫자[all/every/entire/complete(d)/finish(ed)]　거의 숫자[모든/모든/모든/완료된/끝난]

(23) highly[strongly] recommend 강력히 추천하다

(24) agenda for the meeting[conference/session] 회의 의사일정[의제]

　　　itinerary for the trip 여행 일정

(25) earn[gain/develop] reputation　　　명성을 얻다

(26) written ┌ notice[notification] ┐　서면 통지
　　　　　　 └ consent ┘　　　　　　 서면 동의
　　prior notice　　　　　　　　　　　사전 공지[통보]
　　until further notice　　　　　　　추후 공지가 있을 때까지
　　unless otherwise noted[specified/instructed/directed] 별다른 명시가[지정이/지시가/지침이] 없는 한
　　in writing 서면으로

(27) go[come] into effect(=become effective)　효력을 발생하다

(28) ┌ research ┐ ┌ suggest ┐ that ┌ 조사가 ┐ ┌ ～임을 시사하다 ┐
　　 │ survey │ │ reveal │　　│ 설문 조사가 │ │ 밝히다 │
　　 │ study │ │ indicate │　　│ 연구가 │ │ 나타내다 │
　　 └ test ┘ └ show ┘　　└ 실험이 ┘ └ 보여주다 ┘

(29) customer satisfaction　　　　　　고객 만족

(30) customer service representative[desk]　고객 서비스 직원[데스크]

(31) sales representative[associate]　　영업 직원

(32) comply with ～을 준수하다, ～에 부합되다 / compliance with ～에 대한 부합 / deal with ～을 다루다

(33) attribute[ascribe] A to B A를 B의 덕분으로[탓으로] 돌리다

(34) hold a press conference[meeting/conference/seminar/session/party]
　　기자 회견을[회의를/학회를/세미나를/세션을/파티를] 열다[개최하다]

(35) notify[inform/advise/remind] A of B　A에게 B에 관하여 알려주다[상기시키다]
　　brief A on B　　　　　　　　　　 A에게 B에 관하여 간략하게 알려주다

(36) beginning[starting/effective] + 시점　～을 기하여

(37) be comparable[equivalent] to　　～과 필적할 만한

(38) ┌ 증가(increase, rise, expansion) ┐ in
　　 │ 감소(decrease, decline, reduction, fall, drop) │
　　 │ 변화(change, fluctuation) │
　　 └ 경험(experience) ┘

(39) concentrate[focus] on　　　　　　～에 집중하다

(40) depend[rely] on　　　　　　　　　～에 의지[의존]하다

(41) from + 시점 + on(ward)　　　　　～ 이후로

(42) noted[famous/known] for　　　　～으로 유명한

(43) postpone[delay/put off/defer] ～ until　～할 때까지 연기하다[미루다]

TEST 01

[이상적인 시간 배분]
Part 5, 6 15분
Part 7 60분

[빠르고 정확한 문제 해결]
- 1단계: '빈칸 앞뒤'를 본다.
- 2단계: 빈칸 앞뒤를 보고 정답을 알 수 없다면 '문장 전체를 해석'하자.
- 3단계: 문장을 바로 해석할 수 없다면 빠르게 아무 답이나 '선택'하고 다음 문제로 넘어가자

READING TEST

In this Reading test, various texts will be provided for you to read, followed by multiple types of reading comprehension questions. The total duration for the test is 75 minutes. It consists of three parts, with instructions provided at the beginning of each part. You are encouraged to attempt as many questions as you can within the given time.

Make sure to mark your answers on the separate answer sheet. Do not write your answers in your test book.

PART 5

Directions: In the sentences below, a word or phrase is missing. You will find four options below each sentence. Choose the most appropriate answer to fill in the blank, and then mark the letter (A), (B), (C), or (D) on your answer sheet.

101. Ms. Moon noted that Mr. Al-Masri is ------- late for meetings.

(A) little
(B) far
(C) seldom
(D) well

102. The Opelika Lecture Series is ------- by a number of local organizations.

(A) traded
(B) sponsored
(C) explored
(D) achieved

103. Bavarian Motors will ------- its current name even after merging with a competitor.

(A) receive
(B) inquire
(C) grant
(D) retain

104. Mr. Nishimura identified a defect in the strategy ------- requires immediate attention.

(A) whichever
(B) whose
(C) that
(D) who

105. Ms. Chambers strives to make our resources ------- to employees who work remotely.

(A) accesses
(B) accessibility
(C) more accessibly
(D) more accessible

106. Employee handbooks detail the fundamental ------- of the employer-employee relationship.

(A) exercises
(B) elements
(C) similarities
(D) recipes

107. Mr. Bui's letter is in response to the fax and e-mail dated the 10th and 13th of September, -------.

(A) respects
(B) respecting
(C) respective
(D) respectively

108. The wellness workshop at the Community Center serves as a ------- for discussing healthy habits.

(A) selection
(B) ground
(C) vision
(D) forum

109. The inn is ------- located near various restaurants and shops, all within a short walking distance.

(A) widely
(B) quickly
(C) gradually
(D) conveniently

110. It is anticipated that employee performance reviews ------- will be finalized by next Thursday.

(A) ideally
(B) lately
(C) relatively
(D) attractively

111. A courier is delivering the documents Mr. Houston ------- to review and approve by the end of the day.

(A) need
(B) needing
(C) needs
(D) to need

112. Imbriani Architects emphasized that the library ------- a single-story structure to ensure easy access for all.

(A) should remain
(B) that remains
(C) to remain
(D) remaining

113. An independent accounting firm that specializes in charitable foundations is conducting the outside -------.

(A) area
(B) audit
(C) purpose
(D) product

114. ------- in the instructions provided for the device can details about a flashing orange indicator be found.

(A) Someone
(B) Either
(C) While
(D) Nowhere

115. Mr. Tian felt proud to be recognized for ------- dedicated years of contribution to the Wenhardt Company.

(A) he
(B) his
(C) him
(D) himself

116. TRX Industries guarantees on-time delivery of all replacement parts ------- remote the destination may be.

(A) no matter how
(B) insofar as
(C) wherever
(D) in order that

117. The presence of the royal couple at the National Maritime Museum is likely to ------- impact traffic in the vicinity.

(A) previously
(B) dramatically
(C) punctually
(D) sternly

118. In the field of sports medicine, Christie Draper is a recognized therapist, and her services are very ------- priced.

(A) strongly
(B) internally
(C) reasonably
(D) repeatedly

119. To ------- the Adelaide's Apparel store closest to you, choose your state or country from the drop-down menu.

(A) afford
(B) create
(C) locate
(D) provide

120. Ms. Ochoa earned commendation because the quality of her work ------- surpasses even the highest expectations.

(A) consists
(B) consisted
(C) consisting
(D) consistently

GO ON TO THE NEXT PAGE

121. Ms. Rabinowitz suggests that the manufacturing plant should replace the outdated equipment as ------- as possible.

(A) necessarily
(B) definitely
(C) rapidly
(D) predominantly

122. The *Aspen Journal of Cardiology*'s editorial team is ------- about which articles they publish.

(A) prominent
(B) punctual
(C) rigorous
(D) selective

123. Thanks to its innovative features, the Omega X12 is ------- the most advanced smartphone available on the market today.

(A) negatively
(B) doubtfully
(C) sincerely
(D) arguably

124. Policyholders are allowed to terminate their policy whenever they choose, ------- they submit written notice at least 30 days prior.

(A) along with
(B) according to
(C) provided that
(D) regardless of

125. Online communication is an excellent ------- to bring researchers and practitioners together to address practical issues in the field.

(A) technique
(B) approach
(C) instrument
(D) means

126. Industry analysts continue ------- the significance of social media marketing in enhancing brand awareness for fashion designers.

(A) emphasis
(B) to emphasize
(C) are emphasizing
(D) to be emphasized

127. ------- to Brighton Drive will remain restricted to one side street following the commencement of the road repairs next week.

(A) Access
(B) Accesses
(C) Accessible
(D) Accessing

128. Vita Bella Catering seeks ------- who are ready to dedicate themselves to designing engaging social media content on a weekly basis.

(A) those
(B) them
(C) someone
(D) anyone

129. Refrain from placing the digital scale ------- a source of excessive heat, as this could lead to damage of its delicate electronic components.

(A) between
(B) through
(C) despite
(D) near

130. Nearly 70 percent of teachers surveyed indicated that they had received ------- preparation for their roles via Stuggas University's online programs.

(A) adequate
(B) numerous
(C) thankful
(D) adjacent

PART 6

Directions: Review the following texts. In certain sections, there is a missing word, phrase, or sentence. Each question includes four possible answers provided below the text. Choose the most appropriate answer to fill in the blank, and then mark the letter (A), (B), (C), or (D) on your answer sheet.

Questions 131 through 134 refer to the following posting.

Bus Drivers Needed!

The Palm Beach County School District is now recruiting individuals for bus driver positions.

Only part-time roles ------- available. We welcome applications from both novice and
131.
experienced bus drivers. If you have held a valid driver's license for at least five years, we

encourage you to submit an application. -------.
132.

The Palm Beach County School District provides ------- salary levels to all its staff.
133.
-------, we extend an option for bus drivers to supplement their income by taking on
134.
additional routes throughout the academic year. If joining our team interests you, please

contact So-Hee Lee at 212-555-8473 for more information.

---

131. (A) are
(B) were
(C) have been
(D) will have been

132. (A) Application submissions must be
completed by today.
(B) There are chances for career
advancement.
(C) We are prepared to offer any required
training.
(D) School bus drivers play a vital role in
our educational system.

133. (A) compete
(B) competing
(C) competition
(D) competitive

134. (A) If not
(B) In addition
(C) Above all
(D) Once again

Web sites often store small pieces of data, called cookies, on users' devices. Cookies are crucial for many functionalities of a Web site. -------, they enable a Web server to recognize
135.
whether a specific Web site has been accessed previously from a particular device. Without this -------, things like login statuses or items saved in an online shopping cart would not
136.
be remembered. Cookies are also useful for assisting media companies and advertisers in offering content that aligns with users' preferences.

However, one issue ------- cookies is their potential use in monitoring user activity across
137.
multiple Web sites and devices. To address this, some privacy advocates suggest that users modify how cookies are managed. -------.
138.

135. (A) Conversely
(B) For instance
(C) As a consequence
(D) Eventually

136. (A) informs
(B) informing
(C) information
(D) informational

137. (A) regarding
(B) regards
(C) regarded
(D) regardless

138. (A) Alternatively, they allow users to locate cookies.
(B) It includes guidance on how cookies should be used properly.
(C) Thankfully, the majority of Web browsers give users the option to block or remove cookies.
(D) They vary when it comes to cookie management practices.

Social Media Manager for Educational Business Wanted

Brain Quest Studio is a growing company specializing in ------- educational board games for
139.
young adults. We are on the lookout for a creative individual to produce five captivating social
media posts each week. Since our launch one year ago, we have managed our own
advertisements across major platforms. -------. Moreover, due to our focus on other aspects
140.
of running the business, we have not been able to invest sufficient energy in ------- it
141.
online. We are now prepared to entrust this role to a capable individual. This ------- is ideal
142.
for a teacher with marketing expertise who understands the distinctive interests of our
audience. Interested candidates can reach us at jobs@brainqueststudio.ca.

139. (A) innovation
(B) innovative
(C) Innovator
(D) to innovate

140. (A) That said, marketing is not really our
area of expertise.
(B) We are planning to phase out our
product lineup.
(C) Even so, we understand the
importance of social platforms.
(D) Recently, they executed a new
campaign for us.

141. (A) enlarging
(B) promoting
(C) evaluating
(D) acquiring

142. (A) class
(B) location
(C) program
(D) opportunity

From: Member Services <memberservices@atlanticpalette.ca>

To: Anika Patel <apatel972@inbox7.ca>

Date: May 1

Subject: Welcome to The Atlantic Palette

Attachment: Form

Dear Ms. Patel,

We appreciate your decision to join The Atlantic Palette! ------- you will be among the
143.
earliest to hear about captivating art shows, live performances, auctions, and cultural festivals
across Eastern Canada. Your first issue should reach you within a few days, and subsequent
editions will be delivered at the start of each month. -------. Your membership also grants
144.
you unlimited ------- to articles, video content, and other interactive media on our Web site.
145.
Simply log in using your subscriber ID and password, which you will find ------- the
146.
attached enrollment form.

Best regards,

Tekeshi Yamamoto

Customer Representative

---

143. (A) Now
(B) Afterward
(C) Then
(D) Meanwhile

144. (A) If you'd like to place a subscription,
please contact our support line during
regular office hours.
(B) Should your issue not arrive within
seven days, we encourage you to
reach out to us right away.
(C) Creators are welcome to send in
summaries or overviews of their
artistic pieces.
(D) The opening performance is planned
for early June in Toronto.

145. (A) accessing
(B) accesses
(C) accessed
(D) access

146. (A) for
(B) about
(C) on
(D) at

PART 7

Directions: In this part, you will read a variety of texts, such as magazine and newspaper articles, e-mails, and instant messages. Each text or set of texts is followed by a series of questions. Choose the most appropriate answer and mark the letter (A), (B), (C), or (D) on your answer sheet.

Questions 147 through 148 refer to the following form.

WAHLBERG ASSOCIATES, INC.

Product Return Form

Dear Valued Customer:

At Wahlberg Associates, Inc., we take great pride in crafting our games and puzzles with care. However, if your product is defective or if you are dissatisfied for any reason, please send the item back along with the receipt and this completed form. We will either ship a replacement directly from the factory at no additional cost or issue a credit to your account.

Name: Gideon R. Souza

Address: 3049 Maple Street, Springfield, IL 62704

Problem description: Missing components in the item

Action requested: ☑ Send a replacement   ☐ Provide a credit to my account

---

147. What product did Mr. Souza most likely buy?

(A) A bookkeeping manual
(B) An article of apparel
(C) A bicycle
(D) A game

148. What problem is Mr. Souza reporting?

(A) Certain parts were not included.
(B) There were errors in the instructions.
(C) He received an incorrect item.
(D) The item sustained damage during transit.

/// GO ON TO THE NEXT PAGE

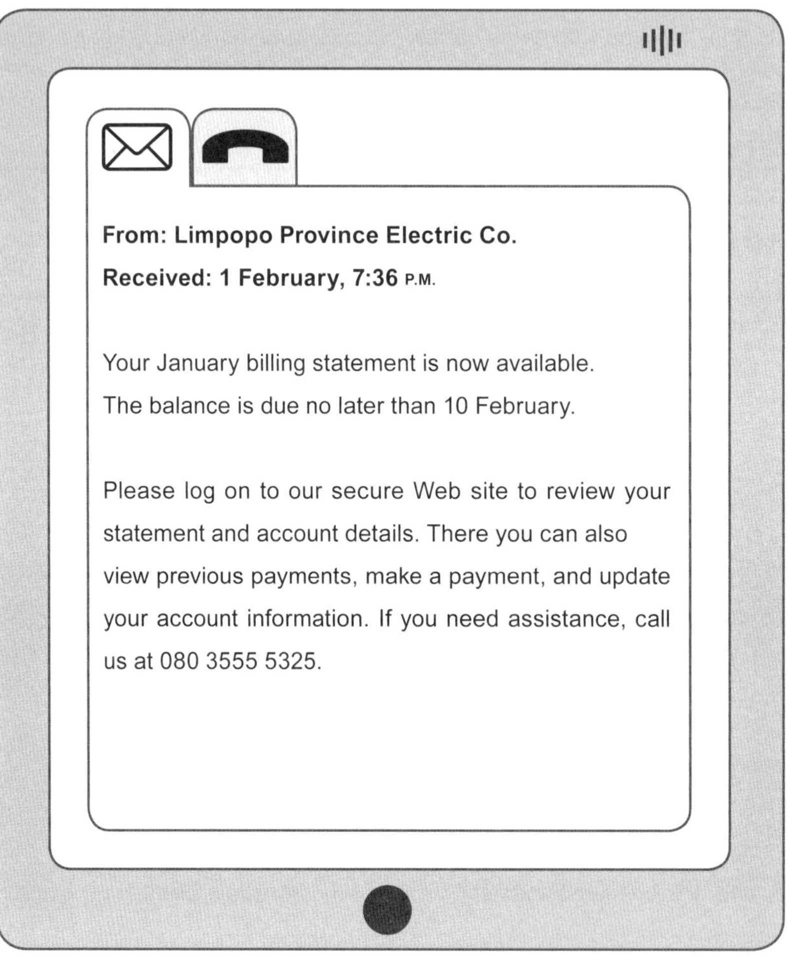

149. What is the purpose of the text message?

(A) To inform the recipient about a bill
(B) To provide details about a password
(C) To resolve a billing issue
(D) To inform about a change in electricity pricing

150. What is the recipient of the text message asked to do?

(A) Submit a purchase request
(B) Access an online account
(C) Set up a new username
(D) Update some payment information

To:	ktang@bloomcent.org
From:	nadined@wyea.org
Date:	February 12
Re:	Inquiry

Dear Mr. Tang,

The Woodville Young Entrepreneurs Alliance (WYEA) is considering reserving a room at the Bloomhill Community Center for an upcoming meeting. This event is scheduled to take place on March 22 between 7:00 and 11:00 in the morning.

We would require seating and tables to accommodate 60 to 90 attendees, along with a laptop, a projector, and a screen. Additionally, we are thinking about hiring a catering service to supply coffee, pastries, and fruit for the attendees. Can you confirm whether it is mandatory to use the Center's in-house catering service, or acceptable to hire an external caterer instead?

Please be so kind as to provide me with the necessary information by Friday afternoon.

Thank you,

Nadine Dupont
Event Coordinator, WYEA

151. Why did Ms. Dupont write the e-mail?

(A) To ask about the availability of a venue
(B) To recommend a new date for an event
(C) To request amendments to a venue's service guidelines
(D) To notify group members of an upcoming event

152. What is indicated about the WYEA meeting?

(A) It happens annually.
(B) It offers refreshments.
(C) It requires participants to pay a fee.
(D) It is organized in the afternoon.

GO ON TO THE NEXT PAGE

FOR IMMEDIATE RELEASE

May 24

www.bradleyinvestments.com

ATLANTA, GA — Bradley Investments hosted a ceremony today to inaugurate its newly constructed office building at 195 South Chippewa Street. The company was founded in Galway, Ireland, twelve years ago. Since its establishment, it has expanded to locations across Europe and opened its African headquarters in Casablanca just last year. The Atlanta office represents the company's first base of operations in North America.

Bradley Investments is a leading firm in the investment industry, focusing on technology and electronics start-ups. Its portfolio of clients includes Arndt Technological Services and Karolin Electronics Superstores, along with other notable companies.

The Atlanta headquarters will manage business operations for clients across both North and South America. Over 600 employees have been hired to work at the new office. For its initial year, Bradley Investments' vice president Lonan O'Brien will oversee operations at the office before returning to Galway.

For further inquiries, contact Maya Wilson from Public Relations at 404-555-0173 or e-mail her at mwilson@bradleyinvestments.com.

---

153. What type of event took place at 195 South Chippewa Street?

(A) A conference about finance
(B) A showcase for electronics
(C) A celebration to mark an opening
(D) A job recruitment event

154. What is stated about Bradley Investments?

(A) It operates in regions across multiple continents.
(B) It is recognized as a pioneer in consumer banking.
(C) Its Atlanta office was constructed by a renowned architectural firm.
(D) Its Atlanta facility has existed for twelve years.

155. What is implied about Mr. O'Brien?

(A) He previously served as the head of Arndt Technological Services.
(B) He is temporarily assigned to the Atlanta office.
(C) He was hired as one of the 600 new staff members.
(D) He started his professional journey in a retail environment.

 **Questions 156 through 157** refer to the following instant-message discussion.

Larissa Kanoa (2:14 P.M.)

We received another delivery that's meant for you.

Takumi Matsuda (2:15 P.M.)

Not again! I can't figure out why this issue persists.

Larissa Kanoa (2:16 P.M.)

I think the confusion comes from the chart on the company Web site. The department addresses are shown together, and Accounting is listed just above Administration.

Takumi Matsuda (2:17 P.M.)

That would make sense; it explains why my name is on the mail but the address belongs to Accounting.

Larissa Kanoa (2:18 P.M.)

Exactly. I'm heading to your building for a meeting with the Legal Department. I'll drop your package off then.

Takumi Matsuda (2:19 P.M.)

Thank you! I'll e-mail Information Technology to request a clearer update to the Web site chart.

---

156. At 2:15 P.M., what does Mr. Matsuda most likely mean when he writes "Not again"?

(A) A package he sent was mistakenly returned to him.
(B) He believes Ms. Kanoa doesn't need to visit his office.
(C) His mail is frequently delivered to the wrong department.
(D) He prefers Ms. Kanoa not to send another follow-up e-mail.

157. What area does Mr. Matsuda work in?

(A) Accounting
(B) Administration
(C) Legal
(D) Information Technology

GO ON TO THE NEXT PAGE

Construction to Add to Traffic

GRANDHAVEN (4 October) - With the construction of multiple new office complexes currently in progress within the central business district, the city's existing traffic challenges are only anticipated to worsen further. City authorities are considering a range of solutions, including the construction of an underground motorway or the expansion of Highway 31 to allow for additional traffic lanes. However, no definitive decisions have been made thus far.

"The current infrastructure is insufficient to handle this volume of vehicles, and it is obvious that action is required," remarked Catherine Radzinski, spokesperson for the highway commission. —[1]—.

"It will take years to finish any large-scale construction initiative, meaning that whatever option we choose will only exacerbate traffic congestion in the short term," Ms. Radzinski added. "That's the main reason we haven't committed to anything yet. The longer we take to craft a comprehensive strategy, the more effectively managed the initiative will hopefully be once it commences." As city officials deliberate over potential options, office workers are growing increasingly agitated. —[2]—.

"Traveling to work has become intolerable for me," complained Philip Hargrove, a lawyer based in the downtown area. "Although my home is located merely 15 kilometers from my workplace, the commute takes more than an hour. —[3]—."

In an effort to mitigate traffic problems for the time being, office administrators are beginning to take matters into their own hands. Some are promoting carpooling among staff members or providing perks to those who commute by bicycle. —[4]—.

---

158. The word "solutions" in paragraph 1, line 6, is closest in meaning to

(A) targets
(B) remedies
(C) appeals
(D) mixtures

159. What reason does Ms. Radzinski give for the highway commission's reluctance to commence a construction project?

(A) Awaiting more financial resources
(B) Difficulty in locating a skilled project manager
(C) Concern about worsening traffic congestion
(D) A large volume of public objections

160. What is indicated about Mr. Hargrove?

(A) He opposes a recently introduced traffic regulation.
(B) He does not support an urban planning suggestion.
(C) He is seeking employment elsewhere downtown.
(D) He feels frustrated with his daily commute.

161. In which of the positions marked [1], [2], [3], and [4] does the following sentence best belong?

"Others are letting their staff work remotely on designated days."

(A) [1]
(B) [2]
(C) [3]
(D) [4]

Keira Vauclair

Keira Vauclair (9:22 A.M.)	Our clients in Taiwan have asked us to organize a video conference to go over the clothing designs.
Miguel Ramos (9:24 A.M.)	Understood. Do we already have a plan?
Keira Vauclair (9:26 A.M.)	I'm arranging it for 8 P.M. tomorrow, our local time, in Room 3B. The later timing is because of the time zone difference between Taipei and Vancouver.
Nora Kravchenko (9:27 A.M.)	Would it be possible to participate in the meeting remotely from home?
Keira Vauclair (9:29 A.M.)	Unfortunately, that's not an option. Our security policy prohibits taking materials out of the office, and the clients are counting on seeing the designs on-site.
Nora Kravchenko (9:30 A.M.)	OK. That makes sense. We now just need Ms. Feldman's permission to work late.
Miguel Ramos (9:32 A.M.)	Let's confirm that with her. Ms. Feldman, we'd like to have a video conference with our Taiwanese clients tomorrow evening. Would it be acceptable for us to stay after regular hours to present the new designs? We plan to use Room 3B as it's equipped with the necessary audiovisual tools.
Jessica Feldman (9:34 A.M.)	Yes, that's fine. I'll notify security so they will keep the building accessible until you're done.
Keira Vauclair (9:35 A.M.)	Thank you, Mr. Ramos, for contacting Ms. Feldman on our behalf.

162. What is the online chat discussion about?

(A) Making a clothing purchase
(B) Organizing a business trip
(C) Scheduling a meeting
(D) Adjusting a project deadline

163. At 9:30 A.M., what does Ms. Kravchenko most likely mean when she writes, "That makes sense"?

(A) She understands the challenges caused by the time zone difference.
(B) She acknowledges improvements in building security protocols.
(C) She recognizes that the task will require her to stay late.
(D) She accepts the reason why the work must be done at the office.

164. What does Ms. Feldman offer to do?

(A) Record a video presentation of the designs
(B) Communicate with some colleagues in Taipei
(C) Ensure the office stays open after hours
(D) Leave extra keys accessible in the workplace

165. Why does Ms. Vauclair express gratitude to Mr. Ramos?

(A) For securing Ms. Feldman's approval
(B) For participating in the video meeting
(C) For preparing the audiovisual equipment
(D) For volunteering to lock up the office

THIS OFFICE TEMPORARILY CLOSED
FOR RENOVATIONS

Kindly note that the Siam branch office of *Bangkok English Newspaper* (BEN) will remain closed during the cool season as renovations are being carried out to enhance the quality of our publishing facilities. Operations at the Siam office are scheduled to resume on March 1.

Additionally, BEN's 2026 Journalism Internship Program will take place at the Silom branch from January 1 to March 1. The program includes internship periods of one week, two weeks, and four weeks, catering to those who wish to gain experience in article writing and editorial work. The Silom branch is conveniently situated directly opposite the Sala Daeng skytrain station on the BTS Silom line.

Bangkok English Newspaper currently boasts a circulation exceeding 100,000 readers, with consistent growth. Moreover, BEN has earned recognition as Thailand's best English newspaper for the past four years, as voted by the editorial team of *Southeast Asia Travel Guide* magazine. For further details, visit www.bangkokenglishnewspaper.or.th or contact us at 02-5532-6841.

166. Where would the notice likely be displayed?

(A) In a job advertisement directory.
(B) On a bulletin board at an academic institution.
(C) At the entrance of a tourist information center.
(D) On the front door of a newspaper branch office.

167. What is the reason for the Siam branch's closure?

(A) The property has been sold.
(B) Remodeling work is underway.
(C) The office is relocating to a different area.
(D) The organization has ceased operations.

168. What is NOT mentioned about BEN?

(A) It is exclusively available on digital platforms.
(B) It operates multiple offices.
(C) It has received compliments from a publication.
(D) It accepts applications for seasonal internship programs.

Questions 169 through 171 refer to the following job advertisement.

Seeking: Pottery Assistants

Earth & Fire, a ceramic production studio located in Stoke-on-Trent, England, is looking to hire two full-time assistants. —[1]—. Successful applicants should possess a strong knowledge of ceramic craftsmanship and be adept at learning and consistently reproducing processes throughout their workday. Attention to detail is vital. —[2]—. At the beginning, assistants will receive close supervision and feedback from the artist and must be receptive to constructive critiques to enhance the quality of their work. Key responsibilities include preparing clay for use, smoothing finished pieces, mixing and applying glazes, and keeping the studio clean at the end of each day. The hourly rate ranges between £11 and £15, depending on experience. —[3]—.

To apply, send your CV and a cover letter to marisol@earthandfire.com. The hiring process starts with a brief phone screening, followed by an in-person working interview for selected candidates. —[4]—. Chosen candidates will be offered a 60-day trial contract, during which the artist will evaluate their skills and determine if they are suitable for a permanent role.

169. What can be inferred about the work?

(A) The tasks require repetitive work.
(B) It offers a flexible work schedule.
(C) No prior knowledge of ceramics is needed.
(D) Supervisory oversight is not part of the role.

170. What is stated about candidates who are chosen for the pottery assistant job?

(A) They are expected to work overtime hours.
(B) They will be hired on a probationary basis initially.
(C) Their interviews will take place in group settings.
(D) They will need to supply their own tools.

171. In which of the positions marked [1], [2], [3], and [4] does the following sentence best belong?

"This will enable them to display their abilities firsthand."

(A) [1]
(B) [2]
(C) [3]
(D) [4]

/// GO ON TO THE NEXT PAGE ▶

<table>
<tr><td>To:</td><td>Employee List</td></tr>
<tr><td>From:</td><td>Selene Jung</td></tr>
<tr><td>Date:</td><td>30 June</td></tr>
<tr><td>Re:</td><td>Updates for the Third Quarter</td></tr>
</table>

First of all, I would like to extend my gratitude to everyone for your hard work during the second quarter - it was truly a collective success. As we look ahead, several personnel changes have been instituted to maintain momentum as we transition into the next quarter.

I am thrilled to share that Chloe Martin has been promoted to the position of Senior Accountant. In the meantime, I've tasked Xiang Wei and his team with temporarily handling Ms. Martin's previous role as Budget Analyst until we finalize recruitment for a permanent successor with the human resources team.

Additionally, as you may already know, Sahil Ahmad retired earlier this month after dedicating over three decades to the company. Taking his place as Credit Risk Analyst is Camilla Salazar. She brings over a decade of professional experience from Irish Credit Bank and is expected to acclimate to her new responsibilities here at Edelboden with ease. I encourage everyone to visit her office in Room 207 to introduce yourselves and offer her a warm welcome.

Sincerely,

Selene Jung, Corporate Finance Manager
Edelboden Company

172. What is the purpose of Ms. Jung's e-mail?

(A) To invite employees to apply for a promotion
(B) To summarize recent changes in staff assignments
(C) To welcome newly joined team members
(D) To explain policy updates regarding hiring

173. According to the e-mail, which position remains vacant?

(A) Senior Accountant
(B) Budget Analyst
(C) Credit Risk Analyst
(D) Corporate Finance Manager

174. Who is no longer part of Edelboden Company?

(A) Ms. Jung
(B) Ms. Martin
(C) Mr. Wei
(D) Mr. Ahmad

175. What does the e-mail say about Ms. Salazar?

(A) She holds a master's degree in finance.
(B) She relocated to Ireland ten years ago.
(C) She has recently joined Edelboden Company.
(D) She will supervise the accounting department.

GO ON TO THE NEXT PAGE

From:	Aaron Pavlovich <pavlovich@oceanviewplazaone.com>
To:	Ganesh De Sousa <gdesousa76@csmailgroup.com>
Date:	Wednesday, April 21, 10:16 A.M.
Re:	Service request

Dear Mr. De Sousa:

I got your service request from April 19 about the flickering hallway light and the malfunctioning dishwasher in your apartment. Typically, I aim to address minor service issues within a day or two after receiving an e-mail request. Apologies for my delayed response. I was occupied yesterday dealing with a water pipe burst on the third floor.

If you would like, I can arrange for my electrician to come and fix your light and dishwasher this week. He is available on April 22 between 2:00 P.M. and 4:00 P.M., or on April 23 between 8:00 A.M. and 10:00 A.M. Please let me know which of these time slots works best for you as soon as possible. If you will not be home during either of these times, let me know if you would like me to grant the electrician access to your apartment, as I have a key.

Regards,

Aaron Pavlovich

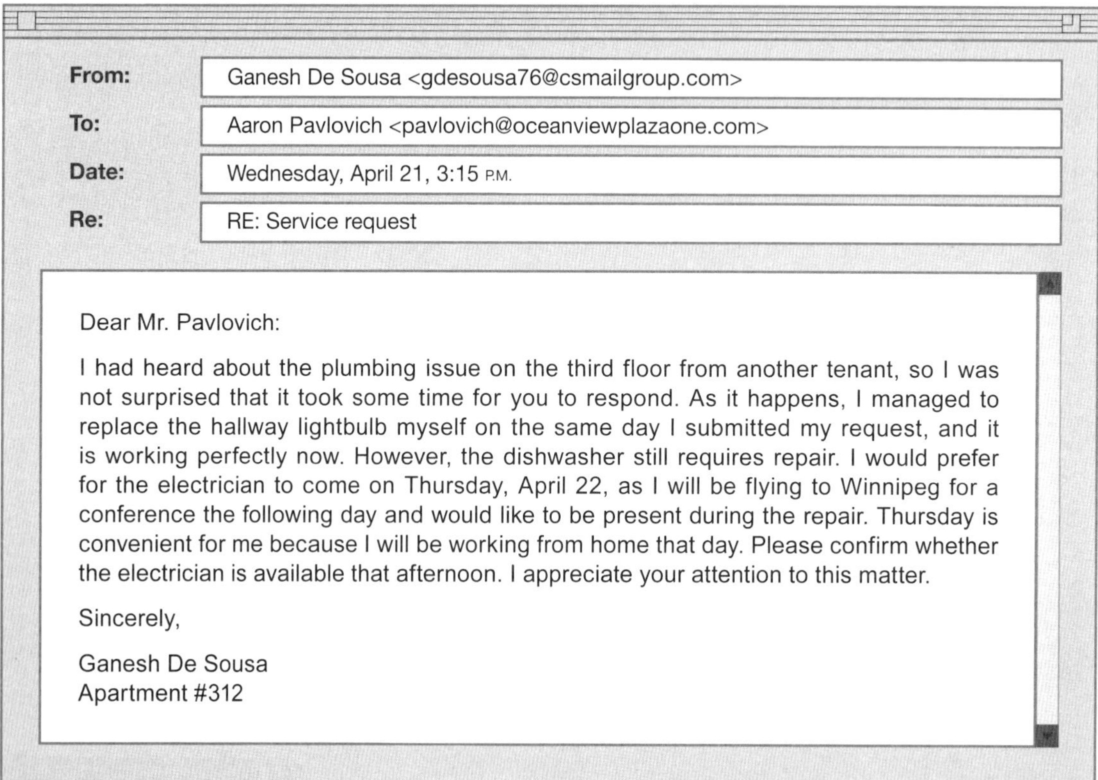

From:	Ganesh De Sousa <gdesousa76@csmailgroup.com>
To:	Aaron Pavlovich <pavlovich@oceanviewplazaone.com>
Date:	Wednesday, April 21, 3:15 P.M.
Re:	RE: Service request

Dear Mr. Pavlovich:

I had heard about the plumbing issue on the third floor from another tenant, so I was not surprised that it took some time for you to respond. As it happens, I managed to replace the hallway lightbulb myself on the same day I submitted my request, and it is working perfectly now. However, the dishwasher still requires repair. I would prefer for the electrician to come on Thursday, April 22, as I will be flying to Winnipeg for a conference the following day and would like to be present during the repair. Thursday is convenient for me because I will be working from home that day. Please confirm whether the electrician is available that afternoon. I appreciate your attention to this matter.

Sincerely,

Ganesh De Sousa
Apartment #312

176. Who most likely is Mr. Pavlovich?

(A) An electrical service provider
(B) The manager of a residential complex
(C) A computer-repair specialist
(D) The supervisor of a plumbing
company

177. According to the first e-mail, why was Mr. Pavlovich's response to Mr. De Sousa delayed?

(A) Mr. Pavlovich was traveling outside
the city.
(B) Mr. Pavlovich was addressing issues
with his computer.
(C) One of Mr. Pavlovich's employees
was absent from work.
(D) Mr. Pavlovich was attending to a more
urgent task.

178. Why does Mr. Pavlovich need information from Mr. De Sousa?

(A) To schedule a repair visit
(B) To deliver a package to his apartment
(C) To issue a reimbursement
(D) To gain access to an account

179. When did Mr. De Sousa resolve the issue with his light?

(A) On April 19
(B) On April 20
(C) On April 21
(D) On April 22

180. According to the second e-mail, what is Mr. De Sousa's plan for April 22?

(A) To return from Vancouver
(B) To participate in a conference
(C) To work remotely from home
(D) To send an e-mail

GO ON TO THE NEXT PAGE

VELVET FORK BISTRO WEEKLY SCHEDULE
December 8-14

	Head Chef	Sous Chef	Receptionist	Waitstaff
Monday	Restaurant Closed			
Tuesday	Myra	Yuriko	Leonardo	Enrique Joshua
Wednesday	Walter	Rajesh	Leonardo	Enrique Asher
Thursday	Myra	Yuriko	Leonardo	Tamara Asher
Friday	Raul	Rajesh	Amira	Tamara Asher
Saturday	Raul	Yuriko	Amira	Joshua Mingxia
Sunday	Myra	Rajesh	Amira	Tania Mingxia

From:	Myra <myra.velvetforkbistro@wavepost.com>
To:	All Staff <staff.velvetforkbistro@wavepost.com>
Date:	Chapelville Food Festival
Re:	December 4

Dear Team,

The Chapelville Food Festival is taking place next week, from December 9 to 14. Chef Julius McCarthy from the Flora Creek Inn Restaurant can no longer attend the event to conduct cooking demonstrations, so I have been asked to step in on his behalf. Yuriko and Asher will come along as my assistants.

Raul has graciously agreed to cover my shifts here at the restaurant next week, and Rajesh will be filling in for Yuriko. Mingxia has volunteered to work in place of Asher on Wednesday, December 10, but Asher's shifts on Thursday and Friday still remain unfilled. Would anyone be available to help out with this? Please let me know as soon as you can.

We are thrilled to be part of the festival this year. It will be a fantastic opportunity to showcase what Velvet Fork Bistro has to offer to the thousands of attendees expected at the event. Although next week will certainly be a busy one, we are confident it will be well worth the effort.

Many thanks!

Myra

181. Why was the e-mail sent?

(A) To encourage people to attend a
   festival
(B) To inform about a change in restaurant
   operating hours
(C) To share news of a head chef's
   retirement
(D) To solicit employees to take on extra
   hours

182. What is indicated about the Chapelville
Food Festival?

(A) It is being held in December for the
   first time.
(B) It will likely be well attended.
(C) It spans two days.
(D) It will take place at the Flora Creek
   Inn Restaurant.

183. According to the e-mail, what benefit
does participating in the festival bring to
Velvet Fork Bistro staff members?

(A) They can come up with new menu
   ideas.
(B) They will be able to publicize the
   restaurant.
(C) They can get a discount on cooking
   utensils.
(D) They can learn new culinary
   techniques.

184. Which group will NOT be affected by a
change in working hours?

(A) Head chefs
(B) Sous chefs
(C) Receptionists
(D) Waitstaff

185. Which day will Raul have off during the
week of December 8–14?

(A) Tuesday
(B) Wednesday
(C) Thursday
(D) Friday

GO ON TO THE NEXT PAGE

From:	Arthur Gaillard
To:	Min-ki Kang
Date:	October 22
Subject:	Follow-up

Dear Mr. Kang:

We had a short discussion following your session at the summer World Energy Transport Congress regarding Lumivault Group potentially organizing a training session for my engineering team at ERS Corporation. We explored two possible topics: one focusing on land-use regulations for pipeline engineers, and the other addressing the environmental impacts of pipelines. I am very keen to bring these sessions to fruition during your visit to Edmonton for the winter conference.

According to the Lumivault Group Web site, your consulting fees are listed as follows: $750 for sessions with up to 10 participants, $1,000 for sessions with up to 20 participants, $1,250 for sessions with up to 30 participants, and $1,500 for sessions with more than 30 participants. Could you please confirm if this information is accurate? I look forward to your swift response.

Sincerely,

Arthur Gaillard

From:	Min-ki Kang
To:	Arthur Gaillard
Date:	October 23
Subject:	RE: Follow-up

Dear Mr. Gaillard:

I would be happy to conduct a session on land-use regulations for your team, and my colleague, Amina Weaver, who specializes in environmental-impact training at our consulting firm, is also available. Since we will be attending the conference on December 7 and 8, there is no guarantee that the sessions will conclude early enough to accommodate an evening workshop on those days. Therefore, it would likely be most practical to arrange for a session either immediately before or directly after the conference.

I am available to conduct the training session on the 6th, while Ms. Weaver, who will remain in Edmonton for a few days after my departure, could deliver her session on the 9th. The training fees mentioned in your e-mail are accurate. Looking ahead, you might find value in additional seminars we provide on topics relevant to environmental engineers, such as promoting environmental sustainability and designing energy-efficient buildings.

Kindly confirm which date and training session would work best for your company. I look forward to your response.

Best,

Min-ki Kang

Training Session Schedule

Session Presenter:	Min-ki Kang
Date:	December 6
Time:	9:00 A.M. – 4:00 P.M. (lunch break 12:00 P.M. – 1:00 P.M.)
Location:	Kingsley Conference Centre Conference Room 15A
Number of Attendees:	Twenty-eight engineers

186. What is the main purpose of the first e-mail?

(A) To confirm attendance at the conference
(B) To inquire about organizing a workshop
(C) To cancel a planned presentation
(D) To request updates to a Web site

187. What can be inferred about ERS Corporation?

(A) It employs a large number of engineers.
(B) It engages external consultants for training purposes.
(C) It serves as a sponsor for an international conference.
(D) It operates out of Edmonton.

188. How much will Lumivault Group charge for the training session in Edmonton?

(A) $750
(B) $1,000
(C) $1,250
(D) $1,500

189. In the second e-mail, the word "guarantee" in paragraph 1, line 3, is closest in meaning to

(A) permission
(B) warranty
(C) notification
(D) assurance

190. According to the schedule, which training session was finalized?

(A) Land-use regulations
(B) Environmental impact
(C) Sustainability strategies
(D) Constructing energy-efficient buildings

GO ON TO THE NEXT PAGE

https://www.auroraalliance.com/membership

Current Promotions for Aurora Alliance Members

From 1 January to 31 June, accumulate rewards points by staying at any of the following Aurora Alliance hotels.

Schneider Grand Hotel, Lucerne, Switzerland Earn 30 points per night for a standard room.	**Ragusa Heritage Hotel, Dubrovnik, Croatia** Earn 70 points per night for a deluxe room.
Lumivien Inn, Salzburg, Austria Opens 1 September! Earn 80 points per night for a standard room.	**Kallistos Suites, Santorini, Greece** Earn 50 points per night for a deluxe room.

Additional Benefits for Members:
• Members are entitled to courtesy bus rides to specific nearby attractions and the main airport. For schedule details, please inquire at the front desk.
• Members can enjoy a 10% reduction in car rental rates when booking with Aditi Rentals.

Redeem Your Points:
• 500 points: Receive 50 percent off a meal valued up to €100 at any restaurant within Aurora Alliance hotels.
• 600 points: Get upgraded to a higher-tier room.
• 1,000 points: Enjoy a complimentary overnight stay at any participating Aurora Alliance hotel.

For more information about promotions and points, visit www.auroraalliance.com/member_rewards.

Aurora Alliance

13 February

Esther Dvorak
124 Meadow Lane
Hawthorn OX4 18B
England

Dear Ms. Dvorak,

We appreciate your recent stay at an Aurora Alliance hotel. Enclosed you will find the Aurora Alliance membership card that you requested during your visit to Lucerne. Your account has been credited with the 30 points earned from your one-night stay. To keep accruing points, please activate your membership card by visiting our Web site at www.auroraalliance.com, selecting "My Account," and following the provided steps.

We look forward to hosting you again in the foreseeable future.

Regards,
Client Care Services
Aurora Alliance

https://www.auroraalliance.com/member_3467184

Ms. Dvorak, thank you for taking the time to complete the survey regarding your stay at Lumivien Inn on 14–15 April. As a token of our gratitude, we have credited your account with 20 bonus points!

Aurora Alliance Membership Card: 2378273
Total Accrued Points: 630

To redeem your points, visit www.auroraalliance.com/member_rewards.

191. What is stated about the services offered by Aurora Alliance hotels?

(A) They feature three different room types.
(B) Guests are provided with complimentary breakfast.
(C) Members receive vouchers for nearby attractions.
(D) Free transport is available for members to local destinations.

192. At what hotel did Ms. Dvorak request a membership card?

(A) Schneider Grand Hotel
(B) Ragusa Heritage Hotel
(C) Lumivien Inn
(D) Kallistos Suites

193. In the letter, the word "keep" in paragraph 1, line 3, is closest in meaning to

(A) place
(B) continue
(C) postpone
(D) retain

194. What most likely true about Ms. Dvorak?

(A) She stayed at a new hotel.
(B) She rented a car from Aditi Rentals.
(C) She was unable to activate her membership card.
(D) She misplaced her membership card.

195. Why was Ms. Dvorak awarded bonus points?

(A) For recommending a courtesy bus
(B) For filling out a questionnaire
(C) For extending her hotel reservation
(D) For checking out earlier than planned

GO ON TO THE NEXT PAGE

From:	Magdalene Graham <mgraham@optivionsystems.com>
To:	Adrian Lindberg <alindberg@casdsn.com>
Subject:	Meeting
Date:	January 8

Dear Mr. Lindberg,

I would like to outline a few topics to cover during our upcoming meeting. Given that the lease for our current building will expire this year, it will be essential to start transitioning to the Windsor Avenue location as soon as the construction is finalized. While our budget for this project is significantly constrained, we remain committed to achieving an aesthetically pleasing design. Additionally, the local neighborhood council requires assurance that the project's impact will be contained, specifically in terms of construction-related dirt and noise, which have the potential to be disruptive for residents and workers in the vicinity.

Our team was impressed with the work they saw on the tour of CAS Design's previous projects within the city, and we are hopeful that we can reach an agreement moving forward.

Sincerely,

Magdalene Graham, President
Optivion Systems

January 10

MEETING MINUTES

Attendees

CAS Design: Adrian Lindberg, Bjorn Norland
Optivion Systems: Magdalene Graham, Lucy Mei

Purpose

Determine the subsequent steps required for the Windsor Avenue construction project.

Decisions

- CAS will investigate the feasibility of constructing additional elements onto the current structure and will prepare a preliminary budget for the project.
- Should the project be deemed too costly to undertake, Optivion Systems will cover the cost of the assessment; otherwise, it will be provided free of charge.
- The entire project must reach completion by the first week in December to ensure adequate time for Optivion Systems to transition all staff into their new headquarters before the year's conclusion.

A Remarkable Transformation

(November 25) - Those familiar with the vacant Sterling Solutions building on Windsor Avenue might find it unbelievable that the majority of that dull, squat structure is still intact. This is due to the fact that the former building is now concealed beneath the striking new national headquarters of Optivion Systems, which is approaching completion. CAS Design managed to incorporate the old building's foundation and some of its existing structure.

"This aspect was crucial as the client aimed to avoid causing disturbance to the community by reducing the noise and dust," explained Bjorn Norland, a design engineer at CAS Design. "Our first step was to examine the structure. From our initial research, we determined that the foundation and the primary support walls could be preserved, which allowed us to attain the client's objective," he added. - By Julia Parmentier

196. In the e-mail, the word "cover" in paragraph 1, line 1, is closest in meaning to

(A) request
(B) discuss
(C) pay for
(D) conceal

197. According to the e-mail, why does Ms. Graham show interest in collaborating with CAS Design?

(A) CAS Design prioritizes eco-friendly construction practices.
(B) CAS Design has previously worked on projects for Optivion Systems.
(C) Ms. Graham wants to support a business from the local community.
(D) Ms. Graham's team appreciates the buildings designed by CAS Design for other companies.

198. What is suggested about the president of Optivion Systems?

(A) She plans to move into a newly constructed office in December.
(B) She serves on the neighborhood council.
(C) She resides in the Windsor Avenue area.
(D) She has prior knowledge or experience with renovating buildings.

199. What does the article imply about Optivion Systems?

(A) It will avoid paying a fee for the evaluation.
(B) It operates as a business owned within the local community.
(C) It overspent its budget on the building project.
(D) It recently rebranded itself from Sterling Solutions.

200. According to Mr. Norland, why were parts of the Windsor Avenue building's original structure retained?

(A) To preserve a structure of historical significance
(B) To comply with a safety regulations
(C) To minimize disruption to the neighborhood
(D) To create an aesthetically pleasing design

This is the end of the test. If you finish before time is called, you may go back to Parts 5, 6, and 7 and check your work.

정답 및 해설 p.2

TEST 02

READING TEST

In this Reading test, various texts will be provided for you to read, followed by multiple types of reading comprehension questions. The total duration for the test is 75 minutes. It consists of three parts, with instructions provided at the beginning of each part. You are encouraged to attempt as many questions as you can within the given time.

Make sure to mark your answers on the separate answer sheet. Do not write your answers in your test book.

PART 5

Directions: In the sentences below, a word or phrase is missing. You will find four options below each sentence. Choose the most appropriate answer to fill in the blank, and then mark the letter (A), (B), (C), or (D) on your answer sheet.

---

101. Only authorized employees ------- permission to access patient records.

(A) are granting
(B) are granted
(C) have been granting
(D) be granted

102. The skilled employees in our division ------- the expertise required to drive rapid growth and success.

(A) enlarge
(B) benefit
(C) contain
(D) possess

103. ------- the tax rate adjustment will gain approval depends on public support.

(A) If
(B) Whether
(C) Though
(D) Either

104. A reception is scheduled to begin in the foyer ------- after Ms. Schuster's presentation concludes.

(A) immediately
(C) lately
(B) mutually
(D) suddenly

105. Ms. Atkin is ------- of reports that fail to incorporate strong research components.

(A) critic
(B) critics
(C) critical
(D) criticize

106. Zephlux, Inc., must expand its workforce if it hopes to ------- all pending orders before the year concludes.

(A) affect
(B) contain
(C) fulfill
(D) mention

107. Managers will not ------- grant employees time off during peak operational months.

(A) generalization
(B) generalize
(C) generally
(D) general

108. The Sheridan Art Museum has ------- invested in software programs to develop more interactive exhibitions.

(A) randomly
(B) roughly
(C) instantly
(D) heavily

109. The hotel manager has offered us -------
that the pool will be ready for use by May.

(A) assurance
(B) assuredly
(C) assuring
(D) assures

110. The store ------- charged Ms. Hong's
credit card twice for the same purchase,
but it promptly corrected the mistake.

(A) uniformly
(B) potentially
(C) inadvertently
(D) functionally

111. *The Regina Daily* will gradually ------- to
provide free subscriptions starting next
month.

(A) cease
(B) ceased
(C) cessation
(D) ceasing

112. ------- its primary competitor, the ergonomic
chair from Lume Living Designs is both
lightweight and available in a range of
colors.

(A) In contrast to
(B) By way of
(C) Instead of
(D) So as

113. We appreciate your so ------- explaining
the enrollment procedures to the new
employees.

(A) being patient
(B) patiently
(C) patience
(D) patient

114. The strategic planning committee advised
that a greater emphasis should be placed
------- research and development in the
upcoming year.

(A) against
(B) during
(C) for
(D) on

115. ------- the affordability of the production
costs, we opted to collaborate with Clifton
Material Co.

(A) Provided
(B) Given
(C) Considering that
(D) Regarding

116. The decorative rugs from Pichon Carpet
are crafted using a ------- of synthetic
and natural materials to achieve a unique
texture and quality.

(A) plan
(B) team
(C) blend
(D) shade

117. The number of shoppers at the store this
holiday is comparable to ------- of the
previous holiday.

(A) that
(B) those
(C) this
(D) they

118. The latest model from Vollmer Motors
boasts a sleek dashboard layout and a
------- interior, providing ample space for
comfort and convenience.

(A) widespread
(B) plenty
(C) prevalent
(D) spacious

119. Oberon Design has a team of nine
architects, ------- earned their degrees
from prestigious universities.

(A) most of whom
(B) some of whose
(C) the reason being
(D) due to them

120. The quarterly revenue reports have been
embarrassingly -------, failing to meet our
projections.

(A) disappointing
(B) disappointed
(C) regretting
(D) pleased

GO ON TO THE NEXT PAGE

121. Major ------- in tourism levels have played a crucial role in shaping the fortunes of Dover Beach's small businesses.

(A) fluctuations
(B) perceptions
(C) narrations
(D) obligations

122. Scientists at TRENIX Electronics will present the wearable devices that ------- have been working on for several years.

(A) they
(B) them
(C) their
(D) theirs

123. The initial estimates for quarterly earnings have already been ------- even though there is still one month left in the quarter.

(A) exceeded
(B) outdated
(C) overdrawn
(D) impressed

124. Acquiring ------- properties as possible can be risky, yet it often proves to be lucrative, yielding substantial financial gains.

(A) as much
(B) as many
(C) so much
(D) so many

125. ------- of the newly developed software solutions, designed to streamline workflow, is available for immediate implementation.

(A) Either
(B) Both
(C) Most
(D) Every

126. Real estate agents assert that ------- to the landscape in the Fremont area will make the neighborhood more attractive to potential homebuyers.

(A) continuations
(B) increments
(C) deviations
(D) enhancements

127. ------- from previous models, the newly redesigned TZ-450 motorcycle offers increased power while maintaining a lighter weight.

(A) Differs
(B) Differently
(C) Difference
(D) Different

128. The proposed development encountered substantial ------- from local residents who voiced their concerns about its potential impact on the community.

(A) condition
(B) prediction
(C) opposition
(D) deduction

129. Fitzroy Bookstores announced a 20 percent drop in net profit this year, which the company ------- to intense competition from Yelland Booksellers, Inc.

(A) accused
(B) presented
(C) disapproved
(D) attributed

130. Customers of Bailey Catering should ------- on the back of this form any special dietary requirements to ensure their needs are properly accommodated.

(A) advise
(B) initiate
(C) specify
(D) permit

PART 6

Directions: Review the following texts. In certain sections, there is a missing word, phrase, or sentence. Each question includes four possible answers provided below the text. Choose the most appropriate answer to fill in the blank, and then mark the letter (A), (B), (C), or (D) on your answer sheet.

Questions 131 through 134 refer to the following press release.

Velisse Perfumes is pleased to share that its latest fragrance, Velvet Bloom, has been

------- Fragrance of the Year by the Global Perfume Society. Each year, the society
131.
considers dozens of entries, and winning this award signifies remarkable prestige within the

industry. This marks the first occasion that -------. of Velisse's fragrances has achieved this
132.
recognition. Velvet Bloom stands out by blending the aroma of freshly picked roses with a hint

of vanilla.

The Velvet Bloom fragrance had a ------- launch earlier this year and remains exclusively
133.
available online. -------.
134.

131. (A) granted
(B) supported
(C) named
(D) founded

132. (A) none
(B) each
(C) others
(D) any

133. (A) limit
(B) limited
(C) limiting
(D) limits

134. (A) The fragrance is set to hit store shelves next month.
(B) A floral scent also took home the award in the previous year.
(C) Its unique packaging has undergone a redesign.
(D) Velisse is in the process of developing a successor to this product.

GO ON TO THE NEXT PAGE

From: Franziska Weber <franziska@franziskasbakery.com>

To: Jin Ha Baek <jhbaek@polyvision.com>

Date: November 27

Subject: Your feedback

Dear Ms. Baek,

We sincerely appreciate you reaching out to Franziska's Bakery with your -------. We are **135.** ------- to share that your idea for caramel banana cupcakes will be incorporated into our **136.** menu starting next month.

As a token of our gratitude, we would love to offer you a complimentary half-dozen cupcakes in any flavor you prefer. To ------- your gift, simply bring this e-mail along when you visit **137.** Franziska's Bakery. -------. We eagerly anticipate welcoming you soon. **138.**

Best regards,

Franziska Weber, Owner

Franziska's Bakery

---

135. (A) suggestion
(B) requirement
(C) complaint
(D) concern

136. (A) delight
(B) delighted
(C) delightful
(D) delights

137. (A) return
(B) exchange
(C) claim
(D) display

138. (A) We're pleased to let you know that the item is available in our inventory.
(B) We hope this small gesture expresses our sincere gratitude.
(C) Kindly get in touch with us to provide the necessary details.
(D) Price details are not included on gift receipts.

Temba Construction Shelters

If you're engaged in the construction industry, you understand how frustrating ------- can be
139.
when unexpected rain forces a project to halt. Not only does this risk inconveniencing clients
due to missed deadlines, but it could also lead to delays in other scheduled projects.

Temba Construction Shelters offer the ------- you require to keep working! These temporary
140.
structures ------- set up directly at your job site. They remain intact throughout your project,
141.
allowing your crew to continue working without disruption, through rain or shine.

Additionally, they help safeguard equipment and materials from moisture, eliminating the risk of
water or mold-related damage. -------. For further details, visit www.tembashelters.com!
142.

---

139. (A) it
(B) one
(C) they
(D) some

140. (A) workers
(B) financing
(C) advice
(D) protection

141. (A) can be
(B) are being
(C) have been
(D) would have been

142. (A) Ensure you specify which repairs are
the most urgent.
(B) Rain will never cause project delays
for you again.
(C) A professional will be dispatched to
your site immediately.
(D) Determining the exact duration of a
project can be challenging.

(September 5) - Beginning October 1, the city of Mableton will implement a new recycling system. Residents will no longer need to sort recyclable materials. -------, they can place all items into a single container.

143.

"This approach is far more streamlined," says Larkin Benson of Mableton Waste Management. "Recycling will be just as simple as throwing things away. -------."

144.

Some skeptics argue that although collection expenses might be lower under the new system, processing costs could increase significantly. "This method may be more ------- for residents," says local resident Daphne Pearson, "but the recyclables will still need to be sorted at a facility. This means the city will incur high processing fees. Eventually, people ------- that the previous system was more effective."

145.

146.

143. (A) Instead
(B) Otherwise
(C) In the meantime
(D) As a rule

144. (A) Staff members have completed extra training for this process.
(B) Observing the outcomes of the system has been intriguing.
(C) The advantages of this change remain uncertain.
(D) Individuals will likely be more inclined to conform.

145. (A) urgent
(B) amusing
(C) convenient
(D) ordinary

146. (A) realized
(B) will realize
(C) would have realized
(D) have been realizing

PART 7

Directions: In this part, you will read a variety of texts, such as magazine and newspaper articles, e-mails, and instant messages. Each text or set of texts is followed by a series of questions. Choose the most appropriate answer and mark the letter (A), (B), (C), or (D) on your answer sheet.

Questions 147 through 148 refer to the following notice.

We are excited to share that Tess Yoon has become part of Stanton Law Firm as an associate attorney. She graduated with top honors from Claridell University Law School, where she specialized in copyright and trademark law. During her studies, she worked as a legal assistant in the university's legal aid office. This past summer, she completed an internship with Davenport and Associates, a law firm that represents authors, musicians, and other professionals in the publishing sector. Ms. Yoon has an outstanding history of service and will be an invaluable asset to our team. Join us this Friday at 2:00 P.M. in the main conference room to extend a warm welcome to her.

147. Where is the notice most likely posted?

(A) In a legal firm
(B) In a talent management agency
(C) In a music production facility
(D) In a publishing house

148. What are staff members invited to do this Friday?

(A) Attend a live music event
(B) Become part of a community service group
(C) Take part in an industry-related seminar
(D) Meet a new colleague

Attention Residents of South Jordan:

The South Jordan Business Directory has grown so large that it now occupies a sizable portion of the neighborhood newsletter. As a result, we will transition to an online format for the directory and discontinue its printed version.

The directory is not yet accessible, but in the upcoming weeks, it will be available at www.southjordan.com. Once it is published, I recommend checking your listing to ensure its accuracy. If you notice outdated information or any broken links, please inform me so that I can update the necessary details.

Thank you,
Leah Langley
South Jordan Neighborhood Council
555-0124

149. What modification is being made to the business directory?

(A) The listings will be condensed.
(B) It will be exclusively available online.
(C) The release schedule will change.
(D) It will expand to include multiple neighborhoods.

150. According to the notice, why might readers contact Ms. Langley?

(A) To request corrections to their listing
(B) To obtain an access code for the directory
(C) To subscribe to a neighborhood newsletter
(D) To propose adjustments to publishing deadlines

<table>
<tr><td colspan="2" align="center">

Workshop: Strengthening Team Dynamics

Date: 27 October
Time: 9:30 A.M. to 5:00 P.M.
Cost: £150 per participant

</td></tr>
<tr><td>**9:30** A.M.</td><td>

Laying the Foundation
Explore critical challenges faced by small business owners. Define both short-term and long-term company objectives and recognize areas in need of improvement.

</td></tr>
<tr><td>**11:00** A.M.</td><td>

Building Collaboration
Gain insights on fostering a cooperative work culture that minimizes unnecessary competition among employees across all levels.

</td></tr>
<tr><td>**12:30** P.M.</td><td>

Lunch Break
Enjoy a complimentary meal with a choice between two entrées: a grilled chicken sandwich served with fresh salad greens or pasta topped with seasonal vegetables.

</td></tr>
<tr><td>**2:00** P.M.</td><td>

Interactive Team Exercises
Engage in practical team-building activities designed for both small and large groups. Exchange ideas with your fellow participants that can be implemented within your own workplace.

</td></tr>
<tr><td>**3:30** P.M.</td><td>

Measuring Success
Discover techniques for assessing the effectiveness of team-building initiatives. Receive useful tips on utilizing common office software to track company performance and improvements.

</td></tr>
</table>

151. For whom is the workshop most likely intended?

(A) Journalists covering business news
(B) Specialists in workforce management
(C) Entrepreneurs operating small businesses
(D) Individuals newly hired at smaller firms

152. What session involves identifying goals?

(A) Laying the Foundation
(B) Building Collaboration
(C) Interactive Team Exercises
(D) Measuring Success

153. What is NOT indicated about the workshop?

(A) Attendance requires a fee.
(B) A meal is included for participants.
(C) It is scheduled as a single-day event.
(D) Newly developed software will be a key focus.

GO ON TO THE NEXT PAGE

Local News

Tuesday, September 1

The Nebula Theater, located on Bradford Street, is set to close at the end of the month. However, the building will not remain vacant for long, as it has been purchased by the Spokane Cinema Society (SCS). According to Aarav Joshi, the Executive Director of SCS, the organization plans to renovate the facility before reopening. He mentioned that all theaters would undergo upgrades, including the replacement of seating, screens, and audio systems. —[1]—.

Mr. Joshi added, "Nonetheless, we will retain one of the original projectors so we can continue screening classic films in their authentic format."

To date, the Nebula Theater primarily showcased independent productions, foreign films, and art house movies. —[2]—. The former owner, Ethan Sattwell, who has recently retired, envisioned the theater as a haven for creative and artistic films. Though he maintained this vision for many years, declining ticket sales led him to the difficult choice of selling the venue. —[3]—.

"It was a tough decision to make," Mr. Sattwell admitted. "I will truly miss running the theater, but I'm glad that SCS plans to revitalize it."

Under new management, the theater will still screen artistic films on select occasions, while expanding its offerings to include more mainstream movies aimed at families and children.

SCS intends to officially reopen the venue on January 12. Additionally, the theater will continue to serve as host for the classic film festival, which begins on the first weekend of February and lasts ten days. The festival will remain unchanged in most aspects, except for one significant update - its name. Previously known as the Bradford Street Film Festival, it will now bear the title of Spokane Cinema Society Film Festival. —[4]—.

154. What is suggested about the Nebula Theater?

(A) It will primarily feature classic film screenings.
(B) It will undergo renovations to install updated equipment.
(C) Its admission prices are expected to rise.
(D) Its planned changes have caused dissatisfaction among patrons.

155. According to the article, what was difficult for Mr. Sattwell?

(A) Securing appropriate technical equipment
(B) Choosing a destination for retirement
(C) Making the decision to sell the theater
(D) Attracting buyers for the establishment

156. What has received a new name?

(A) A cinema venue
(B) A leadership role
(C) A film festival
(D) A cinema society

157. In which of the positions marked [1], [2], [3], and [4] does the following sentence best belong?

"The concession stand has also been refurbished."

(A) [1]
(B) [2]
(C) [3]
(D) [4]

PIONEER TECH SOLUTIONS

As a valued business client, you
- gain access to state-of-the-art technology
- pay solely for the services you utilize, thereby lowering costs for hardware and software
- benefit from our transparent, up-front, and continuous billing system

We offer
- tailored software development and routine upkeep of on-site hardware (requires a one-year agreement)
- management and periodic updates for applications and databases
- data storage, backups, and recovery services
- a around-the-clock support center for prompt issue resolution
- access to our proprietary Pioneer Tech Remote Monitoring (PTRM) platform

158. What is one of the services provided by Pioneer Tech Solutions?

(A) Legal consultation
(B) Office accounting
(C) Facility maintenance
(D) Software production

159. What is stated about regular maintenance of computer systems?

(A) It requires a commitment of at least one year.
(B) It is suggested for older computer models.
(C) It is carried out by external contractors.
(D) It is unavailable to new clients.

GO ON TO THE NEXT PAGE

---

https://www.auroraalliance.com/membership ▶

Work Link 🔗 1266645640

Achieve excellence in your career!

Unlike other companies that require their sales representatives to make countless calls to individuals who are not expecting to be contacted, Prime Shield Insurance allows customers to reach out to us for their insurance needs. Our sales associates handle only inbound sales calls from prospective clients who are already interested in purchasing policies. These roles eliminate the stress of selling on commission.

Participate in our paid sales training program and prepare for the licensing exam to become a certified insurance professional. Successful candidates may be offered a salaried position.

Salary offers will be based on your educational background and work experience. While some college coursework is advantageous, highly motivated high school graduates are also encouraged to apply. Since we operate twenty-four hours a day, seven days a week to serve our customers, we provide a variety of shift options, including a 10% pay increase for late-night and early-morning shifts.

Click "Apply Now" below to seize this opportunity at worklink.com. You will need a valid e-mail address and phone number to complete the application. Qualified applicants will be contacted via phone or e-mail. For inquiries about the application process, call 281-555-0287. We recommend visiting our Web site at primeshieldinsurance.com to learn more about the company before applying.

Apply Now

---

160. What task is described as part of the job?

(A) Meeting commission-based sales goals
(B) Receiving incoming calls from potential policyholders
(C) Working exclusively during unconventional hours
(D) Making calls to individuals unfamiliar with the company

161. According to the advertisement, what is required for a salaried position?

(A) Previous sales experience
(B) Completion of a college degree
(C) References from past employers
(D) Obtaining an insurance license

162. According to the advertisement, why should applicants visit the Prime Shield Web site?

(A) To gain knowledge about Prime Shield Insurance
(B) To submit an application for the sales position
(C) To ask questions about the application process
(D) To check the status of an application

A Lifelong Passion for Books

August 9 - In Ashford Hills and its surrounding areas, Edward Harrison, who has been a professor of Korean literature at Ashford Hills State University for two decades, is perhaps most recognized as the proprietor of The Hidden Chapter, the oldest bookstore in the town. The store is known for two distinctive characteristics: it focuses on rare books and operates exclusively on Saturdays. Apparently, walk-in sales account for only a minor portion of Mr. Harrison's business; the bulk of the store's income comes from orders placed via phone or online by institutions such as universities, museums, and private collectors.

This Sunday, The Hidden Chapter will commemorate its sixtieth year in operation. "When my mother, Melisa, first opened the bookstore six decades ago on Willow Crest Road, just two blocks from here, she likely never imagined it would still be serving the community today," Mr. Harrison remarked. The store still features its original sign above the doorway. Inside, it retains the cozy, living-room-like ambiance it has always had, complete with mismatched tables and chairs. One area of the store is dedicated to books about soccer, reflecting the Harrison family's abiding passion for the sport. On Friday evenings, the store transforms into a casual social gathering spot. Unsurprisingly, attendees often engage in discussions about rare books, literature, and soccer.

Later this month, Mr. Harrison will reach another significant milestone: his retirement from teaching. His retirement does not imply, however, that The Hidden Chapter will expand its hours of operation; it will continue to open only once a week. "I am not leaving one job just to spend more time on another," Mr. Harrison explained. "Rather, the fact that I will no longer need to prepare classes or grade students' papers will allow me to devote more time to my children and grandchildren."

163. Why most likely was the article written?

(A) To attract members to a newly formed book club
(B) To emphasize the advantages of selling rare and unique items
(C) To honor the accomplishments of a prominent local figure
(D) To inform readers about the relocation of an established business

164. What is NOT suggested about Mr. Harrison?

(A) He is about to end his career as an instructor.
(B) He conducts research on Korean literary works.
(C) He has lived in Ashford Hills for nearly two decades.
(D) He takes pleasure in discussing soccer with others.

165. The word "retains" in paragraph 2, line 9, is closest in meaning to

(A) adds to
(B) aligns with
(C) recalls
(D) maintains

166. What is stated about The Hidden Chapter?

(A) It plans to introduce a new section for children's literature.
(B) It will continue to operate with its current schedule.
(C) Its revenue is projected to grow in the coming year.
(D) Its original sign will be replaced later this month.

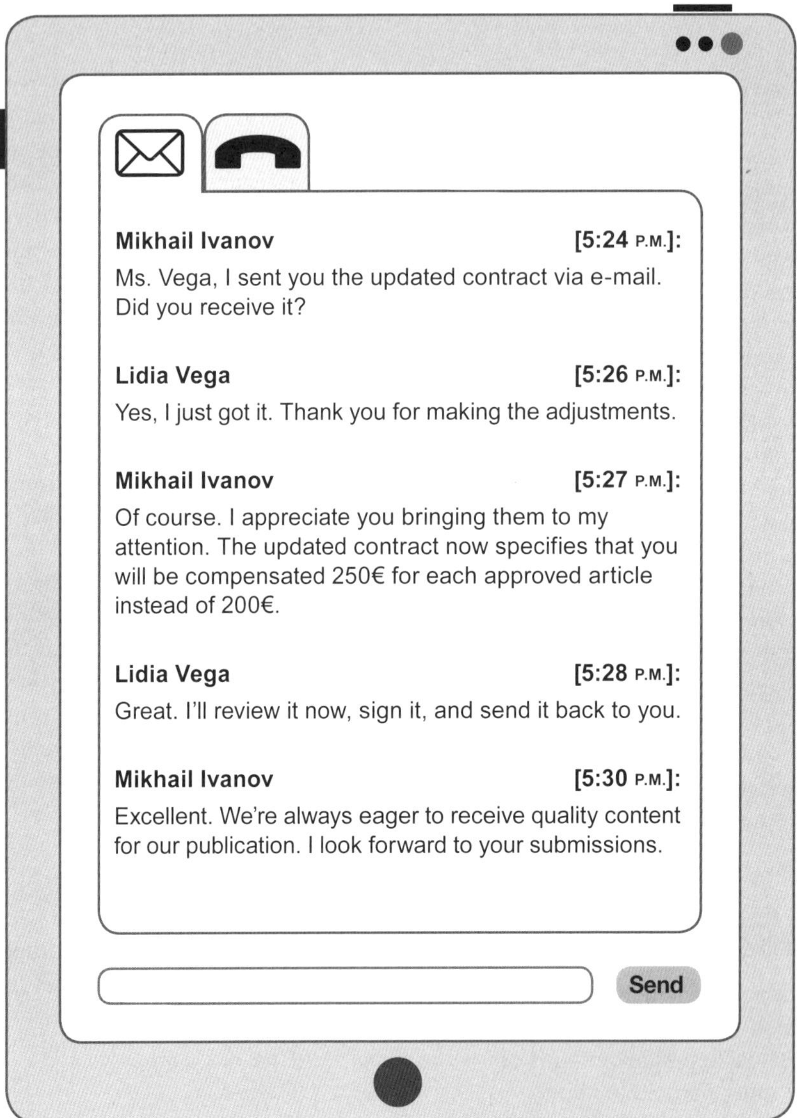

167. At 5:27 P.M., what does Mr. Ivanov mean when he writes, "Of course"?

(A) He was already aware that the e-mail had been received.
(B) He has obtained a signed version of the contract.
(C) He believes the solution to the issue is straightforward.
(D) He was pleased to accommodate a request.

168. Who most likely is Ms. Vega?

(A) An author
(B) An attorney
(C) A financial consultant
(D) A human resources specialist

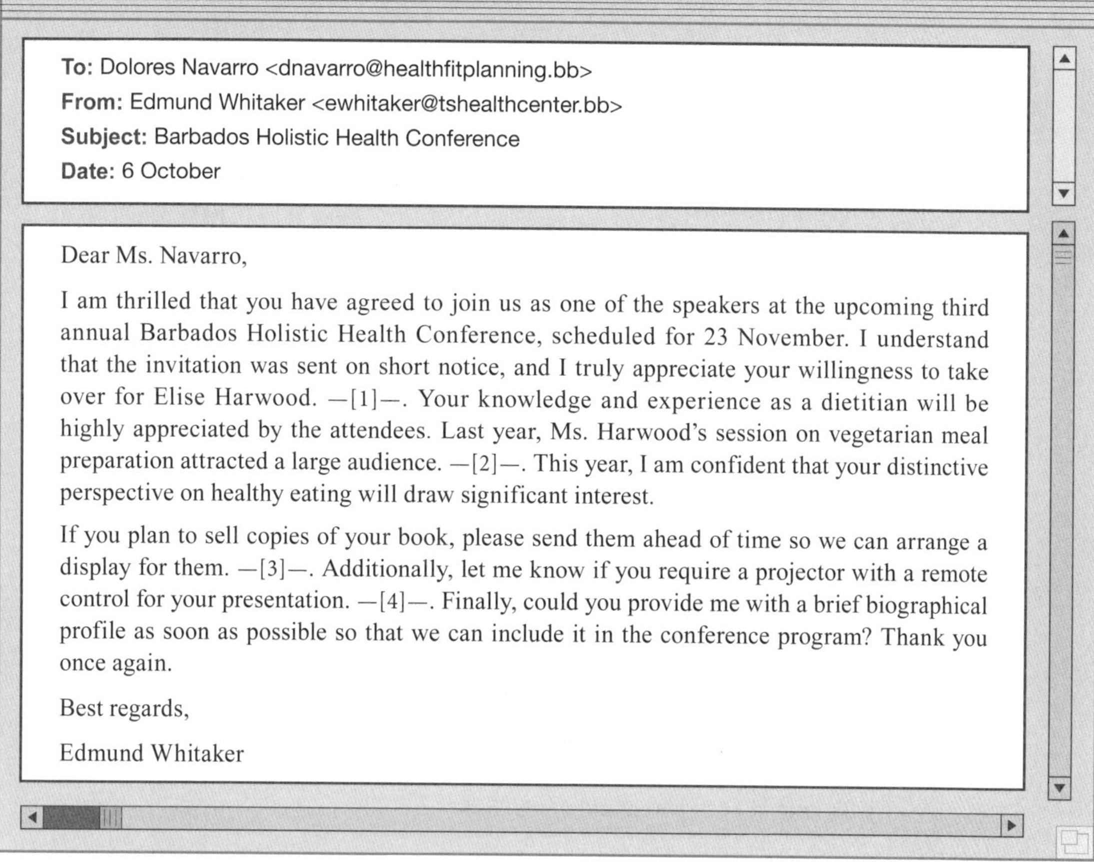

To: Dolores Navarro <dnavarro@healthfitplanning.bb>
From: Edmund Whitaker <ewhitaker@tshealthcenter.bb>
Subject: Barbados Holistic Health Conference
Date: 6 October

Dear Ms. Navarro,

I am thrilled that you have agreed to join us as one of the speakers at the upcoming third annual Barbados Holistic Health Conference, scheduled for 23 November. I understand that the invitation was sent on short notice, and I truly appreciate your willingness to take over for Elise Harwood. —[1]—. Your knowledge and experience as a dietitian will be highly appreciated by the attendees. Last year, Ms. Harwood's session on vegetarian meal preparation attracted a large audience. —[2]—. This year, I am confident that your distinctive perspective on healthy eating will draw significant interest.

If you plan to sell copies of your book, please send them ahead of time so we can arrange a display for them. —[3]—. Additionally, let me know if you require a projector with a remote control for your presentation. —[4]—. Finally, could you provide me with a brief biographical profile as soon as possible so that we can include it in the conference program? Thank you once again.

Best regards,

Edmund Whitaker

169. Why did Mr. Whitaker most likely send the e-mail?

(A) To extend an invitation to Ms. Navarro for an event
(B) To acknowledge Ms. Navarro's acceptance of an offer
(C) To request a suggestion from Ms. Navarro
(D) To recommend rescheduling a session

170. What can be inferred about Ms. Harwood?

(A) She delivered a presentation at the conference the previous year.
(B) She authored a well-known book on nutrition.
(C) She works alongside Ms. Navarro.
(D) She is currently training to become a dietitian.

171. In which of the positions marked [1], [2], [3], and [4] does the following sentence best belong?

"It is absolutely no problem to have visual equipment available."

(A) [1]
(B) [2]
(C) [3]
(D) [4]

Elaine Dietrich | 23 January, 14:36

Blake, has order #8738-3 been shipped yet? If it hasn't, the customer has requested that we include item #736C.

Blake Harlan | 23 January, 14:39

That's a customized silver ring, correct? Typically, the engraving team needs at least three days to add the custom message requested by the customer.

Elaine Dietrich | 23 January, 14:40

Can it be done any faster? The customer needs it as soon as possible.

Blake Harlan | 23 January, 14:42

I'll check with someone from the engraving team to see if it's possible.

Blake Harlan | 23 January, 14:44

Tina, is it possible to expedite the engraving for a ring? It's item #736C, part of order #8738-3.

Tina McAllister | 23 January, 14:45

How quickly do you need it? Would tomorrow be OK?

Elaine Dietrich | 23 January, 14:46

Yes, that works. Thank you both for your assistance!

172. What kind of products does the store sell?

(A) Novels
(B) Accessories
(C) Plants
(D) Home appliances

173. What does the customer want to do?

(A) Modify an order
(B) Update a shipping address
(C) Receive a refund
(D) Select a different delivery option

174. Why does Mr. Harlan contact Ms. McAllister?

(A) To inquire if a task can be completed more quickly than usual
(B) To ask about the shipping schedule for an order
(C) To confirm the timing of a meeting
(D) To alert her to a mistake in a previous message

175. At 14:46, what does Ms. Dietrich most likely mean when she writes, "that works"?

(A) She intends to work overtime tonight.
(B) She is pleased that the machinery is operating properly.
(C) The customer will be content if the item is engraved tomorrow.
(D) Some new products will be selected for a catalog by the end of the day.

GO ON TO THE NEXT PAGE

To:	d.ashcroft@true-sprout.net
From:	nowak@silasfarmsteadweekly.com
Date:	March 12
Subject:	Silas's Farmstead Weekly

Dear Mr. Ashcroft,

For a limited time only, *Silas's Farmstead Weekly* is providing reduced rates on advertisements for businesses that have not yet advertised in our publication. By advertising with *Silas's Farmstead Weekly*, you can connect with a focused audience of over 40,000 agricultural professionals, both in print and online. Don't miss this rare chance to grow your customer base!

Below are the current deals for first-time advertisers, which are valid until April 10. If you would like to book one of these full-color ads, have one of our designers create a personalized ad for you, or request further details, please respond to this e-mail or contact me at 802-555-0214, extension 139. You can find the ad specifications at www.silasfarmsteadweekly.com/ads.

Package	Format	Price (Per Month)
1	One full-page print ad plus 720 × 300 px Web site ad	$1,000
2	One half-page print ad plus 240 × 400 px Web site ad	$725
3	One half-page print ad plus 250 × 250 px Web site ad	$650
4	One quarter-page print ad plus 250 × 250 px Web site ad	$550

Sincerely,

Zofia Nowak
Marketing Coordinator
Silas's Farmstead Weekly

To: nowak@silasfarmsteadweekly.com
From: d.ashcroft@true-sprout.net
Date: March 19
Subject: Re: Silas's Farmstead Weekly

Hello Ms. Nowak,

Thank you for your e-mail. I am interested in placing an ad in *Silas's Farmstead Weekly*. However, I need some clarification regarding the online ad. I checked the specifications on your Web site, but I am still unsure about the location of the ad. Could you let me know exactly where the 240 × 400 ad would appear on your Web site?

Once I receive your response, I will send you an electronic version of the ad along with payment information.

Best regards,

Daniel Ashcroft
Owner, True Sprout Company

176. Why did Ms. Nowak contact Mr. Ashcroft?

(A) To inform him about the launch of a new magazine
(B) To promote a new agricultural product
(C) To notify him of a special promotion
(D) To provide him with a discount on a subscription

177. What can be inferred about *Silas's Farmstead Weekly*?

(A) Its readership has grown recently.
(B) It plans to publish a special edition.
(C) Its advertising prices have gone up.
(D) It produces a magazine with full-color content.

178. What is mentioned about Ms. Nowak?

(A) She works as a graphic designer.
(B) She has collaborated with Mr. Ashcroft in the past.
(C) She is available to offer additional help.
(D) She will not be available in April.

179. In the second e-mail, the word "placing" in paragraph 1, line 1, is closest in meaning to

(A) hiring
(B) running
(C) assigning
(D) estimating

180. What package is Mr. Ashcroft most likely considering?

(A) Package 1
(B) Package 2
(C) Package 3
(D) Package 4

To:	n.krawczyk@plintix.net
From:	i.etim@vintoradigitalmarketing.com
Date:	Monday, January 20
Subject:	Technical Writing Role at Vintora Digital Marketing

Dear Ms. Krawczyk,

Thank you once again for applying to Vintora Digital Marketing. We appreciated the opportunity to speak with you last Thursday and are delighted to extend an invitation for you to join our technical writing team. As discussed, your responsibilities will entail creating user manuals, installation guides, newsletters, and other documents for our technology clients. Your solid background in information technology will be a valuable asset, as it is crucial to comprehend the technical aspects of our clients' products and convey this information in a clear and concise manner.

Your role will commence in February with an in-person training session at our headquarters in Austin, Texas. We aim to schedule this training at a time that accommodates as many new team members as possible, particularly those like you who reside outside of Texas. Kindly reply to this e-mail at your earliest convenience and let us know which weekend in February works best for you.

This is a contract-based position, and apart from the initial training, all work will be conducted remotely during hours of your choosing. As mentioned, your payment will be determined by the complexity of each project you opt to undertake. Alan Fraser, our human resources director, will soon be in touch with the necessary paperwork to complete.

We are excited to collaborate with you!

Best regards,

Iniobong Etim
Vintora Digital Marketing

To:	undisclosed recipients
From:	i.etim@vintoradigitalmarketing.com
Date:	Tuesday, January 21
Subject:	Training Schedule for VDM

Dear Technical Writing Team,

Based on the feedback we received, we have decided that February 22–23 is the most suitable date for the majority of you. Please note that the training will take place from Saturday morning through Sunday afternoon. For those traveling from outside the area, we recommend arriving on Friday. If you wish, we can arrange for you to have dinner with some of our local writers that evening.

All travel expenses will be covered by Vintora Digital Marketing. Further details will be provided soon, but for now, I wanted to inform you of the schedule so you can mark it on your calendars.

Best regards,

Iniobong Etim
Vintora Digital Marketing

181. Why did Ms. Etim contact Ms. Krawczyk?

(A) To offer her a position
(B) To assist her with technical issues
(C) To advertise a writing seminar
(D) To negotiate a salary

182. What information is Ms. Krawczyk requested to provide?

(A) Her academic qualifications
(B) Her availability for a training session
(C) A list of her current clients
(D) A summary of her professional experience

183. What is indicated about the technical writing team members?

(A) They are paid at variable rates.
(B) They have collaborated on previous projects.
(C) They work from the same office location.
(D) They cover their own travel expenses.

184. Why will Mr. Fraser contact Ms. Krawczyk?

(A) To clarify company policies
(B) To make travel arrangements
(C) To issue employment-related documents
(D) To discuss software requirements

185. What will Ms. Krawczyk most likely do on February 21?

(A) Submit a writing project
(B) Travel to Austin
(C) Attend a training session
(D) Meet with Mr. Fraser

GO ON TO THE NEXT PAGE

Isla's Moonlight Tours

☆ ☆ ☆ ☆ ☆

Glasgow, Scotland

Isla's Moonlight Tours is welcoming the autumn season with special pricing - tour packages are now 10% off compared to last year's rates. This limited-time offer is valid for bookings made by September 14. Our autumn getaways depart weekly, but be sure to secure your spot before they're fully booked! Below is a selection of our featured packages.

▶ Dundee and Fort William: This 4-day tour begins in Dundee, a revitalized port city known for its design museums and cutting-edge contemporary art. Enjoy the city's creative energy before heading to Fort William, where you'll explore dramatic Highland landscapes, from Ben Nevis - the UK's highest peak - to the historic beauty of Glencoe and nearby villages.

▶ Stonehaven and the Isle of Mull: This 4-day journey begins in the picturesque coastal town of Stonehaven, which boasts scenic cliffs, winding lanes, and a rich maritime heritage. A highlight of your visit is Dunnottar Castle, perched dramatically atop sea-battered rocks - a perfect blend of history and natural splendor. From there, the tour continues to the serene Isle of Mull, dotted with colorful villages, coastal trails, and sweeping views across tranquil waters. It's a place where quiet charm meets untamed beauty, inviting you to slow down and take in the rhythm of island life.

▶ Kilkenny and Beyond: Take a short trip across the sea to the Emerald Isle and experience the heart of Ireland. Choose from a 3- or 5-day tour starting in the medieval city of Kilkenny, then journey north to Derry, west to Glencolmcille's rugged coastline, and south to the Rock of Cashel - an iconic symbol of Ireland's royal past.

We offer customized tour options for special groups based on duration and preferred attractions.

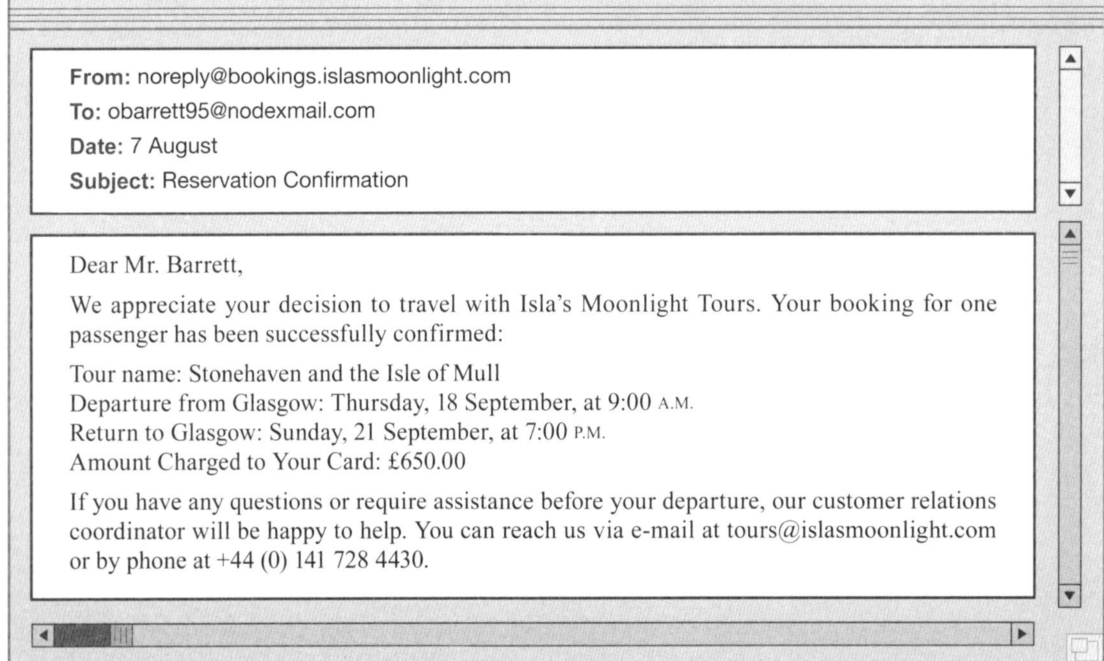

From: noreply@bookings.islasmoonlight.com
To: obarrett95@nodexmail.com
Date: 7 August
Subject: Reservation Confirmation

Dear Mr. Barrett,

We appreciate your decision to travel with Isla's Moonlight Tours. Your booking for one passenger has been successfully confirmed:

Tour name: Stonehaven and the Isle of Mull
Departure from Glasgow: Thursday, 18 September, at 9:00 A.M.
Return to Glasgow: Sunday, 21 September, at 7:00 P.M.
Amount Charged to Your Card: £650.00

If you have any questions or require assistance before your departure, our customer relations coordinator will be happy to help. You can reach us via e-mail at tours@islasmoonlight.com or by phone at +44 (0) 141 728 4430.

Participant feedback

As a photographer, I was thoroughly impressed by the breathtaking scenery and unique locations featured on this tour - genuinely second to none. This company knows how to treat its customers; I'm already looking forward to joining another trip. Our guide, Siobhan O'Malley, was knowledgeable and energetic. As a native of the city we visited, she shared the city's heritage and customs with warmth and familiarity. Her engaging stories taught me a great deal about the area's rich history.

Posted by: Owen Barrett

186. What can be inferred about Isla's Moonlight Tours?

(A) It has recently established additional branches.
(B) It is celebrating a company expansion.
(C) It has introduced new itineraries to meet demand.
(D) It organizes its tours multiple times each month.

187. According to the advertisement, what can Isla's Moonlight Tours offer clients?

(A) Opportunities to interact with artists and actors
(B) Discounts for customers who book repeatedly
(C) A guaranteed maximum tour group size
(D) Tailored travel plans for groups with specific preferences

188. What is implied about Mr. Barrett's tour?

(A) It will last for a total of five days.
(B) It was purchased at a discounted price.
(C) It will not include admission fees for galleries.
(D) It has been specifically designed for historians.

189. In the Web site feedback, the word "treat" in paragraph 1, line 2, is closest in meaning to

(A) serve
(B) pay for
(C) cover
(D) cure

190. What is indicated about Ms. O'Malley?

(A) She is from Stonehaven.
(B) She has recently completed her guide training.
(C) She is fluent in multiple languages.
(D) She is currently enrolled at a local university.

GO ON TO THE NEXT PAGE

<table>
<tr><td colspan="3" align="center">African Council for Industrial & Commercial Development
7th Annual Symposium
Van der Merwe Convention Centre
Cape Town, South Africa
Thursday, 9 October</td></tr>
<tr><td colspan="3" align="center">Tentative Schedule</td></tr>
<tr><td align="center">Time</td><td colspan="2" align="center">Location</td></tr>
<tr><td align="center">9:30 A.M. - 10:00 A.M.</td><td colspan="2" align="center">Welcome Address and Opening Remarks
by ACICD President Linden Mthembu
Langston Jubilee Hall</td></tr>
<tr><td></td><td align="center">Tamarind Room</td><td align="center">Ebony Room</td></tr>
<tr><td align="center">10:30 A.M.- 12:00 P.M.</td><td>Improving Flavor, Texture, and Nutritional Value
- Pieter Van Rooyen</td><td>Setting Standards of Excellence for Safety and Quality
- Anusha Naidoo</td></tr>
<tr><td align="center">1:30 P.M. - 3:00 P.M.</td><td>Revisiting Classic Methods of Food Preservation: Canning and Pickling - Nokuthula Okafor</td><td>Acquiring Automated Machinery For Your Production Facility
- Rohan Mehta</td></tr>
<tr><td align="center">3:30 P.M. - 5:00 P.M.</td><td>Refrigeration and Storage Innovations for Perishables
- Sonja Pretorius</td><td>Optimizing Packaging for Shipping
- Tumelo Mashaba</td></tr>
<tr><td colspan="3">• Please inform Luyanda Mokoena (lmokoena@acicd.org.za) of any required updates to your session details no later than 2 September. The finalized program will be available online at www.acicd.org.za/schedule by 11 September.
• Presenters MUST register for the event. Please visit our Web site, click on the "Registration" tab, and submit the form - remember to check the "Presenter" box. If you intend to recruit during the event, be sure to also fill out the Employer Application found under the "Career Center" tab.
• A limited number of discounted rooms remain at The Montclare Suites - early reservations are strongly encouraged.</td></tr>
</table>

From:	Sonja Pretorius <spretorius6@kbrdev.co.za>
To:	Luyanda Mokoena <lmokoena@acicd.org.za>
Date:	Monday, 28 July 8:50 A.M.
Subject:	Schedule change request

Dear Mr. Mokoena:

Unforeseen circumstances have prevented my colleague, Tumelo Mashaba, from delivering his scheduled presentation. I've been requested to step in as his replacement. However, upon reviewing the latest version of the conference schedule, I realized that Mr. Mashaba's allocated time conflicts with my own. I would appreciate your assistance in resolving this dilemma. Many thanks in advance for your support.

Sincerely,
Sonja Pretorius

Program	Registration	Sponsorships	Comments

https://www.acicd.org.za

At the recent ACICD symposium, I delivered a presentation exploring the intricacies involved in procuring automated equipment. To my delight, the presentation drew a strong turnout, and during the subsequent question-and-answer session, I found myself diving into content I had deliberately omitted, concerned it might be overly technical. Obviously, the audience was far more competent than I had anticipated. In addition, acting in my capacity as a recruiter, I interviewed a dozen promising candidates for a pivotal role at my organization. Overall, this initial experience with the ACICD symposium proved utterly gratifying, and I eagerly await the next one.

- Rohan Mehta

191. What industry is the focus of the conference?

(A) Waste management and repurposing
(B) Food production and processing
(C) Automobile design and engineering
(D) Apparel and textile manufacturing

192. According to the schedule, what are presenters required to do?

(A) Identify themselves as speakers during registration
(B) Specify shipping information for their conference materials
(C) Secure hotel accommodations by September 11
(D) Request a discount code from The Montclare Suites

193. What responsibility has been assigned to Ms. Pretorius?

(A) Arrange a meeting with the event coordinator
(B) Provide a draft of her presentation
(C) Discuss ways of preparing goods for transport
(D) Cancel her colleague's travel arrangements

194. In the review, the word "capacity" in paragraph 1, line 5, is closest in meaning to

(A) position
(B) volume
(C) competence
(D) experience

195. What is probably true about Mr. Mehta?

(A) He recently launched a production facility.
(B) He submitted an Employer Application when registering.
(C) He preferred the recent ACICD symposium over previous ones.
(D) He assumed his subject matter would be easily understood.

GO ON TO THE NEXT PAGE

CARMOSA (November 16) - Officials from Carmosa have begun preliminary discussions about the fate of Marigold Street Bridge, a historic landmark in dire need of upgrades. Though costly restoration options are under discussion, demolition appears increasingly likely due to several contributing factors.

"This isn't a decision we plan to make hastily," explained city planner Miles Pennington. "At this point, replacing the bridge seems to make the most financial sense."

Cost isn't the only concern. Structural engineer Carlos Menendez added that traffic flow is another major issue. "Highway 38 is scheduled to be broadened from four lanes to six, and then the current bridge won't be able to accommodate the increase in traffic. The way I see it, a wider, more modern structure is inevitable."

Residents interested in sharing their input can attend a public listening session at Benton Square next Wednesday at 6:30 P.M.

Letters to the Editor

November 17 - I'm writing to comment on yesterday's article about the Marigold Street Bridge. This bridge is an integral part of Carmosa's cultural identity and it is in the city's best interest to keep it intact. Given the tremendous amount of revenue our city earns each year from cultural heritage tourism, I would argue that the upfront expenses of repairing this historic landmark are justified in the long run.

- Ana Delgado, member of the Carmosa Conservancy (CC)

To:	members@carmosaconservancy.org
From:	diego_morales@carmosaconservancy.org
Date:	November 29
Re:	Update on Marigold Street Bridge

Dear CC Members,

Well done! Due to our strong showing at the recent city council event, and after countless phone calls to city council representatives, it appears that demolition of Marigold Street Bridge is off the table! The Benton Square Herald reported today that the city will now relocate the structure to the Southridge Heritage District, where it will serve as a pedestrian-only bridge.

No doubt this outcome is thanks, in part, to the thoughtful voices you all shared at the gathering last Wednesday.

With gratitude,

Diego Morales
Civic Outreach Manager, Carmosa Conservancy

196. In the article, what is indicated about the city of Carmosa?

(A) It plans to launch a tour program.
(B) It intends to boost municipal spending.
(C) It will begin widening a major highway.
(D) It is enforcing new traffic regulations.

197. What is NOT suggested about Ms. Delgado?

(A) She values a historic landmark.
(B) She collaborated with Mr. Menendez.
(C) She holds a different view from Mr. Pennington.
(D) She read the article published on November 16.

198. In the e-mail, the word "countless" in paragraph 1, line 1, is closest in meaning to

(A) numerous
(B) unrecorded
(C) unimportant
(D) documented

199. Why does Mr. Morales congratulate CC members?

(A) They have elected new representatives.
(B) They have been featured in a recent news piece.
(C) They have helped influence a city council decision.
(D) They have secured additional funding from the municipality.

200. What can be inferred about CC members?

(A) They helped restore a local landmark.
(B) They gather weekly on Wednesdays.
(C) Some of them voiced opinions at Benton Square.
(D) Some of them reside in the Southridge heritage district.

This is the end of the test. If you finish before time is called, you may go back to Parts 5, 6, and 7 and check your work.

정답 및 해설 p.44

TEST 03

[이상적인 시간 배분]
Part 5, 6 15분
Part 7 60분

[빠르고 정확한 문제 해결]
- 1단계: '빈칸 앞뒤'를 본다.
- 2단계: 빈칸 앞뒤를 보고 정답을 알 수 없다면 '문장 전체를 해석'하자.
- 3단계: 문장을 바로 해석할 수 없다면 빠르게 아무 답이나 '선택'하고 다음 문제로 넘어가자

READING TEST

In this Reading test, various texts will be provided for you to read, followed by multiple types of reading comprehension questions. The total duration for the test is 75 minutes. It consists of three parts, with instructions provided at the beginning of each part. You are encouraged to attempt as many questions as you can within the given time.

Make sure to mark your answers on the separate answer sheet. Do not write your answers in your test book.

PART 5

Directions: In the sentences below, a word or phrase is missing. You will find four options below each sentence. Choose the most appropriate answer to fill in the blank, and then mark the letter (A), (B), (C), or (D) on your answer sheet.

101. Hawthorne's cleaning supplies are now available ------- in the nation.

(A) across
(B) everywhere
(C) throughout
(D) previously

102. Owen Pike is ------- the most competent person working in the R&D Department.

(A) considered
(B) appeared
(C) regarded
(D) agreed

103. Amid the surge in construction activity, lumber prices are ------- to increase soon.

(A) covered
(B) sought
(C) limited
(D) bound

104. Most viewers considered the beach scene in Javier Ortega's latest movie genuinely -------.

(A) amusement
(B) amusing
(C) amused
(D) amuse

105. Wearing casual clothing is not regarded as ------- for those attending the Advertising Awards banquet.

(A) useful
(B) complete
(C) significant
(D) appropriate

106. Kindly complete the feedback forms ------- conference organizers can enhance upcoming events.

(A) so that
(B) in order to
(C) because of
(D) as well as

107. The supervisor shared information about employee productivity with ------- on quantifiable results.

(A) emphatic
(B) emphasis
(C) emphasize
(D) emphasized

108. Customers can enjoy this week's special by choosing any two menu items, ------- they like the most.

(A) both
(B) whichever
(C) enough
(D) anybody

109. The unseasonably cold weather has
------- impacted the supply of produce at
neighborhood grocery stores.

(A) adversely
(B) faithfully
(C) consciously
(D) accurately

110. His approach to work is like -------,
apart from the fact that he uses his own
program to process data.

(A) me
(B) myself
(C) mine
(D) my

111. Among the applicants, Ms. Moreno
stands out due to her proven track -------
in boosting sales performance.

(A) retort
(B) regard
(C) record
(D) report

112. CEO Khoury has already ------- to
increase Polyvox Systems' earnings by
20 percent within twelve months.

(A) promised
(B) promise
(C) promising
(D) promises

113. Elarin Soapworks kicked off a marketing
initiative to ------- interest in its latest line
of cleansing products.

(A) consume
(B) generate
(C) endorse
(D) suppose

114. The launch of Gearnova's marketing push
will occur ------- the contract terms are
completely settled.

(A) as well as
(B) other than
(C) rather than
(D) as soon as

115. The inspection of the office building
revealed a few small flaws, but there was
no sign of any ------- damage.

(A) structuring
(B) structural
(C) structurally
(D) structures

116. We will have begun construction on
our new facility in Bangkok ------- we
complete the project in Abu Dhabi.

(A) by the time
(B) as soon as
(C) except when
(D) in the same way

117. At Kessler Automotive, Ms. Morgan
------- the team responsible for installing
refurbished engines into vehicles.

(A) conducts
(B) explains
(C) invests
(D) oversees

118. How ------- a company receives,
documents, and reacts to complaints has
an impact on customer satisfaction.

(A) efficient
(B) efficiently
(C) efficiency
(D) efficiencies

119. Farmers market gatherings are scheduled
every Wednesday from 11 A.M. to 3 P.M.
------- otherwise indicated.

(A) since
(B) neither
(C) unless
(D) toward

120. A synthetic gemstone can look virtually
------- to a mined one to someone without
specialized knowledge.

(A) identical
(B) positive
(C) suitable
(D) convenient

GO ON TO THE NEXT PAGE

121. Considering her strong credentials in international trade law, Ms. Kang was chosen over several other ------- applicants.

(A) promises
(B) to promise
(C) promising
(D) promised

122. A ------- number of user-submitted tech support requests led Cindarelix Corporation to enhance its Web servers.

(A) sole
(B) significant
(C) purposeful
(D) capable

123. Due to the chilly temperatures, Milo's Bicycle Rentals is expected to attract ------- riders over the next few months.

(A) neither
(B) every
(C) fewer
(D) higher

124. The article features a list of recommended cleaning products ------- professionals often use to treat delicate fabrics.

(A) who
(B) whose
(C) which
(D) of which

125. Given the recent surge in electronics purchases, experts believe that the device-to-user ------- will exceed previous forecasts.

(A) division
(B) fraction
(C) part
(D) ratio

126. According to the manufacturer, glass that has special surface treatments might not fuse ------- when combined with other glass types.

(A) completion
(B) completing
(C) completely
(D) completes

127. A new Maplewood Credit Union location will be established downtown, just one mile ------- the institution's main office in the finance hub.

(A) all around
(B) up until
(C) far ahead
(D) away from

128. ------- of local businesses for recognition in the Neighborhood Choice Awards must be submitted to *The Crest Gazette* by November 12.

(A) Subscriptions
(B) Nominations
(C) Supporters
(D) Venues

129. Local authorities must ensure the municipal water system complies with ------- standards for water quality established by federal health agencies.

(A) close
(B) dominant
(C) extended
(D) stringent

130. To mark its ten-year milestone, Sutter & Sons Dry Cleaners plans to ------- the occasion with employee celebrations and special customer promotions.

(A) observe
(B) examine
(C) invite
(D) contain

PART 6

Directions: Review the following texts. In certain sections, there is a missing word, phrase, or sentence. Each question includes four possible answers provided below the text. Choose the most appropriate answer to fill in the blank, and then mark the letter (A), (B), (C), or (D) on your answer sheet.

Questions 131 through 134 refer to the following press release.

Douglas Buchanan, the founder and president of Buchanan's, the largest clothing retailer in Bristol, has announced that he ------- £10,000 to support the city's newly built community
131.
center. The funds derive from ticket sales for a celebration hosted last night at his company's

-------. Mr. Buchanan is scheduled to present a cheque to the center during its official
132.
opening ceremony tomorrow.

------- the last two decades, Mr. Buchanan has organized numerous fund-raising events
133.
benefiting local charities and public services. -------.
134.

131. (A) will donate
(B) donated
(C) might donate
(D) donating

132. (A) museum
(B) hotel
(C) factory
(D) store

133. (A) Despite
(B) Over
(C) Among
(D) Beneath

134. (A) The ceremony to mark the opening is set to start at 10:00 A.M.
(B) The center provides educational programs for both adults and children.
(C) The party held yesterday turned out to be the most successful one to date.
(D) Mr. Buchanan intends to launch a new branch in Sheffield in the upcoming year.

GO ON TO THE NEXT PAGE

KTRX Radio Turns 50!

On December 2, KTRX Radio will mark its 50th year on the air. That's half a century of stimulating -------. Throughout the years, we ------- our audience up-to-the-minute news,
135. **136.**
thought-provoking features, and hit music from across the globe. We're now inviting you to join the celebration at our open house, from 5:00 to 6:30 P.M. on December 2 at our studio on Seventh Street. Come explore our space and witness the behind-the-scenes magic. See how our digital audio technology works in action. -------. Admission is free, but
137.
advance registration is necessary. We look forward to seeing you at this ------- event.
138.

135. (A) concerts
(B) discussions
(C) programming
(D) development

136. (A) offers
(B) offering
(C) will offer
(D) have offered

137. (A) We're preparing to merge with a nearby station in the coming year.
(B) You'll also get the chance to meet some of the hosts you love.
(C) This open house kicks off our line-up of December events.
(D) Our station remains an vital voice in your local community.

138. (A) special
(B) specialize
(C) especially
(D) specialization

Questions 139 through 142 refer to the following article.

March 18 – The Edington City Council has officially signed off on a development agreement with TRAX Developments. As part of the deal, TRAX ------- the 4.5-acre lot located on

139.

Hollister Street. The plan calls for the construction of both office buildings and retail outlets.

Mayor Gavin Dresner expressed his support for the ------- benefits the project is expected

140.

to bring to the community. "We anticipate that 450 permanent full-time jobs will be created as a result," he stated. "It's a relief to see the project finally move forward after numerous

delays." -------. According to TRAX spokesperson Molly Kearney, the development is

141.

projected to take two years, though she warned that unexpected delays could still arise.

"We've submitted our best ------- to the council," she noted, "but it's not possible to foresee all

142.

issues that may emerge."

---

139. (A) to develop
(B) will develop
(C) has developed
(D) could have developed

140. (A) economic
(B) unforeseen
(C) volunteer
(D) frequent

141. (A) Although the city is anxious for construction to get underway, setbacks are common in large-scale commercial endeavors like this one.
(B) Local residents and businesses have voiced legitimate worries regarding potential noise from the building process.
(C) Even though officials had pledged a long-term deal, they might now need to reevaluate that commitment.
(D) The city council is scheduled to review and vote on three architectural design options.

142. (A) argument
(B) background
(C) estimate
(D) combination

GO ON TO THE NEXT PAGE

To: All Staff <staff@orpheusdesign.com>

From: Rosemary Kim <r_kim@orpheusdesign.com>

Date: April 13

Subject: Team Changes

Dear Team,

As shared last month, Roberto Galvani, who has been our art director for an impressive seventeen years, will soon move to Asia. -------, he will embark on the next phase of his
143.
professional journey as an executive director at a Korean marketing agency. After conducting an extensive search for his successor, I am delighted to announce ------- our very own
144.
Selena Pappas will step into the role of art director. -------. Ms. Pappas has been a valued
145.
member of the Orpheus team for ten years, collaborating closely with Mr. Galvani during that time. She will officially assume her new position next week while continuing to work alongside Mr. Galvani until his departure in May. Please take a moment to visit Ms. Pappas's office to

------- her.
146.

Warm regards,

Rosemary Kim

Executive Vice President, Orpheus Design Associates

---

143. (A) Once there
(B) Instead
(C) Nevertheless
(D) For example

144. (A) it
(B) as
(C) that
(D) even

145. (A) The process to recruit someone for her prior role has begun.
(B) Orpheus boasts one of the most imaginative teams in the industry.
(C) At the same time, Mr. Galvani has been working on improving his Korean skills.
(D) We are optimistic that the transition will proceed seamlessly.

146. (A) invite
(B) notify
(C) interview
(D) congratulate

PART 7

Directions: In this part, you will read a variety of texts, such as magazine and newspaper articles, e-mails, and instant messages. Each text or set of texts is followed by a series of questions. Choose the most appropriate answer and mark the letter (A), (B), (C), or (D) on your answer sheet.

Questions 147 through 148 refer to the following invoice.

DreamNest Textiles Co., Ltd.

102-3, Textile Industrial Complex
Hwaseong-si, Gyeonggi-do, 18469
Phone: +82-31-555-7890
E-mail: export@dreamnest.co.kr

Sold To:
Northern Comfort Imports Ltd.
215 Mapleview Drive East
Barrie, Ontario, L4N 0W5

Ship To:
8800 Logistics Parkway
Mississauga, Ontario, L5S 1Y9

Invoice No.: INV-2025-0412
Invoice Date: April 12, 2025
Mode of Shipment: Sea Freight

Order Date: April 10, 2025
Export Date: April 15, 2025
Estimated Delivery Date: May 5, 2025

Item No.	Description	Quantity	Unit Price (USD)	Total Price (USD)
DN-BL001	Premium Cotton Bed Linen Set (Queen)	500 sets	$45.00	$22,500.00
DN-CV002	Microfiber Comforter (King)	300 pcs	$60.00	$18,000.00
			Subtotal	$40,500.00
	International Shipping Invoice		Freight Charges	$2,000.00
			Total Amount Due	$42,500.00

147. When is the purchase scheduled to arrive?

(A) On April 10
(B) On April 12
(C) On April 15
(D) On May 5

148. What is indicated on the invoice?

(A) The order was placed through a Web site.
(B) Payment will be due upon receiving the goods.
(C) Shipping costs are included in the total amount.
(D) The shipment is being sent to multiple locations.

To:	Administrative Staff
From:	Kenta Fujimoto
Date:	February 16
Subject:	Employee Data

As mentioned in the company-wide announcement sent out yesterday, the system used to store employee information has recently been upgraded. All staff members are required to send their most up-to-date résumé to empinfo@takora.com. Additionally, administrative personnel will soon be asked to complete a mandatory questionnaire seeking details about their technical abilities, including:

- Typing speed measured in words per minute

- Proficiency with software tools, such as spreadsheets, word processors, and database systems

If you're unsure of your typing speed and would like to take a timed assessment, please reach out to Lena Vogel at extension 822.

Sincerely,

Kenta Fujimoto
Administrative Manager
Takora Imports Ltd.

149. What is one purpose of the e-mail?

(A) To explain the reorganization of a department
(B) To introduce recently hired staff members
(C) To inform staff about technical training sessions
(D) To notify employees of new requirements

150. According to the e-mail, why might an employee need to get in touch with Ms. Vogel?

(A) To report technical issues
(B) To request a skill evaluation
(C) To inquire about available positions
(D) To schedule a meeting with a senior manager

Norwyn Pharmaceuticals

Norwyn Pharmaceuticals covers travel expenses when staff members are on official business trips. Employees are required to submit lodging requests to the Corporate Travel Department via the company's online travel portal. The form must list the employee's full name, the hotel name and contact information, the check-in and check-out dates, and the purpose for travel.

Once the reservation is finalized and paid for by the Corporate Travel Department, a confirmation number will be issued for the employee to present upon check-in. Although room charges are paid in advance, employees are expected to put any incidental expenses incurred during the trip on their own personal credit card. Employees can submit a reimbursement request for any out-of-pocket expenses after returning from the trip.

151. What is the policy about?

(A) Registering for an employee benefits program
(B) Making arrangements for corporate travel
(C) Applying for a different job assignment
(D) Arranging accommodations for company clients

152. Why must employees have a confirmation number?

(A) To replace a credit card
(B) To qualify for a reduced rate
(C) To eliminate unexpected costs
(D) To validate the hotel arrangement

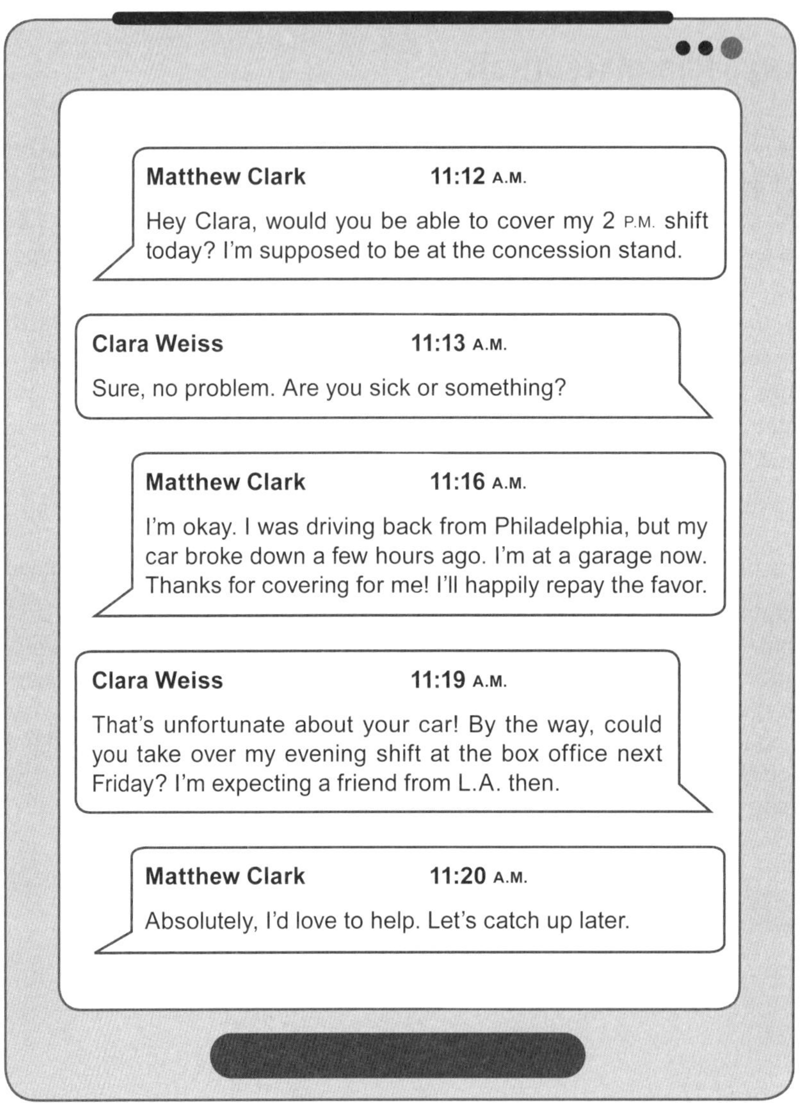

153. Where do Mr. Clark and Ms. Weiss most likely work?

(A) At a restaurant
(B) At a movie theater
(C) At a travel bureau
(D) At an auto repair shop

154. At 11:20 A.M., what does Mr. Clark mean when he writes, "I'd love to help"?

(A) He agrees to work Ms. Weiss's shift.
(B) He intends to cover the repair costs.
(C) He is available to see Ms. Weiss in the afternoon.
(D) He will endorse a request for sick leave.

Questions 155 through 157 refer to the following e-mail.

To:	Camila Navarro <cnavarro@letterly.com>
From:	Rakesh Solanki M <RSolanki@beyondtheresume.com>
Date:	6 November
Subject:	Job Opportunity Available

Dear Ms. Navarro,

We appreciate your decision to join Beyond the Résumé as a client. Our mission is to support you in finding a fulfilling career path. After reviewing the details you shared during our phone conversation, I have identified a job that may be a great fit for you. If the position outlined below interests you, please send me an e-mail today. That way, we can begin drafting a tailored cover letter to accompany your résumé and application.

Position: Office Assistant
Employer: Brookhaven Medical Group
Location: Brookhaven Township

Key Duties:
• Coordinate appointment scheduling
• Generate and send billing statements
• Input patient information into an electronic health records system

Best regards,

Rakesh Solanki, Career Counselor
Beyond the Résumé

155. Why did Mr. Solanki contact Ms. Navarro?

(A) To arrange a job interview
(B) To greet a newly hired worker
(C) To advertise his company's offerings
(D) To notify a client about a job opening

156. What does Mr. Solanki encourage Ms. Navarro to do?

(A) Update her résumé immediately
(B) Let him know her decision promptly
(C) Book a consultation with a physician
(D) Provide him with a list of references

157. What is NOT mentioned as a responsibility of the office assistant?

(A) Checking patients in upon arrival
(B) Mailing out invoices to patients
(C) Managing the calendar for patient visits
(D) Updating medical data

GO ON TO THE NEXT PAGE

PRIVATE SALE

This beautifully maintained 4-bedroom, 3-bathroom residence sits on a 2,400-square-foot elevated site overlooking the Botanical Gardens. It offers easy access to the Central Business District and is well connected to public transit. The interior has been completely renovated, featuring state-of-the-art appliances, brand-new flooring, and central air-conditioning. A detached, refurbished office building is also included on the premises. Private off-street parking is provided.

Property valuation (as of July): $349,000
No agents, please.
Listing ID: BH47219

---

158. What type of property is being advertised?

(A) A garden supply business
(B) A retail space
(C) An office complex
(D) A private house

159. Where is the property located?

(A) Adjacent to an industrial park
(B) Inside an apartment complex
(C) Close to the Botanical Gardens
(D) In a remote rural area

160. What can be inferred about the property?

(A) It is presently under contract.
(B) It may lack a parking garage.
(C) It is being sold via a real estate agency.
(D) Its asking price has been lowered.

Ocean Crest Faces Stormy Skies

by Michelle Ramirez

SAN DIEGO (8 February) - For years, tourists in the know have flocked to the iconic ship-shaped seafood restaurant perched along the historic wharf. —[1]—. Although the Ocean Crest building remains standing, its signature wooden entryway with circular porthole windows has been shuttered. All interior furnishings were auctioned off in October with demolition set to begin in the coming weeks. —[2]—.

However, things are not quite as they appear. Ocean Crest's manager, Daniel Morales, has struck a hard-earned deal with the property developer, Coastal Edge Properties, to reconstruct the restaurant at its current location. —[3]—. According to Mr. Morales, the developers opted to have the building torn down due to the extensive structural damage that would have required costly repairs.

—[4]—. While the rebuilt version will honor the original nautical theme, it will feature more modern architecture in line with Coastal Edge's insistence despite objections from Mr. Morales.

161. What is being reported?

(A) A restaurant has taken on a new name.
(B) A building has transitioned to new ownership.
(C) A ship is going to be reconstructed.
(D) A business intends to resume operations.

162. What does the article imply about Mr. Morales?

(A) He insisted on maintaining the original design.
(B) He is planning to exit the food industry.
(C) He is seeking a new business location.
(D) He converted a ship into a restaurant.

163. In which of the positions marked [1], [2], [3], and [4] does the following sentence best belong?

"Among the items sold was a scale model of the 120-year-old vessel that originally inspired the restaurant's layout."

(A) [1]
(B) [2]
(C) [3]
(D) [4]

GO ON TO THE NEXT PAGE

<table>
<tr><td>To:</td><td>All Staff <team@venturonet.com></td></tr>
<tr><td>From:</td><td>Julia Frankel <jfrankel@venturonet.com></td></tr>
<tr><td>Date:</td><td>November 3</td></tr>
<tr><td>Re:</td><td>Copy Machine Guidelines</td></tr>
</table>

Dear Team,

In an effort to preserve company resources and support eco-friendly practices, we kindly remind you to adhere to office guidelines when using the photocopier. Producing printed materials consumes paper, toner, and other supplies that impact the environment - and also incurs costs. Departments currently pay $0.05 per printed page, and frequent usage can quickly become expensive. To help reduce financial strain and environmental waste, please rely on digital formats whenever feasible.

If hard copies are genuinely required, limit copy machine use to 25 pages per batch. The machine is built for light-duty tasks, and attempting to produce high volumes can lead to wear and tear, increased service needs, and potential replacement expenses. For larger jobs, please submit a request through the Printing Center on the fifth floor. Paper-based order forms are no longer accepted - we now only process requests submitted via the online form available on the staff resources portal. If you need help with accessing the form, please reach out to your department's administrative assistant.

Thank you for your cooperation.

Regards,

Julia Frankel
Operations Coordinator

164. Why did Ms. Frankel send the e-mail?

(A) To inform employees about higher photocopying fees
(B) To introduce a new floor plan for the Printing Center
(C) To remind staff of the current copying policies
(D) To outline repair details for the copy machine

165. What is NOT mentioned as a reason for restricting the number of paper copies?

(A) Minimizing the environmental footprint
(B) Controlling departmental expenses
(C) Improving how quickly documents are distributed
(D) Preventing damage to the machine over time

166. According to the e-mail, when should orders be requested through the Printing Center?

(A) When more than 25 pages are needed
(B) When documents are for future use
(C) When the assistant is unavailable
(D) When the copier requires service

167. How should printing requests be submitted?

(A) Through a phone call to the administrative assistant
(B) By filling out a online form
(C) With a paper order slip
(D) In person at the Printing Center

It is widely understood that Yiran Chen's latest title, *Strategic Risk: Unlocking Potential in Business* (264 pages, Meridian Insight Press, $24.50), was crafted with recent college graduates in mind. The publisher has clearly positioned the book toward younger readers, and its introductory material is geared toward that demographic. Still, the principles elucidated by Ms. Chen resonate with many a well-established business executive. —[1]—. The basic premise of the book is that individuals must be open to smart risk-taking to reach their full potential. As someone who founded and runs a prominent branding agency, I can personally attest to this philosophy.

Learning to embrace risk was not something I mastered instantly. —[2]—. Early in my career, I stuck firmly to my comfort zone and avoided ventures that lacked predictable outcomes. Over time, I came to see that this cautious approach was effectively restricting my company's ability to grow. —[3]—. Only after I began evaluating new ventures carefully and stopped fearing occasional setbacks did my company evolve into the multimillion-dollar enterprise it is today. It was the very shift in thinking that made all the difference, but it took me years to understand.

That is why I am especially glad Ms. Chen is introducing this mindset to the next generation of business leaders. —[4]—. Across eleven thoughtfully written chapters, Ms. Chen showcases the journeys of well-known business figures. Each section ends with reflective prompts that encourage readers to examine their own degree of risk aversion. The final chapter offers a compelling framework for approaching uncertainty with maturity - a message equally valuable to both seasoned professionals and newcomers alike. For me, the book was a timely refresher of insights I have accumulated over the years.

- Anton Becker

168. What is suggested about Mr. Becker in the review?

(A) He does not belong to the group Ms. Chen primarily targeted.
(B) He regularly collects and reviews business-related books.
(C) He works at the same academic institution Ms. Chen graduated from.
(D) He has launched multiple prosperous companies.

169. What does Mr. Becker say is a reason for his own company's growth?

(A) His openness to taking strategic risks
(B) His networking approach within the industry
(C) His emphasis on building a strong brand reputation
(D) His ability to secure outside investment

170. Why does Mr. Becker appreciate Ms. Chen's book?

(A) It inspired him to pursue a new professional path.
(B) It encouraged him to aim for more ambitious goals.
(C) It reaffirmed lessons he gained through experience.
(D) It changed how he measures company achievements.

171. In which of the positions marked [1], [2], [3], and [4] does the following sentence best belong?

"Even worse, my inaction was also making way for more aggressive competitors to dominate the industry landscape."

(A) [1]
(B) [2]
(C) [3]
(D) [4]

GO ON TO THE NEXT PAGE

Leila Demir, 7:45 A.M.

Good morning, team. Once again, when I arrived at the shop early today, all the lights were already on. Has anyone figured out why this keeps happening?

Marco Russo, 7:48 A.M.

I activated the timer just before locking up yesterday afternoon. The lights were supposed to switch off at 5:15 P.M.

Catalina Esparza, 7:51 A.M.

I drove past the store after leaving the post office around 5:40, and I noticed the lights were off.

Leila Demir, 7:53 A.M.

Thanks. Since this has happened every morning for the past three days, it's pretty clear the timer isn't working properly.

Minho Park, 7:54 A.M.

Marco and I both left around 4:45, and I saw him adjust the timer before we exited.

Marco Russo, 8:00 A.M.

You're right - the lights seem to be switching back on earlier than they're supposed to. I'll call BrightFix Electric as soon as I get in for my shift.

Leila Demir, 8:05 A.M.

Please get in touch with the company that installed the system. Their paperwork should be stored in one of the filing drawers. In the meantime, whoever's closing will need to manually switch off each light.

Minho Park, 8:07 A.M.

Yes, I remember filing their invoice back when the installation was done.

Marco Russo, 8:08 A.M.

Got it. I'll take care of it.

172. What is most likely true about Ms. Demir?

(A) She works at a local post office.
(B) She has a flexible work schedule.
(C) She lives close to the shop.
(D) She handles the morning opening shift.

173. Who was the last person to confirm that the shop lights were off?

(A) Ms. Demir
(B) Mr. Russo
(C) Ms. Esparza
(D) Mr. Park

174. At 8:00 A.M., what does Mr. Russo most likely mean when he writes, "You're right"?

(A) He believes that the timer needs to be repaired.
(B) He plans to follow Ms. Demir's instructions about the filing cabinet.
(C) He trusts BrightFix Electric to fix the issue.
(D) He recalls that Mr. Park observed him setting the timer.

175. What is the first thing Mr. Russo will most likely do when he arrives at work?

(A) Make a payment
(B) Install replacement lighting
(C) Complete installation paperwork
(D) Look through some filing drawers

GO ON TO THE NEXT PAGE

Naomi Feldstein
Wexford Steelworks Ltd.
14 Glenmere Close
Dunbridge DN3 8QW

Dear Ms. Feldstein,

The Dunbridge Leisure and Recreation Committee is once again organizing the Shine Dunbridge 8K Fun Run, which will take place on 26 July. Thanks to your company's generosity last year, we raised £21,000, which was used to resurface several pedestrian areas throughout town. This year, our fundraising goal is £24,000, which will be directed toward building new sports courts in Dunbridge's parks.

We're offering four sponsorship packages, each with distinct benefits. Tier 1 requires a contribution of £200, which includes your company logo printed on the back of every race T-shirt. For £400 (Tier 2), your company name will also appear on signage at the starting and ending points. If you commit £800 (Tier 3), your logo will be displayed in all our printed advertisements and event flyers. Lastly, Tier 4 sponsorship, priced at £1,600, includes all previous benefits plus a branded tent space in Hillgrove Park, where the race kicks off.

Please notify me by 2 June regarding your chosen tier. You'll find further details at www.dunbridge.gov.uk/leisure/shinedunbridge. We sincerely appreciate your ongoing support of the Dunbridge community.

Best regards,

David J. Ferreira

To:	Celine Morrison
From:	David Ferreira
Date:	30 May
Subject:	Race Planning Update
Attachment:	📎 WexfordSteelworks_Logo.png

Dear Celine,

I've just received confirmation from Wexford Steelworks. Please add the attached logo image to the printing template for the race T-shirts. Also, Ms. Feldstein asked for the measurements of her company's tent at Hillgrove Park. I'm nearly certain Mr. Desai would know - could you check with him?

We've now heard back from most of the other sponsors. I'll send you the finalized list on 3 June. Meanwhile, could you reach out to a few print vendors for quotes? We'll need twelve 1.5-by-3 metre vinyl banners, thirty-five A2-sized full-colour posters, 250 A4 full-colour flyers, and 600 A4 black-and-white flyers.

Thanks,

David

176. Who most likely is Mr. Ferreira?

(A) A financial consultant
(B) A business owner in Dunbridge
(C) A manager at a print shop
(D) An employee of the city government

177. What is indicated about the race?

(A) A similar event occurred the previous
year.
(B) Only Dunbridge residents are allowed
to enter.
(C) It covers a distance shorter than 3
kilometers.
(D) It will be held on the June 2.

178. Which sponsorship level did Ms. Feldstein
probably agree to?

(A) Tier 1
(B) Tier 2
(C) Tier 3
(D) Tier 4

179. In the e-mail, the word "nearly" in
paragraph 1, line 3, is closest in meaning
to

(A) least
(B) almost
(C) seldom
(D) closely

180. What is one task Mr. Ferreira asked Ms.
Morrison to take care of?

(A) Reserve a promotional tent space
(B) Obtain price estimates from vendors
(C) Place a bulk T-shirt order
(D) Create designs for outdoor signage

GO ON TO THE NEXT PAGE

To:	Zenetron staff
From:	Ingrid Mehta <imehta@pulseinsightgroup.com>
Date:	Thursday, July 7
Subject:	Staff Survey Invitation
Attachment:	Survey Form

Dear Zenetron employees:

Pulse Insight Group, an independent analytics firm based here in Westfield, has been hired by Zenetron to administer a workplace feedback survey. This brief survey includes roughly twenty questions pertaining to topics such as office culture, employee benefits, workspaces, and career development options. Please take a moment to share your honest thoughts.

Responses will remain anonymous-Pulse Insight will not identify your answers by name, and supervisors at Zenetron will not see any individual submissions. However, note that the optional remarks section on the final page will be combined into a single file for management review. If you choose to write a comment and prefer to stay anonymous, avoid mentioning any personal details that may reveal your identity. Also, do not forward this e-mail to others, since each version contains a unique code that prevents duplicate submissions from one individual.

If you have questions or concerns, feel free to reply directly to this message.

Ingrid Mehta
Pulse Insight Group

To:	Zenetron staff
From:	Rafi Qureshi
Date:	Friday, October 14
Subject:	Great News to Share!

Yesterday, the *Westfield Gazette* released its latest rankings titled "Best Workplaces in Westfield," and Zenetron proudly earned number 4 on the list! Out of 180 companies reviewed by a local assessment firm, only 12 were selected for recognition.

We are thrilled to have received this honor-especially since the results stem from the staff survey many of you completed a few months ago. It is amazing to see how much you value your experience at Zenetron, and we truly appreciate all you do to make our company an outstanding place to work.

As you are aware, we will be launching a major recruiting campaign next quarter, so this accolade comes at the perfect time. With this public recognition, we anticipate strong interest among potential candidates before the year wraps up.

Rafi Qureshi
Director of Marketing, Zenetron

181. What is the purpose of the survey mentioned in Ms. Mehta's e-mail?

(A) To evaluate the impact of new workplace policies
(B) To support the development of an advertising campaign
(C) To gather ideas for upcoming product lines
(D) To assess employees' opinions about their work environment

182. What does Ms. Mehta suggest about survey comments?

(A) Every employee is required to submit one.
(B) They will be tied to the names of respondents.
(C) Zenetron supervisors will receive them.
(D) Feedback will be individually mailed to each participant.

183. According to the first e-mail, what should survey recipients avoid doing?

(A) Sending the survey to other team members
(B) Talking about survey content with coworkers
(C) Saving copies on personal devices
(D) Reaching out to Ms. Mehta with questions

184. What is implied about Pulse Insight Group?

(A) It employs the most staff in Westfield.
(B) It was created in the last year.
(C) It works in multiple regional markets.
(D) It issues ratings for many companies.

185. According to Mr. Qureshi, what does Zenetron plan to do in the near future?

(A) Attract new customers
(B) Win more corporate awards
(C) Grow its workforce
(D) Conduct more employee surveys

GO ON TO THE NEXT PAGE

City Chef Wows Crowd

by Gianni Rhee-Kwan

PORTSMONT (24 October)—Last night at Brisa Bistro, a central dining venue, hometown chef Matteo Van der Meer led a live cooking demonstration for a rapt audience. "The event went exceptionally well," said Brisa Bistro proprietor Erin Park. "We sold every seat, and our guests were thoroughly impressed."

Mr. Van der Meer sold his Portsmont restaurant, Matteo's, earlier this summer, and has since taken part in guest chef events at various eateries around the city. "It's refreshing to work without the day-to-day responsibilities of ownership," said Mr. Van der Meer. "I'm enjoying the chance to discover new neighborhoods and engage with different diners."

Details about upcoming appearances can be found at his Web site: www.matteovandermeer.com.

To:	Matteo Van der Meer <matteo@matteovandermeer.com>
From:	Sophie Hanley <sophie.hanley@eletterbox.com>
Re:	Guest Spot Request
Date:	27 October

Dear Mr. Van der Meer,

My name is Sophie Hanley, and I own both Hanley's Table on Riverstone Avenue and Oakwood Eatery on Millcrest Lane. I attended your recent demonstration at Brisa Bistro and was very impressed, to say the least. I am wondering if you'd be available to make a guest appearance at Oakwood Eatery sometime in March or April.

My sister Natalie, who manages a local promotions agency, could help us secure strong visibility and draw in an engaged crowd. We're flexible with scheduling, so please let me know if you'd be interested.

Sincerely,
Sophie Hanley
sophie.hanley@eletterbox.com / (778)-555-8032

To:	Sophie Hanley <sophie.hanley@eletterbox.com>
From:	Matteo Van der Meer <matteo@matteovandermeer.com>
Re:	RE: Guest Spot Request
Date:	28 October

Dear Sophie,

Thank you for your message. I am currently fully booked for both March and April, but I do have a slot open on February 22, which recently became available following a cancellation. If that date would work for your team, I'd be glad to discuss the program and logistics in more detail.

Best regards,

Matteo Van der Meer

186. Who is Ms. Park?

(A) A local journalist
(B) A culinary demonstrator
(C) A restaurant owner
(D) A marketing specialist

187. What is the purpose of Ms. Hanley's e-mail to Mr. Van der Meer?

(A) To apply for a position
(B) To recommend a dining location
(C) To respond to an inquiry
(D) To extend an invitation

188. According to the first e-mail, how did Ms. Hanley learn about Mr. Van der Meer's skills?

(A) She watched one of his demonstrations.
(B) She dined at his former restaurant.
(C) She read an online profile about him.
(D) She saw a print advertisement.

189. Why is Ms. Hanley's sister Natalie mentioned in the first e-mail?

(A) To compliment Mr. Van der Meer's establishment
(B) To suggest that her sister's expertise might be beneficial
(C) To identify who purchased Mr. Van der Meer's restaurant
(D) To imply that her sister's article has provided excellent publicity

190. Where might Mr. Van der Meer perform on February 22?

(A) Matteo's
(B) Brisa Bistro
(C) Hanley's Table
(D) Oakwood Eatery

GO ON TO THE NEXT PAGE

From:	Linnea Haddad
To:	Marketing Department, Barrington Institute of Culinary Arts
Date:	22 February
Subject:	Meeting Summary

Hello Team,

Below is a brief recap of yesterday's meeting discussion:

- Enrollment figures in our professional chef training program continue on an upward trend. Based on student zip codes, it is clear that our outreach to a wider geographic base has paid off. Over 42 percent of new enrollees live 30 or more miles away from the campus. That is a 12 percent increase from last year.

- Conversely, our recreational cooking programs have seen a dip in participation recently. Delphine is working on a digital feedback survey to share with past attendees. Once we gain insight into their current preferences, we will revise the course lineup to suit them.

Our upcoming marketing team meeting is set for 1:30 P.M. next Wednesday.

Linnea

SURVEY

To be entered into a drawing for a free cooking class, please provide your contact information:

Name: Olivia Klein   E-mail address: oklein@vmailer.org

Please select the response that BEST represents your preference:

1. What area of cooking interests you most?
☐ Core cooking methods and skills
☐ Food associated with particular regions
☑ Ingredient handling and usage

2. What might encourage you to sign up for a Barrington Institute class this year?
☐ Reduced course fees
☑ Online course availability
☐ Better scheduling options on site

http://www.barringtonculinaryarts.org

| Home | Chef Certification | **Hobbyist Cooking Classes** | Contact Us |

Early Summer Class Schedule

Essential Kitchen Skills
Just getting started in the kitchen? This foundational course offers hands-on training to help sharpen your knife skills and master cooking basics like roasting, sautéing, and grilling.
June 4–8, 10:00 A.M.–4:00 P.M. $540

NEW! Flavors of the Sea with Renowned Chef Helena Fujimoto
Take a deep dive into seafood cuisine with celebrated culinary expert Helena Fujimoto. Discover preparation methods, flavor pairings, and cooking styles across various regions. All proficiency levels welcome.
June 11–12, 10:00 A.M.–4:00 P.M. $330

Tastes of South America
Spend the day uncovering traditional dishes from Brazil, Peru, Argentina, Colombia, and Chile. Learn classic recipes and new ways to infuse Latin American flair into your cooking. Intermediate and advanced learners only.
June 17, 10:00 A.M.–2:30 P.M. $170

NEW! Global Egg Inspirations
Eggs go far beyond breakfast! In this online-only course, explore their nutritional benefits and cultural versatility through internationally inspired egg-based recipes.
Available starting June 19. $120

---

191. According to the e-mail, what is indicated about the professional training program?

(A) It changed campus locations recently.
(B) It will increase remote learning options.
(C) It has attracted more students lately.
(D) It plans to create a brand-new marketing strategy.

192. In the e-mail, the word "suit" in paragraph 3, line 3, is closest in meaning to

(A) contact
(B) dress
(C) satisfy
(D) flatter

193. What can be inferred about Ms. Klein?

(A) She wants to become a certified professional chef.
(B) She attended a previous cooking class at the institute.
(C) She received a free pass for a culinary class.
(D) She lives farther from the campus than most participants.

194. Which summer class would Ms. Klein most likely be interested in taking?

(A) Essential Kitchen Skills
(B) Flavors of the Sea with Helena Fujimoto
(C) Tastes of South America
(D) Global Egg Inspirations

195. What is NOT true about the class offerings?

(A) All courses are for experienced chefs.
(B) Courses vary in length.
(C) Some courses are being offered for the first time.
(D) One class features a famous culinary instructor.

GO ON TO THE NEXT PAGE

http://www.norwellupholstery.com/product_guide ▶

| Home | **Product Guide** | Place Order | DIY Advice |

Norwell Upholstery Supply

At Norwell Upholstery Supply, we offer a wide selection of cushion foam, available in a variety of densities and price ranges. This handy product guide outlines our four top-rated items to help you select the one that best aligns with your project.

- F10 – Extremely soft. Highly plush but tends to lose its shape and flatten over time. Ideal for items that see infrequent use.
- F20 – Soft. Budget-friendly choice, though less resilient than higher-density options. Becomes softer with continued use.
- F30 – Medium firmness. Our most popular option. Slightly costlier, yet offers excellent comfort, long-term durability, and stands up to frequent use.
- F40 – Very firm. Perfect for dining seating or projects that demand dense support.

Caution: All polyurethane foam products are highly flammable when exposed to open flames.

Custom cutting: Foam is supplied in standard sheet sizes, but shaping it to suit your needs is straightforward. See our instructional video under the "DIY Advice" tab.

Customer Inquiry Form

| **Name:** Hanna Tovarek | **E-mail:** h_tovarek@inboxlane.org | **Phone:** 628-555-0914 |

Message:

I'm renovating a vintage couch and need replacement foam for the cushions. I'm not sure which type to select. I don't want it too stiff, but I also don't want something that sinks too easily. A mid-range firmness sounds ideal. Price isn't really a concern—I'm more focused on longevity, since the couch will get plenty of use. I'd appreciate your guidance. Thank you!

"Norwell has earned my loyalty."
★★★★

If you need high-quality foam for couch cushions, I suggest Norwell Upholstery Supply. As a novice seamstress, I didn't know which kind of padding was best for my upholstery project. The staff at Norwell were incredibly supportive and well-informed, which made the process much easier.

My couch had an unusual shape, but the company's Web site offered all the tools and guidance I needed to tackle those tricky aspects. Just note that Norwell doesn't accommodate custom size orders, so be ready to cut the foam sheets yourself. I only make these purchases occasionally, but Norwell is now my go-to.

Hanna Tovarek (Maple Ridge)

196. On the Web page, what is indicated about Norwell Upholstery Supply's products?

(A) They are considered higher quality than competitors'.
(B) They can catch fire if exposed to heat.
(C) They are often hard to restock.
(D) They are intended primarily for mattresses.

197. What foam type was likely recommended to Ms. Tovarek?

(A) F10
(B) F20
(C) F30
(D) F40

198. What is probably true about Ms. Tovarek?

(A) She operates a home furnishings business.
(B) She asked for a sample of foam material.
(C) She received promotional pricing on an order.
(D) She viewed a tutorial video online.

199. According to the online review, what does Ms. Tovarek appreciate most about Norwell Upholstery Supply?

(A) Their wide range of products
(B) Their efficient shipping system
(C) Their attentive and knowledgeable staff
(D) Their competitive pricing

200. In the online review, the word "accommodate" in paragraph 2, line 2, is closest in meaning to

(A) agree to
(B) make space for
(C) give a refund for
(D) provide lodging to

This is the end of the test. If you finish before time is called, you may go back to Parts 5, 6, and 7 and check your work.

정답 및 해설 p.86

TEST 04

READING TEST

In this Reading test, various texts will be provided for you to read, followed by multiple types of reading comprehension questions. The total duration for the test is 75 minutes. It consists of three parts, with instructions provided at the beginning of each part. You are encouraged to attempt as many questions as you can within the given time.

Make sure to mark your answers on the separate answer sheet. Do not write your answers in your test book.

PART 5

Directions: In the sentences below, a word or phrase is missing. You will find four options below each sentence. Choose the most appropriate answer to fill in the blank, and then mark the letter (A), (B), (C), or (D) on your answer sheet.

101. Trenton Dynamics successfully met its recruitment goals for the third ------- year.

(A) following
(B) consecutive
(C) approximate
(D) absolute

102. To cut down on -------, Eloria Skincare has decided to halve its promotional spending.

(A) values
(B) expenses
(C) customs
(D) refunds

103. Mr. Harris has chosen to lease an apartment for the ------- of his assignment in Liverpool.

(A) collection
(B) duration
(C) capacity
(D) environment

104. The revised proposal was far more detailed ------- the original, especially in its financial projections.

(A) as
(B) than
(C) of
(D) from

105. Ms. Sharma intends to ------- certain terms in her employment contract prior to finalizing the paperwork.

(A) deprive
(B) respond
(C) modify
(D) assure

106. ------- your application has been approved, the bank will deposit the funds into your account.

(A) Although
(B) As soon as
(C) Thereafter
(D) How

107. Mr. Jang has been promoted to Executive Director of Marketing and ------- his new role on April 15.

(A) remains
(B) concerns
(C) assumes
(D) participates

108. Scientists must verify that any modifications to the research setting are not ------- to the experiment.

(A) disrupt
(B) disrupted
(C) disruptive
(D) disrupter

109. Consultants at Virelli Group collaborate with business owners to create ------- marketing strategies.

(A) unavailable
(B) innovative
(C) resolved
(D) convinced

110. Adopting cloud-based accounting tools would streamline Veltrix Solutions' fiscal operations -------.

(A) substantial
(B) substantially
(C) more substantial
(D) substances

111. Earlier this month, the board members voted ------- to implement a new incentive plan for top performers.

(A) commonly
(B) increasingly
(C) critically
(D) unanimously

112. The acclaimed literary publication *Meridian Journal* regularly highlights both seasoned and ------- authors.

(A) emerge
(B) emerging
(C) emerges
(D) to emerge

113. The company welcomes candidate submissions, ------- whether they have worked in digital commerce before.

(A) regardless of
(B) despite that
(C) except for
(D) considering that

114. Due to unforeseen logistical complications, the launch of the new satellite was ------- behind schedule.

(A) marginal
(B) marginally
(C) margin
(D) marginalize

115. Ms. Huang's transition to director of product innovation was finalized more ------- than the company had expected.

(A) partially
(B) ultimately
(C) adequately
(D) swiftly

116. By evaluating the ------- of the equipment in desert terrain, the engineers confirmed its reliability under harsh conditions.

(A) enduring
(B) endurance
(C) endures
(D) endure

117. Many job seekers submit applications to Dentra Solutions because it provides ------- opportunities for career advancement.

(A) outgrown
(B) outlying
(C) outstretched
(D) outstanding

118. ------- of lacquered hardwood materials, these coat racks offer both strength and eco-friendly appeal.

(A) Made
(B) Making
(C) To make
(D) They are made

119. Ms. Takahashi's supervisors believe she deserves special ------- for her achievements during the recent sales initiative.

(A) recognition
(B) accomplishment
(C) capability
(D) balance

120. Mr. Novak has the qualifications required and so has appointed ------- to the Bravell Partners negotiations.

(A) he
(B) his
(C) him
(D) himself

GO ON TO THE NEXT PAGE

121. ------- a downturn in the economy, the automotive sector achieved a 17 percent increase in revenue this year.

(A) Except
(B) Toward
(C) Pending
(D) Despite

122. In her debut business venture, Olympic medalist Dana Whitaker launched ------- brand of athletic footwear for women.

(A) her own
(B) she
(C) hers
(D) herself

123. Linton General Hospital's finance office is available to ------- any inquiries you may have about your invoice.

(A) address
(B) respond
(C) attend
(D) appeal

124. Brighttel sales representatives are ------- to learn about competitors' products and their promotional strategies.

(A) encourage
(B) encourages
(C) encouraged
(D) encouraging

125. Use our editing software ------- features allow users to produce illustrations with professional-level precision.

(A) whom
(B) which
(C) whose
(D) that

126. Management was notified yesterday that the arrival of the shipment sent to the Seoul office ------- due to a customs issue.

(A) being delayed
(B) would be delayed
(C) has been delayed
(D) have delayed

127. ------- acknowledging their financial intentions, individuals should submit thorough documentation to their financial advisor.

(A) In addition to
(B) Provided that
(C) In order to
(D) So that

128. Most of the equipment in the storage room, along with several outdated monitors, ------- still in good condition despite years of use.

(A) is
(B) are
(C) being
(D) have been

129. Naomi Tanaka, a leading authority in sustainable land development, will serve as the ------- speaker at the Seventh Agroforestry Symposium.

(A) successive
(B) principal
(C) maximum
(D) immediate

130. Recent studies show that a growing number of individuals are taking up video production and editing as an ------- for expressing their creativity.

(A) entry
(B) outcome
(C) outlet
(D) obstacle

PART 6

Directions: Review the following texts. In certain sections, there is a missing word, phrase, or sentence. Each question includes four possible answers provided below the text. Choose the most appropriate answer to fill in the blank, and then mark the letter (A), (B), (C), or (D) on your answer sheet.

Questions 131 through 134 refer to the following product review.

I was ------- to try powdered milk, as I doubted it would taste anything like fresh milk.
131.
However, when my neighborhood grocery store ran out of regular milk last week, I opted to

give Lunara Milk a shot. I was ------- surprised.
132.

-------. Eventually, I used a high-speed blender and prepared a larger batch. This method
133.
requires additional time, but the result is a smooth and flavorful milk. I would absolutely

recommend -------, even with the extra steps involved.
134.

I will probably purchase fresh milk on my next shopping trip, but I will make sure to keep

some Lunara Milk stocked at home. Unlike fresh milk, it can be stored for years without

refrigeration.

— Marisol Delgado

131. (A) hesitated
(B) hesitant
(C) hesitates
(D) hesitation

132. (A) rarely
(B) remotely
(C) probably
(D) pleasantly

133. (A) I will not repeat that error in the future.
(B) A bigger grocery store might have offered more choices.
(C) Achieving the ideal texture was tricky at first.
(D) Lunara Milk works well as a substitute in many dishes.

134. (A) it
(B) several
(C) them
(D) some

GO ON TO THE NEXT PAGE

A forthcoming analysis from the National Farming Outlook Council forecasts that soy output is expected to decline next year for the first time in two decades. -------, grain yields are
135.
projected to rise. Industry specialists familiar with the findings say the primary drivers of these

------- are newly imposed regulations and recent breakthroughs in agricultural technology.
136.
-------. Soy prices could skyrocket, while abundant grain supplies help stabilize the cost of
137.
wheat, corn, and rice. Some market observers believe that an ------- shift toward soy
138.
alternatives will soon become evident.

135. (A) To summarize
(B) For example
(C) In contrast
(D) Likewise

136. (A) purchases
(B) decisions
(C) tractors
(D) changes

137. (A) Shoppers may soon notice the impact at checkout counters.
(B) The Council was financially supported by multiple eco-focused organizations.
(C) Agricultural machinery costs have surged significantly in recent years.
(D) Nutrition experts advocate for a varied eating pattern.

138. (A) anticipation
(B) anticipating
(C) anticipated
(D) anticipate

To: Daniela Ruiz <druiz@solsticekitchen.com>

From: Julian Ortega <jortega@auroradininggroup.com>

Re: Assistant Chef Opportunity

Date: August 11

Dear Ms. Ruiz,

We appreciate your interest in and interview for the Assistant Chef role at Aurora Dining Group. We were surprised by the volume of applications we received. -------, we chose to meet **139.** with seven candidates in total. Ultimately, we selected an exceptionally experienced chef ------- several prestigious culinary awards. **140.**

-------. We are eager to reconnect with you about another opportunity in our kitchen team. **141.**

If you are -------, feel free to reach me at 646-555-7824, or simply reply to this message. **142.** Thank you.

Julian Ortega

---

139. (A) Instead
(B) As a result
(C) On the contrary
(D) In the meantime

140. (A) that is receiving
(B) the reception of
(C) who has received
(D) whose reception is

141. (A) That said, we were genuinely impressed by your qualifications.
(B) Our culinary team had been excited to meet you.
(C) Additionally, we are planning updates to our dining space.
(D) We will soon be introducing new items to our food selection.

142. (A) worried
(B) occupied
(C) interested
(D) determined

To: All Staff <staff@lexfordglobal.com>

From: Fatima Elmasry <f.elmasry@lexfordglobal.com>

Date: October 3

Subject: Mandatory Training Session

To All Staff:

Ongoing developments in technology ------- continuous challenges in handling our **143.** organization's information. At Lexford Global Counsel, we are committed to protecting ------- **144.** our internal data and the sensitive information of our clients. That is why we have teamed up with SecureSphere, a top-rated data protection company based in Africa. They will be conducting this ------- training, and all staff members have already been registered. The **145.** more informed we are, the more secure and, ultimately, more effective we become.

Please set aside 60 minutes to complete the training, which must be finished by November 15. -------. **146.**

Best regards,

Fatima Elmasry

Director of Information Technology

---

143. (A) present
(B) to present
(C) are presented
(D) presenting

144. (A) either
(B) both
(C) not only
(D) as though

145. (A) financial
(B) fitness
(C) security
(D) electrical

146. (A) Participation in this session is entirely voluntary for each team member.
(B) Your involvement will help our Web site appear more inviting to visitors.
(C) You will soon get an e-mail with a link to begin the training module.
(D) Our prosperity depends on how well we make use of the data we gather.

PART 7

Directions: In this part, you will read a variety of texts, such as magazine and newspaper articles, e-mails, and instant messages. Each text or set of texts is followed by a series of questions. Choose the most appropriate answer and mark the letter (A), (B), (C), or (D) on your answer sheet.

Questions 147 through 148 refer to the following text message.

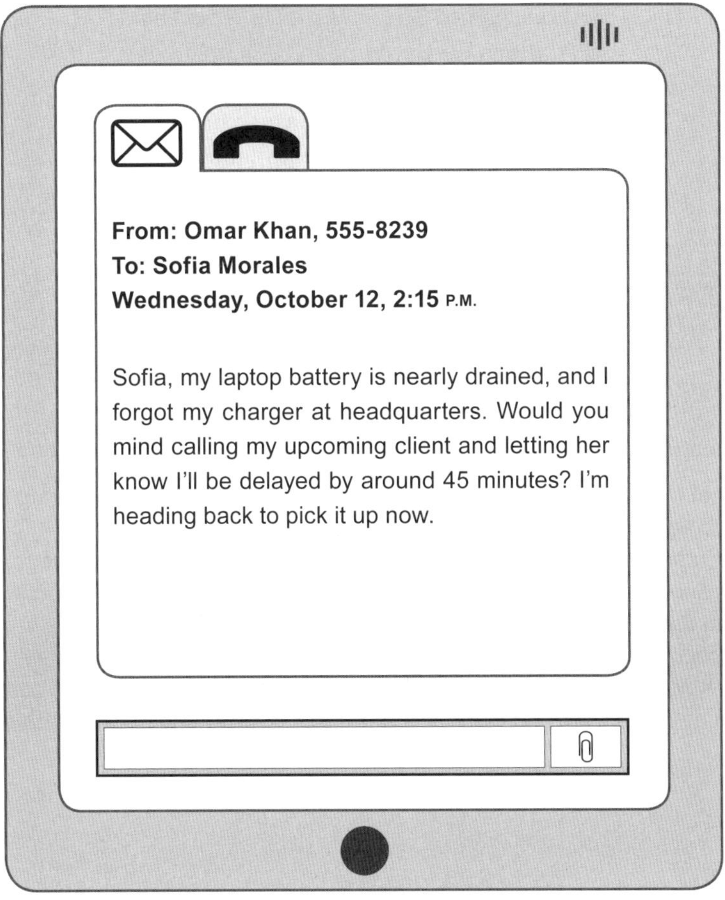

147. Why did Mr. Khan send the text message to Ms. Morales?

(A) To check whether his charger was located
(B) To ask her to contact a customer
(C) To remind her to plug in a device
(D) To verify the location of a meeting

148. What will Mr. Khan probably do next?

(A) Search for his computer
(B) Return to his workplace
(C) Purchase a new charger
(D) Contact technical support

GO ON TO THE NEXT PAGE

City Highlights

The owner of Golden Leaf Café, Lucia Delgado, has finalized a lease for a second dining location at 318 Maple Avenue. The site, adjacent to Orion Playhouse, previously housed a branch of Crescent Bank. Her new venture, named Soluna Bistro, is set to begin operations on September 12. Initially, the bistro will only be open in the evenings. The goal is to build a customer base—particularly among theatergoers—before launching a lunch menu. Ms. Delgado's first successful eatery, Golden Leaf Café, is situated on Riverbend Road, near the Eastwood Farmers' Market bus stop. Head Chef Rafael Costa will manage both establishments.

149. What is the purpose of the article?

(A) To highlight the achievements of a real estate agent
(B) To inform readers about the launch of a new business
(C) To explain the relocation of a dining establishment
(D) To share news about a business changing ownership

150. What is indicated about Soluna Bistro?

(A) It will begin offering lunch service on September 12.
(B) It is located close to a public transportation route.
(C) It is Ms. Delgado's first venture in the restaurant industry.
(D) It aims to attract customers who attend nearby theater shows.

Questions 151 through 153 refer to the following memo.

To: All staff at Strathmore Design Studio
From: Douglas Fairchild, Senior Partner
Re: Upcoming All-Staff Meeting
Date: 5 April

To All Staff,

On Thursday, 11 April, we will be welcoming a special guest to our all-staff meeting in room 407. Anja Lindström, a senior architect at Vestergaard & Co. in Oslo, will be joining us. She has been with the firm for the past six years, and she led the design of Nordhavn Pavilion in Oslo as well as the Sundström Tower in Helsinki. Both structures have received international recognition for their sleek and innovative architecture. Before making a name for herself in Scandinavia, Ms. Lindström spent ten years working in Chicago at Morrison & Tate Architecture. It was during her time at Morrison & Tate that I had the opportunity to collaborate with her on several notable projects. Ms. Lindström will be visiting us here in York next week and has kindly agreed to speak at our meeting about some of her internationally acclaimed design work. We strongly urge all staff to attend.

151. What does the memo discuss?

(A) Plans to launch a new office location
(B) The hiring of a new employee
(C) Recommendations for a design proposal
(D) An architect's professional accomplishments

152. What does Mr. Fairchild mention about Ms. Lindström?

(A) She will contribute to one of his firm's upcoming projects.
(B) She is preparing to establish her own company.
(C) She is a former colleague of his.
(D) She is in the process of relocating to a different city.

153. Where is Strathmore Design Studio based?

(A) In York
(B) In Chicago
(C) In Helsinki
(D) In Oslo

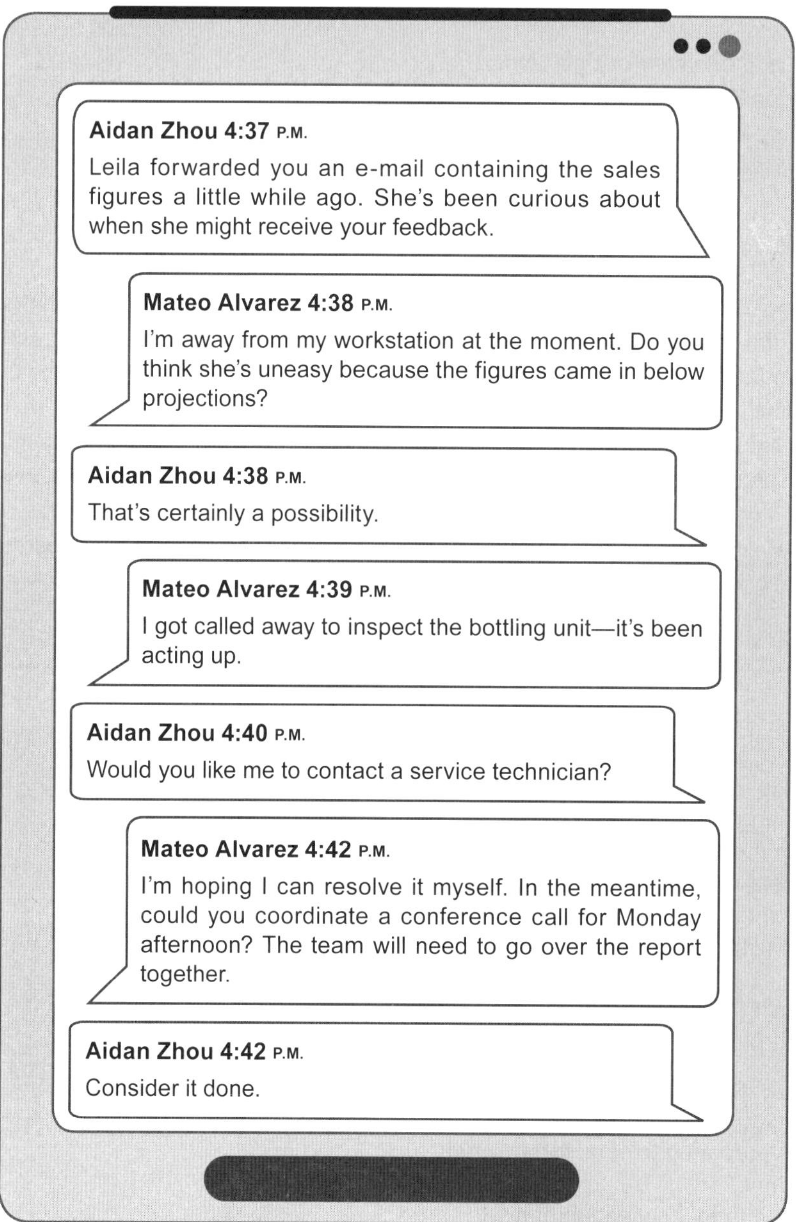

154. At 4:38 P.M., what does Mr. Alvarez most likely mean when he writes, "I'm away from my workstation at the moment"?

(A) He has already left for the day.
(B) He will be unable to attend a scheduled meeting.
(C) He is currently in Mr. Zhou's office.
(D) He is not in a position to reply to Leila at the moment.

155. What task is Mr. Zhou asked to do?

(A) Examine some documentation
(B) Organize a team meeting
(C) Finalize travel arrangements
(D) Troubleshoot a piece of machinery

Questions 156 through 158 refer to the following letter.

Marisol Art Gallery
78 Coral Vista Drive
Kingston KN 07
www.marisolgallery.jm

17 January

Mr. Malik Bennett
22 Pelican Bay Road
Montego Bay MB 03
Jamaica

Dear Mr. Bennett:

As a valued member of the Marisol Art Gallery, you will soon be able to enjoy the benefits of our Member Appreciation Month promotions. —[1]—. From 1 to 28 February, members will receive an additional 15 percent discount on all items in the gift shop. Members will also be treated to a complimentary coffee or tea with any meal purchased in the café. Furthermore, those who register as first-time members by 28 February will receive a 10 percent reduction on their membership fee. —[2]—. We encourage you to invite your friends to visit our Web site and enroll.

—[3]—. Each Saturday evening during the month, our third-floor galleries—normally closed to the public—will be open until 8:30 P.M. These galleries showcase sculptures and paintings by contemporary Jamaican artists. Selected pieces from these collections can also be viewed online.

—[4]—. We look forward to welcoming you soon.

Warm regards,

Tiana Morgan

Tiana Morgan
Director of Member Services

156. What is true about the Marisol Art Gallery facility?

(A) It includes a restaurant.
(B) It will be closed for a month.
(C) It will feature photographic exhibits.
(D) It offers studio space for art instruction.

157. According to the letter, what change will occur on Saturdays?

(A) Admission will be waived.
(B) Additional galleries will be accessible.
(C) Gift shop hours will be extended.
(D) Jamaican artwork will be available for purchase.

158. In which of the positions marked [1], [2], [3], and [4] does the following sentence best belong?

"February is an especially good time to explore the gallery for yet another reason."

(A) [1]
(B) [2]
(C) [3]
(D) [4]

To:	Isabella Hartley <ihartley@novaterraentertainment.ca>
From:	Mei-Ling Zhang <mzhang@novaterraentertainment.sg>
Date:	Novaterra's milestone celebration
Subject:	14 July
Attachment:	🖉 Opening Gala Invitation

Dear Executive Director Hartley,

Preparations are well underway for Novaterra Entertainment's commemoration of forty years in Singapore, with a lineup of high-profile engagements and a diverse media campaign already in motion. The opening gala is scheduled to take place at the Celestia Regent Hotel in Singapore City on 5 September. We would be delighted to have you join us as our guest of honour. You'll find a formal invitation attached.

In addition, we've just finalized promotional arrangements for a series of in-store anniversary campaigns that will roll out intermittently throughout the remainder of the calendar year. Each phase will be preceded by a press release to ensure optimal visibility. I'll be sending you a comprehensive timeline once all details have been confirmed.

Sincerely,

Mei-Ling Zhang
Regional Communications Lead, Novaterra Entertainment

159. What is the purpose of the e-mail?

(A) To request information about promotional discounts
(B) To verify a hotel booking for an upcoming event
(C) To accept an invitation to a formal dinner
(D) To outline marketing initiatives related to an anniversary

160. What does Ms. Zhang promise to send later?

(A) An updated version of the invitation
(B) A detailed calendar of scheduled activities
(C) A finalized travel agenda
(D) A summary of recent retail performance

Storm ZR Stalls Before the Storm

By Lucia Ramirez

On Thursday, Kaito Engineering, the firm currently manufacturing Thunderline motorcycles, announced a postponement in the launch of its upcoming Storm ZR model. Industry competitors reacted with astonishment to the announcement. —[1]—. Meanwhile, Thunderline enthusiasts took to social media en masse, voicing their disappointment over the cancellation of the highly anticipated April release.

The decision to incorporate a hybrid engine—combining gasoline and electric power—is to blame for the delay. According to Kaito Engineering, the initial prototype was deemed unsuitable due to its excessive bulk and weight. The hybrid system's design would have necessitated a significantly larger motorcycle body than originally intended. Engineers also raised concerns over its insufficient power output. —[2]—.

Beyond the technical setbacks, the Thunderline production facility, which had previously been optimized for earlier models, is currently ill-equipped to manufacture the Storm ZR hybrid. —[3]—. The company will need to invest in new machinery, and the assembly floor must be reconfigured to accommodate the updated specifications.

Just last year, Kaito Engineering was widely praised by motorcycle enthusiasts for rescuing Thunderline from financial collapse. What a contrast a single year can make. —[4]—.

161. What is indicated about Kaito Engineering?

(A) It holds ownership of the Thunderline motorcycle brand.
(B) It intends to offer a model at a discounted rate.
(C) It is relocating its corporate headquarters.
(D) It will introduce a new motorcycle in April.

162. What is NOT mentioned as a flaw with the power system?

(A) It is excessively heavy.
(B) Its production cost is exorbitant.
(C) It fails to achieve optimal performance.
(D) It demands structural expansion.

163. Why will the factory undergo renovations?

(A) It must comply with updated regulations.
(B) It has not been modernized in over ten years.
(C) It had been set up for older models.
(D) It cannot produce multiple models simultaneously.

164. In which of the positions marked [1], [2], [3], and [4] does the following sentence best belong?

"Now they will need to regain the goodwill of these prospective buyers."

(A) [1]
(B) [2]
(C) [3]
(D) [4]

Marco Alvarez [7:42 A.M.] Ms. Ito, tomorrow's weather report is calling for heavy rain, so the roofing job on your hotel's new wing will need to be put on hold.

Naoko Ito [7:43 A.M.] Does that mean no work at all tomorrow?

Marco Alvarez [7:43 A.M.] Not necessarily. My team can assist Jordan Kim's crew with reinforcing the support beams inside the older section of the building.

Naoko Ito [7:44 A.M.] How long do you think that will take?

Marco Alvarez [7:44 A.M.] Let me check in with him.

Marco Alvarez [7:45 A.M.] Jordan, any idea how close you are to wrapping up your current task?

Jordan Kim [7:47 A.M.] We were on track until this morning, but the structural engineer came by and gave us some updates. We'll probably have to work late for the next few days.

Marco Alvarez [7:48 A.M.] How would you feel about my crew jumping in to help tomorrow?

Jordan Kim [7:49 A.M.] That'd be perfect! We might even be able to finish in a single day.

Naoko Ito [7:51 A.M.] So your team will only need access to the older building?

Marco Alvarez [7:52 A.M.] Yes, just for tomorrow. Would it be okay if they parked their vehicles in front of that section?

Naoko Ito [7:54 A.M.] No problem. There should be enough spots near the main entrance. Just remind them not to drive onto the lawn.

165. What does Mr. Alvarez say will cause an interruption in tomorrow's work?

(A) Equipment malfunction
(B) A shipment arriving late
(C) Unfavorable weather conditions
(D) Not enough crew members available

166. At 7:47 A.M., what does Mr. Kim most likely mean when he writes, "We'll probably have to work late for the next few days"?

(A) His crew has not been reporting to the site on time.
(B) His team plans to leave early on Wednesday.
(C) His workers are assigned to multiple locations.
(D) His project has become more complicated.

167. Who most likely is Ms. Ito?

(A) A landscape architect
(B) A hotel manager
(C) A logistics supervisor
(D) A roofing contractor

168. What is one topic Mr. Alvarez inquires about?

(A) Which entrance his team should use
(B) How to get to the older building
(C) The construction timeline for the new wing
(D) Whether parking will be available

GO ON TO THE NEXT PAGE

InsightPilot

Discover the Data That Drives Your Business

InsightPilot is a robust, next-generation platform built to simplify the creation and administration of surveys. Our intuitive cloud-based interface helps you build surveys efficiently and monitor responses in real time.

You asked—we delivered. InsightPilot includes the most requested features:

- A guided, step-by-step system for building surveys from start to finish
- A wide variety of question formats, including multiple choice, true/false, and open-ended, with expert tips on usage
- A curated collection of sample questions proven to capture meaningful insights
- Multiple fast and simple distribution options (e-mail, social media, and more)
- Real-time summaries and detailed analytics for instant reporting

Visit www.insightpilot.com to explore more.

169. How would a business most likely use InsightPilot?

(A) To conduct market research
(B) To build custom software applications
(C) To design promotional graphics
(D) To compile annual financial statements

170. What is implied about the creators of InsightPilot?

(A) They were led by a software developer.
(B) They feature user testimonials on their Web site.
(C) They are known for manufacturing durable products.
(D) They incorporated customer input during development.

171. What is NOT mentioned as a feature of InsightPilot?

(A) A guided setup process
(B) Prewritten survey questions
(C) Visual charts and graphs for results
(D) Tips for easy survey distribution

Questions 172 through 175 refer to the following notice.

Greenbay National Park Authority (GNPA)

Greenbay National Park encompasses both the coastal mainland and Greenbay Island. Please be aware that new restrictions are now in force regarding access to the island during the upcoming summer season. Visitors who are not part of an authorized tour group will be prohibited from making landfall on Greenbay Island. This policy also applies to individuals attempting to reach the island independently using private boats or other watercraft. While such individuals may anchor offshore and observe the island from the water, they must not step onto the island itself.

The GNPA offers official guided boat tours to the island every day of the year. Tours depart every two hours, beginning at 8:00 in the morning, with the final tour leaving at 4:00 in the afternoon. However, during the summer months—December through March—the last tour is extended to 6:00 P.M. To reserve a spot, call (08) 9456 3271. Each tour includes a short visit to the island, where guests can view bird-nesting areas under the supervision of a GNPA park ranger, who serves as an authorized escort.

Booking and Payment Details
- Each tour is capped at 20 participants. If your group includes fewer than 15 people, GNPA reserves the right to add other guests to your tour.
- Admission is $30 per adult (ages 12 and up) and $20 per child (under age 12).
- A nonrefundable deposit of $7 per person is required to secure group reservations. This deposit will be credited toward your total admission cost.
- If your party fails to arrive at the scheduled time, GNPA reserves the right to shorten the tour as needed to avoid interfering with subsequent tours. Rescheduling is not available.

172. What is announced in the notice?

(A) A newly introduced visitor service
(B) A recently constructed tourist attraction
(C) A newly implemented rule
(D) A revised fee structure

173. What is indicated about visiting Greenbay Island?

(A) Guests are cautioned against disturbing nesting birds.
(B) Walking tours require a guide's presence.
(C) Swimming near the island is not allowed.
(D) Viewing the island from a boat requires joining an official tour.

174. What is NOT mentioned about the GNPA's tours?

(A) There is a limit on the number of attendees.
(B) Advance payment might be necessary.
(C) Tour hours differ depending on the season.
(D) Overnight excursions are available.

175. According to the notice, what might occur if a group arrives late for a scheduled tour?

(A) The tour could be canceled.
(B) The duration could be under two hours.
(C) The cost could increase.
(D) The tour might be rescheduled.

GO ON TO THE NEXT PAGE

Welcome to Event Forge

| REVIEWS | **HOME** | SERVICES | ORDER TICKETS |

Event Forge — your trusted online partner for professional ticket printing!
We have produced tickets for thousands of occasions, from music festivals and athletic competitions to trade expos and more. Whatever your event, we will help you craft a ticket that reflects its unique character.

Step 1: Design Your Ticket
Browse our collection of elegant templates by choosing a category. You can easily adjust the text to reflect your event details. For those seeking greater control over the color scheme, typography, imagery, and layout, download our Event Forge Designer Suite. This complimentary software empowers users to customize every visual element of their ticket beyond the default templates.

Step 2: Select Quantity
Whether you need just a few or several thousand, Event Forge accommodates orders of all sizes. Bulk discounts apply — the more you order, the less you pay per ticket.

Quantity	Price per ticket
100–500	45 cents
501–1,000	35 cents
1,001–3,000	25 cents
3,001 or more	20 cents

Step 3: Add an Invisible Verification Stamp
For an additional 5 cents per ticket, you may opt to include a discreet invisible verification stamp printed in ultraviolet ink, visible only under black light. This feature enhances the authenticity of your tickets and helps prevent counterfeiting.

Step 4: Submit Your Order
Standard orders are processed within three business days, though larger requests may require additional time. We recommend placing your order well in advance of your event to ensure timely delivery.

Welcome to Event Forge

| **REVIEWS** | HOME | SERVICES | ORDER TICKETS |

★★★★★ *I'm thrilled we chose Event Forge!*

I manage a small independent venue called Linden Hall, and we recently ordered 3,000 tickets from Event Forge. We opted not to include the invisible verification stamp but did install the free design software to customize the layout and incorporate our venue's logo. The final product was outstanding! Several patrons complimented us on the new look, and we were especially impressed by the prompt delivery. Last year, we ordered from a local vendor here in Fairhaven, and the tickets took six weeks to arrive. In contrast, Event Forge—despite being located across the country—delivered our order in just four business days!

— **Elliot Ramirez**

176. According to the Web page, what does the free software enable users to do?

(A) Customize ticket visuals
(B) Confirm event attendees
(C) Maintain a company Web site
(D) Access customer databases

177. What is stated on the Web page about Event Forge?

(A) It provides multiple ticket dimensions.
(B) It offers an optional security feature.
(C) It uses a distinct numbering scheme.
(D) It operates several retail outlets.

178. What is indicated about Mr. Ramirez?

(A) He paid twenty-five cents per ticket.
(B) He requested expedited processing.
(C) He used a default template.
(D) He received more tickets than he ordered.

179. What is suggested about the Linden Hall?

(A) It is located in Fairhaven.
(B) It is planning a logo redesign.
(C) It recently lowered admission prices.
(D) It distributes tickets via postal mail.

180. According to the review, why does Mr. Ramirez prefer Event Forge over previous vendor?

(A) It offers more competitive pricing.
(B) It ships internationally.
(C) It uses superior printing technology.
(D) It processes orders more efficiently.

GO ON TO THE NEXT PAGE

To:	Claire Katsaros <ckatsaros@capitalhorizon.net>
From:	Eleni Stavros <e.stavros@velvetstride.com>
Date:	January 18
Re:	Updated Business Plan
Attachment:	🗋 Stavros_UpdatedPlan

Dear Ms. Katsaros,

I truly appreciate your assistance in helping me secure financial support for my upcoming venture. After reviewing your comments, I have revised my proposal accordingly. Per your recommendation, I have included a section that identifies our expected customer population. You will find the updated version attached. I believe this finalizes all the documentation required for my loan submission. Should you need any additional information, please feel free to reach out.

I'm eager to receive your formal confirmation regarding my application.

Regards,

Eleni Stavros

Revised Business Plan: Velvet Stride

Section 1. Objective
The Apollo Avenue area has evolved into a vibrant district filled with eateries, retail outlets, and entertainment venues. Velvet Stride aims to fill a noticeable gap among the existing apparel stores. Our shop will specialize in women's footwear and fashion accessories. We are dedicated to delivering stylish, high-quality shoes at affordable prices in a welcoming, customer-focused setting.

Section 2. Intended Customer Base
Velvet Stride will cater to professional women employed nearby. With numerous office buildings located within walking distance, we expect many customers to frequent during lunch breaks or after work. On weekends, we anticipate attracting shoppers and diners who come to the area for leisure and entertainment.

Section 3. Projected Schedule
Our grand opening is planned for June 15. Below are the estimated deadlines for each phase:
March 1 Finalize lease agreement and acquire business license
April 5   Renovate interior and set up product displays
May 10   Advertise job openings, conduct interviews, and hire team members
June 12 Stock inventory and prepare for launch

Section 4. Financial Overview
Please refer to the attached projection sheet for a breakdown of estimated expenditures and anticipated profits.

181. Why did Ms. Stavros send the e-mail?

(A) To congratulate someone on a recent promotion
(B) To provide steps for obtaining a business license
(C) To offer guidance to a new entrepreneur
(D) To address a specific recommendation

182. In the e-mail, the word "secure" in paragraph 1, line 1, is closest in meaning to

(A) protect
(B) acquire
(C) assure
(D) affix

183. Which part of the business plan was newly included?

(A) Section 1
(B) Section 2
(C) Section 3
(D) Section 4

184. What type of business is Ms. Stavros planning to launch?

(A) A gourmet restaurant
(B) A staffing agency
(C) A beauty parlor
(D) A shoe boutique

185. According to the business plan, what information was submitted separately?

(A) Personal recommendation letters
(B) A list of contracted vendors
(C) Financial projections detailing expenditures
(D) An inventory catalog

▶ ◀   https://www.vistaformofficeconcepts.com/ | ▼

| PHOTO GALLERY | **HOME** | BROWSE | ORDER FORM | CONTACT US |

VistaForm Office Concepts

Welcome to our Web site! Browse our inventory to visualize office setups that are both modern and functional. We have proudly served the KwaZulu-Natal region for over 20 years, and you can count on our high quality furnishings to truly set your workspace apart.

We always offer the following deals:
• Free shipping and handling for first-time customers
• Special discounts for schools and nonprofit organizations (call for details)

From:	Daniel Mokoena [dmokoena@oakandledger.co.za]
To:	Lerato Ndlovu [lndlovu@oakandledger.co.za]
Date:	14 June
Subject:	Office furniture proposal

Hi, Lerato,

After doing some research, I'd like to recommend VistaForm Office Concepts for the desks and other items we'll need for our office upgrade. Although we haven't ordered from them before, they provided references that included glowing feedback.

For the main work zone, I suggest we go with a larger desk model—ten units—along with matching file cabinets and bookshelves. For the upstairs team and interns, a more compact desk style would be suitable.

If you're on board with this plan, I'd like to place the order soon so that delivery happens while most of our staff are attending the conference in Richmond. Unfortunately, the workspace will look a bit chaotic as we clear out the old furniture and await the new pieces.

Let me know what you think of the proposal I've outlined above.

Best,

Daniel

Order code: R8427Z
Contact: Daniel Mokoena, (031) 774–2186
Delivery to: Oak & Ledger Associates, 88 Constitution Avenue, Pietermaritzburg 3201
Delivery window: 04–06 July, 08:30–16:30

Quantity	Product ID	Description
10	VED4421	Vista Executive Desk
10	TFC2210	Trimline File Cabinet; brushed charcoal
3	BQ3095	Booknest Shelving Unit; brushed charcoal
5	FD5127	Flexform Desk

Note: *Due to high demand, Product BQ3095 is currently unavailable at our Howick location. These units will be delivered to your office directly from our production facility, so they will be shipped into Pietermaritzburg from Durban rather than from Howick. This may result in a delay of one to three days. We will make every effort to deliver the full order on the same day.*

186. What is indicated about VistaForm Office Concepts?

(A) It offers help with designing office layouts.
(B) It grants special deals to educational institutions.
(C) It has recently diversified its product line.
(D) It has recently launched a new store.

187. What is probably true about Oak & Ledger Associates' furniture order?

(A) Its delivery expenses will be waived.
(B) It contains an item that has been discontinued.
(C) It missed the deadline for July delivery.
(D) It includes some furniture selected by interns.

188. Why does Mr. Mokoena probably prefer to schedule a delivery during a particular period of time?

(A) He expects to get an extra discount.
(B) He wants the furniture ready for an important meeting.
(C) He requires more time to discard outdated items.
(D) He strives to minimize disruption for his colleagues.

189. What furniture product will most likely be located on the upper story at Oak & Ledger Associates?

(A) Vista Executive Desk
(B) Trimline File Cabinets
(C) Booknest Shelving Unit
(D) Flexform Desks

190. According to the form, where is the furniture manufactured?

(A) Pietermaritzburg
(B) Durban
(C) Richmond
(D) Howick

From:	Matteo Ricci <mricci@villagusto.com>
To:	Chiara Bianchi <cbianchi@villagusto.com>
Date:	Tuesday, June 7
Subject:	Preview Dinner Planning

Hi Chiara,

Can you believe Mr. Martin will be arriving in less than three weeks? His column will be published in the Liberty Gazette, so we must ensure that our offerings reflect the very essence of Villa Gusto. To gather input on the dishes we'll present to him, I've decided we should host a preview dinner next Friday evening.

I've been thinking about the menu. Let's include a hearty vegetarian entrée that can truly hold its own. That way, we can showcase our plant-based creativity. I also suggest featuring our steamed shellfish dish, which has been a customer favorite lately. I'm adamant about including the new specialty pizzas we've been developing for the summer menu. That is, of course, assuming the brick oven installation is finalized by then. And let's not forget our fruit-based desserts—they're always well received by critics. Naturally, I trust your judgment as our Executive Chef to finalize the selections.

One more thing—I'd love for our preview dinner guests to have the opportunity to tour the kitchen. Let me know your thoughts and how best to coordinate that.

Thanks,

Matteo

VILLA GUSTO

PREVIEW DINNER MENU
Saturday, June 17

Smoked salmon canapés with dill créme

Butter-roasted halibut with lemon zest

Grilled eggplant steak in
tangy tomato-lemon glaze

Steamed mussels and prawns
in coconut saffron broth

Tuscan-style roasted chicken with
cannellini beans and wilted arugula

Glazed almond peach tart

Guest Feedback Card

Name: *Isabella Moreau*

Please share your thoughts on the preview dinner at Villa Gusto.

The eggplant dish had a lovely sweetness, though the sauce was a bit too acidic for my taste. The halibut was absolutely divine—perfectly cooked and seasoned. The Tuscan chicken was tender, but lacked depth of flavor. As for the tart, it was pleasant, though slightly overbaked. I was impressed by the sleek layout of your kitchen. I'm eager to try the new brick-oven pizzas once they're available. It's a shame they weren't ready for tonight's dinner.

191. What is the purpose of the preview dinner?

(A) To prepare for a visit from a culinary journalist
(B) To choose dishes for a regional food festival
(C) To evaluate a new chef's performance
(D) To test items for the weekly specials

192. In the e-mail, the word "hearty" in paragraph 2, line 1, is closest in meaning to

(A) genuine
(B) abundant
(C) satisfying
(D) inventive

193. What is true about the preview dinner menu?

(A) It lists complimentary dishes for guests.
(B) It includes a dessert Mr. Ricci suggested.
(C) It was served inside the restaurant's kitchen.
(D) It is a recurring weekly event.

194. Which menu item was most likely Ms. Moreau's favorite?

(A) The halibut
(B) The tart
(C) The eggplant
(D) The chicken

195. What is implied about the brick oven?

(A) It is too large for the kitchen space.
(B) It requires technical repairs.
(C) It did not pass a safety inspection.
(D) It has not been completed yet.

/// **GO ON TO THE NEXT PAGE**

To:	Interns
From:	Dr. Farah Almasi
Date:	Guest Lecture Series
Subject:	September 18

Dear team,

Exciting update! Ms. Hana Takeda has confirmed her participation in our Guest Lecture Series this fall. As part of your student internship duties, please arrange her lodging here at the university for October 15–17 and ensure all necessary documentation is completed and approved so that she can receive her honorarium. Also, reserve a venue for her talk—I suggest the Emerson Forum since it can accommodate the largest audience, but any room in the economics wing will suffice.

Once Ms. Takeda sends her abstract, one of you should design a flyer and post it in the usual spots around the building. I trust the five of you will coordinate without any issues. Much appreciated!

Dr. Almasi
Professor, Langford School of Economics

Langford School of Economics

Guest Lecture Series Presents:

Ms. Hana Takeda
Chief Strategy Officer, Sendai Capital Partners, Japan

Building Resilient Entrepreneurial Finance Models
October 16, 4:00 P.M.
The Mirae Room

In recent years, traditional banks have tightened lending policies to reduce exposure to risk. This practice has contributed to unfavorable market dynamics. How can financial institutions balance risk management with the need to support entrepreneurs? One promising approach that is gaining in popularity is alternative finance. I will offer an overview of this practice, present compelling findings from a joint study by Sendai Capital Partners and Langford School of Economics, and explore how this innovation could revive the global financial sector.

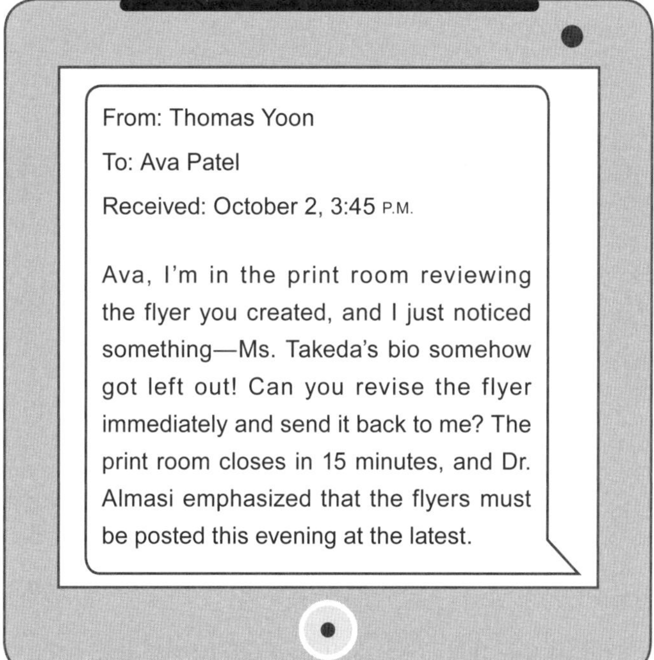

196. What can be inferred about the Mirae Room?

(A) It is located outside the economics building.
(B) It houses all the events in the Guest Lecture Series.
(C) It has a smaller capacity than the Emerson Forum.
(D) It is available for use on October 17.

197. In the e-mail, the word "issues" in paragraph 2, line 2, is closest in meaning to

(A) conflicts
(B) periodicals
(C) distributions
(D) offspring

198. What is Ms. Takeda's presentation about?

(A) A new trend in the banking industry
(B) A career opportunity in the finance field
(C) Unconventional methods of data collection
(D) Characteristics of successful entrepreneurs

199. What problem does Mr. Yoon mention?

(A) A name has been spelled incorrectly.
(B) The flyer is missing some information.
(C) The flyer will not be posted by the deadline.
(D) The venue for the presentation is currently unavailable.

200. Who most likely is Ms. Patel?

(A) A technician in the print room
(B) An executive assistant to Ms. Takeda
(C) A speaker from the Guest Lecture Series
(D) A student at Langford School of Economics

This is the end of the test. If you finish before time is called, you may go back to Parts 5, 6, and 7 and check your work.

정답 및 해설 p.126

Notes

TEST

05

[이상적인 시간 배분]
Part 5, 6 15분
Part 7   60분

[빠르고 정확한 문제 해결]
- 1단계: '빈칸 앞뒤'를 본다.
- 2단계: 빈칸 앞뒤를 보고 정답을 알 수 없다면 '문장 전체를
         해석'하자.
- 3단계: 문장을 바로 해석할 수 없다면 빠르게 아무 답이나
         '선택'하고 다음 문제로 넘어가자

READING TEST

In this Reading test, various texts will be provided for you to read, followed by multiple types of reading comprehension questions. The total duration for the test is 75 minutes. It consists of three parts, with instructions provided at the beginning of each part. You are encouraged to attempt as many questions as you can within the given time.

Make sure to mark your answers on the separate answer sheet. Do not write your answers in your test book.

PART 5

Directions: In the sentences below, a word or phrase is missing. You will find four options below each sentence. Choose the most appropriate answer to fill in the blank, and then mark the letter (A), (B), (C), or (D) on your answer sheet.

101. Outgoing packages must be addressed ------- to avoid delivery issues.

(A) correct
(B) correcting
(C) correctly
(D) corrected

102. Our team ------- in the policy meeting last Tuesday, but we had a scheduling conflict.

(A) can participate
(B) must have participated
(C) should participate
(D) would have participated

103. Chef Zhang's culinary program is ------- to be broadcast on public television next month.

(A) given
(B) scheduled
(C) found
(D) considered

104. Input from residents regarding the proposed Mapleview Market ------- by local officials.

(A) seeking
(B) sought
(C) was sought
(D) used to seek

105. The journalist for ------- the award was named had investigated several intriguing cases.

(A) when
(B) that
(C) whom
(D) whoever

106. The warranty for Corvella cookware does not cover any damage caused by ------- use of the product.

(A) concise
(B) equivalent
(C) submissive
(D) improper

107. To meet the high standards, the quality control team conducts ------- evaluations of each item.

(A) exhaust
(B) exhausted
(C) exhaustion
(D) exhaustive

108. All straps ------- the equipment onto the platform need to be inspected thoroughly before use.

(A) securing
(B) secured
(C) secures
(D) secure

109. The regulation ------- that all elevators
be inspected annually does not apply to
private residences.

(A) require
(B) requires
(C) required
(D) requirement

110. When Golden Hearth Bakery upgraded to
larger delivery trucks, each one was -------
white and brown.

(A) changed
(B) painted
(C) alternated
(D) transferred

111. Virell Research Center gains -------
from having staff scientists with strong
interdisciplinary backgrounds.

(A) jointly
(B) immensely
(C) evenly
(D) impulsively

112. Morocco's two leading airlines have
------- to finalize the specifics of their joint
initiative to boost tourism.

(A) yet
(B) up
(C) until
(D) else

113. The series of workshops that -------
scheduled for next month focuses on
sustainable business practices.

(A) is
(B) are
(C) has
(D) have

114. Prices for electronics and home décor
items ------- on our Web site are subject
to updates without prior notice.

(A) listed
(B) have listed
(C) list
(D) will list

115. Ms. Kapoor stands out among the
applicants ------- she has an impressive
track record of driving sales growth.

(A) while
(B) so
(C) because
(D) however

116. Once the necessary protocols -------, the
clinical trial is supposed to proceed to the
next phase without delay.

(A) have implemented
(B) have been implemented
(C) being implemented
(D) will be implemented

117. Veltrix Automotive has not ------- any
setbacks in manufacturing or shipments
to retail partners this quarter.

(A) exerted
(B) submitted
(C) represented
(D) experienced

118. How ------- a company receives,
documents, and reacts to complaints has
an impact on customer satisfaction.

(A) efficient
(B) efficiently
(C) efficiency
(D) efficiencies

119. Atwell & Pierce CPAs provides a year-
end financial overview as ------- of its
standard bookkeeping package.

(A) piece
(B) division
(C) section
(D) part

120. The ------- of the newly developed
inventory system has notably affected our
approach to resource management.

(A) habit
(B) adoption
(C) trade
(D) reservation

GO ON TO THE NEXT PAGE

121. At Fresh Basket, shoppers are encouraged to ask for help rather than take items down from high shelves -------.

(A) themselves
(B) their own
(C) them
(D) their

122. After extensive deliberation, the designers chose to abandon the vivid orange gown ------- a more subdued alternative.

(A) favorable
(B) out of favor
(C) favorite
(D) in favor of

123. ------- preparing correspondence for clients, make sure to use the updated letterhead provided by the association.

(A) When
(B) During
(C) Meanwhile
(D) Yet

124. The initial agreements with Mariton Freight Services have just been shredded because they ------- exactly ten years ago today.

(A) submitted
(B) violated
(C) expired
(D) invalidated

125. While the instructions were somewhat confusing, the updated application ------- remained simple to navigate for novices.

(A) it
(B) itself
(C) themselves
(D) them

126. Following a strategic 15 percent price reduction, sales of Vireon television units surged ------- across key markets.

(A) accidentally
(B) expressively
(C) dramatically
(D) eagerly

127. The finance committee of the organization firmly opposes ------- any potentially high-risk investments during this fiscal year.

(A) making
(B) is making
(C) to make
(D) make

128. Although there was a ------- in the economy, the electronics sector managed to achieve a 20 percent increase in profits this year.

(A) protocol
(B) longevity
(C) drawback
(D) downturn

129. The current ------- of seasonal decorations at Merriton Celebrations Co. suggests that the company is fully equipped for the holiday surge.

(A) proposal
(B) inventory
(C) consideration
(D) commitment

130. The corporate legal department has ------- finished its assessment of company bylaws and anticipates submitting a proposal for improvements tomorrow.

(A) slightly
(B) frequently
(C) nearly
(D) continually

PART 6

Directions: Review the following texts. In certain sections, there is a missing word, phrase, or sentence. Each question includes four possible answers provided below the text. Choose the most appropriate answer to fill in the blank, and then mark the letter (A), (B), (C), or (D) on your answer sheet.

Questions 131 through 134 refer to the following e-mail.

From: Pacific Horizon Airways

To: Margaret Brennan

Date: 12 July

Subject: Your flight reservation

Dear Ms. Brennan,

We appreciate your decision to fly with Pacific Horizon Airways and your utilizing our digital booking and check-in platform. -------. To make your experience smoother when checking
131.
luggage and clearing the security checkpoints, we recommend printing your boarding pass at home. This will help guarantee your ------- arrival at the departure gate.
132.
While you're at the airport, ------- advantage of the secure wireless network available at our
133.
Horizon Retreat Lounge for a modest fee of just $12 NZD. You can easily arrange this

------- using our booking system prior to your travel date.
134.
Sincerely,

The team at Pacific Horizon Airways

131. (A) Kindly sign in to initiate the procedure.
(B) Our airline serves destinations across six continents.
(C) You'll have access to onboard wireless Internet.
(D) Your reservation has been successfully processed.

132. (A) timely
(B) quiet
(C) near
(D) together

133. (A) taking
(B) taken
(C) take
(D) took

134. (A) repair
(B) inspection
(C) journey
(D) service

From: Rivera, Sofia

Sent: Thursday, December 11, 10:42 A.M.

To: Company Staff

Subject: Travel Reimbursement Guidelines and Receipt Requirements

Good morning, everyone.

Just a reminder: When submitting a travel reimbursement request, you must include itemized receipts for all purchases. This policy ------- to costs related to meals, lodging, airfare, local
135.
transportation, and other travel-related expenses. Credit card receipts by themselves do not offer complete ------- of the specific products or services you paid for. We have recently
136.
received several reimbursement submissions from ------- who used their personal credit
137.
cards during business trips. -------. Without detailed receipts, we are unable to process
138.
reimbursement payments. Please be sure to keep this in mind.

Sofia Rivera, Director of Accounting

---

135. (A) applies
(B) apply
(C) is applying
(D) had applied

136. (A) document
(B) documented
(C) documenting
(D) documentation

137. (A) visitors
(B) suppliers
(C) customers
(D) employees

138. (A) Regrettably, the company does not cover costs for leisure activities.
(B) Sadly, they only turned in credit card receipts.
(C) The majority of the charges pertained to office supplies.
(D) It's common for staff to use personal credit cards while traveling.

Martelli Named CEO at DentaraLink

DentaraLink Group, a nationwide alliance of dental service providers, has announced that industry veteran Giancarlo Martelli will serve as its incoming CEO. "Mr. Martelli shares our ------- to excellence and growth, and we are so pleased to have him take us forward," said
139.
board member Luca Moretti.

Mr. Martelli brings 18 years of experience in expanding medical practices. He previously served as CEO of Solvia Surgery Centers and led its growth into 24 states. -------. "I -------
140.   **141.**
thrilled to move DentaraLink into new markets and grow the organization," said Mr. Martelli.

Headquartered in Tucson, DentaraLink collaborates with dentists ------- the country to deliver
142.
management and operational support services.

---

139. (A) committed
(B) commitment
(C) commit
(D) committee

140. (A) MedHire Solutions will be retained to oversee the recruitment process.
(B) That experience was accessible to all DentaraLink executives.
(C) Earnings rose by 12 percent during his leadership period.
(D) The consolidation came as a surprise to many in the dental industry.

141. (A) am
(B) was
(C) had been
(D) have been

142. (A) among
(B) along
(C) into
(D) throughout

Questions 143 through 146 refer to the following press release.

FOR IMMEDIATE RELEASE

Contact: Jean lau, 604-555-0273

Ulsan Gains Momentum

SINGAPORE (December 1)-Kim Heng Offshore & Marine (KHOM) ------- a 30 percent
143.
interest in the Ulsan offshore wind farm project. This was a critical component in the financing
of Ulsan, which will be the largest offshore wind farm in Korea. During the pilot period of the
project, two turbines were erected. -------. The total number of turbines in the Ulsan project
144.
will be enough to power a small urban area.

"We are delighted to offer assistance to the key players in a project of such consequence,"
said Thomas Tan, the CEO of KHMO. "Not only is Ulsan on track to become a major wind
farm in Asia, ------- the involvement of international sponsors will also set a new precedent
145.
for projects of this nature. We hope this will stimulate future ------- in the region."
146.

143. (A) was acquired
(B) has acquired
(C) is acquiring
(D) will acquire

144. (A) KHOM funds turbines on wind farms
in other countries, too.
(B) The wind farms will encounter some
challenges in the foreseeable future.
(C) Fifty more units will be constructed in
the subsequent phase of the project.
(D) Multiple companies chose not to
finance supplemental turbines.

145. (A) as
(B) or
(C) so
(D) but

146. (A) travel
(B) events
(C) regulations
(D) investment

PART 7

Directions: In this part, you will read a variety of texts, such as magazine and newspaper articles, e-mails, and instant messages. Each text or set of texts is followed by a series of questions. Choose the most appropriate answer and mark the letter (A), (B), (C), or (D) on your answer sheet.

Questions 147 through 148 refer to the following instructions.

How to Execute a Global Reset

Initiating a global reset on your television's remote-control unit will erase all personalized configurations and reinstate the default operational parameters as defined by the manufacturer. To carry out this procedure, adhere to the following sequence:

Step 1
Depress and hold the POWER button for six seconds, then release it.

Step 2
Tap the left ARROW button. A brief auditory signal will confirm the action.

Step 3
Press the CLEAR button. The red indicator light located at the top should extinguish. If it remains illuminated, press the button again prior to advancing to step 4.

Step 4
Enter your designated user code. A green light will blink, signifying that the global reset has successfully restored the standard settings.

If desired, you may now proceed to reconfigure the remote in order to customize its functionality to suit your preferences.

147. What do the instructions explain?

(A) How to remotely activate lighting features
(B) How to eliminate customized configurations from the device
(C) How to initiate subscription to additional television content
(D) How to enhance the visual resolution of the display

148. According to the instructions, which step might require repetition?

(A) Step 1
(B) Step 2
(C) Step 3
(D) Step 4

GO ON TO THE NEXT PAGE

Notice to All Employees of Halston & Avery

Please be advised that the staff kitchen will be inaccessible from November 3 through November 7. During this interval, the space will undergo repainting, and both a new dishwasher and refrigerator will be installed. Kindly refrain from entering the kitchen for any reason—including preparing beverages such as tea or coffee—while work is in progress. To accommodate your refreshment needs, a temporary beverage station will be available in the foyer of the office. We appreciate your understanding and cooperation during this brief renovation period.

149. What is one purpose of the notice?

(A) To promote the launch of a company-sponsored café
(B) To request that staff maintain cleanliness in the kitchen
(C) To inform employees of scheduled upgrades to kitchen facilities
(D) To declare a temporary closure of the office building

150. What will be provided in the foyer?

(A) A catered midday meal
(B) A registration list for kitchen access
(C) Packaged snacks available for purchase
(D) Tea and coffee for employee use

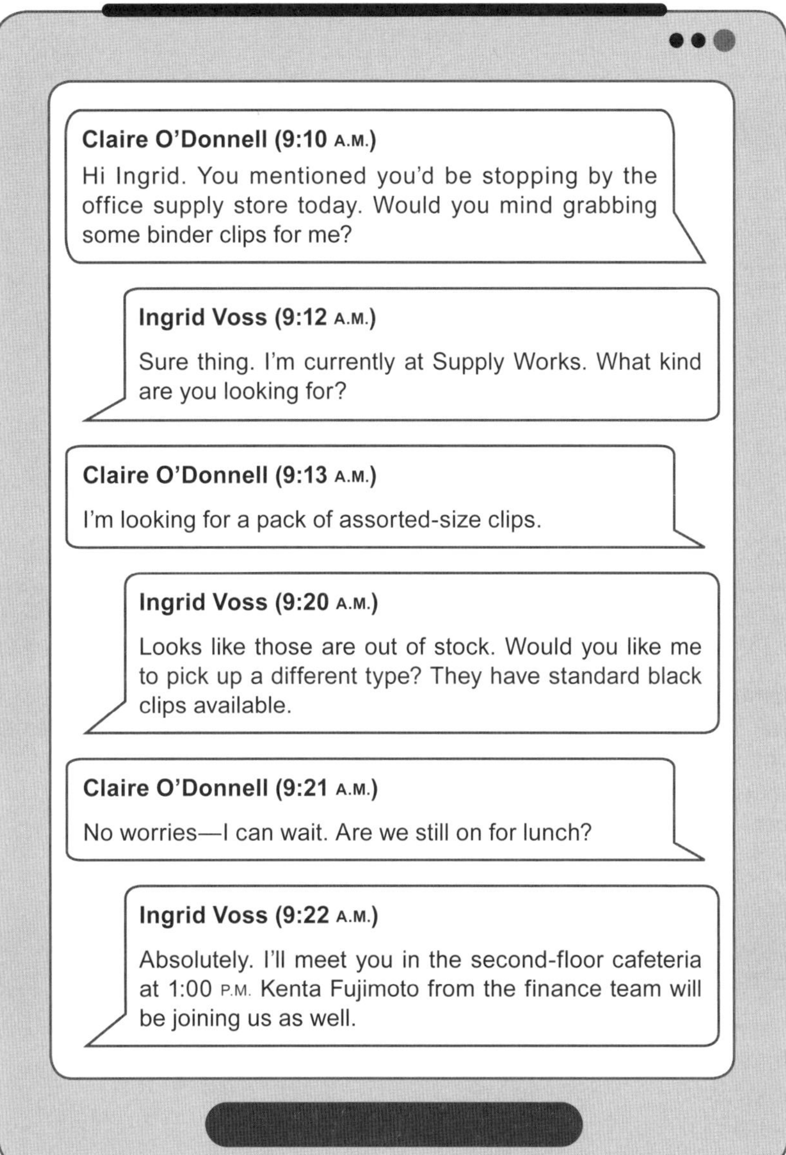

151. At 9:21 A.M., what does Ms. O'Donnell most likely mean when she writes, "I can wait"?

(A) She is not feeling very hungry at the moment.
(B) She wants only assorted-size clips.
(C) She expects Ms. Voss to continue searching for the item.
(D) She plans to reschedule her meeting with Mr. Fujimoto.

152. What is probably true about the writers?

(A) They work in the same office building.
(B) They typically commute to work together.
(C) They are employed at an office supply store.
(D) They are late for a business luncheon.

GO ON TO THE NEXT PAGE

Lunaria Threads—Your Go-To Name in Style!

For a limited period, enjoy savings of up to 40 percent off on all purchases!
This offer remains valid through October 31.

LunariaThreads.com is your trusted hub for fashion on the Web, featuring thousands of selections in women's and children's apparel. Browse our digital catalog to discover the latest trends in outerwear such as coats and jackets, as well as dresses, tops, skirts, swimwear, sleepwear, shoes, and accessories.

And now, we are bringing fashion into your living space with a brand-new line of interior design products. Visit LunariaThreads.com today to explore our newest offerings in home décor.

Take advantage of our long-standing free shipping policy on all orders exceeding $60.00.

153. What is being advertised?

(A) A department store's rebranding initiative
(B) A recently enhanced fashion Web site
(C) A promotional discount for online shoppers
(D) A revision to the company's delivery terms

154. Based on the advertisement, what will happen on November 1?

(A) Customers will be charged regular prices.
(B) A new section for children's fashion will launch.
(C) Shoppers will become eligible for complimentary gifts.
(D) Shipping fees will be reduced across all orders.

155. What is being introduced for the first time?

(A) Home-decorating items
(B) Outerwear
(C) Children's clothing
(D) Footwear

Warm Welcome & Special Thanks

(March 12) — Readers of the *Selat Courier* may have noticed a new name added to the newspaper's masthead. We are delighted to introduce Lina Hartono as our very first intern reporter.

Ms. Hartono recently relocated to Surabaya, having studied English and journalism in Australia. For her initial assignment, she investigated the current difficulties facing our country's agriculture sector from a global perspective. Her debut article on this topic is featured in this issue.

The introduction of internships is another way we aim to fulfill our educational mission. Over the past 18 months, the *Selat Courier* has been sustained primarily through financial support from local academic institutions. Our publication now strives not only to keep the community informed, but also to serve career-development purposes.

One positive outcome of this new direction is the growing number of students who contribute to the paper in various capacities. The editor would like to extend sincere gratitude to all the students who volunteer their time each month— including those who ensure the print edition reaches the doorsteps of our subscribers promptly every week.

156. What is mentioned about the intern position?

(A) It is a new addition to the publication.
(B) It involves travel abroad.
(C) It is based in Australia.
(D) It requires a degree in journalism.

157. What is implied about Ms. Hartono?

(A) She is an experienced interpreter.
(B) She is contributing a series of articles.
(C) She will assist in recruiting future interns.
(D) She previously worked in the agriculture sector.

158. What is indicated about the *Selat Courier*?

(A) It is provided free of charge to locals.
(B) It is delivered by volunteers.
(C) It is published in several languages.
(D) It receives funding from advertisements.

MEMO

From: Naomi Sakamoto, Food Safety Supervisor
To: All Staff

Maintaining proper hygiene is a year-round responsibility for all food handlers, but it becomes even more critical during the approaching cold and flu season. Viruses may linger on surfaces like countertops and cutting boards, travel via hands, and eventually find their way onto utensils and serving dishes. To reduce the risk of spreading illness, every employee involved in food preparation or delivery must practice thorough handwashing before handling any food or related tools. Guidelines on the proper handwashing technique have been posted at the kitchen entrance, inside the restrooms, and in the meeting room adjacent to the lobby. Please follow these instructions diligently to help ensure a safe and sanitary work environment.

Naomi

159. What is the primary focus of the memo?

(A) How to properly treat symptoms of a seasonal illness
(B) The importance of practicing a hygiene protocol
(C) A review of the company's sick-leave procedures
(D) Instructions for operating new kitchen appliances

160. What items are most likely mentioned in the posted guidelines?

(A) Hand cleanser and disposable towels
(B) Cooking oil and vinegar
(C) Napkins and tablecloths
(D) Mixing bowls and measuring cups

To:	Team@bradleyworks.com
From:	Elliot Turner, Workplace Operations Lead
Date:	15 March
Subject:	Desks Incoming

Dear team,

We're excited to announce that all staff desks will soon be upgraded to new hybrid models that support both sitting and standing work styles. These desks are scheduled to arrive on 22 March. —[1]—. I've arranged for the delivery to take place early in the morning before regular hours so it won't interrupt your workflow. —[2]—. To help facilitate the transition, please ensure that all contents of your current desk—including any personal items—are transferred into a cardboard box on 21 March.

You can learn more about the desk model we selected by visiting www.hartleyfurnishings.co.uk/hybrid09. —[3]—. Based on my research, this model stood out as the most intuitive and user-friendly. You can easily alter its height by flipping a latch and pressing a button.

Many of you have expressed interest in hybrid desks for quite some time, so I'm thrilled we're making this happen. This upgrade is just one of several initiatives management plans to implement this year to make Bradley Works a more comfortable and health-conscious workplace. —[4]—.

Warm regards,

Elliot Turner

---

161. What should employees do to assist with the delivery process?

(A) Pack up their belongings
(B) Gather cardboard containers
(C) Finish their tasks before lunch
(D) Remove furniture from their workspaces

162. What was the main reason the desk model was chosen?

(A) It offers ample storage space.
(B) It is simple to adjust.
(C) It can be shipped quickly.
(D) It is the most budget-friendly option.

163. In which of the positions marked [1], [2], [3], and [4] does the following sentence best belong?

"We're happy to hear any additional suggestions you might have."

(A) [1]
(B) [2]
(C) [3]
(D) [4]

GO ON TO THE NEXT PAGE

Emily Novak [10:02 A.M.]
Hi, everyone. When we met last week, I asked you to come up with ideas to raise awareness about the community garden program. Has anyone made any progress?

Ryan Goodwin [10:03 A.M.]
I got in touch with Daniel Chen from *Metro Pulse*, our local newspaper. You might be familiar with his column, "Urban Life".

Michael Landon [10:04 A.M.]
The one that's published on Thursdays? I never miss it!

Ryan Goodwin [10:05 A.M.]
He has a strong online following as well. He's interested in interviewing me for an upcoming issue. That'll happen next week.

Emily Novak [10:05 A.M.]
That's great news. Will you be discussing the garden program as a whole?

Ryan Goodwin [10:06 A.M.]
I told Daniel that we're currently surveying garden members about water access concerns. So he wants to center the article around that topic.

Michael Landon [10:07 A.M.]
Lena and I are compiling the survey findings. Emily, I'm about to send you a draft. Once you've approved it, I'll upload it to our Web site.

Emily Novak [10:08 A.M.]
Perfect. I'll review it later today.

164. What is indicated about Ms. Novak?

(A) She was absent from last week's meeting.
(B) She recently came back from traveling.
(C) She disagrees with Ryan Goodwin's suggestion.
(D) She assigned a task to her colleagues.

165. Who is Mr. Chen?

(A) A municipal employee
(B) A journalist from the local press
(C) A potential hire
(D) A gardening specialist

166. At 10:04 A.M., what does Mr. Landon most likely mean when he writes, "I never miss it"?

(A) He enjoys joining in community events.
(B) He consistently finishes his work on time.
(C) He is a subscriber to *Metro Pulse*.
(D) He regularly reads a column.

167. What does Mr. Landon indicate he plans to do?

(A) Carry out a survey
(B) Post a document online
(C) Prepare questions for an interview
(D) Work on improving water access

Associate Publicist Opening
Silverpine Publishing House

Silverpine Publishing House publishes a wide range of contemporary titles, including fiction, nonfiction, and poetry. Among our fiction authors are Julian Mercer, Thomas Ellery, and Camila Ortega. —[1]—. Our nonfiction catalog primarily features books on personal finance, travel writing, wellness, and digital culture.

We are currently hiring an associate publicist to join our dynamic team. —[2]—. The successful candidate will assist senior staff and also take the lead on publicity campaigns for our authors. Responsibilities include coordinating and managing author events such as book signings, festival appearances, and both domestic and international speaking engagements.

Ideal applicants should have three to four years of experience in trade publishing, either in a publicity or editorial capacity. —[3]—. Candidates must demonstrate strong familiarity with social media platforms used in publishing, proficiency in word-processing tools, excellent written and verbal communication skills, and commendable attention to detail. —[4]—.

If this opportunity aligns with your background, please submit a cover letter and résumé no later than November 12 to careers@silverpinepublishing.com.

168. What is the purpose of the notice?

(A) To advertise an upcoming recruitment event
(B) To communicate changes in upper-level staffing to employees
(C) To motivate recent graduates to pursue internships
(D) To invite eligible candidates to apply for a position

169. What do Mr. Mercer and Ms. Ortega have in common?

(A) They contribute to books on digital culture.
(B) They are signed to the same publisher.
(C) They organize literary events.
(D) They have participated in international speaking engagements.

170. What is listed as one of the responsibilities of an associate publicist?

(A) Scheduling author appearances
(B) Maintaining word processing software
(C) Interviewing prospective interns
(D) Attending industry conventions

171. In which of the positions marked [1], [2], [3], and [4] does the following sentence best belong?

"Two professional references from these positions are required."

(A) [1]
(B) [2]
(C) [3]
(D) [4]

To:	Eliza Morton <emorton@greenridgegroup.co.au>
From:	Nolan Barrett <nbarrett@skyreachmedia.co.au>
Subject:	New Service
Date:	April 12

Dear Ms. Morton,

Regarding your recent order, before we process it, I wanted to inform you of an exciting opportunity. Skyreach Media is now offering an additional method for engaging with your customers: automated text messages. We are combining our distinctive lawn advertisements with the latest mobile technology to provide a swift, straightforward approach to expanding your client base. We've successfully aided numerous property rental agents in your vicinity and are currently providing free trials to new members.

Our automated text-messaging service starts with a few basic steps.

1. Navigate to our Web site, skyreachmedia.co.au, select the Registration page, and then New User. You will then be guided through our simple and efficient registration to set up an account.

2. Once your account is activated, you can begin entering the automated responses intended for interested renters. Be sure to include comprehensive details about each property. You also have the option to incorporate images, audio recordings, videos, and links to external Web sites.

3. Designate a unique keyword for each property. This keyword is what prospective renters will text to obtain more information about a rental unit. It should not be excessively long or challenging to spell, and it must be easy for clients to recall.

4. Afterwards, simply wait. Those searching for apartments will pass by the location, spot the keyword, and upon texting it, instantly access the message you have programmed!

Your complimentary trial includes us producing fresh rental signs for one of your properties so that your advertisements incorporate the keyword. Should you contact me before Wednesday, I will also extend the order to cover two additional properties. Thus, in addition to a month of our text-messaging service, you'll acquire updated signs for three rental units, all entirely free of charge. Once the trial period ends, you may choose from six reasonably priced packages, including the option of dispatching daily updates to preferred customers.

I eagerly await your reply!

Nolan Barrett

172. What can be inferred regarding Ms. Morton?

(A) She is interested in securing a property to rent.
(B) She works professionally as a property rental agent.
(C) She has recently purchased a new mobile telephone.
(D) She frequently dispatches text messages.

173. What is indicated about Skyreach Media?

(A) It is a company that was recently founded.
(B) It fills orders with speed.
(C) It offers a novel service.
(D) It underwent a recent merger with another business.

174. What is mentioned about the automated responses?

(A) They are not identical for all properties.
(B) They can be forwarded to an e-mail address.
(C) They incorporate images captured by Skyreach Media.
(D) They compel apartment seekers to establish a password.

175. According to the e-mail, why should Ms. Morton communicate with Mr. Barrett before Wednesday?

(A) To extend her current plan
(B) To discuss pricing details
(C) To arrange property tours
(D) To take advantage of complimentary services

GO ON TO THE NEXT PAGE

This week's highlight

Featured this week is the documentary series *Blueprints Uncovered*, which, following lengthy editing and multiple delays caused by production setbacks, is at last hitting television screens. This four-episode journey, directed by Karim Haddad and Eleanor Ashcroft, uncovers lesser-known facts behind some of the most celebrated architectural landmarks across the globe. Viewers who admire actor and comedian Colin Radcliffe will be pleased to know he serves as the host, bringing both insight and humor to the narration. Produced by Erik Thorsen, the series is slated to appear on the Insight Sphere channel according to the schedule below.

EPISODE	AIRDATE

1. "Against All Odds"   June 5

This opening episode transports us to Ancient Egypt, where builders overcame formidable structural challenges to create enduring monuments.

2. "Hands That Built History"   June 12

Without the benefit of modern machinery, medieval craftsmen in Europe constructed towering cathedrals that would dominate the cityscape for centuries.

3. "The Shape of Now"   June 19

Here, we explore the elegance of contemporary architecture and uncover gripping narratives behind the design and execution of today's most iconic buildings.

4. "Beyond the Skyline"   June 26

The final installment looks ahead to concepts still in the making: revolutionary skyscraper designs, nature-inspired structures with reduced footprints, and other architectural marvels poised to grace future cities.

Freya Lindholm ★ ★ ★ ★ ★

After watching the premiere of *Blueprints Uncovered*, I'm absolutely hooked! Radcliffe does a tremendous job recounting the story; he's informative but also entertaining. The free companion booklet, available on Insight Sphere's Web site, should not be overlooked-it's packed with extra details about the buildings featured in the show and is indispensable for anyone eager to dive deeper into the subject.

176. What is indicated about the making of the program?

(A) It was a very costly process.
(B) It was prolonged past the initial timeline.
(C) It was financed by multiple sponsors.
(D) It involved a considerable number of producers.

177. Who appears in the documentary?

(A) Mr. Haddad
(B) Ms. Ashcroft
(C) Mr. Radcliffe
(D) Mr. Thorsen

178. What episode highlights themes related to modern urban planning?

(A) Episode 1
(B) Episode 2
(C) Episode 3
(D) Episode 4

179. When did Ms. Lindholm most likely view the program?

(A) On June 5
(B) On June 12
(C) On June 19
(D) On June 26

180. What does Ms. Lindholm recommend doing?

(A) Purchasing movies starring a specific actor
(B) Visiting the architectural sites shown in the series
(C) Accessing supplementary content online
(D) Watching other documentaries by the same director

GO ON TO THE NEXT PAGE

To:	Daniel Solano <solano@selvaverdeeco.com>
From:	Natalia Vetrova <nvetrova@pacificroutes.com>
Subject:	New Booking Request
Date:	July 18

Good afternoon, Mr. Solano,

I thoroughly appreciated our collaboration again, alongside you and all the staff at Selva Verde Eco Lodge. My clients found the rain forest tour to be very enjoyable. The couple who stayed in the Heliconia Bungalow commented that the view of the tropical garden from their room was breathtaking.

At this time, I wish to secure a booking for a new client, Min-jae Park. Please make the following arrangements for Mr. Park and his companion:
Arrival: August 14 (please arrange airport shuttle service)
Departure: August 17 (shuttle service also requested)
Room type: Double occupancy
Tour type: Guided rain forest hike (5-hour tour)

Flight information:
Savannalink Airways Flight SL312 from Incheon, arriving at 4:10 P.M. August 14
Savannalink Airways Flight SL309 to Incheon, departing at 10:30 A.M. August 17

Thank you again for the exceptional care you provide to my clients.

Natalia Vetrova
Travel Consultant, Pacific Routes

To:	Natalia Vetrova <nvetrova@pacificroutes.com>
From:	Daniel Solano <solano@selvaverdeeco.com>
Subject:	Park Reservation Confirmation
Date:	July 19

Ms. Vetrova,

Thank you for your message and for passing along such positive remarks from your clients.

The information about Mr. Park's reservation is as follows. Kindly be aware of our limited room options. The room we booked for him is marginally more expensive, with single rooms being the sole other choices.

Check-in date:	August 14
Check-out date:	August 17
Room:	Heliconia Bungalow
Rate:	$160 USD/night Total: $480 USD (excluding tax)
Tour type:	Guided Rain Forest Hike; August 15, 7:30 A.M. to 12:30 P.M.
Tour fee:	$85 USD

Please note that the transportation between the airport and the lodge has been arranged. The bill must be settled in full no later than August 10.

We treasure the ongoing business we conduct with Pacific Routes. Should you have any questions or concerns, please don't hesitate to reach out to me.

Daniel Solano
Guest Services, Selva Verde Eco Lodge

181. Why did Ms. Vetrova write to Mr. Solano?

(A) To recommend a new tour destination
(B) To inquire about flight information
(C) To provide assistance to a client
(D) To make a revision to an itinerary

182. What is suggested about Pacific Routes?

(A) It has a history of commercial activity
    with Selva Verde Eco Lodge.
(B) Its expertise lies in rain forest locales.
(C) It is situated in proximity to Selva
    Verde Eco Lodge.
(D) It is under Ms. Vetrova's ownership.

183. What does Mr. Park request?

(A) A loyal customer discount
(B) A booking confirmation
(C) A dining package
(D) A conveyance solution

184. What is indicated about Mr. Park?

(A) He has visited Selva Verde Eco Lodge
    on an earlier occasion.
(B) He will occupy a room that faces a
    garden.
(C) He has traveled in the company of Mr.
    Solano.
(D) He intends to travel by himself.

185. By when does Mr. Solano anticipate the
payment will be made?

(A) July 19
(B) August 10
(C) August 14
(D) August 17

http://www.clearhavencleaning.com

CLEARHAVEN CLEANING

298 Pine Hollow Road, Boulder, CO 80302

About Us	**Home**	Testimonials	Rates	Contact Us

Clearhaven Cleaning delivers comprehensive cleaning solutions that cater to both domestic and commercial clientele. We have maintained exceptional service at competitive prices for more than 15 years.

Beyond our standard offerings, we provide a premium cleaning option that utilizes all-natural, odor-free cleaning practices as well as products formulated to lessen allergens.

Clients may opt for weekly, biweekly, or monthly service plans, and we are happy to accommodate custom scheduling preferences. Our cleaning team is known for its punctuality in both arrival and completion. We provide a money-back guarantee if you are not entirely content.

Contact us to schedule a complimentary on-site assessment and quote. Call 1-303-555-0192 or head to our Web site at www.clearhavencleaning.com. Make sure to visit our testimonials page to read glowing reviews from our numerous satisfied clients.

To:	support@clearhavencleaning.com
From:	lharper@moduloformstudio.com
Re:	Cleaning Service Concern
Date:	November 9

To Whom It May Concern,

My company's premises were cleaned by Clearhaven Cleaning, whom I employed. Your advertisement, coupled with the strong recommendations from clients on your site, led me to believe I would be entirely pleased with your performance. Regrettably, that was not the case. I had explicitly requested your premium treatment, but your cleaning personnel neglected to provide it. Evidently, an issue arose. I am contemplating discontinuing the next scheduled appointment.

Lydia Harper
Moduloform Studio

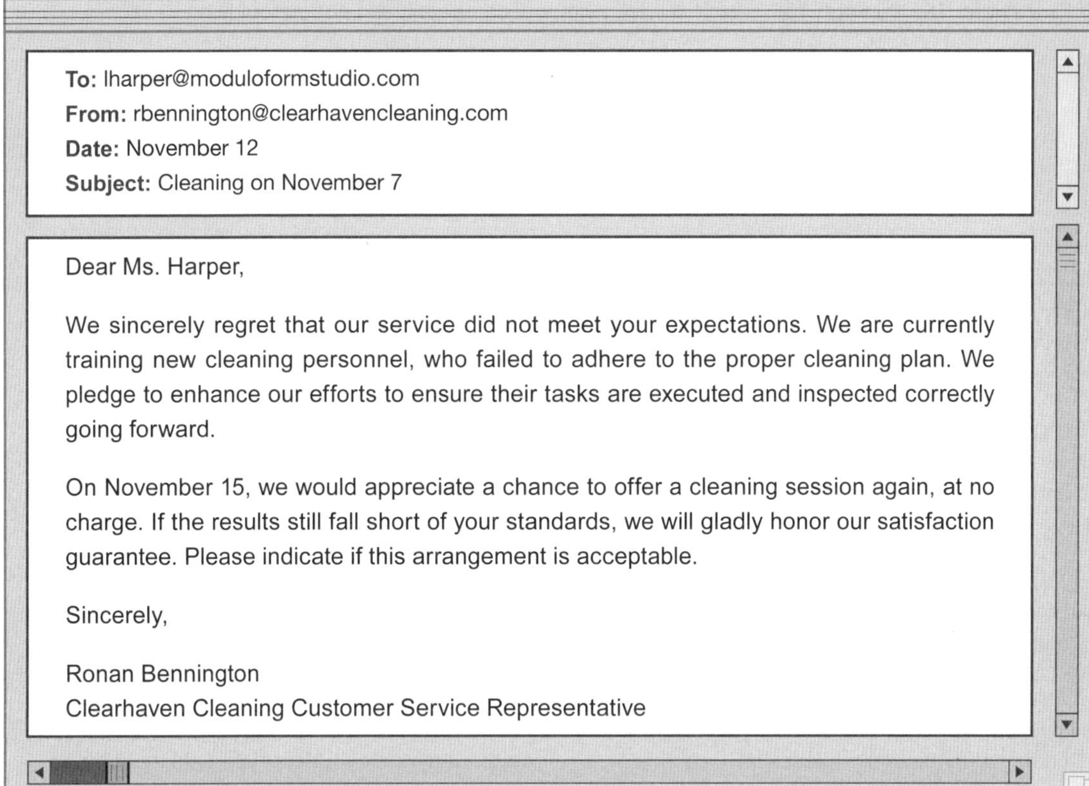

To: lharper@moduloformstudio.com
From: rbennington@clearhavencleaning.com
Date: November 12
Subject: Cleaning on November 7

Dear Ms. Harper,

We sincerely regret that our service did not meet your expectations. We are currently training new cleaning personnel, who failed to adhere to the proper cleaning plan. We pledge to enhance our efforts to ensure their tasks are executed and inspected correctly going forward.

On November 15, we would appreciate a chance to offer a cleaning session again, at no charge. If the results still fall short of your standards, we will gladly honor our satisfaction guarantee. Please indicate if this arrangement is acceptable.

Sincerely,

Ronan Bennington
Clearhaven Cleaning Customer Service Representative

186. What is indicated about Clearhaven Cleaning?

(A) It was recently established.
(B) It manufactures its own line of cleaning products.
(C) It delivers free in-person evaluations.
(D) It has just launched residential services.

187. What is implied about Ms. Harper?

(A) She investigated other cleaners before contacting Clearhaven Cleaning.
(B) She was referred to Clearhaven Cleaning by a acquaintance.
(C) She is seeking employment at Clearhaven Cleaning.
(D) She read customer feedback online prior to hiring Clearhaven Cleaning.

188. In the first e-mail, the word "case" in paragraph 1, line 3, is closest in meaning to

(A) argument
(B) instance
(C) situation
(D) investigation

189. Why did Ms. Harper express her dissatisfaction in writing?

(A) The office floors were not polished.
(B) The office kitchenette was not sterilized.
(C) The cleaners omitted shampooing the carpets.
(D) The cleaners did not employ eco-friendly products.

190. What commitment does Mr. Bennington make if Ms. Harper remains unsatisfied after November 15?

(A) To reimburse her expenses
(B) To devise an updated cleaning strategy
(C) To assign different cleaning employees
(D) To offer a reduced rate on subsequent cleaning work

Waikiki Monarch Hotel

Scheduled activities for guests in August

Start time for all activities is 10:00 A.M. at the Guest Services desk in the lobby.

Activity and instructor/guide	Description
Every Tuesday Surfing lesson Conducted by Kalani Kealoha	Master the art of surfing in Waikiki. Should be an adept swimmer. $60 per person. All participants must be 12 years or older.
Every Wednesday Hawaiian flower crafts Conducted by Elina Aquino	Your instructor will provide you with guidance in creating a lei: an ornamental Hawaiian flower garland or necklace. All supplies included. $12 per person.
Every Thursday History tour Conducted by Leilani Ogawa	This 2-hour walking tour will provide participants with an insight into Waikiki's history. No charge.
Every Friday Hawaiian cookery class Conducted by head chef Jessica Chen	Learn how to prepare authentic Hawaiian cuisine. (Lessons can be tailored to focus solely on vegetarian recipes.) All participants must be 12 years or older. $25 per person.

Visit the Guest Services desk for more information and to sign up.

To:	Guest Services Staff <gsstaff@waikikimonarchhotel.com>
From:	Soo-Min Lee <smlee@waikikimonarchhotel.com>
Date:	August 17
Subject:	Update

Hi all,

This month's program of guest activities needs to be revised. Elina Aquino and Jessica Chen will be away August 20-26. I will lead Elina's activities and Astrid Geensen will lead Jessica's. Everything will return to normal on August 27, when Elina and Jessica both return.

Sincerely,

Soo-Min Lee
Guest Services Director, Waikiki Monarch Hotel

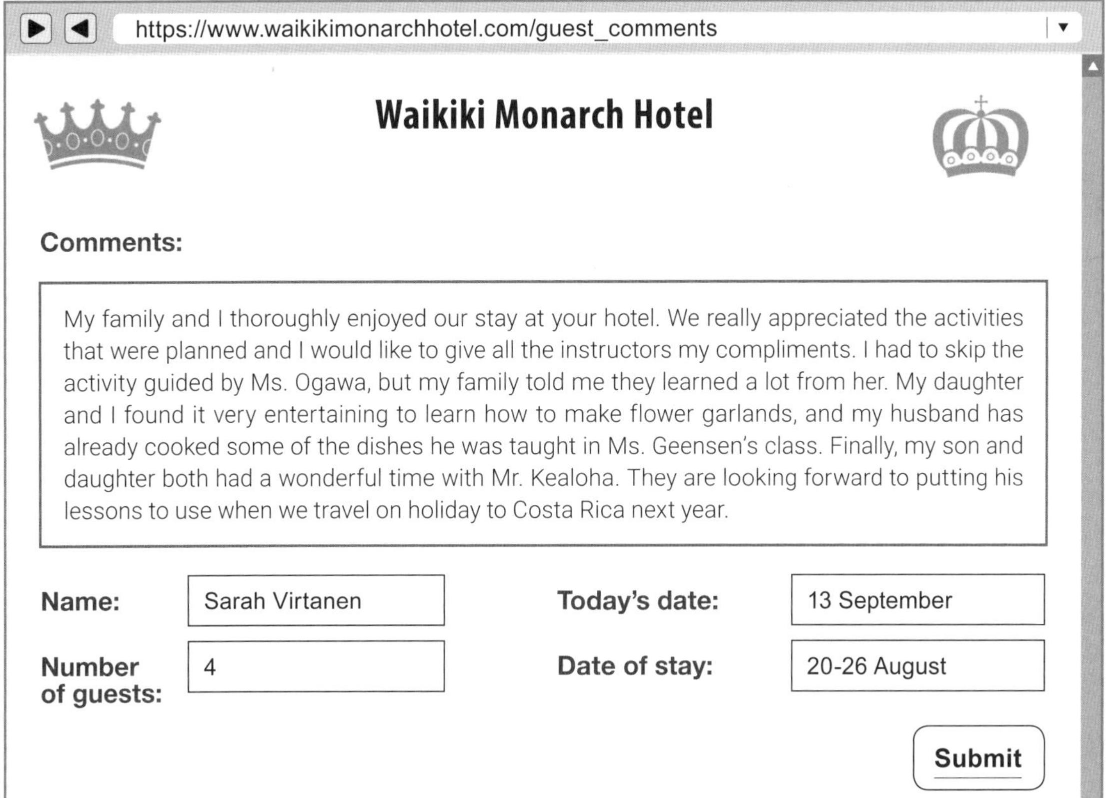

191. What activity can be customized?

(A) Tuesday's activity
(B) Wednesday's activity
(C) Thursday's activity
(D) Friday's activity

192. What is the purpose of the e-mail?

(A) To welcome two new employees
(B) To address a guest inquiry
(C) To make changes to a schedule
(D) To arrange training sessions for staff

193. In the comment form, the word "skip" in paragraph 1, line 2, is closest in meaning to

(A) jump
(B) miss
(C) pay for
(D) look over

194. Who taught the course enjoyed by Ms. Virtanen and her daughter?

(A) Ms. Aquino
(B) Ms. Lee
(C) Ms. Ogawa
(D) Ms. Chen

195. What are Ms. Virtanen's children planning to do in Costa Rica?

(A) Go surfing
(B) Learn traditional crafts
(C) Take a walking tour
(D) Try local food

GO ON TO THE NEXT PAGE

Redwood National Park Trails

Friendship Ridge Loop - *8.5 Kilometers*
Enjoy views of the Klamath River from the summit of Friendship Ridge. This path, of moderate difficulty, entails a steady incline to the summit of the ridge, followed by a well-defined trail that loops back and descends to the north parking lot.

Ossagon Slope - *6 Kilometers*
Trek up the side of Ossagon Ridge. This challenging trail features rocky terrain and intermittent steep climbs, providing scenic views of Orick Palisades Valley. The trailhead is located 100 meters to the south of the ranger station.

River's Edge - *6.7 Kilometers*
This trail stretches along the bank of the Klamath River. Starting at the north parking lot, the level trail leads to Orick Palisades Park.

Trillium Falls Trail - *3 Kilometers*
This leisurely trail commences at the rear of the main pavilion and extends through the Redwood Forest before culminating at Trillium Falls. Picnic and barbeque areas are scattered along the route.

To:	Nature Explorers Club
From:	Anne Zelnikova
Date:	Nature hike on Saturday
Re:	September 12
Attachment:	❏ Map

Hi, everyone

The nature hike this month is set for Saturday at 6:00 A.M. Since a number of people during our last trip to Fern Canyon expressly mentioned their desire to view the Klamath River, we decided to meet up at Redwood National Park this month. Please arrive in the north parking lot by 5:45 A.M. I have attached a park map for your reference. Don't forget to pack a lunch and plenty of water. Our hike will last approximately 5–6 hours.

See you on Saturday!

Anne

NOTICE

Posted September 14

The River's Edge trail has been closed due to flooding caused by recent rain storms and will not reopen until further notice. Please refrain from traveling on this trail and locations adjacent to the Klamath River bank until the floodwaters recede. The north parking lot was also affected by the floodwaters, and is currently under construction. Kindly leave your automobile in the east parking lot and follow the Ranger Path to reach the trailheads.

196. How long is the trail that goes up Ossagon Ridge?

(A) 3 kilometers
(B) 6 kilometers
(C) 6.7 kilometers
(D) 8.5 kilometers

197. In the e-mail, the phrase "expressly" in paragraph 1, line 2, is closest in meaning to

(A) affectionately
(B) correctly
(C) specifically
(D) totally

198. Where will Nature Explorers Club members likely hike?

(A) On Friendship Ridge Loop
(B) On Ossagon Slope
(C) On River's Edge
(D) On Trillium Falls Trail

199. What is indicated about Redwood National Park?

(A) It offers guided nature walks.
(B) It has multiple parking areas.
(C) It provides food for purchase.
(D) It opens at 6:00 A.M.

200. What will Nature Explorers Club members likely do upon arriving at the park?

(A) See Trillium Falls
(B) Eat at the pavilion
(C) Purchase a trail map
(D) Walk along Ranger Path

This is the end of the test. If you finish before time is called, you may go back to Parts 5, 6, and 7 and check your work.

정답 및 해설 p.166

◆ 각 TEST를 풀고 난 후, 맞은 개수를 세어 점수를 환산해 보세요.

READING Raw Score (맞은 개수)	READING Scaled Score (환산 점수)
96–100	460–495
91–95	425–490
86–90	400–465
81–85	375–440
76–80	340–415
71–75	310–390
66–70	285–370
61–65	255–340
56–60	230–310
51–55	200–275
46–50	170–245
41–45	140–215
36–40	115–180
31–35	95–150
26–30	75–120
21–25	60–95
16–20	45–75
11–15	30–55
6–10	10–40
1–5	5–30
0	5–15

자르는 선

Answer Sheet

TEST 01

READING (PART 5~7)									
1	Ⓐ Ⓑ Ⓒ Ⓓ	21	Ⓐ Ⓑ Ⓒ Ⓓ	41	Ⓐ Ⓑ Ⓒ Ⓓ	61	Ⓐ Ⓑ Ⓒ Ⓓ	81	Ⓐ Ⓑ Ⓒ Ⓓ
2	Ⓐ Ⓑ Ⓒ Ⓓ	22	Ⓐ Ⓑ Ⓒ Ⓓ	42	Ⓐ Ⓑ Ⓒ Ⓓ	62	Ⓐ Ⓑ Ⓒ Ⓓ	82	Ⓐ Ⓑ Ⓒ Ⓓ
3	Ⓐ Ⓑ Ⓒ Ⓓ	23	Ⓐ Ⓑ Ⓒ Ⓓ	43	Ⓐ Ⓑ Ⓒ Ⓓ	63	Ⓐ Ⓑ Ⓒ Ⓓ	83	Ⓐ Ⓑ Ⓒ Ⓓ
4	Ⓐ Ⓑ Ⓒ Ⓓ	24	Ⓐ Ⓑ Ⓒ Ⓓ	44	Ⓐ Ⓑ Ⓒ Ⓓ	64	Ⓐ Ⓑ Ⓒ Ⓓ	84	Ⓐ Ⓑ Ⓒ Ⓓ
5	Ⓐ Ⓑ Ⓒ Ⓓ	25	Ⓐ Ⓑ Ⓒ Ⓓ	45	Ⓐ Ⓑ Ⓒ Ⓓ	65	Ⓐ Ⓑ Ⓒ Ⓓ	85	Ⓐ Ⓑ Ⓒ Ⓓ
6	Ⓐ Ⓑ Ⓒ Ⓓ	26	Ⓐ Ⓑ Ⓒ Ⓓ	46	Ⓐ Ⓑ Ⓒ Ⓓ	66	Ⓐ Ⓑ Ⓒ Ⓓ	86	Ⓐ Ⓑ Ⓒ Ⓓ
7	Ⓐ Ⓑ Ⓒ Ⓓ	27	Ⓐ Ⓑ Ⓒ Ⓓ	47	Ⓐ Ⓑ Ⓒ Ⓓ	67	Ⓐ Ⓑ Ⓒ Ⓓ	87	Ⓐ Ⓑ Ⓒ Ⓓ
8	Ⓐ Ⓑ Ⓒ Ⓓ	28	Ⓐ Ⓑ Ⓒ Ⓓ	48	Ⓐ Ⓑ Ⓒ Ⓓ	68	Ⓐ Ⓑ Ⓒ Ⓓ	88	Ⓐ Ⓑ Ⓒ Ⓓ
9	Ⓐ Ⓑ Ⓒ Ⓓ	29	Ⓐ Ⓑ Ⓒ Ⓓ	49	Ⓐ Ⓑ Ⓒ Ⓓ	69	Ⓐ Ⓑ Ⓒ Ⓓ	89	Ⓐ Ⓑ Ⓒ Ⓓ
10	Ⓐ Ⓑ Ⓒ Ⓓ	30	Ⓐ Ⓑ Ⓒ Ⓓ	50	Ⓐ Ⓑ Ⓒ Ⓓ	70	Ⓐ Ⓑ Ⓒ Ⓓ	90	Ⓐ Ⓑ Ⓒ Ⓓ
11	Ⓐ Ⓑ Ⓒ Ⓓ	31	Ⓐ Ⓑ Ⓒ Ⓓ	51	Ⓐ Ⓑ Ⓒ Ⓓ	71	Ⓐ Ⓑ Ⓒ Ⓓ	91	Ⓐ Ⓑ Ⓒ Ⓓ
12	Ⓐ Ⓑ Ⓒ Ⓓ	32	Ⓐ Ⓑ Ⓒ Ⓓ	52	Ⓐ Ⓑ Ⓒ Ⓓ	72	Ⓐ Ⓑ Ⓒ Ⓓ	92	Ⓐ Ⓑ Ⓒ Ⓓ
13	Ⓐ Ⓑ Ⓒ Ⓓ	33	Ⓐ Ⓑ Ⓒ Ⓓ	53	Ⓐ Ⓑ Ⓒ Ⓓ	73	Ⓐ Ⓑ Ⓒ Ⓓ	93	Ⓐ Ⓑ Ⓒ Ⓓ
14	Ⓐ Ⓑ Ⓒ Ⓓ	34	Ⓐ Ⓑ Ⓒ Ⓓ	54	Ⓐ Ⓑ Ⓒ Ⓓ	74	Ⓐ Ⓑ Ⓒ Ⓓ	94	Ⓐ Ⓑ Ⓒ Ⓓ
15	Ⓐ Ⓑ Ⓒ Ⓓ	35	Ⓐ Ⓑ Ⓒ Ⓓ	55	Ⓐ Ⓑ Ⓒ Ⓓ	75	Ⓐ Ⓑ Ⓒ Ⓓ	95	Ⓐ Ⓑ Ⓒ Ⓓ
16	Ⓐ Ⓑ Ⓒ Ⓓ	36	Ⓐ Ⓑ Ⓒ Ⓓ	56	Ⓐ Ⓑ Ⓒ Ⓓ	76	Ⓐ Ⓑ Ⓒ Ⓓ	96	Ⓐ Ⓑ Ⓒ Ⓓ
17	Ⓐ Ⓑ Ⓒ Ⓓ	37	Ⓐ Ⓑ Ⓒ Ⓓ	57	Ⓐ Ⓑ Ⓒ Ⓓ	77	Ⓐ Ⓑ Ⓒ Ⓓ	97	Ⓐ Ⓑ Ⓒ Ⓓ
18	Ⓐ Ⓑ Ⓒ Ⓓ	38	Ⓐ Ⓑ Ⓒ Ⓓ	58	Ⓐ Ⓑ Ⓒ Ⓓ	78	Ⓐ Ⓑ Ⓒ Ⓓ	98	Ⓐ Ⓑ Ⓒ Ⓓ
19	Ⓐ Ⓑ Ⓒ Ⓓ	39	Ⓐ Ⓑ Ⓒ Ⓓ	59	Ⓐ Ⓑ Ⓒ Ⓓ	79	Ⓐ Ⓑ Ⓒ Ⓓ	99	Ⓐ Ⓑ Ⓒ Ⓓ
20	Ⓐ Ⓑ Ⓒ Ⓓ	40	Ⓐ Ⓑ Ⓒ Ⓓ	60	Ⓐ Ⓑ Ⓒ Ⓓ	80	Ⓐ Ⓑ Ⓒ Ⓓ	100	Ⓐ Ⓑ Ⓒ Ⓓ

RC 시험시간: 75분

맞은 문제 개수: ______ / 100

자르는 선

Answer Sheet

TEST 02

READING (PART 5~7)									
1	Ⓐ Ⓑ Ⓒ Ⓓ	21	Ⓐ Ⓑ Ⓒ Ⓓ	41	Ⓐ Ⓑ Ⓒ Ⓓ	61	Ⓐ Ⓑ Ⓒ Ⓓ	81	Ⓐ Ⓑ Ⓒ Ⓓ
2	Ⓐ Ⓑ Ⓒ Ⓓ	22	Ⓐ Ⓑ Ⓒ Ⓓ	42	Ⓐ Ⓑ Ⓒ Ⓓ	62	Ⓐ Ⓑ Ⓒ Ⓓ	82	Ⓐ Ⓑ Ⓒ Ⓓ
3	Ⓐ Ⓑ Ⓒ Ⓓ	23	Ⓐ Ⓑ Ⓒ Ⓓ	43	Ⓐ Ⓑ Ⓒ Ⓓ	63	Ⓐ Ⓑ Ⓒ Ⓓ	83	Ⓐ Ⓑ Ⓒ Ⓓ
4	Ⓐ Ⓑ Ⓒ Ⓓ	24	Ⓐ Ⓑ Ⓒ Ⓓ	44	Ⓐ Ⓑ Ⓒ Ⓓ	64	Ⓐ Ⓑ Ⓒ Ⓓ	84	Ⓐ Ⓑ Ⓒ Ⓓ
5	Ⓐ Ⓑ Ⓒ Ⓓ	25	Ⓐ Ⓑ Ⓒ Ⓓ	45	Ⓐ Ⓑ Ⓒ Ⓓ	65	Ⓐ Ⓑ Ⓒ Ⓓ	85	Ⓐ Ⓑ Ⓒ Ⓓ
6	Ⓐ Ⓑ Ⓒ Ⓓ	26	Ⓐ Ⓑ Ⓒ Ⓓ	46	Ⓐ Ⓑ Ⓒ Ⓓ	66	Ⓐ Ⓑ Ⓒ Ⓓ	86	Ⓐ Ⓑ Ⓒ Ⓓ
7	Ⓐ Ⓑ Ⓒ Ⓓ	27	Ⓐ Ⓑ Ⓒ Ⓓ	47	Ⓐ Ⓑ Ⓒ Ⓓ	67	Ⓐ Ⓑ Ⓒ Ⓓ	87	Ⓐ Ⓑ Ⓒ Ⓓ
8	Ⓐ Ⓑ Ⓒ Ⓓ	28	Ⓐ Ⓑ Ⓒ Ⓓ	48	Ⓐ Ⓑ Ⓒ Ⓓ	68	Ⓐ Ⓑ Ⓒ Ⓓ	88	Ⓐ Ⓑ Ⓒ Ⓓ
9	Ⓐ Ⓑ Ⓒ Ⓓ	29	Ⓐ Ⓑ Ⓒ Ⓓ	49	Ⓐ Ⓑ Ⓒ Ⓓ	69	Ⓐ Ⓑ Ⓒ Ⓓ	89	Ⓐ Ⓑ Ⓒ Ⓓ
10	Ⓐ Ⓑ Ⓒ Ⓓ	30	Ⓐ Ⓑ Ⓒ Ⓓ	50	Ⓐ Ⓑ Ⓒ Ⓓ	70	Ⓐ Ⓑ Ⓒ Ⓓ	90	Ⓐ Ⓑ Ⓒ Ⓓ
11	Ⓐ Ⓑ Ⓒ Ⓓ	31	Ⓐ Ⓑ Ⓒ Ⓓ	51	Ⓐ Ⓑ Ⓒ Ⓓ	71	Ⓐ Ⓑ Ⓒ Ⓓ	91	Ⓐ Ⓑ Ⓒ Ⓓ
12	Ⓐ Ⓑ Ⓒ Ⓓ	32	Ⓐ Ⓑ Ⓒ Ⓓ	52	Ⓐ Ⓑ Ⓒ Ⓓ	72	Ⓐ Ⓑ Ⓒ Ⓓ	92	Ⓐ Ⓑ Ⓒ Ⓓ
13	Ⓐ Ⓑ Ⓒ Ⓓ	33	Ⓐ Ⓑ Ⓒ Ⓓ	53	Ⓐ Ⓑ Ⓒ Ⓓ	73	Ⓐ Ⓑ Ⓒ Ⓓ	93	Ⓐ Ⓑ Ⓒ Ⓓ
14	Ⓐ Ⓑ Ⓒ Ⓓ	34	Ⓐ Ⓑ Ⓒ Ⓓ	54	Ⓐ Ⓑ Ⓒ Ⓓ	74	Ⓐ Ⓑ Ⓒ Ⓓ	94	Ⓐ Ⓑ Ⓒ Ⓓ
15	Ⓐ Ⓑ Ⓒ Ⓓ	35	Ⓐ Ⓑ Ⓒ Ⓓ	55	Ⓐ Ⓑ Ⓒ Ⓓ	75	Ⓐ Ⓑ Ⓒ Ⓓ	95	Ⓐ Ⓑ Ⓒ Ⓓ
16	Ⓐ Ⓑ Ⓒ Ⓓ	36	Ⓐ Ⓑ Ⓒ Ⓓ	56	Ⓐ Ⓑ Ⓒ Ⓓ	76	Ⓐ Ⓑ Ⓒ Ⓓ	96	Ⓐ Ⓑ Ⓒ Ⓓ
17	Ⓐ Ⓑ Ⓒ Ⓓ	37	Ⓐ Ⓑ Ⓒ Ⓓ	57	Ⓐ Ⓑ Ⓒ Ⓓ	77	Ⓐ Ⓑ Ⓒ Ⓓ	97	Ⓐ Ⓑ Ⓒ Ⓓ
18	Ⓐ Ⓑ Ⓒ Ⓓ	38	Ⓐ Ⓑ Ⓒ Ⓓ	58	Ⓐ Ⓑ Ⓒ Ⓓ	78	Ⓐ Ⓑ Ⓒ Ⓓ	98	Ⓐ Ⓑ Ⓒ Ⓓ
19	Ⓐ Ⓑ Ⓒ Ⓓ	39	Ⓐ Ⓑ Ⓒ Ⓓ	59	Ⓐ Ⓑ Ⓒ Ⓓ	79	Ⓐ Ⓑ Ⓒ Ⓓ	99	Ⓐ Ⓑ Ⓒ Ⓓ
20	Ⓐ Ⓑ Ⓒ Ⓓ	40	Ⓐ Ⓑ Ⓒ Ⓓ	60	Ⓐ Ⓑ Ⓒ Ⓓ	80	Ⓐ Ⓑ Ⓒ Ⓓ	100	Ⓐ Ⓑ Ⓒ Ⓓ

RC 시험시간: 75분

맞은 문제 개수: ______ / 100

자르는 선 ✂

Answer Sheet

TEST

READING (PART 5~7)

RC 시험시간: 75분

맞은 문제 개수: ______ / 100

TEST 05

READING (PART 5~7)

RC 시험시간: 75분

맞은 문제 개수: ______ / 100

▌ 이교희

2009년에 강남에서 강의를 시작하며 정기 토익에서 10회 만점을 달성했다. 가장 효율적인 문제 풀이 방식을 제시하는 깔끔한 강의로 수강생들의 호응을 얻었으며, 각종 인터넷 강의로도 수많은 수험생들과 만났다. 강사이자 저자로서 끊임없이 축적해 온 연구의 결실을 '토익 마법 – 2주의 기적 실전편'을 통해 함께 즐겨보자.

약력

● 학원

광주광역시 제제 외국어학원 대표 강사
파고다 외국어학원 토익 일타 강사(신촌, 종로)
현, 안산 이지어학원 토익 대표 강사

● 인터넷 강의

ujeje.com
Cracking TOEIC
파고다스타 '이교희의 탑토익 족보공개'

● 저서

토익 마법 2주의 기적 실전편 1 RC (2026)
토익 마법 2주의 기적 실전편 1 LC (2026)
토익 마법 2주의 기적 990 RC (2024)
토익 마법 2주의 기적 990 LC (2024)
토익 마법 2주의 기적 RC (2022)
토익 마법 2주의 기적 LC (2022)
시나공 토익 950 실전 모의고사 (2012)
파고다 외국어학원 월간 모의고사 해설

토익 마법 2주의 기적 실전편1 RC

2026. 2. 18. 초 판 1쇄 인쇄
2026. 2. 25. 초 판 1쇄 발행

지은이 ｜ 이교희
펴낸이 ｜ 이종춘
펴낸곳 ｜ BM (주)도서출판 **성안당**
주소 ｜ 04032 서울시 마포구 양화로 127 첨단빌딩 3층(출판기획 R&D 센터)
｜ 10881 경기도 파주시 문발로 112 파주 출판 문화도시(제작 및 물류)
전화 ｜ 02) 3142-0036
｜ 031) 950-6300
팩스 ｜ 031) 955-0510
등록 ｜ 1973. 2. 1. 제406-2005-000046호
출판사 홈페이지 ｜ www.cyber.co.kr
ISBN ｜ 978-89-315-8345-8 (13740)
정가 ｜ **19,800원**

이 책을 만든 사람들
책임 ｜ 최옥현
진행 ｜ 김은주
편집 · 교정 ｜ 김은주, 박가현
영문 검수 ｜ Thomas Giammarco
본문 디자인 ｜ 신인남
표지 디자인 ｜ 임흥순
홍보 ｜ 김계향, 임진성, 김주승, 최정민
국제부 ｜ 이선민, 조혜란
마케팅 ｜ 구본철, 차정욱, 오영일, 나진호, 강호묵
마케팅 지원 ｜ 장상범
제작 ｜ 김유석

■ **도서 A/S 안내**

성안당에서 발행하는 모든 도서는 저자와 출판사, 그리고 독자가 함께 만들어 나갑니다.
좋은 책을 펴내기 위해 많은 노력을 기울이고 있습니다. 혹시라도 내용상의 오류나 오탈자 등이
발견되면 **"좋은 책은 나라의 보배"**로서 우리 모두가 함께 만들어 간다는 마음으로 연락주시기
바랍니다. 수정 보완하여 더 나은 책이 되도록 최선을 다하겠습니다.
성안당은 늘 독자 여러분들의 소중한 의견을 기다리고 있습니다. 좋은 의견을 보내주시는 분께는
성안당 쇼핑몰의 포인트(3,000포인트)를 적립해 드립니다.

잘못 만들어진 책이나 부록 등이 파손된 경우에는 교환해 드립니다.

토익마법 RC

2주의 기적

실전편1

해설집

BM (주)도서출판 성안당

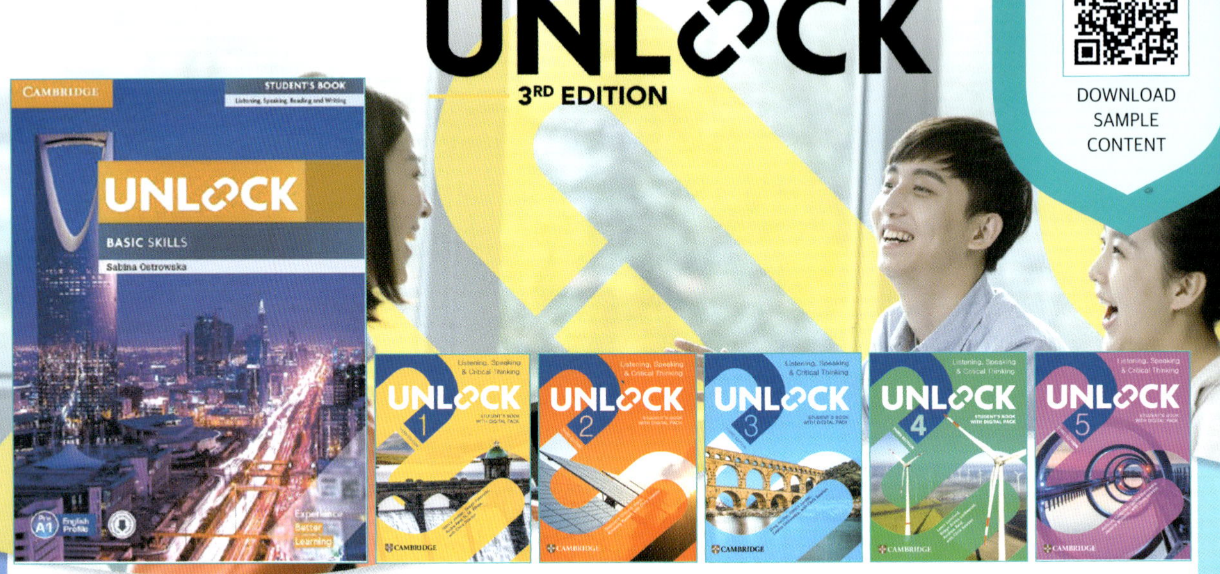

www.cambridge.org/unlock

비판적 사고력을 여는 첫걸음, **Unlock** 시리즈!

학습에서의 이해부터 분석까지, 균형 잡힌 사고를 키우는 최적의 코스입니다.
언어 학습 초기부터 학문적 맥락에서 비판적 사고를 할 수 있도록 이끌어 줍니다.

- **Critical Thinking Skills** 측정 목표와 자기 평가를 통한 비판적 사고 기술 습득

- **Video Content** 비디오 강의를 통해 학문, 시사 및 일반 관심사 등 다양한 콘텐츠로 동기 부여

- **Cambridge English Corpus** 수십억 단어로 구성된 캠브리지 코퍼스로 실제로 사용되는
  언어를 제공함으로써 적합한 콘텐츠의 최신 언어 학습

- **Cambridge One** 캠브리지 학습관리 플랫폼인 Cambridge One에서 추가 학습 및 다운로드
  - eBook, Class audio, Video, Digital Workbook with videos, Teacher Resources
  - 읽기 및 듣기 자료, 대학 수업용 자료, 테스트

The digital resources

Presentation Plus | Interactive eBook with Audio and Video | Video | Downloadable Audio | Teacher Training

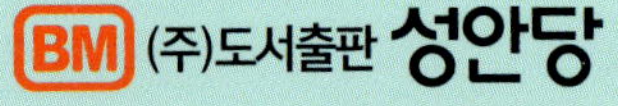

도서문의 031-950-6394

토익마법

2주의 기적

실전편1 RC

해설집

BM (주)도서출판 성안당

➡ **Answer**

101	(C)	111	(C)	121	(C)	131	(A)	141	(B)	151	(A)	161	(D)	171	(D)	181	(D)	191	(D)
102	(B)	112	(A)	122	(D)	132	(C)	142	(D)	152	(B)	162	(C)	172	(B)	182	(B)	192	(A)
103	(D)	113	(B)	123	(D)	133	(D)	143	(A)	153	(C)	163	(D)	173	(B)	183	(B)	193	(B)
104	(C)	114	(D)	124	(C)	134	(B)	144	(B)	154	(A)	164	(C)	174	(D)	184	(C)	194	(A)
105	(D)	115	(B)	125	(D)	135	(B)	145	(D)	155	(B)	165	(A)	175	(C)	185	(B)	195	(B)
106	(B)	116	(A)	126	(B)	136	(C)	146	(C)	156	(C)	166	(D)	176	(B)	186	(B)	196	(B)
107	(D)	117	(B)	127	(A)	137	(A)	147	(D)	157	(B)	167	(B)	177	(D)	187	(B)	197	(D)
108	(D)	118	(C)	128	(A)	138	(C)	148	(A)	158	(B)	168	(A)	178	(A)	188	(C)	198	(A)
109	(D)	119	(C)	129	(D)	139	(B)	149	(A)	159	(C)	169	(A)	179	(A)	189	(D)	199	(A)
110	(A)	120	(D)	130	(A)	140	(A)	150	(B)	160	(D)	170	(B)	180	(C)	190	(A)	200	(C)

PART 5

101

Ms. Moon noted that Mr. Al-Masri is ------- late for meetings.

(A) little
(B) far
(C) seldom
(D) well

Ms. Moon은 Mr. Al-Masri가 회의에 거의 늦지 않는 다는 점을 언급했다.

어휘 note 언급하다

해설 현재 시제 동사 is를 수식하여 "늦는 일이 거의 없다."라는 뜻이 되도록 빈도 부사 (C) seldom을 선택하는 게 알맞다. (A) little은 빈도를 나타내는 부사가 아니며, (B) far는 보통 비교급 형용사/부사를 수식한다. (D) well은 형용사를 수식하는 경우 '충분히'라는 뜻이다.

102

The Opelika Lecture Series is ------- by a number of local organizations.

(A) traded
(B) sponsored
(C) explored
(D) achieved

Opelika 강연 시리즈는 여러 지역 단체들의 후원을 받는다.

어휘 trade 거래하다, 교환하다 sponsor 후원하다 explore 탐험하다, 탐구하다

해설 Lecture Series is ------- by a number of local organizations(강연 시리즈가 여러 지역 단체들에 의해 [(A) 교환된다 (B) 후원받는다 (C) 탐구된다 (D) 달성된다]).의 의미를 자연스럽게 만들어 주는 동사를 정답으로 선택해야 한다.

103

Bavarian Motors will ------- its current name even after merging with a competitor.

(A) receive
(B) inquire
(C) grant
(D) retain

Bavarian Motors는 경쟁사와 합병한 후에도 현재 이름을 유지할 것이다.

어휘 retain 유지하다, 보유하다 merge 합병하다 competitor 경쟁사 inquire 문의하다 grant 수여하다

해설 빈칸 앞뒤 will ------- its current name(현재의 이름을 [(A) 받을 것이다 (B) 문의할 것이다 (C) 수여할 것이다 (D) 유지할 것이다])의 의미를 자연스럽게 만들어 주는 동사가 정답이다.

104

Mr. Nishimura identified a defect in the strategy ------- requires immediate attention.

(A) whichever
(B) whose
(C) that
(D) who

Mr. Nishimura는 즉각적인 주의가 필요한 그 전략의 결함을 밝혀냈다.

어휘 identify 밝히다, 규명하다 defect 결함 strategy 전략 immediate 즉각적인 attention 주의, 관심

해설 빈칸 앞뒤 a defect in the strategy ------- requires만 보면 정답을 알 수 있다. 복합 관계대명사는 선행사가 없을 때 쓰이므로 (A)는 정답이 될 수 없다. 선행사 a defect in the strategy는 사람이 아니므로 (D) who도 오답이다. 빈칸 바로 뒤에 동사가 있을 때는 주격 관계대명사가 정답이라는 사실을 기억하자.

105

Ms. Chambers strives to make our resources ------- to employees who work remotely.

(A) accesses
(B) accessibility
(C) more accessibly
(D) more accessible

Ms. Chambers는 원격으로 근무하는 직원들이 우리 자료를 더 쉽게 이용할 수 있도록 노력한다.

어휘 strive 노력하다, 애쓰다 resources 자원, 자료 accessibility 접근 가능성 accessible 접근[이용] 가능한 remotely 원격으로

해설 빈칸 앞에서 동사 make를 발견해야 한다. find, make, keep, consider 같은 5형식 동사가 보이면 목적격 보어 자리에 형용사를 넣어야 한다.

106

Employee handbooks detail the fundamental ------- of the employer-employee relationship.

(A) exercises
(B) elements
(C) similarities
(D) recipes

직원 안내서는 고용주와 직원 관계의 근본적인 요소들을 상세히 설명한다.

어휘 handbook 안내서, 편람 detail 상세히 설명하다 fundamental 근본적인 element 요소, 성분

해설 the fundamental ------- of the employer-employee relationship(고용주와 직원 관계의 근본적인 [(A) 운동 (B) 요소 (C) 유사성 (D) 조리법])의 의미를 자연스럽게 만들어 주는 명사가 정답이다.

107

Mr. Bui's letter is in response to the fax and e-mail dated the 10th and 13th of September, -------.

(A) respects
(B) respecting
(C) respective
(D) respectively

Mr. Bui의 편지는 각각 9월 10일과 13일로 되어 있는 팩스와 이메일에 대한 답변입니다.

어휘 in response to ~에 대한 답변으로 date A B(날짜) A에 B(날짜)를 적다 respective 각각의

해설 dated the 10th and 13th of September가 앞에 있는 명사 the fax and e-mail을 수식하고 있으며, the fax – the 10th, the e-mail – the 13th의 대응 관계를 나타내기 위해 부사 respectively가 필요하다.

108

The wellness workshop at the Community Center serves as a ------- for discussing healthy habits.

(A) selection
(B) ground
(C) vision
(D) forum

지역 문화 센터에서 하는 웰빙 워크숍은 건강한 습관을 논하기 위한 공개 토론장의 역할을 한다.

어휘 wellness 웰빙, 건강 serve as ~의 역할을 하다 forum 포럼, 공개 토론(장)

해설 The wellness workshop ... serves as a ------- for discussing healthy habits(웰빙 워크숍은 건강한 습관을 논하기 위한 [(A) 선택 (B) 땅 / 근거 (C) 비전 (D) 공개 토론장]의 역할을 한다).를 자연스러운 문장으로 만들어 주는 명사가 정답이다.

109

The inn is ------- located near various restaurants and shops, all within a short walking distance.

(A) widely　　　　　　　　　(B) quickly
(C) gradually　　　　　　　**(D) conveniently**

그 호텔은 다양한 식당과 상점 근처에 편리하게 위치해 있으며, 모두 걸어서 갈 수 있는 짧은 거리에 있다.

어휘 widely 널리, 광범위하게　gradually 점차, 서서히　conveniently 편리하게　within a short walking distance 걸어서 갈 수 있는 짧은 거리에

해설 항상 짝을 이루어 출제되는 어휘 문제는 암기하고 있다가 재빨리 정답을 선택할 수 있도록 하자. be ------- located[situated]가 보이면 정답은 무조건 conveniently, perfectly, ideally 중 하나다.

110

It is anticipated that employee performance reviews ------- will be finalized by next Thursday.

(A) ideally　　　　　　　(B) lately
(C) relatively　　　　　　　(D) attractively

직원 성과 평가는 이상적으로는 다음 주 목요일까지 마무리될 것으로 예상됩니다.

어휘 anticipate 기대하다　performance review 성과 평가　ideally 이상적으로　lately 최근에　relatively 상대적으로, 비교적　finalize 마무리하다, 완결하다

해설 employee performance reviews ------- will be finalized by next Thursday(직원 성과 평가는 [(A) 이상적으로 (B) 최근에 (C) 상대적으로 (D) 매력적으로] 다음 주 목요일까지 마무리될 것이다)가 자연스러운 문장이 되는 부사를 정답으로 선택해야 한다.

111

A courier is delivering the documents Mr. Houston ------- to review and approve by the end of the day.

(A) need　　　　　　　　　(B) needing
(C) needs　　　　　　　　(D) to need

택배 기사가 Mr. Houston이 오늘 안으로 검토하고 승인해야 할 문서를 배달하고 있다.

어휘 courier 택배 기사　approve 승인하다

해설 빈칸 뒤에 to review and approve의 목적어가 없으므로 the documents 뒤에 목적격 관계대명사 which/that이 생략되어 있음을 파악할 수 있다. 그렇다면 관계대명사 절 안에 동사가 없으므로 빈칸에는 동사 (A)나 (C)가 들어가야 한다. 주어 Mr. Houston이 단수 명사이므로 단수 동사를 선택하자.

112

Imbriani Architects emphasized that the library ------- a single-story structure to ensure easy access for all.

(A) should remain　　　　(B) that remains
(C) to remain　　　　　　　(D) remaining

Imbriani Architects는 도서관이 모든 사람이 쉽게 접근할 수 있도록 단층 구조로 유지되어야 한다고 강조했다.

어휘 single-story structure 단층 구조　ensure 보장하다, 확실하게 하다　access 접근

해설 [(A) 동사 (B) 주격 관계대명사 + 동사 (C) 준동사 (D) 준동사] that절에 동사가 없으므로 빈칸에 동사를 넣어야 한다. (B)에 동사가 있지만 이 선택지를 고르면 수식어구인 관계대명사 that이 이끄는 절 전체의 동사는 없는 것이 된다.

113

An independent accounting firm that specializes in charitable foundations is conducting the outside -------.

(A) area　　　　　　　　　**(B) audit**
(C) purpose　　　　　　　　(D) product

자선 재단을 전문으로 하는 별도의 회계 법인이 외부 감사를 실시하고 있다.

어휘 independent (기관, 단체가) 독립된, 별개의　accounting firm 회계 법인　specialize in ~을 전문으로 하다　charitable foundation 자선 재단　audit 회계 감사

해설 is conducting the outside -------(외부 [(A) 영역을 (B) 회계 감사를 (C) 목적을 (D) 상품을] 실시하고 있다)를 의미상 자연스러운 어구로 만들어 주는 명사가 정답이다.

114

------- in the instructions provided for the device can details about a flashing orange indicator be found.

(A) Someone
(B) Either
(C) While
(D) Nowhere

장치에 제공된 설명서 어디에서도 깜박이는 주황색 표시등에 대한 세부 사항을 찾을 수 없습니다.

어휘 nowhere 아무 데도 (~ 없다), 어디에도 (~ 않다) instructions 지침, 사용 설명서 flash 깜빡이다 indicator 표시등

해설 can details about a flashing orange indicator be found에서 주어와 동사가 도치되었다는 것을 발견해야 한다. little, seldom, hardly, rarely, scarcely, never, in no way, nowhere, no sooner 같은 부정어로 시작하는 문장에서는 도치가 일어난다.

115

Mr. Tian felt proud to be recognized for ------- dedicated years of contribution to the Wenhardt Company.

(A) he
(B) his
(C) him
(D) himself

Mr. Tian은 Wenhardt 사(社)에 헌신한 수년간의 공로를 인정받아 자랑스러웠다.

어휘 be recognized for ~으로 인정받다 dedicated 헌신적인 contribution 공헌

해설 빈칸 앞뒤 for ------- dedicated years of contribution만 보면 정답을 알 수 있다. 명사 앞에 빈칸이 있으면 소유격 대명사가 정답이다.

116

TRX Industries guarantees on-time delivery of all replacement parts ------- remote the destination may be.

(A) no matter how
(B) insofar as
(C) wherever
(D) in order that

TRX Industries는 목적지가 아무리 멀리 떨어져 있더라도 모든 교체 부품의 정시 배송을 보장합니다.

어휘 on-time 정시의 replacement part 교체 부품 no matter how 아무리 ~해도 insofar as ~하는 한에 있어서는 in order that ~하기 위해 remote 먼, 멀리 떨어진 destination 목적지

해설 빈칸 뒤에 있는 형용사 remote에 주목하자. 네 개의 선택지 모두 부사절 접속사로 사용할 수 있지만 바로 뒤에 형용사나 부사를 붙여서 사용하는 것은 (A) no matter how밖에 없다.

117

The presence of the royal couple at the National Maritime Museum is likely to ------- impact traffic in the vicinity.

(A) previously
(B) dramatically
(C) punctually
(D) sternly

왕족 부부가 국립 해양 박물관을 방문하는 것은 인근 교통에 크게 영향을 미칠 것으로 보인다.

어휘 presence (행사나 장소에) 방문, 참석 royal 왕실의 maritime 해양의 be likely to-V ~할 것 같다 vicinity 부근, 근처 previously 사전에 dramatically 극적으로, 크게 punctually 시간을 잘 지켜서 sternly 엄격하게

해설 빈칸 앞뒤 is likely to ------- impact([(A) 사전에 (B) 크게 (C) 시간을 엄수하여 (D) 엄격하게] 영향을 미칠 가능성이 있다)를 자연스러운 어구로 만들어 줄 부사를 정답으로 선택해야 한다.

118

In the field of sports medicine, Christie Draper is a recognized therapist, and her services are very ------- priced.

(A) strongly
(B) internally
(C) reasonably
(D) repeatedly

스포츠 의학 분야에서 Christie Draper는 인정받는 치료사이며 그녀의 서비스는 가격이 매우 합리적이다.

어휘 field 분야, 영역 recognize (사실, 중요성 등을) 인정하다 therapist 치료사 internally 내부적으로 reasonably priced 합리적인 가격인 repeatedly 반복해서

해설 항상 짝을 이루어 출제되는 어휘는 암기하고 있다가 재빨리 정답을 선택하자. 보통 형용사 어휘 문제로 출제되는데, price나 rate 앞에 빈칸이 있으면 무조건 reasonable이나 affordable이 정답이다. 과거분사 priced 앞이 빈칸이면 부사 reasonably나 affordably가 정답이다.

To ------- the Adelaide's Apparel store closest to you, choose your state or country from the drop-down menu.
(A) afford
(B) create
(C) locate
(D) provide

가장 가까운 Adelaide's Apparel 매장을 찾으려면 드롭다운 메뉴에서 거주하는 주나 국가를 선택하십시오.

어휘 afford 제공하다 locate 찾아내다 drop-down menu 드롭다운 메뉴(클릭하면 아래로 확장되어 뜨는 선택 메뉴)

해설 To------- the Adelaide's Apparel store closest to you(가장 가까운 Adelaide's Apparel 매장을 [(A) 제공하려면 (B) 만들려면 (C) 찾으려면 (D) 제공하려면])의 의미를 가장 자연스럽게 만들어 주는 동사가 어느 것인지 생각해 보자.

Ms. Ochoa earned commendation because the quality of her work ------- surpasses even the highest expectations.
(A) consists
(B) consisted
(C) consisting
(D) consistently

Ms. Ochoa는 작업의 품질이 일관되게 최고 기대치마저 뛰어넘었기 때문에 칭찬을 받았다.

어휘 earn (존경, 칭찬 등을) 받다 commendation 칭찬, 찬사 consist (of와 함께) ~으로 구성되다 consistently 일관되게, 한결같이 surpass 뛰어넘다, 능가하다

해설 빈칸 앞뒤 the quality of her work ------- surpasses만 보면 정답을 알 수 있다. '주어 + ------- + 동사' 유형의 문제에서는 빈칸 뒤 동사를 수식하는 부사가 정답이다.

Ms. Rabinowitz suggested that the manufacturing plant should replace the outdated equipment as ------- as possible.
(A) necessarily
(B) definitely
(C) rapidly
(D) predominantly

Ms. Rabinowitz는 제조 공장이 구식 장비를 되도록 빨리 교체할 것을 제안했다.

어휘 manufacturing plant 제조 공장 outdated 구식의 necessarily 불가피하게 definitely 확실히 rapidly 빠르게, 급속하게 predominantly 대부분, 주로

해설 빈칸 앞뒤 as ------- as possible(되도록 [(A) 불가피하게 (B) 확실히 (C) 빨리 (D) 대부분])를 의미가 통하게 만들어 주는 부사는 하나밖에 없다.

The *Aspen Journal of Cardiology*'s editorial team is ------- about which articles they publish.
(A) prominent
(B) punctual
(C) rigorous
(D) selective

Aspen 심장의학 저널의 편집팀은 어느 논문을 게재할 것인지에 대해 선택이 까다롭다.

어휘 journal (학술) 잡지 cardiology 심장학 editorial 편집(상)의 prominent 저명한 punctual 시간을 잘 지키는 rigorous 철저한, 엄격한 selective 까다롭게[꼼꼼하게] 선택하는 article (학술지의) 논문 publish 게재하다

해설 학술지에 게재할 글을 까다롭게 선택한다는 내용의 문장이므로 내용에 가장 알맞은 형용사는 (D) selective이다.

Thanks to its innovative features, the Omega X12 is ------- the most advanced smartphone available on the market today.
(A) negatively
(B) doubtfully
(C) sincerely
(D) arguably

혁신적인 기능들 덕분에 Omega X12는 현재 시중에 나온 스마트폰 중에서 거의 틀림없이 가장 앞선 제품이라 할 만하다.

어휘 innovative 혁신적인 feature (특징적인) 기능 doubtfully 의심스럽다는 듯이 arguably 거의 틀림없이, 가장 ~이라고 할 만한 advanced 진보한, 앞선

해설 빈칸 앞뒤를 잘 보자. the Omega X12 is ------- the most advanced smartphone(Omega X12는 [(A) 부정적으로 (B) 의심스럽다는 듯이 (C) 진심으로 (D) 거의 틀림없이] 가장 진보한 스마트폰이다)를 자연스러운 문장으로 만들어주는 부사를 선택해야 한다.

124

Policyholders are allowed to terminate their policy whenever they choose, ------- they submit written notice at least 30 days prior.

(A) along with
(B) according to
(C) provided that
(D) regardless of

보험 가입자는 최소 30일 전에 통지서를 제출한다면 원할 때 언제든지 계약을 종료하는 것이 허용된다.

어휘 policyholder 보험 계약자[가입자] terminate 종료하다 policy 보험 계약 along with ~와 함께 provided that (만약) ~이라면 regardless of ~에 관계없이 written notice 통지서 prior 전에, 앞서

해설 [(A) 전치사구 (B) 전치사구 (C) 부사절 접속사 (D) 전치사구] 빈칸 뒤에 절이 있으므로 부사절 접속사를 선택해야 한다.

125

Online communication is an excellent ------- to bring researchers and practitioners together to address practical issues in the field.

(A) technique
(B) approach
(C) instrument
(D) means

온라인 커뮤니케이션은 연구자들과 실무자들을 한데 모아 현장의 실질적인 문제들을 해결하는 탁월한 수단이다.

어휘 instrument 기구 means 수단, 방법 bring together ~을 한데 모으다 practitioner (전문직) 실무자 address 다루다, 해결하다

해설 온라인 커뮤니케이션을 '접근법(approach)'으로 표현하는 것은 적절하지만 approach 뒤에는 to부정사가 아니라 전치사 to를 사용해야 한다. 온라인 커뮤니케이션을 '기술/기법(technique)'의 일종으로 보는 것도 가능하지만 이 문장의 문맥에는 맞지 않다. instrument는 물리적인 '기구'를 주로 뜻하는데, 비유적으로 사용할 수도 있지만, 이 문장에서는 자연스럽지 않다. 온라인 커뮤니케이션을 문제 해결의 '수단/방법(means)'이라고 일컫는 것이 문맥에 맞다.

126

Industry analysts continue ------- the significance of social media marketing in enhancing brand awareness for fashion designers.

(A) emphasis
(B) to emphasize
(C) are emphasizing
(D) to be emphasized

업계 분석가들은 패션 디자이너들의 브랜드 인지도를 높이는 데 소셜 미디어 마케팅의 중요성을 계속해서 강조하고 있다.

어휘 significance 중요성 enhance (질, 가치 등을) 높이다, 향상시키다 brand awareness 브랜드 인지도

해설 문장에 이미 continue라는 동사가 있으므로 빈칸에 또 다른 동사 (C) are emphasizing을 넣을 수는 없다. 빈칸 뒤에 목적어 the significance가 있는데, 명사가 목적어를 취하는 법은 없으므로 (A) emphasis를 넣을 수도 없다. to부정사 (B)나 (D) 중 정답을 골라야 하므로 능동태와 수동태의 구분을 요구하는 문제다. 빈칸 뒤에 목적어가 있을 때는 능동태가 정답이다.

127

------- to Brighton Drive will remain restricted to one side street following the commencement of the road repairs next week.

(A) Access
(B) Accesses
(C) Accessible
(D) Accessing

다음 주에 도로 공사가 시작된 이후에 Brighton Drive 진입은 한쪽 차로로 제한될 것이다.

어휘 access 진입, 통행; 진입하다, 이용하다 restricted 제한된 following ~ 후에 commencement 시작, 개시

해설 빈칸이 주어 자리이므로 명사 (A)나 (B)와 동명사 (D)가 들어갈 수 있다. 그러나 동사 access가 타동사이므로 빈칸에 동명사 (D)를 넣으려면 뒤에 목적어가 있어야 한다. 또한 access는 추상 명사이므로 복수형 (B)를 사용할 수도 없다.

128

Vita Bella Catering seeks ------- who are ready to dedicate themselves to designing engaging social media content on a weekly basis.

(A) those   (B) them
(C) someone   (D) anyone

Vita Bella Catering은 매주 매력적인 소셜 미디어 콘텐츠를 디자인하는 일에 헌신할 준비가 된 사람들을 찾고 있습니다.

어휘 catering 출장 요리 seek 찾다, 구하다 dedicate oneself to ~에 전념하다, 헌신하다 engaging 사람을 끌어당기는, 매력적인 content 내용

해설 빈칸 뒤에 who로 시작하는 구문, 분사 구문, 형용사구, 전치사구가 보이면 정답은 항상 those나 anyone이다. (A)와 (D) 중에서 주격 관계대명사의 선행사로서 관계대명사 다음에 나오는 동사 are의 수와 일치하는 복수 대명사 those가 정답이다.

129

Refrain from placing the digital scale ------- a source of excessive heat, as this could lead to damage of its delicate electronic components.

(A) between   (B) through
(C) despite   **(D) near**

디지털 저울을 과량의 열이 나오는 곳 가까이에 두는 것을 삼가세요. 이는 민감한 전자 부품에 손상을 초래할 수 있습니다.

어휘 refrain from ~을 삼가다 scale 저울 excessive 과도한 lead to ~으로 이어지다 delicate 민감한 component 부품

해설 빈칸 앞뒤 placing the digital scale ------- a source of excessive heat(디지털 저울을 과도한 열의 원천 ~에 두는 것)만 보면 적절한 전치사가 어느 것인지 알 수 있다.

130

Nearly 70 percent of teachers surveyed indicated that they had received ------- preparation for their roles via Stuggas University's online programs.

(A) adequate   (B) numerous
(C) thankful   (D) adjacent

조사에 응한 교사들의 약 70퍼센트가 Stuggas 대학교의 온라인 프로그램을 통해 직무에 대비한 충분한 준비 교육을 받았다고 밝혔다.

어휘 survey 의견을 조사하다 indicate (의견을) 밝히다 adequate 충분한, 적절한 adjacent 인접한 role 직무 via ~을 통해

해설 일단 (B) numerous는 복수 명사 앞에 사용해야 하므로 제외하자. '------- preparation([(A) 충분한 (C) 감사하는 (D) 인접한] 준비)'의 의미를 자연스럽게 해주는 형용사가 정답이다.

PART 6

Questions 131 through 134 refer to the following posting.

Bus Drivers Needed!

The Palm Beach County School District is now recruiting individuals for bus driver positions. Only part-time roles **131**are available. We welcome applications from both novice and experienced bus drivers. If you have held a valid driver's license for at least five years, we encourage you to submit an application. **132**We are prepared to offer any required training.

The Palm Beach County School District provides **133**competitive salary levels to all its staff. **134**In addition, we extend an option for bus drivers to supplement their income by taking on additional routes throughout the academic year. If joining our team interests you, please contact So-Hee Lee at 212-555-8473 for more information.

131-134번 문제는 다음 구인 광고에 관한 것입니다.

버스 운전기사 모집!

Palm Beach County 교육청이 현재 버스 운전기사 자리에 지원할 분들을 모집하고 있습니다. 파트타임 자리만 가능합니다. 초보자와 경력 버스 기사 모두의 지원을 환영합니다. 최소 5년 이상 유효한 운전면허를 보유하고 있다면 지원서를 제출하시기 바랍니다. 저희는 어떤 필요한 교육이든 제공할 준비가 되어 있습니다.

Palm Beach County 교육청은 모든 직원들에게 경쟁력 있는 수준의 급여를 제공합니다. 또한 버스 기사가 학기 내내 추가 노선을 맡음으로써 수입을 보충할 수 있는 옵션도 제공합니다. 저희 팀에 합류할 의향이 있으시면 212-555-8473으로 So-Hee Lee에게 연락하셔서 추가 정보를 받으시기 바랍니다.

어휘 school district 교육구, 교육청 recruit 모집하다, 채용하다 individuals (조직의) 구성원, 사람들 role 자리, 직무 novice 초보자 experienced 경험이 많은 we encourage you to-V ~하시기 바랍니다 competitive 경쟁력 있는, 뒤지지 않는 extend (공적으로, 정중하게) 제공하다 supplement 보충하다 take on ~을 맡다 academic year 학년도

131-134

131 **(A) are** (B) were (C) have been (D) will have been	**133** (A) compete (B) competing (C) competition **(D) competitive**
132 (A) Application submissions must be completed by today. (B) There are chances for career advancement. **(C) We are prepared to offer any required training.** (D) School bus drivers play a vital role in our educational system.	**134** (A) If not **(B) In addition** (C) Above all (D) Once again

131 **해설** 바로 앞 문장에서 현재 버스 기사를 모집하고 있다고(now recruiting) 했으므로, 부연 설명이 되는 이 문장의 시제도 현재 시제가 되어야 한다.

132 (A) 지원서 제출은 오늘까지 완료되어야 합니다.

(B) 승진의 기회가 있습니다.

(C) 저희는 어떤 필요한 교육이든 제공할 준비가 되어 있습니다.

(D) 스쿨버스 기사들은 우리의 교육 시스템에서 매우 중요한 역할을 합니다.

어휘 submission 제출 career advancement 승진 vital 매우 중요한, 없어서는 안 될

해설 앞에 있는 두 문장의 내용을 보자. 5년 이상 운전면허를 보유하기만 했다면 초보자이든 경력자이든 상관없이 지원을 환영한다는 내용이므로, 초보자가 지원할 경우 필요하다면 적절한 교육을 제공하겠다는 말이 이어지는 것이 자연스럽다.

133 **해설** 빈칸 앞뒤 provides ------- salary levels를 보면 정답을 알 수 있다. 명사 앞에 빈칸이 있을 때는 형용사가 정답이다.

134 **어휘** if not 그렇지 않다면 above all 무엇보다, 특히

해설 앞 문장에서 경쟁력 있는 수준의 급여(competitive salary levels)를 약속하면서 금전상의 장점을 언급하고 있는데, 이어지는 문장에서 부수입원 (an option for bus drivers to supplement their income)에 대해 설명하면서 같은 종류의 장점을 추가로 알려주고 있다.

📝 **Questions 135 through 138** refer to the following article.

Web sites often store small pieces of data, called cookies, on users' devices. Cookies are crucial for many functionalities of a Web site. [135]For instance, they enable a Web server to recognize whether a specific Web site has been accessed previously from a particular device. Without this [136]information, things like login statuses or items saved in an online shopping cart would not be remembered. Cookies are also useful for assisting media companies and advertisers in offering content that aligns with users' preferences.

However, one issue [137]regarding cookies is their potential use in monitoring user activity across multiple Web sites and devices. To address this, some privacy advocates suggest that users modify how cookies are managed. [138]Thankfully, the majority of Web browsers give users the option to block or remove cookies.

135-138번 문제는 다음 기사에 관한 것입니다.

웹 사이트들은 종종 쿠키라고 불리는 작은 데이터 조각들을 사용자의 장치에 저장한다. 쿠키는 웹 사이트의 여러 기능에 매우 중요하다. 예를 들어 쿠키는 특정 기기에서 특정 웹 사이트에 이전에 접속한 적이 있는지 웹 서버가 인식할 수 있게 해 준다. 이 정보가 없다면 로그인 상태나 온라인 쇼핑 카트에 담긴 품목 같은 것들이 기억되지 않을 것이다. 쿠키는 또한 미디어 기업들이나 광고주들이 사용자의 취향에 맞는 콘텐츠를 제공하도록 돕는 데도 유용하다.

그러나 쿠키와 관련한 한 가지 문제는 다수의 웹 사이트들과 장치들에 걸친 사용자의 활동을 감시하는 데 사용될 가능성이 있다는 것이다. 이것을 해결하기 위해 몇몇 개인정보 보호 옹호론자들은 사용자가 쿠키 관리 방식을 변경할 것을 제안한다. 다행히도 대다수의 웹브라우저들은 사용자에게 쿠키를 차단하거나 삭제할 수 있는 옵션을 제공한다.

어휘 crucial 결정적인, 매우 중요한 functionality 기능 enable ~할 수 있게 하다 access 접속하다 previously 전에 status 상태 advertiser 광고주 align with (기준, 목표, 관점 등에) 맞추다 regarding ~에 관한 monitor 감시하다 address 다루다, 해결하다 advocate 옹호자, 지지자 thankfully 다행히도

135-138

135 (A) Conversely	**137** (A) regarding
(B) For instance	(B) regards
(C) As a consequence	(C) regarded
(D) Eventually	(D) regardless
136 (A) informs	**138** (A) Alternatively, they allow users to locate cookies.
(B) informing	(B) It includes guidance on how cookies should be used properly.
(C) information	**(C) Thankfully, the majority of Web browsers give users the option to block or remove cookies.**
(D) informational	(D) They vary when it comes to cookie management practices.

135 **어휘** conversely 반대로, 역으로 as a consequence 결과적으로 eventually 결국

해설 쿠키가 웹 사이트의 여러 기능에 매우 중요하다는(Cookies are crucial for many functionalities of a Web site.) 문장에 이어 쿠키의 역할의 예를 서술하는(they enable a Web server to recognize whether a specific Web site has been accessed previously from a particular device.) 문장이 나오고 있다.

136 **어휘** informational 정보를 제공하는

해설 전치사 Without의 목적어가 되면서 지시형용사 this의 수식을 받는 자리이므로 명사가 들어가야 한다.

137 **해설** 빈칸 앞뒤 one issue ------- cookies가 '쿠키에 관한 한 가지 문제점'이라는 의미가 되도록 전치사 (A) regarding을 선택하자.

138 (A) 대안으로 그들은 사용자가 쿠키를 찾아내도록 해준다.
(B) 거기에는 쿠키의 적절한 사용법에 대한 지침이 포함된다.
(C) 다행히도 대다수의 웹브라우저들은 사용자에게 쿠키를 차단하거나 삭제할 수 있는 옵션을 제공한다.
(D) 그것들은 쿠키 관리 관행에 있어서 각기 다르다.

어휘 alternatively 대안으로 locate (~의 위치를) 찾아내다 guidance 안내, 지침 properly 적절하게 vary 각기 다르다 when it comes to ~에 대해서라면 practice 관행

해설 앞 문장에서 쿠키 관리 방식의 변경을 언급하고 있으므로(users modify how cookies are managed) 이어지는 문장에서는 쿠키의 차단이나 삭제에 대해 말하는 것이(the option to block or remove cookies) 문맥상 자연스럽다.

Questions 139 through 142 refer to the following job advertisement.

Social Media Manager for Educational Business Wanted

Brain Quest Studio is a growing company specializing in ¹³⁹innovative educational board games for young adults. We are on the lookout for a creative individual to produce five captivating social media posts each week. Since our launch one year ago, we have managed our own advertisements across major platforms. ¹⁴⁰That said, marketing is not really our area of expertise. Moreover, due to our focus on other aspects of running the business, we have not been able to invest sufficient energy in ¹⁴¹promoting it online. We are now prepared to entrust this role to a capable individual. This ¹⁴²opportunity is ideal for a teacher with marketing expertise who understands the distinctive interests of our audience. Interested candidates can reach us at jobs@brainqueststudio.ca.

139-142번 문제는 다음 구인 광고에 관한 것입니다.

교육업체 소셜 미디어 관리자 구함

Brain Quest Studio는 청년들을 위한 혁신적인 교육용 보드게임을 전문으로 하며 성장하는 기업입니다. 저희는 매주 다섯 편의 매력적인 소셜 미디어 게시물을 제작할 창의적인 사람을 찾고 있습니다. 1년 전 창립 이후 저희는 주요 플랫폼에 자체적으로 광고를 제작하여 운영해 왔습니다. 그렇기는 하지만 마케팅이 저희의 전문 영역이 아닙니다. 더욱이 저희는 사업 운영의 다른 측면에 집중하느라 온라인 홍보에 충분한 에너지를 쏟지 못했습니다. 이제는 이 역할을 유능한 분에게 맡길 준비가 되어 있습니다. 이 기회는 마케팅 전문 지식을 갖추고 있으면서 저희 이용자들의 독특한 관심사를 이해하는 교사에게 이상적입니다. 관심 있는 지원자는 jobs@brainqueststudio.ca로 연락 주시기 바랍니다.

어휘 specialize in ~을 전문으로 하다 innovative 혁신적인 be on the lookout for ~을 세심히 살피다, 찾다 captivating 마음을 사로잡는, 매혹적인 post 게시물 manage (어떻게든) 해내다 that said 그렇다고는 해도 expertise 전문 지식 moreover 게다가, 더욱이 aspect 측면 invest 투자하다, 쏟다 sufficient 충분한 promote 홍보하다 entrust 맡기다 capable 유능한 distinctive 독특한 audience 타깃층, 이용자

139-142

139 (A) innovation
   (B) innovative
   (C) Innovator
   (D) to innovate

140 **(A) That said, marketing is not really our area of expertise.**
   (B) We are planning to phase out our product lineup.
   (C) Even so, we understand the importance of social platforms.
   (D) Recently, they executed a new campaign for us.

141 (A) enlarging
   (B) promoting
   (C) evaluating
   (D) acquiring

142 (A) class
   (B) location
   (C) program
   (D) opportunity

139 **해설** 빈칸 앞뒤 in ------- educational board games를 보고 정답을 선택하자. 명사 앞에 빈칸이 있으면 형용사가 정답이다.

140 (A) 그렇기는 하지만 마케팅이 우리의 전문 영역이라고 할 수는 없습니다.
   (B) 저희는 제품들을 단계적으로 중단할 계획입니다.
   (C) 그렇다 할지라도 저희는 소셜 플랫폼의 중요성은 이해합니다.
   (D) 최근에는 그들이 새 캠페인을 시행했습니다.

   어휘 phase out ~을 단계적으로 중단하다, 철수하다 lineup 제품 구성[종류] execute 집행하다, 시행하다

   해설 빈칸 뒤에서 첨가 내용을 나타내는 부사 Moreover에 이어 회사가 홍보 업무를 외부 인력에게 맡기려고 하는 이유를 설명하고 있으므로(due to our focus on other aspects of running the business, we have not been able to invest sufficient energy in promoting it online.), 빈칸에서는 이러한 조치의 또 다른 이유가 서술되는 것이 알맞다.

141 **어휘** enlarge 확대하다 evaluate 평가하다 acquire 습득하다, 얻다

   해설 구인 광고를 통해 구하고자 하는 사람이 마케팅 담당자이므로 해당 문장에서는 사업을 홍보하는 일에 충분한 에너지를 쏟지 못한다고(we have not been able to invest sufficient energy in promoting it online) 말하는 게 문맥상 자연스럽다.

142 **해설** 'This -------'는 이 글에서 광고하고 있는 일자리를 가리킨다.

Questions 143 through 146 refer to the following e-mail.

From: Member Services <memberservices@atlanticpalette.ca>
To: Anika Patel <apatel972@inbox7.ca>
Date: May 1
Subject: Welcome to The Atlantic Palette
Attachment: Form

Dear Ms. Patel,

We appreciate your decision to join *The Atlantic Palette*! **¹⁴³Now** you will be among the earliest to hear about captivating art shows, live performances, auctions, and cultural festivals across Eastern Canada. Your first issue should reach you within a few days, and subsequent editions will be delivered at the start of each month. **¹⁴⁴Should your issue not arrive within seven days, we encourage you to reach out to us right away.** Your membership also grants you unlimited **¹⁴⁵access** to articles, video content, and other interactive media on our Web site. Simply log in using your subscriber ID and password, which you will find **¹⁴⁶on** the attached enrollment form.

Best regards,

Tekeshi Yamamoto
Customer Representative

143–146번 문제는 다음 이메일에 관한 것입니다.

발신: Member Services
　　　〈memberservices@atlanticpalette.ca〉
수신: Anika Patel 〈apatel972@inbox7.ca〉
날짜: 5월 1일
제목: The Atlantic Palette에 오신 것을 환영합니다
첨부 파일: 서식

　Ms. Patel께,

*The Atlantic Palette*에 가입해 주셔서 감사합니다! 이제 당신은 캐나다 동부 전역에서 있는 매력적인 미술 전시회와 라이브 공연, 경매, 문화 축제 등의 소식을 가장 먼저 접하게 될 것입니다. 첫 호는 며칠 내로 도착할 것이고, 이후의 간행물은 매월 초에 배송됩니다. 7일 이내에 잡지가 도착하지 않을 경우 즉시 저희에게 연락해 주시기 바랍니다. 회원 자격으로 저희 홈페이지에서 기사와 동영상 콘텐츠, 기타 쌍방향 미디어에 무제한 접속이 가능합니다. 구독자 ID와 비밀번호를 사용하여 로그인만 하시면 되고, 이 정보는 첨부된 등록 서식에서 찾으실 수 있습니다.

이만 줄입니다.

고객 서비스 담당자
Tekeshi Yamamoto

어휘 attachment 첨부 파일 captivating 마음을 사로잡는, 매혹적인 auction 경매 issue (잡지, 신문 등의) 호(號) subsequent 그 다음의, 이후의 edition 판(版), 간행(잡지 등의) 호(號) reach out to (제안, 의견을 위해) ~에게 연락하다, 접근하다 right away 즉시, 곧바로 grant (권리 등을) 부여하다 access 이용 권리 content 내용 interactive 상호 교류 방식의, 쌍방향의 simply 그저 ~하기만 하면 되어 subscriber 구독자 enrollment 등록 customer representative 고객 서비스 담당자

143-146

143 (A) **Now**
　　(B) Afterward
　　(C) Then
　　(D) Meanwhile

145 (A) accessing
　　(B) accesses
　　(C) accessed
　　(D) **access**

144 (A) If you'd like to place a subscription, please contact our support line during regular office hours.
　　(B) **Should your issue not arrive within seven days, we encourage you to reach out to us right away.**
　　(C) Creators are welcome to send in summaries or overviews of their artistic pieces.
　　(D) The opening performance is planned for early June in Toronto.

146 (A) for
　　(B) about
　　(C) **on**
　　(D) at

143 ⟶**어휘** afterward 그 후에 meanwhile 그동안, 그사이

⟶**해설** 앞 문장 We appreciate your decision to join *The Atlantic Palette*!를 읽으면 신규 가입자에게 보내는 이메일임을 알 수 있으므로 "이제부터 당신은 이러이러한 서비스를 받게 됩니다."라고 말하는 게 상황에 알맞다.

144 (A) 구독을 원하신다면 업무 시간에 저희 고객 지원 서비스로 연락 주시기 바랍니다.
(B) 7일 이내에 잡지가 도착하지 않을 경우 즉시 저희에게 연락해 주시기 바랍니다.
(C) 창작자들이 자신의 예술 작품 요약이나 개요를 제출하셔도 좋습니다.
(D) 개막 공연은 6월 초에 Toronto에서 열릴 예정입니다.

⟶**어휘** place a subscription 구독하다 line 전화 서비스 we encourage you to-V ~해 주시기 바랍니다 be welcome to-V (기꺼이) ~해도 좋다 send in ~을 제출하다 summary 요약, 개요 overview 개관, 개요 be planned for ~으로 예정되어 있다

⟶**해설** 앞 문장에서 잡지가 매월 초에 배송될 것이라고 말하고 있으므로(subsequent editions will be delivered at the start of each month), 배송되지 않을 경우의 조치 사항을 안내하는 것이 부연 설명으로 알맞다.

145 ⟶**해설** 빈칸에 4형식 동사 grants의 직접 목적어가 되면서 형용사 unlimited의 수식을 받을 명사가 들어가야 한다. (B)와 (D)가 모두 명사이지만 access는 셀 수 없는 명사이므로 단수형으로 써야 한다.

146 ⟶**해설** 구독자 ID와 비밀번호가 등록 서식 '위에' 적혀 있으므로 전치사 on이 필요하다. 참고로 선택지에 in이 있다면 그것도 정답이 될 수 있다.

Questions 147 through 148 refer to the following form.

WAHLBERG ASSOCIATES, INC.
Product Return Form

Dear Valued Customer:

[147]At Wahlberg Associates, Inc., we take great pride in crafting our games and puzzles with care. However, if your product is defective or if you are dissatisfied for any reason, please send the item back along with the receipt and this completed form. We will either ship a replacement directly from the factory at no additional cost or issue a credit to your account.

Name: Gideon R. Souza
Address: 3049 Maple Street, Springfield, IL 62704
[148]Problem description: Missing components in the item
Action requested: ☑ Send a replacement
　　　　　　　　　　 ☐ Provide a credit to my account

147-148번 문제는 다음 서식에 관한 것입니다.

(주) WAHLBERG ASSOCIATES
반품 신청서

소중한 고객님께:

(주) Wahlberg Associates는 게임과 퍼즐을 정성을 다해 제작하는 데 큰 자부심이 있습니다. 그러나 상품에 결함이 있거나 어떤 이유로든 만족하지 못하셨다면 영수증과 이 작성 양식을 함께 첨부하여 반품하시기 바랍니다. 추가 비용 없이 공장에서 직접 교체 상품을 배송해 드리거나 계정에 적립금을 발행해 드리겠습니다.

이름: Gideon R. Souza
주소: 3049 Maple Street, Springfield, IL 62704
반품 사유: 제품에 부품이 누락되어 있음
요청 사항: ☑ 교체 상품 배송
　　　　　　 ☐ 계정에 적립금 발행

어휘 take pride in ~을 자랑스럽게 여기다 craft (공들여) 제작하다 with care 주의 깊게, 정성을 다해 defective 결함이 있는 dissatisfied 만족하지 못하는 along with ~과 함께 complete (서식을) 기입하다, 작성하다 ship 배송하다, 발송하다 replacement 대신하는 것 issue 발급하다, 지급하다 credit 입금액, 적립금 account 계정 component 부품

147

What product did Mr. Souza most likely buy?

(A) A bookkeeping manual
(B) An article of apparel
(C) A bicycle
(D) A game

Mr. Souza는 어떤 상품을 구입했겠는가?

(A) 장부 기입 매뉴얼
(B) 의복 한 벌
(C) 자전거
(D) 게임

어휘 bookkeeping 부기, 장부 기입 article (물건) 한 가지, 한 점 apparel 의류, 의복

해설 첫 문장에 (주) Wahlberg Associates는 게임과 퍼즐을 제작하는 회사라고 나와 있다.

148

What problem is Mr. Souza reporting?

(A) Certain parts were not included.
(B) There were errors in the instructions.
(C) He received an incorrect item.
(D) The item sustained damage during transit.

Mr. Souza는 어떤 문제를 알리는가?

(A) 어떤 부품이 포함되지 않았다.
(B) 설명서에 실수가 있었다.
(C) 주문한 것과 다른 제품을 받았다.
(D) 제품이 운송 중에 손상을 입었다.

어휘 part 부품 instructions 설명서 incorrect 틀린, 잘못된 sustain (손상, 피해 등을) 입다, 당하다 transit 운송

해설 반품 사유가 누락된 부품(missing components)이라고 적혀 있다.

Questions 149 through 150 refer to the following text message.

From: Limpopo Province Electric Co.
Received: 1 February, 7:36 P.M.

[149]Your January billing statement is now available. The balance is due no later than 10 February.

[150]Please log on to our secure Web site to review your statement and account details. There you can also view previous payments, make a payment, and update your account information. If you need assistance, call us at 080 3555 5325.

149-150번 문제는 다음 문자 메시지에 관한 것입니다.

발신: Limpopo 주 전기 회사
수신: 2월 1일 오후 7:36

1월 청구서가 확인 가능합니다. 지불 잔액은 2월 10일까지 납부하셔야 합니다.
당사의 보안 웹 사이트에 로그인해서 청구서와 계정 상세 정보를 확인하시기 바랍니다. 웹 사이트에서는 또한 이전 결제 기록 조회, 대금 결제, 계정 정보 갱신도 하실 수 있습니다. 도움이 필요하시면 080 3555 5325로 전화하시기 바랍니다.

어휘 province (행정구역) 주(州) electric 전기의 billing statement 청구 명세서 balance 지불 잔액 due 지불해야 하는 no later than 늦어도 ~까지 secure 안전한, 보안이 철저한 review (간단히) 확인하다 statement 명세서 account 계정 update 갱신하다

149

What is the purpose of the text message?
(A) To inform the recipient about a bill
(B) To provide details about a password
(C) To resolve a billing issue
(D) To inform about a change in electricity pricing

문자 메시지의 목적은 무엇인가?
(A) 수신자에게 청구서에 대해 알려주는 것
(B) 비밀번호에 대한 세부 사항을 알려주는 것
(C) 청구서 발부의 문제를 해결하는 것
(D) 전기 요금 책정의 변경에 대해 알려주는 것

어휘 recipient 수신자 resolve 해결하다 billing 청구서 발부 pricing 가격 책정

해설 지문의 주제나 목적은 대부분 도입부에서 알 수 있다. 첫 두 문장 Your January billing statement is now available. The balance is due no later than 10 February.를 읽고 바로 정답을 선택하자.

150

What is the recipient of the text message asked to do?
(A) Submit a purchase request
(B) Access an online account
(C) Set up a new username
(D) Update some payment information

문자 메시지의 수신자는 무엇을 하도록 요구받는가?
(A) 구매 청구서를 제출한다
(B) 온라인 계정에 접속한다
(C) 새 사용자 이름을 설정한다
(D) 결제 정보를 갱신한다

어휘 access 접속하다 set up ~을 설정하다 update 갱신하다

해설 Please log on to our secure Web site가 패러프레이즈 되어 있는 문장이 정답이다.

🔲 **Questions 151 through 152** refer to the following e-mail.

To: ktang@bloomcent.org
From: nadined@wyea.org
Date: February 12
Re: Inquiry

Dear Mr. Tang,

151 The Woodville Young Entrepreneurs Alliance (WYEA) is considering reserving a room at the Bloomhill Community Center for an upcoming meeting. This event is scheduled to take place on March 22 between 7:00 and 11:00 in the morning.

We would require seating and tables to accommodate 60 to 90 attendees, along with a laptop, a projector, and a screen. **152**Additionally, we are thinking about hiring a catering service to supply coffee, pastries, and fruit for the attendees. Can you confirm whether it is mandatory to use the Center's in-house catering service, or acceptable to hire an external caterer instead?

Please be so kind as to provide me with the necessary information by Friday afternoon.

Thank you,

Nadine Dupont
Event Coordinator, WYEA

151-152번 문제는 다음 이메일에 관한 것입니다.

수신: ktang@bloomcent.org
발신: nadined@wyea.org
날짜: 2월 12일
제목: 문의

Mr. Tang께,

Woodville 청년 기업가 연합(WYEA)은 다가오는 회의를 위해 Bloomhill 지역 문화 회관에서 룸을 예약하고자 합니다. 이번 행사는 3월 22일 오전 7시부터 11시까지 있을 예정입니다.

60~90명의 참석자를 수용할 수 있는 좌석 및 테이블과 함께 노트북, 프로젝터, 스크린이 필요하게 될 것입니다. 아울러 출장 연회 서비스를 고용하여 참석자들에게 커피와 페이스트리, 과일을 제공하는 것을 생각 중입니다. 문화 회관 자체 연회 서비스를 이용하는 것이 의무인지, 아니면 외부 출장 연회 업체를 고용하는 것이 허용되는지 확인해 주시겠습니까?

필요한 정보를 금요일 오후까지 제공해 주시기 바랍니다.

고맙습니다.

Nadine Dupont
WYEA 행사 진행자

어휘 Re: ~과 관련하여(regarding) inquiry 문의 entrepreneur 기업가 alliance 연합 community center 지역 문화 회관 upcoming 다가오는, 곧 있을 take place (행사, 회의가) 열리다 seating 좌석 accommodate 수용하다 attendee 참석자 projector 프로젝터, 영사기 catering 출장 요리 mandatory 의무적인 in-house 내부의, 자체의 acceptable 허용되는 external 외부의 caterer 출장 연회 업체 please be so kind as to-V ~해 주시면 감사하겠습니다 coordinator 진행자

151

Why did Ms. Dupont write the e-mail?

(A) To ask about the availability of a venue
(B) To recommend a new date for an event
(C) To request amendments to a venue's service guidelines
(D) To notify group members of an upcoming event

Ms. Dupont은 왜 이메일을 썼는가?

(A) 어떤 장소의 이용 가능 여부에 대해 묻기 위해
(B) 행사의 새 날짜를 추천하기 위해
(C) 어떤 장소의 서비스 지침에 대한 수정을 요구하기 위해
(D) 단체 구성원들에게 다가오는 행사에 대해 통보하기 위해

어휘 availability 이용 가능성 venue 장소, 개최지 amendment 수정 guidelines 지침, 가이드라인 notify ~에게 알리다, 통보하다

해설 글의 주제나 목적은 도입부에서 알 수 있다. 첫 문장 The Woodville Young Entrepreneurs Alliance (WYEA) is considering reserving a room at the Bloomhill Community Center for an upcoming meeting.을 읽고 바로 정답을 선택하자.

152

What is indicated about the WYEA meeting?

(A) It happens annually.
(B) It offers refreshments.
(C) It requires participants to pay a fee.
(D) It is organized in the afternoon.

WYEA 회의에 대하여 무엇이 언급되어 있는가?

(A) 매년 열린다.
(B) 다과를 제공한다.
(C) 참석자들에게 참가비 지불을 요구한다.
(D) 오후에 개최된다.

어휘 indicate 나타내다, 언급하다 annually 매년 refreshments (행사의) 다과, 간단한 음식 organize (행사를) 조직하다, 개최하다

해설 두 번째 문단에 we are thinking about hiring a catering service to supply coffee, pastries, and fruit for the attendees.를 읽으면서 coffee, pastries, and fruit을 refreshments로 바꾸어 놓았음을 파악하고 정답을 고르자.

Questions 153 through 155 refer to the following press release.

FOR IMMEDIATE RELEASE
May 24
www.bradleyinvestments.com

ATLANTA, GA – [153]Bradley Investments hosted a ceremony today to inaugurate its newly constructed office building at 195 South Chippewa Street. [154]The company was founded in Galway, Ireland, twelve years ago. Since its establishment, it has expanded to locations across Europe and opened its African headquarters in Casablanca just last year. The Atlanta office represents the company's first base of operations in North America.

Bradley Investments is a leading firm in the investment industry, focusing on technology and electronics start-ups. Its portfolio of clients includes Arndt Technological Services and Karolin Electronics Superstores, along with other notable companies.

The Atlanta headquarters will manage business operations for clients across both North and South America. Over 600 employees have been hired to work at the new office. [155]For its initial year, Bradley Investments' vice president Lonan O'Brien will oversee operations at the office before returning to Galway.

For further inquiries, contact Maya Wilson from Public Relations at 404-555-0173 or e-mail her at mwilson@bradleyinvestments.com.

153-155번 문제는 다음 보도 자료에 관한 것입니다.

즉시 보도하여 주시기 바랍니다
5월 24일
www.bradleyinvestments.com

ATLANTA, GA – Bradley Investments는 오늘 South Chippewa 가(街) 195번지에 새로 건설된 사무용 건물의 개관을 기념하는 행사를 가졌다. 이 회사는 12년 전 아일랜드 Galway에 설립되었다. 설립 이후 유럽 전역의 여러 곳으로 확장해 왔으며 작년에는 Casablanca에 아프리카 본부를 세웠다. Atlanta 지점은 이 회사의 첫 북미 운영 거점이다.

Bradley Investments 투자업계를 선도하는 기업으로서 기술 및 전자 분야 신생 기업들에 집중하고 있다. 고객 포트폴리오에는 Arndt Technological Services와 Karolin Electronics Superstores를 비롯한 기타 여러 유명 기업들이 포함된다.

Atlanta 본부는 북미와 남미 모두에 걸쳐 고객들의 사업 운영을 관리할 것이다. 600명 이상의 직원들이 새 지점에서 근무하기 위해 채용되었다. 첫해 동안은 Bradley Investments의 부회장 Lonan O'Brien이 지점 운영을 관리하다가 Galway로 돌아갈 것이다.

추가 문의는 전화 404-555-0173이나 이메일 mwilson@bradleyinvestments.com으로 홍보팀 Maya Wilson에게 연락하면 된다.

어휘 release 공식 발표 host 개최하다, 주최하다 inaugurate (건물의) 개관을 선언하다 found 설립하다 establishment 설립 headquarters 본부, 본사 represent ~이다 base 근거지, 거점 leading 주요한, 선도하는 firm 회사, 기업 electronics 전자 산업 start-up 신생 기업 along with ~에 덧붙여, ~을 비롯해 notable 유명한, 주목할 만한 operation 운영, 영업 initial 처음의 vice president 부사장, 부회장 oversee 감독하다, 관리하다 inquiry 문의, 질문 public relations 홍보

153

What type of event took place at 195 South Chippewa Street?	South Chippewa 가(街)에서 어떤 유형의 행사가 있었는가?
(A) A conference about finance	(A) 금융에 관한 학술 대회
(B) A showcase for electronics	(B) 전자 제품 공개 행사
(C) A celebration to mark an opening	(C) 개업 기념행사
(D) A job recruitment event	(D) 채용 행사

어휘 conference 학술 대회 showcase 공개 행사 celebration 축해[기념] 행사 mark 기념하다, 축하하다 recruitment 신규 모집[채용]

해설 첫 문장에서 a ceremony to inaugurate its newly constructed office building의 뜻을 알면 정답을 선택할 수 있다.

154

What is stated about Bradley Investments?	Bradley Investments에 대해 무엇이 언급되는가?
(A) It operates in regions across multiple continents.	(A) 여러 대륙에 걸친 지역들에서 운영된다.
(B) It is recognized as a pioneer in consumer banking.	(B) 소비자 금융 분야의 개척자로 인정받는다.
(C) Its Atlanta office was constructed by a renowned architectural firm.	(C) Atlanta 지점이 유명한 건축 회사에 의해 건설되었다.
(D) Its Atlanta facility has existed for twelve years.	(D) Atlanta 시설이 12년 동안 존재했다.

어휘 operate 운영되다 continent 대륙 recognize 인정하다 pioneer 선구자, 개척자 consumer banking 소비자 금융 renowned 유명한, 저명한 architectural firm 건축 회사

해설 첫 문단을 읽어 보면 Bradley Investments는 현재 유럽과 아프리카, 북미에서 지점들을 운영하고 있다.

155

What is implied about Mr. O'Brien?	Mr. O'Brien에 관하여 무엇이 암시되어 있는가?
(A) He previously served as the head of Arndt Technological Services.	(A) 과거에 Arndt Technological Services의 책임자로 근무했다.
(B) He is temporarily assigned to the Atlanta office.	(B) 임시로 Atlanta 지점에 배정되었다.
(C) He was hired as one of the 600 new staff members.	(C) 600명의 신입 직원들 중 한 명으로 채용되었다.
(D) He started his professional journey in a retail environment.	(D) 소매업 분야에서 경력을 시작했다.

어휘 previously 이전에, 과거에 serve 근무하다 head (조직의) 장(長), 책임자 temporarily 임시로 professional journey 직업의 여정, 경력 retail 소매의 environment 업계, 분야

해설 For its initial year, Bradley Investments' vice president Lonan O'Brien will oversee operations at the office before returning to Galway.에서 정답을 알 수 있다. Lonan O'Brien은 Atlanta 본부의 운영 첫해에만 임시로 근무한 후 다시 Galway로 돌아갈 것이다.

Questions 156 through 157 refer to the following instant-message discussion.

Larissa Kanoa (2:14 P.M.)
[156]We received another delivery that's meant for you.

Takumi Matsuda (2:15 P.M.)
[Not again!] [156]I can't figure out why this issue persists.

Larissa Kanoa (2:16 P.M.)
[157]I think the confusion comes from the chart on the company Web site. [157]The department addresses are shown together, and Accounting is listed just above Administration.

Takumi Matsuda (2:17 P.M.)
That would make sense; [157]it explains why my name is on the mail but the address belongs to Accounting.

Larissa Kanoa (2:18 P.M.)
Exactly. I'm heading to your building for a meeting with the Legal Department. I'll drop your package off then.

Takumi Matsuda (2:19 P.M.)
Thank you! I'll e-mail Information Technology to request a clearer update to the Web site chart.

156–157번 문제는 다음 메신저 대화에 관한 것입니다.

Larissa Kanoa (오후 2:14)
당신에게 가야 할 배달물이 또 우리에게 왔어요.

Takumi Matsuda (오후 2:15)
또요! 왜 이런 문제가 지속되는지 알 수가 없네요.

Larissa Kanoa (오후 2:16)
회사 홈페이지에 있는 차트에서 혼동이 오는 것 같아요. 부서 주소들이 다 나오는데, 회계 부서가 총무부 바로 위에 기재되어 있거든요.

Takumi Matsuda (오후 2:17)
그게 말이 되네요. 그거면 왜 우편물에 내 이름이 쓰여 있는데 주소는 회계 부서로 되어 있는지 설명이 돼요.

Larissa Kanoa (오후 2:18)
딱 그거죠. 법무 팀과 회의가 있어서 그쪽 건물로 갈 거예요. 소포는 그때 전달할게요.

Takumi Matsuda (오후 2:19)
고마워요! IT 부서에 이메일을 보내서 홈페이지 차트를 더 명확하게 업데이트해 달라고 요청해야겠어요.

어휘 be meant for ~을 대상으로 하다 Not again! 또야! figure out ~을 알아내다 persist 계속되다, 지속되다 confusion 혼동 accounting 회계 list (목록에) 올리다, 기재하다 administration 총무부 make sense 이해할 만하다, 말이 되다 head (특정 장소로) 향하다, 가다 legal 법률의 drop off ~을 맡기다, 전달하다

156

At 2:15 P.M., what does Mr. Matsuda most likely mean when he writes "Not again"?

(A) A package he sent was mistakenly returned to him.
(B) He believes Ms. Kanoa doesn't need to visit his office.
(C) His mail is frequently delivered to the wrong department.
(D) He prefers Ms. Kanoa not to send another follow-up e-mail.

오후 2시 15분에 Mr. Matsuda는 "또요!"라고 쓸 때 무엇을 의미하겠는가?

(A) 자기가 보낸 소포가 착오로 반송되었다.
(B) Ms. Kanoa가 자기 사무실을 방문할 필요는 없다고 생각한다.
(C) 자기 우편물이 자주 다른 부서로 배송된다.
(D) Ms. Kanoa가 후속 이메일을 보내지 않기를 바란다.

어휘 mistakenly 착오로 frequently 자주, 빈번히 prefer *sb* to-V (가급적) ~가 ~하기를 바라다 follow-up 후속의, 잇달은

해설 We received another delivery that's meant for you.라는 Ms. Kanoa의 말에 대한 반응이 Not again!이다. 게다가 이어지는 문장에서 이런 일이 반복되고 있다고(this issue persists) 말하고 있으므로, Not again!은 우편물 오배송이 자주 발생하고 있다는 뜻으로 하는 말이다.

157

What area does Mr. Matsuda work in?

(A) Accounting
(B) Administration
(C) Legal
(D) Information Technology

Mr. Matsuda는 어느 분야에 종사하는가?

(A) 회계
(B) 총무
(C) 법무
(D) 정보기술

해설 회사 홈페이지 차트에(the chart on the company Web site) 회계 부서와 총무부의 주소가 있는데(Accounting is listed just above Administration), 이름은 Mr. Matsuda라고 적혀 있으면서 주소는 회계 부서로 되어 있는 실수가 일어난다고 말하고 있으므로(my name is on the mail but the address belongs to Accounting.), Mr. Matsuda가 근무하는 부서는 회계 부서가 아니라 총무부이다.

Construction to Add to Traffic

GRANDHAVEN (4 October) - With the construction of multiple new office complexes currently in progress within the central business district, the city's existing traffic challenges are only anticipated to worsen further. [158]City authorities are considering a range of solutions, including the construction of an underground motorway or the expansion of Highway 31 to allow for additional traffic lanes. However, no definitive decisions have been made thus far.

"The current infrastructure is insufficient to handle this volume of vehicles, and it is obvious that action is required," remarked Catherine Radzinski, spokesperson for the highway commission. — [1] —.

[159]"It will take years to finish any large-scale construction initiative, meaning that whatever option we choose will only exacerbate traffic congestion in the short term," Ms. Radzinski added. "That's the main reason we haven't committed to anything yet. The longer we take to craft a comprehensive strategy, the more effectively managed the initiative will hopefully be once it commences." As city officials deliberate over potential options, office workers are growing increasingly agitated. — [2] —.

[160]"Traveling to work has become intolerable for me," complained Philip Hargrove, a lawyer based in the downtown area. "Although my home is located merely 15 kilometers from my workplace, the commute takes more than an hour. — [3] —."

In an effort to mitigate traffic problems for the time being, office administrators are beginning to take matters into their own hands. [161]Some are promoting carpooling among staff members or providing perks to those who commute by bicycle. — [4] —.

158-161번 문제는 다음 기사에 관한 것입니다.

공사로 교통량 증가 전망

GRANDHAVEN (10월 4일) – 현재 중심 업무 지구에서 다수의 신규 사무 단지 공사가 진행 중인 가운데, 기존의 시의 교통 문제는 더욱 악화되기만 할 것으로 예상된다. 시 당국은 지하 고속도로 건설이나 추가 차선 확보가 가능한 31번 고속도로 확장 등을 포함한 여러 가지 해결책을 고려 중이다. 그러나 아직까지 확정된 결정은 내려지지 않았다.

고속도로 위원회 대변인 Catherine Radzinski는 "현재의 인프라는 이 정도의 차량들을 감당하기에는 불충분하며, 조치가 필요한 것은 분명합니다."라고 말했다.

"어떤 대규모 건설 프로젝트이든 완료하는데 수년이 걸리며, 어떤 옵션을 선택하든 단기적으로는 교통 혼잡을 악화시킬 뿐임을 뜻합니다."라고 그는 덧붙였다. "이것이 우리가 아직 어느 것도 착수하겠다고 약속하지 못한 주요 이유입니다. 종합 전략을 짜는 데 시간을 들일수록, 프로젝트가 시작되면 더 효과적으로 운영되기를 희망하고 있습니다." 시 공무원들이 가능한 옵션들에 대해 심사숙고하는 동안 직장인들은 점점 더 평정심을 잃어가고 있다.

중심가에서 근무하는 변호사 Philip Hargrove는 "출퇴근이 이제는 참을 수 없는 지경이 되어 버렸어요."라고 불평했다. "저희 집이 직장에서 불과 15킬로미터 떨어진 곳에 있는데도 통근에 한 시간이 넘게 걸립니다."

당분간이라도 교통 문제를 완화하려는 노력으로 사무실 관리자들이 직접 나서기 시작했다. 일부는 직원들 사이에 카풀을 장려하거나 자전거로 통근하는 사람들에게 특전을 제공하고 있다.

어휘 add to ~을 증가시키다 multiple 다수의 complex 건물 단지 in progress 진행 중인 central business district 중심 업무 지구 existing 지금 있는, 기존의 worsen 악화되다 authorities 당국 underground 지하의 motorway 고속도로 allow for ~을 가능하게 하다 definitive 최종적인, 확정적인 thus far 지금까지 infrastructure 인프라, 사회 기반 시설 insufficient 불충분한 volume 총량 remark 언급하다 spokesperson 대변인 commission 위원회 large-scale 대규모의 initiative 계획, 프로젝트 exacerbate 악화시키다 congestion 혼잡 in the short term 단기적으로 add 덧붙여 말하다 commit to (착수, 실행을 확실히) 약속하다 craft 정교하게 만들다 comprehensive 포괄적인, 종합적인 strategy 전략 hopefully +V ~되기를 바라다 commence 시작되다 deliberate over ~에 대해 심사숙고하다 potential 가능성이 있는 agitated 평정심을 잃은 travel to work 출퇴근하다 intolerable 참을 수 없는 based in ~에 기반을 둔 merely 그저, 단지 commute 통근, 출퇴근 길; 통근하다 in an effort to-V ~하려는 노력으로 mitigate 완화하다, 경감하다 for the time being 당분간, 일시적으로 administrator 운영자, 관리자 take matters into one's own hands (해결에) 직접 나서다 promote 장려하다 perks 특전, 특혜

158

The word "solutions" in paragraph 1, line 6, is closest in meaning to

(A) targets
(B) remedies
(C) appeals
(D) mixtures

첫 문단 여섯 번째 줄의 단어 "solutions"와 의미상 가장 가까운 것은

(A) 목표
(B) 해결책
(C) 호소, 간청
(D) 혼합물

🔹해설 solutions가 '해결책'이라는 뜻으로 사용되면 (B) remedies와, '용액'이라는 뜻으로 사용되면 (D) mixtures와 동의어가 될 수 있다. 본문에서는 지하 고속 도로 건설이나 고속도로 확장 같은 '해결책'이라는 의미다.

159

What reason does Ms. Radzinski give for the highway commission's reluctance to commence a construction project?

(A) Awaiting more financial resources
(B) Difficulty in locating a skilled project manager
(C) Concern about worsening traffic congestion
(D) A large volume of public objections

Ms. Radzinski는 고속도로 위원회가 건설 프로젝트 시작하기를 꺼리는 것에 대해 어떤 이유를 대는가?

(A) 더 많은 재정적 자원에 대한 기대
(B) 노련한 프로젝트 관리자를 찾기 어려움
(C) 악화되는 교통 혼잡에 대한 우려
(D) 대중의 많은 반대

🔹어휘 reluctance 내키지 않음, 꺼림 await 기다리다, 기대하다 locate 찾아내다 skilled 노련한, 유능한 objection 반대, 이의

🔹해설 세 번째 문단에 있는 Radzinski 대변인의 말을 인용한 부분에서 정답을 알 수 있다. 대규모 건설 프로젝트로 인해 단기적으로 교통 혼잡이 가중될 것을 우려하기 때문이다(It will take years to finish any large-scale construction initiative, meaning that whatever option we choose will only exacerbate traffic congestion in the short term).

160

What is indicated about Mr. Hargrove?

(A) He opposes a recently introduced traffic regulation.
(B) He does not support an urban planning suggestion.
(C) He is seeking employment elsewhere downtown.
(D) He feels frustrated with his daily commute.

Mr. Hargrove에 대해 무엇이 언급되어 있는가?

(A) 최근에 도입된 교통 규정에 반대한다.
(B) 도시 계획 제안을 지지하지 않는다.
(C) 중심가 다른 곳에서 직장을 구하고 있다.
(D) 매일 통근 때문에 짜증이 난다.

🔹어휘 oppose 반대하다 seek employment 직장을 구하다 elsewhere 다른 곳에서 frustrated 짜증이 난, 속이 타는

🔹해설 네 번째 문단에서 정답을 알 수 있다. 직장까지 이동하는 것이 참을 수 없는 지경이라고 말하면서(Traveling to work has become intolerable for me.) 겨우 15킬로미터 떨어진 직장까지 한 시간이 넘게 걸린다는(Although my home is located merely 15 kilometers from my workplace, the commute takes more than an hour.) 부연 설명을 제공하고 있다.

161

In which of the positions marked [1], [2], [3], and [4] does the following sentence best belong?

"Others are letting their staff work remotely on designated days."

(A) [1]
(B) [2]
(C) [3]
(D) [4]

다음 문장은 [1], [2], [3], [4]로 표시된 자리 중 어느 곳에 가장 잘 어울리는가?

"또 일부는 직원들이 지정된 요일에 원격으로 근무하도록 하고 있다."

🔹어휘 remotely 원격으로 designate 지정하다

🔹해설 주어진 문장에 들어 있는 Others가 앞 문장과 이 문장을 연결시켜 주는 키워드다. Others로 시작하는 문장 앞에는 Some으로 시작하는 문장이 짝을 이루며 있는 것이 자연스럽다.

Keira Vauclair (9:22 A.M.)
162Our clients in Taiwan have asked us to organize a video conference to go over the clothing designs.

Miguel Ramos (9:24 A.M.)
162Understood. Do we already have a plan?

Keira Vauclair (9:26 A.M.)
162I'm arranging it for 8 P.M. tomorrow, our local time, in Room 3B. The later timing is because of the time zone difference between Taipei and Vancouver.

Nora Kravchenko (9:27 A.M.)
163Would it be possible to participate in the meeting remotely from home?

Keira Vauclair (9:29 A.M.)
163Unfortunately, that's not an option. Our security policy prohibits taking materials out of the office, and the clients are counting on seeing the designs on-site.

Nora Kravchenko (9:30 A.M.)
OK. [That makes sense.] 165We now just need Ms. Feldman's permission to work late.

Miguel Ramos (9:32 A.M.)
Let's confirm that with her. 164Ms. Feldman, we'd like to have a video conference with our Taiwanese clients tomorrow evening. Would it be acceptable for us to stay after regular hours to present the new designs? We plan to use Room 3B as it's equipped with the necessary audiovisual tools.

Jessica Feldman (9:34 A.M.)
164Yes, that's fine. I'll notify security so they will keep the building accessible until you're done.

Keira Vauclair (9:35 A.M.)
165Thank you, Mr. Ramos, for contacting Ms. Feldman on our behalf.

162-165번 문제는 다음 온라인 채팅 대화에 관한 것입니다.

Keira Vauclair (오전 9:22)
대만 고객들이 옷 디자인을 검토할 수 있게 화상 회의를 준비해 달라고 요청했어요.

Miguel Ramos (오전 9:24)
알겠어요. 회의 계획을 잡았나요?

Keira Vauclair (오전 9:26)
우리 시각으로 내일 저녁 8시에 3B 회의실에서 하도록 준비하려고요. 늦은 시간으로 하는 이유는 Taipei와 Vancouver 사이의 시차 때문입니다.

Nora Kravchenko (오전 9:27)
집에서 원격으로 회의에 참여하는 게 가능할까요?

Keira Vauclair (오전 9:29)
안타깝게도 그건 불가능해요. 우리 보안 정책은 자료를 사무실 밖으로 가지고 나가는 걸 금지하고 있는데, 고객들은 현장에서 디자인 보는 것을 기대하고 있거든요.

Nora Kravchenko (오전 9:30)
알겠어요. 이해가 돼요. 이제 야근을 하기 위해 Ms. Feldman의 허가만 있으면 되겠네요.

Miguel Ramos (오전 9:32)
그녀에게 확인해 보죠. Ms. Feldman, 내일 저녁에 대만 고객들과 화상 회의를 하려고 합니다. 새 디자인을 보여주기 위해 정규 근무 시간 이후에 남아 있어도 괜찮을까요? 필요한 시청각 장치가 설치되어 있어서 3B 회의실을 사용할 계획입니다.

Jessica Feldman (오전 9:34)
네, 좋습니다. 끝날 때까지 건물을 계속 이용할 수 있도록 보안 팀에 알려 둘게요.

Keira Vauclair (오전 9:35)
대표로 Ms. Feldman께 연락해 주셔서 고맙습니다, Mr. Ramos.

어휘 video conference 화상 회의 go over ~을 자세히 검토하다 arrange 준비하다, 마련하다 time zone (표준) 시간대 remotely 원격으로 prohibit 금지하다 materials 자료 count on 기대하다 on-site 현장에서 make sense 이해할 만하다, 말이 되다 permission 허가 acceptable 허용될 만한, 괜찮은 present 보여주다 be equipped with ~이 설치되어 있다 audiovisual 시청각의 accessible 사용 가능한 on one's behalf ~를 대표하여, 대신하여

162

What is the online chat discussion about?	온라인 채팅 대화는 무엇에 관한 것인가?
(A) Making a clothing purchase	(A) 의류 구매하기
(B) Organizing a business trip	(B) 출장 준비하기
(C) Scheduling a meeting	(C) 회의 일정 잡기
(D) Adjusting a project deadline	(D) 프로젝트 기한 조정하기

어휘 make a purchase 구매하다 adjust 조정하다

해설 지문의 주제는 거의 항상 도입부에서 알 수 있다. Ms. Vauclair와 Mr. Ramos가 주고받는 대화를 읽으면 고객과의 회의 일정 잡는 것에 관한 이야기임을 알 수 있다(Our clients in Taiwan have asked us to organize a video conference / Do we already have a plan? / I'm arranging it for 8 P.M. tomorrow, our local time, in Room 3B).

163

At 9:30 A.M., what does Ms. Kravchenko most likely mean when she writes, "That makes sense"?	오전 9시 30분에 Ms. Kravchenko는 "이해가 돼요." 라고 쓸 때 무엇을 의미하겠는가?
(A) She understands the challenges caused by the time zone difference.	(A) 시차 때문에 생기는 어려움을 이해한다.
(B) She acknowledges improvements in building security protocols.	(B) 건물 보안 규정이 개선되었음을 인정한다.
(C) She recognizes that the task will require her to stay late.	(C) 업무 때문에 야근하게 될 것을 인식하고 있다.
(D) She accepts the reason why the work must be done at the office.	(D) 업무가 사무실에서 이루어져야 하는 이유를 수긍한다.

어휘 challenge (긍정적) 어려움 time zone (같은 표준시를 쓰는) 시간대 acknowledge 인정하다 protocol 통신규약, 규정 recognize 인정하다, 인식하다

해설 That makes sense.는 집에서 회의에 참석하는 것이 가능한지 묻는 질문 Would it be possible to participate in the meeting remotely from home?과 그렇게 할 수 없는 이유를 설명하는 대답 Our security policy prohibits taking materials out of the office, and the clients are counting on seeing the designs on-site.에 이어서 나오는 말이므로, 반드시 회사에 남아서 회의를 해야 하는 이유를 납득하고 있음을 보여주고 있다.

164

What does Ms. Feldman offer to do?	Ms. Feldman은 무엇을 해주겠다고 제안하는가?
(A) Record a video presentation of the designs	(A) 디자인에 대한 영상 발표를 녹화한다
(B) Communicate with some colleagues in Taipei	(B) Taipei에 있는 동료들과 연락한다
(C) Ensure the office stays open after hours	(C) 근무 시간 이후에도 사무실이 열려 있도록 한다
(D) Leave extra keys accessible in the workplace	(D) 사무실에 여분의 열쇠를 사용하도록 해 둔다

어휘 ensure 보장하다, 확실하게 하다

해설 내일 저녁에 화상 회의를 하기 위해 정규 근무 시간 이후에 회사에 남아 있도록 허가해 달라는 요청을 받은(we'd like to have a video conference with our Taiwanese clients tomorrow evening. Would it be acceptable for us to stay after regular hours ...?) Ms. Feldman은 야간에 회의가 다 끝날 때까지 건물을 이용할 수 있게 해 주겠다고 약속한다(I'll notify security so they will keep the building accessible until you're done).

165

Why does Ms. Vauclair express gratitude to Mr. Ramos?	Ms. Vauclair는 왜 Mr. Ramos에게 감사를 표하는가?
(A) For securing Ms. Feldman's approval	(A) Ms. Feldman의 허가를 받아 주어서
(B) For participating in the video meeting	(B) 화상 회의에 참석해 주어서
(C) For preparing the audiovisual equipment	(C) 시청각 장비를 준비해 주어서
(D) For volunteering to lock up the office	(D) 사무실을 잠그겠다고 자원해 주어서

어휘 gratitude 감사, 고마움 secure 확보하다, 얻어내다 approval 승인, 허가

해설 Ms. Vauclair는 Mr. Ramos에게 Ms. Feldman에게 연락해 주어서(for contacting Ms. Feldman) 고맙다고 말하는데, Mr. Ramos가 Ms. Feldman에게 연락한 이유는 근무 시간이 끝난 후에도 회사에 남아 있도록 허가를 받기 위해서였다(We now just need Ms. Feldman's permission to work late).

[166]**THIS OFFICE TEMPORARILY CLOSED FOR RENOVATIONS**

[166 167 168(B)]Kindly note that the Siam branch office of *Bangkok English Newspaper* (BEN) will remain closed during the cool season as renovations are being carried out to enhance the quality of our publishing facilities. Operations at the Siam office are scheduled to resume on March 1.

[168(B)(D)]Additionally, BEN's 2026 Journalism Internship Program will take place at the Silom branch from January 1 to March 1. The program includes internship periods of one week, two weeks, and four weeks, catering to those who wish to gain experience in article writing and editorial work. The Silom branch is conveniently situated directly opposite the Sala Daeng skytrain station on the BTS Silom line.

Bangkok English Newspaper currently boasts a circulation exceeding 100,000 readers, with consistent growth. [168(C)]Moreover, BEN has earned recognition as Thailand's best English newspaper for the past four years, as voted by the editorial team of *Southeast Asia Travel Guide* magazine. For further details, visit www.bangkokenglishnewspaper.or.th or contact us at 02-5532-6841.

166-168번 문제는 다음 안내문에 관한 것입니다.

개조 공사를 위해 임시로 사무실을 닫습니다

Bangkok English Newspaper (BEN) Siam 지사가 출판 시설의 품질 향상을 위해 개조 공사가 실시됨에 따라 서늘한 계절 동안 문을 닫게 되었음에 유의하시기 바랍니다. Siam 지사의 운영은 3월 1일에 재개될 예정입니다.

또한, BEN의 2026년 저널리즘 인턴 프로그램이 1월 1일부터 3월 1일까지 Silom 지사에서 열립니다. 이 프로그램에는 1주, 2주, 4주 인턴 과정이 있으며, 기사 작성과 편집 업무의 경험을 얻고자 하는 사람들에게 맞추어 제공됩니다. Silom 지사는 BTS Silom 노선 Sala Daeng 스카이트레인 역 바로 맞은편에 위치해 있어 편리합니다.

*Bangkok English Newspaper*는 현재 꾸준한 증가세 속에 10만 명이 넘는 구독자 수를 자랑합니다. 또한 BEN은 *Southeast Asia Travel Guide* 지(誌) 편집 팀이 선정한 지난 4년간 태국 최고의 영자 신문으로 인정받았습니다. 자세한 사항은 www.bangkokenglishnewspaper.or.th를 방문하시거나 02-5532-6841로 연락하시기 바랍니다.

어휘 temporarily 임시로 kindly +V ~해 주시기 바랍니다 carry out ~을 실시하다 enhance 향상시키다 facilities 시설, 설비 resume 재개하다 cater to ~에게 맞춰 제공되다 editorial 편집의 situated 위치한, 자리한 opposite ~의 맞은편에 currently 현재 boast 자랑하다 circulation (판매) 부수, 유통량 exceed 초과하다, 능가하다 consistent 꾸준한 earn (명성, 존경 등을) 얻다, 받다 recognition (업적, 공로의) 인정 voted *sth* (투표를 통해) ~으로 선정된 further details (더) 자세한 사항

166

Where would the notice likely be displayed?

(A) In a job advertisement directory
(B) On a bulletin board at an academic institution
(C) At the entrance of a tourist information center
(D) On the front door of a newspaper branch office

안내문은 어디에 게시되어 있겠는가?

(A) 구인 광고 안내 책자에
(B) 교육 기관의 게시판에
(C) 관광 안내소 입구에
(D) 신문사 지사 정문에

어휘 display 게시하다, 비치하다 directory 안내 책자 academic institution 교육 기관

해설 안내문 제목 THIS OFFICE TEMPORARILY CLOSED FOR RENOVATIONS를 보면 사무실 정문에 붙어 있을 글이라는 것을 알 수 있으며, 첫 문장 Kindly note that the Siam branch office of *Bangkok English Newspaper* (BEN) will remain closed during the cool season을 통해 이 사무실은 *Bangkok English Newspaper*의 Siam 지사임을 알 수 있다.

167

What is the reason for the Siam branch's closure?

(A) The property has been sold.
(B) Remodeling work is underway.
(C) The office is relocating to a different area.
(D) The organization has ceased operations.

Siam 지사가 폐쇄된 이유는 무엇인가?

(A) 건물이 팔렸다.
(B) 리모델링이 진행 중이다.
(C) 사무실이 다른 지역으로 이전할 것이다.
(D) 기관이 운영을 중단했다.

어휘 closure 폐쇄 property 건물, 부동산 underway 진행 중인 relocate 이전하다 cease 중단하다 operation 운영, 활동

해설 첫 문장에서 사무실이 문을 닫은 이유를 as renovations are being carried out이라고 알려주고 있다.

What is NOT mentioned about BEN?

(A) It is exclusively available on digital platforms.
(B) It operates multiple offices.
(C) It has received compliments from a publication.
(D) It accepts applications for seasonal internship programs.

BEN에 대해 언급되지 않은 사항은 무엇인가?

(A) 디지털 플랫폼에서만 이용할 수 있다.
(B) 다수의 사무실을 운영한다.
(C) 한 출판물에서 칭찬을 받았다.
(D) 계절 인턴 프로그램에 대한 신청을 받는다.

어휘 exclusively 오로지, 오직 ~만 operate 운영하다 compliment 칭찬

해설 첫 문단 첫 문장 Kindly note that the Siam branch office of *Bangkok English Newspaper* (BEN) will remain closed와 두 번째 문단의 첫 문장 Additionally, BEN's 2026 Journalism Internship Program will take place at the Silom branch from January 1 to March 1.를 읽으면 BEN은 최소 두 개의 지사를 운영하고 있다는 사실을 파악할 수 있다. 또한 같은 문장에서 계절 인턴 프로그램을 진행할 예정이라는 점도 알 수 있다. (B)와 (D)를 제거하자. 세 번째 문단에는 BEN이 한 잡지사 편집 팀의 투표에 의해 수년 동안 가장 좋은 영자신문으로 인정받아 왔다는 내용이 있다(BEN has earned recognition as Thailand's best English newspaper for the past four years, as voted by the editorial team of *Southeast Asia Travel Guide* magazine). 여기서 (C)를 제거하자.

📑 **Questions 169 through 171** refer to the following job advertisement.

169–171번 문제는 다음 구인 광고에 관한 것입니다.

Seeking: Pottery Assistants

Earth & Fire, a ceramic production studio located in Stoke-on-Trent, England, is looking to hire two full-time assistants. —[1]—. [169]Successful applicants should possess a strong knowledge of ceramic craftsmanship and be adept at learning and consistently reproducing processes throughout their workday. Attention to detail is vital. —[2]—. At the beginning, assistants will receive close supervision and feedback from the artist and must be receptive to constructive critiques to enhance the quality of their work. Key responsibilities include preparing clay for use, smoothing finished pieces, mixing and applying glazes, and keeping the studio clean at the end of each day. The hourly rate ranges between £11 and £15, depending on experience. —[3]—.

To apply, send your CV and a cover letter to marisol@earthandfire.com. [171]The hiring process starts with a brief phone screening, followed by an in-person working interview for selected candidates. —[4]—. [170]Chosen candidates will be offered a 60-day trial contract, during which the artist will evaluate their skills and determine if they are suitable for a permanent role.

모집: 도자기 제작 보조원

잉글랜드 Stoke-on-Trent에 위치한 도자기 제작 스튜디오 Earth & Fire가 두 명의 정규직 조수를 채용하려고 합니다. 합격한 지원자는 도자기 세공 기술에 대한 탄탄한 지식을 보유하고, 업무 시간 내내 제작 과정을 배워서 일관되게 반복해 내는 데 능숙해야 합니다. 세밀함은 필수입니다. 초기에 조수는 작가로부터 면밀한 관리와 피드백을 받게 되며 작업의 질을 향상시키기 위한 건설적인 비판을 수용할 수 있어야 합니다. 주요 업무에는 사용할 점토 준비하기, 완성된 작품 다듬기, 유약 혼합하여 바르기, 매일 퇴근할 때 스튜디오 청소하기 등이 있습니다. 시급 범위는 경력에 따라 11파운드에서 15파운드 사이입니다.

지원하려면 이력서와 자기소개서를 marisol@earthandfire.com으로 보내시기 바랍니다. 채용 절차는 간단한 전화 심사로 시작되며, 선별된 지원자들을 대상으로 대면 실무 면접이 이어집니다. 합격한 지원자에게는 60일간의 수습 계약을 제안하며, 이 기간 동안 작가가 지원자의 역량을 평가하여 정규직에 적합한지를 판단합니다.

어휘 seek 찾다, 구하다 be looking to-V ~하려고 하다 successful (지원에) 합격한 craftsmanship 세공 기술 adept 능숙한 consistently 일관되게 reproduce 다시 만들어 내다, 재현하다 throughout ~ 동안 내내 workday 업무 시간 vital 매우 중요한, 필수적인 close 면밀한 supervision 감독, 관리 receptive 수용적인, 잘 받아들이는 constructive 건설적인 critique 비평, 비판 responsibility (담당) 업무 apply 바르다, 지원하다 glaze 유약 hourly rate 시급 range 범위가 ~이다 depending on ~에 따라 CV(curriculum vitae) 이력서 cover letter 자기소개서 screening 검사, 심사 A be followed by B A에 뒤이어 B가 뒤따르다[이어지다] in-person 직접의, 대면의 trial 시험의, 수습의 evaluate 평가하다 skill 기술, 역량 determine 결정하다, 판단하다 permanent 정규직의, 상임의

What can be inferred about the work?

(A) The tasks require repetitive work.
(B) It offers a flexible work schedule.
(C) No prior knowledge of ceramics is needed.
(D) Supervisory oversight is not part of the role.

일자리에 관하여 무엇을 추론할 수 있는가?

(A) 업무가 반복적인 작업을 요한다.
(B) 유연한 근무 일정을 제공한다.
(C) 도자기 공예에 대한 사전 지식이 필요 없다.
(D) 관리 감독은 업무의 일부가 아니다.

어휘 infer 추론하다 repetitive 반복적인 flexible 유연한 prior 이전의, 사전의 ceramics 도자기 공예 supervisory 감독의, 관리의 oversight 감독, 관리

해설 지원자의 자격 요건으로 근무 시간 내내 제작 과정을 일관되게 재현하는 능력(adept at learning and consistently reproducing processes throughout their workday)을 언급하고 있다. 일관되게 재현한다는 것은 같은 업무가 반복된다는 것을 암시한다.

What is stated about candidates who are chosen for the pottery assistant job?

(A) They are expected to work overtime hours.
(B) They will be hired on a probationary basis initially.
(C) Their interviews will take place in group settings.
(D) They will need to supply their own tools.

도자기 제작 조수 자리에 합격한 지원자에 대해 무엇이 언급되어 있는가?

(A) 시간외 근무를 할 것이 기대된다.
(B) 처음에는 수습으로 채용될 것이다.
(C) 면접이 그룹으로 있을 것이다.
(D) 자기 연장을 준비해야 한다.

어휘 state 밝히다, 언급하다 overtime hours 시간외 근무 probationary 수습의 on a ~ basis ~ 기준으로 initially 처음에 take place (상황, 활동 등이) 진행되다 setting 환경 supply 공급하다, 제공하다

해설 합격자는 60일 동안 수습 계약을 맺고 일하며 정규직으로 채용되기에 알맞은 역량을 갖추었는지 평가받는다(Chosen candidates will be offered a 60-day trial contract, during which the artist will evaluate their skills and determine if they are suitable for a permanent role).

In which of the positions marked [1], [2], [3], and [4] does the following sentence best belong?

"This will enable them to display their abilities firsthand."

(A) [1]
(B) [2]
(C) [3]
(D) [4]

다음 문장은 [1], [2], [3], [4]로 표시된 자리 중 어느 곳에 가장 잘 어울리는가?

"이것이 그들로 하여금 직접 자신의 능력을 내보일 수 있게 해줄 것입니다."

어휘 display 드러내다, 나타내다 firsthand 직접, 바로

해설 자신의 능력을 직접 펼쳐 보일 수 있는 기회에 해당하는 표현은 두 번째 문단의 두 번째 문장에 들어 있는 an in-person working interview(직접 실무 면접)이다. 따라서 문맥이 가장 자연스러워지는 자리는 [4]이다.

Questions 172 through 175 refer to the following e-mail.

To: Employee List
From: Selene Jung
Date: 30 June
Re: Updates for the Third Quarter

First of all, I would like to extend my gratitude to everyone for your hard work during the second quarter - it was truly a collective success. [172]As we look ahead, several personnel changes have been instituted to maintain momentum as we transition into the next quarter.

[173]I am thrilled to share that Chloe Martin has been promoted to the position of Senior Accountant. In the meantime, I've tasked Xiang Wei and his team with temporarily handling Ms. Martin's previous role as Budget Analyst until we finalize recruitment for a permanent successor with the human resources team.

Additionally, as you may already know, [174] [175]Sahil Ahmad retired earlier this month after dedicating over three decades to the company. [175]Taking his place as Credit Risk Analyst is Camilla Salazar. She brings over a decade of professional experience from Irish Credit Bank and is expected to acclimate to her new responsibilities here at Edelboden with ease. I encourage everyone to visit her office in Room 207 to introduce yourselves and offer her a warm welcome.

Sincerely,

Selene Jung, Corporate Finance Manager
Edelboden Company

172-175번 문제는 다음 이메일에 관한 것입니다.

수신: 전 직원
발신: Selene Jung
날짜: 6월 30일
제목: 3분기 업데이트

우선 2분기 동안의 노고에 대해 모든 분들께 감사를 표하고 싶습니다. 진정 공동의 성과였습니다. 미래를 내다보는 이 시점에 다음 분기로 넘어가며 여세를 유지하기 위해 몇몇 인사 변동이 시행되었습니다.

Chloe Martin이 수석 회계사 자리로 승진했다는 소식을 공유하게 되어 매우 기쁩니다. 그동안 우리가 인사팀과 함께 정규 후임자 채용을 마무리할 때까지 Xiang Wei와 그의 팀에게 Ms. Martin이 전에 맡았던 예산 분석관 직무를 임시로 담당하도록 맡겼습니다.

또한 아마 이미 아시겠지만, 30년이 넘는 시간을 회사에 헌신한 Sahil Ahmad가 이달 초에 은퇴했습니다. 그의 신용 위험도 분석관 자리는 Camilla Salazar가 맡을 것입니다. 그녀는 아일랜드 신용 은행에서 전문가로서 10년이 넘는 경력을 쌓았으며 이곳 Edelboden에서도 쉽게 새 업무에 적응할 것으로 기대합니다. 모두 207호에 있는 그녀의 사무실을 방문해서 자기소개도 하시고 따뜻한 환영 인사도 건네시기 바랍니다.

진심을 담아,

기업 재무 관리자 Selene Jung
Edelboden Company

어휘 Re: (편지에서) ~에 관하여, 제목 quarter 분기 extend (환영, 감사 등을) 전하다, 표현하다 gratitude 감사, 고마움 collective 집단의, 공동의 look ahead 앞을 내다보다 personnel 직원, 인원 institute 도입하다, 시행하다 maintain 유지하다 momentum 기세, 여세 transition 변천하다, 전환하다 thrilled to-V ~해서 매우 기쁜 accountant 회계사 in the meantime 그동안 task A with B A에게 B를 맡기다 temporarily 일시적으로, 임시로 analyst 분석가 finalize 마무리하다 recruitment 채용, 모집 permanent (채용에서) 정규의 successor 후임자 dedicate (시간, 노력 등을) 바치다 credit risk 신용 위험(도) bring experience 경력을 쌓다 acclimate to ~에 적응하다 with ease 쉽게

172

What is the purpose of Ms. Jung's e-mail?

(A) To invite employees to apply for a promotion
(B) To summarize recent changes in staff assignments
(C) To welcome newly joined team members
(D) To explain policy updates regarding hiring

Ms. Jung이 보낸 이메일의 목적은 무엇인가?

(A) 직원들에게 승진 지원을 권유하는 것
(B) 직원 배치의 최근 변화를 요약하는 것
(C) 새로 합류한 팀원들을 환영하는 것
(D) 채용에 대한 정책 갱신을 설명하는 것

어휘 invite 권하다 summarize 요약하다 assignment 배정, 할당 regarding ~에 대한

해설 글의 목적은 언제나 도입부에 나타난다. 첫 문단 마지막 문장에서 several personnel changes have been instituted라고 말하면서 이어지는 내용이 인사 변동에 관한 것임을 예고하고 있다.

According to the e-mail, which position remains vacant?

(A) Senior Accountant
(B) Budget Analyst
(C) Credit Risk Analyst
(D) Corporate Finance Manager

이메일에 따르면 어느 자리가 비어 있는 상태인가?

(A) 수석 회계사
(B) 예산 분석관
(C) 신용 위험도 분석관
(D) 기업 재무 관리자

어휘 vacant 비어 있는, 공석인 budget 예산 corporate 기업의

해설 두 번째 문단을 읽어 보면 Chloe Martin이 승진하면서(Chloe Martin has been promoted) 원래 그녀가 맡고 있던 예산 분석관 업무는 Xiang Wei와 그의 팀에게 맡겨졌다(I've tasked Xiang Wei and his team with temporarily handling Ms. Martin's previous role as Budget Analyst). 그런데 이것은 영구 후임자를 채용할 때까지의 임시 조치(until we finalize recruitment for a permanent successor)이므로 현재 예산 분석관 자리는 비어 있다고 할 수 있다.

Who is no longer part of Edelboden Company?

(A) Ms. Jung
(B) Ms. Martin
(C) Mr. Wei
(D) Mr. Ahmad

더 이상 Edelboden 사(社)의 일원이 아닌 사람은 누구인가?

(A) Ms. Jung
(B) Ms. Martin
(C) Mr. Wei
(D) Mr. Ahmad

해설 세 번째 문단에서 Sahil Ahmad가 은퇴했다고 알려주고 있다(Sahil Ahmad retired earlier this month).

What does the e-mail say about Ms. Salazar?

(A) She holds a master's degree in finance.
(B) She relocated to Ireland ten years ago.
(C) She has recently joined Edelboden Company.
(D) She will supervise the accounting department.

이메일은 Ms. Salazar에 대해 무엇이라고 말하는가?

(A) 금융학 석사 학위를 보유하고 있다.
(B) 10년 전에 아일랜드로 이주했다.
(C) 최근에 Edelboden 사(社)에 합류했다.
(D) 회계 부서를 관리할 것이다.

어휘 master's degree 석사 학위 relocate 이동하다 supervise 감독하다, 관리하다 accounting 회계

해설 Ms. Salazar는 이달 초에 은퇴한 Sahil Ahmad(Sahil Ahmad retired earlier this month) 대신 신용 위험도 분석관 자리를 맡아 Edelboden 사(社)에 합류했다(Taking his place as Credit Risk Analyst is Camilla Salazar). 그녀에 대한 간단한 소개 후에(She brings over a decade of professional experience from Irish Credit Bank and is expected to acclimate to her new responsibilities here at Edelboden with ease.) 사무실에 들러 첫 인사를 나눌 것을 권장하고 있으므로(I encourage everyone to visit her office in Room 207 to introduce yourselves and offer her a warm welcome.), Ms. Salazar는 최근에 Edelboden 사(社)에 합류했다는 문장을 정답으로 선택하는 것이 타당하다.

From: Aaron Pavlovich <pavlovich@oceanviewplazaone.com>
To: Ganesh De Sousa <gdesousa76@csmailgroup.com>
Date: Wednesday, April 21, 10:16 A.M.
Re: Service request

Dear Mr. De Sousa:

[176][179]I got your service request from April 19 about the flickering hallway light and the malfunctioning dishwasher in your apartment. Typically, I aim to address minor service issues within a day or two after receiving an e-mail request. [177]Apologies for my delayed response. I was occupied yesterday dealing with a water pipe burst on the third floor.

[178]If you would like, I can arrange for my electrician to come and fix your light and dishwasher this week. He is available on April 22 between 2:00 P.M. and 4:00 P.M., or on April 23 between 8:00 A.M. and 10:00 A.M. Please let me know which of these time slots works best for you as soon as possible. If you will not be home during either of these times, let me know if you would like me to grant the electrician access to your apartment, as I have a key.

Regards,

Aaron Pavlovich

From: Ganesh De Sousa <gdesousa76@csmailgroup.com>
To: Aaron Pavlovich <pavlovich@oceanviewplazaone.com>
Date: Wednesday, April 21, 3:15 P.M.
Subject: RE: Service request

Dear Mr. Pavlovich:

I had heard about the plumbing issue on the third floor from another tenant, so I was not surprised that it took some time for you to respond. [179]As it happens, I managed to replace the hallway lightbulb myself on the same day I submitted my request, and it is working perfectly now. However, the dishwasher still requires repair. [180]I would prefer for the electrician to come on Thursday, April 22, as I will be flying to Winnipeg for a conference the following day and would like to be present during the repair. [180]Thursday is convenient for me because I will be working from home that day. Please confirm whether the electrician is available that afternoon. I appreciate your attention to this matter.

Sincerely,

Ganesh De Sousa
Apartment #312

발신: Aaron Pavlovich
〈pavlovich@oceanviewplazaone.com〉
수신: Ganesh De Sousa
〈gdesousa76@csmailgroup.com〉
날짜: 4월 21일 수요일 오전 10:16
제목: 서비스 요청

Mr. De Sousa께:

아파트 내의 깜빡거리는 복도 전등과 오작동하는 식기세척기에 관한 4월 19일 귀하의 서비스 요청을 받았습니다. 보통 가벼운 서비스 문제는 이메일 요청을 받은 후 하루나 이틀 내에 처리해 드리려고 합니다. 답변이 지연되어 사과드립니다. 어제 3층에서 수도관 파열을 처리하느라 바빴습니다.

원하신다면 저의 전기기사가 이번 주에 방문하여 전등과 식기세척기를 고치도록 준비해 드리겠습니다. 기사는 4월 22일 오후 2시부터 4시까지, 혹은 4월 23일 오전 8시부터 10시까지 시간을 낼 수 있습니다. 이 중 어느 시간대가 가장 좋으신지 되도록 빨리 알려주시기 바랍니다. 두 시간대 모두 집에 계시지 않는다면, 저에게 열쇠가 있으니 기사가 아파트에 출입하도록 허용해 줘도 되는지 알려주시기 바랍니다.

이만 줄입니다.

Aaron Pavlovich

발신: Ganesh De Sousa
〈gdesousa76@csmailgroup.com〉
수신: Aaron Pavlovich
〈pavlovich@oceanviewplazaone.com〉
날짜: 4월 21일 수요일 오후 3:15
제목: RE: 서비스 요청

Mr. Pavlovich께:

3층 배관 문제에 대해서는 다른 주민에게 들었기 때문에 답변에 시간이 조금 걸린 것은 놀랍지 않았습니다. 마침 복도 전구는 요청서를 제출한 당일에 제가 직접 교체해서, 지금 완벽하게 작동하고 있습니다. 그러나 식기세척기는 여전히 수리가 필요합니다. 전기 기사분이 4월 22일 목요일에 오시면 더 좋겠습니다. 그 다음 날 회의 때문에 Winnipeg으로 가는 비행기를 타야 하는데 수리하는 중에 집에 있고 싶거든요. 목요일은 제가 재택근무를 하기 때문에 편리하기도 합니다. 기사님이 그날 오후에 시간이 되시는지 확인 부탁드립니다. 이 문제에 대해 신경 써 주셔서 고맙습니다.

진심을 담아,

Ganesh De Sousa
312호 아파트

어휘1 flicker 깜박이다 hallway 복도 malfunction 오작동하다 dishwasher 식기세척기 typically 일반적으로, 보통 address (문제 등을) 다루다,
처리하다 occupied 바쁜, 몰두한 burst 파열 electrician 전기 기사 time slot 시간대 grant 승인하다, 허가하다

어휘2 plumbing 배관 (설비) tenant 세입자 as it happens 마침, 우연히도 lightbulb 전구 present 그 자리에 있는 confirm 확인하다

176

Who most likely is Mr. Pavlovich?	Mr. Pavlovich는 누구겠는가?
(A) An electrical service provider	(A) 전기 서비스 제공업자
(B) The manager of a residential complex	(B) 주거 단지 관리인
(C) A computer-repair specialist	(C) 컴퓨터 수리 전문가
(D) The supervisor of a plumbing company	(D) 배관 설비 회사 관리자

어휘 electrical 전기의 residential complex 주거 단지

해설 첫 번째 이메일의 첫 문장을 읽으면 정답을 알 수 있다. Mr. Pavlovich는 고장 난 아파트 시설의 수리 요청을 받는 사람, 즉 아파트 관리인이다(I got your service request from April 19 about the flickering hallway light and the malfunctioning dishwasher in your apartment).

177

According to the first e-mail, why was Mr. Pavlovich's response to Mr. De Sousa delayed?	첫 번째 이메일에 따르면 Mr. Pavlovich가 Mr. De Sousa에게 보내는 답장은 왜 지연되었는가?
(A) Mr. Pavlovich was traveling outside the city.	(A) Mr. Pavlovich가 외지 출장 중이었다.
(B) Mr. Pavlovich was addressing issues with his computer.	(B) Mr. Pavlovich가 컴퓨터 문제를 처리하고 있었다.
(C) One of Mr. Pavlovich's employees was absent from work.	(C) Mr. Pavlovich의 직원 중 한 명이 결근했다.
(D) Mr. Pavlovich was attending to a more urgent task.	(D) Mr. Pavlovich가 더 긴급한 업무를 처리하고 있었다.

어휘 attend to ~을 처리하다, 신경 쓰다 urgent 긴급한

해설 답장이 늦은 것에 대해 사과하면서(Apologies for my delayed response.) 3층 수도관 파열이라는 더 긴급한 문제의 처리를 이유로 대고 있다(I was occupied yesterday dealing with a water pipe burst on the third floor).

178

Why does Mr. Pavlovich need information from Mr. De Sousa?	Mr. Pavlovich는 왜 Mr. De Sousa로부터 정보가 필요한가?
(A) To schedule a repair visit	(A) 수리 방문의 일정을 잡기 위해서
(B) To deliver a package to his apartment	(B) 아파트로 소포를 배달하기 위해서
(C) To issue a reimbursement	(C) 환급금을 지불하기 위해서
(D) To gain access to an account	(D) 계좌에 대한 접속 권한을 얻기 위해서

어휘 issue 발급하다, 발행하다 reimbursement 환급

해설 Mr. Pavlovich가 Mr. De Sousa에게 요구하는 정보는 4월 22일 오후와 4월 23일 오전 중 어느 때가 알맞은가 하는 것이다(... on April 22 between 2:00 P.M. and 4:00 P.M., or on April 23 between 8:00 A.M. and 10:00 A.M. Please let me know which of these time slots works best for you). 이 정보가 필요한 이유는 전기 기사의 수리 방문 일정을 잡아야 하기 때문이다(I can arrange for my electrician to come and fix your light and dishwasher this week).

179

When did Mr. De Sousa resolve the issue with his light?

(A) On April 19
(B) On April 20
(C) On April 21
(D) On April 22

Mr. De Sousa는 언제 전등 문제를 해결했는가?

(A) 4월 19일에
(B) 4월 20일에
(C) 4월 21일에
(D) 4월 22일에

해설 두 번째 이메일에서 Mr. De Sousa는 서비스를 요청한 당일에 복도 전구를 교체하는 데 성공했고 지금은 조명이 잘 작동한다고 말한다(I managed to replace the hallway lightbulb myself on the same day I submitted my request, and it is working perfectly now). 첫 번째 이메일 첫 문장을 보면 Mr. De Sousa가 조명과 관련하여 서비스를 요청한 날은 4월 19일이다(I got your service request from April 19 about the flickering hallway light and the malfunctioning dishwasher in your apartment). 두 문장의 내용을 연계하여 정답을 알아내자.

180

According to the second e-mail, what is Mr. De Sousa's plan for April 22?

(A) To return from Vancouver
(B) To participate in a conference
(C) To work remotely from home
(D) To send an e-mail

두 번째 이메일에 따르면 Mr. De Sousa의 4월 22일 계획은 무엇인가?

(A) Vancouver에서 돌아온다
(B) 회의에 참석한다
(C) 재택으로 근무한다
(D) 이메일을 보낸다

어휘 remotely 원격으로

해설 두 번째 이메일에서 Mr. De Sousa는 전기 기사가 4월 22일 목요일에 방문해 주기를 바란다고 말하는데(I would prefer for the electrician to come on Thursday, April 22), 그 다음 문장에서 이 날을 원하는 이유를 재택근무를 하기 때문이라고 설명한다(Thursday is convenient for me because I will be working from home that day).

VELVET FORK BISTRO WEEKLY SCHEDULE
December 8-14

	Head Chef	Sous Chef	Receptionist	Waitstaff
Monday	Restaurant Closed			
Tuesday	¹⁸⁵Myra	Yuriko	Leonardo	Enrique Joshua
Wednesday	Walter	Rajesh	Leonardo	Enrique Asher
Thursday	¹⁸⁵Myra	Yuriko	Leonardo	Tamara Asher
Friday	¹⁸⁵Raul	Rajesh	Amira	Tamara Asher
Saturday	¹⁸⁵Raul	Yuriko	Amira	Joshua Mingxia
Sunday	¹⁸⁵Myra	Rajesh	Amira	Tania Mingxia

181–185번 문제는 다음 일정표와 이메일에 관한 것입니다.

VELVET FORK BISTRO 주간 일정
12월 8일 ~ 14일

	주방장	부주방장	프런트 담당	서빙팀
월요일	식당 휴무			
화요일	Myra	Yuriko	Leonardo	Enrique Joshua
수요일	Walter	Rajesh	Leonardo	Enrique Asher
목요일	Myra	Yuriko	Leonardo	Tamara Asher
금요일	Raul	Rajesh	Amira	Tamara Asher
토요일	Raul	Yuriko	Amira	Joshua Mingxia
일요일	Myra	Rajesh	Amira	Tania Mingxia

From: Myra <myra.velvetforkbistro@wavepost.com>
To: All Staff <staff.velvetforkbistro@wavepost.com>
Subject: Chapelville Food Festival
Date: December 4

Dear Team,

The Chapelville Food Festival is taking place next week, from December 9 to 14. Chef Julius McCarthy from the Flora Creek Inn Restaurant can no longer attend the event to conduct cooking demonstrations, so I have been asked to step in on his behalf. Yuriko and Asher will come along as my assistants.

¹⁸⁴ ¹⁸⁵Raul has graciously agreed to cover my shifts here at the restaurant next week, and Rajesh will be filling in for Yuriko. Mingxia has volunteered to work in place of Asher on Wednesday, December 10, ¹⁸¹but Asher's shifts on Thursday and Friday still remain unfilled. Would anyone be available to help out with this? Please let me know as soon as you can.

We are thrilled to be part of the festival this year. ¹⁸² ¹⁸³It will be a fantastic opportunity to showcase what Velvet Fork Bistro has to offer to the thousands of attendees expected at the event. Although next week will certainly be a busy one, we are confident it will be well worth the effort.

Many thanks!

Myra

발신: Myra
  〈myra.velvetforkbistro@wavepost.com〉
수신: 전 직원
  〈staff.velvetforkbistro@wavepost.com〉
제목: Chapelville 음식 축제
날짜: 12월 4일

팀원 여러분께,

Chapelville 음식 축제가 다음 주 12월 9일부터 14일까지 열립니다. Flora Creek 호텔 레스토랑의 Julius McCarthy 셰프가 더 이상 행사에 참석해 요리 시연을 진행할 수 없게 되어 제가 그를 대신해서 나서 달라는 요청을 받았습니다. Yuriko와 Asher가 조수로 동행할 겁니다.

Raul이 흔쾌히 다음 주에 식당에서 제 근무를 대신하기로 했으며, Rajesh가 Yuriko를 대신해 줄 것입니다. Mingxia가 12월 10일 수요일에 Ashe 대신해서 일하기로 자원했는데, Asher의 목요일과 금요일 근무는 아직 채워지지 않은 상태입니다. 도움을 줄 수 있는 분이 있을까요? 되도록 빨리 알려 주시기 바랍니다.

올해 축제의 일원으로 참여하게 되어 정말 기쁩니다. 행사에 올 것으로 예상되는 수천 명의 참가자들에게 Velvet Fork Bistro가 제공하는 것을 선보일 훌륭한 기회가 될 것입니다. 확실히 다음 주가 바쁜 한 주가 되기는 하겠지만, 우리는 이것이 노력을 들일 만한 가치가 있을 것이라 확신합니다.

정말 고맙습니다!

Myra

어휘1 sous chef 부주방장 receptionist 프런트 직원 waitstaff (전체) 서빙 직원

어휘2 inn 작은 호텔 demonstration 시연 step in (돕기 위해) 나서다 on one's behalf ~을 대신하여 come along 함께 가다[오다] graciously 너그럽게, 흔쾌히 shift (교대) 근무 cover (남의 일을) 대신하다 fill in for ~를 대신해 일하다 in place of ~을 대신하여 unfilled 채워지지 않은, 비어 있는 help out with ~을 도와주다 showcase 선보이다, 소개하다 well worth + N[V-ing] ~할 만한 가치가 있는

181

Why was the e-mail sent?	이메일은 왜 발송되었는가?
(A) To encourage people to attend a festival (B) To inform about a change in restaurant operating hours (C) To share news of a head chef's retirement **(D) To solicit employees to take on extra hours**	(A) 사람들에게 축제 참여를 권장하기 위해 (B) 식당 영업시간 변경에 대해 알리기 위해 (C) 주방장의 은퇴 소식을 공유하기 위해 (D) 직원들에게 추가 근무 시간을 맡아 달라고 요청하기 위해

어휘 operating hour 영업시간 retirement 은퇴 solicit 요청하다 take on (일, 책임 등을) 떠맡다

해설 첫 번째와 두 번째 문단을 읽어 보면 다음 주에 음식 축제에 참여하기 위해 세 명의 직원이 식당을 비우게 된 상황이다. 대부분의 근무 시간은 대체 인력이 확보되었는데, 목요일과 금요일에 Asher 대신 근무할 사람은 아직 찾지 못했다(but Asher's shifts on Thursday and Friday still remain unfilled). 이메일을 보낸 목적은 이것에 대한 도움을 구하는 것(Would anyone be available to help out with this?), 즉 추가 근무를 맡아 줄 직원을 구하는 것이다.

182

What is indicated about the Chapelville Food Festival?	Chapelville 음식 축제에 대해 무엇이 나타나 있는가?
(A) It is being held in December for the first time. **(B) It will likely be well attended.** (C) It spans two days. (D) It will take place at the Flora Creek Inn Restaurant.	(A) 최초로 12월에 열리고 있다. (B) 아마 참석자가 많을 것이다. (C) 이틀에 걸쳐 진행된다. (D) Flora Creek 호텔 레스토랑에서 열릴 것이다.

어휘 well attended 많은 사람이 참석한 span (특정 기간)에 걸쳐 이어지다

해설 행사에 참여하는 사람이 수천 명일 것으로 예상되고 있다(the thousands of attendees expected at the event).

183

According to the e-mail, what benefit does participating in the festival bring to Velvet Fork Bistro staff members?	이메일에 따르면 축제에 참가하는 것은 Velvet Fork Bistro 직원들에게 어떤 혜택을 가져다주는가?
(A) They can come up with new menu ideas. **(B) They will be able to publicize the restaurant.** (C) They can get a discount on cooking utensils. (D) They can learn new culinary techniques.	(A) 새 메뉴 아이디어를 생각해낼 수 있다. (B) 식당을 홍보할 수 있을 것이다. (C) 조리 도구 할인을 받을 수 있다. (D) 새로운 요리 기법을 배울 수 있다.

어휘 come up with (아이디어, 해결책 등을) 생각해내다 publicize 홍보하다 cooking utensil 조리 도구 culinary 요리의

해설 수천 명의 사람들에게 식당의 매력을 뽐낼 수 있는 환상적인 기회(It will be a fantastic opportunity to showcase what Velvet Fork Bistro has to offer to the thousands of attendees expected at the event.), 즉 홍보를 위한 더할 나위 없는 기회라고 평가하고 있다.

184

Which group will NOT be affected by a change in working hours?	근무 시간 변경에 영향을 받지 않는 것은 어느 그룹인가?
(A) Head chefs (B) Sous chefs **(C) Receptionists** (D) Waitstaff	(A) 주방장들 (B) 부주방장들 (C) 프런트 담당자들 (D) 서빙 팀

해설 이메일의 두 번째 문단을 읽어 보면 근무 시간이 변경되는 사람들은 주방장 Myra와 Raul, 부주방장 Yuriko와 Rajesh, 서빙 직원 Mingxia와 Asher이다(Raul has graciously agreed to cover my(Myra's) shifts here at the restaurant next week, and Rajesh will be filling in for Yuriko. Mingxia has volunteered to work in place of Asher on Wednesday, December 10). 이 내용을 토대로 일정표를 보면 근무 시간 변경이 없는 팀은 프런트 담당자들이다.

Which day will Raul have off during the week of December 8–14?

(A) Tuesday
(B) Wednesday
(C) Thursday
(D) Friday

Raul은 12월 8일~14일 주간의 어느 요일에 휴무일을 가질 것인가?

(A) 화요일
(B) 수요일
(C) 목요일
(D) 금요일

어휘 off 휴무일

해설 Raul은 음식 축제가 있는 주간에 Myra의 근무를 대신 하게 된다(Raul has graciously agreed to cover my shifts here at the restaurant next week). 일정표에서 Myra의 이름을 Raul로 바꿔 보면, Raul이 근무하지 않는 날은 수요일이라는 것을 알 수 있다.

Questions 186 through 190 refer to the following e-mails and schedule.

From: Arthur Gaillard
To: Min-ki Kang
Date: October 22
Subject: Follow-up

Dear Mr. Kang:

[186][187]We had a short discussion following your session at the summer World Energy Transport Congress regarding Lumivault Group potentially organizing a training session for my engineering team at ERS Corporation. We explored two possible topics: one focusing on land-use regulations for pipeline engineers, and the other addressing the environmental impacts of pipelines. I am very keen to bring these sessions to fruition during your visit to Edmonton for the winter conference.

According to the Lumivault Group Web site, your consulting fees are listed as follows: $750 for sessions with up to 10 participants, $1,000 for sessions with up to 20 participants, [188]$1,250 for sessions with up to 30 participants, and $1,500 for sessions with more than 30 participants. Could you please confirm if this information is accurate? I look forward to your swift response.

Sincerely,

Arthur Gaillard

From: Min-ki Kang
To: Arthur Gaillard
Date: October 23
Subject: RE: Follow-up

Dear Mr. Gaillard:

[190]I would be happy to conduct a session on land-use regulations for your team, and my colleague, Amina Weaver, who specializes in environmental-impact training at our consulting firm, is also available. Since we will be attending the conference on December 7 and 8, [189]there is no guarantee that the sessions will conclude early enough to accommodate an evening workshop on those days. Therefore, it would likely be most practical to arrange for a session either immediately before or directly after the conference.

186-190번 문제는 다음 이메일들과 일정표에 관한 것입니다.

발신: Arthur Gaillard
수신: Min-ki Kang
날짜: 10월 22일
제목: 후속 논의

Mr. Kang께:

하계 국제 에너지 수송 학회에서 선생님의 발표 후에 Lumivault Group이 저희 ERS 사(社)의 엔지니어링 팀을 위한 교육 세션을 진행할 가능성에 대해 간단히 논의했었습니다. 두 개의 가능한 주제를 검토했죠. 하나는 수송관 엔지니어들을 대상으로 하는 토지 사용 규정을 중점적으로 다룬 것이고, 나머지 하나는 수송관이 환경에 미치는 영향을 다루는 것이었습니다. 저는 선생님이 동계 학회를 위해 Edmonton을 방문하시는 동안 이 교육 세션들이 실현되기를 매우 바라고 있습니다.

Lumivault Group 홈페이지에 따르면 귀사의 컨설팅 비는 다음과 같이 명시되어 있습니다. 참가자 최대 10명인 세션은 750달러, 참가자 최대 20명은 1,000달러, 참가자 최대 30명은 1,250달러, 참가자 30명이 넘는 세션은 1,500달러. 이 정보가 정확한 것인지 확인해 주시겠습니까? 빠른 답변 기다리겠습니다.

진심을 담아,

Arthur Gaillard

발신: Min-ki Kang
수신: Arthur Gaillard
날짜: 10월 23일
제목: RE: 후속 논의

Mr. Gaillard께:

귀사의 팀을 대상으로 토지 사용 규정에 대한 교육을 실시하게 되어 기쁘게 생각하며, 저희 컨설팅 회사에서 환경 영향 교육을 전문으로 하는 제 동료 Amina Weaver도 시간을 낼 수 있습니다. 저희가 12월 7일과 8일에 학회에 참석하기 때문에 그날 세션들이 당일에 저녁 워크숍을 열 수 있을 만큼 일찍 끝날지는 확실히 약속드릴 수 없습니다. 따라서 교육 일정을 학회 직전이나 직후로 잡는 것이 가장 현실적일 것입니다.

^{190}I am available to conduct the training session on the 6th, while Ms. Weaver, who will remain in Edmonton for a few days after my departure, could deliver her session on the 9th. ^{188}The training fees mentioned in your e-mail are accurate. Looking ahead, you might find value in additional seminars we provide on topics relevant to environmental engineers, such as promoting environmental sustainability and designing energy-efficient buildings.

Kindly confirm which date and training session would work best for your company. I look forward to your response.

Best,

Min-ki Kang

저는 6일에 시간을 내서 교육 세션을 진행할 수 있고, Ms. Weaver는 제가 떠난 후 며칠 동안 Edmonton에 남을 예정이라 9일에 교육을 진행할 수 있습니다. 귀하의 이메일에 언급된 수강료는 정확합니다. 추후에는 환경 지속 가능성 증진이나 에너지 효율이 좋은 건물 설계 등 환경 공학자들과 관련된 주제로 저희가 제공하는 추가 세미나들도 유익하다고 생각하실 것 같습니다.

어떤 날짜와 교육 세션이 귀사에 가장 좋을지 확인 부탁드립니다. 답장 기다리겠습니다.

행운이 가득하기를,

Min-ki Kang

Training Session Schedule	
^{190}Session Presenter:	Min–ki Kang
^{190}Date:	December 6
Time:	9:00 A.M. – 4:00 P.M. (lunch break 12:00 P.M. – 1:00 P.M.)
Location:	Kingsley Conference Centre Conference Room 15A
^{188}Number of Attendees:	Twenty-eight engineers

교육 일정	
교육 강사:	Min–ki Kang
날짜:	12월 6일
시간:	오전 9:00 – 오후 4:00 (점심시간 오후 12:00 – 오후 1:00)
장소:	Kingsley 콘퍼런스 센터 15A 회의실
참가자 수:	엔지니어 28명

어휘1 follow-up 후속 조치 transport 운송, 수송 congress 회의, 학회 potentially ~할 가능성이 있게 organize (행사를) 조직하다, 진행하다 explore 모색하다, 검토하다 regulation 규정 pipeline 수송관 address (문제 등을) 다루다, 처리하다 keen 열망하는 bring *sth* to fruition ~을 실현시키다 list 열거하다, 나열하다 as follows 다음과 같이 accurate 정확한 look forward to ~을 기대하다 swift 빠른, 신속한

어휘2 guarantee 보장, 확약 conclude 끝나다, 종료되다 accommodate (요구를) 수용하다 practical 현실적인 arrange for 일정을 잡다, 준비하다 immediately 즉시 deliver a session 교육을 진행하다 look ahead 앞일[미래를] 내다보다 find value in ~이 유익하다고 생각하다 relevant to ~과 관련된 promote 촉진하다, 증진시키다 sustainability 지속 가능성 efficient 효율적인 kindly +V ~해 주시기 바랍니다, ~을 부탁드립니다

186

What is the main purpose of the first e-mail?

(A) To confirm attendance at the conference
(B) To inquire about organizing a workshop
(C) To cancel a planned presentation
(D) To request updates to a Web site

첫 번째 이메일의 주요 목적은 무엇인가?

(A) 학회 참석을 확인하는 것
(B) 워크숍 개최에 대해 문의하는 것
(C) 계획된 발표를 취소하는 것
(D) 홈페이지 갱신을 요청하는 것

어휘 attendance 참석 inquire 문의하다

해설 글의 주제나 목적은 항상 도입부에서 알 수 있다. 첫 문단을 읽어 보면 ERS 사(社)의 대표가 컨설팅 회사 대표에게 자기 회사 엔지니어들을 위한 교육을 요청하고 있음을 알 수 있다.

187

What can be inferred about ERS Corporation? (A) It employs a large number of engineers. **(B) It engages external consultants for training purposes.** (C) It serves as a sponsor for an international conference. (D) It operates out of Edmonton.	ERS 사(社)에 대해 무엇을 추론할 수 있는가? (A) 많은 수의 엔지니어들을 고용한다. (B) 교육 목적으로 외부 컨설턴트들을 고용한다. (C) 국제 학술대회의 후원사 역할을 한다. (D) Edmonton을 거점으로 운영된다.

어휘 infer 추론하다 engage 고용하다 external 외부의 serve as ~의 역할을 하다 sponsor 후원업체 operate out of ~을 거점으로 운영되다

해설 첫 번째 이메일 첫 문단을 읽어 보면, ERS 사(社)가 Lumivault Group이라는 컨설팅 회사에 교육을 의뢰하고 있으므로, ERS 사(社)는 직원들의 교육을 외부 컨설턴트들에게 맡긴다는 내용의 문장이 정답임을 알 수 있다.

188

How much will Lumivault Group charge for the training session in Edmonton? (A) $750 (B) $1,000 **(C) $1,250** (D) $1,500	Lumivault Group은 Edmonton에서 하는 교육에 얼마를 부과할 것인가? (A) 750달러 (B) 1,000달러 (C) 1,250달러 (D) 1,500달러

해설 첫 번째 이메일에서 Mr. Gaillard는 Lumivault Group 홈페이지에서 21~30명의 참가자를 대상으로 하는 교육은 요금이 1,250달러임을 확인했다고 말한다($1,250 for sessions with up to 30 participants). Mr. Kang은 답장에서 이 내용이 정확하다고 확인해 준다(The training fees mentioned in your e-mail are accurate). 교육 일정표를 보면 참가하는 엔지니어가 28명이므로 Lumivault Group은 이 교육에 대해 1,250달러를 부과할 것이다.

189

In the second e-mail, the word "guarantee" in paragraph 1, line 3, is closest in meaning to (A) permission (B) warranty (C) notification **(D) assurance**	두 번째 이메일에서 첫 문단 세 번째 줄의 단어 "guarantee"와 의미상 가장 가까운 것은 (A) 허가 (B) 보증서 (C) 통지 (D) 장담, 보장

해설 guarantee는 '고장, 파손 등에 대한 제품의 보증'이라는 뜻과 '보장, 확약'이라는 뜻이 있으므로 동의어가 될 수 있는 단어는 (B) warranty와 (D) assurance이다. 문맥상 there is no guarantee that the sessions will conclude early enough to accommodate an evening workshop on those days.에서는 '보장, 확약'이라는 뜻으로 사용된다.

190

According to the schedule, which training session was finalized? **(A) Land-use regulations** (B) Environmental impact (C) Sustainability strategies (D) Constructing energy-efficient buildings	일정표에 따르면 어느 교육 모임이 최종 확정되었는가? (A) 토지 사용 규정 (B) 환경적 영향 (C) 지속 가능성 전략 (D) 에너지 효율성이 좋은 건물의 건설

해설 두 번째 이메일 첫 문장을 보면 Mr. Kang은 토지 사용 규정에 대한 교육을(I would be happy to conduct a session on land-use regulations for your team), Ms. Weaver는 환경적 영향에 대한 교육을 담당한다(Amina Weaver, who specializes in environmental-impact training at our consulting firm, is also available). 두 번째 문단을 보면 Mr. Kang은 12월 6일에(I am available to conduct the training session on the 6th), Ms. Weaver는 다른 날짜에 교육을 주재할 수 있다(Ms. Weaver, ... could deliver her session on the 9th). 일정표를 보면 강사는 Mr. Kang, 교육 날짜는 12월 6일이므로, 주제는 토지 사용 규정이라고 추론할 수 있다.

Questions 191 through 195 refer to the following Web pages and letter.

Current Promotions for Aurora Alliance Members

From 1 January to 31 June, accumulate rewards points by staying at any of the following Aurora Alliance hotels.

[192]**Schneider Grand Hotel, Lucerne, Switzerland** Earn 30 points per night for a standard room.	**Ragusa Heritage Hotel, Dubrovnik, Croatia** Earn 70 points per night for a deluxe room.
[194]**Lumivien Inn, Salzburg, Austria** Opens 1 September! Earn 80 points per night for a standard room.	**Kallistos Suites, Santorini, Greece** Earn 50 points per night for a deluxe room.

Additional Benefits for Members:

- [191]Members are entitled to courtesy bus rides to specific nearby attractions and the main airport. For schedule details, please inquire at the front desk.
- Members can enjoy a 10% reduction in car rental rates when booking with Aditi Rentals.

Redeem Your Points:

- 500 points: Receive 50 percent off a meal valued up to €100 at any restaurant within Aurora Alliance hotels.
- 600 points: Get upgraded to a higher-tier room.
- 1,000 points: Enjoy a complimentary overnight stay at any participating Aurora Alliance hotel.

For more information about promotions and points, visit www.auroraalliance.com/member_rewards.

---

13 February

Esther Dvorak
124 Meadow Lane
Hawthorn OX4 18B
England

Dear Ms. Dvorak,

We appreciate your recent stay at an Aurora Alliance hotel. [192]Enclosed you will find the Aurora Alliance membership card that you requested during your visit to Lucerne. Your account has been credited with the 30 points earned from your one-night stay. [193]To keep accruing points, please activate your membership card by visiting our Web site at www.auroraalliance.com, selecting "My Account," and following the provided steps.

191-195번 **문제**는 다음 웹 페이지들과 편지에 관한 것입니다.

Aurora Alliance 회원을 위한 진행 프로모션

1월 1일부터 6월 31일까지 다음 Aurora Alliance 호텔 중 어느 곳에서든 투숙하시고 보상 포인트를 쌓으세요.

Schneider Grand 호텔, 스위스 Lucerne 스탠다드 룸 1박에 30포인트를 받으세요.	Ragusa Heritage 호텔, 크로아티아 Dubrovnik 디럭스 룸 1박에 70포인트를 받으세요.
Lumivien 호텔, 오스트리아 Salzburg 9월 1일 오픈! 스탠다드 룸 1박에 80포인트를 받으세요.	Kallistos 스위트 호텔, 그리스 Santorini 디럭스 룸 1박에 50포인트를 받으세요.

회원 추가 혜택:

- 회원은 특정 인근 명소들과 주요 공항까지 무료 셔틀버스 탑승 혜택이 주어집니다. 자세한 일정에 대해서는 프런트에 문의하시기 바랍니다.
- 회원은 Aditi Rentals에서 예약 시 자동차 대여 요금에서 10퍼센트 할인을 받을 수 있습니다.

포인트 사용:

- 500 포인트: Aurora Alliance 호텔 내 모든 식당에서 최대 100유로로 상당의 식사에 50퍼센트 할인을 받으세요.
- 600 포인트: 더 높은 등급의 객실로 업그레이드하세요.
- 1,000 포인트: Aurora Alliance 모든 참여 호텔에서 무료 1박을 즐기세요.

프로모션과 포인트에 대한 자세한 사항은 www.auroraalliance.com/member_rewards를 방문하세요.

2월 13일

잉글랜드
Hawthorn OX4 18B
Meadow Lane 124번지
Esther Dvorak

Ms. Dvorak께,

최근 Aurora Alliance 호텔에 묵어 주셔서 고맙습니다. Lucerne을 방문하셨을 때 신청하신 Aurora Alliance 회원 카드를 동봉해 드립니다. 1박 하시면서 받으신 30포인트를 계정에 적립해 드렸습니다. 포인트 적립을 계속 하려면 홈페이지 www.auroraalliance.com를 방문해서 "내 계정"을 선택하고 안내되는 절차에 따라서 회원 카드를 활성화하시기 바랍니다.

We look forward to hosting you again in the foreseeable future.

Regards,
Client Care Services
Aurora Alliance

가까운 시일 내에 다시 모시게 되기를 기대합니다.

이만 줄입니다.
Aurora Alliance
고객 지원 부서

---

194 195 Ms. Dvorak, thank you for taking the time to complete the survey regarding your stay at Lumivien Inn on 14–15 April. As a token of our gratitude, we have credited your account with 20 bonus points!

Aurora Alliance Membership Card: 2378273
Total Accrued Points: 630

To redeem your points, visit www.auroraalliance.com/member_rewards.

Ms. Dvorak, 시간을 내서 4월 14일~15일 Lumivien 호텔 투숙에 관한 설문 조사를 작성해 주셔서 고맙습니다. 감사의 표시로 보너스 포인트 20점을 계정에 적립해 드렸습니다!

Aurora Alliance 회원 카드: 2378273
총 누적 포인트: 630

포인트를 사용하시려면 www.auroraalliance.com/member_rewards를 방문하시기 바랍니다.

어휘1 alliance 연합, 제휴 accumulate 모으다, 축적하다 reward 보상 be entitled to ~에 대한 권리가[자격이] 있다 courtesy bus (호텔, 전시장 등의) 무료 셔틀버스 specific 특정한 nearby 근처의, 인근의 attraction 명소, 관광지 inquire 문의하다 reduction 할인 rate 요금, 가격 redeem (쿠폰, 포인트 등을) 사용하다 off 할인하여 valued 가치가 ~인 tier 등급, 단계 complimentary 무료의

어휘2 Enclosed you will find ~을 동봉해 드립니다 credit A with B A에 B를 입금하다 accrue 누적하다, 축적하다 activate 활성화하다 host (손님을) 접대하다 in the foreseeable future 가까운 시일 내에

어휘3 complete 작성하다 regarding ~에 관한 token 상징, 표시

191

What is stated about the services offered by Aurora Alliance hotels?

(A) They feature three different room types.
(B) Guests are provided with complimentary breakfast.
(C) Members receive vouchers for nearby attractions.
(D) Free transport is available for members to local destinations.

Aurora Alliance 호텔들이 제공하는 서비스에 대해 무엇이 언급되어 있는가?

(A) 세 가지의 객실 유형을 포함한다.
(B) 투숙객들에게 무료 아침식사가 제공된다.
(C) 회원들이 인근 명소들의 이용권을 받는다.
(D) 회원들이 현지 목적지까지 무료 교통편을 이용할 수 있다.

어휘 feature 포함하다, 특징으로 하다 voucher 상품권, 이용권 destination 목적지

해설 첫 번째 웹 페이지에 회원들을 위한 추가 혜택으로(Additional Benefits for Members) 호텔 인근 몇몇 명소들까지 무료 셔틀버스 탑승이 언급되고 있다 (Members are entitled to courtesy bus rides to specific nearby attractions and the main airport).

192

At what hotel did Ms. Dvorak request a membership card?

(A) Schneider Grand Hotel
(B) Ragusa Heritage Hotel
(C) Lumivien Inn
(D) Kallistos Suites

Ms. Dvorak은 어느 호텔에서 회원 카드를 신청했는가?

(A) Schneider Grand 호텔
(B) Ragusa Heritage 호텔
(C) Lumivien 호텔
(D) Kallistos 스위트 호텔

해설 편지에 따르면 Ms. Dvorak은 Lucerne을 방문했을 때 회원 카드를 신청했는데(Enclosed you will find the Aurora Alliance membership card that you requested during your visit to Lucerne.), 첫 번째 웹 페이지 안내에 따르면 Lucerne에 있는 호텔은 Schneider Grand 호텔이다(Schneider Grand Hotel, Lucerne, Switzerland).

In the letter, the word "keep" in paragraph 1, line 3, is closest in meaning to (A) place **(B) continue** (C) postpone (D) retain	편지에서 첫 문단 세 번째 줄의 단어 "keep"과 의미 상 가장 가까운 것은 (A) 두다, 놓다 (B) 계속하다 (C) 연기하다 (D) 유지하다, 보유하다

해설 keep의 동의어가 될 수 있는 것은 (B) continue와 (D) retain인데, To keep accruing points는 '포인트 적립을 계속 하려면'이라는 뜻이다.

What most likely is true about Ms. Dvorak? **(A) She stayed at a new hotel.** (B) She rented a car from Aditi Rentals. (C) She was unable to activate her membership card. (D) She misplaced her membership card.	Ms. Dvorak에 대해 무엇이 사실이겠는가? (A) 새 호텔에 묵었다. (B) Aditi Rentals에서 자동차를 대여했다. (C) 회원 카드를 활성화할 수 없었다. (D) 회원 카드를 잃어버렸다.

어휘 misplace 잘못 두다, 잃어버리다

해설 두 번째 웹 페이지에 Ms. Dvorak은 4월에 Lumivien에 묵었다고 나와 있는데(your stay at Lumivien Inn on 14 - 15 April), 첫 번째 웹 페이지에 Lumivien 호텔은 9월에 개업한다고 소개되어 있으므로(Opens 1 September!), Ms. Dvorak은 개업한지 7개월밖에 안 된 새 호텔을 이용한 것이다.

Why was Ms. Dvorak awarded bonus points? (A) For recommending a courtesy bus **(B) For filling out a questionnaire** (C) For extending her hotel reservation (D) For checking out earlier than planned	Ms. Dvorak은 왜 보너스 포인트를 지급받았는가? (A) 무료 셔틀버스를 추천해 주어서 (B) 설문지를 작성해 주어서 (C) 호텔 예약을 연장해 주어서 (D) 계획보다 일찍 체크아웃해 주어서

어휘 fill out ~을 작성하다, 기입하다 questionnaire 설문지 extend 연장하다

해설 시간을 내서 설문지를 작성해 준 것에 대한 감사의 표시로 보너스 포인트 20점이 계정에 적립되었다(Ms. Dvorak, thank you for taking the time to complete the survey regarding your stay at Lumivien Inn on 14 - 15 April. As a token of our gratitude, we have credited your account with 20 bonus points!).

Questions 196 through 200 refer to the following e-mail, meeting notes, and article.

From: Magdalene Graham <mgraham@optivionsystems.com>
To: Adrian Lindberg <alindberg@casdsn.com>
Subject: Meeting
Date: January 8

Dear Mr. Lindberg,

[196]I would like to outline a few topics to cover during our upcoming meeting. Given that the lease for our current building will expire this year, it will be essential to start transitioning to the Windsor Avenue location as soon as the construction is finalized. While our budget for this project is significantly constrained, we remain committed to achieving an aesthetically pleasing design. Additionally, the local neighborhood council requires assurance that the project's impact will be contained, specifically in terms of construction-related dirt and noise, which have the potential to be disruptive for residents and workers in the vicinity.

[197]Our team was impressed with the work they saw on the tour of CAS Design's previous projects within the city, and we are hopeful that we can reach an agreement moving forward.

Sincerely,

Magdalene Graham, President
Optivion Systems

January 10

MEETING MINUTES

Attendees
CAS Design: Adrian Lindberg, Bjorn Norland
Optivion Systems: Magdalene Graham, Lucy Mei

Purpose
Determine the subsequent steps required for the Windsor Avenue construction project.

Decisions
- [199]CAS will investigate the feasibility of constructing additional elements onto the current structure and will prepare a preliminary budget for the project.
- [199]Should the project be deemed too costly to undertake, Optivion Systems will cover the cost of the assessment; otherwise, it will be provided free of charge.
- [198]The entire project must reach completion by the first week in December to ensure adequate time for Optivion Systems to transition all staff into their new headquarters before the year's conclusion.

196–200번 문제는 다음 이메일과 회의록, 기사에 관한 것입니다.

발신: Magdalene Graham
　　　〈mgraham@optivionsystems.com〉
수신: Adrian Lindberg 〈alindberg@casdsn.com〉
제목: 회의
날짜: 1월 8일

Mr. Lindberg께,

다가오는 회의에서 다룰 몇몇 주제에 대해 간략하게 말씀드리고자 합니다. 저희가 현재 사용하고 있는 건물의 임대차 계약이 올해 만료된다는 점을 고려하면, 공사가 마무리되는 대로 Windsor 대로 지점으로 이전을 시작하는 것이 필수입니다. 이 프로젝트를 위한 예산이 상당히 제한되어 있지만, 미적으로 만족스러운 설계를 구현하려는 의지는 확고합니다. 또한 지역 주민 회의에서는 특히 인근 주민과 근로자에게 방해가 될 가능성이 있는 공사 관련 먼지와 소음 면에서 프로젝트의 영향이 제한될 것이라는 보장을 요구하고 있습니다.

저희 팀은 시내에서 CAS Design의 이전 프로젝트들을 둘러보면서 작업물에 깊은 인상을 받았습니다. 앞으로의 진행에서 합의에 도달할 수 있기를 기대합니다.

진심을 담아,

회장 Magdalene Graham
Optivion Systems

1월 10일

회의록

참석자
CAS Design: Adrian Lindberg, Bjorn Norland
Optivion Systems: Magdalene Graham, Lucy Mei

목적
Windsor 대로 건설 프로젝트에 필요한 다음 단계를 정한다.

결정 사항
- CAS가 현재의 구조물 위에 추가 요소를 건설할 수 있는 타당성을 조사하고 프로젝트의 예비 예산안을 마련한다.
- 프로젝트 착수에 비용이 너무 많이 든다고 판단한다면, Optivion Systems가 평가 비용을 부담하며, 그렇지 않은 경우 평가는 무료로 제공된다.
- Optivion Systems가 연말 전에 전 직원을 새 본사로 이동시킬 수 있도록 충분한 시간을 확보하기 위해 프로젝트 전체는 12월 첫째 주까지 완료되어야 한다.

A Remarkable Transformation

(November 25) - Those familiar with the vacant Sterling Solutions building on Windsor Avenue might find it unbelievable that the majority of that dull, squat structure is still intact. [199]This is due to the fact that the former building is now concealed beneath the striking new national headquarters of Optivion Systems, which is approaching completion. CAS Design managed to incorporate the old building's foundation and some of its existing structure.

[200]"This aspect was crucial as the client aimed to avoid causing disturbance to the community by reducing the noise and dust," explained Bjorn Norland, a design engineer at CAS Design. "Our first step was to examine the structure. [200]From our initial research, we determined that the foundation and the primary support walls could be preserved, which allowed us to attain the client's objective," he added. - By Julia Parmentier

놀라운 변화

(11월 25일) – Windsor 대로의 비어 있는 Sterling Solutions 건물에 익숙한 사람들은 그 땅딸막하고 칙칙한 건물 대부분이 여전히 남아 있다는 사실이 믿기지 않을 수도 있다. 이것은 기존의 건물이 완공이 임박한 Optivion Systems의 인상적인 새 전국 본사 아래에 감추어져 있기 때문이다. CAS Design이 이전 건물의 토대와 기존 구조의 일부를 통합해냈다.

"이 점은 매우 중요했습니다. 고객사가 소음과 먼지를 줄여 지역 사회에 피해를 주지 않는 것을 목표로 삼았기 때문이죠."라고 CAS Design의 설계사 Bjorn Norland가 설명했다. 그는 덧붙여 말했다. "첫 단계는 기존 구조를 검사하는 것이었습니다. 초기 조사를 통해 토대와 주요 지지벽을 보존할 수 있다고 판단을 내렸고, 이를 통해 고객사의 목표를 달성할 수 있었습니다."

어휘1 outline 간략하게 설명하다, 정리하다 given that ~을 고려하면 lease 임대차 계약 expire 만료되다 transition 변화하다, 전환하다 significantly 상당히, 크게 constrain 제한하다 committed 확고한 aesthetically 미적으로 pleasing 만족스러운, 기분 좋은 neighborhood council 지역 주민 회의 assurance 장담, 보장 contain 억제하다, 제한하다 specifically 특히 in terms of ~ 면에서 dirt 먼지 potential 가능성 disruptive 지장을 주는, 방해하는 vicinity 부근, 근처 impressed 깊은 인상을 받은 moving forward 앞으로

어휘2 minutes 회의록 determine (결)정하다 subsequent 그 다음의, 이후의 investigate 조사하다 feasibility 실현 가능성, 타당성 element 요소 preliminary 예비의, 잠정적인 deem ~라고 판단하다, 간주하다 costly 많은 비용이 드는 undertake ~에 착수하다 cover ~의 비용을 대다 assessment 평가 otherwise 그렇지 않으면 free of charge 무료로 completion 완성, 완료 adequate 충분한, 적절한 transition 옮기다 conclusion 종결

어휘3 remarkable 놀라운, 주목할 만한 transformation 변화, 전환 majority 대부분 dull 칙칙한 squat 땅딸막한 structure 구조, 건축물 intact 손상되지 않은, 온전한 conceal 감추다, 숨기다 striking 강렬한, 인상적인 manage to-V (어려움에도) ~을 해내다 incorporate 포함해 넣다, 통합하다 foundation 기초, 토대 existing 기존의 crucial 매우 중요한 aim to-V ~하는 것을 목표로 하다 disturbance 피해, 지장 examine 검사하다 initial 초기의 determine 결정하다, 판단하다 primary 주요한 support 버팀목 preserve 보존하다, 유지하다 attain 달성하다 objective 목표, 목적

196

In the e-mail, the word "cover" in paragraph 1, line 1, is closest in meaning to

(A) request
(B) discuss
(C) pay for
(D) conceal

이메일에서 첫 문단 첫 번째 줄의 단어 "cover"와 의미상 가장 가까운 것은

(A) 요청하다
(B) 논의하다
(C) 지불하다
(D) 감추다

해설 cover를 '덮다, 가리다'라는 뜻으로 사용하면 (D) conceal이, '(책, 연설 등에서) 다루다'의 뜻으로 사용하면 (B) discuss가, '비용을 대다'의 뜻으로 사용하면 (C) pay for가 동의어가 될 수 있다. 본문에서는 회의 주제로 다룬다는 뜻으로 사용했다(topics to cover during our upcoming meeting).

197

According to the e-mail, why does Ms. Graham show interest in collaborating with CAS Design?

(A) CAS Design prioritizes eco-friendly construction practices.
(B) CAS Design has previously worked on projects for Optivion Systems.
(C) Ms. Graham wants to support a business from the local community.
(D) Ms. Graham's team appreciates the buildings designed by CAS Design for other companies.

이메일에 따르면 Ms. Graham은 왜 CAS Design과 협업에 관심을 보이는가?

(A) CAS Design은 친환경 건설 방식을 우선시한다.
(B) CAS Design은 이전에 Optivion Systems를 위한 프로젝트를 맡은 적이 있다.
(C) Ms. Graham이 지역 사회의 기업을 지원하고 싶어 한다.
(D) Ms. Graham의 팀이 CAS Design이 다른 회사들을 위해 설계한 건물들을 높이 평가한다.

어휘 prioritize 우선시하다 eco-friendly 친환경적인 practice 관행, 방식 appreciate 높이 평가하다

해설 이메일 마지막에 나오는 Our team was impressed with the work they saw on the tour of CAS Design's previous projects within the city를 읽고 이 부분이 패러프레이즈된 문장을 정답으로 선택해야 한다.

198

What is suggested about the president of Optivion Systems?

(A) She plans to move into a newly constructed office in December.
(B) She serves on the neighborhood council.
(C) She resides in the Windsor Avenue area.
(D) She has prior knowledge or experience with renovating buildings.

Optivion Systems의 회장에 대해 무엇이 암시되어 있는가?

(A) 12월에 새로 건설된 사무실로 이사할 계획이다.
(B) 지역 주민 회의에서 재직한다.
(C) Windsor 대로 지역에 거주한다.
(D) 건물 개조에 대한 사전 지식이나 경험이 있다.

어휘 reside in ~에 거주하다

해설 회의록에서 마지막 결정 사항을 보면, Optivion Systems의 전 직원이 연말 전에 새 건물에 들어가도록 하기 위해 공사는 12월 첫째 주까지 완료되어야 한다고 나와 있다(The entire project must reach completion by the first week in December to ensure adequate time for Optivion Systems to transition all staff into their new headquarters before the year's conclusion). 다르게 말하면 Optivion Systems의 회장이 12월 중에 직원들을 데리고 새 사무실로 옮겨 입주할 것이다.

199

What does the article imply about Optivion Systems?

(A) It will avoid paying a fee for the evaluation.
(B) It operates as a business owned within the local community.
(C) It overspent its budget on the building project.
(D) It recently rebranded itself from Sterling Solutions.

기사는 Optivion Systems에 대해 무엇을 암시하는가?

(A) 평가에 대한 수수료를 지불하지 않을 것이다.
(B) 지역 사회 내에 소유주가 있는 사업체로 운영된다.
(C) 건물 프로젝트에 예산을 초과하여 지출했다.
(D) 최근에 Sterling Solutions에서 브랜드를 변경했다.

어휘 avoid 피하다, 하지 않다 evaluation 평가 operate 운영되다 overspend 초과 지출하다 rebrand 브랜드를 변경하다

해설 먼저 회의록 내용을 기억하자. 결정 사항에 CAS가 기존 건축물 위에 새 건축물을 얹는 것이 가능한 일인지 조사한다고 나와 있다(CAS will investigate the feasibility of constructing additional elements onto the current structure and will prepare a preliminary budget for the project). 프로젝트 비용이 많이 들면 조사 비용을 Optivion Systems가 댄다(Should the project be deemed too costly to undertake, Optivion Systems will cover the cost of the assessment). 즉 기존 건축물 활용이 불가능해서 비용이 더 드는 경우에는 조사비를 Optivion Systems가 부담한다는 것이다. 그러나 활용이 가능하다면 조사 비용 부담은 CAS의 몫이 된다(otherwise, it will be provided free of charge). 이제 기사를 읽어 보면 전에 서 있던 건물이 Optivion Systems의 새 본사 건물 아래에 감추어졌다는 내용이 나오고(the former building is now concealed beneath the striking new national headquarters of Optivion Systems), 이어지는 문장에서 옛 건물의 토대와 일부분이 새 건물에 포함되었다고 말하고 있다(CAS Design managed to incorporate the old building's foundation and some of its existing structure). CAS가 기존 건축물을 활용하는 데 성공했으므로, 즉 프로젝트 비용이 과도하게 많이 드는 상황이 아니므로, 조사 비용은 Optivion Systems가 댈 필요가 없게 되는 것이다.

200

According to Mr. Norland, why were parts of the Windsor Avenue building's original structure retained?

(A) To preserve a structure of historical significance
(B) To comply with a safety regulations
(C) To minimize disruption to the neighborhood
(D) To create an aesthetically pleasing design

Mr. Norland의 말에 따르면 왜 Windsor 대로 건물의 원래 구조 중 일부가 보존되었는가?

(A) 역사적 의미가 있는 건축물을 보존하기 위해
(B) 안전 규정을 따르기 위해
(C) 지역에 미치는 방해를 최소화하기 위해
(D) 미적으로 만족스러운 설계를 하기 위해

어휘 retain 유지하다 significance 의미, 중요성 comply with ~을 따르다 minimize 최소화하다 disruption 지장, 방해

해설 기사에 나오는 인터뷰 인용문에서 Mr. Norland는 고객의 목표가 지역에 방해를 유발하지 않는 것이었다고 밝힌다(the client aimed to avoid causing disturbance to the community). 그리고 이어지는 문장에서 기존 건물의 토대와 버팀벽들을 보존함으로써 고객의 목표를 달성할 수 있었다고 말한다(we determined that the foundation and the primary support walls could be preserved, which allowed us to attain the client's objective).

➡ Answer

101	(B)	111	(A)	121	(A)	131	(C)	141	(A)	151	(C)	161	(D)	171	(D)	181	(A)	191	(B)
102	(D)	112	(A)	122	(A)	132	(D)	142	(B)	152	(A)	162	(A)	172	(B)	182	(B)	192	(A)
103	(B)	113	(B)	123	(A)	133	(B)	143	(A)	153	(D)	163	(C)	173	(A)	183	(A)	193	(C)
104	(A)	114	(D)	124	(B)	134	(A)	144	(D)	154	(B)	164	(C)	174	(A)	184	(C)	194	(A)
105	(C)	115	(B)	125	(A)	135	(A)	145	(C)	155	(C)	165	(D)	175	(C)	185	(B)	195	(B)
106	(C)	116	(C)	126	(D)	136	(B)	146	(B)	156	(C)	166	(B)	176	(C)	186	(D)	196	(C)
107	(C)	117	(A)	127	(D)	137	(C)	147	(A)	157	(A)	167	(D)	177	(D)	187	(D)	197	(B)
108	(D)	118	(D)	128	(C)	138	(B)	148	(D)	158	(D)	168	(A)	178	(C)	188	(B)	198	(A)
109	(A)	119	(A)	129	(D)	139	(A)	149	(B)	159	(A)	169	(B)	179	(B)	189	(A)	199	(C)
110	(C)	120	(A)	130	(C)	140	(D)	150	(A)	160	(B)	170	(A)	180	(B)	190	(A)	200	(C)

PART 5

101

Only authorized employees ------- permission to access patient records.

(A) are granting
(B) are granted
(C) have been granting
(D) be granted

허가받은 직원들에게만 환자 기록에 접근하는 권한이 부여된다.

어휘 authorize 승인하다, 허가하다 grant (권리 등을) 부여하다, 허가하다 permission (접근) 권한, 허가 access (정보 등에) 접근하다

해설 [(A) 능동태 (B) 수동태 (C) 능동태 (D) 수동태] 대표적인 4형식 동사 grant는 능동태로 사용할 때는 목적어가 2개, 수동태일 때는 목적어가 하나만 있다. 빈칸 뒤에 목적어가 하나만 있으므로 수동태 (B)나 (D) 중 정답을 선택해야 하는데, 이 문장에서는 (D)와 같은 동사원형을 사용해야 할 이유가 없다. 4형식 동사들은 3형식으로도 사용할 수 있으므로, 정답을 고른 후에 동사를 수동태로 사용하는 게 의미상 자연스러운지 해석을 통해 확인하고 넘어가자.

102

The skilled employees in our division ------- the expertise required to drive rapid growth and success.

(A) enlarge
(B) benefit
(C) contain
(D) possess

숙련된 우리 부서 직원들은 빠른 성장과 성공을 이끄는 데 필요한 전문 지식을 소유하고 있다.

어휘 skilled 숙련된, 노련한 division 부서 enlarge 확대하다 benefit 이익을 가져다주다 contain (특정 내용을) 담고 있다, (성분을) 포함하다, 함유하다 possess 소유하다, 소지하다 expertise 전문 지식 drive 촉진하다, 이끌다 rapid 빠른, 급속한

해설 빈칸 앞뒤 The skilled employees in our division ------- the expertise(숙련된 우리 부서 직원들은 전문 지식을 [(A) 확대한다 (B) 이득을 준다 (C) 담고 있다 (D) 소유하고 있다])의 의미를 자연스럽게 해주는 동사를 정답으로 선택해야 한다.

103

------- the tax rate adjustment will gain approval depends on public support.

(A) If
(B) Whether
(C) Though
(D) Either

세율 조정안이 승인을 받을지는 대중의 지지에 달려 있다.

어휘 tax rate 세율 adjustment 조정, 수정 approval 승인

해설 ------- the tax rate adjustment will gain approval이 이 문장의 주어인 명사절이므로 빈칸에는 명사절 접속사가 들어가야 한다. 명사절 접속사로 가장 많이 사용되는 것은 that이며, 그밖에 whether, 의문사, 복합 관계대명사가 들어갈 수 있다. if도 명사절 접속사로 사용할 수 있지만, 해당 절이 주어일 때는 안 되며, 주로 구어체 문장에 사용하기 때문에 Part 5에서는 정답으로 등장하지 않는다.

104

A reception is scheduled to begin in the foyer ------- after Ms. Schuster's presentation concludes.

(A) immediately　　(B) lately
(C) mutually　　(D) suddenly

Ms. Schuster의 프레젠테이션이 종료된 직후에 로비에서 리셉션이 시작될 예정입니다.

어휘 foyer 로비 lately 최근에 mutually 서로, 상호 간에 conclude 끝나다, 종료되다

해설 매년 여러 번 출제되는 문제이므로 반드시 짝을 이루어 기억해 두자. '------- after(ward) [thereafter / before]'가 보이면 정답은 무조건 promptly, shortly, immediately, right, soon, just 중 하나다.

105

Ms. Atkin is ------- of reports that fail to incorporate strong research components.

(A) critic　　(B) critics
(C) critical　　(D) criticize

Ms. Atkin은 탄탄한 연구 요소를 포함하지 못하는 보고서에 대해 비판적이다.

어휘 critic 비평가, 평론가 critical 비판적인 criticize 비판하다, 비난하다 fail to-V ~하지 못하다 incorporate 포함해 넣다 component 구성 요소

해설 be동사 뒤 주격 보어 자리에는 언제나 형용사가 정답이다. 보어 자리에는 명사도 들어갈 수 있지만 (A) critic은 보통 명사이기 때문에 앞에 관사가 있어야 하고, (B) critics는 복수 명사이므로 동사와 수가 일치되지 않는다. 토익에서 be동사 뒤에 빈칸이 있는 품사 문제에서는 명사가 정답으로 출제되지 않는다. 항상 형용사를 정답으로 선택하자.

106

Zephlux, Inc., must expand its workforce if it hopes to ------- all pending orders before the year concludes.

(A) affect　　(B) contain
(C) fulfill　　(D) mention

Zephlux 사(社)는 올해가 가기 전에 모든 미결 주문을 완료하려면 인원을 확충해야 한다.

어휘 workforce 인력 fulfill 이행하다, 완료하다 pending 미결의, 보류 중인

해설 빈칸 앞뒤 if it hopes to ------- all pending orders(아직 이행되지 않은 모든 주문을 [(A) 영향을 미치 (B) 함유하 (C) 완료하 (D) 언급하]고자 한다면)의 의미를 자연스럽게 만들어 주는 동사가 정답이다.

107

Managers will not ------- grant employees time off during peak operational months.

(A) generalization　　(B) generalize
(C) generally　　(D) general

관리자들은 보통 업무가 가장 바쁜 시기에는 직원들에게 휴가를 허용하지 않을 것이다.

어휘 generalize 일반화하다 time off 휴가 peak 가장 바쁜 operational 운영상의, 영업상의

해설 '조동사 + ------- + 동사원형'이 보이면 부사가 정답이다. 'be + ------- + 형용사', be + ------- + p.p., be + ------- + V-ing, have + ------- + p.p.도 모두 부사가 들어가는 자리로 기억하고 있어야 한다.

108

The Sheridan Art Museum has ------- invested in software programs to develop more interactive exhibitions.

(A) randomly　　(B) roughly
(C) instantly　　**(D) heavily**

Sheridan 미술관은 더 많은 체험형 전시회를 개발하기 위해 소프트웨어 프로그램에 많이 투자해 왔다.

 randomly 무작위로, 임의로 roughly 대략적으로, 대충 instantly 즉각, 곧바로 heavily 많이, 대량으로 interactive 상호 교류 방식의, 쌍방향의

 빈칸 앞뒤 has ------ invested([(A) 무작위로 (B) 대충 (C) 즉각 (D) 많이] 투자해 왔다)의 의미를 자연스럽게 만들어 주는 부사가 정답이다.

109

The hotel manager has offered us ------- that the pool will be ready for use by May.

(A) assurance　　　　　(B) assuredly
(C) assuring　　　　　　(D) assures

호텔 지배인은 수영장이 5월까지는 사용 준비가 될 것이라고 우리에게 장담했다.

 assurance 장담, 보장 assuredly 확실히, 틀림없이

 4형식 동사 has offered 뒤에 간접 목적어 us가 있으므로 그 뒤 빈칸에는 직접 목적어가 될 명사가 들어가야 한다.

110

The store ------- charged Ms. Hong's credit card twice for the same purchase, but it promptly corrected the mistake.

(A) uniformly　　　　　(B) potentially
(C) inadvertently　　　(D) functionally

상점에서 본의 아니게 Ms. Hong의 신용 카드에 같은 구매에 두 번 비용을 부과했지만, 곧바로 실수를 바로잡았다.

 uniformly 동일하게, 균일하게 potentially 잠재적으로 inadvertently 본의 아니게, 무심결에 functionally 기능적으로, 실용적으로 charge 요금을 부과하다 promptly 곧바로, 즉시 correct 고치다, 바로잡다

 The store ------- charged Ms. Hong's credit card twice for the same purchase(상점에서 [(A) 동일하게 (B) 잠재적으로 (C) 본의 아니게 (D) 기능적으로] Ms. Hong의 신용 카드에 같은 구매에 대해 두 번 비용을 부과했다)의 의미를 자연스럽게 해주는 부사가 정답이다.

111

The Regina Daily will gradually ------- to provide free subscriptions starting next month.

(A) cease　　　　　　(B) ceased
(C) cessation　　　　　(D) ceasing

The Regina Daily는 다음 달부터 무료 구독 제공을 점차 중단할 것이다.

 gradually 점차, 서서히 cease 중단하다, 중지하다 cessation 중지, 휴지

 빈칸 앞뒤 will gradually ------- to provide만 보면 정답을 알 수 있다. 조동사 뒤에는 동사원형이 들어가야 한다.

112

------- its primary competitor, the ergonomic chair from Lume Living Designs is both lightweight and available in a range of colors.

(A) In contrast to　　　(B) By way of
(C) Instead of　　　　　(D) So as

주요 경쟁업체와는 대조적으로 Lume Living Designs의 인체공학 의자는 가벼우면서 다양한 색상으로 이용할 수 있다.

 in contrast to ~과 대조적으로 by way of ~을 통해 primary 주요한 competitor 경쟁자, 경쟁 상대 ergonomic 인체공학적인

 so as는 to부정사와 함께 사용해야 '~하기 위해서'라는 의미가 되므로 여기서는 제외한다. 의미상 its primary competitor를 목적어로 취할 수 있는 것은 (A)와 (C)인데, 주절의 내용이 경쟁사 제품과의 차별점에 대한 설명이므로 정답으로는 (A)가 알맞다.

113

We appreciate your so ------- explaining the enrollment procedures to the new employees.

(A) being patient　　　　**(B) patiently**
(C) patience　　　　　　(D) patient

큰 인내심을 갖고 신입 사원들에게 등록 절차를 설명해 주셔서 고맙습니다.

 enrollment 등록 procedure 절차

 빈칸 앞뒤 your so ------- explaining를 보면 정답을 알 수 있다. 빈칸은 뒤에 있는 동명사를 수식한다. 준동사를 수식하는 것을 부사다.

114

The strategic planning committee advised that a greater emphasis should be placed ------- research and development in the upcoming year.

(A) against
(B) during
(C) for
(D) on

전략 기획 위원회는 다가오는 해에는 연구 개발에 더 많은 중점을 두어야 한다고 조언했다.

어휘 strategic 전략적인 place emphasis on ~을 강조하다, ~에 중점을 두다 upcoming 다가오는, 곧 있을

해설 place[put] emphasis on(~을 강조하다, ~에 중점을 두다)을 통째로 기억하고 있으면 빈칸에 들어가야 할 전치사를 알 수 있다.

115

------- the affordability of the production costs, we opted to collaborate with Clifton Material Co.

(A) Provided
(B) Given
(C) Considering that
(D) Regarding

생산 원가의 저렴함을 감안하여 Clifton Material 사(社)와 협력하는 쪽을 선택했습니다.

어휘 provided (that) ~이라는 조건으로 given ~을 고려하여 considering that ~이라는 점을 고려하여 regarding ~에 관하여 affordability 저렴함 opt to-V ~하는 것을 선택하다 collaborate with ~와 협력하다

해설 [(A) 접속사 (B) 접속사 / 전치사 (C) 접속사 (D) 전치사] 부사절 접속사 뒤에는 절이 있어야 한다. 빈칸 뒤에 명사구가 있으므로 전치사인 (B)와 (D) 중 정답을 선택해야 한다. 문장의 의미를 자연스럽게 해주는 것은 (B)이다.

116

The decorative rugs from Pichon Carpet are crafted using a ------- of synthetic and natural materials to achieve a unique texture and quality.

(A) plan
(B) team
(C) blend
(D) shade

Pichon Carpet의 장식용 깔개는 합성 및 천연 소재의 혼합물을 사용하여 제작되어 독특한 질감과 품질을 갖추게 되었다.

어휘 craft 공들여 만들다, 제작하다 blend 혼합(물), 융합(물) shade 그늘, 차양, 색조 synthetic 합성의, 인조의 texture 질감, 촉감 quality 품질

해설 빈칸 앞뒤 are crafted using a ------- of synthetic and natural materials(합성 및 천연 소재의 [(A) 계획 (B) 팀 (C) 혼합물 (D) 색조]을 사용하여 만들었다)의 의미를 자연스럽게 해주는 명사를 정답으로 선택해야 한다.

117

The number of shoppers at the store this holiday is comparable to ------- of the previous holiday.

(A) that
(B) those
(C) this
(D) they

이번 휴일의 매장 쇼핑객 수는 지난 휴일의 수와 비슷하다.

어휘 comparable 비교할 만한, 견줄 만한, 비슷한

해설 전치사구가 빈칸 뒤에서 수식하고 있을 때는(특히 전치사가 of인 경우가 많다.) 무조건 that이나 those를 정답으로 고르자. 선택지에 두 대명사가 모두 있을 때는 앞부분을 읽어서 빈칸이 가리키는 명사가 단수인지 복수인지 알아보아야 한다. 빈칸이 가리키는 명사가 단수 명사 number이므로 (A)가 정답이다.

118

The latest model from Vollmer Motors boasts a sleek dashboard layout and a ------- interior, providing ample space for comfort and convenience.

(A) widespread
(B) plenty
(C) prevalent
(D) spacious

Vollmer 자동차의 최신 모델은 세련된 대시보드 설계와 널찍한 내부 공간을 가지고 있어 안락함과 편리함을 위한 풍부한 공간을 제공한다.

 boast 자랑하다, 자랑할 만한 ~을 갖고 있다 **sleek** 미끈한, 세련된 **dashboard** 대시보드, 자동차 계기판 **layout** 배치, 설계 **widespread** 널리 퍼진, 광범위한 **plenty** 풍부한, 충분한 **prevalent** 보편화된, 유행하는 **spacious** 널찍한, 넓은 **ample** 풍부한, 넉넉한

 (B) plenty는 한정사로 명사 앞에 사용할 수 있지만 빈칸 앞에 한정사 a가 있어 함께 사용할 수 없으므로 제외하자. 빈칸 앞뒤 a ------- interior ([(A) 널리 퍼진 (C) 유행하는 (D) 널찍한] 내부 공간)를 의미상 자연스럽게 만들어 주는 형용사를 정답으로 선택해야 한다.

119

Oberon Design has a team of nine architects, ------- earned their degrees from prestigious universities.

(A) most of whom　　　(B) some of whose
(C) the reason being　　　(D) due to them

Oberon Design에는 9명의 건축가로 구성된 팀이 있는데, 그들 중 대다수는 명문 대학교에서 학위를 취득했다.

 architect 건축가 **earn** 획득하다, 취득하다 **degree** 학위 **prestigious** 권위 있는, 명망 높은

 (C) the reason being은 의미상, (D) due to them은 구조상 빈칸에 들어갈 수 없다. 토익에서는 선택지 중 두 개 이상이 관계사로 구성되면 십중팔구 관계사가 정답이다. (A)와 (B) 중 정답을 선택해야 하는데, 소유격 관계대명사 whose 뒤에는 항상 명사가 있어야 하므로 (A)가 정답이다. 보통 이 유형의 문제가 출제될 때는 whom을 빈칸으로 출제한다. '수량 표현(all[most / half / some / one / 숫자 / none]) of' 뒤 빈칸에는 목적격 관계대명사가 정답이라고 기억해 두자.

120

The quarterly revenue reports have been embarrassingly -------, failing to meet our projections.

(A) disappointing　　　(B) disappointed
(C) regretting　　　(D) pleased

분기별 수익 보고서는 창피할 정도로 실망스러웠으며, 우리의 예상치를 충족시키지 못했다.

 quarterly 분기의 **revenue** 수입, 수익 **embarrassingly** 난처하게, 창피하게 **meet** 충족시키다 **projection** 예상, 추정

 빈칸에 어떤 분사를 넣어야 할지 선택하는 문제에서 빈칸이 주격 보어 자리일 때는 주어와 분사의 원형이 의미상 능동 관계인지 수동 관계인지 보면 된다. (B), (C), (D)는 모두 주어가 사람일 때 자연스럽게 사용할 수 있는 것들이다.

121

Major ------- in tourism levels have played a crucial role in shaping the fortunes of Dover Beach's small businesses.

(A) fluctuations　　　(B) perceptions
(C) narrations　　　(D) obligations

관광 수요의 큰 변동이 Dover Beach 소규모 사업체들의 운명을 형성하는 데 결정적인 역할을 해 왔다.

 fluctuation 변동, 등락 **perception** 인식, 이해 **narration** 서술, 기술 **obligation** 의무(감), 책임(감) **tourism** 관광업 **play a crucial role in** ~에서 결정적인 역할을 하다 **shape** 형성하다 **fortune** 운명

 '증가(increase, rise, expansion), 감소(decrease, reduction, drop, fall), 변화(change, fluctuation), 경험(experience)' 같은 단어들은 자주 전치사 in과 함께 사용한다. 반대로 전치사가 빈칸으로 출제되는 경우도 많으니 '증가, 감소, 변화, 경험' 뒤에는 무조건 in이 정답이라고 암기해 두는 게 좋다.

122

Scientists at TRENIX Electronics will present the wearable devices that ------- have been working on for several years.

(A) they　　　(B) them
(C) their　　　(D) theirs

TRENIX 전자의 과학자들은 수년간 개발해 온 웨어러블 기기들을 발표할 것이다.

 electronics 전자 (산업) **present** 발표하다, 선보이다

 빈칸은 that절의 주어 자리이므로 주격 대명사와 소유대명사가 들어갈 수 있다. 소유대명사는 빈칸이 가리키는 대상이 '소유격 대명사 + 명사'의 형태일 때 정답이 된다. 이 문제에서는 문장 앞부분의 Scientists를 가리키므로 주격 대명사 (A) they가 알맞다.

123

The initial estimates for quarterly earnings have already been ------- even though there is still one month left in the quarter.

(A) exceeded　　　　(B) outdated
(C) overdrawn　　　　(D) impressed

분기별 수익에 대한 초기 추정치가 분기가 아직 한 달이 남아 있음에도 불구하고 이미 초과 달성되었다.

어휘 initial 최초의, 초기의　estimate 추정(치), 추산(치)　quarterly 분기의　earnings 수입, 이익　exceed 초과하다, 넘다　outdated 오래된, 흐름에 뒤처진　overdrawn 초과 인출의, 마이너스 대출의

해설 The initial estimates for quarterly earnings have already been -------(처음의 분기별 수익 추산치는 이미 [(A) 초과 달성되었다 (B) 흐름이 뒤처진 것이었다 (C) 초과 인출되었다 (D) 깊은 인상을 받았다])의 의미를 자연스럽게 만들어 주는 분사가 정답이다.

124

Acquiring ------- properties as possible can be risky, yet it often proves to be lucrative, yielding substantial financial gains.

(A) as much　　　　**(B) as many**
(C) so much　　　　(D) so many

되도록 많은 부동산을 취득하는 것은 위험할 수 있지만, 종종 수익성이 높다는 것이 입증되며 상당한 재정적 이익을 창출한다.

어휘 acquire 획득하다, 취득하다　property 부동산, 건물　risky 위험한, 모험적인　lucrative 고수익의, 돈벌이가 되는　yield (수익을) 내다, 창출하다　substantial (수량이) 상당한, 꽤 많은　gain 이익, 이득

해설 빈칸 뒤에 있는 as possible과 짝을 이루어 원급 비교 문장이 되어야 하므로 (A)와 (B) 중 정답을 선택해야 하는데, much는 항상 셀 수 없는 명사 앞에, many는 항상 복수 명사 앞에 사용한다는 점을 생각하면 된다.

125

------- of the newly developed software solutions, designed to streamline workflow, is available for immediate implementation.

(A) Either　　　　(B) Both
(C) Most　　　　(D) Every

업무의 흐름을 효율화하도록 설계된 새로 개발된 소프트웨어 솔루션 중 어느 것이든 즉시 도입이 가능하다.

어휘 streamline 효율화하다, 간소화하다　workflow 업무의 흐름　immediate 즉시의, 즉각의　implementation 도입, 시행

해설 one[each / either / neigher] of 뒤에 '복수 명사 + 단수 동사'가 온다. (B) Both와 (C) Most를 사용하려면 동사가 복수형 are이어야 한다. (D) Every는 명사 앞에서 한정사로만 사용할 수 있다.

126

Real estate agents assert that ------- to the landscape in the Fremont area will make the neighborhood more attractive to potential homebuyers.

(A) continuations　　　　(B) increments
(C) deviations　　　　**(D) enhancements**

부동산 중개업자들은 Fremont 지역 조경의 개선이 지역을 잠재 주택 구입자들에게 더 매력적인 곳으로 만들어 줄 것이라고 단언한다.

어휘 real estate agent 부동산 중개업자　assert 단언하다, 단호히 주장하다　continuation 연결[연장] 부분　increment 인상(분), 증가(분)　deviation 일탈, 벗어남　enhancement 향상, 개선　neighborhood 지역, 동네

해설 ------- to the landscape in the Fremont area will make the neighborhood more attractive(Fremont 지역 조경의 [(A) 연결 부분이 (B) 증가분이 (C) 일탈이 (D) 개선이] 지역을 더 매력적인 곳으로 만들어 줄 것이다.)의 의미를 가장 자연스럽게 해주는 명사가 정답이다.

127

------- from previous models, the newly redesigned TZ-450 motorcycle offers increased power while maintaining a lighter weight.

(A) Differs
(B) Differently
(C) Difference
(D) Different

이전 모델들과는 달리 새롭게 재설계된 TZ-450 오토바이는 더 가벼운 무게를 유지하면서 더 강력한 출력을 제공한다.

어휘 maintain 유지하다, 지속하다

해설 이 문장은 부사절 As it is different from previous models를 분사구문으로 전환한 것이다. 접속사와 주어를 제거하고 동사를 현재분사로 바꾸면 Being different from previous models가 되는데, 분사구문이 Being으로 시작되는 경우에는 Being을 생략할 수 있다.

128

The proposed development encountered substantial ------- from local residents who voiced their concerns about its potential impact on the community.

(A) condition
(B) prediction
(C) opposition
(D) deduction

제안된 개발 사업은 지역 사회에 미칠 잠재적 영향에 대해 우려를 표명하는 주민들로부터 큰 반대에 부딪혔다.

어휘 encounter ~에 직면하다, 부딪히다 substantial 상당한, 꽤 많은 opposition 반대, 저항 deduction 공제, 차감 voice 표명하다 concern 걱정거리, 우려

해설 빈칸 앞뒤 encountered substantial ------- from local residents(주민들로부터 큰 [(A) 상태에 (B) 예측에 (C) 반대에 (D) 공제에] 부딪혔다.)의 의미를 자연스럽게 만들어 주는 명사가 정답이다.

129

Fitzroy Bookstores announced a 20 percent drop in net profit this year, which the company ------- to intense competition from Yelland Booksellers, Inc.

(A) accused
(B) presented
(C) disapproved
(D) attributed

Fitzroy Bookstores는 올해 20퍼센트의 순이익 하락을 발표했는데, 이것을 Yelland Booksellers와의 치열한 경쟁에서 기인한 것으로 보았다.

어휘 net profit 순이익, 순익 accuse 고소하다, 비난하다 disapprove (제안 등에) 반대하다 attribute A to B A를 B에서 기인한 것으로 여기다 intense 치열한

해설 '~을 ~에서 기인한 것으로 여기다'라는 뜻으로 attribute[ascribe] A to B를 기억하자. 의미와 용법이 비슷한 credit A to B(A를 B에게 돌리다)도 함께 기억해 두자.

130

Customers of Bailey Catering should ------- on the back of this form any special dietary requirements to ensure their needs are properly accommodated.

(A) advise
(B) initiate
(C) specify
(D) permit

Bailey 케이터링의 고객은 필요 사항이 적절히 반영되도록 이 양식 뒷면에 특별한 식이 요구 사항을 명시해야 한다.

어휘 catering 출장 요리, 케이터링 initiate 시작하다, 착수하다 specify 명시하다, 구체적으로 지정하다 dietary 식사의, 식생활의 properly 적절하게, 제대로 accommodate 받아들이다, 반영하다

해설 should ------- on the back of this form any special dietary requirements(이 양식 뒷면에 특별한 식이 요구 사항을 [(A) 조언해야 (B) 시작해야 (C) 명시해야 (D) 허용해야] 합니다.)를 의미상 자연스럽게 만들어 주는 동사가 정답이다.

PART 6

Questions 131 through 134 refer to the following press release.

Velisse Perfumes is pleased to share that its latest fragrance, Velvet Bloom, has been [131]named Fragrance of the Year by the Global Perfume Society. Each year, the society considers dozens of entries, and winning this award signifies remarkable prestige within the industry. This marks the first occasion that [132]any of Velisse's fragrances has achieved this recognition. Velvet Bloom stands out by blending the aroma of freshly picked roses with a hint of vanilla.

The Velvet Bloom fragrance had a [133]limited launch earlier this year and remains exclusively available online. [134]The fragrance is set to hit store shelves next month.

131-134번 문제는 다음 보도 자료에 관한 것입니다.

Velisse Perfumes가 최신 향수 Velvet Bloom이 세계 향수 협회가 정하는 올해의 향수로 선정되었다는 소식을 기쁘게 나누고 있다. 협회는 매년 수십 개의 출품작들을 심사하며, 이 상을 받는 것은 업계 내에서 주목할 만한 명성을 의미한다. Velisse의 향수 제품이 이러한 인정을 받는 것은 이번이 처음이다. Velvet Bloom은 갓 수확한 장미향과 바닐라의 은은한 향이 혼합되어 돋보이는 제품이다.

Velvet Bloom 향수는 올 초에 제한적으로 출시되었으며 아직까지는 온라인으로만 구입할 수 있다. 다음 달에는 매장에도 입점할 예정이다.

어휘 latest 최신의 fragrance 향수 name 선정하다 society 협회 consider 심사하다, 검토하다 entry 응모작, 출품작 signify 의미하다, 나타내다 remarkable 놀랄 만한, 주목할 만한 prestige 명성, 명예 mark 기념하다 occasion 경우, 때 recognition 인정, 표창 stand out 눈에 띄다, 돋보이다 blend 섞다, 혼합하다 aroma 향기 freshly picked 갓[방금] 딴, 수확한 a hint of 아주 약간의, 은은한 exclusively 독점적으로, 전적으로 set to-V ~할 준비가 된 hit (시장, 상점에) 나오다, 출시되다

131-134

131 (A) granted (B) supported **(C) named** (D) founded	**133** (A) limit **(B) limited** (C) limiting (D) limits
132 (A) none (B) each (C) others **(D) any**	**134 (A) The fragrance is set to hit store shelves next month.** (B) A floral scent also took home the award in the previous year. (C) Its unique packaging has undergone a redesign. (D) Velisse is in the process of developing a successor to this product.

131 **어휘** grant (권리 등을) 부여하다 name 선정하다 found 설립하다, 창설하다

해설 수동태이면서 뒤에 명사 Fragrance of the Year가 있으므로 4형식 동사 (A)나 5형식 동사 (C) 중 정답을 선택해야 한다. 의미상 '올해의 향수로 선정되었다'가 자연스럽다.

132 **해설** the first occasion that ------- of Velisse's fragrances has achieved this recognition이 'Velisse의 향수 중 어느 것이라도 이러한 표창을 받은 첫 경우'라는 의미가 되도록 (D) any를 선택하는 것이 알맞다.

133 **해설** 형용사가 들어가야 하는 명사 앞 빈칸에 형용사 역할의 분사를 넣어야 한다. 현재분사 (C)와 과거분사 (B) 중 빈칸과 명사 launch는 의미상 수동의 관계이므로(제한된 출시) 과거분사가 정답이다.

134 (A) 다음 달에는 매장 선반에도 출시될 예정이다.
(B) 꽃향기는 전년도에도 상을 받았다.
(C) 독특한 포장은 재디자인을 거쳤다.
(D) Velisse는 이 제품의 후속 제품을 개발 중이다.

어휘 floral 꽃의 scent 향기 take home an award 상을 받다 undergo 거치다 successor 후속 제품

해설 앞 문장이 상품의 판매 방식에 대해 말하고 있으므로(exclusively available online) 이어지는 문장도 상품의 또 다른 판매 방식을 언급하는 것이 부연 설명으로 알맞다.

From: Franziska Weber <franziska@franziskasbakery.com>
To: Jin Ha Baek <jhbaek@polyvision.com>
Date: November 27
Subject: Your feedback

Dear Ms. Baek,

We sincerely appreciate you reaching out to Franziska's Bakery with your [135]suggestion. We are [136]delighted to share that your idea for caramel banana cupcakes will be incorporated into our menu starting next month.

As a token of our gratitude, we would love to offer you a complimentary half-dozen cupcakes in any flavor you prefer. To [137]claim your gift, simply bring this e-mail along when you visit Franziska's Bakery. [138]We hope this small gesture expresses our sincere gratitude. We eagerly anticipate welcoming you soon.

Best regards,

Franziska Weber, Owner
Franziska's Bakery

135–138번 문제는 다음 이메일에 관한 것입니다.

발신: Franziska Weber
〈franziska@franziskasbakery.com〉
수신: Jin Ha Baek 〈jhbaek@polyvision.com〉
날짜: 11월 27일
제목: 귀하의 피드백

Ms. Baek께

Franziska 베이커리에 연락해 주셔서 진심으로 감사합니다. 캐러멜 바나나 컵케이크를 만들자는 고객님의 아이디어가 다음 달부터 저희 메뉴에 포함될 것이라는 소식을 알려 드리게 되어 기쁩니다.

감사의 표시로 무료 컵케이크 6개를 선호하시는 맛으로 제공해 드리고자 합니다. 선물을 받으시려면 Franziska 베이커리를 방문하실 때 이 이메일을 지참해 주세요. 이 작은 표현으로 저희의 진심 어린 감사가 전달되기를 바랍니다. 조만간 고객님을 맞이하게 되기를 간절히 기대합니다.

이만 줄입니다.

Franziska 베이커리
사장 Franziska Weber

어휘 reach out to (제안, 의견을 위해) ~에게 연락하다, 접근하다 incorporate 포함해 넣다 token 표시, 증표 gratitude 감사, 고마움 complimentary 무료의 claim 청구하다, 신청하다 eagerly 열렬히, 간절히 anticipate 기대하다

135-138

135 (A) suggestion (B) requirement (C) complaint (D) concern	**137** (A) return (B) exchange **(C) claim** (D) display
136 (A) delight **(B) delighted** (C) delightful (D) delights	**138** (A) We're pleased to let you know that the item is available in our inventory. **(B) We hope this small gesture expresses our sincere gratitude.** (C) Kindly get in touch with us to provide the necessary details. (D) Price details are not included on gift receipts.

135 **해설** 빈칸에 들어갈 명사는 다음 문장에 나오는 your idea for caramel banana cupcakes를 가리키는 것이어야 한다.

136 **해설** '~하게 되어 기쁘다'라는 뜻으로 be glad[happy / pleased / delighted / thrilled / overjoyed] to-V를 기억해야 한다.

137 **해설** 앞 문장에서 감사의 표시로 무료 컵케이크를 제공하겠다고 했으므로, 이메일을 제시하는 것은 이 혜택을 청구하는 방법이다.

138 (A) 제품이 재고로 있음을 알려 드리게 되어 기쁩니다.

(B) 이 작은 표현으로 저희의 진심 어린 감사가 전달되기를 바랍니다.

(C) 저희와 연락하셔서 필요한 세부 사항을 알려 주시기 바랍니다.

(D) 가격 세부 사항은 선물 영수증에 포함되지 않습니다.

어휘 inventory 재고 kindly 부디 get in touch with ~와 연락하다

해설 앞선 두 문장에서 감사의 표시로(As a token of our gratitude) 무료 컵케이크를 제공하겠다고 말하고 있으므로(to offer you a complimentary half-dozen cupcakes), 선물(this small gesture)과 감사(our sincere gratitude)를 언급하는 문장이 이어지는 것이 문맥상 자연스럽다.

Questions 139 through 142 refer to the following advertisement.

Temba Construction Shelters

If you're engaged in the construction industry, you understand how frustrating [139]it can be when unexpected rain forces a project to halt. Not only does this risk inconveniencing clients due to missed deadlines, but it could also lead to delays in other scheduled projects.

Temba Construction Shelters offer the [140]protection you require to keep working! These temporary structures [141]can be set up directly at your job site. They remain intact throughout your project, allowing your crew to continue working without disruption, through rain or shine. Additionally, they help safeguard equipment and materials from moisture, eliminating the risk of water or mold-related damage. [142]Rain will never cause project delays for you again. For further details, visit www.tembashelters.com!

139-142번 문제는 다음 광고에 관한 것입니다.

Temba 건설 현장 보호막

건설업에 종사하신다면, 예상치 못한 비로 인해 프로젝트가 중단될 수밖에 없을 때 얼마나 좌절감이 느껴지는지 이해하실 것입니다. 이것은 기한을 지키지 못해 고객에게 불편을 끼칠 위험이 있을 뿐만 아니라 일정이 잡혀 있는 다른 프로젝트들의 지연으로 이어질 수도 있습니다.

Temba 건설 현장 보호막은 작업을 계속하기 위해 필요한 보호를 제공합니다! 이 임시 구조물은 작업 현장에 바로 설치할 수 있습니다. 이것은 프로젝트 기간 내내 손상되지 않은 상태로 비가 오든 화창하든 작업반이 방해받지 않고 업무를 계속할 수 있게 합니다. 더욱이 이것은 장비와 자재를 습기로부터 보호하도록 도와주어 물이나 곰팡이와 관련된 손상의 위험을 없애 주기도 합니다. 비가 프로젝트 지연을 유발하는 일은 절대 다시 없을 것입니다. 자세한 내용은 www.tembashelters.com을 방문해 주세요!

어휘 shelter (임시) 구조물, 보호막 be engaged in ~에 종사하다 frustrating 좌절감을 주는 unexpected 예상치 못한 force (어쩔 수 없이) ~하게 만들다 halt 중지되다, 중단되다 risk V-ing ~할 위험이 있다 inconvenience ~에게 불편을 끼치다 lead to (특정 결과)로 이어지다 temporary 임시의 structure 구조물, 건축물 directly 바로, 즉시 set up ~을 세우다 intact 손상되지 않은, 파손되지 않은 crew 팀, 조, 반 disruption 지장, 방해 additionally 더욱이 safeguard 보호하다, 지키다 moisture 수분, 습기 eliminate 제거하다, 없애다 mold 곰팡이

139-142

139 (A) it
   (B) one
   (C) they
   (D) some

141 (A) can be
   (B) are being
   (C) have been
   (D) would have been

140 (A) workers
   (B) financing
   (C) advice
   (D) protection

142 (A) Ensure you specify which repairs are the most urgent.
   (B) Rain will never cause project delays for you again.
   (C) A professional will be dispatched to your site immediately.
   (D) Determining the exact duration of a project can be challenging.

139 해설 (B), (C), (D)는 모두 무언가를 가리키는 대명사들인데, 빈칸은 특정 대상을 가리키지 않는다. 비인칭 주어 it을 사용하는 것이 알맞다.

140 해설 앞 문단의 내용이 건설 현장에 내리는 비로 인한 어려움을 설명하고 있으므로, 광고 상품은 소비자가 중단 없이 공사를 계속 하기 위한 비로부터의 보호를 제공하는 것이어야 한다.

141 해설 광고의 일부로서 상품의 사용법을 설명하는 문장이므로 "직접 작업 현장에 설치할 수 있습니다."라고 현재 시제로 말하는 것이 알맞다.

142 (A) 어느 수리가 가장 긴급한 것인지 반드시 명시해 주세요.
(B) 비가 프로젝트 지연을 유발하는 일은 절대 다시 없을 것입니다.
(C) 전문가가 즉시 현장에 파견될 것입니다.
(D) 프로젝트의 정확한 지속 기간을 확정하는 것은 어렵습니다.

어휘 specify 명시하다, 구체적으로 지정하다 urgent 긴급한, 다급한 dispatch 파견하다 determine 알아내다, 확정하다 duration 지속 기간 challenging 힘 드는, 어려운

해설 비가 올 때도 공사를 중단하지 않고 계속 할 수 있게 해주는 상품을 소개하는 광고이므로, 관련 내용을 언급하는 문장으로 마무리하는 것이 알맞다.

(September 5) - Beginning October 1, the city of Mableton will implement a new recycling system. Residents will no longer need to sort recyclable materials. [143]Instead, they can place all items into a single container.

"This approach is far more streamlined," says Larkin Benson of Mableton Waste Management. "Recycling will be just as simple as throwing things away. [144]Individuals will likely be more inclined to conform."

Some skeptics argue that although collection expenses might be lower under the new system, processing costs could increase significantly. "This method may be more [145]convenient for residents," says local resident Daphne Pearson, "but the recyclables will still need to be sorted at a facility. This means the city will incur high processing fees. Eventually, people [146]will realize that the previous system was more effective."

143-146번 문제는 다음 기사에 관한 것입니다.

(9월 5일) – 10월 1일부터 Mableton 시는 새 재활용 시스템을 시행한다. 주민들은 더 이상 재활용 물품을 분류할 필요가 없다. 대신 모든 물품을 하나의 수거 함에 넣을 수 있다.

"이 방식은 훨씬 더 간소화되어 있습니다."라고 Mableton 폐기물 관리국의 Larkin Benson은 말한다. "재활용이 물건을 버리는 것만큼 간단해질 겁니다. 사람들이 더 쉽게 준수할 가능성이 높습니다."

일부 회의론자들은 새 시스템 하에서 수거 비용은 낮아질지 몰라도 처리 비용은 상당히 증가할 수 있다고 주장한다. 지역 주민 Daphne Pearson은 말한다. "이 방식이 주민들에게는 더 편리할 수 있겠지만, 재활용품은 여전히 시설에서 분류해야 할 거예요. 이것은 시가 높은 처리 요금을 부담하게 된다는 것을 의미하죠. 결국 사람들은 이전 시스템이 더 효과적이었다는 것을 깨닫게 될 겁니다."

어휘 implement 실행하다, 이행하다 resident 주민 sort 분류하다 recyclable 재활용할 수 있는, 재생 가능한 container 용기, 통, 그릇 streamline 효율화하다, 간소화하다 likely 아마도 inclined to-V ~하는 경향이 있는, ~하기 쉬운 conform 따르다, 준수하다 skeptic 회의론자 argue 주장하다 significantly 상당히 recyclables 재활용품 incur (비용을) 부담하다

143-146

143 (A) **Instead**
(B) Otherwise
(C) In the meantime
(D) As a rule

145 (A) urgent
(B) amusing
(C) convenient
(D) ordinary

144 (A) Staff members have completed extra training for this process.
(B) Observing the outcomes of the system has been intriguing.
(C) The advantages of this change remain uncertain.
(D) Individuals will likely be more inclined to conform.

146 (A) realized
(B) will realize
(C) would have realized
(D) have been realizing

143 **어휘** otherwise 그렇지 않으면[않았으면] in the meantime 그동안(에), 그사이 as a rule 일반적으로, 통상

해설 앞뒤 문장을 읽어 보면 재활용품을 분류하는 대신(no longer need to sort recyclable materials) 한 수거함에 모은다는(place all items into a single container) 내용이므로, 두 문장을 이어 주기에 알맞은 부사는 (A) Instead이다.

144 (A) 직원들은 이 절차를 위해 추가로 교육을 이수했습니다.
(B) 이 시스템의 결과를 관찰하는 것은 흥미로웠습니다.
(C) 이러한 변화의 장점은 여전히 불확실합니다.
(D) 사람들이 더 쉽게 준수할 가능성이 높습니다.

어휘 outcome 결과 intriguing 흥미로운, 호기심을 자극하는 advantage 장점, 이점

해설 앞 문장의 내용이 새 재활용 시스템의 장점을 설명하는 것이므로(Recycling will be just as simple as throwing things away.), 이어지는 문장도 또 다른 장점을 언급하는 것이 부연 설명으로 알맞다.

145 **어휘** amusing 재미있는 ordinary 평범한, 보통의

해설 기사에서 소개되고 있는 새 방식은 재활용품을 분류하지 않고(no longer need to sort recyclable materials) 한 수거함에 모으는 것이므로(place all items into a single container), 주민들에게는 더 편리하다고 평가하는 것이 적절하다.

146 **해설** 새 재활용 시스템이 시행된 후에 사람들이 깨닫게 될 내용을 예상하는 내용의 문장이므로 문맥상 미래 시제로 말하는 것이 알맞다.

Questions 147 through 148 refer to the following notice.

147-148번 문제는 다음 공지문에 관한 것입니다.

[147]We are excited to share that Tess Yoon has become part of Stanton Law Firm as an associate attorney. She graduated with top honors from Claridell University Law School, where she specialized in copyright and trademark law. During her studies, she worked as a legal assistant in the university's legal aid office. This past summer, she completed an internship with Davenport and Associates, a law firm that represents authors, musicians, and other professionals in the publishing sector. Ms. Yoon has an outstanding history of service and will be an invaluable asset to our team. [148]Join us this Friday at 2:00 P.M. in the main conference room to extend a warm welcome to her.

Tess Yoon이 법무 법인 Stanton의 소속 변호사로서 일원이 되었다는 소식을 기쁘게 나누고자 합니다. 그녀는 Claridell 대학교 로스쿨을 최우등으로 졸업했으며, 저작권법과 상표법을 전공했습니다. 학업 기간 동안에는 대학교 법률 지원 센터에서 법률 보조원으로 근무했습니다. 지난 여름에는 작가들과 음악가들, 기타 출판 분야의 전문가들을 대리하는 법무 법인 Davenport and Associates에서 인턴 과정을 마쳤습니다. Ms. Yoon은 뛰어난 근무 경력을 갖추고 있으며 우리 팀의 매우 소중한 자산이 될 것입니다. 이번 주 금요일 오후 2시에 대회의실에 모여서 따뜻하게 환영해 주시기 바랍니다.

어휘 associate attorney 소속 변호사 with honors (졸업 때에) 우등으로, 우수한 성적으로 specialize in ~을 전문으로, 전공하다 copyright 저작권 trademark (등록) 상표 legal aid 법률 지원 represent (법정에서) ~을 대리하다, 변호하다 sector 부문, 분야 outstanding 뛰어난, 걸출한 service 근무 (기간) invaluable 아주 유용한, 매우 소중한 asset 자산, 재산 extend (환영 등을) 전하다, (동정 등을) 나타내다

147

Where is the notice most likely posted?

(A) In a legal firm
(B) In a talent management agency
(C) In a music production facility
(D) In a publishing house

이 공지문은 어디에 게시되어 있겠는가?

(A) 법률 회사에
(B) 연예 기획사에
(C) 음반 제작 시설에
(D) 출판사에

해설 첫 문장에 회사 이름이 Stanton Law Firm이라고 나와 있고, 변호사의 입사를 알리고 있다(We are excited to share that Tess Yoon has become part of Stanton Law Firm as an associate attorney).

148

What are staff members invited to do this Friday?

(A) Attend a live music event
(B) Become part of a community service group
(C) Take part in an industry-related seminar
(D) Meet a new colleague

직원들에게 이번 주 금요일에 무엇을 하도록 권하는가?

(A) 라이브 음악 행사에 참석한다
(B) 지역 봉사 단체의 일원이 된다
(C) 업계 관련 세미나에 참여한다
(D) 새 동료를 만난다

해설 마지막 문장에서 금요일 오후에 대회의실에서 신입 변호사를 환영하는 모임을 갖자고 권하고 있다(Join us this Friday at 2:00 P.M. in the main conference room to extend a warm welcome to her).

Questions 149 through 150 refer to the following notice.

Attention Residents of South Jordan:

[149]The South Jordan Business Directory has grown so large that it now occupies a sizable portion of the neighborhood newsletter. As a result, we will transition to an online format for the directory and discontinue its printed version.

The directory is not yet accessible, but in the upcoming weeks, it will be available at www.southjordan.com. Once it is published, [150]I recommend checking your listing to ensure its accuracy. If you notice outdated information or any broken links, please inform me so that I can update the necessary details.

Thank you,
Leah Langley
South Jordan Neighborhood Council
555-0124

149-150번 문제는 다음 공지문에 관한 것입니다.

South Jordan 주민 여러분 주목해 주세요.

South Jordan 사업체 주소록이 너무 커져서 현재 지역 소식지의 상당 부분을 차지하고 있습니다. 그 결과 우리는 명부를 온라인 판으로 전환하고 인쇄 버전을 중단하기로 했습니다.

아직은 주소록에 접할 수 없지만, 앞으로 몇 주 후에는 www.southjordan.com에서 이용할 수 있습니다. 게시되고 나면 본인의 기재 사항이 정확한지 내용을 확인해 보시기를 권장합니다. 오래된 정보나 잘못된 링크를 발견하시면 저에게 알려 주셔서 필요한 세부 사항을 갱신하겠습니다.

고맙습니다.
South Jordan 주민 자치 위원회
Leah Langley
555-0124

어휘 directory 명부, 주소록 occupy (공간을) 차지하다 sizable (수, 양 등이) 상당한 portion 부분, 일부 neighborhood 동네, 지역 transition 전환하다, 변경하다 format (서적의) 판형 discontinue (생산, 제조 등을) 중단하다 accessible 쉽게 얻을[이용할] 수 있는 upcoming 다가오는, 곧 있을 listing 표[명부]의 기재 사항 accuracy 정확성 outdated (정보, 수치가) 오래된, 해묵은

149

What modification is being made to the business directory?

(A) The listings will be condensed.
(B) It will be exclusively available online.
(C) The release schedule will change.
(D) It will expand to include multiple neighborhoods.

사업체 명부에 어떤 변경이 이루어질 것인가?

(A) 기재 사항이 요약될 것이다.
(B) 온라인으로만 이용할 수 있게 될 것이다.
(C) 발표 일정이 변경될 것이다.
(D) 확대되어 다수의 지역을 아우를 것이다.

어휘 modification 수정, 변경 condense 요약하다, (~의 길이를) 줄이다 exclusively 독점적으로, 전적으로 release 공개, 발표

해설 사업체 명부가 소식지에 실을 수 없을 만큼 너무 커졌기 때문에(The South Jordan Business Directory has grown so large that it now occupies a sizable portion of the neighborhood newsletter.), 온라인 형식으로만 발간하고 인쇄 버전을 중단한다는 소식을 전하고 있다(we will transition to an online format for the directory and discontinue its printed version).

150

According to the notice, why might readers contact Ms. Langley?

(A) To request corrections to their listing
(B) To obtain an access code for the directory
(C) To subscribe to a neighborhood newsletter
(D) To propose adjustments to publishing deadlines

공지문에 따르면 독자는 왜 Ms. Langley에게 연락하겠는가?

(A) 기재 사항의 수정을 요구하기 위해
(B) 주소록의 접속 코드를 획득하기 위해
(C) 지역 소식지를 구독하기 위해
(D) 발간 기한의 조정을 제안하기 위해

어휘 correction 정정, 수정 access 접근, 접속 subscribe to ~을 구독하다 adjustment 조정, 조절, 수정

해설 명부의 기재 사항을 확인한 후에(I recommend checking your listing to ensure its accuracy.) 잘못된 정보가 있다면 연락해서 갱신을 요청하라고 권하고 있다(If you notice outdated information or any broken links, please inform me so that I can update the necessary details).

Workshop: Strengthening Team Dynamics	
[153(C)]**Date**: 27 October	
Time: 9:30 A.M. to 5:00 P.M.	
[153(A)]**Cost**: £150 per participant	
9:30 A.M.	*Laying the Foundation* [151]Explore critical challenges faced by small business owners. [152]Define both short-term and long-term company objectives and recognize areas in need of improvement.
11:00 A.M.	*Building Collaboration* [151]Gain insights on fostering a cooperative work culture that minimizes unnecessary competition among employees across all levels.
12:30 P.M.	[153(B)]*Lunch Break* Enjoy a complimentary meal with a choice between two entrées: a grilled chicken sandwich served with fresh salad greens or pasta topped with seasonal vegetables.
2:00 P.M.	*Interactive Team Exercises* Engage in practical team-building activities designed for both small and large groups. Exchange ideas with your fellow participants that can be implemented within your own workplace.
3:30 P.M.	*Measuring Success* Discover techniques for assessing the effectiveness of team-building initiatives. Receive useful tips on utilizing common office software to track company performance and improvements.

워크숍: 팀 소통 강화하기	
날짜: 10월 27일	
시간: 오전 9:30 – 오후 5:00	
비용: 참가자 1인당 150파운드	
오전 9:30	*기초 다지기* 소규모 기업 소유주가 직면한 중대한 과제를 탐색한다. 기업의 장단기 목표를 규정하고 개선이 필요한 부분을 알아본다.
오전 11:00	*협력 관계 구축하기* 모든 직급에 걸쳐 직원 간의 불필요한 경쟁을 최소화하는 협력적인 직장 문화를 조성하는 일에 대한 식견을 얻는다.
오후 12:30	*점심시간* 두 가지 주 요리 중 선택하여 무료 식사를 즐기세요. 신선한 샐러드용 녹색 채소와 함께 제공되는 그릴 치킨 샐러드 / 제철 채소가 얹어진 파스타
오후 2:00	*상호 교류 팀 활동* 소규모 및 대규모 그룹에 알맞게 짜여진 실용적인 단합 활동에 참여한다. 동료 참가자들과 직장 내에서 시행할 만한 아이디어를 교환한다.
오후 3:30	*성과 측정하기* 팀워크 프로젝트의 효과를 평가하는 기법을 알아본다. 기업의 성과와 개선 사항을 추적하기 위한 일반 사무용 소프트웨어 활용의 유용한 팁을 얻는다.

어휘 agenda (회의) 일정표 strengthen 강화하다, 공고히 하다 dynamics (조직의) 소통 방식, 인간관계 explore 탐구하다, 탐색하다 critical 결정적인, 중대한 face 직면하다 define 정의하다, 명확히 규정하다 short-term 단기의 long-term 장기의 objective 목표, 목적 recognize 인식하다, 알아보다 in need of ~이 필요한 insight 식견 foster 조성하다, 발전시키다 level 지위, 계층 complimentary 무료의 entrée 앙트레(식단의 중심이 되는 주요리) greens 녹색 채소 topped with ~이 얹힌, 뿌려진 seasonal 제철의 interactive 상호 교류 방식의, 쌍방향의 engage in ~에 참여하다, 참가하다 implement 실행하다, 이행하다 measure 측정하다 success 성공, 성과 assess 평가하다, 판단하다 effectiveness 효능, 효과 team-building 팀워크 initiative 계획, 프로젝트 utilize 활용하다, 이용하다 track 추적하여 조사하다[기록하다]

151

For whom is the workshop most likely intended?

(A) Journalists covering business news
(B) Specialists in workforce management
(C) Entrepreneurs operating small businesses
(D) Individuals newly hired at smaller firms

워크숍은 누구를 대상으로 하겠는가?

(A) 비즈니스 뉴스를 취재하는 언론인들
(B) 인력 관리 전문가들
(C) 소규모 사업체를 운영하는 기업가들
(D) 작은 회사에 새로 채용된 사람들

어휘 journalist 언론인, 기자 cover 취재하다, 보도하다 entrepreneur 기업가, 사업가 operate 운영하다 firm 회사, 기업

해설 이 워크숍에서 참가자가 할 일이 소규모 사업체 운영자가 겪는 어려움 알아보기(Explore critical challenges faced by small business owners.), 기업의 목표 정하고 개선할 부분 파악하기(Define both short-term and long-term company objectives and recognize areas in need of improvement.), 협력적인 직장 문화 조성하는 법 배우기(Gain insights on fostering a cooperative work culture that minimizes unnecessary competition among employees across all levels.) 등인 것을 보면 작은 사업체를 운영하는 기업가들을 대상으로 하고 있다는 것을 알 수 있다.

152

What session involves identifying goals?

(A) Laying the Foundation
(B) Building Collaboration
(C) Interactive Team Exercises
(D) Measuring Success

어느 세션이 목표를 파악하는 내용을 포함하는가?

(A) 기초 다지기
(B) 협력 관계 구축하기
(C) 상호 교류 팀 활동
(D) 성과 측정하기

어휘 identify 파악하다, 식별하다

해설 오전 9시 30분에 있는 '기초 다지기' 시간에 기업의 목표를 정한다고 나와 있다(Define both short-term and long-term company objectives and recognize areas in need of improvement).

153

What is NOT indicated about the workshop?

(A) Attendance requires a fee.
(B) A meal is included for participants.
(C) It is scheduled as a single-day event.
(D) Newly developed software will be a key focus.

워크숍에 대해 언급되지 않은 것은 무엇인가?

(A) 참석에는 참가비가 필요하다.
(B) 참가자들을 위해 식사가 포함된다.
(C) 하루 행사로 예정되어 있다.
(D) 새로 개발된 소프트웨어가 핵심 주제가 될 것이다.

어휘 attendance 출석, 참석 scheduled 예정된

해설 일정표에 참가 비용(Cost: £150 per participant)과 12시 30분에 있는 점심시간(*Lunch Break*), 하루뿐인 행사 날짜(Date: 27 October)가 나와 있다. 소프트웨어에 대해 배우기는 하겠지만, 소프트웨어 자체가 워크숍의 핵심 주제는 아니다.

Local News
Tuesday, September 1

The Nebula Theater, located on Bradford Street, is set to close at the end of the month. However, the building will not remain vacant for long, as it has been purchased by the Spokane Cinema Society (SCS). According to Aarav Joshi, the Executive Director of SCS, [154][157]the organization plans to renovate the facility before reopening. He mentioned that all theaters would undergo upgrades, including the replacement of seating, screens, and audio systems. —[1]—.

Mr. Joshi added, "Nonetheless, we will retain one of the original projectors so we can continue screening classic films in their authentic format."

To date, the Nebula Theater primarily showcased independent productions, foreign films, and art house movies. —[2]—. The former owner, Ethan Sattwell, who has recently retired, envisioned the theater as a haven for creative and artistic films. Though he maintained this vision for many years, [155]declining ticket sales led him to the difficult choice of selling the venue. —[3]—.

"It was a tough decision to make," Mr. Sattwell admitted. "I will truly miss running the theater, but I'm glad that SCS plans to revitalize it."

Under new management, the theater will still screen artistic films on select occasions, while expanding its offerings to include more mainstream movies aimed at families and children.

SCS intends to officially reopen the venue on January 12. Additionally, the theater will continue to serve as host for the classic film festival, which begins on the first weekend of February and lasts ten days. The festival will remain unchanged in most aspects, except for one significant update - its name. [156]Previously known as the Bradford Street Film Festival, it will now bear the title of Spokane Cinema Society Film Festival. —[4]—.

154-157번 문제는 다음 기사에 관한 것입니다.

지역 소식
9월 1일 화요일

Bradford 가(街)에 있는 Nebula 극장이 이달 말에 문을 닫을 예정이다. 그러나 이 건물이 오랫동안 비어 있지는 않을 전망인데, Spokane 영화 협회(SCS)가 매입했기 때문이다. SCS 전무이사 Aarav Joshi에 따르면 기관은 재개관 전에 이 시설을 개조할 예정이다. 그는 모든 상영관이 개선될 것이라고 말했는데, 여기에는 좌석과 스크린, 음향 시스템의 교체가 포함된다.

Mr. Joshi는 "그렇기는 하지만, 고전 영화를 원본 형식 그대로 계속해서 상영할 수 있도록 기존의 영사기 중 하나는 유지할 겁니다."라고 덧붙였다.

지금까지 Nebula 극장은 독립 영화와 해외 영화, 예술 영화를 주로 소개해 왔다. 최근에 은퇴한 전 소유주 Ethan Sattwell은 이 극장을 창의적이고 예술적인 영화들의 안식처로 구상해 왔다. 여러 해 동안 이러한 비전을 고수했지만, 감소하는 티켓 판매량은 그를 이 장소의 매각이라는 어려운 선택으로 이끌었다.

Mr. Sattwell은 "하기 어려운 결정이었죠."라고 인정했다. "극장을 운영하던 때가 정말 그립겠지만, SCS가 이곳에 새로운 활력을 불어넣을 계획을 가지고 있어 기쁩니다."

새 경영진 하에서 극장은 특정 시기에 계속 예술 영화를 상영하겠지만, 상영 작품을 확대하여 가족과 어린이들을 겨냥한 주류 영화를 더 많이 포함할 것이다.

SCS는 1월 12일에 이 장소를 공식 재개관할 계획이다. 추가적으로 극장은 고전 영화 축제의 주최자 역할도 계속할 것인데, 영화제는 2월 첫째 주에 시작하여 열흘 동안 계속된다. 영화제는 대부분의 면에서 변함이 없을 것이지만, 한 가지 중요한 변화만 예외인데, 그것은 이름이다. 전에는 Bradford 가(街) 영화제라고 알려져 있던 이 축제는 이제 Spokane 영화 협회 영화제라는 타이틀을 갖게 될 것이다.

어휘 set to-V ~할 준비가 된 vacant 비어 있는 society 협회 executive director 전무 이사 mention ~라고 말하다 undergo 거치다 nonetheless 그럼에도 불구하고 retain 유지하다, 보유하다 projector 영사기 screen 상영하다 authentic 원본 그대로의, 정통 방식의 format 형식, 방식 to date 지금까지 showcase 소개하다, 선보이다 independent 독립의 production 제작된 작품 art house (영화가) 예술적인, 실험적인 envision 구상하다, 상상하다 haven 안식처, 피난처 declining 감소하는, 쇠퇴하는 venue 개최지, 장소 admit 인정하다, 시인하다 revitalize 다시 활성화하다, 새로운 활력을 불어넣다 management 경영진 select 엄선한, 특정한 occasion 경우, 시기 offering 작품, 프로그램 mainstream 주류의, 대세의 aim 겨냥하다, 조준하다 serve as ~의 역할을 하다 host 주최자 last 계속되다, 지속되다 aspect 일면, 측면 significant 중요한, 의미 있는 bear (이름, 직함 등을) 가지다

154

What is suggested about the Nebula Theater?

(A) It will primarily feature classic film screenings.
(B) It will undergo renovations to install updated equipment.
(C) Its admission prices are expected to rise.
(D) Its planned changes have caused dissatisfaction among patrons.

Nebula 극장에 관하여 무엇이 시사되어 있는가?

(A) 고전 영화 상영을 주요 특징으로 삼을 것이다.
(B) 개조 공사를 거쳐 최신 장비를 설치할 것이다.
(C) 입장 가격이 인상될 것으로 예상된다.
(D) 계획된 변화가 고객들 사이에 불만을 유발했다.

어휘 primarily 주로 feature 특징으로 삼다 screening 상영 equipment 장비 admission 입장 dissatisfaction 불만(족) patron 고객

해설 첫 문단을 읽어 보면 SCS가 극장을 인수한 후에 개조 공사가 계획되어 있고(the organization plans to renovate the facility before reopening.), 이 공사에는 여러 장비의 교체가 포함된다고 말하고 있다(He mentioned that all theaters would undergo upgrades, including the replacement of seating, screens, and audio systems).

155

According to the article, what was difficult for Mr. Sattwell?

(A) Securing appropriate technical equipment
(B) Choosing a destination for retirement
(C) Making the decision to sell the theater
(D) Attracting buyers for the establishment

기사에 따르면 Mr. Sattwell에게 어려운 점은 무엇이었는가?

(A) 적절한 기술 장비를 확보하는 것
(B) 은퇴 후 행선지를 선택하는 것
(C) 극장을 팔 결심을 하는 것
(D) 시설의 매수자들을 유치하는 것

어휘 secure 확보하다, 얻어내다 destination 행선지 retirement 은퇴 attract 유치하다 establishment 시설

해설 세 번째 문단에서 Mr. Sattwell은 감소하는 티켓 판매량 때문에 극장을 팔 결심을 했는데, 이것은 어려운 선택이었다고 말하고 있다(declining ticket sales led him to the difficult choice of selling the venue).

156

What has received a new name?

(A) A cinema venue
(B) A leadership role
(C) A film festival
(D) A cinema society

무엇이 새 이름을 얻었는가?

(A) 영화 상영 장소
(B) 지도부 역할
(C) 영화제
(D) 영화 협회

해설 기사 마지막 문장을 보면 영화제 이름이 the Bradford Street Film Festival에서 Spokane Cinema Society Film Festival로 바뀐다고 알려주고 있다.

157

In which of the positions marked [1], [2], [3], and [4] does the following sentence best belong?

"The concession stand has also been refurbished."

(A) [1]
(B) [2]
(C) [3]
(D) [4]

다음 문장은 [1], [2], [3], [4]로 표시된 자리 중 어느 곳에 가장 잘 어울리는가?

"구내매점도 재단장되었다."

어휘 concession stand 구내매점 refurbish 재단장하다

해설 시설의 재단장을 언급하고 있으므로 첫 문단에서 시설 개조 공사를 말하는 the organization plans to renovate the facility before reopening. He mentioned that all theaters would undergo upgrades, including the replacement of seating, screens, and audio systems. 뒤에 들어가는 것이 알맞다.

PIONEER TECH SOLUTIONS

As a valued business client, you
- gain access to state-of-the-art technology
- pay solely for the services you utilize, thereby lowering costs for hardware and software
- benefit from our transparent, up-front, and continuous billing system

We offer
- [158]tailored software development and [159]routine upkeep of on-site hardware (requires a one-year agreement)
- management and periodic updates for applications and databases
- data storage, backups, and recovery services
- an around-the-clock support center for prompt issue resolution
- access to our proprietary Pioneer Tech Remote Monitoring (PTRM) platform

158–159번 문제는 다음 안내 책자 페이지에 관한 것입니다.

PIONEER TECH SOLUTIONS

귀사는 소중한 기업 고객으로서
- 최첨단 기술을 이용하실 수 있습니다.
- 오직 사용한 서비스에 대해서만 지불함으로써 하드웨어 및 소프트웨어 비용을 낮춥니다.
- 투명한 사전 고지되는 청구 시스템의 혜택을 지속적으로 누립니다.

저희는 제공합니다.
- 맞춤 소프트웨어 개발 및 현장 하드웨어 정기 유지 보수(1년 계약 필요)
- 애플리케이션과 데이터베이스의 관리 및 주기적인 업데이트
- 데이터 보관 및 백업, 복구 서비스
- 신속한 문제 해결을 위한 24시간 지원 센터
- 독점 Pioneer Tech 원격 모니터링(PTRM) 플랫폼에 대한 접근

어휘 valued 귀중한, 소중한 gain access to ~을 이용할 수 있게 되다 state-of-the-art 첨단의, 최신의 solely 오로지 thereby 그 결과, 그에 따라 lower 내리다, 낮추다 benefit from ~에서 이익을 얻다 transparent 투명한, 숨김없는 up-front 선불의, 사전 고지된 billing 청구서 발부 tailored 맞춤의 routine (늘 하던 대로) 일상적인, 정례적인 upkeep 유지, 보존 on-site 현장의 agreement 협정, 계약 periodic 정기적인, 주기적인 storage 보관, 저장 recovery 복구 around-the-clock 24시간 계속되는, 밤낮 없는 prompt 신속한, 조속한 resolution 해결 proprietary 전용의, 독점의 remote 원격 조작의 monitor 감독하다, 감시하다

158

What is one of the services provided by Pioneer Tech Solutions?

(A) Legal consultation
(B) Office accounting
(C) Facility maintenance
(D) Software production

Pioneer Tech Solutions가 제공하는 서비스 중 하나는 무엇인가?

(A) 법률 자문
(B) 기업 회계
(C) 시설 관리
(D) 소프트웨어 제작

해설 제공하는 서비스로 맞춤 소프트웨어 개발(tailored software development)을 소개하고 있다.

159

What is stated about regular maintenance of computer systems?

(A) It requires a commitment of at least one year.
(B) It is suggested for older computer models.
(C) It is carried out by external contractors.
(D) It is unavailable to new clients.

컴퓨터 시스템의 정기 유지 보수에 관하여 무엇이 언급되어 있는가?

(A) 최소 1년의 약정을 요한다.
(B) 오래된 컴퓨터 모델에 권장한다.
(C) 외부 계약자에 의해 실시된다.
(D) 신규 고객은 이용할 수 없다.

어휘 maintenance 유지 보수 commitment 약속, 약정 carry out ~을 행하다, 실시하다 external 외부의 unavailable 이용할 수 없는

해설 지문에 나오는 routine upkeep of on-site hardware가 문제에서는 regular maintenance of computer systems라고 패러프레이즈 되어 있음을 파악해야 한다. 1년 이상의 계약을 요하는 서비스이다(requires a one-year agreement).

Questions 160 through 162 refer to the following job advertisement.

Achieve excellence in your career!

Unlike other companies that require their sales representatives to make countless calls to individuals who are not expecting to be contacted, Prime Shield Insurance allows customers to reach out to us for their insurance needs. [160]Our sales associates handle only inbound sales calls from prospective clients who are already interested in purchasing policies. These roles eliminate the stress of selling on commission.

Participate in our paid sales training program and [161]prepare for the licensing exam to become a certified insurance professional. Successful candidates may be offered a salaried position.

Salary offers will be based on your educational background and work experience. While some college coursework is advantageous, highly motivated high school graduates are also encouraged to apply. Since we operate twenty-four hours a day, seven days a week to serve our customers, we provide a variety of shift options, including a 10% pay increase for late-night and early-morning shifts.

Click "Apply Now" below to seize this opportunity at worklink. com. You will need a valid e-mail address and phone number to complete the application. Qualified applicants will be contacted via phone or e-mail. For inquiries about the application process, call 281-555-0287. [162]We recommend visiting our Web site at primeshieldinsurance.com to learn more about the company before applying.

Apply Now

160-162번 문제는 다음 구인 광고에 관한 것입니다.

커리어에 날개를 달아 보세요!

연락 받기를 기대하지 않는 사람들에게 무수히 많은 전화를 걸도록 영업 사원들에게 요구하는 다른 회사들과 달리, Prime Shield 보험에서는 고객들이 보험이 필요할 때 우리에게 연락하도록 합니다. 저희 영업 사원들은 이미 보험 가입에 관심이 있는 잠재 고객들로부터 오는 판매 전화만 처리합니다. 이 자리에서는 수수료를 기반으로 판매하는 스트레스가 없습니다.

유급 영업 교육 프로그램에 참여해서 공인 보험 전문가 자격증 시험에 대비하세요. 합격자는 고정급 자리를 제안받을 수 있습니다.

급여 제안은 학력과 경력을 근거로 합니다. 대학 과정을 이수했다면 유리하겠지만, 동기 부여가 잘 되어 있는 고졸자에게도 지원을 권장합니다. 우리는 주 7일 24시간 내내 운영하여 고객들에게 서비스를 제공하기 때문에 다양한 교대 근무 옵션이 있으며, 여기에는 야간 및 새벽 근무에 대한 10퍼센트 급여 인상이 포함됩니다.

아래의 '지금 지원하기'를 클릭하셔서 worklink.com에서 이 기회를 잡으세요. 지원서 작성에는 유효한 이메일 주소와 전화번호가 필요합니다. 자격을 갖춘 지원자는 전화나 이메일로 연락드리겠습니다. 지원 절차에 대한 문의는 281-555-0287로 전화하시기 바랍니다. 지원하시기 전에 홈페이지 primeshieldinsurance.com을 방문하셔서 회사에 대해 더 알아보실 것을 권장합니다.

지금 지원하기

어휘 sales representative[associate] 영업 사원 countless 무수히 많은 reach out to (제안, 의견을 위해) ~에게 연락하다. 접근하다 inbound 들어오는 prospective client 잠재 고객 policy 보험 계약, 보험 증서 eliminate 제거하다. 없애다 on commission 수수료 기반으로 paid 유급의, 보수를 받는 certified 공인의, 자격증의 successful candidate 합격자 salaried 고정급을 받는 coursework 수업 활동 advantageous 유리한, 이로운 motivated 동기가 부여된, 의욕이 넘치는 a variety of 다양한 shift (교대제의) 근무 (시간) seize 붙잡다. 움켜잡다 valid 유효한 complete 작성하다 qualified 자격을 갖춘 via ~을 통해서, ~을 매개로 inquiry 문의, 질문

What task is described as part of the job?

(A) Meeting commission-based sales goals
(B) Receiving incoming calls from potential policyholders
(C) Working exclusively during unconventional hours
(D) Making calls to individuals unfamiliar with the company

이 직무의 일부로 어떤 업무가 설명되고 있는가?

(A) 수수료 기반의 영업 목표 달성하기
(B) 잠재 보험 가입자로부터 걸려 오는 전화 받기
(C) 통상적이지 않은 시간대에만 일하기
(D) 회사에 익숙하지 않은 사람들에게 전화 걸기

어휘 meet a goal 목표를 달성하다 commission (판매) 수수료 policyholder 보험 계약자, 피보험자 unconventional 통상적이지 않은

해설 첫 문단에서 영업 사원이 할 일로 보험 가입에 관심 있는 사람으로부터 걸려 오는 전화 받기를 언급하고 있다(Our sales associates handle only inbound sales calls from prospective clients).

According to the advertisement, what is required for a salaried position?

(A) Previous sales experience
(B) Completion of a college degree
(C) References from past employers
(D) Obtaining an insurance license

광고에 따르면 고정급을 받는 자리에 요구되는 것은 무엇인가?

(A) 이전의 영업 경력
(B) 대학 학위 과정 이수
(C) 과거 고용주의 추천서
(D) 보험 면허 취득

어휘 completion 이수 degree 학위 reference 추천서

해설 두 번째 문단에 면허 발급 시험에 합격하면 고정급 받는 자리를 제안받을 수 있다는 조건이 나와 있다(prepare for the licensing exam to become a certified insurance professional. Successful candidates may be offered a salaried position).

According to the advertisement, why should applicants visit the Prime Shield Web site?

(A) To gain knowledge about Prime Shield Insurance
(B) To submit an application for the sales position
(C) To ask questions about the application process
(D) To check the status of an application

광고에 따르면 지원자는 왜 Prime Shield 홈페이지를 방문해야 하는가?

(A) Prime Shield 보험사에 대해 알아보기 위해
(B) 영업직 지원서를 제출하기 위해
(C) 지원 절차에 대해 질문하기 위해
(D) 지원 처리 상황을 확인하기 위해

어휘 status (처리) 상태, 상황

해설 마지막 문장에서 지원하기 전에 회사 홈페이지에 들어가서 회사에 대해 더 알아볼 것을 권하고 있다(We recommend visiting our Web site at primeshieldinsurance.com to learn more about the company before applying).

Questions 163 through 166 refer to the following article.

A Lifelong Passion for Books

August 9 - [163] [164(B)]In Ashford Hills and its surrounding areas, Edward Harrison, who has been a professor of Korean literature at Ashford Hills State University for two decades, is perhaps most recognized as the proprietor of The Hidden Chapter, the oldest bookstore in the town. The store is known for two distinctive characteristics: it focuses on rare books and operates exclusively on Saturdays. Apparently, walk-in sales account for only a minor portion of Mr. Harrison's business; the bulk of the store's income comes from orders placed via phone or online by institutions such as universities, museums, and private collectors.

[163]This Sunday, The Hidden Chapter will commemorate its sixtieth year in operation. "When my mother, Melisa, first opened the bookstore six decades ago on Willow Crest Road, just two blocks from here, she likely never imagined it would still be serving the community today," Mr. Harrison remarked. The store still features its original sign above the doorway. Inside, [165]it retains the cozy, living-room-like ambiance it has always had, complete with mismatched tables and chairs. [164(D)]One area of the store is dedicated to books about soccer, reflecting the Harrison family's abiding passion for the sport. On Friday evenings, the store transforms into a casual social gathering spot. Unsurprisingly, attendees often engage in discussions about rare books, literature, and soccer.

[163] [164(A)]Later this month, Mr. Harrison will reach another significant milestone: his retirement from teaching. [166]His retirement does not imply, however, that The Hidden Chapter will expand its hours of operation; it will continue to open only once a week. "I am not leaving one job just to spend more time on another," Mr. Harrison explained. "Rather, the fact that I will no longer need to prepare classes or grade students' papers will allow me to devote more time to my children and grandchildren."

163-166번 문제는 다음 기사에 관한 것입니다.

책을 향한 평생의 열정

8월 9일 – Edward Harrison은 Ashford Hills 주립 대학교에서 20년 동안 한국 문학 교수로 재직해 왔지만, Ashford Hills와 주변 지역에서 그는 아마 마을에서 가장 오래된 서점 The Hidden Chapter의 주인으로 가장 많이 알려져 있다. 서점은 두 가지 독특한 특징으로 유명한데, 희귀 서적을 중점적으로 다루며 토요일에만 운영된다. 실제로 매장 내 방문 판매는 Mr. Harrison의 사업에서 작은 부분만 차지하는 것 같다. 서점 수입의 대부분은 대학교나 박물관 같은 기관들과 개인 수집가들에 의한 전화나 온라인에 의한 주문에서 나온다.

이번 일요일에 The Hidden Chapter는 운영 60주년을 기념할 예정이다. Mr. Harrison은 "60년 전 여기서 딱 두 블록 거리에 있는 Willow Crest 길에 서점을 처음 열었을 때 저희 어머니 Melisa는 이곳이 오늘날에도 여전히 지역 사회에 서비스를 제공하고 있을 것이라고는 아마 전혀 상상하지도 못 하셨을 거예요."라고 말했다. 서점은 출입구 위에 원래부터 있던 간판을 아직도 달아 놓고 있다. 내부에는 항상 그래 왔던 아늑하고 거실 같은 분위기를 유지하고 있으며 짝이 맞지 않는 테이블과 의자들을 갖추고 있다. 서점의 한 구역은 축구에 관한 책들에 할애됨으로써 스포츠에 대한 Harrison 가문의 변함없는 열정을 반영하고 있다. 금요일 저녁이면 서점은 격식 없는 사교 모임 장소로 변신한다. 놀랄 것도 없이 참석자들은 자주 희귀 서적과 문학, 축구에 대한 토론에 참여한다. 이달 하순에 Mr. Harrison은 또 다른 중요한 이정표에 다다르는데, 바로 교수직 은퇴이다. 그러나 그의 퇴직이 The Hidden Chapter의 영업 시간이 늘어난다는 뜻은 아니다. 서점은 계속해서 일주일에 한 번씩만 문을 열 것이다. Mr. Harrison은 "단지 한가지 일에 더 많은 시간을 쓰기 위해 다른 일을 그만두는 것은 아닙니다."라고 설명했다. "그보다는 제가 더 이상 수업을 준비하거나 학생들의 과제를 채점할 필요가 없다는 사실이 더 많은 시간을 자식들과 손자들에게 쓸 수 있게 해 줄 것입니다."

어휘 lifelong 평생의, 평생 지속되는 recognized as ~으로 인정받은, 알려진 proprietor 소유주, 주인 distinctive 독특한, 특유의 rare 희귀한, 진귀한 operate 운영되다 apparently 보아하니 (~인 것 같다), 실제로 walk-in sale (직접) 방문 판매 account for (부분, 비율을) 차지하다 portion 부분, 일부 the bulk of 대부분의 place an order 주문을 하다 institution 기관, 협회 commemorate 기념하다 in operation 운영하는 likely 아마도 remark ~이라고 말하다, 언급하다 feature (눈에 띄게) 보여주다 doorway 출입구 retain 유지하다, 간직하다 cozy 아늑한, 포근한, 편안한 ambiance 분위기 complete with ~을 갖춘, ~을 완비하고 있는 mismatched 어울리지 않는, 짝이 맞지 않는 dedicate[devote] A to B A(장소, 시간, 돈 등)를 B에 할애하다 reflect 반영하다, 나타내다 abiding 지속적인, 변함없는 transform into ~으로 완전히 바뀌다[변화하다] casual 격식을 차리지 않은 unsurprisingly 놀랄 것도 없이 engage in ~에 참여하다, 참가하다 milestone 이정표 retirement 은퇴, 퇴직 expand 확장하다, 늘리다 rather 그보다는

Why most likely was the article written?

(A) To attract members to a newly formed book club
(B) To emphasize the advantages of selling rare and unique items
(C) **To honor the accomplishments of a prominent local figure**
(D) To inform readers about the relocation of an established business

기사는 왜 쓰여졌겠는가?

(A) 새로 만들어진 독서 클럽에 회원을 유치하기 위해
(B) 희귀하고 독특한 제품을 판매하는 장점을 강조하기 위해
(C) 지역 저명인사의 업적을 조명하기 위해
(D) 독자들에게 오래된 사업체의 이전을 알리기 위해

어휘 advantage 장점, 이점 honor (업적을) 기리다, 기념하다, 조명하다 prominent 저명한, 유력한 relocation 이전 established 오래된, 오래 유지된

해설 첫 문장에서 20년간 주립 대학교에서 문학을 가르친 교수이자 지역에서 가장 오래된 서점의 운영자인 Edward Harrison을 소개하고 있으며(In Ashford Hills and its surrounding areas, Edward Harrison, who has been a professor of Korean literature at Ashford Hills State University for two decades, is perhaps most recognized as the proprietor of The Hidden Chapter, the oldest bookstore in the town.), 두 번째 문단에서는 이 사람이 운영하는 서점이 60주년을 맞이하고 있음을 알리고 있다(This Sunday, The Hidden Chapter will commemorate its sixtieth year in operation). 마지막 문단에서는 교수직에서 퇴직한다는 Mr. Harrison의 계획을 밝히고 있다(Later this month, Mr. Harrison will reach another significant milestone: his retirement from teaching). 이러한 내용을 종합해 보면 기사의 목적은 지역 저명인사의 삶을 조명하는 것이다.

What is NOT suggested about Mr. Harrison?

(A) He is about to end his career as an instructor.
(B) He conducts research on Korean literary works.
(C) **He has lived in Ashford Hills for nearly two decades.**
(D) He takes pleasure in discussing soccer with others.

Mr. Harrison에 관하여 나타나 있지 않은 사항은 무엇인가?

(A) 강사로서의 경력을 끝내려는 참이다.
(B) 한국 문학 작품에 대한 연구를 한다.
(C) Ashford Hills에서 거의 20년 동안 살았다.
(D) 다른 사람들과 축구에 대해 논하는 것에서 즐거움을 느낀다.

어휘 be about to-V 막 ~하려는 참이다 literary 문학의

해설 첫 문장에 들어 있는 Edward Harrison, who has been a professor of Korean literature at Ashford Hills State University for two decades를 읽으면서 선택지 (B)를 지우자. 두 번째 문단에서 One area of the store is dedicated to books about soccer, ~ attendees often engage in discussions about rare books, literature, and soccer.를 읽어 보면 (D)를 지울 수 있다. 마지막 문단에서 Later this month, Mr. Harrison will reach another significant milestone: his retirement from teaching.를 읽으면 (A)를 지우고 정답을 알아낼 수 있다.

The word "retains" in paragraph 2, line 9, is closest in meaning to

(A) adds to
(B) aligns with
(C) recalls
(D) **maintains**

두 번째 문단 아홉 번째 줄의 단어 "retains"와 의미상 가장 가까운 것은

(A) ~을 추가하다
(B) ~과 일렬이 되다
(C) 기억해내다
(D) 유지하다

해설 retain은 '유지하다'와 '기억하다'라는 뜻이 있으므로 (C), (D)와 동의어가 될 수 있다. it retains the cozy, living-room-like ambiance it has always had는 서점이 늘 가져 왔던 아늑하고 거실 같은 분위기를 여전히 유지하고 있다는 뜻이다.

What is stated about The Hidden Chapter?

(A) It plans to introduce a new section for children's literature.
(B) **It will continue to operate with its current schedule.**
(C) Its revenue is projected to grow in the coming year.
(D) Its original sign will be replaced later this month.

The Hidden Chapter에 관하여 무엇이 언급되어 있는가?

(A) 어린이 문학을 위한 새 코너를 도입할 계획이다.
(B) 계속해서 현재의 일정대로 운영될 것이다.
(C) 내년에 수입이 증가할 것으로 예상된다.
(D) 이달 하순에 원래의 간판이 교체될 것이다.

어휘 state 언급하다 revenue 수입 be projected to-V ~할 것으로 예상되다 sign 간판

해설 The Hidden Chapter는 Mr. Harrison이 교수직에서 은퇴한 후에도 계속해서 일주일에 한 번만 문을 열 것이다(His retirement does not imply, however, that The Hidden Chapter will expand its hours of operation; it will continue to open only once a week).

Questions 167 through 168 refer to the following text-message chain.

Mikhail Ivanov [5:24 P.M.]:
Ms. Vega, I sent you the updated contract via e-mail. Did you receive it?

Lidia Vega [5:26 P.M.]:
Yes, I just got it. [167]Thank you for making the adjustments.

Mikhail Ivanov [5:27 P.M.]:
[Of course.] [167]I appreciate you bringing them to my attention. [168]The updated contract now specifies that you will be compensated 250€ for each approved article instead of 200€.

Lidia Vega [5:28 P.M.]:
Great. I'll review it now, sign it, and send it back to you.

Mikhail Ivanov [5:30 P.M.]:
Excellent. [168]We're always eager to receive quality content for our publication. I look forward to your submissions.

167-168번 문제는 다음 문자 메시지 대화에 관한 것입니다.

Mikhail Ivanov [오후 5:24]:
Ms. Vega, 갱신된 계약서를 이메일로 보내 드렸습니다. 받으셨나요?

Lidia Vega [오후 5:26]:
네, 방금 받았어요. 조정해 주셔서 감사합니다.

Mikhail Ivanov [오후 5:27]:
당연히 해 드려야죠. 사안을 저에게 알려 주셔서 고맙습니다. 이제 갱신된 계약서에는 승인된 기사마다 200유로가 아니라 250유로를 받는다고 명시되어 있습니다.

idia Vega [오후 5:28]:
좋습니다. 지금 검토하고 사인해서 보내 드릴게요.

Mikhail Ivanov [오후 5:30]:
네. 저희는 언제나 출판물에 실을 우수한 콘텐츠를 기대합니다. 보내 주실 원고 기대하겠습니다.

어휘 make an adjustment 조정하다　bring *sth* to one's attention ~을 ~에게 알리다　specify 명시하다　compensate (보수, 급료를) 지불하다　be eager to-V 간절히 ~하고 싶어하다, 기대하다　quality 우수한, 높은 품질의　content 내용, 주제　publication 출판물, 간행물　submission 제출물, 제출 서류

167

At 5:27 P.M., what does Mr. Ivanov mean when he writes, "Of course"?

(A) He was already aware that the e-mail had been received.
(B) He has obtained a signed version of the contract.
(C) He believes the solution to the issue is straightforward.
(D) He was pleased to accommodate a request.

오후 5시 27분에 "당연히 해 드려야죠."라고 쓸 때 Mr. Ivanov는 무엇을 의미하는가?

(A) 이메일이 수령되었음을 이미 알고 있었다.
(B) 서명된 계약서를 받았다.
(C) 문제의 해결책이 간단하다고 생각한다.
(D) 요청을 기꺼이 수용했다.

어휘 straightforward 간단한, 쉬운　accommodate 수용하다, 받아들이다

해설 주어진 문장 앞에는 수정 작업에 대한 감사 인사가 나오고 있고(Thank you for making the adjustments.), 이어지는 문장은 사안을 알려준 것에 대해 고맙다고 말하고 있다(I appreciate you bringing them to my attention). 문맥상 Mr. Ivanov가 Ms. Vega의 수정 요청을 기꺼운 마음으로 받아들였다고 추론할 수 있다.

168

Who most likely is Ms. Vega?

(A) An author
(B) An attorney
(C) A financial consultant
(D) A human resources specialist

Ms. Vega는 누구겠는가?

(A) 작가
(B) 변호사
(C) 재무 컨설턴트
(D) 인사 담당자

해설 Ms. Vega가 기사 한 편당 250유로를 받는다는 내용과(you will be compensated 250€ for each approved article instead of 200€.) 그녀가 제출하는 원고가 Mr. Ivanov의 회사가 펴낼 출판물에 실릴 것이라는 사실을 통해(We're always eager to receive quality content for our publication. I look forward to your submissions.) Ms. Vega의 직업은 작가라고 추론할 수 있다.

To: Dolores Navarro <dnavarro@healthfitplanning.bb>
From: Edmund Whitaker <ewhitaker@tshealthcenter.bb>
Subject: Barbados Holistic Health Conference
Date: 6 October

Dear Ms. Navarro,

[169]I am thrilled that you have agreed to join us as one of the speakers at the upcoming third annual Barbados Holistic Health Conference, scheduled for 23 November. I understand that the invitation was sent on short notice, [169]and I truly appreciate your willingness to take over for Elise Harwood. —[1]—. Your knowledge and experience as a dietitian will be highly appreciated by the attendees. [170]Last year, Ms. Harwood's session on vegetarian meal preparation attracted a large audience. —[2]—. This year, I am confident that your distinctive perspective on healthy eating will draw significant interest.

If you plan to sell copies of your book, please send them ahead of time so we can arrange a display for them. —[3]—. Additionally, [171]let me know if you require a projector with a remote control for your presentation. —[4]—. Finally, could you provide me with a brief biographical profile as soon as possible so that we can include it in the conference program? Thank you once again.

Best regards,

Edmund Whitaker

169-171번 문제는 다음 이메일에 관한 것입니다.

수신: Dolores Navarro
〈dnavarro@healthfitplanning.bb〉
발신: Edmund Whitaker
〈ewhitaker@tshealthcenter.bb〉
제목: Barbados 전인 건강 학회
날짜: 10월 6일

Ms. Navarro께,

11월 23일로 예정되어 있는 제3회 연례 Barbados 전인 건강 학회에 발표자로 합류하는 데 동의해 주셔서 매우 기쁩니다. 미리 알려 드리지 못하고 갑자기 초대장이 발송된 터라 Elise Harwood를 대신해 주시기로 한 것에 대해 진심으로 감사드립니다. 영양학자로서 귀하의 지식과 경험은 참석자들에게 큰 도움이 될 것입니다. 작년에 Ms. Harwood의 채식 식사 준비에 관한 세션이 많은 청중을 끌어 모았습니다. 올해는 건강한 식습관에 대한 귀하의 독특한 관점이 상당한 관심을 끌 것이라고 확신합니다.

저술하신 책을 판매할 계획이시면 진열 공간을 마련하도록 미리 보내 주시기 바랍니다. 또한 프레젠테이션을 위해 리모컨이 있는 프로젝터가 필요하시면 알려 주세요. 마지막으로 학회 프로그램 책자에 실을 수 있도록 가능한 빨리 간단한 약력을 제공해 주시겠습니까? 다시 한 번 고맙습니다.

이만 줄입니다.

Edmund Whitaker

어휘 holistic 전인적인 thrilled 크게 기뻐하는 on short notice 충분한 예고 없이, 갑자기, 급하게 willingness 기꺼이 하는 마음, 의향 take over 넘겨받다, (이어서) 대신하다 dietitian 영양학자, 영양사 be highly appreciated (공적 문구에서) 감사를 받다, 크게 도움이 되다 attendee 참석자 session (활동의) 기간, 시간 confident 확신하는, 굳게 믿는 distinctive 독특한, 특유의 perspective 시각, 관점 significant 상당한 copy (책, 잡지 등의) 한 부 ahead of time 미리, 사전에 arrange 준비하다, 마련하다 projector 프로젝터, 영사기 remote control 리모컨 biographical profile 약력 program 프로그램 책자, 일정 안내표

169

Why did Mr. Whitaker most likely send the e-mail?

(A) To extend an invitation to Ms. Navarro for an event
(B) To acknowledge Ms. Navarro's acceptance of an offer
(C) To request a suggestion from Ms. Navarro
(D) To recommend rescheduling a session

Mr. Whitaker는 왜 이메일을 보냈겠는가?

(A) Ms. Navarro를 행사에 초대하기 위해
(B) Ms. Navarro의 제안 수락에 감사하기 위해
(C) Ms. Navarro에게 의견을 요청하기 위해
(D) 회의 일정 변경을 권하기 위해

어휘 extend an invitation to ~를 초대하다 acknowledge (공적으로) 감사를 표하다

해설 첫 두 문장 I am thrilled that you have agreed to join us as one of the speakers at the upcoming third annual Barbados Holistic Health Conference, ~ and I truly appreciate your willingness to take over for Elise Harwood.를 읽어 보면 Ms. Navarro가 Ms. Harwood를 대신하여 학회 발표를 준비해 달라는 부탁을 수락했고, Mr. Whitaker는 이에 대한 감사를 표하기 위해 이메일을 보냈다.

170

What can be inferred about Ms. Harwood?

(A) She delivered a presentation at the conference the previous year.
(B) She authored a well-known book on nutrition.
(C) She works alongside Ms. Navarro.
(D) She is currently training to become a dietitian.

Ms. Harwood에 관하여 무엇을 추론할 수 있는가?

(A) 전년도에 학회에서 프레젠테이션을 했다.
(B) 잘 알려진 영양학에 대한 책을 저술했다.
(C) Ms. Navarro와 함께 근무한다.
(D) 현재 영양학자가 되기 위해 교육을 받고 있다.

어휘 deliver a presentation 프레젠테이션을 하다 author 저술하다 alongside ~와 함께

해설 Last year, Ms. Harwood's session on vegetarian meal preparation attracted a large audience(작년에는 채식주의 식사 준비에 관하여 Ms. Harwood가 진행한 시간이 많은 청중을 끌어 모았습니다).를 통해 정답을 알 수 있다.

171

In which of the positions marked [1], [2], [3], and [4] does the following sentence best belong?

"It is absolutely no problem to have visual equipment available."

(A) [1]
(B) [2]
(C) [3]
(D) [4]

다음 문장은 [1], [2], [3], [4]로 표시된 자리 중 어느 곳에 가장 잘 어울리는가?

"시각 장비를 이용할 수 있게 해 드리는 것은 전혀 문제가 없습니다."

해설 주어진 문장에 visual equipment라는 키워드가 있으므로 a projector를 언급하고 있는 let me know if you require a projector with a remote control for your presentation.에 대한 부연 설명으로 알맞다.

Elaine Dietrich | 23 January, 14:36
[173]Blake, has order #8738-3 been shipped yet? [172]If it hasn't, the customer has requested that we include item #736C.

Blake Harlan | 23 January, 14:39
[172]That's a customized silver ring, correct? Typically, the engraving team needs at least three days to add the custom message requested by the customer.

Elaine Dietrich | 23 January, 14:40
Can it be done any faster? The customer needs it as soon as possible.

Blake Harlan | 23 January, 14:42
I'll check with someone from the engraving team to see if it's possible.

Blake Harlan | 23 January, 14:44
[174][175]Tina, is it possible to expedite the engraving for a ring? It's item #736C, part of order #8738-3.

Tina McAllister | 23 January, 14:45
How quickly do you need it? [175]Would tomorrow be OK?

Elaine Dietrich | 23 January, 14:46
Yes, [that works.] Thank you both for your assistance!

172-175번 문제는 다음 문자 메시지 대화에 관한 것입니다.

Elaine Dietrich | 1월 23일, 14:36
Blake, #8738-3 주문품 이미 발송되었나요? 아직 안 나갔으면, 고객이 #736C 제품을 포함해 달라고 요청하셨어요.

Blake Harlan | 1월 23일, 14:39
그거 맞춤 은반지 맞죠? 보통 각인 팀에서 고객이 요청한 맞춤 메시지를 추가하는 데는 최소 3일이 필요해요.

Elaine Dietrich | 1월 23일, 14:40
조금이라도 더 빨리 할 수 있을까요? 고객 측에서 되도록 빨리 필요하다는데요.

Blake Harlan | 1월 23일, 14:42
각인 팀에게 확인해서 가능한지 알아볼게요.

Blake Harlan | 1월 23일, 14:44
Tina, 반지 각인 작업을 더 신속히 처리하는 게 가능할까요? #736C 제품인데 #8738-3 주문에 포함되는 거예요.

Tina McAllister | 1월 23일, 14:45
얼마나 빨리 필요하신데요? 내일이면 괜찮을까요?

Elaine Dietrich | 1월 23일, 14:46
네, 그거면 돼요. 두 사람 모두 도와줘서 고마워요!

어휘 ship 운송하다 customized 맞춤형의 typically 보통, 일반적으로 engraving 각인 custom 맞춤의, 주문 제작한 expedite 촉진하다, 더 신속하게 처리하다 work 문제없다, 좋다

172

What kind of products does the store sell?
(A) Novels
(B) Accessories
(C) Plants
(D) Home appliances

상점이 어떤 종류의 상품을 판매하는가?
(A) 소설
(B) 액세서리
(C) 식물
(D) 가전제품

해설 고객이 어떤 제품을 요구했는데(the customer has requested that we include item #736C.), 그게 맞춤 제작 은반지이다(That's a customized silver ring, correct?) 여기서 정답을 알 수 있다.

173

What does the customer want to do?	고객은 무엇을 하고 싶은가?
(A) Modify an order (B) Update a shipping address (C) Receive a refund (D) Select a different delivery option	(A) 주문을 변경한다 (B) 배송 주소를 갱신한다 (C) 환불을 받는다 (D) 다른 배송 옵션을 선택한다

어휘 modify 수정하다, 변경하다　shipping 운송, 수송

해설 첫 문장을 읽어 보면 고객은 이미 주문한 제품에 다른 것을 추가하고 싶어 한다(Blake, has order #8738-3 been shipped yet? If it hasn't, the customer has requested that we include item #736C). 즉 고객이 원하는 것은 주문을 변경하는 것이다.

174

Why does Mr. Harlan contact Ms. McAllister?	Mr. Harlan은 왜 Ms. McAllister에게 연락하는가?
(A) To inquire if a task can be completed more quickly than usual (B) To ask about the shipping schedule for an order (C) To confirm the timing of a meeting (D) To alert her to a mistake in a previous message	(A) 작업을 평소보다 빨리 완료할 수 있는지 문의하기 위해 (B) 주문품의 배송 일정에 대해 묻기 위해 (C) 회의 시간을 확인하기 위해 (D) 이전 메시지에 있던 실수에 대해 주의를 환기시키기 위해

어휘 alert A to B A에게 B에 대한 주의를 환기시키다

해설 Mr. Harlan은 Ms. McAllister에게 is it possible to expedite the engraving for a ring(반지 각인 작업을 더 신속히 처리하는 게 가능할까요)?라고 묻고 있다. 동사 expedite가 무슨 뜻인지 알면 정답을 선택할 수 있다.

175

At 14:46, what does Ms. Dietrich most likely mean when she writes, "that works"?	Ms. Dietrich가 14시 46분에 "그거면 돼요."라고 쓸 때 무엇을 의미하겠는가?
(A) She intends to work overtime tonight. (B) She is pleased that the machinery is operating properly. **(C) The customer will be content if the item is engraved tomorrow.** (D) Some new products will be selected for a catalog by the end of the day.	(A) 오늘 저녁에 야근할 생각이다. (B) 기계가 제대로 작동하고 있어서 기쁘다. (C) 내일 제품에 각인이 된다면 고객이 만족할 것이다. (D) 카탈로그에 실을 신제품들이 오늘 중에 선정될 것이다.

어휘 machinery 기계(류)　operate 작동되다, 가동되다　content 만족하는　engrave 새기다

해설 반지 각인 작업을 더 신속히 처리해 달라는 Mr. Harlan의 요청에 대해(is it possible to expedite the engraving for a ring?) Ms. McAllister가 "내일이면 괜찮을까요(Would tomorrow be OK)?"라고 반문했고, 여기에 "그거면 돼요(that works)."라고 대답한 것이므로, 각인 작업이 내일 완료된다면 고객이 만족할 것이라는 뜻이 된다.

To: d.ashcroft@true-sprout.net
From: nowak@silasfarmsteadweekly.com
Date: March 12
Subject: Silas's Farmstead Weekly

Dear Mr. Ashcroft,

[176]For a limited time only, *Silas's Farmstead Weekly* is providing reduced rates on advertisements for businesses that have not yet advertised in our publication. By advertising with *Silas's Farmstead* Weekly, you can connect with a focused audience of over 40,000 agricultural professionals, both in print and online. Don't miss this rare chance to grow your customer base!

Below are the current deals for first-time advertisers, which are valid until April 10. [177]If you would like to book one of these full-color ads, have one of our designers create a personalized ad for you, or [178]request further details, [177]please respond to this e-mail or contact me at 802-555-0214, extension 139. You can find the ad specifications at www.silasfarmsteadweekly.com/ads.

Package	Format	Price (Per Month)
1	One full-page print ad plus 720 × 300 px Web site ad	$1,000
[180]2	[180]One half-page print ad plus 240 × 400 px Web site ad	$725
3	One half-page print ad plus 250 × 250 px Web site ad	$650
4	One quarter-page print ad plus 250 × 250 px Web site ad	$550

Sincerely,

Zofia Nowak
Marketing Coordinator
Silas's Farmstead Weekly

To: nowak@silasfarmsteadweekly.com
From: d.ashcroft@true-sprout.net
Date: March 19
Subject: Re: Silas's Farmstead Weekly

Hello Ms. Nowak,

Thank you for your e-mail. [179]I am interested in placing an ad in *Silas's Farmstead Weekly*. However, I need some clarification regarding the online ad. I checked the specifications on your Web site, but I am still unsure about the location of the ad. [180]Could you let me know exactly where the 240 × 400 ad would appear on your Web site?

Once I receive your response, I will send you an electronic version of the ad along with payment information.

176-180번 문제는 다음 이메일들에 관한 것입니다.

수신: d.ashcroft@true-sprout.net
발신: nowak@silasfarmsteadweekly.com
날짜: 3월 12일
제목: Silas's Farmstead Weekly

Mr. Ashcroft께,

한정 기간 동안만 *Silas's Farmstead Weekly*가 아직 저희 출판물에 광고하신 적이 없는 사업체에 광고 할인 요금을 제공해 드립니다. *Silas's Farmstead Weekly*에 광고를 내시면 4만 명 이상의 농업 전문 독자층과 지면과 인터넷을 통해 연결될 수 있습니다. 고객층을 넓힐 이 흔치 않은 기회를 놓치지 마세요!

아래는 첫 광고주를 위한 현재 할인 혜택이며 4월 10일까지 유효합니다. 전면 칼라 광고 중 하나를 예약하거나, 디자이너가 맞춤형 광고를 제작해 주길 원하거나, 또는 추가 정보를 요청하고 싶으시다면, 이 이메일에 답장하시거나 802-555-0214(내선 139)로 연락 주시기 바랍니다. 광고의 사양은 www.silasfarmsteadweekly.com/ads 에서 확인하실 수 있습니다.

패키지	구성	가격 (월당)
1	전면 지면 광고 + 720 × 300 픽셀 웹사이트 광고	1,000달러
2	1/2면 지면 광고 + 240 × 400 픽셀 웹사이트 광고	725달러
3	1/2면 지면 광고 + 250 × 250 픽셀 웹사이트 광고	650달러
4	1/4면 지면 광고 + 250 × 250 픽셀 웹사이트 광고	550달러

진심을 담아,

Silas's Farmstead Weekly
마케팅 책임자
Zofia Nowak

수신: nowak@silasfarmsteadweekly.com
발신: d.ashcroft@true-sprout.net
날짜: 3월 19일
제목: Re: Silas's Farmstead Weekly

안녕하세요, Ms. Nowak,

이메일 고맙습니다. *Silas's Farmstead Weekly*에 광고를 내는 데 관심이 있습니다. 그러나 온라인 광고에 관하여 명확한 설명이 좀 필요합니다. 홈페이지에서 사양을 확인했지만, 여전히 광고의 위치를 잘 모르겠습니다. 240×400 광고가 정확히 홈페이지 어디에 게재되는지 알려 주시겠습니까?

답장을 받자마자 결제 정보와 함께 광고의 전자 파일을 보내 드리겠습니다.

<table>
<tr><td>

Best regards,

Daniel Ashcroft
Owner, True Sprout Company

</td><td>

이만 줄입니다.

True Sprout Company 사장
Daniel Ashcroft

</td></tr>
</table>

어휘1 rate 요금 focused 집중하는, 전문으로 하는 audience 독자층 agricultural 농업의 in print (책, 신문 등에) 실려, 인쇄되어 rare 드문, 흔치 않은 customer base 고객층 deal 특별 제안, 혜택 advertiser 광고주 personalized 맞춤형의 extension 내선 번호 specification 사양, 세부 지침

어휘2 place an advertisement 광고를 내다 clarification 명확한 regarding ~에 관하여 unsure 확신이 없는, 잘 모르는 location 위치 along with ~와 함께 payment 결제, 지불

176

<table>
<tr><td>

Why did Ms. Nowak contact Mr. Ashcroft?

(A) To inform him about the launch of a new magazine
(B) To promote a new agricultural product
(C) To notify him of a special promotion
(D) To provide him with a discount on a subscription

</td><td>

Ms. Nowak는 왜 Mr. Ashcroft에게 연락했는가?

(A) 새 잡지 발간에 대해 알려 주기 위해
(B) 새 농업 제품을 홍보하기 위해
(C) 특별 판촉 행사에 대해 알려 주기 위해
(D) 구독 할인을 제공하기 위해

</td></tr>
</table>

어휘 launch 출시, 발간 notify 알리다, 통보하다 subscription 구독

해설 Ms. Nowak이 Mr. Ashcroft에게 연락한 이유는 그녀가 보낸 이메일 첫 문장에서 알 수 있다. 자사 잡지에 처음으로 광고를 내는 사업주에게 할인 혜택을 주는(*Silas's Farmstead Weekly* is providing reduced rates on advertisements for businesses that have not yet advertised in our publication.) 특별 판촉 행사에 대해 알려 주고 있다.

177

<table>
<tr><td>

What can be inferred about *Silas's Farmstead Weekly*?

(A) Its readership has grown recently.
(B) It plans to publish a special edition.
(C) Its advertising prices have gone up.
(D) It produces a magazine with full-color content.

</td><td>

*Silas's Farmstead Weekly*에 관하여 무엇을 추론할 수 있는가?

(A) 최근에 독자 수가 늘어났다.
(B) 특별판을 출간할 계획이다.
(C) 광고 가격이 인상되었다.
(D) 전면 컬러 콘텐츠로 잡지를 제작한다.

</td></tr>
</table>

어휘 readership 독자층, 독자 수

해설 첫 이메일 두 번째 문단에서 총천연색 광고를 예약하려면 연락 달라고 말하는 문장에서 정답을 알 수 있다(If you would like to book one of these full-color ads, ~ please respond to this e-mail or contact me at 802-555-0214, extension 139).

178

<table>
<tr><td>

What is mentioned about Ms. Nowak?

(A) She works as a graphic designer.
(B) She has collaborated with Mr. Ashcroft in the past.
(C) She is available to offer additional help.
(D) She will not be available in April.

</td><td>

Ms. Nowak에 관하여 무엇이 언급되어 있는가?

(A) 그래픽 디자이너로 일한다.
(B) 과거에 Mr. Ashcroft와 협업한 적이 있다.
(C) 추가로 도움을 제공할 수 있다.
(D) 4월에는 시간이 없다.

</td></tr>
</table>

어휘 collaborate 협업하다 available 시간을 낼 수 있는, 형편[여건]이 되는

해설 첫 이메일 두 번째 문단에서 더 자세한 사항을 알고 싶으면 연락 달라고 말하는 문장에서 정답을 알 수 있다(request further details, please respond to this e-mail or contact me at 802-555-0214, extension 139).

179

<table>
<tr><td>

In the second e-mail, the word "placing" in paragraph 1, line 1, is closest in meaning to

(A) hiring
(B) running
(C) assigning
(D) estimating

</td><td>

두 번째 이메일 첫 문단 첫 번째 줄의 단어 "placing"과 의미상 가장 가까운 것은

(A) 고용하기
(B) (광고를) 내기
(C) 배정하기
(D) 추정하기

</td></tr>
</table>

180

What package is Mr. Ashcroft most likely considering? (A) Package 1 **(B) Package 2** (C) Package 3 (D) Package 4	Mr. Ashcroft는 어느 패키지 상품을 고려하고 있겠는가? (A) 패키지 1 (B) 패키지 2 (C) 패키지 3 (D) 패키지 4

Questions 181 through 185 refer to the following e-mails.

181–185번 **문제**는 다음 두 이메일에 관한 것입니다.

To: n.krawczyk@plintix.net
From: i.etim@vintoradigitalmarketing.com
Date: Monday, January 20
Subject: Technical Writing Role at Vintora Digital Marketing

Dear Ms. Krawczyk,

Thank you once again for applying to Vintora Digital Marketing. [181]We appreciated the opportunity to speak with you last Thursday and are delighted to extend an invitation for you to join our technical writing team. As discussed, your responsibilities will entail creating user manuals, installation guides, newsletters, and other documents for our technology clients. Your solid background in information technology will be a valuable asset, as it is crucial to comprehend the technical aspects of our clients' products and convey this information in a clear and concise manner.

[182][185]Your role will commence in February with an in-person training session at our headquarters in Austin, Texas. We aim to schedule this training at a time that accommodates as many new team members as possible, [185]particularly those like you who reside outside of Texas. Kindly reply to this e-mail at your earliest convenience [182]and let us know which weekend in February works best for you.

This is a contract-based position, and apart from the initial training, all work will be conducted remotely during hours of your choosing. [183]As mentioned, your payment will be determined by the complexity of each project you opt to undertake. [184]Alan Fraser, our human resources director, will soon be in touch with the necessary paperwork to complete.

We are excited to collaborate with you!

수신: n.krawczyk@plintix.net
발신: i.etim@vintoradigitalmarketing.com
날짜: 1월 20일 월요일
제목: Vintora Digital Marketing 기술 문서 작성 직무

Ms. Krawczyk께,

Vintora Digital Marketing에 지원해 주셔서 다시 한 번 감사드립니다. 지난주 목요일에 이야기 나눌 기회가 있어 감사하며 저희 기술 문서 작성 팀에 함께해 주시기를 제안드리게 되어 매우 기쁩니다. 논의한 바와 같이, 업무에는 기술 관련 고객사를 위한 사용자 매뉴얼, 설치 가이드, 회보 및 기타 문서 작성이 포함될 것입니다. 귀하의 탄탄한 정보 기술 배경은 소중한 자산이 될 것입니다. 고객사의 제품에 대한 기술적 측면을 이해하여 그 정보를 명확하고 간결하게 전달하는 일이 매우 중요하기 때문입니다.

직무는 2월에 텍사스 Austin에 있는 본사에서 있을 대면 교육으로 시작됩니다. 저희는 가능한 한 많은 신입 팀원들, 특히 귀하와 같이 텍사스 외부에 거주하는 사람들에게 맞출 수 있는 시간에 이 교육의 일정을 잡고자 합니다. 가급적 빠른 시간 내에 이메일에 답장하셔서 2월 어느 주말이 가장 좋으신지 알려 주시기 바랍니다.

이 직무는 계약직이며, 첫 교육을 제외하고 모든 업무는 원격으로 선택한 시간에 이루어집니다. 말씀드렸다시피 지급 금액은 맡기로 한 각 프로젝트의 난이도에 따라 정해집니다. 인사부장 Alan Fraser가 작성해야 하는 필수 서류를 가지고 곧 연락드릴 것입니다.

귀하와 함께 일하게 되어 매우 기대됩니다!

Best regards,

Iniobong Etim
Vintora Digital Marketing

이만 줄입니다.

Iniobong Etim
Vintora Digital Marketing

To: undisclosed recipients
From: i.etim@vintoradigitalmarketing.com
Date: Tuesday, January 21
Subject: Training Schedule for VDM

Dear Technical Writing Team,

Based on the feedback we received, [185]we have decided that February 22–23 is the most suitable date for the majority of you. Please note that the training will take place from Saturday morning through Sunday afternoon. For those traveling from outside the area, we recommend arriving on Friday. If you wish, we can arrange for you to have dinner with some of our local writers that evening.

All travel expenses will be covered by Vintora Digital Marketing. Further details will be provided soon, but for now, I wanted to inform you of the schedule so you can mark it on your calendars.

Best regards,

Iniobong Etim
Vintora Digital Marketing

수신: 비공개
발신: i.etim@vintoradigitalmarketing.com
날짜: 1월 21일 화요일
제목: VDM 교육 일정

기술문서 작성 팀원 여러분께,

수신한 피드백에 근거하여 2월 22, 23일이 여러분 대다수에게 가장 알맞은 날짜라는 결론을 내렸습니다. 교육이 토요일 오전부터 일요일 오후까지 이어진다는 점에 유의하시기 바랍니다. 외지에서 오시는 분들께는 금요일에 도착하시기를 권장합니다. 원하시는 분들은 그날 저녁에 이 지역 작가 몇 분과 저녁 식사를 하시도록 준비해 드릴 수 있습니다.

모든 이동 경비는 Vintora Digital Marketing이 부담합니다. 추후에 자세한 사항이 곧 제공되겠지만, 일단 지금은 일정을 알려 드리며, 일정표에 표시해 주시기 바랍니다.

이만 줄입니다.

Iniobong Etim
Vintora Digital Marketing

어휘1 technical writing (매뉴얼과 같은) 기술 문서 작성 extend an invitation 초대하다, 제안하다 responsibility (담당) 업무 entail 수반하다, 포함하다 installation 설치 solid 확고한, 견실한, 굳건한 background 배경, 소양, 이력 asset 자산, 재산 crucial 결정적인, 매우 중요한 comprehend 이해하다, 파악하다 aspect 일면, 측면 convey (정보, 생각 등을) 전달하다, 전하다 concise 간결한, 간명한 manner 방식, 방법 commence 시작되다 in-person 직접의 headquarters 본사 aim to–V ~하는 것을 목표로 하다, ~할 생각이다 accommodate (요구나 일정을) ~에 맞추다 particularly 특히 reside 거주하다 kindly 제발, 부디 at your earliest convenience 가급적 빠른 시간 내에 work for ~에게 문제없다, 좋다 contract-based position 계약직 apart from ~을 제외하고는, ~을 빼고는 initial 최초의, 초기의 remotely 원격으로, 멀리에서 determine 확정하다 complexity 복잡함, 난이도 opt to–V ~하는 것을 선택하다 undertake 떠맡다, 착수하다 in touch 연락하는 complete 기입하다, 작성하다

어휘2 undisclosed 공개되지 않은 recipient 수령자, 수취인 suitable 알맞은 take place (계획된 일이) 일어나다 travel 이동하다; 이동 arrange for *sb* to–V ~가 ~하도록 준비하다 cover (비용을) 치르다, 부담하다 mark 표시하다

181

Why did Ms. Etim contact Ms. Krawczyk?

(A) To offer her a position
(B) To assist her with technical issues
(C) To advertise a writing seminar
(D) To negotiate a salary

Ms. Etim은 왜 Ms. Krawczyk에게 연락했는가?

(A) 자리를 제안하기 위해
(B) 기술적인 문제를 돕기 위해
(C) 작문 세미나를 광고하기 위해
(D) 급여를 협상하기 위해

어휘 negotiate 협상하다

해설 첫 번째 이메일의 두 번째 문장 We appreciated the opportunity to speak with you last Thursday and are delighted to extend an invitation for you to join our technical writing team.에서 지난주에 면접을 본 지원자에게 합격을 통보하고 있음을 알 수 있다.

What information is Ms. Krawczyk requested to provide?

(A) Her academic qualifications
(B) Her availability for a training session
(C) A list of her current clients
(D) A summary of her professional experience

Ms. Krawczyk는 어떤 정보를 제공하라고 요청받는가?

(A) 학력 사항
(B) 교육 시간 가능 날짜
(C) 현재 고객들의 명단
(D) 직업 경력 요약

어휘 academic qualifications 학력 사항[요건] availability 시간을 낼 수 있음 summary 요약, 개요 professional 직업의

해설 Ms. Krawczyk는 새 직장에서의 직무는 2월에 대면 교육으로 시작하게 되는데(Your role will commence in February with an in-person training session), 2월 몇째 주말에 시간을 낼 수 있는지 Ms. Etim에게 알려 주어야 한다(let us know which weekend in February works best for you).

What is indicated about the technical writing team members?

(A) They are paid at variable rates.
(B) They have collaborated on previous projects.
(C) They work from the same office location.
(D) They cover their own travel expenses.

기술문서 작성 팀원들에 관하여 무엇인 언급되어 있는가?

(A) 변동 급여를 지급받는다.
(B) 이전의 프로젝트들에서 협업해 왔다.
(C) 같은 지사에서 근무한다.
(D) 자신의 이동 경비를 부담한다.

어휘 variable 가변적인, 변동의 rate 임금, 요금 location 장소

해설 첫 번째 이메일 마지막 문단에 작성을 맡은 문서의 난이도에 따라 원고료가 정해진다는 설명이 나온다(your payment will be determined by the complexity of each project you opt to undertake). 즉 기술지원 팀원들은 매 프로젝트마다 다른 급여를 지급받을 수 있다.

Why will Mr. Fraser contact Ms. Krawczyk?

(A) To clarify company policies
(B) To make travel arrangements
(C) To issue employment-related documents
(D) To discuss software requirements

Mr. Fraser는 왜 Ms. Krawczyk에게 연락할 것인가?

(A) 회사 정책을 명확히 설명하기 위해
(B) 여행을 준비하기 위해
(C) 고용 관련 문서를 발급하기 위해
(D) 소프트웨어 요구 사항을 논하기 위해

어휘 clarify 명확하게 설명하다 arrangement 준비, 마련 issue 발급하다

해설 첫 번째 이메일 마지막 문장에서 인사부장 Mr. Fraser가 신입 직원이 작성해야 하는 서류를 준비해서 곧 연락할 것이라고 알려 주고 있다(Alan Fraser, our human resources director, will soon be in touch with the necessary paperwork to complete).

What will Ms. Krawczyk most likely do on February 21?

(A) Submit a writing project
(B) Travel to Austin
(C) Attend a training session
(D) Meet with Mr. Fraser

Ms. Krawczyk는 2월 21일에 무엇을 하겠는가?

(A) 작성한 프로젝트 문서를 제출한다
(B) Austin으로 이동한다
(C) 교육에 참석한다
(D) Mr. Fraser와 만난다

해설 두 번째 이메일에 따르면 2월 22일과 23일 이틀에 걸쳐 교육이 진행될 것인데, 이 날들은 토요일과 일요일이다(we have decided that February 22 - 23 is the most suitable date for the majority of you. Please note that the training will take place from Saturday morning through Sunday afternoon). 그러므로 교육을 받기 위해 외지에서 오는 사람들에게 오라고 권장하는 금요일은 2월 21일이다(For those traveling from outside the area, we recommend arriving on Friday). 첫 번째 이메일 두 번째 문단에 나오는 those like you who reside outside of Texas를 보면 Ms. Krawczyk가 바로 이 외지에서 오는 사람에 해당한다는 것을 알 수 있다. 같은 문단 첫 문장에는 교육은 본사가 있는 텍사스 Austin에서 있을 예정이다(Your role will commence in February with an in-person training session at our headquarters in Austin, Texas). 내용을 종합해 보면 텍사스 외부에 거주하는 Ms. Krawczyk는 Ms. Etim의 권고에 따라 2월 21일 금요일에 Austin으로 이동할 가능성이 높다.

Questions 186 through 190 refer to the following advertisement, e-mail, and Web site feedback.

Isla's Moonlight Tours
Glasgow, Scotland

Isla's Moonlight Tours is welcoming the autumn season with special pricing - [188]tour packages are now 10% off compared to last year's rates. This limited-time offer is valid for bookings made by September 14. [186]Our autumn getaways depart weekly, but be sure to secure your spot before they're fully booked! Below is a selection of our featured packages.

Dundee and Fort William: This 4-day tour begins in Dundee, a revitalized port city known for its design museums and cutting-edge contemporary art. Enjoy the city's creative energy before heading to Fort William, where you'll explore dramatic Highland landscapes, from Ben Nevis - the UK's highest peak - to the historic beauty of Glencoe and nearby villages.

Stonehaven and the Isle of Mull: This 4-day journey begins in the picturesque coastal town of Stonehaven, which boasts scenic cliffs, winding lanes, and a rich maritime heritage. A highlight of your visit is Dunnottar Castle, perched dramatically atop sea-battered rocks - a perfect blend of history and natural splendor. From there, the tour continues to the serene Isle of Mull, dotted with colorful villages, coastal trails, and sweeping views across tranquil waters. It's a place where quiet charm meets untamed beauty, inviting you to slow down and take in the rhythm of island life.

Kilkenny and Beyond: Take a short trip across the sea to the Emerald Isle and experience the heart of Ireland. Choose from a 3- or 5-day tour starting in the medieval city of Kilkenny, then journey north to Derry, west to Glencolmcille's rugged coastline, and south to the Rock of Cashel - an iconic symbol of Ireland's royal past.

[187]**We offer customized tour options for special groups based on duration and preferred attractions.**

From: noreply@bookings.islasmoonlight.com
To: obarrett95@nodexmail.com
[188]Date: 7 August
Subject: Reservation Confirmation

Dear Mr. Barrett,

We appreciate your decision to travel with Isla's Moonlight Tours. Your booking for one passenger has been successfully confirmed:

186-190번 문제는 다음 광고와 이메일, 웹 사이트 피드백에 관한 것입니다.

Isla's Moonlight Tours
스코틀랜드 Glasgow

Isla's Moonlight Tours가 특가 행사로 가을을 맞이합니다. 현재 투어 패키지 상품들이 작년 요금에 비하여 10퍼센트 할인되고 있습니다. 이 한정 할인은 9월 14일까지 이루어지는 예약에 유효합니다. 가을 여행은 매주 출발하지만 예약이 다 차기 전에 반드시 자리를 확보하세요! 아래는 행사에 포함되는 패키지 상품들 중 선별된 것입니다.

Dundee와 Fort William: 이 4일 일정의 관광은 디자인 박물관과 최첨단 현대 미술로 유명하고, 다시 활기를 찾은 항구 도시 Dundee에서 시작합니다. 도시의 창의적인 에너지를 즐기시다가 Fort William으로 가시면 영국에서 가장 높은 봉우리인 Ben Nevis부터 Glencoe와 인근 마을들의 역사적인 아름다움에 이르기까지 Highland의 감동적인 풍경을 체험하실 수 있습니다.

Stonehaven와 Mull 섬: 이 4일 일정의 여행은 그림 같은 해안 마을 Stonehaven에서 시작됩니다. Stonehaven은 아름다운 절벽과 구불구불한 길, 풍부한 해양 유산을 자랑합니다. 방문의 하이라이트는 Dunnottar 성인데, 파도에 깍인 바위 꼭대기에 웅장하게 자리 잡고 있어서 역사와 자연의 장관이 완벽하게 조화를 이루고 있습니다. 투어는 거기서 평화로운 섬 Mull로 계속됩니다. 이곳은 다채로운 마을들과 해변 길, 잔잔한 바다 위로 탁 트인 전망이 여기저기 퍼져 있습니다. 이곳은 고요한 매력이 야생의 아름다움과 만나는 곳으로서 당신에게 발걸음을 늦추고 섬 생활의 리듬에 몸을 맡겨 보라고 권합니다.

Kilkenny와 그 너머: 바다를 건너 에메랄드 섬으로 짧은 여행을 떠나 아일랜드의 심장을 경험하세요. 중세 도시 Kilkenny에서 출발하는 3일 혹은 5일 관광을 선택하셔서 북쪽으로 Derry를 향해, 서쪽 Glencolmcille의 울퉁불퉁한 해안선으로, 남쪽에 있는 과거 아일랜드 왕가의 상징 Rock of Cashel로 여행합니다.

기간과 선호하는 명소에 따라 특별 그룹을 위한 맞춤 관광 옵션을 제공합니다.

발신: noreply@bookings.islasmoonlight.com
수신: obarrett95@nodexmail.com
날짜: 8월 7일
제목: 예약 확인

Mr. Barrett께,

Isla's Moonlight Tours와 함께 여행하기로 결정해 주셔서 고맙습니다. 승객 1인 예약이 확정되었습니다.

[190]Tour name: Stonehaven and the Isle of Mull
Departure from Glasgow: Thursday, 18 September, at 9:00 A.M.
Return to Glasgow: Sunday, 21 September, at 7:00 P.M.
Amount Charged to Your Card: £650.00

If you have any questions or require assistance before your departure, our customer relations coordinator will be happy to help. You can reach us via e-mail at tours@islasmoonlight.com or by phone at +44 (0) 141 728 4430.

투어명: Stonehaven와 Mull 섬
Glasgow 출발: 9월 18일 목요일 오전 9시
Glasgow 복귀: 9월 21일 일요일 오후 7시
카드 청구 금액: 650파운드

출발 전 질문이나 도움이 필요하시면 고객 관리 담당자가 기꺼이 도와드립니다. 이메일 tours@islasmoonlight.com이나 전화 +44 (0) 141 728 4430으로 연락 주시기 바랍니다.

Participant feedback

As a photographer, I was thoroughly impressed by the breathtaking scenery and unique locations featured on this tour - genuinely second to none. [189]This company knows how to treat its customers; I'm already looking forward to joining another trip. Our guide, Siobhan O'Malley, was knowledgeable and energetic. [190]As a native of the city we visited, she shared the city's heritage and customs with warmth and familiarity. Her engaging stories taught me a great deal about the area's rich history.

Posted by: Owen Barrett

참가자 피드백

사진작가로서 저는 이 투어에서 선보인 숨이 멎을 만큼 멋진 경치와 독특한 장소들에 정말 깊은 인상을 받았습니다. 정말 비길 데가 없습니다. 이 회사는 고객을 대하는 법을 알고 있습니다. 벌써 다음 여행에 참여하는 게 기대됩니다. 가이드 Siobhan O'Malley는 해박하고 활기가 넘쳤습니다. 우리가 방문한 도시 출신자인 그녀는 도시의 문화유산과 풍습에 대해 따뜻하고 친근하게 알려 주었습니다. 빠져들게 하는 그녀의 이야기는 저에게 이 지역의 풍부한 역사에 대해 많은 것을 가르쳐 주었습니다.

게시자: Owen Barrett

어휘1 pricing 가격 설정 off 할인하여 rate 요금 offer (한시적인) 할인, 가격 인하 getaway 짧은 여행 spot 자리 feature 특별히 포함하다 revitalize 다시 활성화하다, 새로운 활력을 불어넣다 cutting-edge 최첨단의 contemporary 현대의 head 향하다, 가다 isle 섬 picturesque 그림 같은, 그림처럼 예쁜 boast 자랑하다 scenic 경치가 좋은, 장관의 winding 구불구불한 lane 샛길, 골목(길) maritime 해양의 heritage (문화)유산 perched (높은 곳에) 위치한, 자리한 atop ~의 꼭대기에 sea-battered 파도와 바람에 깎인 blend (보기 좋거나 유용한) 조합 splendor (경치, 건축물 등의) 장려함, 장관 serene 평화로운, 고요한 dotted with ~이 퍼져 있는 sweeping 확 트인 tranquil 고요한, 평온한 untamed 길들이지 않은, 야생의 Emerald Isle 아일랜드(Ireland)의 별칭 medieval 중세(시대)의 rugged 울퉁불퉁한 coastline 해안선 iconic 표상으로 쓰이는, 상징성을 지닌 customized 맞춤형의 duration 지속 기간 attraction 명소

어휘2 coordinator 조정자, 담당자

어휘3 thoroughly 완전히, 전적으로 breathtaking 숨이 멎을 정도로 멋진[놀라운] genuinely 진정으로, 진심으로 second to none 비길 데 없는, 최고인 knowledgeable 해박한, 박식한 a native of ~의 출신자 familiarity 친숙함 engaging 매력적인, 빠져들게 하는 a great deal 많이, 상당한 정도로 post 게시하다

186

What can be inferred about Isla's Moonlight Tours?
(A) It has recently established additional branches.
(B) It is celebrating a company expansion.
(C) It has introduced new itineraries to meet demand.
(D) It organizes its tours multiple times each month.

Isla's Moonlight Tours에 관하여 무엇을 추론할 수 있는가?
(A) 최근에 추가로 지점들을 설립했다.
(B) 회사의 확장을 기념하고 있다.
(C) 수요를 충족시키기 위해 새 여행 일정을 도입했다.
(D) 매달 여러 차례 투어를 준비한다.

어휘 expansion 확장 itinerary 여행 일정 meet demand 수요를 충족시키다 organize (행사, 활동 등을) 준비하다, 조직하다

해설 가을 여행이 매주 출발하도록 일정을 잡아 놓았으므로, 최소 매달 네 번 이상은 있는 것이다(Our autumn getaways depart weekly).

187

According to the advertisement, what can Isla's Moonlight Tours offer clients?

(A) Opportunities to interact with artists and actors
(B) Discounts for customers who book repeatedly
(C) A guaranteed maximum tour group size
(D) Tailored travel plans for groups with specific preferences

광고에 따르면 Isla's Moonlight Tours는 고객들에게 무엇을 제공할 수 있는가?

(A) 예술가 및 배우들과 교류할 기회
(B) 반복해서 예약하는 고객들을 위한 할인
(C) 최대 투어 그룹 인원 보장
(D) 특정 선호도가 있는 그룹 맞춤형 여행 계획

어휘 interact 교류하다 guarantee 장담하다, 보장하다 tailored 맞춤의 specific 특정의 preference 선호

해설 광고 마지막 줄이 기간이나 선호하는 명소에 따라 맞춤 투어를 제공한다는 내용이다(We offer customized tour options for special groups based on duration and preferred attractions).

188

What is implied about Mr. Barrett's tour?

(A) It will last for a total of five days.
(B) It was purchased at a discounted price.
(C) It will not include admission fees for galleries.
(D) It has been specifically designed for historians.

Mr. Barrett의 여행에 관하여 무엇이 암시되어 있는가?

(A) 총 5일 동안 계속될 것이다.
(B) 할인가로 구입되었다.
(C) 미술관 입장료는 포함되지 않을 것이다.
(D) 특히 역사학자들을 위해 설계되었다.

어휘 last 계속되다, 지속되다 admission fee 입장료 specifically 특히 historian 역사가, 역사학자

해설 광고문 도입부에서 9월 14일 전에 투어를 예약하면 10퍼센트 할인을 받을 수 있다고 나와 있는데(tour packages are now 10% off compared to last year's rates. This limited-time offer is valid for bookings made by September 14.), 예약 확인 이메일 작성 날짜가 8월 7일이다(Date: 7 August). Mr. Barrett은 기한이 되기 전에 예약했으므로 할인가로 상품을 구매했다고 할 수 있다.

189

In the Web site feedback, the word "treat" in paragraph 1, line 2, is closest in meaning to

(A) serve
(B) pay for
(C) cover
(D) cure

웹 사이트 피드백 첫 문단 두 번째 줄의 단어 "treat"와 의미상 가장 가까운 것은

(A) (직원이 손님을) 응대하다
(B) ~의 값을 지불하다
(C) (책, 연설 등이) ~을 다루다
(D) 치료하다

해설 treat가 '(사람을) 대하다, 대우하다'의 뜻으로는 (A)와, '한턱내다'의 뜻이면 (B)와, '(주제, 소재 등을) 다루다, 논의하다'의 뜻이면 (C)와, '치료하다의 뜻이면 (D)와 동의어가 된다. This company knows how to treat its customers는 "이 회사는 고객을 대하는 법을 알고 있습니다."라는 뜻이다.

190

What is indicated about Ms. O'Malley?

(A) She is from Stonehaven.
(B) She has recently completed her guide training.
(C) She is fluent in multiple languages.
(D) She is currently enrolled at a local university.

Ms. O'Malley에 관하여 무엇이 언급되었는가?

(A) Stonehaven 출신이다.
(B) 최근에 가이드 교육을 마쳤다.
(C) 여러 언어에 유창하다.
(D) 현재 지역 대학교에 등록되어 있다.

해설 피드백에서 Mr. Barrett이 투어 가이드 Ms. O'Malley는 자신이 방문한 도시 출신자라고 말하고 있는데(As a native of the city we visited), 이메일에 나와 있는 일정표를 보면 방문 도시는 Stonehaven이다(Tour name: Stonehaven and the Isle of Mull). 두 부분을 연계하여 생각하면 Ms. O'Malley가 Stonehaven 출신이라는 것을 알 수 있다.

Questions 191 through 195 refer to the following schedule, e-mail, and review.

191–195번 문제는 다음 일정표와 이메일, 후기에 관한 것입니다.

African Council for Industrial & Commercial Development
7th Annual Symposium
Van der Merwe Convention Centre
Cape Town, South Africa
Thursday, 9 October

Tentative Schedule	
Time	**Location**
9:30 A.M. – 10:00 A.M.	Welcome Address and Opening Remarks by ACICD President Linden Mthembu Langston Jubilee Hall

Time	Tamarind Room	Ebony Room
10:30 A.M. – 12:00 A.M.	191 Improving Flavor, Texture, and Nutritional Value – Pieter Van Rooyen	Setting Standards of Excellence for Safety and Quality – Anusha Naidoo
1:30 P.M. – 3:00 P.M.	Revisiting Classic Methods of Food Preservation: Canning and Pickling – Nokuthula Okafor	Acquiring Automated Machinery For Your Production Facility – Rohan Mehta
3:30 P.M. – 5:00 P.M.	Refrigeration and Storage Innovations for Perishables – Sonja Pretorius	193 Optimizing Packaging for Shipping – Tumelo Mashaba

- Please inform Luyanda Mokoena (lmokoena@acicd.org.za) of any required updates to your session details no later than 2 September. The finalized program will be available online at www.acicd.org.za/schedule by 11 September.
- 192 Presenters MUST register for the event. Please visit our Web site, click on the "Registration" tab, and submit the form – remember to check the "Presenter" box. 195 If you intend to recruit during the event, be sure to also fill out the Employer Application found under the "Career Center" tab.
- A limited number of discounted rooms remain at The Montclare Suites – early reservations are strongly encouraged.

아프리카 상공업 진흥 위원회
제7회 연례 심포지엄
Van der Merwe 컨벤션 센터
남아프리카 공화국 Cape Town
10월 9일 목요일

잠정 일정		
시간	장소	
오전 9:30 – 오전 10:00	환영 연설 및 인사말 ACICD 회장 Linden Mthembu Langston 기념관	
	Tamarind 회의실	Ebony 회의실
오전 10:30 – 오후 12:00	풍미, 식감 및 영양 가치의 향상 – Pieter Van Rooyen	안전 및 품질 우수성의 기준 세우기 – Anusha Naidoo
오후 1:30 – 오후 3:00	식품 보존의 고전적 방식 재조명: 통조림과 절임 – Nokuthula Okafor	생산 시설을 위한 자동화 기계 도입 – Rohan Mehta
오후 3:30 – 오후 5:00	신선 식품을 위한 냉장 및 보관의 혁신 – Sonja Pretorius	운송을 위한 포장 최적화 – Tumelo Mashaba

- 담당 세션의 정보에 변경이 필요하면 늦어도 9월 2일까지 Luyanda Mokoena (lmokoena@acicd.org.za)에게 알려 주시기 바랍니다. 최종 프로그램은 9월 11일까지 www.acicd.org.za/schedule에서 이용할 수 있게 하겠습니다.
- 발표자도 행사에 등록해야 합니다. 홈페이지를 방문하셔서 '등록' 탭을 클릭하고 서식을 제출하시기 바랍니다. '발표자' 상자에 체크하시는 것을 잊지 마세요. 행사 기간에 인재 채용을 계획 중이라면 '취업 센터' 탭에서 찾을 수 있는 고용주 신청서도 반드시 작성해 주세요.
- The Montclare Suites에 할인 객실이 한정된 수만 남아 있으니, 조기 예약을 강력히 권장합니다.

From: Sonja Pretorius <spretorius6@kbrdev.co.za>
To: Luyanda Mokoena <lmokoena@acicd.org.za>
Date: Monday, 28 July 8:50 A.M.
Subject: Schedule change request

Dear Mr. Mokoena:

193 Unforeseen circumstances have prevented my colleague, Tumelo Mashaba, from delivering his scheduled presentation. I've been requested to step in as his replacement. However, upon

발신: Sonja Pretorius 〈spretorius6@kbrdev.co.za〉
수신: Luyanda Mokoena 〈lmokoena@acicd.org.za〉
날짜: 7월 28일 월요일 오전 8:50
제목: 일정 변경 요청

Mr. Mokoena께:

예기치 못한 사정 때문에 제 동료 Tumelo Mashaba가 예정된 프레젠테이션을 할 수 없게 되었습니다. 제가 그를 대신하여 도와달라고 요청받았습니다.

reviewing the latest version of the conference schedule, I realized that Mr. Mashaba's allocated time conflicts with my own. I would appreciate your assistance in resolving this dilemma. Many thanks in advance for your support.

Sincerely,
Sonja Pretorius

그러나 최신 학회 일정을 확인해 보니 Mr. Mashaba 에게 배정된 시간이 제 시간과 겹친다는 것을 알게 되었습니다. 이 문제를 해결하도록 도와주시면 고맙 겠습니다. 지원에 대해 미리 깊이 감사드립니다.

진심을 담아,
Sonja Pretorius

Program | Registration | Sponsorships | **Comments**

At the recent ACICD symposium, I delivered a presentation exploring the intricacies involved in procuring automated equipment. To my delight, the presentation drew a strong turnout, and during the subsequent question-and-answer session, I found myself diving into content I had deliberately omitted, concerned it might be overly technical. Obviously, the audience was far more competent than I had anticipated. In addition, [194 195]acting in my capacity as a recruiter, I interviewed a dozen promising candidates for a pivotal role at my organization. Overall, this initial experience with the ACICD symposium proved utterly gratifying, and I eagerly await the next one.

- Rohan Mehta

프로그램 | 등록 | 후원 | **의견**

최근 ACICD 심포지엄에서 자동화 장비를 조달하는 데 수반되는 복잡한 사항들을 살펴보는 프레젠테이 션을 했습니다. 기쁘게도 프레젠테이션은 많은 참석 자들의 관심을 끌어들였으며, 이어진 질의응답 시간 에는 제가 지나치게 전문적일까봐 우려해서 의도적 으로 제외했던 내용들까지 깊이 있게 설명하게 되었 습니다. 확실히 청중들이 제가 기대했던 것보다 훨 씬 더 실력이 있었습니다. 게다가 채용 담당자 역할 로 자사의 핵심 직무에 지원한 유망한 후보자 10여 명의 면접까지 볼 수 있었습니다. 전체적으로 이번 ACICD 심포지엄에서의 첫 경험은 완전히 만족스러 웠으며 다음 행사가 정말 기다려집니다.

– Rohan Mehta

어휘1 tentative 잠정적인 address 연설 remarks (연설, 강연 등에서의) 발언 jubilee (25주년, 50주년 등의) 기념제, 축제 texture (음식 등의) 질감 nutritional 영양의 revisit 재고하다, 다시 논의하다 classic 고전적인, 유행을 타지 않는 preservation 보존 acquire 획득하다, 도입하다 refrigeration 냉장 storage 보관, 저장 perishables 잘 상하는 식품, 신선 (유지 필수) 식품 optimize 최적화하다, 최대한 효율화하다 shipping 운송, 수송 no later than 늦어도 ~까지 presenter 강연자, 발표자 intend to-V ~할 생각이다, ~할 계획이다 recruit 모집하다, 채용하다 be sure to-V 반드시 ~하다 fill out ~을 작성하다 strongly encourage 강력히 권장하다

어휘2 unforeseen 뜻밖의, 예기치 못한 circumstances 상황, 사정 prevent 막다 deliver a presentation 프레젠테이션을 하다 step in 돕고 나서다 replacement 대체할 사람 upon + ~ing ~하자마자 allocate 할당하다, 배정하다 conflict (약속, 계획 등이) 겹치다 resolve 해결하다 in advance 미리

어휘3 sponsorship 후원 comment 의견, 논평 explore 살펴보다, 검토하다 intricacies 복잡한 사항 involve 수반하다 procure 조달하다 to one's delight ~에게 기쁘게도 turnout 참석자 수 subsequent 그 다음의, 이후의 find oneself ~ing ~하고 있음을 알게 되다 dive into ~에 몰입하다, 깊게 다루다 deliberately 의도적으로, 고의로 omit 누락하다, 제외하다 overly 지나치게, 과도하게 obviously 확실히, 분명히 competent 유능한, 실력 있는 in one's capacity as ~의 지위[역할]로 promising 장래가 촉망되는, 전도유망한 pivotal 중추적인, 핵심적인 utterly 완전히, 전적으로 gratifying 만족스러운, 기쁘게 하는 await 기다리다, 기대하다

191

What industry is the focus of the conference?

(A) Waste management and repurposing
(B) Food production and processing
(C) Automobile design and engineering
(D) Apparel and textile manufacturing

학술 대회의 주제는 어느 업계인가?

(A) 폐기물 처리 및 용도 전환
(B) 식품 생산 및 가공
(C) 자동차 디자인 및 엔지니어링
(D) 의류 및 직물 제조

어휘 focus 핵심, 주제 conference 학술 대회 repurpose 용도를 변경하다 processing 가공

해설 일정표에서 Improving Flavor, Texture, and Nutritional Value(풍미, 식감 및 영양학적 가치 향상시키기) 같은 프레젠테이션 제목을 보면 학술 대회의 초 점은 식품업계에 있음을 알 수 있다.

According to the schedule, what are presenters required to do?

(A) Identify themselves as speakers during registration
(B) Specify shipping information for their conference materials
(C) Secure hotel accommodations by September 11
(D) Request a discount code from The Montclare Suites

일정표에 따르면 발표자는 무엇을 해야 하는가?

(A) 등록할 때 자신이 발표자임을 알린다
(B) 학회 자료의 운송 정보를 명시한다
(C) 9월 11일까지 호텔 숙박을 확보한다
(D) The Montclare Suites에 할인 코드를 요청한다

어휘 be required to–V ~해야 한다, ~하는 것이 요구되다 identify A as B A가 B임을 알려주다 secure 확보하다, 얻어내다 accommodations 숙박 시설

해설 발표자도 등록해야 한다고 강조하면서 등록하는 방법과 발표자임을 표시해야 한다는 사실까지 알려주고 있다(Presenters MUST register for the event. Please visit our Web site, click on the "Registration" tab, and submit the form – remember to check the "Presenter" box).

What responsibility has been assigned to Ms. Pretorius?

(A) Arrange a meeting with the event coordinator
(B) Provide a draft of her presentation
(C) Discuss ways of preparing goods for transport
(D) Cancel her colleague's travel arrangements

Ms. Pretorius에게 어떤 업무가 맡겨졌는가?

(A) 행사 담당자와 회의 일정을 잡는다
(B) 프레젠테이션 자료 초안을 제공한다
(C) 상품 수송 준비 방법을 논한다
(D) 동료의 출장 일정을 취소한다

어휘 assign (책임, 업무 등을) 부여하다, 맡기다 draft 초안, 초고 transport 운송, 수송 arrangement 준비, 일정

해설 이메일에서 Ms. Pretorius는 프레젠테이션을 할 수 없게 된 Tumelo Mashaba의 대체자가 되어 달라는 요청을 받았다고 말한다(Unforeseen circumstances have prevented my colleague, Tumelo Mashaba, from delivering his scheduled presentation. I've been requested to step in as his replacement). 일정표를 보면 Tumelo Mashaba가 하기로 예정되어 있던 프레젠테이션 제목이 '운송을 위한 포장 최적화(Optimizing Packaging for Shipping)'이다. 두 지문의 내용을 연계하면 정답을 알 수 있다.

In the review, the word "capacity" in paragraph 1, line 5, is closest in meaning to

(A) position
(B) volume
(C) competence
(D) experience

후기에서 첫 문단 다섯 번째 줄의 단어 "capacity"와 의미상 가장 가까운 것은

(A) 지위
(B) 용량
(C) 능력
(D) 경험

해설 capacity가 '지위'라는 뜻으로 사용된다면 (A)가 동의어다. 그러나 '용량', '능력'이라는 뜻도 있기 때문에 문맥에 따라 (B)와 (C)도 동의어가 될 수 있다. 경험을 쌓으면 능력이 생기므로 문맥에 따라서는 (D)도 동의어가 될 수 있다. acting in my capacity as a recruiter는 '채용 담당자의 자격으로', 직역하면 '채용 담당자의 지위에서 행동하여'라는 뜻이다.

What is probably true about Mr. Mehta?

(A) He recently launched a production facility.
(B) He submitted an Employer Application when registering.
(C) He preferred the recent ACICD symposium over previous ones.
(D) He assumed his subject matter would be easily understood.

Mr. Mehta에 관하여 무엇이 사실이겠는가?

(A) 최근에 생산 시설을 개설했다.
(B) 등록할 때 고용주 신청서를 제출했다.
(C) 최근 ACICD 심포지엄이 이전 것보다 낫다고 생각한다.
(D) 자신의 주제가 쉽게 이해될 것이라고 생각했다.

어휘 launch 개시하다, 시작하다 assume 추정하다 subject matter 주제

해설 Mr. Mehta는 후기에서 채용을 위해 10여 명의 지원자 면접을 봤다고 진술하는데(acting in my capacity as a recruiter, I interviewed a dozen promising candidates for a pivotal role at my organization.), 일정표에 나오는 안내에 따르면 심포지엄 기간 동안 인원 채용을 원하는 참가자는 고용주 신청서를 작성해야 한다(If you intend to recruit during the event, be sure to also fill out the Employer Application found under the "Career Center" tab). 두 지문의 내용을 연계하면 Mr. Mehta는 고용주 신청서를 제출했다고 추론할 수 있다.

Questions 196 through 200 refer to the following article, opinion letter, and e-mail.

CARMOSA (November 16) - Officials from Carmosa have begun preliminary discussions about the fate of Marigold Street Bridge, a historic landmark in dire need of upgrades. Though costly restoration options are under discussion, demolition appears increasingly likely due to several contributing factors.

"This isn't a decision we plan to make hastily," [197(C)]explained city planner Miles Pennington. "At this point, replacing the bridge seems to make the most financial sense."

Cost isn't the only concern. Structural engineer Carlos Menendez added that traffic flow is another major issue. [196]"Highway 38 is scheduled to be broadened from four lanes to six, and then the current bridge won't be able to accommodate the increase in traffic. The way I see it, a wider, more modern structure is inevitable."

[200]Residents interested in sharing their input can attend a public listening session at Benton Square next Wednesday at 6:30 P.M.

Letters to the Editor

[197(D)]November 17 - I'm writing to comment on yesterday's article about the Marigold Street Bridge. [197(A)]This bridge is an integral part of Carmosa's cultural identity and it is in the city's best interest to keep it intact. Given the tremendous amount of revenue our city earns each year from cultural heritage tourism, I would argue that the upfront expenses of repairing this historic landmark are justified in the long run.
- Ana Delgado, member of the Carmosa Conservancy (CC)

To: members@carmosaconservancy.org
From: diego_morales@carmosaconservancy.org
Date: November 29
Subject: Update on Marigold Street Bridge

Dear CC Members,

[199]Well done! Due to our strong showing at the recent city council event, [198]and after countless phone calls to city council representatives, it appears that demolition of Marigold Street Bridge is off the table! *The Benton Square Herald* reported today that the city will now relocate the structure to the Southridge Heritage District, where it will serve as a pedestrian-only bridge.

CARMOSA (11월 16일) – Carmosa 시 관계자들은 개선이 절실히 필요한 역사적 랜드마크 Marigold 가(街) 다리의 운명에 대해 예비 논의를 시작했다. 많은 비용이 드는 복원 옵션도 논의 중이기는 하지만, 여러 요인 때문에 철거가 점점 더 가능성이 높아 보인다.

도시계획가 Miles Pennington은 "이것은 서둘러 결정할 사안이 아닙니다."라고 설명했다. "현재로서는 교량을 교체하는 것이 재정적으로 가장 타당한 것으로 보입니다."

비용이 유일한 우려 사항은 아니다. 구조 공학자 Carlos Menendez는 교통의 흐름도 또 다른 주요 이슈라고 덧붙인다. "38번 고속도로가 4차선에서 6차선으로 확장될 예정인데, 그렇게 되면 현재의 다리는 교통량 증가를 수용하지 못할 겁니다. 제가 보기에는 더 넓고 더 현대적인 구조물이 불가피합니다."

의견을 나누고자 하는 주민들은 다음 주 수요일 저녁 6시 30분에 Benton 광장에서 열리는 공청회에 참석할 수 있다.

독자 투고

11월 17일 – Marigold 가(街) 다리에 대한 어제 기사에 대해 의견을 내고자 글을 씁니다. 이 다리는 Carmosa의 문화적 정체성에 필수적인 부분이며 온전하게 유지하는 것이 도시에 가장 이익이 됩니다. 우리 시가 매년 문화유산 관광으로 올리는 막대한 수익을 감안하여 이 역사적인 랜드마크를 수리하는 데 드는 초기 비용은 장기적으로 충분히 정당하다고 주장합니다.
– Carmosa 보존 협회(CC) 회원 Ana Delgado

수신: members@carmosaconservancy.org
발신: diego_morales@carmosaconservancy.org
날짜: 11월 29일
제목: Marigold 가(街) 다리에 대한 업데이트

CC 회원 여러분께,

정말 수고하셨습니다! 최근 시 의회 행사에서 우리가 보인 강력한 활약상 덕분에, 그리고 시 의회 대표들에게 셀 수 없이 많은 전화를 건 끝에, Marigold 가(街) 다리의 철거가 안건에서 제외된 것으로 보입니다! *The Benton Square Herald*는 오늘 시가 이제 이 구조물을 Southridge 문화유산 지구로 옮겨, 보행자 전용 교량으로 사용될 것이라고 보도했습니다.

[200]No doubt this outcome is thanks, in part, to the thoughtful voices you all shared at the gathering last Wednesday.

With gratitude,

Diego Morales
Civic Outreach Manager, Carmosa Conservancy

틀림없이 이러한 결과는 어느 정도 지난주 수요일 모임에서 여러분 모두가 내 주신 진심 어린 목소리 덕분입니다.

고마움을 담아,

Carmosa 보존 협회 시민 지원 매니저
Diego Morales

어휘1 official (고위) 공무원 preliminary 예비의, 사전의 fate 운명 in dire need of ~이 절실히 필요한 costly 값비싼, 많은 비용이 드는 restoration 복원 demolition 철거, 해체 increaingly 점점 더 likely 있을 법한, 가능성이 있는 contributing factor (원인이 되는) 요인, 요소 hastily 서둘러서, 급하게 make sense 타당하다, 말이 되다 the way I see it 내가 보기에는 structure 구조물, 건축물 inevitable 불가피한, 필연적인 input 의견 public listening 공청회

어휘2 comment on ~에 대해 의견을 말하다, 논평하다 integral 필수적인 identity 정체성 in one's best interest ~에게 가장 도움이 되는 intact 손상되지 않은, 온전한 given ~을 고려해 볼 때 tremendous 막대한, 엄청난 upfront 선불의 justified 정당한, 근거 있는 in the long run 장기적으로 conservancy 보존 협회, 보호 단체

어휘3 Well done! 수고하셨어요! showing 실력 발휘, 활약상 countless 무수한, 셀 수 없이 많은 representative 대의원 off the table (더이상, 이제는) 협의 대상이 아닌 relocate 이전하다, 옮기다 district 지구(地區), 지역 pedestrian 보행자 outcome 결과 in part 부분적으로는, 어느 정도는 thoughtful 사려 깊은, 진지하고 성의 있는 gratitude 감사, 고마움 civic 시민의 outreach (지역 주민에 대한) 봉사 활동, 원조 사업

196

In the article, what is indicated about the city of Carmosa?

(A) It plans to launch a tour program.
(B) It intends to boost municipal spending.
(C) It will begin widening a major highway.
(D) It is enforcing new traffic regulations.

기사에서 Carmosa 시에 관하여 무엇이 언급되어 있는가?

(A) 관광 프로그램을 시작할 계획이다.
(B) 시의 지출을 확대할 계획이다.
(C) 주요 고속도로 확장을 시작할 것이다.
(D) 새 교통 규정을 시행하고 있다.

어휘 boost 증대하다, 확대하다 municipal 지방자치체의, 시의 widen 폭을 넓히다 enforce (법, 규칙 등을) 시행하다 regulation 규정

해설 기사 세 번째 문단에서 현재 4차선인 38번 고속도로가 6차선으로 확장될 예정이라고 말하고 있다(Highway 38 is scheduled to be broadened from four lanes to six).

197

What is NOT suggested about Ms. Delgado?

(A) She values a historic landmark.
(B) She collaborated with Mr. Menendez.
(C) She holds a different view from Mr. Pennington.
(D) She read the article published on November 16.

Ms. Delgado에 관하여 나타나 있지 않은 사항은 무엇인가?

(A) 역사적 랜드마크를 가치 있게 여긴다.
(B) Mr. Menendez와 협력했다.
(C) Mr. Pennington과 다른 관점을 지니고 있다.
(D) 11월 16일에 게재된 기사를 읽었다.

어휘 value 중요하게 여기다

해설 사설에서 Ms. Delgado는 역사적 랜드마크인 Marigold 가(街) 다리가 시의 문화적 정체성의 필수적인 부분이라고 평가하면서(This bridge is an integral part of Carmosa's cultural identity) 이곳은 보존되어야 한다고 주장하고 있다(it is in the city's best interest to keep it intact). 이 문장을 읽으면서 (A)를 지우자. 그런데 기사를 읽어 보면 구조 공학자 Mr. Pennington은 이 다리를 교체하는 것, 즉 기존의 다리를 없애는 것이 타당한 결정이라고 말한다(replacing the bridge seems to make the most financial sense). 이로써 두 사람이 견해가 서로 대치된다는 것을 확인할 수 있으므로 여기서 (C)를 지우자. 사설은 11월 17일에 작성되었는데, Ms. Delgado는 '어제' 기사를 읽고 글을 쓴다고 말하고 있으므로(November 17 – I'm writing to comment on yesterday's article about the Marigold Street Bridge.), 11월 16일 기사를 읽었음을 알 수 있다. 여기서 (D)를 지우자.

198

In the e-mail, the word "countless" in paragraph 1, line 1, is closest in meaning to

(A) numerous
(B) unrecorded
(C) unimportant
(D) documented

이메일 첫 문단 첫 번째 줄의 단어 "countless"와 의미상 가장 가까운 것은

(A) 수많은
(B) 기록되지 않은
(C) 중요하지 않은
(D) 문서로 기록된

해설 단어의 뜻을 정확이 모르는 사람을 유추의 함정에 빠뜨리는 문제다. countless는 셀 수 없어서 기록할 수 없다(unrecorded)나 너무 적어서 중요하지 않다(unimportant)라는 뜻이 아니다. '셀 수 없이 많은, 무수한'이라는 뜻을 알아야 동의어를 선택할 수 있다.

199

Why does Mr. Morales congratulate CC members?

(A) They have elected new representatives.
(B) They have been featured in a recent news piece.
(C) They have helped influence a city council decision.
(D) They have secured additional funding from the municipality.

Mr. Morales은 왜 CC 회원들에게 축하 인사를 전하는가?

(A) 새 대의원들을 선출했다.
(B) 최근 뉴스 기사에서 특집으로 다루어졌다.
(C) 시 의회의 결정에 영향을 미치는 데 도움을 주었다.
(D) 시 자치 단체에서 추가 자금을 확보했다.

어휘 congratulate 축하 인사를 전하다 representative 대의원 feature 특집으로 다루다 funding 기금. 자금 municipality 지방 자치 단체

해설 이메일을 Well done!이라는 축하의 말로 시작하는데, 이유는 회원들이 시 의회 행사에서 활약하고, 시 의원들과 많은 통화를 한 덕분에, 즉 의회에 영향력을 행사한 덕분에 교량 철거 안건이 부결되었기 때문이다(Due to our strong showing at the recent city council event, and after countless phone calls to city council representatives, it appears that demolition of Marigold Street Bridge is off the table!). No doubt this outcome is thanks, in part, to the thoughtful voices you all shared at the gathering last Wednesday.

200

What can be inferred about CC members?

(A) They helped restore a local landmark.
(B) They gather weekly on Wednesdays.
(C) Some of them voiced opinions at Benton Square.
(D) Some of them reside in the Southridge heritage district.

CC 회원들에 관하여 무엇을 추론할 수 있는가?

(A) 지역의 랜드마크를 복원하도록 도왔다.
(B) 매주 수요일마다 모인다.
(C) 일부가 Benton 광장에서 의견을 냈다.
(D) 일부는 Southridge 문화유산 지구에 거주한다.

어휘 voice (의견을) 표명하다 reside 거주하다 heritage (문화)유산 district 지구(地區), 지역

해설 이메일 마지막 문장에서 회원들이 지난 수요일 모임에서 목소리를 냈다고 말하고 있는데(No doubt this outcome is thanks, in part, to the thoughtful voices you all shared at the gathering last Wednesday.), 기사 마지막 문단을 읽으면 이 모임이 Benton 광장에서 열린 공청회였음을 알 수 있다(Residents interested in sharing their input can attend a public listening session at Benton Square next Wednesday at 6:30 P.M.). 주민들이 의견을 내도록 기획된 공청회이므로, CC 회원들이 Benton 광장에서 열린 이 행사에서 많은 의견을 냈을 것이라고 추론할 수 있다.

TEST 03

➡ Answer

101	(B)	111	(C)	121	(C)	131	(A)	141	(A)	151	(B)	161	(D)	171	(C)	181	(D)	191	(C)
102	(A)	112	(A)	122	(B)	132	(D)	142	(C)	152	(D)	162	(A)	172	(D)	182	(C)	192	(C)
103	(D)	113	(B)	123	(C)	133	(B)	143	(A)	153	(B)	163	(B)	173	(C)	183	(A)	193	(B)
104	(B)	114	(D)	124	(C)	134	(C)	144	(C)	154	(A)	164	(C)	174	(A)	184	(D)	194	(D)
105	(D)	115	(B)	125	(D)	135	(C)	145	(D)	155	(D)	165	(C)	175	(D)	185	(C)	195	(A)
106	(A)	116	(A)	126	(C)	136	(D)	146	(D)	156	(B)	166	(A)	176	(D)	186	(C)	196	(B)
107	(B)	117	(D)	127	(D)	137	(B)	147	(D)	157	(A)	167	(B)	177	(A)	187	(D)	197	(C)
108	(B)	118	(B)	128	(B)	138	(A)	148	(C)	158	(D)	168	(A)	178	(D)	188	(A)	198	(D)
109	(A)	119	(C)	129	(D)	139	(B)	149	(D)	159	(C)	169	(A)	179	(B)	189	(B)	199	(C)
110	(C)	120	(A)	130	(A)	140	(A)	150	(B)	160	(B)	170	(C)	180	(B)	190	(D)	200	(A)

PART 5

101

Hawthorne's cleaning supplies are now available ------- in the nation.

(A) across
(B) everywhere
(C) throughout
(D) previously

Hawthorne 청소용품은 현재 전국 어디서나 이용하실 수 있습니다.

어휘 supplies 용품, 비품 previously 이전에

해설 (A)와 (C)는 전치사로서 목적어가 필요하므로 뒤에 in the nation 같은 전치사구가 나올 수 없다. 현재 이용할 수 있다고(are now available) 말하고 있으므로 (D) previously를 사용하는 것도 알맞지 않다.

102

Owen Pike is ------- the most competent person working in the R&D Department.

(A) considered
(B) appeared
(C) regarded
(D) agreed

Owen Pike는 연구 개발 부서에서 가장 유능한 사람으로 여겨진다.

어휘 competent 유능한, 실력 있는 R&D (research and development) (기업 등의) 연구 개발

해설 5형식 동사 (A) considered를 사용해야 수동태 동사 뒤에 목적격 보어로 명사가 나오는 구조(is considered the most competent person)가 될 수 있다. (C) regard는 같은 의미로 사용하려면 뒤에 전치사 as가 필요하다. 명사를 목적격 보어로 사용하는 동사 name, appoint, call, make 등이 수동태로 출제될 수 있다.

103

Amid the surge in construction activity, lumber prices are ------- to increase soon.

(A) covered
(B) sought
(C) limited
(D) bound

건설 활동이 급증하는 가운데 목재 가격은 곧 상승할 가능성이 크다.

어휘 amid ~하는 가운데, ~의 와중에 surge 급증 lumber 목재 cover (비용을) 대다 seek 찾다, 구하다 bound 꼭 ~할 것 같은, ~할 가능성이 큰

해설 be bound to-V(~할 가능성이 크다, 틀림없이 ~할 것이다)를 알고 있으면 빈칸 앞뒤 lumber prices are ------- to increase soon를 보면서 정답을 파악할 수 있다.

104

Most viewers considered the beach scene in Javier Ortega's latest movie genuinely -------.

(A) amusement
(B) amusing
(C) amused
(D) amuse

대부분의 관람객들은 Javier Ortega의 최신 영화에 나오는 해변 장면이 정말로 재미있다고 생각했다.

어휘 latest 최신의 genuinely 진심으로, 정말로

해설 consider, find, make, keep 동사는 형용사를 목적격 보어로 사용하는 5형식 동사로 자주 시험에 등장한다. 선택지에 형용사가 없으므로 형용사를 대신할 분사를 선택해야 한다. 현재분사 (B)와 과거분사 (C) 중 정답을 선택해야 하는데, 목적격 보어이므로 목적어와의 관계가 능동인지 수동인지 보면 된다. 즉, 해변 장면(the beach scene)이 '즐겁게 해주는' 것인지 '즐거움을 받는' 것인지 생각해야 한다. 해변 장면이 관람객들을 '즐겁게 해주는' 것이므로 능동의 의미가 있는 현재분사가 정답이다.

105

Wearing casual clothing is not regarded as ------- for those attending the Advertising Awards banquet.

(A) useful
(B) complete
(C) significant
(D) appropriate

평상복을 입는 것은 광고 대상 시상식 연회에 참석하는 사람들에게는 적절하다고 여겨지지 않는다.

어휘 regard A as B A를 B로 여기다 significant 중요한, 의미 있는 appropriate 적절한, 적합한 banquet 연회, 축하연

해설 시상식에 참석하는 사람에 캐주얼한 복장을 하는 것은 아무래도 '적절하지' 않다.

106

Kindly complete the feedback forms ------- conference organizers can enhance upcoming events.

(A) so that
(B) in order to
(C) because of
(D) as well as

학회 주최 측에서 앞으로 있을 행사를 개선할 수 있도록 피드백 서식을 작성해 주시기 바랍니다.

어휘 kindly (명령문에서) 제발, 부디 complete 기입하다, 작성하다 conference 회의, 학회 organizer 기획자, 주최자 enhance 개선하다 upcoming 다가오는, 곧 있을

해설 토익에서는 빈칸 위에 '주어 + can[may/will] + 동사'가 보이면 언제나 so (that)이 정답이라는 사실을 기억하고 빠르게 정답을 선택하자. (B) in order to 뒤에는 동사원형이 있어야 한다. (C) because of는 전치사이므로 뒤에 목적어가 나와야 한다. (D) as well as 뒤에는 '주어 + 동사'가 사용되지 않는다.

107

The supervisor shared information about employee productivity with ------- on quantifiable results.

(A) emphatic
(B) emphasis
(C) emphasize
(D) emphasized

관리자는 수량화할 수 있는 결과를 강조하며 직원 생산성에 대한 정보를 공유했다.

어휘 supervisor 관리자 productivity 생산성 quantifiable 수량화할 수 있는, 계량화할 수 있는

해설 빈칸 앞뒤 with ------- on만 보면 정답을 알 수 있다. 전치사 뒤에는 목적어가 있어야 하므로 명사가 정답이다.

108

Customers can enjoy this week's special by choosing any two menu items, ------- they like the most.

(A) both
(B) whichever
(C) enough
(D) anybody

고객들은 메뉴에서 어느 것을 가장 좋아하든 두 가지 품목을 선택함으로써 이 주의 특별 요리를 즐길 수 있다.

어휘 special (음식점의) 특별 요리

해설 '완성된 문장 + ------- + 주어 + 동사'의 구조가 보이면 앞에 있는 완성된 문장이 주절, 빈칸 이후로는 부사절이다. 빈칸에는 부사절 접속사가 들어가야 한다. whichever 같은 복합 관계대명사나 복합 관계부사가 부사절 접속사로 사용된다.

The unseasonably cold weather has ------- impacted the supply of produce at neighborhood grocery stores.

(A) adversely
(B) faithfully
(C) consciously
(D) accurately

계절에 맞지 않게 추운 날씨가 지역 내 식료품점들의 농산물 공급에 매우 부정적인 영향을 미쳤다.

어휘 unseasonably 계절에 맞지 않게 adversely 부정적으로, 불리하게 faithfully 충실하게, 성실하게 consciously 의식적으로 impact ~에 큰 영향을 미치다 supply 공급 produce 농산물 neighborhood 지역, 동네

해설 빈칸 앞뒤 cold weather has ------- impacted the supply of produce(추운 날씨가 농산물 공급에 매우 [(A) 부정적으로 (B) 충실하게 (C) 의식적으로 (D) 정확하게] 영향을 미쳤다)의 의미를 자연스럽게 만들어 주는 부사가 정답이다.

110

His approach to work is like -------, apart from the fact that he uses his own program to process data.

(A) me
(B) myself
(C) mine
(D) my

업무에 대한 그의 접근법은 데이터를 처리하기 위해 자기가 만든 프로그램을 사용한다는 사실만 제외하고 내 것과 같다.

어휘 approach 접근법, 방법 apart from ~을 제외하고는

해설 전치사 like의 목적어 자리에는 목적격 대명사뿐만 아니라 소유대명사나 재귀대명사도 들어갈 수 있으므로 문장 앞부분을 잘 읽어 보고 결정해야 한다. "그의 접근법은 나의 접근법과 같다."라는 문장이므로 빈칸에는 my approach를 대신할 소유대명사가 사용되는 것이 적절하다.

111

Among the applicants, Ms. Moreno stands out due to her proven track ------- in boosting sales performance.

(A) retort
(B) regard
(C) record
(D) report

지원자들 사이에서 Ms. Moreno가 매출 성과를 향상시킨 검증된 실적으로 인해 눈에 띈다.

어휘 applicant 지원자 stand out 두드러지다, 눈에 띄다 due to ~ 때문에 track record 실적, 성과 retort 되받아치는 말, 응수 regard 존중, 존경 boost 증대시키다 performance 성과, 실적

해설 어휘력이 생명이다. 빈칸 앞에 있는 track을 보는 순간 함께 사용하여 복합명사를 만들 수 있는 단어는 (C) record밖에 없다는 사실을 알아야 한다.

112

CEO Khoury has already ------- to increase Polyvox Systems' earnings by 20 percent within twelve months.

(A) promised
(B) promise
(C) promising
(D) promises

CEO Khoury는 12개월 이내에 Polyvox Systems의 수익을 20퍼센트 증가시키겠다고 이미 약속했다.

어휘 earnings 수입, 이익

해설 has already -------가 문장의 동사이다. has가 포함된 현재완료형이므로 빈칸에는 과거분사가 들어가야 한다.

Elarin Soapworks kicked off a marketing initiative to ------- interest in its latest line of cleaning products.

(A) consume
(B) generate
(C) endorse
(D) suppose

Elarin Soapworks는 최신 청소 제품군에 대한 관심을 불러일으키기 위한 마케팅 프로젝트를 시작했다.

어휘 kick off ~을 시작하다 initiative 계획, 프로젝트 generate 일으키다, 발생시키다 endorse 승인하다, 지지하다 suppose 생각하다, 간주하다 line 제품군

해설 빈칸 앞뒤 to ------- interest in (관심을 [(A) 소비하다 (B) 불러일으키다 (C) 승인하다 (D) 간주하다])의 의미를 자연스럽게 만들어 주는 동사가 정답이다.

114

The launch of Gearnova's marketing push will occur ------- the contract terms are completely settled.

(A) as well as
(B) other than
(C) rather than
(D) as soon as

Gearnova 사(社) 마케팅 캠페인의 개시는 계약 조건이 완전히 합의되자마자 이루어질 것이다.

어휘 launch 개시, 착수 push (사업에서) 추진, 활동, 캠페인 other than ~ 외에 rather than ~ 보다는, ~ 대신에 terms 조항, 조건 settle 확정하다, ~에 합의하다

해설 (A), (B), (C)는 모두 뒤에 '주어 + 동사' 구조가 올 수 없는 것들이다. 빈칸 뒤의 구조만 보고 빠른 속도로 부사절 접속사를 정답으로 선택하자.

115

The inspection of the office building revealed a few small flaws, but there was no sign of any ------- damage.

(A) structuring
(B) structural
(C) structurally
(D) structures

사무실 건물의 점검으로 몇몇 작은 결함이 드러나기는 했지만, 구조적 손상의 징후는 없었다.

어휘 inspection 검사, 점검 reveal 밝히다, 드러내다 flaw 결함 sign 조짐, 징후 structural 구조의, 구조적인 structure 구조; 구성하다, 조직하다

해설 빈칸 앞뒤 any ------- damage만 보면 정답을 알 수 있다. 명사 앞 빈칸에는 형용사가 정답이다. 선택지에 형용사가 보이지 않을 때는 분사를 고르자. 형용사와 분사가 모두 있을 때는 대부분 형용사가 정답이다.

116

We will have begun construction on our new facility in Bangkok ------- we complete the project in Abu Dhabi.

(A) by the time
(B) as soon as
(C) except when
(D) in the same way

Abu Dhabi 프로젝트를 완료할 때쯤이면 Bangkok의 새 시설 공사는 이미 시작되었을 것이다.

어휘 by the time ~할 때쯤에는 (이미)

해설 이 문제는 선택지가 서로 다른 시제의 동사들로 구성된 시제 문제이다. 'by + 미래 시점', 'as of + 미래 시점', 'by the time + 주어 + 현재 시제 동사' 같은 부사구나 부사절이 보이면 주절에는 미래완료 시제 동사가 들어가야 한다. 반대로 이 문장처럼 주절이 미래완료 시제라면 방금 열거한 세 가지 구조들을 만들어 주자.

117

At Kessler Automotive, Ms. Morgan ------- the team responsible for installing refurbished engines into vehicles.

(A) conducts
(B) explains
(C) invests
(D) oversees

Kessler Automotive에서 Ms. Morgan은 차량에 수리된 엔진 설치를 담당하는 팀을 감독한다.

어휘 oversee 감독하다 responsible for ~을 담당하는 install 설치하다 refurbish 재단장하다, 재정비하다 vehicle 차량

해설 빈칸 앞뒤 Ms. Morgan ------- the team responsible(Ms. Morgan은 ~을 담당하는 팀을 [(A) 실시한다 (B) 설명한다 (C) 투자한다 (D) 감독한다])의 의미를 자연스럽게 만들어 주는 동사가 정답이다.

118

How ------- a company receives, documents, and reacts to complaints has an impact on customer satisfaction.

(A) efficient
(B) efficiently
(C) efficiency
(D) efficiencies

기업이 불만 사항을 접수하고 기록하여 응대하는 일을 얼마나 효율적으로 하는지가 고객 만족도에 영향을 미친다.

어휘 document 기록하다 have an impact on ~에 영향을 미치다

해설 How ------- a company receives, documents, and reacts to complaints가 문장의 주어가 되는 명사절이고 3형식 문장 구조이다. 품사 문제에서 완성된 절에 빈칸이 보이면 부사가 정답이다.

119

Farmers market gatherings are scheduled every Wednesday from 11 A.M. to 3 P.M. ------- otherwise indicated.

(A) since
(B) neither
(C) unless
(D) toward

별다른 안내가 없는 한 농산물 직판장 행사는 매주 수요일 오전 11시부터 오후 3시로 예정되어 있다.

어휘 farmers market 농산물 직판장 gathering 모임 indicate 나타내다, 알리다

해설 항상 짝을 이루어 출제되는 어휘 문제는 암기하고 있다가 재빨리 정답을 선택할 수 있도록 하자. unless[if not] otherwise indicated[noted / specified / instructed / directed](별다른 명시[지시]가 없는 한)은 자주 문제로 출제되는 표현이며, 주로 unless[if not]이나 otherwise가 빈칸으로 주어진다.

120

A synthetic gemstone can look virtually ------- to a mined one to someone without specialized knowledge.

(A) identical
(B) positive
(C) suitable
(D) convenient

인조 보석은 전문 지식이 없는 사람에게는 채굴된 것과 거의 똑같아 보일 수 있다.

어휘 synthetic 합성의, 인조의 gemstone 보석, 준보석 virtually 거의, 사실상 identical 동일한, 똑같은 mine 채굴하다, 캐내다 specialized 전문의, 전문화된

해설 A synthetic gemstone can look virtually ------- to a mined one(인조 보석은 채굴된 것과 거의 [(A) 똑같아 (B) 긍정적으로 (C) 알맞아 (D) 편리해] 보인다)의 의미를 자연스럽게 만들어 주는 형용사가 정답이다.

121

Considering her strong credentials in international trade law, Ms. Kang was chosen over several other ------- applicants.

(A) promises
(B) to promise
(C) promising
(D) promised

국제 무역법 분야에서의 우수한 자격을 고려하여 Ms. Kang은 여러 유망한 지원자들을 제치고 선발되었다.

어휘 considering ~을 고려하여 credentials 자격, 업적 promising 장래가 촉망되는, 유망한

해설 빈칸 앞뒤 other ------- applicants만 보면, 명사 앞에 빈칸이 있으므로 형용사가 들어갈 자리라는 것을 알 수 있다. 선택지에 형용사가 없으므로 형용사를 대신하는 분사 (C)와 (D) 중 정답을 선택해야 하는데, 현재분사와 과거분사를 구별해야 하는 문제에서 항상 현재분사만 선택해야 하는 동사들을 암기해 두면 문제를 쉽게 해결할 수 있다. challenging, demanding, rewarding, missing, opposing, promising, outstanding, verifying, misleading

122

A ------- number of user-submitted tech support requests led Cindarelix Corporation to enhance its Web servers.

(A) sole
(B) significant
(C) purposeful
(D) capable

사용자들이 제출한 상당수의 기술 지원 요청서가 Cindarelix 사(社)로 하여금 웹 서버를 개선하게 했다.

어휘 sole 유일한, 단 하나뿐인 significant (수량이) 상당한 purposeful 목적이 뚜렷한

해설 항상 짝을 이루어 출제되는 어휘 문제는 암기하고 있다가 재빨리 정답을 선택하자. 토익 시험에서 40여 년 동안 빈칸 앞뒤가 A ------- number of로 구성되면 정답은 언제나 limited, large, great, good, significant, increasing, growing 중 하나였다.

123

Due to the chilly temperatures, Milo's Bicycle Rentals is expected to attract ------- riders over the next few months.

(A) neither
(B) every
(C) fewer
(D) higher

쌀쌀한 기온 때문에 Milo 자전거 대여소는 앞으로 몇 달 동안 이용객을 덜 끌어 모을 것으로 예상된다.

어휘 chilly (날씨가) 쌀쌀한 rental 임대, 대여 attract 끌어 모으다 rider (자전거, 오토바이 등을) 타는 사람

해설 (D) higher는 의미상 riders와 어울리지 않으므로 제외한다. (A)와 (B)는 모두 뒤에 단수 명사가 와야 한다. 복수 명사 앞에 쓸 수 있는 것은 (a) few(er)이다.

124

The article features a list of recommended cleansing products
------ professionals often use to treat delicate fabrics.

(A) who
(B) whose
(C) which
(D) of which

기사는 전문가들이 섬세한 직물을 다루기 위해 자주 사용하는 추천 세척 제품의 목록을 특집으로 다룬다.

어휘 feature 특집으로 다루다 cleanse 세척하다, 세정하다 delicate 섬세한, 연약한 fabric 직물

해설 빈칸 뒤에 타동사 use의 목적어가 없으므로 목적격 관계대명사가 정답이다.

125

Given the recent surge in electronics purchases, experts believe
that the device-to-user ------ will exceed previous forecasts.

(A) division
(B) fraction
(C) part
(D) ratio

전문가들은 최근 전자 제품 구입의 급증을 감안하면 기기 대 사용자 비율이 이전 예상치를 초과할 것으로 전망하고 있다.

어휘 given ~을 고려하면 surge 급증 believe 판단하다, 예상하다 division 분할, 분배 fraction 분수(分數) ratio 비(比), 비율 exceed 초과하다 forecast 예상, 예측

해설 빈칸 앞뒤 the device-to-user ------ will exceed previous forecasts(기기 대 사용자 [(A) 분할 (B) 분수 (C) 부분 (D) 비율]이 이전 예상치를 초과할 것이다)의 의미를 자연스럽게 만들어 주는 명사가 정답이다.

126

According to the manufacturer, glass that has special surface
treatments might not fuse ------ when combined with other
glass types.

(A) completion
(B) completing
(C) completely
(D) completes

제조업체에 따르면 특수 표면 처리가 된 유리는 다른 유형의 유리와 결합할 때 완전히 융합되지 않을 수 있다.

어휘 treatment (화학 약품 등의) 처리(법) fuse 융합되다, 하나로 합쳐지다 combine 결합하다

해설 빈칸 앞뒤 might not fuse ------ when combined with other glass types를 보면 동사 fuse가 1형식 자동사로 사용되었음을 알 수 있다. 빠른 문제 풀이를 위해 '1형식 자동사 + ------', '타동사 + 목적어 + ------' 같은 것들은 부사가 들어갈 자리라고 기억해 두자.

127

A new Maplewood Credit Union location will be established
downtown, just one mile ------ the institution's main office in
the finance hub.

(A) all around
(B) up until
(C) far ahead
(D) away from

Maplewood 신용 조합의 새 지점은 시내에 설립될 것인데, 금융 중심지에 있는 기관 본사에서 겨우 1마일 떨어진 곳이다.

어휘 credit union 신용 조합 location 지점, 사업장 all around ~의 사방에(서) up until (어떤 시점)까지 institution 기관 main office 본사, 본점 hub 중심(지)

해설 빈칸 앞뒤 just one mile ------ the institution's main office가 '기관 본사에서 겨우 1마일 떨어진 곳에 있는'이라는 의미가 되어야 자연스럽다.

------ of local businesses for recognition in the Neighborhood Choice Awards must be submitted to *The Crest Gazette* by November 12.

(A) Subscriptions (B) **Nominations**
(C) Supporters (D) Venues

Neighborhood Choice Awards 표창을 위한 지역 사업체의 후보 추천은 11월 12일까지 The Crest Gazette에 제출해야 한다.

> **어휘** nomination 후보 추천 venue 개최지, 장소 recognition 표창, 인정 Gazette ~ 신문(신문 이름)

> **해설** ------ of local businesses for recognition(표창을 위한 지역 사업체의 [(A) 구독 (B) 후보 추천 (C) 후원자 (D) 장소])의 의미를 자연스럽게 만들어 주는 명사를 정답으로 선택해야 한다.

129

Local authorities must ensure the municipal water system complies with ------ standards for water quality established by federal health agencies.

(A) close (B) dominant
(C) extended (D) **stringent**

지역 당국은 지자체의 상수도 시스템이 연방 보건 기구가 제정한 엄격한 수질 기준을 준수하도록 해야 한다.

> **어휘** authorities 당국, 당국자 municipal 지방 자치 단체의, 시[군/읍]의 comply with (법률, 규칙 등을) 준수하다, 따르다 dominant 지배적인, 우세한 stringent 엄격한, 엄중한 establish 확립하다, 제정하다 federal 연방 정부의, 연방의 agency (특히 정부의) 기관, ~국(局)

> **해설** 빈칸 앞뒤 complies with ------ standards for water quality([(A) 가까운 (B) 지배적인 (C) 연장된 (D) 엄격한] 수질 기준을 준수하다)의 의미를 자연스럽게 만들어 주는 형용사가 정답이다.

130

To mark its ten-year milestone, Sutter & Sons Dry Cleaners plans to ------ the occasion with employee celebrations and special customer promotions.

(A) **observe** (B) examine
(C) invite (D) contain

Sutter & Sons 세탁소는 설립 10주년을 축하하기 위해 임직원 축하 행사와 고객 특별 프로모션으로 이 날을 기념할 계획이다.

> **어휘** mark 기념하다, 축하하다 milestone 중대 시점[단계] observe (공휴일, 기념일 등을) 지내다, 기념하다 occasion (특정한) 경우, 때

> **해설** 빈칸 앞뒤 plans to ------ the occasion with employee celebrations(임직원 축하 행사로 이 날을 [(A) 기념할 (B) 살펴볼 (C) 초대할 (D) 담을] 계획이다)의 의미를 자연스럽게 만들어 주는 동사가 정답이다.

PART 6

Questions 131 through 134 refer to the following press release.

Douglas Buchanan, the founder and president of Buchanan's, the largest clothing retailer in Bristol, has announced that he [131]will donate £10,000 to support the city's newly built community center. The funds derived from ticket sales for a celebration hosted last night at his company's [132]store. Mr. Buchanan is scheduled to present a cheque to the center during its official opening ceremony tomorrow.

[133]Over the last two decades, Mr. Buchanan has organized numerous fund-raising events benefiting local charities and public services. [134]The party held yesterday turned out to be the most successful one to date.

131-134번 문제는 다음 보도 자료에 관한 것입니다.

Bristol 최대의 의류 소매업체 Buchanan's의 창업주이자 회장인 Douglas Buchanan이 시에 새로 지어진 지역 문화 회관을 후원하기 위해 10,000파운드를 기부하겠다고 발표했다. 자금은 어제 저녁에 자사 매장에서 주최된 축하 행사의 티켓 판매에서 나왔다. Mr. Buchanan은 내일 공식 개관식에서 회관에 수표를 증정할 예정이다.

지난 20년 동안 Mr. Buchanan은 지역의 자선 단체와 공공 서비스를 돕기 위한 수많은 기금 마련 행사를 주최해 왔다. 어제 열린 파티는 지금까지 했던 것 중 가장 성공적인 것으로 평가받았다.

> **어휘** founder 창립자, 창업자 retailer 소매상 community center 지역 문화 회관 derive from ~에서 나오다, 유래하다 host 개최하다, 주최하다 present 수여하다, 증정하다 cheque(= check) 수표 organize 조직하다, 주최하다 fund-raising 기금 모금[조성] benefit 이익이 되다, 도움을 주다 charity 자선(사업) turn out ~으로 밝혀지다, 판명되다 to date 현재까지, 지금까지

131-134

131 **(A) will donate**
(B) donated
(C) might donate
(D) donating

132 (A) museum
(B) hotel
(C) factory
(D) store

133 (A) Despite
(B) Over
(C) Among
(D) Beneath

134 (A) The ceremony to mark the opening is set to start at 10:00 A.M.
(B) The center provides educational programs for both adults and children.
(C) The party held yesterday turned out to be the most successful one to date.
(D) Mr. Buchanan intends to launch a new branch in Sheffield in the upcoming year.

131 > **해설** 빈칸에 that절의 동사가 들어가야 하므로 준동사인 (D)는 제외한다. 문맥을 고려하여 시제를 선택해야 한다. 이어지는 내용을 읽어 보면 내일 지역 문화 회관에 수표를 증정할 것이라고 진술이 나오므로(Mr. Buchanan is scheduled to present a cheque to the center during its official opening ceremony tomorrow.) 미래 시제가 정답이다.

132 > **해설** 앞에 나오는 내용을 읽어 보면 Buchanan's는 의류 소매업체(clothing retailer)이므로 자사가 소유하고 있으면서 축하 파티를 열기에 알맞은 장소는 매장이다.

133 > **해설** 항상 짝을 이루어 출제되는 어휘 문제는 암기하고 있다가 재빨리 정답을 선택하자. 'Over[For / In] the last[past / next / following] + 기간'은 시험에 매우 자주 등장하는 어구로서 전치사와 형용사가 모두 빈칸으로 출제될 수 있다. 빈칸 앞뒤를 보자마자 정답을 고를 수 있도록 반드시 암기해 두자.

134 (A) 개관을 기념하는 행사가 오전 10시에 시작될 예정이다.
(B) 그 회관은 성인과 어린이 모두를 위한 교육 프로그램을 제공한다.
(C) 어제 열린 파티는 지금까지 했던 것 중 가장 성공적인 것으로 평가받았다.
(D) Mr. Buchanan은 내년에 Sheffield에 새 지사를 차릴 생각이다.

> **어휘** mark 기념하다, 축하하다 be set to-V ~할 예정이다 launch 개시하다, 시작하다

> **해설** 앞 문장에서 그동안 많은 기금 마련 행사를 열어 왔다는 말을 하고 있으므로(Mr. Buchanan has organized numerous fund-raising events) 이어지는 문장은 이러한 행사에 관련된 내용이어야 문맥이 자연스럽다.

KTRX Radio Turns 50!

On December 2, KTRX Radio will mark its 50th year on the air. That's half a century of stimulating [135]programming. Throughout the years, we [136]have offered our audience up-to-the-minute news, thought-provoking features, and hit music from across the globe. We're now inviting you to join the celebration at our open house, from 5:00 to 6:30 P.M. on December 2 at our studio on Seventh Street. Come explore our space and witness the behind-the-scenes magic. See how our digital audio technology works in action. [137]You'll also get the chance to meet some of the hosts you love. Admission is free, but advance registration is necessary. We look forward to seeing you at this [138]special event.

135–138번 문제는 다음 안내문에 관한 것입니다.

KTRX 라디오가 50살이 됩니다!

12월 2일에 KTRX 라디오가 방송 50주년을 기념합니다. 반세기 동안의 흥미진진한 프로그램 편성이었습니다. 50년 내내 저희는 청취자 여러분께 가장 최신의 뉴스와 깊이 있는 특집 프로그램, 전 세계 히트 음악을 제공해 왔습니다. 이제 공개 참관 행사에 오셔서 축하 행사에 함께해 주시기를 청합니다. 행사는 12월 2일 저녁 5시부터 6시 30분까지 7번가에 있는 저희 스튜디오에서 진행됩니다. 저희의 현장을 둘러보시면서 무대 뒤에서 벌어지는 마법을 직접 경험해 보세요. 디지털 오디오 기술이 어떻게 작동하는지 확인해 보세요. 여러분이 사랑하시는 진행자 몇 명을 만나 볼 기회도 갖게 됩니다. 입장은 무료이지만, 사전 등록은 필수입니다. 이번 특별 행사에서 만나 뵙기를 고대합니다.

어휘 turn (어떤 나이가) 되다 on the air 방송 중인 stimulating 흥미를 불러일으키는 programming 프로그램 편성 up-to-the-minute 가장 최신의 thought-provoking 깊이 생각하게 하는, 시사하는 바가 큰 feature 특집 (프로그램) open house 오픈 하우스, 공개 참관 행사 explore 답사하다, 둘러보다 witness (사건, 변화를) 경험하다, 보다 behind-the-scenes 무대 뒤에서(의) in action 활동하는, 작동하는 host 사회자, 진행자 admission 입장 advance 사전(事前)의

135-138

135 (A) concerts
(B) discussions
(C) programming
(D) development

136 (A) offers
(B) offering
(C) will offer
(D) have offered

137 (A) We're preparing to merge with a nearby station in the coming year.
(B) You'll also get the chance to meet some of the hosts you love.
(C) This open house kicks off our line-up of December events.
(D) Our station remains an vital voice in your local community.

138 **(A) special**
(B) specialize
(C) especially
(D) specialization

135 **해설** 바로 이어지는 문장에서 그동안 뉴스, 특집 방송, 음악 등 다양한 프로그램을 송출해 왔다고 말하고 있으므로(we have offered our audience up-to-the-minute news, thought-provoking features, and hit music from across the globe.) 이것을 표현하기에 적절한 말은 '반세기 동안의 흥미진진한 프로그램 편성(half a century of stimulating programming)'이다.

136 **해설** 주어가 we이므로 단수 동사인 (A)는 사용할 수 없고, 동사가 필요하므로 준동사인 (B)도 빈칸에 들어갈 수 없다. (C)와 (D) 중 알맞은 시제의 동사를 선택해야 하는데, 문맥상 Throughout the years는 지난 50년을 의미하므로 현재완료 시제가 알맞다.

137 (A) 저희는 내년에 인근 방송국과 합병할 준비를 하고 있습니다.
(B) 여러분이 사랑하시는 진행자 몇 명을 만나 볼 기회도 갖게 됩니다.
(C) 이번 공개 참관 행사로 12월 행사 일정이 시작됩니다.
(D) 저희 방송국은 지역 사회에서 여전히 중요한 목소리를 내고 있습니다.

어휘 merge 합병하다 nearby 근처의 kick off ~을 시작하다 line-up (행사) 목록, 일정 vital 매우 중요한, 없어서는 안 될

해설 앞에 있는 두 문장에서 공개 참관 행사에서 볼 수 있는 것들을 나열하고 있으므로(the behind-the-scenes magic, digital audio technology), 이어지는 문장에서도 행사에서 만나 볼 수 있는 라디오 진행자들을 언급하는 것이 적절하다.

138 **해설** 빈칸 앞뒤 this ------- event만 보면 정답을 알 수 있다. 명사 앞에 빈칸이 있으므로 형용사를 선택해야 한다.

Questions 139 through 142 refer to the following article.

139–142번 문제는 다음 기사에 관한 것입니다.

March 18 – The Edington City Council has officially signed off on a development agreement with TRAX Developments. As part of the deal, TRAX [139]will develop the 4.5-acre lot located on Hollister Street. The plan calls for the construction of both office buildings and retail outlets. Mayor Gavin Dresner expressed his support for the [140]economic benefits the project is expected to bring to the community. "We anticipate that 450 permanent full-time jobs will be created as a result," he stated. "It's a relief to see the project finally move forward after numerous delays." [141]Although the city is anxious for construction to get underway, setbacks are common in large-scale commercial endeavors like this one. According to TRAX spokesperson Molly Kearney, the development is projected to take two years, though she warned that unexpected delays could still arise. "We've submitted our best [142]estimate to the council," she noted, "but it's not possible to foresee all issues that may emerge."

3월 18일 – Edington 시 의회가 TRAX Developments와의 개발 협정을 공식 승인했다. 합의의 일환으로 TRAX는 Hollister 가(街)에 있는 4.5에이커 규모의 부지를 개발할 것이다. 계획에는 사무용 건물과 소매상점 모두의 건설이 포함된다. 시장 Gavin Dresner는 이 프로젝트가 지역 사회에 가져다 줄 것으로 예상되는 경제적 혜택에 대해 지지를 표명했다. 그는 "우리는 결과적으로 450개의 상근 정규직 일자리가 창출될 것으로 내다보고 있습니다."라고 말했다. "여러 번 지연된 끝에 마침내 프로젝트가 진행되는 것을 보게 되어 안심입니다." 시에서는 공사가 시작되기를 몹시 바라고 있지만, 이것과 같은 대규모 상업 개발 사업에서 차질이 생기는 것이 흔한 일이다. TRAX 대변인 Molly Kearney는 개발 공사에 2년이 걸릴 것으로 예상된다고 말했지만, 예기치 못한 지연이 여전히 발생할 수 있다고 미리 일러두기도 했다. 그녀는 "저희가 최선의 추정치를 의회에 제출하기는 했습니다만, 발생할 수 있는 모든 문제를 예상한다는 것은 가능하지 않습니다."라고 말했다.

어휘 sign off on (서명으로) ~을 승인하다 agreement 협정, 계약 deal 계약, 합의 acre 에이커 (토지 면적 단위) lot (특정 용도의) 부지, 터 call for (공적으로) ~을 포함하다, 예정하다 retail outlet 소매점 benefit 이득, 혜택 as a result 결과적으로 relief 안도, 안심 be anxious for ~을 몹시 바라다 get underway 시작되다 setback 차질 large-scale 대규모의 endeavor (특정 목적의 지속적) 활동, 사업 spokesperson 대변인 project 예상하다, 예측하다 warn (걱정하거나 놀라지 않게) 일러두다 arise 발생하다, 일어나다 estimate 추정(치), 추산(치) note 언급하다 foresee 예견하다, 예상하다 emerge 생겨나다, 발생하다

139-142

139 (A) to develop
(B) will develop
(C) has developed
(D) could have developed

140 (A) economic
(B) unforeseen
(C) volunteer
(D) frequent

141 (A) Although the city is anxious for construction to get underway, setbacks are common in large-scale commercial endeavors like this one.
(B) Local residents and businesses have voiced legitimate worries regarding potential noise from the building process.
(C) Even though officials had pledged a long-term deal, they might now need to reevaluate that commitment.
(D) The city council is scheduled to review and vote on three architectural design options.

142 (A) argument
(B) background
(C) estimate
(D) combination

139 **해설** 문장에 동사가 필요하므로 준동사인 (A)는 제외하자. 알맞은 시제의 동사를 선택해야 하는데, 앞 문장에서 개발 협정이 승인되었다고 진술하고 있으므로(The Edington City Council has officially signed off on a development agreement with TRAX Developments.), 개발 공사는 앞으로 있을 일이므로 미래 시제가 알맞다.

140 **해설** 뒤에 이어지는 인용문에서 일자리 창출을 언급하고 있으므로(We anticipate that 450 permanent full-time jobs will be created as a result), 시장이 환영하는 것은 프로젝트가 지역 사회에 가져다 줄 경제적 혜택(economic benefits)이다.

141 (A) 시에서는 공사가 시작되기를 몹시 바라고 있지만, 이것과 같은 대규모 상업 프로젝트에서 차질이 생기는 것이 흔한 일이다.
(B) 지역 주민들과 사업체들은 건축 과정에서 나올 수 있는 소음에 대해 타당한 우려를 표명했다.
(C) 공무원들은 장기 계약을 약속했지만 이제는 그 약속을 재평가해야 할지도 모른다.
(D) 시 의회는 세 개의 건축 설계 옵션을 검토하고 투표할 예정이다.

➡️**해설** 앞 문장에서는 여러 번의 지연이 있은 후에야(after numerous delays) 프로젝트가 진행되고 있음을 알려주고 있고, 빈칸 뒤에 이어지는 문장에서도 앞으로도 예상치 못한 지연이 있을 수 있다고 말하고 있다(unexpected delays could still arise). 중간에 들어가는 문장에서도 지연과 관련된 진술이어야 문맥이 자연스럽다.

142 ➡️**어휘** argument 주장 background 배경, 소양, 이력

➡️**해설** 빈칸 뒤 but 이후의 문장이 어떤 문제가 생겨서 다시 공사가 지연될지 알 수 없다는 내용이므로(but it's not possible to foresee all issues that may emerge), 문맥상 빈칸은 앞 문장에서 말하는 개발에 걸리는 2년(two years)을 가리킨다. 이것을 대신할 수 있는 단어는 '추산치'이다.

📰 **Questions 143 through 146** refer to the following e-mail.

143-146번 문제는 다음 이메일에 관한 것입니다.

To: All Staff <staff@orpheusdesign.com>
From: Rosemary Kim <r_kim@orpheusdesign.com>
Date: April 13
Subject: Team Changes

Dear Team,

As shared last month, Roberto Galvani, who has been our art director for an impressive seventeen years, will soon move to Asia. [143]Once there, he will embark on the next phase of his professional journey as an executive director at a Korean marketing agency. After conducting an extensive search for his successor, I am delighted to announce [144]that our very own Selena Pappas will step into the role of art director. [145]We are optimistic that the transition will proceed seamlessly. Ms. Pappas has been a valued member of the Orpheus team for ten years, collaborating closely with Mr. Galvani during that time. She will officially assume her new position next week while continuing to work alongside Mr. Galvani until his departure in May. Please take a moment to visit Ms. Pappas's office to [146]congratulate her.

Warm regards,

Rosemary Kim
Executive Vice President, Orpheus Design Associates

수신: 전직원 〈staff@orpheusdesign.com〉
발신: Rosemary Kim 〈r_kim@orpheusdesign.com〉
날짜: 4월 13일
제목: 팀 변동

팀원 여러분께,

지난달에 공유한 바와 같이 무려 17년 동안 우리의 아트 디렉터였던 Roberto Galvani가 곧 아시아로 옮겨 갑니다. 그곳에 가서 그는 한국의 마케팅 대행사의 전무 이사로서 경력의 다음 단계를 시작할 것입니다. 후임자를 찾기 위해 광범위한 검토를 실시한 끝에 우리 회사의 Selena Pappas가 아트 디렉터 자리를 맡게 되었음을 발표하게 되어 기쁩니다. 우리는 이번 인수인계가 매끄럽게 진행될 것임을 낙관합니다. Ms. Pappas는 10년 동안 Orpheus 팀의 중요한 일원이었으며, 그 기간 동안 Mr. Galvani와 긴밀히 협력해 왔습니다. 그녀는 다음 주에 공식적으로 새 직책을 맡게 되며 5월에 Mr. Galvani가 떠날 때까지 계속해서 함께 일할 예정입니다. 잠시 시간을 내어 Ms. Pappas의 사무실을 방문하셔서 축하 인사를 건네시기 바랍니다.

따뜻한 마음을 전합니다.

Rosemary Kim
Orpheus Design Associates 수석 부사장

143 (A) Once there
(B) Instead
(C) Nevertheless
(D) For example

144 (A) it
(B) as
(C) that
(D) even

145 (A) The process to recruit someone for her prior role has begun.
(B) Orpheus boasts one of the most imaginative teams in the industry.
(C) At the same time, Mr. Galvani has been working on improving his Korean skills.
(D) We are optimistic that the transition will proceed seamlessly.

146 (A) invite
(B) notify
(C) interview
(D) congratulate

143 해설 아시아로 떠나는 것과(will soon move to Asia) 새로운 여정을 시작하는 것은(he will embark on the next phase of his professional journey) 순차적으로 일어나는 일이므로, 두 문장을 이어주는 부사로는 (A) Once there가 알맞다.

144 해설 빈칸 뒤에 있는 절이 동사 announce의 목적어이므로 명사절이다. 빈칸에는 명사절 접속사가 들어가야 한다.

145 (A) 그녀의 이전 직책을 맡을 사람을 채용하는 절차가 시작되었습니다.
(B) Orpheus는 업계에서 가장 창의적인 팀 중 하나임을 자랑합니다.
(C) 동시에 Mr. Galvani는 한국어 능력을 향상시키기 위해 힘써 왔습니다.
(D) 우리는 이번 인수인계가 매끄럽게 진행될 것임을 낙관합니다.

어휘 prior 이전의 boast 자랑하다 imaginative 창의적인 at the same time 동시에

해설 앞 문장에서는 Selena Pappas가 후임자로 낙점되었다고 말하면서(our very own Selena Pappas will step into the role of art director.) 빈칸 뒤에는 Ms. Pappas가 오랫동안 Mr. Galvani와 긴밀한 협력 관계에 있었음을 언급하고 있으므로(collaborating closely with Mr. Galvani during that time), 빈칸에는 담당자의 전환 과정이 원활할 것이라는 내용이 알맞다.

146 해설 새 아트 디렉터로 임명된 Ms. Pappas의 사무실을 방문해서 하기에 가장 적절한 행동은 축하 인사를 건네는 것이다.

Questions 147 through 148 refer to the following invoice.

147-148번 문제는 다음 청구서에 관한 것입니다.

DreamNest Textiles Co., Ltd.
102-3, Textile Industrial Complex
Hwaseong-si, Gyeonggi-do, 18469
Phone: +82-31-555-7890
E-mail: export@dreamnest.co.kr

Sold To:
Northern Comfort Imports Ltd.
215 Mapleview Drive East
Barrie, Ontario, L4N 0W5

Ship To:
8800 Logistics Parkway
Mississauga, Ontario, L5S 1Y9

Invoice No.: INV-2025-0412
Invoice Date: April 12, 2025
Mode of Shipment:
Sea Freight

Order Date: April 10, 2025
Export Date: April 15, 2025
147Estimated Delivery Date:
May 5, 2025

Item No.	Description	Quantity	Unit Price (USD)	Total Price (USD)
DN-BL001	Premium Cotton Bed Linen Set (Queen)	500 sets	$45.00	$22,500.00
DN-CV002	Microfiber Comforter (King)	300 pcs	$60.00	$18,000.00
International Shipping Invoice			148Subtotal	$40,500.00
			148Freight Charges	$2,000.00
			148Total Amount Due	$42,500.00

DreamNest Textiles Co., Ltd.
102-3, 섬유 산업 단지
Hwaseong-si, Gyeonggi-do, 18469
전화: +82-31-555-7890
이메일: export@dreamnest.co.kr

구매자:
Northern Comfort Imports Ltd.
215 Mapleview Drive East
Barrie, Ontario, L4N 0W5

배송지:
8800 Logistics Parkway
Mississauga, Ontario, L5S 1Y9

청구서 번호:
INV-2025-0412
청구서 작성일:
2025년 4월 12일
운송 방식:
해상 화물

주문 날짜:
2025년 4월 10일
수출 날짜:
2025년 4월 15일
예상 도착일:
2025년 5월 5일

제품 번호	품목	수량	단가 (USD)	총액 (USD)
DN-BL001	프리미엄 코튼 침구 세트(퀸)	500 세트	45.00달러	22,500.00달러
DN-CV002	극세사 이불(킹)	300개	60.00달러	18,000.00달러
국제 배송 청구서			소계	40,500.00달러
			화물 운임	2,000.00달러
			지불 총액	42,500.00달러

어휘 textiles 섬유 산업 industrial complex 산업 단지 ship 운송하다, 배송하다 invoice 청구서, 명세서 mode 방식, 방법 shipment 운송, 배송(품) freight 화물 description 품목, 항목 설명 quantity 양, 수량 unit (완성 제품의) 한 개 premium 고급의 bed linen 리넨 침구 세트 microfiber 극세사 comforter 깃털 이불 subtotal 소계(小計) due 지불해야 하는

147

When is the purchase scheduled to arrive?

(A) On April 10
(B) On April 12
(C) On April 15
(D) On May 5

구입품은 언제 도착할 예정인가?

(A) 4월 10일
(B) 4월 12일
(C) 4월 15일
(D) 5월 5일

해설 송장에 예상 도착 날짜가 5월 5일이라고 나와 있다(Estimated Delivery Date: May 5, 2025).

148

What is indicated on the invoice?

(A) The order was placed through a Web site.
(B) Payment will be due upon receiving the goods.
(C) Shipping costs are included in the total amount.
(D) The shipment is being sent to multiple locations.

청구서에는 무엇이 나타나 있는가?

(A) 주문은 웹 사이트를 통해 이루어졌다.
(B) 대금은 상품을 받자마자 지불할 것이다.
(C) 운송료는 총액에 포함되어 있다.
(D) 배송품을 여러 장소로 보낼 것이다.

어휘 place an order 주문하다 upon ~하자마자 shipping costs 운송료, 배송비 multiple 여럿의, 다수의

해설 소계(subtotal) 40,500달러와 화물 운임(freight charges) 2,000달러를 합한 총액(total amount due)이 42,500달러이다.

Questions 149 through 150 refer to the following e-mail.

To: Administrative Staff
From: Kenta Fujimoto
Date: February 16
Subject: Employee Data

As mentioned in the company-wide announcement sent out yesterday, the system used to store employee information has recently been upgraded. [149]All staff members are required to send their most up-to-date résumé to empinfo@takora.com. Additionally, administrative personnel will soon be asked to complete a mandatory questionnaire seeking details about their technical abilities, including:

• Typing speed measured in words per minute
• Proficiency with software tools, such as spreadsheets, word processors, and database systems

[150]If you're unsure of your typing speed and would like to take a timed assessment, please reach out to Lena Vogel at extension 822.

Sincerely,

Kenta Fujimoto
Administrative Manager
Takora Imports Ltd.

149-150번 문제는 다음 이메일에 관한 것입니다.

수신: 총무부 직원들
발신: Kenta Fujimoto
날짜: 2월 16일
제목: 직원 데이터

어제 회사 전체에 발송된 공지에 나와 있다시피, 직원 정보를 보관하는 데 사용하는 시스템이 최근에 업그레이드되었습니다. 모든 직원들은 최신 이력서를 empinfo@takora.com로 보내야 합니다. 또한 총무부 직원 여러분에게는 다음과 같은 기술 능력에 대한 세부 정보를 파악하는 필수 설문지를 작성하라는 요청이 곧 있을 예정입니다.

• 분당 단어 수로 측정된 타이핑 속도
• 스프레드시트, 워드프로세서, 데이터베이스 시스템 등 소프트웨어 도구 사용 능력

자신의 타이핑 속도가 확실하지 않아서 시간을 재며 평가받고 싶다면 내선 822번으로 Lena Vogel에게 연락하시기 바랍니다.

진심을 담아,

Takora Imports Ltd.
총무부장
Kenta Fujimoto

어휘 administrative 관리의, 행정의, 총무의 company-wide 전사적인 send out ~을 발송하다 up-to-date 최신의 personnel 직원 complete 작성하다, 기입하다 mandatory 의무적인, 필수적인 questionnaire 설문지 seek 얻으려고 하다 measure 측정하다, 재다 proficiency 능숙, 사용 능력 timed 시한의, 시간이 정해진 assessment 평가 extension 내선

149

What is one purpose of the e-mail?

(A) To explain the reorganization of a department
(B) To introduce recently hired staff members
(C) To inform staff about technical training sessions
(D) To notify employees of new requirements

이메일의 목적 중 하나는 무엇인가?

(A) 부서 재편성에 대해 설명하는 것
(B) 최근에 채용된 직원들을 소개하는 것
(C) 직원들에게 기술 교육에 대해 알리는 것
(D) 직원들에게 새 요구 사항에 대해 알리는 것

어휘 reorganization 재조직, 재편성 notify 알리다

해설 이메일의 목적은 회사에 이력서를 제출해야 한다는 요구 사항과(All staff members are required to send their most up-to-date résumé to empinfo@takora.com.) 설문지 작성 요청이 있을 예정임을 알리는 것이다(Additionally, administrative personnel will soon be asked to complete a mandatory questionnaire).

150

According to the e-mail, why might an employee need to get in touch with Ms. Vogel?

(A) To report technical issues
(B) To request a skill evaluation
(C) To inquire about available positions
(D) To schedule a meeting with a senior manager

이메일에 따르면 직원은 왜 Ms. Vogel과 연락해야 하겠는가?

(A) 기술적인 문제를 보고하기 위해
(B) 능력 평가를 요청하기 위해
(C) 채용 중인 직책에 대해 문의하기 위해
(D) 고위 관리자와의 회의 일정을 잡기 위해

어휘 get in touch with ~와 연락하다 evaluation 평가

해설 타이핑 속도를 평가받고 싶은 직원이 Ms. Vogel에게 연락해야 한다(If you're unsure of your typing speed and would like to take a timed assessment, please reach out to Lena Vogel at extension 822).

Norwyn Pharmaceuticals

[151]Norwyn Pharmaceuticals covers travel expenses when staff members are on official business trips. Employees are required to submit lodging requests to the Corporate Travel Department via the company's online travel portal. The form must list the employee's full name, the hotel name and contact information, the check-in and check-out dates, and the purpose for travel.

[152]Once the reservation is finalized and paid for by the Corporate Travel Department, a confirmation number will be issued for the employee to present upon check-in. Although room charges are paid in advance, employees are expected to put any incidental expenses incurred during the trip on their own personal credit card. Employees can submit a reimbursement request for any out-of-pocket expenses after returning from the trip.

151–152번 문제는 다음 방침에 관한 것입니다.

Norwyn 제약

Norwyn 제약은 직원이 공식 출장 중일 때 출장비를 를 부담한다. 직원은 회사 온라인 출장 포털을 통해 출장 지원팀에 숙박 신청서를 제출해야 한다. 서식에 는 직원 성명, 호텔 이름과 연락처, 체크인 및 체크아 웃 날짜, 출장 목적이 기재되어야 한다.

출장 지원팀에서 예약을 확정하고 비용을 지불하면, 직원에게 체크인 시 제시해야 하는 확인 번호가 발급 된다. 객실 요금은 사전에 지불되지만, 출장 중 발생 하는 부수 경비는 직원이 개인 신용 카드로 결제해야 한다. 직원은 출장에서 돌아온 후 자기 부담 경비에 대한 환급 요청서를 제출할 수 있다.

어휘 pharmaceuticals 제약 회사　cover (비용을) 부담하다　be required to-V ~하는 것이 요구되다, ~해야 한다　lodging 숙박　corporate 기업의, 회사의　via ~을 통해서　list (목록에) 올리다, 기재하다　contact information 연락처　finalize 확정하다　issue 발급하다　present 제시하다, 보여주다　in advance 미리　put *sth* on one's credit card ~을 신용 카드로 결제하다　incidental 부수적인　incur 초래하다, 발생시키다　reimbursement 상환, 환급　out-of-pocket 자기 부담의

151

What is the policy about?

(A) Registering for an employee benefits program
(B) Making arrangements for corporate travel
(C) Applying for a different job assignment
(D) Arranging accommodations for company clients

방침은 무엇에 관한 것인가?

(A) 직원 복리 후생 프로그램에 등록하기
(B) 출장 준비하기
(C) 다른 업무에 지원하기
(D) 회사 고객을 위한 숙박 시설 마련하기

어휘 benefits 복리 후생　make arrangements for ~을 준비하다, 마련하다　accommodations 숙박 시설

해설 첫 문단을 읽어 보면 회사가 출장비를 부담하기 위해(Norwyn Pharmaceuticals covers travel expenses) 숙박 신청서를 제출해야 한다는 사실을 말하 고 있고(Employees are required to submit lodging requests) 신청서에 기재해야 하는 내용이 나열되어 있다(The form must list the ...). 지문이 설명 하는 것은 출장을 준비하는 방법이다.

152

Why must employees have a confirmation number?

(A) To replace a credit card
(B) To qualify for a reduced rate
(C) To eliminate unexpected costs
(D) To validate the hotel arrangement

직원은 왜 확인 번호가 있어야 하는가?

(A) 신용 카드를 교체하기 위해
(B) 할인 요금의 자격을 얻기 위해
(C) 예상치 못한 비용을 없애기 위해
(D) 호텔 예약을 입증하기 위해

어휘 confirmation 확인　qualify for ~을 얻을 자격이 있다　rate 요금　eliminate 제거하다, 없애다　validate 증명하다, 입증하다

해설 회사 출장 지원팀이 예약을 확정하고 숙박비를 지불하고 나면 직원에게 확인 번호가 지급되는데, 직원은 이 번호를 호텔에 제시하여 예약 투숙객임을 입증해야 한다(Once the reservation is finalized and paid for by the Corporate Travel Department, a confirmation number will be issued for the employee to present upon check–in).

Questions 153 through 154 refer to the following text-message chain.

Matthew Clark 11:12 A.M.
Hey Clara, would you be able to cover my 2 P.M. shift today? [153]I'm supposed to be at the concession stand.

Clara Weiss 11:13 A.M.
Sure, no problem. Are you sick or something?

Matthew Clark 11:16 A.M.
I'm okay. I was driving back from Philadelphia, but my car broke down a few hours ago. I'm at a garage now. Thanks for covering for me! I'll happily repay the favor.

Clara Weiss 11:19 A.M.
That's unfortunate about your car! By the way, [153 154]could you take over my evening shift at the box office next Friday? I'm expecting a friend from L.A. then.

Matthew Clark 11:20 A.M.
Absolutely, [154]I'd love to help. Let's catch up later.

153–154번 문제는 다음 문자 메시지 대화에 관한 것입니다. .

Matthew Clark 오전 11:12
Clara, 오늘 오후 2시 근무를 대신해 줄 수 있겠어요? 구내매점 근무를 해야 해서요.

Clara Weiss 오전 11:13
물론이죠, 문제없어요. 어디 아파요?

Matthew Clark 오전 11:16
몸은 괜찮아요. Philadelphia에서 차로 돌아오는 길이었는데, 몇 시간 전에 차가 고장 나 버렸어요. 지금 정비소예요. 대신 근무해 줘서 고마워요. 이번 일 꼭 갚을게요.

Clara Weiss 오전 11:19
차 문제는 안타깝네요! 그나저나 다음 주 금요일에 매표소에서 제 저녁 근무를 대신 맡아 줄 수 있나요? 그때 L.A.에서 친구가 오기로 되어 있거든요.

Matthew Clark 오전 11:20
당연하죠, 꼭 도와주고 싶어요. 나중에 다시 얘기해요.

> **어휘** cover 대신하다 shift 교대 근무 (시간) be supposed to-V ~해야 한다 concession stand 구내매점 break down 고장 나다 garage 자동차 정비소 cover for ~를 대신해 일하다 repay 갚다, 보답하다 favor 호의, 친절 unfortunate 안타까운 take over ~을 넘겨받다, 대신 맡다 box office 매표소 expect ~가 오기로 되어 있다 catch up 밀린 얘기를 나누다

153

Where do Mr. Clark and Ms. Weiss most likely work?

(A) At a restaurant
(B) At a movie theater
(C) At a travel bureau
(D) At an auto repair shop

Mr. Clark와 Ms. Weiss는 어디에서 근무하겠는가?

(A) 식당에서
(B) 극장에서
(C) 여행사에서
(D) 자동차 정비소에서

> **해설** 화자들이 근무하는 곳에 구내매점(concession stand)과 매표소(box office)가 있다는 사실을 통해 이곳이 극장임을 추론할 수 있다.

154

At 11:20 A.M., what does Mr. Clark mean when he writes, "I'd love to help"?

(A) He agrees to work Ms. Weiss's shift.
(B) He intends to cover the repair costs.
(C) He is available to see Ms. Weiss in the afternoon.
(D) He will endorse a request for sick leave

오전 11시 20분에 Mr. Clark이 "꼭 도와주고 싶어요."라고 쓸 때 무엇을 의미하는가?

(A) Ms. Weiss의 근무를 맡는 데 동의한다.
(B) 수리 비용을 부담할 생각이다.
(C) 오후에 Ms. Weiss를 만날 시간이 있다.
(D) 병가 신청을 승인할 것이다.

> **어휘** intend to-V ~할 생각이다, 계획이다 available 시간이 있는 endorse 승인하다 sick leave 병가

> **해설** 저녁 매표소 근무를 대신 해 달라는(could you take over my evening shift at the box office next Friday?) 부탁에 대한 대답이므로 Ms. Weiss의 일을 대신 맡는 데 동의한다는 뜻으로 하는 말이다.

To: Camila Navarro <cnavarro@letterly.com>
From: Rakesh Solanki M <RSolanki@beyondtheresume.com>
Date: 6 November
155Subject: Job Opportunity Available

Dear Ms. Navarro,

We appreciate your decision to join Beyond the Résumé as a client. Our mission is to support you in finding a fulfilling career path. After reviewing the details you shared during our phone conversation, 155I have identified a job that may be a great fit for you. 156If the position outlined below interests you, please send me an e-mail today. That way, we can begin drafting a tailored cover letter to accompany your résumé and application.

Position: Office Assistant
Employer: Brookhaven Medical Group
Location: Brookhaven Township

Key Duties:
157(C)• Coordinate appointment scheduling
157(B)• Generate and send billing statements
157(D)• Input patient information into an electronic health records system

Best regards,

Rakesh Solanki, Career Counselor
Beyond the Résumé

155-157번 문제는 다음 이메일에 관한 것입니다.

수신: Camila Navarro 〈cnavarro@letterly.com〉
발신: Rakesh Solanki M
　　　〈RSolanki@beyondtheresume.com〉
날짜: 11월 6일
제목: 채용 기회 안내

Ms. Navarro께,

Beyond the Résumé에 고객으로 가입해 주셔서 고맙습니다. 저희의 목표는 귀하가 만족스러운 직업 진로를 찾아 나갈 수 있도록 지원하는 것입니다. 전화 통화 중에 공유해 주신 세부 정보를 검토해 본 후에 귀하에게 매우 적합할 것 같은 자리를 찾아냈습니다. 아래에 설명한 직무에 관심이 있으시면 오늘 저에게 이메일을 보내 주시기 바랍니다. 그렇게 해주시면 이력서 및 지원서에 첨부할 맞춤형 자기소개서의 초안 작성을 시작할 수 있습니다.

직책: 사무 보조원
고용주: Brookhaven Medical Group
위치: Brookhaven Township

주요 업무:
• 진료 예약 일정 조율하기
• 청구 명세서 작성 및 발송
• 전자 건강 기록 시스템에 환자 정보 입력

이만 줄입니다.

Beyond the Résumé
취업 상담사 Rakesh Solanki

어휘 mission (기업의) 목적, 목표 fulfilling 만족감[성취감]을 주는 career path 직업 진로 details 세부 정보 identify 찾다, 발견하다 great fit 매우 잘 맞는 것 outline 간략하게 설명하다, 정리하다 that way 그렇게 하면 draft 초안을 잡다 tailored 맞춤의, 딱 알맞은 cover letter 자기소개서 accompany ~과 함께 제공하다, 첨부하다 duty 직무, 업무 coordinate 조율하다, 조정하다 generate 만들어 내다 billing statement 청구 명세서 input 입력하다 electronic 전자의 career counselor 직업 상담사

155

Why did Mr. Solanki contact Ms. Navarro?

(A) To arrange a job interview
(B) To greet a newly hired worker
(C) To advertise his company's offerings
(D) To notify a client about a job opening

Mr. Solanki는 왜 Ms. Navarro에게 연락했는가?

(A) 취업 면접을 준비하기 위해
(B) 새로 채용된 직원을 환영하기 위해
(C) 자기 회사의 제공 상품을 광고하기 위해
(D) 고객에게 채용 공고를 알리기 위해

어휘 arrange 준비하다, 마련하다 greet 인사하다, 환영하다 offering 제공된 것 job opening 채용 공고

해설 이메일의 제목이 Job Opportunity Available인 것만 보아도 정답을 알 수 있다. 이메일 본문에서도 고객에게 적합해 보이는 일자리를 찾았다고 알리고 있다(I have identified a job that may be a great fit for you).

156

What does Mr. Solanki encourage Ms. Navarro to do?

(A) Update her résumé immediately
(B) Let him know her decision promptly
(C) Book a consultation with a physician
(D) Provide him with a list of references

Mr. Solanki는 Ms. Navarro에게 무엇을 하라고 권하는가?

(A) 즉시 이력서를 갱신한다
(B) 결정한 사항을 지체 없이 알린다
(C) 의사와 진료 예약을 잡다
(D) 신원 보증인 명단을 제공한다

어휘 update 갱신하다, 업데이트하다 promptly 신속하게, 지체 없이 book 예약하다 consultation (의사의) 진료 physician 의사 reference 추천인, 신원 보증인

해설 추천하는 일자리에 지원할 의향이 있다면 오늘 중에 연락을 달라고 요청하고 있다(If the position outlined below interests you, please send me an e-mail today).

157

What is NOT mentioned as a responsibility of the office assistant?

(A) Checking patients in upon arrival
(B) Mailing out invoices to patients
(C) Managing the calendar for patient visits
(D) Updating medical data

사무 보조원의 업무로 언급되지 않은 것은 무엇인가?

(A) 환자가 도착했을 때 접수 받기
(B) 환자들에게 청구서 발송하기
(C) 환자 방문 일정 관리하기
(D) 의료 데이터 갱신하기

어휘 check in 등록 절차를 밟다 upon ~하자마자 calendar 일정, 스케줄

해설 사무 보조원의 업무로 나열된 것은 진료 예약 편성하기와(Coordinate appointment scheduling) 청구 명세서 작성 및 발송(Generate and send billing statements), 전자 건강 기록 시스템에 환자 정보 입력하기이다(Input patient information into an electronic health records system). 방문 환자의 접수를 받는 일은 언급되어 있지 않다.

PRIVATE SALE

[158][159]This beautifully maintained 4-bedroom, 3-bathroom residence sits on a 2,400-square-foot elevated site overlooking the Botanical Gardens. It offers easy access to the Central Business District and is well connected to public transit. The interior has been completely renovated, featuring state-of-the-art appliances, brand-new flooring, and central air-conditioning. A detached, refurbished office building is also included on the premises. [160]Private off-street parking is provided.

Property valuation (as of July): $349,000
No agents, please.
Listing ID: BH47219

158–160번 문제는 다음 광고에 관한 것입니다.

개인 매물

잘 관리된 방 4개, 욕실 3개의 이 주택은 식물원이 내려다보이는 2,400 제곱피트 규모의 높은 지대에 자리하고 있습니다. 중심 상업 지구에 쉽게 접근할 수 있으며 대중교통과도 잘 연결되어 있습니다. 내부는 완전히 개조되어 최첨단 가전제품과 새 바닥재, 중앙 냉방 장치를 포함하고 있습니다. 경내에는 재단장한 사무실 건물이 본채와 분리되어 포함되어 있습니다. 도로 밖 전용 주차 공간도 제공됩니다.

부동산 감정가 (7월 기준): 349,000달러
중개업자 사절입니다.
매물 ID: BH47219

어휘 beautifully 훌륭하게, 잘 maintain 유지 관리하다 residence 주택, 거주지 square foot 제곱 피트 elevated (주변이나 지면보다) 높은 site 부지, 지대 overlook ~가 내려다보이다 botanical garden 식물원 access 접근 central business district 중심 상업 지구 public transit 대중교통 feature 특별히 포함하다 state-of-the-art 최첨단의, 최신식의 appliance 가전제품 brand-new 완전 새 것인 flooring 바닥재 detached (건물 등이) 독립된 refurbish 재단장하다 premises (건물이 포함된) 경내, 구내, 부지 off-street 도로에서 떨어진 property 부동산, 건물 valuation (평가된) 가치, 가치액 as of ~ 기준, ~ 현재 agent 대리인, 중개상 listing (목록의) 항목

158

What type of property is being advertised?

(A) A garden supply business
(B) A retail space
(C) An office complex
(D) A private house

어떤 유형의 부동산이 광고되고 있는가?

(A) 정원용품 사업체
(B) 소매업 장소
(C) 사무 단지
(D) 개인 주택

해설 첫 문장에서 매물을 잘 관리된 방 4개, 욕실 3개가 있는 주택이라고 소개하고 있다(This beautifully maintained 4-bedroom, 3-bathroom residence).

159

Where is the property located?

(A) Adjacent to an industrial park
(B) Inside an apartment complex
(C) Close to the Botanical Gardens
(D) In a remote rural area

부동산은 어디에 위치해 있는가?

(A) 산업 단지에 인접한 곳에
(B) 아파트 단지 내부에
(C) 식물원 가까이에
(D) 외딴 전원 지역에

어휘 adjacent to ~에 인접한 industrial park 산업 단지, 공단 complex 건물 단지 remote 외딴, 외진 rural 시골의, 전원의

해설 첫 문장에서 이 집은 식물원이 내려다보이는 곳에 있다고 알려주고 있다(This beautifully maintained 4-bedroom, 3-bathroom residence sits on a 2,400-square-foot elevated site overlooking the Botanical Gardens).

160

What can be inferred about the property?

(A) It is presently under contract.
(B) It may lack a parking garage.
(C) It is being sold via a real estate agency.
(D) Its asking price has been lowered.

부동산에 관하여 무엇을 추론할 수 있는가?

(A) 현재 계약 기간 중이다.
(B) 실내 주차장은 없을 수 있다.
(C) 부동산 중개업소를 통해 매매되고 있다.
(D) 호가가 낮아졌다.

어휘 infer 추론하다 presently 현재에, 지금 parking garage 실내 주차장, 차고 real estate agency 부동산 중개업소 asking price 호가(呼價), (팔려는 사람의) 제시 가격 lower 내리다, 낮추다

해설 광고 마지막에 길가에 차를 세울 필요가 없도록 도로 밖 전용 주차 공간이 제공된다고 쓰여 있는데(Private off-street parking is provided.), 이것이 반드시 실내 차고가 있음을 의미하는 것은 아니다.

Questions 161 through 163 refer to the following article.

Ocean Crest Faces Stormy Skies
by Michelle Ramirez

SAN DIEGO (8 February) - For years, [162]tourists in the know have flocked to the iconic ship-shaped seafood restaurant perched along the historic wharf. —[1]—. [161]Although the Ocean Crest building remains standing, its signature wooden entryway with circular porthole windows has been shuttered. [163]All interior furnishings were auctioned off in October with demolition set to begin in the coming weeks. —[2]—.

However, things are not quite as they appear. [161]Ocean Crest's manager, Daniel Morales, has struck a hard-earned deal with the property developer, Coastal Edge Properties, to reconstruct the restaurant at its current location. —[3]—. According to Mr. Morales, the developers opted to have the building torn down due to the extensive structural damage that would have required costly repairs.

—[4]—. While the rebuilt version will honor the original nautical theme, [162]it will feature more modern architecture in line with Coastal Edge's insistence despite objections from Mr. Morales.

161-163번 문제는 다음 기사에 관한 것입니다.

Ocean Crest 폭풍을 맞이하다
Michelle Ramirez

SAN DIEGO (2월 8일) – 수년간, 소식에 밝은 관광객들은 역사적인 부두에 자리한, 배 모양의 상징적인 해산물 식당에 몰려들었다. Ocean Crest 건물은 여전히 서 있지만, 둥근 현창이 달린 대표적인 나무 출입구는 폐쇄되었다. 내부 가구는 10월에 모두 경매에 부쳐졌으며, 몇 주 안에 철거가 시작될 예정이다. 그러나 상황은 겉보기와는 다르다. Ocean Crest의 운영자 Daniel Morales는 부동산 개발업체 Coastal Edge Properties와 현재의 자리에 식당을 재건하기로 어렵게 합의를 보았다. Mr. Morales에 따르면 개발업자들은 고비용 수리를 요하는 광범위한 구조적 손상 때문에 건물을 철거하는 쪽을 택했다. 다시 지어지는 식당은 기존의 선박 테마를 유지하지만, Mr. Morales 측의 반대에도 불구하고 Coastal Edge의 강력한 요구에 따라 현대적인 건축 양식을 특징으로 할 것이다.

어휘 face 직면하다 stormy 폭풍우가 몰아치는 in the know 잘 아는, 소식에 밝은 flock 몰려들다 iconic 표상으로 쓰이는, 상징성을 지닌 perched ~에 위치한 wharf 부두 signature 대표하는, ~하면 떠오르는 entryway 입구, 현관 circular 원형의, 둥근 porthole (선박, 항공기 측면의) 현창, 둥근 창 shutter 폐업하다, 폐쇄하다 furnishings 가구, 비품, 세간 auction off ~을 경매에 부치다 demolition 철거, 해체 set to-V ~할 예정인 not quite as they appear 겉보기와는 다른 strike a deal 거래를 맺다, 합의를 보다 hard-earned 어렵게 얻은 property 부동산, 건물 opt to-V ~하는 것을 선택하다 tear down (tore-torn) (건물 등을) 헐다, 철거하다 extensive 광범위한 structural 구조적인 costly 많은 비용이 드는 honor 존중하다, 보존하다 nautical 선박의, 항해의 theme 주제, 테마 feature 특징으로 삼다 in line with ~에 따라, 맞추어 insistence 주장, 강력한 요구 objection 반대

161

What is being reported?

(A) A restaurant has taken on a new name.
(B) A building has transitioned to new ownership.
(C) A ship is going to be reconstructed.
(D) A business intends to resume operations.

무엇이 보도되고 있는가?

(A) 식당이 새 이름을 갖게 되었다.
(B) 건물이 새 소유주에게로 넘어갔다.
(C) 배가 복원될 것이다.
(D) 사업체가 영업을 재개할 계획이다.

어휘 take on (특성·이름·역할 등을) 갖게 되다 transition to ~으로 전환되다, 넘어가다 resume 재개하다 operation 운영, 영업

해설 첫 문단에서 식당 정문이 폐쇄되어 있고, 철거가 예정된 상태에서 모든 집기가 경매에 부쳐졌다는 내용(its signature wooden entryway with circular porthole windows has been shuttered. All interior furnishings were auctioned off in October with demolition set to begin in the coming weeks.)으로 식당 운영을 중단되었음을 알 수 있다. 그러나 두 번째 문단에는 식당 운영자가 부동산 개발 업체와 식당을 재건하기로 했다는 내용이 나온다 (Ocean Crest's manager, Daniel Morales, has struck a hard-earned deal with the property developer, Coastal Edge Properties, to reconstruct the restaurant at its current location). 따라서 기사가 보도하는 내용은 사업체의 영업 재개 계획이다.

162

What does the article imply about Mr. Morales?

(A) He insisted on maintaining the original design.
(B) He is planning to exit the food industry.
(C) He is seeking a new business location.
(D) He converted a ship into a restaurant.

기사는 Mr. Morales에 관하여 무엇을 암시하는가?

(A) 원래의 디자인을 유지할 것을 주장했다.
(B) 식품업계를 떠날 계획이다.
(C) 새 사업 장소를 찾고 있다.
(D) 배를 개조하여 식당으로 만들었다.

어휘 insist on ~을 주장하다 exit 빠져나가다, 떠나다 seek 찾다, 구하다 convert 개조하다, 전환하다

163

In which of the positions marked [1], [2], [3], and [4] does the following sentence best belong?

"Among the items sold was a scale model of the 120-year-old vessel that originally inspired the restaurant's layout."

(A) [1]
(B) [2]
(C) [3]
(D) [4]

다음 문장은 [1], [2], [3], [4]로 표시된 자리 중 어느 곳에 가장 잘 어울리는가?

"팔린 물건들 중에는 처음에 식당의 설계에 영감을 준 120년 된 선박의 축소 모형도 있었다."

📧 **Questions 164 through 167** refer to the following e-mail.

164–167번 문제는 다음 이메일에 관한 것입니다.

To: All Staff <team@venturonet.com>
From: Julia Frankel <jfrankel@venturonet.com>
Date: November 3
164Re: Copy Machine Guidelines

Dear Team,

In an effort to preserve company resources and support eco-friendly practices, 164we kindly remind you to adhere to office guidelines when using the photocopier. Producing printed materials consumes paper, toner, and other supplies that impact the environment - and also incurs costs. Departments currently pay $0.05 per printed page, and frequent usage can quickly become expensive. 165(A)(B)To help reduce financial strain and environmental waste, please rely on digital formats whenever feasible.

165(D) 166If hard copies are genuinely required, limit copy machine use to 25 pages per batch. The machine is built for light-duty tasks, and attempting to produce high volumes can lead to wear and tear, increased service needs, and potential replacement expenses. 166 167For larger jobs, please submit a request through the Printing Center on the fifth floor. Paper-based order forms are no longer accepted - 167we now only process requests submitted via the online form available on the staff resources portal. If you need help with accessing the form, please reach out to your department's administrative assistant.

Thank you for your cooperation.

Regards,

Julia Frankel
Operations Coordinator

수신: 전 직원 〈team@venturonet.com〉
발신: Julia Frankel 〈jfrankel@venturonet.com〉
날짜: 11월 3일
제목: 복사기 사용 지침

팀원 여러분께,

회사 자원을 보존하고 환경 친화적 관행을 지지하려는 시도로 복사기를 사용할 때 사무실 지침을 준수해 주시기 바랍니다. 인쇄 자료를 만드는 것은 환경에 큰 영향을 미치는 종이와 토너 및 기타 비품을 소비하며 비용을 발생시키기도 합니다. 각 부서는 현재 인쇄비로 페이지당 0.05달러를 내고 있으며, 잦은 사용은 빠르게 비용이 쌓이게 됩니다. 재정적 부담과 환경 낭비를 줄이기 위해 가능하다면 디지털 형식을 사용하시기 바랍니다.

출력 인쇄물이 정말로 필요하다면 복사기 사용을 회당 25페이지로 제한해 주시기 바랍니다. 기계가 소량 복사에 맞도록 만들어져 있어서 대량 출력을 시도하면 마모 발생과 수리 횟수 증가, 때로는 교체를 위한 지출로 이어질 수 있습니다. 대량 복사를 하려면 5층에 있는 인쇄 센터를 통해 신청서를 제출하시기 바랍니다. 종이 양식의 신청서는 더 이상 받지 않습니다. 현재는 직원 자료 포털에서 이용할 수 있는 온라인 서식을 통해 제출된 신청만 처리합니다. 서식 이용에 도움이 필요하다면 부서 행정 담당자에게 도움을 연락하시기 바랍니다.

협조 고맙습니다.

이만 줄입니다.

운영 책임자
Julia Frankel

어휘 guidelines 지침, 가이드라인 in an effort to-V ~하려는 시도로 eco-friendly 친환경적인 practice 관행 we kindly remind *sb* to-V ~해 주시기 바랍니다 adhere to ~을 준수하다 photocopier 복사기 frequent 빈번한, 잦은 strain 부담, 압박 format 형식, 방식 feasible 실행 가능한 hard copy 하드 카피, 출력물 genuinely 정말로 batch 1회분 light-duty 경량용의 attempt 시도하다 lead to ~으로 이어지다 wear and tear 마모 replacement 교체 access 접속하다, 이용하다 assistant (지원) 담당자

164

Why did Ms. Frankel send the e-mail?

(A) To inform employees about higher photocopying fees
(B) To introduce a new floor plan for the Printing Center
(C) To remind staff of the current copying policies
(D) To outline repair details for the copy machine

Ms. Frankel은 왜 이메일을 보냈는가?

(A) 직원들에게 높아진 복사비를 알리기 위해
(B) 인쇄 센터의 새 배치도를 소개하기 위해
(C) 직원들에게 현재의 복사 방침을 상기시키기 위해
(D) 복사기 수리 정보를 설명하기 위해

어휘 photocopy 복사하다 floor plan 평면도, 배치도

해설 일단 제목 Re: Copy Machine Guidelines만 읽어도 정답을 알 수 있다. 또한 첫 문장에서도 복사기 사용에 대한 지침을 준수할 것을 촉구하고 있다 (we kindly remind you to adhere to office guidelines when using the photocopier).

165

What is NOT mentioned as a reason for restricting the number of paper copies?

(A) Minimizing the environmental footprint
(B) Controlling departmental expenses
(C) Improving how quickly documents are distributed
(D) Preventing damage to the machine over time

복사 매수를 제한하는 이유로 언급되지 않는 것은 무엇인가?

(A) 환경에 미치는 영향을 최소화하는 것
(B) 부서의 지출을 통제하는 것
(C) 문서가 배포되는 속도를 개선하는 것
(D) 시간이 지나면서 기계 손상을 방지하는 것

어휘 restrict 제한하다, 규제하다 environmental footprint 환경 발자국 (인간의 활동이 환경에 미치는 악영향) distribute 배포하다, 분배하다

해설 재정적인 부담과 환경에 악영향을 미치는 낭비를 줄이기 위해 되도록 디지털 문서를 이용하고(To help reduce financial strain and environmental waste, please rely on digital formats whenever feasible.) 복사 매수는 25부로 제한하라는 내용을 읽으면서(limit copy machine use to 25 pages per batch.) (A)와 (B)를 제거해야 한다. 다량의 복사는 기계의 마모를 초래한다는 내용을 읽으면서(and attempting to produce high volumes can lead to wear and tear) (D)도 제거하자.

166

According to the e-mail, when should orders be requested through the Printing Center?

(A) When more than 25 pages are needed
(B) When documents are for future use
(C) When the assistant is unavailable
(D) When the copier requires service

이메일에 따르면 언제 인쇄 센터를 통한 주문이 있어야 하는가?

(A) 25페이지 이상이 필요할 때
(B) 문서가 향후 사용을 위한 것일 때
(C) 담당자가 부재중일 때
(D) 복사기에 점검이 필요할 때

해설 복사기 사용은 회당 25페이지로 제한하고(limit copy machine use to 25 pages per batch.) 다량의 복사가 필요할 때는 인쇄 센터를 통해 신청서를 제출하라고 지시하고 있다(For larger jobs, please submit a request through the Printing Center on the fifth floor). 인쇄 센터에 도움을 구하는 경우는 25페이지 이상의 인쇄가 필요할 때이다.

167

How should printing requests be submitted?

(A) Through a phone call to the administrative assistant
(B) By filling out a online form
(C) With a paper order slip
(D) In person at the Printing Center

인쇄 신청서는 어떻게 제출해야 하는가?

(A) 행정 담당자와의 통화를 통해
(B) 온라인 서식을 작성함으로써
(C) 종이 주문서로
(D) 직접 인쇄 센터로 가서

어휘 fill out ~을 작성하다 order slip 주문서 in person 직접, 몸소

해설 다량의 복사는 인쇄 센터에 신청해야 하는데(For larger jobs, please submit a request through the Printing Center on the fifth floor), 이때 신청은 온라인 서식을 통해서만 할 수 있다(we now only process requests submitted via the online form available on the staff resources portal).

[168]It is widely understood that Yiran Chen's latest title, *Strategic Risk: Unlocking Potential in Business* (264 pages, Meridian Insight Press, $24.50), was crafted with recent college graduates in mind. The publisher has clearly positioned the book toward younger readers, and its introductory material is geared toward that demographic. Still, the principles elucidated by Ms. Chen resonate with many a well-established business executive. — [1] —. The basic premise of the book is that individuals must be open to smart risk-taking to reach their full potential. [168]As someone who founded and runs a prominent branding agency, I can personally attest to this philosophy.

Learning to embrace risk was not something I mastered instantly. — [2] —. [169][171]Early in my career, I stuck firmly to my comfort zone and avoided ventures that lacked predictable outcomes. [171]Over time, I came to see that this cautious approach was effectively restricting my company's ability to grow. — [3] —. [169]Only after I began evaluating new ventures carefully and stopped fearing occasional setbacks did my company evolve into the multimillion-dollar enterprise it is today. It was the very shift in thinking that made all the difference, but it took me years to understand.

That is why I am especially glad Ms. Chen is introducing this mindset to the next generation of business leaders. — [4] —. Across eleven thoughtfully written chapters, Ms. Chen showcases the journeys of well-known business figures. Each section ends with reflective prompts that encourage readers to examine their own degree of risk aversion. The final chapter offers a compelling framework for approaching uncertainty with maturity - a message equally valuable to both seasoned professionals and newcomers alike. [170]For me, the book was a timely refresher of insights I have accumulated over the years.

- Anton Becker

Yiran Chen의 신간, *전략적 리스크: 비즈니스 잠재력 깨우기*(264페이지, Meridian Insight 출판사, 24.50 달러)는 최근 대학 졸업생들을 염두에 두고 집필되었다고 널리 알려져 있다. 출판사는 분명 이 책을 젊은 독자층을 겨냥하여 기획하였으며, 도입부 내용도 그 고객층에 적합하도록 구성되어 있다. 그럼에도 Ms. Chen이 명확히 설명한 원칙들은 이미 자리를 잡은 많은 경영자들에게서도 공감을 얻고 있다. 이 책의 기본 전제는 개인이 잠재력을 최대한 발휘하려면 현명한 위험 감수에 열려 있어야 한다는 것이다. 유명 브랜드 전략 전문 회사를 설립하여 운영하고 있는 사람으로서 나는 이러한 철학을 직접 입증할 수 있다.

위험을 수용하는 법을 배운다는 것은 즉시 통달할 수 있는 것은 아니었다. 경력 초기에 나는 익숙한 영역에 머물며 결과를 예측할 수 없는 모험은 피했다. 시간이 지나며 이러한 조심스러운 접근법이 사실상 내 회사의 성장 가능성을 제한하고 있다는 것을 알게 되었다. 새로운 시도를 주의 깊게 평가하기 시작하고 가끔 있을 수 있는 실패를 두려워하지 않게 되자 우리 회사는 오늘날의 모습인 수백만 달러 규모의 기업으로 성장할 수 있었다. 모든 차이를 만들어낸 것은 바로 이 생각의 전환이었지만, 이것을 깨닫는 데 수년이 걸렸다.

바로 이 점 때문에 Ms. Chen이 다음 세대 비즈니스 리더들에게 이러한 사고방식을 소개하고 있다는 사실이 특히 더 반갑다. 깊이 있게 쓰여진 11개의 챕터를 통해 Ms. Chen은 유명 기업인들의 여정을 소개한다. 각 부분은 독자가 자신의 위험 회피 성향 정도를 점검하도록 독려하는 성찰형 유도 질문으로 마무리된다. 마지막 챕터는 성숙한 자세로 불확실성에 접근하도록 매우 설득력 있는 틀을 제공하는데, 이것은 경험이 풍부한 전문가나 사회 초년생 모두에게 똑같이 가치 있는 메시지이다. 나에게 이 책은 수년에 걸쳐 쌓아 온 통찰을 되새길 수 있는 시의적절한 계기가 되었다.

— Anton Becker

어휘 title 서적, 출판물 strategic 전략적인, 계획적인 press 출판사 craft (정성 들여) 만들다, 구성하다 with *sth* in mind ~을 염두에 두고, ~을 고려하여 publisher 출판사 position A toward B A를 B에 맞춰 설정하다 introductory 서두의 material 자료, 내용 be geared to(ward) ~에 적합하도록 만들다, ~를 대상으로 삼다 demographic 특정 인구 집단, 고객층 principle 원칙, 기본 개념 elucidate 명확히 설명하다 resonate with ~의 공감을 얻다 well-established 안정된, 자리를 잡은 premise 전제 prominent 유명한, 두드러진 branding agency 브랜드 전략 회사 attest to ~을 입증하다, 증언하다 embrace 수용하다 master 통달하다 instantly 즉시, 순식간에 stick to ~을 고수하다, 계속 유지하다 firmly 확고히 comfort zone 편안한 상황, 익숙한 영역 venture (모험적인) 사업, 시도 outcome 결과 cautious 신중한, 조심스러운 effectively 사실상, 실질적으로 restrict 제한하다, 제약하다 evaluate 평가하다 fear 두려워하다 occasional 가끔의 setback 좌절, 실패 evolve 발전하다, 성장하다 enterprise 기업, 사업체 shift 변화, 전환 mindset 사고방식 thoughtfully 신중하게, 깊이 있게 showcase 소개하다, 보여주다 figure 인물 reflective 성찰적인, 반성하는 prompt 유도 질문 degree 정도, 수준 aversion 혐오감, 회피 성향 compelling 강력한, 매우 설득력 있는 framework 틀, 체계 maturity 성숙, 숙련됨 seasoned 노련한, 경험이 풍부한 newcomer 초보자, 사회 초년생 alike 똑같이 timely 시의적절한, 알맞은 시점의 refresher 상기시키는 것, 되새기는 것 insight 통찰력 accumulate 쌓다, 축적하다

168

What is suggested about Mr. Becker in the review?

(A) He does not belong to the group Ms. Chen primarily targeted.
(B) He regularly collects and reviews business-related books.
(C) He works at the same academic institution Ms. Chen graduated from.
(D) He has launched multiple prosperous companies.

서평에서 Mr. Becker에 관하여 무엇이 암시되어 있는가?

(A) Ms. Chen이 주로 대상으로 삼은 집단에는 속하지 않는다.
(B) 정기적으로 비즈니스 관련 서적을 수집하고 평가한다.
(C) Ms. Chen이 졸업한 곳과 같은 교육 기관에서 근무한다.
(D) 여러 성공적인 기업을 창업했다.

어휘 academic institution 교육 기관, 학교 launch 시작하다, 출범시키다 prosperous 번창하는, 성공적인

해설 Ms. Chen의 신간 서적은 지금 막 대학을 졸업한 청년들을 대상으로 하는 책인데(Yiran Chen's latest title, *Strategic Risk: Unlocking Potential in Business* (264 pages, Meridian Insight Press, $24.50), was crafted with recent college graduates in mind.), Mr. Becker는 이미 성공을 거둔 기업가이다(As someone who founded and runs a prominent branding agency).

169

What does Mr. Becker say is a reason for his own company's growth?

(A) His openness to taking strategic risks
(B) His networking approach within the industry
(C) His emphasis on building a strong brand reputation
(D) His ability to secure outside investment

Mr. Becker는 자신의 기업이 성장한 이유가 무엇이라고 말하는가?

(A) 전략적 위험을 감수하는 개방성
(B) 업계 내 인맥 구축 전략
(C) 강력한 브랜드 평판 구축 강조
(D) 외부 투자를 이끌어 내는 능력

어휘 networking 인맥 구축[형성] approach 접근법, 전략 emphasis 강조 reputation 명성, 평판 secure 확보하다, 얻어내다

해설 두 번째 문단에서 정답을 알 수 있다. 경력 초기에 Mr. Becker는 위험을 회피하는 유형의 기업가였으며(Early in my career, I stuck firmly to my comfort zone and avoided ventures that lacked predictable outcomes.) 그의 회사의 성장은 실패를 두려워하지 않고 주의 깊게 모험을 시도하기 시작한 이후에 가능했다고 진술하고 있다(Only after I began evaluating new ventures carefully and stopped fearing occasional setbacks did my company evolve into the multimillion–dollar enterprise it is today).

170

Why does Mr. Becker appreciate Ms. Chen's book?

(A) It inspired him to pursue a new professional path.
(B) It encouraged him to aim for more ambitious goals.
(C) It reaffirmed lessons he gained through experience.
(D) It changed how he measures company achievements.

Mr. Becker는 왜 Ms. Chen의 책을 높이 평가하는가?

(A) 직업에서 새로운 진로를 추구하도록 영감을 주었다.
(B) 더 야심찬 목표를 세우도록 독려했다.
(C) 경험을 통해 얻은 교훈을 재확인시켜 주었다.
(D) 기업의 성과를 측정하는 방식을 바꾸어 주었다.

어휘 appreciate 높이 평가하다 aim for ~을 목표로 하다 ambitious 야심찬 reaffirm 재확인하다 achievement 성과, 업적

해설 마지막 문장에서 수년 동안의 경험을 통해 축적한 통찰을 되새기는 좋은 계기가 되었다는 말을 하고 있다(For me, the book was a timely refresher of insights I have accumulated over the years).

171

In which of the positions marked [1], [2], [3], and [4] does the following sentence best belong?

"Even worse, my inaction was also making way for more aggressive competitors to dominate the industry landscape."

(A) [1]
(B) [2]
(C) [3]
(D) [4]

다음 문장은 [1], [2], [3], [4]로 표시된 자리 중 어느 곳에 가장 잘 어울리는가?

"설상가상으로 아무 행동도 하지 않는 나의 태도는 더 공격적인 경쟁업체들에게 업계 판도를 장악할 수 있는 길을 열어 주고 있기도 했다."

어휘 even worse 더 안 좋은 것. 설상가상으로 inaction 행동하지 않음 make way for ~에게 길을 열어주다. ~이 자리를 차지하게 하다 aggressive 공격적인. 적극적인 competitor 경쟁자 dominate 지배하다. 장악하다 industry landscape (비유적) 산업 환경. 업계 판도

해설 my inaction이라는 키워드가 가리키는 것은 위험 감수를 피하며 안전지대에 머무르는 태도이다(Early in my career, I stuck firmly to my comfort zone and avoided ventures that lacked predictable outcomes). 또한 '설상가상으로(Even worse)'라고 말했으므로 바로 앞에 자신의 기업 운영상의 또 다른 부정적인 측면이 진술되어야 한다. 이러한 내용으로 알맞은 것은 회사의 성장이 제한되었다는 문장이다(Over time, I came to see that this cautious approach was effectively restricting my company's ability to grow). 주어진 문장과 앞뒤 문장을 연결시켜 주는 키워드를 파악하면 어느 자리에 들어가는 게 알맞은지 파악할 수 있다.

Questions 172 through 175 refer to the following text-message chain.

172–175번 문제는 다음 문자 메시지 대화에 관한 것입니다.

Leila Demir, 7:45 A.M.
Good morning, team. [172]Once again, when I arrived at the shop early today, all the lights were already on. Has anyone figured out why this keeps happening?

Leila Demir, 오전 7:45
좋은 아침입니다. 팀원 여러분. 또 다시, 제가 아침 일찍 매장에 도착했을 때 모든 조명이 이미 켜져 있더군요. 왜 이런 일이 계속 일어나는지 알아낸 사람 있나요?

Marco Russo, 7:48 A.M.
[173]I activated the timer just before locking up yesterday afternoon. The lights were supposed to switch off at 5:15 P.M.

Marco Russo, 오전 7:48
제가 어제 오후에 문을 잠그기 직전에 타이머를 작동시켰어요. 조명은 오후 5시 15분에 꺼지도록 설정되었습니다.

Catalina Esparza, 7:51 A.M.
I drove past the store after leaving the post office around 5:40, [173]and I noticed the lights were off.

Catalina Esparza, 오전 7:51
제가 5시 40분경에 차를 몰고 우체국에서 나온 후에 매장을 지나쳐 갔는데, 조명이 꺼져 있는 걸 봤어요.

Leila Demir, 7:53 A.M.
Thanks. Since this has happened every morning for the past three days, [174]it's pretty clear the timer isn't working properly.

Leila Demir, 오전 7:53
고마워요. 이런 일이 지난 3일 동안 아침마다 발생한 것으로 봐서 타이머가 제대로 작동하지 않고 있는 게 분명하군요.

Minho Park, 7:54 A.M.
[173]Marco and I both left around 4:45, and I saw him adjust the timer before we exited.

Minho Park, 오전 7:54
Marco와 제가 4시 45분쯤에 함께 퇴근했는데, 나가기 전에 그가 타이머를 조정하는 걸 봤어요.

Marco Russo, 8:00 A.M.
[You're right] - [174]the lights seem to be switching back on earlier than they're supposed to. I'll call BrightFix Electric as soon as I get in for my shift.

Marco Russo, 오전 8:00
맞습니다. 조명이 설정된 시간보다 일찍 다시 켜지고 있는 것 같아요. 제 근무 시간에 출근하자마자 BrightFix Electric에 전화할게요.

Leila Demir, 8:05 A.M.
[175]Please get in touch with the company that installed the system. Their paperwork should be stored in one of the filing drawers. In the meantime, whoever's closing will need to manually switch off each light.

Leila Demir, 오전 8:05
시스템을 설치해 준 회사에 연락해 주세요. 그 업체의 서류가 파일 서랍 중 한 군데에 보관되어 있을 겁니다. 그동안은 누구든 마감하는 사람이 수동으로 각 조명을 꺼 주셔야겠습니다.

Minho Park, 8:07 A.M.
Yes, I remember filing their invoice back when the installation was done.

Minho Park, 오전 8:07
네, 설치가 완료되었던 당시에 청구서를 정리했던 기억이 나네요.

Marco Russo, 8:08 A.M.
[175]Got it. I'll take care of it.

Marco Russo, 오전 8:08
알겠습니다. 제가 처리할게요.

어휘 figure out ~을 알아내다. 이해하다 activate 작동시키다. 활성화하다 properly 제대로 adjust 조정하다 shift 근무조, 교대 근무 get in touch with ~와 연락하다 in the meantime 그동안에는. 그 사이에 manually 수동으로, 손으로 file 서류를 정리하다. 서류철에 넣다

172

What is most likely true about Ms. Demir?

(A) She works at a local post office.
(B) She has a flexible work schedule.
(C) She lives close to the shop.
(D) She handles the morning opening shift.

Ms. Demir에 관하여 무엇이 사실이겠는가?

(A) 지역의 우체국에서 근무한다.
(B) 근무 일정이 탄력적이다.
(C) 매장 가까운 곳에 산다.
(D) 오전 개점 시간 근무를 담당한다.

어휘 flexible 융통성 있는, 탄력적인 handle (업무를) 처리하다, 담당하다

해설 7시 45분의 when I arrived at the shop early today, all the lights were already on(제가 아침 일찍 가게에 도착했을 때 보니 모든 조명이 이미 켜져 있더군요.)은 원래 Ms. Demir가 출근한 이후에 매장 조명이 켜져야 한다는 것을 의미한다. 즉 Ms. Demir는 개점 시간 근무를 담당하고 있다.

173

Who was the last person to confirm that the shop lights were off?

(A) Ms. Demir
(B) Mr. Russo
(C) Ms. Esparza
(D) Mr. Park

매장 조명이 꺼져 있는 것을 확인한 마지막 사람은 누구인가?

(A) Ms. Demir
(B) Mr. Russo
(C) Ms. Esparza
(D) Mr. Park

해설 Mr. Russo는 퇴근할 때 조명이 꺼지도록 타이머를 설정했고(I activated the timer just before locking up yesterday afternoon.), Mr. Park은 Mr. Russo 와 함께 퇴근했다(Marco and I both left around 4:45). 그러므로 두 사람은 조명이 켜져 있을 때 퇴근했다. 이런 내용의 보고를 받고 있는 것으로 보아 Ms. Demir는 이 직원들보다 일찍 퇴근했다. 즉 Ms. Demir도 조명이 켜져 있을 때 퇴근했다. 조명이 꺼져 있는 것을 보았다고 말하는 사람은 Ms. Esparza밖에 없다(and I noticed the lights were off).

174

At 8:00 A.M., what does Mr. Russo most likely mean when he writes, "You're right"?

(A) He believes that the timer needs to be repaired.
(B) He plans to follow Ms. Demir's instructions about the filing cabinet.
(C) He trusts BrightFix Electric to fix the issue.
(D) He recalls that Mr. Park observed him setting the timer.

오전 8시에 Mr. Russo가 "맞습니다."라고 쓸 때, 이는 무엇을 의미하겠는가?

(A) 타이머를 수리할 필요가 있다고 생각한다.
(B) 파일 수납장에 관하여 Ms. Demir의 지시를 따를 계획이다.
(C) BrightFix Electric이 문제를 해결할 것이라고 믿는다.
(D) Mr. Park이 자신이 타이머 설정하는 것을 보았다고 기억한다.

어휘 instructions 지시 (사항) recall 기억하다

해설 부연 설명이 the lights seem to be switching back on earlier than they're supposed to(조명이 설정된 시간보다 일찍 다시 켜지고 있는 것 같아요.)인 것으로 보아 You're right은 7시 53분에 Ms. Demir가 말한 it's pretty clear the timer isn't working properly(타이머가 제대로 작동하지 않고 있는 게 분명하군요.)에 대한 대답이다. 즉 Mr. Russo는 Ms. Demir와 같이 타이머가 제대로 작동하지 않고 있으므로 수리가 필요하다고 생각하고 있다.

175

What is the first thing Mr. Russo will most likely do when he arrives at work?

(A) Make a payment
(B) Install replacement lighting
(C) Complete installation paperwork
(D) Look through some filing drawers

Mr. Russo가 직장에 도착했을 때 처음으로 할 일은 무엇이겠는가?

(A) 대금을 지불한다
(B) 교체 조명을 설치한다
(C) 설치 서류를 작성한다
(D) 파일 서랍을 살펴본다

어휘 complete 작성하다 install 설치하다 lighting 조명 look through (서랍, 주머니 등을) 살펴보다

해설 8시 8분에 Mr. Russo가 말하는 Got it. I'll take care of it(알겠습니다. 제가 처리할게요.)는 8시 5분에 Ms. Demir가 말한 Please get in touch with the company that installed the system. Their paperwork should be stored in one of the filing drawers(시스템을 설치해 준 회사에 연락해 주세요. 서류가 파일 서랍 중 한 군데에 보관되어 있을 겁니다.)에 대한 대답이다. Mr. Russo는 출근하자마자 파일 서랍을 뒤져 서류를 찾아내서 시스템을 설치해 준 회사에 연락할 것이다.

Dear Ms. Feldstein,

[176] [177]The Dunbridge Leisure and Recreation Committee is once again organizing the Shine Dunbridge 8K Fun Run, which will take place on 26 July. [177]Thanks to your company's generosity last year, [176]we raised £21,000, which was used to resurface several pedestrian areas throughout town. This year, our fundraising goal is £24,000, which will be directed toward building new sports courts in Dunbridge's parks.

We're offering four sponsorship packages, each with distinct benefits. Tier 1 requires a contribution of £200, which includes your company logo printed on the back of every race T-shirt. For £400 (Tier 2), your company name will also appear on signage at the starting and ending points. If you commit £800 (Tier 3), your logo will be displayed in all our printed advertisements and event flyers. [178]Lastly, Tier 4 sponsorship, priced at £1,600, includes all previous benefits plus a branded tent space in Hillgrove Park, where the race kicks off.

Please notify me by 2 June regarding your chosen tier. You'll find further details at www.dunbridge.gov.uk/leisure/shinedunbridge. We sincerely appreciate your ongoing support of the Dunbridge community.

Best regards,
David J. Ferreira

To: Celine Morrison
From: David Ferreira
Date: 30 May
Subject: Race Planning Update
Attachment: WexfordSteelworks_Logo.png

Dear Celine,

I've just received confirmation from Wexford Steelworks. Please add the attached logo image to the printing template for the race T-shirts. [178]Also, Ms. Feldstein asked for the measurements of her company's tent at Hillgrove Park. [179]I'm nearly certain Mr. Desai would know - could you check with him?

We've now heard back from most of the other sponsors. I'll send you the finalized list on 3 June. [180]Meanwhile, could you reach out to a few print vendors for quotes? We'll need twelve 1.5-by-3 metre vinyl banners, thirty-five A2-sized full-colour posters, 250 A4 full-colour flyers, and 600 A4 black-and-white flyers.

Thanks,

David

176-180번 문제는 다음 편지와 이메일에 관한 것입니다.

Ms. Feldstein께,

Dunbridge 여가 레크리에이션 위원회가 다시 한 번 Shine Dunbridge 8K Fun Run 행사를 주최합니다. 행사는 7월 26일에 열립니다. 지난해 귀사의 아낌없는 후원 덕분에 우리는 21,000파운드를 모금했으며, 이 금액은 도시 여러 곳의 보행자 도로를 재포장하는 데 사용되었습니다. 올해 우리의 모금 목표액은 24,000파운드이며, Dunbridge의 공원들 내에 새 스포츠 경기장을 짓는 데 사용될 것입니다.

네 가지 후원 패키지를 제공하며, 각각 뚜렷한 혜택이 있습니다. 1단계는 200파운드의 기부를 요하며 이것으로 모든 경주 티셔츠 뒷면에 귀사의 로고가 새겨집니다. 400파운드를 내시면(2단계) 출발점과 결승점에 있는 안내판에도 귀사의 이름이 나옵니다. 800파운드를 약속하시면(3단계) 모든 인쇄 광고와 행사 전단지에 귀사의 로고가 표시됩니다. 마지막으로 1,600파운드의 4단계 후원은 이 모든 혜택과 더불어 경주가 시작되는 Hillgrove 공원에 귀사의 브랜드가 표시된 텐트 공간이 포함됩니다.

선택하신 후원 단계에 관하여 6월 2일까지 저에게 알려 주시기 바랍니다. 더 자세한 사항은 www.dunbridge.gov.uk/leisure/shinedunbridge에서 확인하실 수 있습니다. Dunbridge 지역 사회에 대한 지속적인 지원에 진심으로 고맙습니다.

이만 줄입니다.
David J. Ferreira

수신: Celine Morrison
발신: David Ferreira
날짜: 5월 30일
제목: 경주 기획 업데이트
첨부파일: WexfordSteelworks_Logo.png

Celine,

방금 Wexford Steelworks로부터 확인을 받았어요. 첨부된 로고 이미지를 경주 티셔츠 인쇄 서식에 추가해 주세요. 그리고 Ms. Feldstein이 Hillgrove 공원에 설치될 자기 회사 텐트의 크기를 알려 달라고 하셨어요. Mr. Desai가 알고 있을 것이 거의 확실한데, 그에게 확인해 주겠어요?

이제 대부분의 다른 후원 업체들로부터도 답장을 받았어요. 최종 확정된 명단은 6월 3일에 보내 줄게요. 그사이에 몇몇 인쇄업체들에 연락해서 견적을 받아 주겠어요? 우리는 1.5×3미터 비닐 현수막 12장과 A2 크기의 전면 컬러 포스터 35장, A4 크기의 컬러 전단지 250장, A4 크기의 흑백 전단지 600장이 필요해요.

고마워요.

David

176

Who most likely is Mr. Ferreira?

(A) A financial consultant
(B) A business owner in Dunbridge
(C) A manager at a print shop
(D) An employee of the city government

Mr. Ferreira는 누구겠는가?

(A) 재무 컨설턴트
(B) Dunbridge 지역의 사업주
(C) 인쇄소 운영자
(D) 시 정부 직원

해설 Mr. Ferreira는 'Dunbridge 여가 레크리에이션 위원회'에 소속되어 있으며(The Dunbridge Leisure and Recreation Committee is once again organizing the Shine Dunbridge 8K Fun Run), 이 위원회가 모금한 돈은 지역의 도로를 개선하는 데 사용되었다(we raised £21,000, which was used to resurface several pedestrian areas throughout town). 소속 기관명과 기관이 하는 업무를 통해 Mr. Ferreira는 시 공무원이라고 추론할 수 있다.

177

What is indicated about the race?

(A) A similar event occurred the previous year.
(B) Only Dunbridge residents are allowed to enter.
(C) It covers a distance shorter than 3 kilometers.
(D) It will be held on the June 2.

경주에 관하여 무엇이 나타나 있는가?

(A) 전년도에 유사한 행사가 있었다.
(B) 오직 Dunbridge 주민만 참가할 수 있다.
(C) 3킬로미터가 안 되는 거리를 아우른다.
(D) 6월 2일에 열릴 것이다.

해설 첫 문장에서 다시 한 번(once again) 대회가 열린다고 말하고 있으므로 이 행사는 처음 개최되는 것이 아님을 알 수 있고, 이어지는 문장의 Thanks to your company's generosity last year를 통해 이 행사가 작년에도 있었음을 알 수 있다.

178

Which sponsorship level did Ms. Feldstein probably agree to?

(A) Tier 1
(B) Tier 2
(C) Tier 3
(D) Tier 4

Ms. Feldstein은 어느 후원 단계를 선택했겠는가?

(A) 1단계
(B) 2단계
(C) 3단계
(D) 4단계

해설 편지에서 4단계 후원 패키지를 선택하면 Hillgrove 공원에 회사 브랜드가 표시된 텐트를 설치해 주겠다고 제안하고 있는데(Tier 4 sponsorship, priced at £1,600, includes all previous benefits plus a branded tent space in Hillgrove Park), 이메일에 Ms. Feldstein이 자기 회사 텐트의 크기에 대해 문의했다는 진술이 있다(Ms. Feldstein asked for the measurements of her company's tent at Hillgrove Park). 양쪽의 내용을 연계하여 추론하면 Ms. Feldstein은 4단계 후원을 약정했다.

179

In the e-mail, the word "nearly" in paragraph 1, line 3, is closest in meaning to

(A) least
(B) almost
(C) seldom
(D) closely

이메일에서 첫 문단 세 번째 줄의 단어 "nearly"와 의미상 가장 가까운 것은

(A) 가장 적게
(B) 거의
(C) 거의 ~ 않는
(D) 긴밀하게, 밀접하게

해설 이메일에 등장하는 nearly certain은 거의 확실하다는 뜻이므로 nearly와 의미상 가장 가까운 것은 '거의'라는 뜻의 almost이다. nearly나 closely를 거리에 관련된 단어로 착각하여 오답을 고르지 않도록 주의하자.

What is one task Mr. Ferreira asked Ms. Morrison to take care of?

(A) Reserve a promotional tent space
(B) Obtain price estimates from vendors
(C) Place a bulk T-shirt order
(D) Create designs for outdoor signage

Mr. Ferreira가 Ms. Morrison에게 처리하기를 요구한 한 가지 업무는 무엇인가?

(A) 홍보용 텐트 공간을 예약한다
(B) 판매사로부터 가격 견적을 받는다
(C) 티셔츠를 대량으로 주문한다
(D) 옥외 안내판을 디자인한다

어휘 estimate 견적 vendor 판매자, 공급업체 bulk 대량의

해설 인쇄 업체 몇 군데에 연락해서 견적을 받아 달라고 부탁하고 있다(could you reach out to a few print vendors for quotes?).

Questions 181 through 185 refer to the following e-mails.

181-185번 문제는 다음 두 이메일에 관한 것입니다.

To: Zenetron staff
From: Ingrid Mehta <imehta@pulseinsightgroup.com>
Date: Thursday, July 7
Subject: Staff Survey Invitation
Attachment: Survey Form

Dear Zenetron employees,

[184]Pulse Insight Group, an independent analytics firm based here in Westfield, has been hired by Zenetron to administer a workplace feedback survey. [181]This brief survey includes roughly twenty questions pertaining to topics such as office culture, employee benefits, workspaces, and career development options. Please take a moment to share your honest thoughts.

Responses will remain anonymous - Pulse Insight will not identify your answers by name, and supervisors at Zenetron will not see any individual submissions. [182]However, note that the optional remarks section on the final page will be combined into a single file for management review. If you choose to write a comment and prefer to stay anonymous, avoid mentioning any personal details that may reveal your identity. [183]Also, do not forward this e-mail to others, since each version contains a unique code that prevents duplicate submissions from one individual.

If you have questions or concerns, feel free to reply directly to this message.

Ingrid Mehta
Pulse Insight Group

수신: Zenetron 직원들
발신: Ingrid Mehta
　　　〈imehta@pulseinsightgroup.com〉
날짜: 7월 7일 목요일
제목: 직원 설문 참여 요청
첨부파일: 설문 조사 서식

Zenetron 직원 여러분께,

이곳 Westfield에 본사를 두고 있는 독립 분석 기업 Pulse Insight Group은 Zenetron으로부터 직장 피드백 설문 조사를 실시해 달라는 의뢰를 받았습니다. 이 간단한 설문 조사는 직장 문화와 직원 복리 후생, 업무 공간, 경력 개발 기회와 같은 주제에 관련된 약 20개의 질문을 포함하고 있습니다. 잠시 시간을 내셔서 여러분의 솔직한 생각을 공유해 주시기 바랍니다.

응답은 익명으로 처리됩니다. Pulse Insight는 이름으로 답변을 식별하지 않으며 Zenetron의 관리자들은 어떠한 개별 제출물도 볼 수 없습니다. 그러나 선택 사항인 마지막 페이지에 있는 의견란은 경영진의 검토를 위해 하나의 파일로 합쳐질 것입니다. 의견 작성을 선택하고 익명으로 남기를 원하신다면 신원을 드러내는 개인적인 사항의 언급은 피하시기 바랍니다. 또한 한 사람이 중복 제출하지 못하도록 각 설문지마다 고유 코드가 포함되어 있으므로 이 이메일을 다른 사람에게 전달하지 마시기 바랍니다.

질문이나 우려 사항이 있으시면 이 메시지에 직접 답장해 주시기 바랍니다.

Ingrid Mehta
Pulse Insight Group

To: Zenetron staff
From: Rafi Qureshi
Date: Friday, October 14
Subject: Great News to Share!

[184]Yesterday, the *Westfield Gazette* released its latest rankings titled "Best Workplaces in Westfield," and Zenetron proudly earned number 4 on the list! Out of 180 companies reviewed by a local assessment firm, only 12 were selected for recognition.

We are thrilled to have received this honor -[184]especially since the results stem from the staff survey many of you completed a few months ago. It is amazing to see how much you value your experience at Zenetron, and we truly appreciate all you do to make our company an outstanding place to work.

[185]As you are aware, we will be launching a major recruiting campaign next quarter, so this accolade comes at the perfect time. With this public recognition, we anticipate strong interest among potential candidates before the year wraps up.

Rafi Qureshi
Director of Marketing, Zenetron

수신: Zenetron 직원들
발신: Rafi Qureshi
날짜: 10월 14일 금요일
제목: 기쁜 소식을 전합니다!

*Westfield Gazette*가 어제 "Westfield 최고의 직장"이라는 제목의 최신 순위를 발표했는데, Zenetron이 자랑스럽게도 명단에서 4위를 차지했습니다! 지역 평가 기관이 검토한 180개의 기업 중 단 12개 기업만이 인정 대상으로 선정되었습니다.

이러한 영예를 얻은 것이 특별히 기쁜 것은 이 결과가 여러분 중 상당수가 몇 달 전에 작성한 직원 설문 조사에서 나온 것이기 때문입니다. 여러분이 Zenetron에서의 근무 경험을 얼마나 가치 있게 여기는지 알게 되어 놀랍고, 여러분이 우리 회사를 훌륭한 일터로 만들기 위해 해주신 모든 일에 대해 진심으로 고맙습니다.

여러분도 아시다시피 우리가 다음 분기에 대규모 채용 캠페인을 시작하기 때문에 이번 수상은 절묘한 시기에 이루어졌다고 할 수 있습니다. 이러한 공적인 인정으로 인해 올해가 가기 전에 잠재적인 지원자들로부터 많은 관심이 있을 것으로 기대합니다.

Zenetron 마케팅 부장
Rafi Qureshi

어휘1 independent 독립의 analytics 분석 firm 회사 based ~에 위치한, 기반을 둔 hire (업체에) 의뢰하다 administer 실시하다, 관리하다 roughly 대략 pertaining to ~과 관련된 benefits 복지, 혜택 anonymous 익명인 identify 식별하다 submission 제출 remark 발언, 언급 combine 결합하다 management 경영진 comment 의견 reveal 드러내다 identity 신원 forward 전달하다 unique code 고유 코드 prevent 막다 duplicate 중복의

어휘2 Gazette ~ 신문(신문 이름) select A for B A를 B로 선정하다 recognition 인정, 표창 thrilled 기뻐하는 stem from ~에서 비롯되다 value 소중히 여기다 outstanding 뛰어난 recruiting 채용 accolade 상, 영예 wrap up 마무리되다

181

What is the purpose of the survey mentioned in Ms. Mehta's e-mail?

(A) To evaluate the impact of new workplace policies
(B) To support the development of an advertising campaign
(C) To gather ideas for upcoming product lines
(D) To assess employees' opinions about their work environment

---

Ms. Mehta의 이메일에서 언급된 설문 조사의 목적은 무엇인가?

(A) 새 사내 정책의 영향을 평가하는 것
(B) 광고 캠페인 개발을 지원하는 것
(C) 곧 출시될 제품군에 대한 아이디어를 모으는 것
(D) 업무 환경에 대한 직원들의 의견을 파악하는 것

어휘 line 제품군 assess 파악하다, 평가하다

해설 첫 문단에서 정답을 알 수 있다. 직장 문화, 복리 후생, 업무 공간, 경력 개발 기회(office culture, employee benefits, workspaces, and career development options) 등에 대한 직원들의 의견을 구하고 있다(Please take a moment to share your honest thoughts).

What does Ms. Mehta suggest about survey comments?

(A) Every employee is required to submit one.
(B) They will be tied to the names of respondents.
(C) Zenetron supervisors will receive them.
(D) Feedback will be individually mailed to each participant.

Ms. Mehta는 설문 조사 의견에 대해 무엇을 제안하는가?

(A) 모든 직원이 하나씩 제출해야 한다.
(B) 의견이 응답자의 이름과 연결될 것이다.
(C) Zenetron의 관리자들이 받을 것이다.
(D) 피드백이 각 참여자에게 개별적으로 우편 발송될 것이다.

어휘 comment 의견 tie 연결하다 respondent 응답자 participant 참가자

해설 설문 조사 마지막 페이지에 적게 되는 직원들의 의견은 경영진에게 제공하겠다고 알려주고 있다(note that the optional remarks section on the final page will be combined into a single file for management review).

According to the first e-mail, what should survey recipients avoid doing?

(A) Sending the survey to other team members
(B) Talking about survey content with coworkers
(C) Saving copies on personal devices
(D) Reaching out to Ms. Mehta with questions

첫 번째 이메일에 따르면 설문지 수신자는 무엇을 피해야 하는가?

(A) 설문지를 다른 팀원들에게 보내는 것
(B) 설문 내용에 대해 동료와 이야기하는 것
(C) 개인 장치에 사본을 저장하는 것
(D) 질문이 있을 때 Ms. Mehta에게 연락하는 것

어휘 recipient 수신자 content 내용

해설 이메일 말미에 설문지가 첨부된 이메일을 다른 사람에게 전달하지 말라는 당부가 나온다(do not forward this e-mail to others).

What is implied about Pulse Insight Group?

(A) It employs the most staff in Westfield.
(B) It was created in the last year.
(C) It works in multiple regional markets.
(D) It issues ratings for many companies.

Pulse Insight Group에 관하여 무엇이 암시되어 있는가?

(A) Westfield에서 가장 많은 직원을 고용한다.
(B) 작년에 설립되었다.
(C) 여러 지역 시장에서 활동한다.
(D) 많은 기업에 대한 평가를 발표한다.

어휘 employ 고용하다 issue 발표하다 rating 평점, 등급

해설 첫 번째 이메일 첫 문장에서 Pulse Insight Group이 Zenetron의 의뢰를 받아 직원 설문 조사를 실시한다고 말하고 있다(Pulse Insight Group, an independent analytics firm based here in Westfield, has been hired by Zenetron to administer a workplace feedback survey). 두 번째 이메일 첫 문장에서는 Zenetron이 지역에서 가장 일하기 좋은 직장 중 하나로 선정되었다는 소식을 전하고 있다(Yesterday, the *Westfield Gazette* released its latest rankings titled "Best Workplaces in Westfield," and Zenetron proudly earned number 4 on the list!) 이 결과는 몇 달 전에 실시된 직원 설문 조사에서 나온 것이다(especially since the results stem from the staff survey many of you completed a few months ago). 이 조사는 바로 첫 번째 이메일에서 Pulse Insight Group이 Zenetron 직원을 대상으로 실시한 것이고, 두 번째 이메일을 통해 Pulse Insight Group이 180개의 기업들을 평가했다는(Out of 180 companies reviewed by a local assessment firm, only 12 were selected for recognition) 것을 추론할 수 있다.

According to Mr. Qureshi, what does Zenetron plan to do in the near future?

(A) Attract new customers
(B) Win more corporate awards
(C) Grow its workforce
(D) Conduct more employee surveys

Mr. Qureshi에 따르면 Zenetron은 가까운 미래에 무엇을 할 계획인가?

(A) 신규 고객을 유치한다
(B) 더 많은 기업상을 수상한다
(C) 인력을 확충한다
(D) 더 많은 직원 설문 조사를 실시한다

해설 마지막 문단에서 다음 분기에 채용 캠페인을 시작한다고 말하고 있다(we will be launching a major recruiting campaign next quarter).

Questions 186 through 190 refer to the following article and e-mails.

City Chef Wows Crowd
by Gianni Rhee-Kwan

PORTSMONT (24 October)—Last night at Brisa Bistro, a central dining venue, hometown chef Matteo Van der Meer led a live cooking demonstration for a rapt audience. "The event went exceptionally well," [186]said Brisa Bistro proprietor Erin Park. "We sold every seat, and our guests were thoroughly impressed."

Mr. Van der Meer sold his Portsmont restaurant, Matteo's, earlier this summer, and has since taken part in guest chef events at various eateries around the city. "It's refreshing to work without the day-to-day responsibilities of ownership," said Mr. Van der Meer. "I'm enjoying the chance to discover new neighborhoods and engage with different diners." Details about upcoming appearances can be found at his Web site: www.matteovandermeer.com.

To: Matteo Van der Meer <matteo@matteovandermeer.com>
From: Sophie Hanley <sophie.hanley@eletterbox.com>
Re: Guest Spot Request
Date: 27 October

Dear Mr. Van der Meer,

My name is Sophie Hanley, and I own both Hanley's Table on Riverstone Avenue and Oakwood Eatery on Millcrest Lane. [188]I attended your recent demonstration at Brisa Bistro and was very impressed, to say the least. [187][190]I am wondering if you'd be available to make a guest appearance at Oakwood Eatery sometime in March or April.

[189]My sister Natalie, who manages a local promotions agency, could help us secure strong visibility and draw in an engaged crowd. We're flexible with scheduling, so please let me know if you'd be interested.

Sincerely,
Sophie Hanley
sophie.hanley@eletterbox.com / (778)-555-8032

186–190번 문제는 다음 기사와 두 이메일에 관한 것입니다.

지역 출신 요리사, 군중을 사로잡다
Gianni Rhee-Kwan

PORTSMONT(10월 24일) 어제 저녁 도심의 식당 Brisa Bistro에서 지역 출신 요리사 Matteo Van der Meer가 몰입한 관객을 대상으로 라이브 요리 시연을 진행했다. Brisa Bistro 소유주 Erin Park은 "행사가 전에 없이 잘 진행되었어요."라고 말했다. "모든 좌석이 매진되었고, 손님들은 완전히 감명받았습니다."

Mr. Van der Meer은 올여름 초에 Portsmont에 자신의 식당 Matteo's를 처분하고 이후 도시 곳곳의 여러 식당에서 초청 요리사 행사에 참여해 오고 있다. Mr. Van der Meer는 "소유주의 일상적인 업무에서 벗어나 일하는 것은 참 신선합니다."라고 말했다. "새로운 동네를 발견하고 다양한 손님들과 교류할 기회가 있어서 즐거워요." 다가오는 출연 일정에 대한 세부 정보는 홈페이지 www.matteovandermeer.com에서 확인할 수 있다.

수신: Matteo Van der Meer
　　　〈matteo@matteovandermeer.com〉
발신: Sophie Hanley
　　　〈sophie.hanley@eletterbox.com〉
제목: 게스트 출연 요청
날짜: 10월 27일

　Mr. Van der Meer께,

제 이름은 Sophie Hanley이며, Riverstone 대로에 있는 Hanley's Table과 Millcrest 길에 있는 Oakwood Eatery를 운영하고 있습니다. 최근 Brisa Bistro에서 하신 시연회에 참석했는데 조금도 과장하지 않고 정말 감명 깊었습니다. 3월이나 4월 중에 Oakwood Eatery에서 게스트로 출연할 시간이 되시는지 궁금합니다.

제 여동생이 Natalie가 이 지역에서 홍보 대행사를 운영하고 있는데, 강력한 노출도를 확보하고 참여도가 높은 사람들을 끌어들이도록 도와줄 수 있습니다. 일정은 조정이 가능하니 관심이 있으시다면 알려 주시기 바랍니다.

진심을 담아,
Sophie Hanley
sophie.hanley@eletterbox.com / (778)-555-8032

To: Sophie Hanley <sophie.hanley@eletterbox.com> From: Matteo Van der Meer <matteo@matteovandermeer.com> Re: RE: Guest Spot Request Date: 28 October Dear Sophie, Thank you for your message. [190]I am currently fully booked for both March and April, but I do have a slot open on February 22, which recently became available following a cancellation. If that date would work for your team, I'd be glad to discuss the program and logistics in more detail. Best regards, Matteo Van der Meer	수신: Sophie Hanley 〈sophie.hanley@eletterbox.com〉 발신: Matteo Van der Meer 〈matteo@matteovandermeer.com〉 제목: RE: 게스트 출연 요청 날짜: 10월 28일 Sophie께, 메시지 고맙습니다. 현재 3월과 4월은 모두 예약이 다 차 있지만, 2월 22일에는 최근 취소로 인해 생긴 비는 시간이 있습니다. 이 날짜가 귀하의 팀에게도 괜찮다면 프로그램과 세부 계획에 대해 더 자세히 논의하고 싶습니다. 이만 줄입니다. Matteo Van der Meer

어휘1 wow 감탄시키다 bistro 작은 레스토랑 venue 장소 demonstration 시연 rapt 몰두한 go well 잘 진행되다 exceptionally 전에 없이, 예외적으로 proprietor 소유주 thoroughly 완전히, 전적으로 impressed 감명 받은 eatery 식당 refreshing 참신하고 재미있는 ownership 소유주 neighborhood 지역, 동네 engage with ~와 교류하다 diner 식사하는 손님 appearance 출연, 등장

어휘2 Re: ~에 관하여(regarding) spot 출연 to say the least 조금도 과장하지 않고 available to-V ~할 시간을 낼 수 있는 make an appearance 출연하다 visibility 노출도 engaged 참여도가 높은, 적극적인

어휘3 fully booked 예약이 꽉 찬 slot 시간대, 자리 following ~ 후에 cancellation 취소 work for *sb* ~에게 괜찮다 logistics 세부 (실행) 계획

186

Who is Ms. Park? (A) A local journalist (B) A culinary demonstrator **(C) A restaurant owner** (D) A marketing specialist	Ms. Park은 누구인가? (A) 지역의 언론인 (B) 요리 시연자 (C) 식당 소유주 (D) 마케팅 전문가

해설 기사 첫 문단에 Ms. Park은 식당 소유주(Brisa Bistro proprietor Erin Park)라고 나와 있다.

187

What is the purpose of Ms. Hanley's e-mail to Mr. Van der Meer? (A) To apply for a position (B) To recommend a dining location (C) To respond to an inquiry **(D) To extend an invitation**	Ms. Hanley가 Mr. Van der Meer에게 보낸 이메일의 목적은 무엇인가? (A) 어떤 자리에 지원하기 위해 (B) 식사 장소를 추천하기 위해 (C) 문의에 응답하기 위해 (D) 초청을 제안하기 위해

어휘 inquiry 문의 extend 주다, 베풀다

해설 이메일 첫 문단에서 자신이 운영하는 식당에 게스트로 출연해 달라고 요청하고 있다(I am wondering if you'd be available to make a guest appearance at Oakwood Eatery sometime in March or April).

188

According to the first e-mail, how did Ms. Hanley learn about Mr. Van der Meer's skills?

(A) She watched one of his demonstrations.
(B) She dined at his former restaurant.
(C) She read an online profile about him.
(D) She saw a print advertisement.

첫 번째 이메일에 따르면 Ms. Hanley는 Mr. Van der Meer의 기술에 대해 어떻게 알게 되었는가?

(A) 시연회를 관람했다.
(B) 전에 그가 운영하던 식당에서 식사했다.
(C) 그에 대한 온라인 소개를 읽었다.
(D) 인쇄 광고를 보았다.

어휘 profile 프로필, 간략한 소개

해설 첫 문단에서 Mr. Van der Meer의 최근 시연회를 보고 깊은 감명을 받았다고 말하고 있다(I attended your recent demonstration at Brisa Bistro and was very impressed, to say the least).

189

Why is Ms. Hanley's sister Natalie mentioned in the first e-mail?

(A) To compliment Mr. Van der Meer's establishment
(B) To suggest that her sister's expertise might be beneficial
(C) To identify who purchased Mr. Van der Meer's restaurant
(D) To imply that her sister's article has provided excellent publicity

첫 번째 이메일에서 Ms. Hanley의 여동생 Natalie는 왜 언급되는가?

(A) Mr. Van der Meer의 사업장을 칭찬하기 위해
(B) 여동생의 전문성이 도움이 될 수 있음을 시사하기 위해
(C) 누가 Mr. Van der Meer의 식당을 매입했는지 밝히기 위해
(D) 여동생의 기사로 인한 홍보 효과가 컸음을 암시하기 위해

어휘 compliment 칭찬하다 establishment 시설 beneficial 유익한 identify 확인하다 publicity 홍보

해설 여동생이 홍보 대행사를 운영하고 있기 때문에, 그녀의 광고 전문 지식이 행사를 대중들에게 알리고 관객을 끌어 모으는 데 도움이 될 것이라고 말하고 있다(My sister Natalie, who manages a local promotions agency, could help us secure strong visibility and draw in an engaged crowd).

190

Where might Mr. Van der Meer perform on February 22?

(A) Matteo's
(B) Brisa Bistro
(C) Hanley's Table
(D) Oakwood Eatery

Mr. Van der Meer는 2월 22일에 어디에서 공연하겠는가?

(A) Matteo's
(B) Brisa Bistro
(C) Hanley's Table
(D) Oakwood Eatery

해설 첫 번째 이메일에서 Ms. Hanley가 Mr. Van der Meer에게 3월이나 4월에 Oakwood Eatery에서 쇼에 출연해 달라고 요청했는데(I am wondering if you'd be available to make a guest appearance at Oakwood Eatery sometime in March or April), 답장을 읽어 보면 3, 4월에는 시간을 낼 수 없고, 대신 2월 22일에 출연할 수 있다고 말하고 있다(I am currently fully booked for both March and April, but I do have a slot open on February 22). 장소에 대한 언급이 더 이상 없는 것으로 보아, 만약 합의가 잘 이루어진다면 Mr. Van der Meer은 2월 22일에 처음에 요청받은 대로 Oakwood Eatery에서 요리 시연을 할 것이라고 짐작할 수 있다.

From: Linnea Haddad
To: Marketing Department, Barrington Institute of Culinary Arts
Date: 22 February
Subject: Meeting Summary

Hello Team,

Below is a brief recap of yesterday's meeting discussion:

- [191]Enrollment figures in our professional chef training program continue on an upward trend. Based on student zip codes, it is clear that our outreach to a wider geographic base has paid off. Over 42 percent of new enrollees live 30 or more miles away from the campus. That is a 12 percent increase from last year.

- Conversely, our recreational cooking programs have seen a dip in participation recently. [193]Delphine is working on a digital feedback survey to share with past attendees. [192]Once we gain insight into their current preferences, we will revise the course lineup to suit them.

Our upcoming marketing team meeting is set for 1:30 P.M. next Wednesday.

Linnea

SURVEY

To be entered into a drawing for a free cooking class, please provide your contact information:

[193]Name: Olivia Klein
E-mail address: oklein@vmailer.org

Please select the response that BEST represents your preference:

1. What area of cooking interests you most?
☐ Core cooking methods and skills
☐ Food associated with particular regions
☑ Ingredient handling and usage

2. [194]What might encourage you to sign up for a Barrington Institute class this year?
☐ Reduced course fees
☑ [194]Online course availability
☐ Better scheduling options on site

191-195번 문제는 다음 이메일과 설문 조사, 수업 일정에 관한 것입니다.

발신: Linnea Haddad
수신: Barrington 요리 예술원 마케팅부
날짜: 2월 22일
제목: 회의 요약

팀원 여러분, 안녕하세요.

아래는 어제 회의에서 논의한 사항의 간략한 요약입니다.

– 전문 요리사 양성 프로그램의 등록 수치가 지속적으로 상승세에 있다. 학생들의 우편 번호를 근거로 보았을 때 더 넓은 지역으로 홍보한 것이 성과를 거둔 것이 분명하다. 42퍼센트가 넘는 신규 등록자들이 캠퍼스에서 30마일 이상 떨어진 곳에 살고 있다. 이것은 작년보다 12퍼센트 증가한 것이다.

– 반대로 취미 요리 프로그램은 최근 참가자 수가 감소했다. Delphine이 과거 참가자들을 대상으로 한 디지털 피드백 설문 조사를 작성하고 있다. 일단 그들이 현재 선호하는 사항을 파악하고 나면 그에 맞게 코스 구성을 수정할 것이다.

다음 마케팅 팀 회의는 다음 주 수요일 오후 1시 30분으로 예정되어 있습니다.

Linnea

설문 조사

무료 요리 수업 추첨에 참여하시려면 연락처를 제공해 주시기 바랍니다.

이름: Olivia Klein
이메일 주소: oklein@vmailer.org

선호하는 사항을 가장 잘 나타내는 응답을 선택해 주세요.

1. 요리의 어느 분야에 가장 관심 있으신가요?
☐ 기본 요리 방식과 기법
☐ 특정 지역과 관련된 음식
☑ 재료 취급 및 사용법

2. 올해 무엇이 Barrington 요리 예술원 강좌에 등록하도록 귀하를 유도할 수 있을까요?
☐ 수업료 인하
☑ 온라인 수업 이용 가능성
☐ 더 나은 현장 수업 일정 옵션

Home | Chef Certification | **Hobbyist Cooking Classes** | Contact Us

Early Summer Class Schedule

Essential Kitchen Skills
Just getting started in the kitchen? This foundational course offers hands-on training to help sharpen your knife skills and master cooking basics like roasting, sautéing, and grilling.
[195(B)]June 4 – 8, 10:00 A.M.– 4:00 P.M. $540

[195(C)(D)]NEW! Flavors of the Sea with Renowned Chef Helena Fujimoto
Take a deep dive into seafood cuisine with celebrated culinary expert Helena Fujimoto. Discover preparation methods, flavor pairings, and cooking styles across various regions. All proficiency levels welcome.
[195(B)]June 11–12, 10:00 A.M.– 4:00 P.M. $330

Tastes of South America
Spend the day uncovering traditional dishes from Brazil, Peru, Argentina, Colombia, and Chile. Learn classic recipes and new ways to infuse Latin American flair into your cooking. Intermediate and advanced learners only.
[195(B)]June 17, 10:00 A.M.– 2:30 P.M. $170

[195(C)]NEW! Global Egg Inspirations
Eggs go far beyond breakfast! [194]In this online-only course, explore their nutritional benefits and cultural versatility through internationally inspired egg-based recipes.
[195(B)]Available starting June 19. $120

홈 | 요리사 자격증 과정 | **취미 요리 수업** | 문의하기

초여름 수업 일정

기초 주방 기술
요리를 처음 시작하시나요? 이 기초 코스는 칼 다루는 기술을 연마하고 굽기, 볶음, 그릴 요리 같은 기본기를 숙달하도록 도와드리는 실습 교육을 제공합니다.
6월 4~8일, 오전 10시 ~ 오후 4시, 540달러

신설! 유명 요리사 Helena Fujimoto와 함께하는 바다의 맛
유명 요리 전문가 Helena Fujimoto와 함께 해산물 요리의 세계에 깊이 빠져들어 보세요. 다양한 지역의 조리법과 맛의 조합, 요리 스타일을 발견해 보세요. 숙련도에 상관없이 환영합니다.
6월 11~12일 오전 10시 ~ 오후 4시, 330달러

남미의 맛
브라질, 페루, 아르헨티나, 콜롬비아, 칠레의 전통 요리를 탐구하며 하루를 보내 보세요. 여러분의 요리에 라틴아메리카의 감각을 불어넣어 주는 고전적 조리법과 새로운 방식을 배워 보세요. 중급 및 상급 수강생 전용.
6월 17일 오전 10시 ~ 오후 2시 30분, 170달러

신설! 세계의 달걀 요리
달걀은 아침 식사만을 위한 것이 아닙니다! 이 온라인 전용 강좌에서 국제적으로 영감받은 달걀 기반 조리법을 통해 달걀의 영양학적 이점과 문화적 다용도성에 대해 탐구해 보세요.
6월 19일부터 수강 가능. 120달러

어휘1 institute 전문학교 culinary 요리의 summary 요약 recap 요약, 개요 enrollment 등록 figure 수치 upward 상승하는 zip code 우편 번호 outreach 퍼짐, 도달 geographic 지리적인 pay off 성과를 거두다 enrollee 등록자 conversely 반대로 recreational 취미의 dip 감소 attendee 참가자 gain insight into ~에 대한 통찰을 얻다. ~을 파악하다 preference 선호(하는 것) revise 수정하다 lineup 구성 suit ~에 맞다 be set for ~으로 예정되다

어휘2 be entered into ~에 참가하다. 응모하다 drawing 추첨 represent 나타내다 core 핵심의 associated with ~과 관련된 handling 다루는 방식, 취급 usage 사용 sign up for ~에 등록하다 on site 현장의

어휘3 certification 자격증 hobbyist 취미로 하는 사람 foundational 기초적인 hands-on 실습의 sharpen 연마하다 roast 굽다 sauté 볶다 grill 석쇠에 굽다 renowned 유명한 take a dive into ~을 깊이 탐구하다 cuisine 요리 celebrated 유명한 preparation (음식의) 준비, 조리 pairing 조합 proficiency 숙련도 uncover 밝혀내다, 탐구하다 infuse 불어넣다 flair 재능, (독특한) 멋 intermediate 중급의 advanced 고급의 go far beyond ~을 훨씬 넘어가다 explore 조사하다, 탐구하다 nutritional 영양의 benefit 이점 versatility 다목적성

191

According to the e-mail, what is indicated about the professional training program?

(A) It changed campus locations recently.
(B) It will increase remote learning options.
(C) It has attracted more students lately.
(D) It plans to create a brand-new marketing strategy.

이메일에 따르면 전문 교육 프로그램에 관하여 무엇이 나타나 있는가?

(A) 최근에 캠퍼스 위치를 변경했다.
(B) 원격 학습 옵션을 늘릴 것이다.
(C) 최근에 더 많은 학생을 유치했다.
(D) 완전히 새로운 마케팅 계획을 수립할 계획이다.

어휘 remote 원격의 attract 끌어들이다 lately 최근에

해설 요약된 회의 내용의 첫 항목으로 전문 요리사 양성 과정 등록자 수의 지속적인 상승세를 언급하고 있다(Enrollment figures in our professional chef training program continue on an upward trend).

In the e-mail, the word "suit" in paragraph 3, line 3, is closest in meaning to

(A) contact
(B) dress
(C) satisfy
(D) flatter

이메일에서 세 번째 문단 세 번째 줄의 단어 "suit"와 의미상 가장 가까운 것은

(A) 연락하다
(B) 옷을 입히다
(C) 충족시키다
(D) 돋보이게 하다

해설 Once we gain insight into their current preferences, we will revise the course lineup to suit them.(일단 그들이 현재 선호하는 사항을 파악하고 나면 그에 맞게 코스 구성을 수정할 것이다.)에서 suit는 '～에 알맞다'라는 뜻이므로 satisfy로 대신할 수 있다. suit가 옷에 관련된 단어로도 사용될 수 있기 때문에 역시 옷과 관련된 단어인 (B)나 (D)를 정답으로 고르지 않도록 단어의 의미와 용법을 정확히 알고 있어야 한다.

What can be inferred about Ms. Klein?

(A) She wants to become a certified professional chef.
(B) She attended a previous cooking class at the institute.
(C) She received a free pass for a culinary class.
(D) She lives farther from the campus than most participants.

Ms. Klein에 관하여 무엇을 추론할 수 있는가?

(A) 공인 전문 요리사가 되기를 원한다.
(B) 기관에서 전에 요리 수업을 들었다.
(C) 요리 수업 무료 수강권을 받았다.
(D) 대부분의 참가자들보다 캠퍼스에서 더 먼 곳에 산다.

어휘 certified 공인된

해설 이메일에서 과거 수강생들을 대상으로 하는 설문 조사를 준비하고 있다고 했으므로(Delphine is working on a digital feedback survey to share with past attendees.) 설문에 참여하고 있는 Ms. Klein은 전에 이 기관에서 수업을 들은 사람임을 추론할 수 있다.

Which summer class would Ms. Klein most likely be interested in taking?

(A) Essential Kitchen Skills
(B) Flavors of the Sea with Helena Fujimoto
(C) Tastes of South America
(D) Global Egg Inspirations

Ms. Klein는 어느 여름 강좌를 듣는 데 관심이 있겠는가?

(A) 기초 주방 기술
(B) Helena Fujimoto와 함께 하는 바다의 맛
(C) 남미의 맛
(D) 세계의 달걀 요리

해설 설문 조사에서 요리 수업 등록을 위해 바라는 점을 묻는 질문에 대해(What might encourage you to sign up for a Barrington Institute class this year?) 온라인 수업을 원한다고 답했는데(Online course availability), 수업 일정에 온라인으로 제공되는 수업은(In this online-only course) Global Egg Inspirations이다.

What is NOT true about the class offerings?

(A) All courses are for experienced chefs.
(B) Courses vary in length.
(C) Some courses are being offered for the first time.
(D) One class features a famous culinary instructor.

강좌에 관하여 사실이 아닌 것은 무엇인가?

(A) 모든 코스가 경험 많은 요리사를 위한 것이다.
(B) 코스마다 길이가 다르다.
(C) 어떤 코스는 처음으로 제공된다.
(D) 한 강좌는 유명 요리 강사를 출연시킨다.

어휘 offering 강의 과목, 강좌 experienced 경험이 많은 vary 다양하다 feature 출연시키다 instructor 강사

해설 우선 수업 일정에서 각 강좌가 제공되는 날짜와 시간을 보며 (B)를 제거해야 한다. 강좌명에 NEW!가 포함된 것들이 있으므로 (C)도 제거한다. 유명 요리사 Helena Fujimoto를 강사로 초빙한 강좌도 있으므로 (D)도 제거하면 정답을 알 수 있다.

Questions 196 through 200 refer to the following Web page, online form, and online review.

Home | **Product Guide** | Place Order | DIY Advice

Norwell Upholstery Supply

At Norwell Upholstery Supply, we offer a wide selection of cushion foam, available in a variety of densities and price ranges. This handy product guide outlines our four top-rated items to help you select the one that best aligns with your project.

- F10 – Extremely soft. Highly plush but tends to lose its shape and flatten over time. Ideal for items that see infrequent use.
- F20 – Soft. Budget-friendly choice, though less resilient than higher-density options. Becomes softer with continued use.
- [197]F30 – Medium firmness. Our most popular option. Slightly costlier, yet offers excellent comfort, long-term durability, and stands up to frequent use.
- F40 – Very firm. Perfect for dining seating or projects that demand dense support.

Caution: [196]All polyurethane foam products are highly flammable when exposed to open flames.

Custom cutting: [198]Foam is supplied in standard sheet sizes, but shaping it to suit your needs is straightforward. See our instructional video under the "DIY Advice" tab.

Customer Inquiry Form

Name: Hanna Tovarek
E-mail: h_tovarek@inboxlane.org
Phone: 628-555-0914
Message:
I'm renovating a vintage couch and need replacement foam for the cushions. I'm not sure which type to select. I don't want it too stiff, but I also don't want something that sinks too easily. [197]A mid-range firmness sounds ideal. Price isn't really a concern—I'm more focused on longevity, since the couch will get plenty of use. I'd appreciate your guidance. Thank you!

196–200번 문제는 다음 웹 페이지와 온라인 서식, 온라인 후기에 관한 것입니다.

홈 | **제품 안내** | 주문하기 | DIY 팁

Norwell Upholstery Supply

Norwell Upholstery Supply는 다양한 쿠션용 발포 고무를 제공하며, 여러 밀도와 가격대로 이용할 수 있습니다. 이 유용한 제품 안내는 가장 인기 있는 네 가지 제품을 소개함으로써 당신의 프로젝트에 가장 잘 맞는 것을 선택하도록 도와드립니다.

- F10 – 매우 부드러움. 매우 푹신하지만 시간이 지남에 따라 모양이 사라지고 납작해질 수 있음. 자주 사용하지 않는 물건에 알맞음.
- F20 – 부드러움. 밀도가 더 높은 제품에 비해 탄력은 떨어지지만 비용 부담이 적은 선택. 지속적으로 사용하면 더 부드러워짐.
- F30 – 중간 정도의 단단함. 가장 인기 있는 선택. 비용은 약간 더 많이 들지만, 탁월한 편안함과 장기간의 내구성을 보이며 잦은 사용을 견뎌냄.
- F40 – 매우 단단함. 식탁 좌석이나 고밀도 쿠션을 요하는 프로젝트에 안성맞춤.

주의: 모든 폴리우레탄 발포 고무 제품은 개방된 불에 노출될 때 가연성이 매우 높습니다.

맞춤 절단: 발포 고무는 표준 낱장 크기로 공급되지만, 필요에 맞게 모양을 잡는 일은 간단합니다. "DIY 팁" 탭을 클릭하여 안내 동영상을 보세요.

고객 문의 서식

이름: Hanna Tovarek
이메일: h_tovarek@inboxlane.org
전화: 628-555-0914
메시지:
빈티지 소파 하나를 개조하고 있어서 쿠션으로 쓸 교체용 발포 고무가 필요합니다. 어떤 유형을 선택해야 할지 모르겠네요. 너무 뻣뻣한 것은 원하지 않지만, 너무 쉽게 꺼지는 것도 별로입니다. 중간 정도의 단단함이 딱 좋을 것 같습니다. 가격은 별로 중요하지 않습니다. 저는 소파를 많이 사용할 것이기 때문에, 수명에 더 신경을 씁니다. 안내해 주시면 감사하겠습니다. 고맙습니다!

"Norwell has earned my loyalty."

If you need high-quality foam for couch cushions, I suggest Norwell Upholstery Supply. As a novice seamstress, I didn't know which kind of padding was best for my upholstery project. [199]The staff at Norwell were incredibly supportive and well-informed, which made the process much easier.

[198]My couch had an unusual shape, but the company's Web site offered all the tools and guidance I needed to tackle those tricky aspects. [200]Just note that Norwell doesn't accommodate custom size orders, so be ready to cut the foam sheets yourself. I only make these purchases occasionally, but Norwell is now my go-to.

"이제부터 Norwell만 이용합니다."

소파 쿠션용으로 고품질의 발포 고무가 필요하다면 Norwell Upholstery Supply를 추천합니다. 재봉 초보자라서 소파 커버를 씌울 때 어떤 종류의 패딩이 가장 좋을지 몰랐어요. Norwell의 직원들은 매우 열심히 도와주고 전문적이어서, 작업이 훨씬 더 쉬워졌습니다.

제 소파는 모양이 특이하지만, 회사 홈페이지에서 그러한 까다로운 측면을 다루는 데 필요한 모든 툴과 안내를 제공해 주었습니다. Norwell이 맞춤 사이즈 주문은 받지 않는다는 점만 유의하시고, 발포 고무 시트를 직접 자를 준비를 하시기 바랍니다. 이러한 구매는 가끔씩만 하지만, Norwell은 이제 제가 가장 먼저 찾는 곳이 되었습니다.

어휘1 upholstery (의자, 소파 등의) 커버, 덮개 foam (의자, 매트리스의) 발포 고무 density 밀도 handy 유용한 top-rated 가장 인기 있는, 최고로 꼽히는 align with ~에 알맞다 plush 푹신한 tend to-V ~하기 쉽다 flatten 납작해지다 infrequent 드문 budget-friendly 비용 부담이 적은 resilient 탄력 있는 firmness 단단함 costly 비용이 많이 드는 durability 내구성 stand up to ~을 견디다 frequent 빈번한, 잦은 firm 단단한 seating 좌석 dense 고밀도의 polyurethane 폴리우레탄 flammable 불에 잘 타는 open flame (덮개나 보호 장치 없이) 노출된 불 custom 주문 제작의 shape 모양을 만들다 suit one's needs ~의 필요에 맞추다 straightforward 간단한 instructional 안내의, 사용 설명의 DIY(do-it-yourself) 직접 하기

어휘2 inquiry 문의 vintage 고풍스러운 couch 소파 stiff 뻣뻣한 longevity 수명 guidance 안내, 지도

어휘3 loyalty 충성 novice 초보자 seamstress 여성 재봉사 incredibly 대단히, 엄청나게 supportive 지원하는, 도와주는 well-informed 해박한, 전문적인 unusaul 특이한 tackle 대처하다, 다루다 tricky 까다로운 aspect 측면 accommodate 수용하다 occasionally 가끔 go-to 가장 먼저 찾는 것, 단골

196

On the Web page, what is indicated about Norwell Upholstery Supply's products?

(A) They are considered higher quality than competitors'.
(B) They can catch fire if exposed to heat.
(C) They are often hard to restock.
(D) They are intended primarily for mattresses.

웹 페이지에서 Norwell Upholstery Supply의 제품에 관하여 무엇이 나타나 있는가?

(A) 경쟁업체들의 제품보다 고품질인 것으로 여겨진다.
(B) 열에 노출되면 불이 붙을 수 있다.
(C) 종종 재입고가 어렵다.
(D) 주로 매트리스용이다.

어휘 competitor 경쟁업체 catch fire 불이 붙다 restock 재입고하다

해설 불에 노출되면 가연성이 매우 높다는 주의 사항이 나와 있다(All polyurethane foam products are highly flammable when exposed to open flames).

197

What foam type was likely recommended to Ms. Tovarek?
(A) F10
(B) F20
(C) F30
(D) F40

Ms. Tovarek에게 어떤 발포 고무 유형이 추천되었겠는가?
(A) F10
(B) F20
(C) F30
(D) F40

해설 Ms. Tovarek은 문의 서식에 중간 정도의 단단함을 원하며 싼 가격보다는 수명이 긴 것을 선호한다고, 또한 소파를 많이 사용할 것이라고 말한다(A mid-range firmness sounds ideal. Price isn't really a concern—I'm more focused on longevity, since the couch will get plenty of use). Norwell Upholstery Supply의 제품 안내를 읽어 보면 F30이 중간 정도의 단단함을 갖고 있으며, 약간 비싸지만 내구성이 좋고 잦은 사용을 견뎌낼 수 있는 제품이다(F30 - Medium firmness. Our most popular option. Slightly costlier, yet offers excellent comfort, long-term durability, and stands up to frequent use). Ms. Tovarek은 이 제품을 추천받았을 것이라고 추론할 수 있다.

198

What is probably true about Ms. Tovarek?

(A) She operates a home furnishings business.
(B) She asked for a sample of foam material.
(C) She received promotional pricing on an order.
(D) She viewed a tutorial video online.

Ms. Tovarek에 관하여 무엇이 사실이겠는가?

(A) 가정용 가구 사업체를 운영한다.
(B) 발포 고무 견본을 요청했다.
(C) 주문에 대해 판촉용 가격 혜택을 받았다.
(D) 온라인으로 사용 지침 동영상을 시청했다.

어휘 operate 운영하다 furnishings 가구 tutorial (컴퓨터의) 사용 지침서

해설 Ms. Tovarek은 평가에서 Norwell이 맞춤 제작 주문을 받지 않기 때문에 발포 고무 시트를 필요한 모양으로 자르는 것은 스스로 해야 한다는 점을 언급하면서(Just note that Norwell doesn't accommodate custom size orders, so be ready to cut the foam sheets yourself.) 작업에 필요한 지원을 회사 홈페이지에서 받을 수 있었다고 말한다(My couch had an unusual shape, but the company's Web site offered all the tools and guidance I needed to tackle those tricky aspects). 웹 페이지 마지막 문단에서 회사가 제공하는 동영상이 시트를 필요한 모양에 맞게 자르는 법을 알려준다(Foam is supplied in standard sheet sizes, but shaping it to suit your needs is straightforward. See our instructional video under the "DIY Advice" tab). 두 지문의 내용을 연계시키면 Ms. Tovarek이 사용 지침 영상을 시청했음을 추론할 수 있다.

199

According to the online review, what does Ms. Tovarek appreciate most about Norwell Upholstery Supply?

(A) Their wide range of products
(B) Their efficient shipping system
(C) Their attentive and knowledgeable staff
(D) Their competitive pricing

온라인 후기에 따르면 Ms. Tovarek이 Norwell Upholstery Supply에 대하여 무엇을 가장 높게 평가하는가?

(A) 매우 다양한 제품
(B) 효율적인 배송 시스템
(C) 배려 있고 박식한 직원들
(D) 경쟁력 있는 가격 책정

어휘 appreciate 진가를 인정하다 shipping 운송, 수송 attentive 배려하는, 친절한 knowledgeable 박식한 competitive 경쟁력 있는 pricing 가격 책정

해설 고객을 돕는 일에 열심이고 지식이 풍부한 직원들 덕분에 작업이 훨씬 수월해졌다고 칭찬하고 있다(The staff at Norwell were incredibly supportive and well-informed, which made the process much easier).

200

In the online review, the word "accommodate" in paragraph 2, line 2, is closest in meaning to

(A) agree to
(B) make space for
(C) give a refund for
(D) provide lodging to

온라인 후기에서 두 번째 문단 두 번째 줄의 단어 "accommodate"와 의미상 가장 가까운 것은

(A) ~에 찬성하다, 응하다
(B) ~을 위한 공간을 만들다
(C) ~을 환불해 주다
(D) ~에게 숙박을 제공하다

해설 accommodate는 '(요구를) 수용하다', '(공간에 사람이나 물건을) 수용하다', '~에게 숙박을 제공하다' 같은 의미가 있으므로 (C)를 제외한 모든 선택지가 동의어가 될 가능성이 있다. Norwell doesn't accommodate custom size orders는 Norwell이 맞춤 제작 주문을 받지 않는다는 뜻이므로 accommodate를 대신할 수 있는 말은 (A) agree to이다.

TEST 04

➡ **Answer**

101	(B)	111	(D)	121	(D)	131	(B)	141	(A)	151	(D)	161	(A)	171	(C)	181	(D)	191	(A)
102	(B)	112	(B)	122	(A)	132	(D)	142	(C)	152	(C)	162	(B)	172	(C)	182	(B)	192	(C)
103	(B)	113	(A)	123	(A)	133	(C)	143	(A)	153	(A)	163	(C)	173	(B)	183	(B)	193	(B)
104	(B)	114	(B)	124	(C)	134	(A)	144	(B)	154	(D)	164	(D)	174	(D)	184	(D)	194	(A)
105	(C)	115	(D)	125	(C)	135	(C)	145	(C)	155	(B)	165	(C)	175	(B)	185	(C)	195	(D)
106	(B)	116	(B)	126	(B)	136	(D)	146	(C)	156	(A)	166	(D)	176	(A)	186	(B)	196	(C)
107	(C)	117	(D)	127	(A)	137	(A)	147	(B)	157	(B)	167	(D)	177	(B)	187	(A)	197	(A)
108	(C)	118	(A)	128	(A)	138	(C)	148	(B)	158	(C)	168	(D)	178	(A)	188	(D)	198	(A)
109	(B)	119	(D)	129	(B)	139	(B)	149	(B)	159	(D)	169	(A)	179	(A)	189	(D)	199	(B)
110	(B)	120	(D)	130	(C)	140	(C)	150	(D)	160	(B)	170	(D)	180	(D)	190	(B)	200	(D)

PART 5

101

Trenton Dynamics successfully met its recruitment goals for the third ------- year.

(A) following
(B) **consecutive**
(C) approximate
(D) absolute

Trenton Dynamics는 3년 연속으로 채용 목표를 성공적으로 달성했다.

어휘 meet 달성하다 recruitment 채용 consecutive 연속적인 approximate 대략의

해설 항상 짝을 이루어 출제되는 어휘 문제는 암기하고 있다가 재빨리 정답을 선택하자. for the + 서수 + ------- + year[month]가 보이면 정답은 항상 consecutive이다.

102

To cut down on -------, Eloria Skincare has decided to halve its promotional spending.

(A) values
(B) **expenses**
(C) customs
(D) refunds

Eloria Skincare는 비용을 절감하기 위해 홍보비 지출을 절반으로 줄이기로 결정했다.

어휘 cut down on ~을 줄이다 customs 관세 halve 절반으로 줄이다 promotional 홍보의 spending 지출

해설 홍보비 지출을 줄이는 것은 회사 운영 '비용'을 절감하기 위한 조치이다.

103

Mr. Harris has chosen to lease an apartment for the ------- of his assignment in Liverpool.

(A) collection
(B) **duration**
(C) capacity
(D) environment

Mr. Harris는 Liverpool에서의 업무 기간 동안 아파트를 임대하기로 했다.

어휘 lease 임대하다, 임차하다 duration 기간 capacity 용량, 수용력 assignment 수행 업무

해설 빈칸 앞뒤 to lease an apartment for the ------- of his assignment(업무의 [(A) 수집을 위해 (B) 기간 동안 (C) 용량을 위해 (D) 환경을 위해] 아파트를 임차하다]의 의미를 자연스럽게 만들어 주는 명사가 정답이다.

104

The revised proposal was far more detailed ------- the original, especially in its financial projections.

(A) as
(B) than
(C) of
(D) from

수정된 기획안은 원안보다 훨씬 더 상세했으며, 특히 재정 예상 부분에서 그랬다.

어휘 revise 수정하다 proposal 제안서, 기획안 projection 예상, 추정

해설 수정된 기획안이 원안'보다' 더 자세하다고 말해야 한다. 비교급 형용사/부사 뒤에는 항상 than이 따라다닌다.

105

Ms. Sharma intends to ------- certain terms in her employment contract prior to finalizing the paperwork.

(A) deprive
(B) respond
(C) modify
(D) assure

Ms. Sharma는 서류 작업을 마무리하기 전에 근로 계약서의 일부 조항을 수정할 생각이다.

어휘 intend to-V ~할 생각[계획]이다 deprive 빼앗다 modify 수정하다 assure 보장하다 terms 조항, 조건 prior to ~하기 전에

해설 deprive는 deprive A of B의 형태로 사용하며, respond는 자동사이기 때문에 바로 뒤에 목적어가 올 수 없다. assure는 성공, 승리 등을 나타내는 단어를 목적어로 취한다. 계약서 조항을 수정한다고 말하는 것이 자연스럽다.

106

------- your application has been approved, the bank will deposit the funds into your account.

(A) Although
(B) As soon as
(C) Thereafter
(D) How

신청서가 승인되는 즉시 은행은 자금을 귀하의 계좌에 입금할 것입니다.

어휘 thereafter 그 이후에 approve 승인하다 deposit 입금하다

해설 쉼표 앞부분이 부사절이므로 빈칸에는 부사절 접속사인 (A)나 (B)가 들어갈 수 있다. (C)는 부사이고, 의문사인 (D)는 명사절 접속사이다. 문장 해석이 어렵다면, 시간 부사절에서는 미래 시제를 사용할 수 없고 대신 현재(완료) 시제가 사용된다는 사실을 기억하자. 주절이 미래 시제인 것을 보면 쉼표 앞은 현재완료 시제가 미래 사건을 나타내는 시간 부사절임을 알 수 있다.

107

Mr. Jang has been promoted to Executive Director of Marketing and ------- his new role on April 15.

(A) remains
(B) concerns
(C) assumes
(D) participates

Mr. Jang은 마케팅 부서 전무 이사로 승진했으며, 4월 15일에 새 직책을 맡는다.

어휘 executive director 전무 이사 concern 관련되다 assume (직책을) 맡다

해설 승진한 중역이 4월 15일에 새 직책을 맡게 된다고 말하는 것이 자연스럽다. (D) participates는 의미상 말이 되는 것 같지만 전치사 in과 함께 사용해야 한다.

108

Scientists must verify that any modifications to the research setting are not ------- to the experiment.

(A) disrupt
(B) disrupted
(C) disruptive
(D) disrupter

과학자들은 연구 환경에 대한 어떤 변경도 실험에 방해되지 않는다는 것을 확인해야 한다.

어휘 verify 확인하다 modification 수정, 변경 setting 환경 disrupt 방해하다 disruptive 방해가 되는 disrupter 방해 요소 experiment 실험

해설 be동사 뒤 주격 보어 자리에는 형용사가 정답이다. 주격 보어 자리에는 명사도 들어갈 수 있지만 토익에서는 항상 형용사만 정답으로 출제된다. 선택지에 형용사가 없을 때는 형용사를 대신할 수 있는 분사가 정답이다. 형용사와 분사가 모두 있을 때는 거의 대부분 형용사가 정답이다.

109

Consultants at Virelli Group collaborate with business owners to create ------- marketing strategies.

(A) unavailable　　　　　　　　**(B) innovative**
(C) resolved　　　　　　　　　(D) convinced

Virelli Group의 컨설턴트들은 사업주들과 협력하여 혁신적인 마케팅 전략을 수립한다.

어휘 unavailable 이용할 수 없는　collaborate 협력하다　innovative 혁신적인　resolved 굳게 결심한, 단호한　convinced 확신하는　strategy 전략

해설 항상 짝을 이루어 출제되는 어휘 문제는 암기하고 있다가 재빨리 정답을 선택하자. '------- + marketing strategy[solution / design]'가 보이면 항상 innovative나 creative가 정답이다. 참고로 (C)나 (D)는 명사 앞에는 사용할 수 없으며, (A)도 명사 앞에 사용되는 일은 거의 없고 대부분 보어로 사용한다.

110

Adopting cloud-based accounting tools would streamline Veltrix Solutions' fiscal operations -------.

(A) substantial　　　　　　　**(B) substantially**
(C) more substantial　　　　　(D) substances

클라우드 기반의 회계 도구를 채택하면 Veltrix Solutions의 재정 운영이 상당히 간소화될 것이다.

어휘 adopt 채택하다　accounting 회계　streamline 간소화하다　fiscal 재정의　operation 운영　substantial 상당한　substance 물질

해설 완성된 문장 구조가 보이면 빈칸에 부사가 들어가야 한다. '타동사 + 목적어 + -------'은 매우 자주 출제되는 구조이므로 기억해 두자. 3형식 문장이 완성되어 있으므로 부사가 정답이다.

111

Earlier this month, the board members voted ------- to implement a new incentive plan for top performers.

(A) commonly　　　　　　　　(B) increasingly
(C) critically　　　　　　　　　**(D) unanimously**

이달 초, 이사회는 투표를 통해 최고 성과자들을 위한 새 인센티브 계획을 시행할 것을 만장일치로 결정했다.

어휘 board 이사회　vote 투표하다　critically 비판적으로　unanimously 만장일치로　implement 시행하다　plan 계획, 안(案)　top performer 최고 성과자

해설 빈칸 앞뒤 voted ------- to implement(투표를 통하여 시행할 것을 [(A) 흔히 (B) 점점 더 (C) 비판적으로 (D) 만장일치로] 결정했다)의 의미를 자연스럽게 만들어 주는 부사가 정답이다.

112

The acclaimed literary publication *Meridian Journal* regularly highlights both seasoned and ------- authors.

(A) emerge　　　　　　　　　**(B) emerging**
(C) emerges　　　　　　　　　(D) to emerge

호평받는 문학 출판물인 *Meridian Journal*은 베테랑 작가들과 신진 작가들을 모두 정기적으로 조명한다.

어휘 acclaimed 호평받는　publication 출판물　highlight 강조하다, 조명하다　seasoned 경험이 많은, 노련한　emerge 부상하다, 부각되다　emerging 신흥의, 떠오르는　author 작가, 저자

해설 빈칸 앞뒤에 and, or, but, so, yet 같은 등위접속사가 보이면 병렬 구조를 생각해야 한다. 토익에서는 대부분 and를 이용한 문제가 출제된다. and 앞에 형용사 seasoned가 있으므로 뒤에도 형용사가 필요하다.

113

The company welcomes candidate submissions, ------- whether they have worked in digital commerce before.

(A) regardless of　　　　　(B) despite that
(C) except for　　　　　　　　(D) considering that

그 회사는 이전에 디지털 상거래 분야에서 일한 경험이 있는지 여부와 관계없이 지원을 환영한다.

어휘 candidate submissions 지원　regardless of ~에 관계없이　despite ~에도 불구하고　considering that ~을 고려하면

해설 접속사 whether로 시작하는 명사절 바로 앞에 또 다른 접속사인 (B)나 (D)가 들어갈 수는 없다. 경력 여부에 상관없이 지원을 받는다는 뜻의 문장이 되도록 전치사를 선택해야 한다.

114

Due to unforeseen logistical complications, the launch of the new satellite was ------ behind schedule.

(A) marginal
(B) **marginally**
(C) margin
(D) marginalize

예기치 못한 물류상의 문제로 인해, 새 위성의 발사는 일정보다 약간 늦춰졌다.

어휘 unforeseen 예기치 못한 logistical 물류의 complication 복잡한 문제 launch 발사 satellite (인공)위성 marginal 미미한 margin 여유, 차이 marginalize 소외시키다 behind schedule 예정보다 늦은

해설 전치사구를 수식하는 품사는 부사이다. 전치사구, to부정사, 동명사, 분사, 관사, 소유격 (대)명사 등을 수식하는 자리가 빈칸이면 모두 부사가 정답이라고 알고 있어야 한다.

115

Ms. Huang's transition to director of product innovation was finalized more ------ than the company had expected.

(A) partially
(B) ultimately
(C) adequately
(D) **swiftly**

Ms. Huang이 제품 혁신 책임자 자리로 전환되는 일은 회사의 예상보다 더 신속하게 마무리되었다.

어휘 transition 이동, 전환 director 이사, 책임자 innovation 혁신 partially 부분적으로 ultimately 궁극적으로 adequately 충분하게, 적합하게 swiftly 신속하게

해설 빈칸 앞뒤 was finalized more ------ than the company had expected(회사의 예상보다 더 [(A) 부분적으로 (B) 궁극적으로 (C) 충분하게 (D) 신속하게] 마무리되었다)의 의미를 자연스럽게 만들어 주는 부사가 정답이다.

116

By evaluating the ------ of the equipment in desert terrain, the engineers confirmed its reliability under harsh conditions.

(A) enduring
(B) **endurance**
(C) endures
(D) endure

사막 지형에서 장비의 내구성을 평가함으로써, 엔지니어들은 그것이 혹독한 환경에서도 신뢰할 수 있음을 확인했다.

어휘 evaluate 평가하다 endurance 내구성, 지구력 endure 견디다 desert 사막 terrain 지형 reliability 신뢰성 harsh 혹독한

해설 관사와 전치사 사이에 빈칸 있을 때는 주저 말고 명사를 정답으로 선택해야 한다.

117

Many job seekers submit applications to Dentra Solutions because it provides ------ opportunities for career advancement.

(A) outgrown
(B) outlying
(C) outstretched
(D) **outstanding**

많은 구직자들이 Dentra Solutions에 지원서를 제출하는 이유는 그곳이 경력 발전을 위한 훌륭한 기회를 제공하기 때문이다.

어휘 outgrow ~보다 더 커지다 outlying 외딴, 외진 outstretched 쭉 뻗은 outstanding 뛰어난

해설 빈칸 앞뒤 it provides ------ opportunities for career advancement(경력 발전을 위한 [(A) 맞지 않게 된 (B) 외딴 (C) 쭉 뻗은 (D) 훌륭한] 기회를 제공한다)의 의미를 자연스럽게 만들어 주는 형용사가 정답이다.

118

------ of lacquered hardwood materials, these coat racks offer both strength and eco-friendly appeal.

(A) **Made**
(B) Making
(C) To make
(D) They are made

래커를 칠한 경목 재료로 만들어진 이 코트 걸이들은 튼튼함과 친환경적인 매력을 모두 제공한다.

어휘 lacquer 래커 칠을 하다 hardwood 경목, 경재(활엽수에서 얻은 단단한 목재) coat rack 코트 걸이 appeal 매력

해설 원래 쉼표 앞은 부사절이므로 '접속사 + 주어 + 동사'의 구조이지만, 선택지를 살펴보면 접속사와 주어가 없으므로 분사 구문이 되어야 한다. (A)와 (B) 중 알맞은 분사를 선택해야 하는데, 주절의 주어와 동사 make의 관계가 능동인지 수동인지 보면 된다. 코트 걸이가 '만들어지는' 것이므로 과거분사가 정답이다.

119

Ms. Takahashi's supervisors believe she deserves special ------- for her achievements during the recent sales initiative.

(A) recognition　　　　(B) accomplishment
(C) capability　　　　　　(D) balance

Ms. Takahashi의 상사들은 그녀가 최근 영업 프로젝트 동안의 성과에 대해 특별한 인정을 받을 만하다고 생각한다.

어휘 deserve ~을 받을 만하다 recognition 인정 capability 능력 initiative 계획, 프로젝트

해설 빈칸 앞뒤 she deserves special ------- for her achievements(성과에 대해 [(A) 인정 (B) 업적 (C) 능력 (D) 균형]을 받을 만하다)의 의미를 자연스럽게 만들어 주는 명사가 정답이다.

120

Mr. Novak has the qualifications required and so has appointed ------- to the Bravell Partners negotiations.

(A) he　　　　　　　　(B) his
(C) him　　　　　　　　**(D) himself**

Mr. Novak은 필요한 능력을 갖추고 있어서 Bravell Partners와의 협상에 자기 자신을 임명했다.

어휘 qualification 자격 요건, 능력 appoint 임명하다 negotiation 협상

해설 빈칸이 동사 has appointed의 목적어 자리이므로 목적격 대명사 (C), 소유대명사 (B), 재귀대명사 (D)가 모두 들어갈 수 있다. Mr. Novak가 자기 자신을 임명했으므로 목적어로 재귀대명사가 필요하다. 행위의 주체와 목적어가 같은 대상이면 재귀대명사가 정답이라는 사실을 기억하자.

121

------- a downturn in the economy, the automotive sector achieved a 17 percent increase in revenue this year.

(A) Except　　　　　　　(B) Toward
(C) Pending　　　　　　　**(D) Despite**

경기 하강에도 불구하고, 자동차 분야는 올해 17%의 수익 증가를 달성했다.

어휘 pending ~을 기다리는 동안, ~이 있을 때까지 downturn (경기) 하강 sector 분야, 부문

해설 부사구에 downturn, 주절에 increase라는 서로 상반되는 뜻의 단어가 있는 것을 보면 적절한 전치사를 선택할 수 있다.

122

In her debut business venture, Olympic medalist Dana Whitaker launched ------- brand of athletic footwear for women.

(A) her own　　　　　　(B) she
(C) hers　　　　　　　　(D) herself

올림픽 메달리스트 Dana Whitaker는 첫 벤처 사업에서 자체 여성용 운동화 브랜드를 출시했다.

어휘 debut 첫 등장, 첫걸음의 launch 출시하다 athletic footwear 운동화

해설 인칭대명사 문제에서 명사 앞에 빈칸이 있으면 소유격이 정답이다. 선택지에 소유격이 보이지 않으면 one's own을 고르자. own은 소유격을 강조하는 형용사이다.

123

Linton General Hospital's finance office is available to ------- any inquiries you may have about your invoice.

(A) address　　　　　　(B) respond
(C) attend　　　　　　　(D) appeal

Linton 종합병원의 재무과는 청구서에 대해 할 수 있는 어떤 문의든 답해드릴 수 있습니다.

어휘 general hospital 종합병원 address (문제, 질문 등을) 다루다 appeal 항소하다 inquiry 문의 invoice 청구서

해설 respond와 appeal은 자동사이기 때문에 바로 뒤에 목적어가 올 수 없다. any inquiries를 목적어로 취할 수 있는 동사를 정답으로 선택하자.

124

Brighttel sales representatives are ------- to learn about competitors' products and their promotional strategies.

(A) encourage
(B) encourages
(C) encouraged
(D) encouraging

Brighttel의 영업 사원들은 경쟁사의 제품과 홍보 전략에 대해 학습하도록 권장받는다.

어휘 sales representative 영업 사원 competitor 경쟁자, 경쟁 업체 promotional 홍보의

해설 빈칸이 be동사 뒤에 있으므로 분사인 (C)나 (D)가 들어가야 한다. 즉 능동태와 수동태를 구분하는 문제이다. 빈칸 뒤에 목적어가 있으면 능동태, 없으면 수동태를 선택하면 된다. encourage는 to부정사를 목적격 보어로 사용함을 알고 있어야 한다. 빈칸 뒤에 목적격 보어인 to부정사가 있고 목적어가 없으므로 수동태 문장이 되도록 과거분사를 정답으로 골라야 한다. to부정사를 목적격 보어로 사용하는 5형식 동사인 enable, allow, encourage, persuade, advise, ask, request, require, expect, invite, cause는 반드시 암기해 두자.

125

Use our editing software ------- features allow users to produce illustrations with professional-level precision.

(A) whom
(B) which
(C) whose
(D) that

여러 기능들로 전문가 수준의 삽화를 제작할 수 있는 저희의 편집 소프트웨어를 사용하세요.

어휘 feature 기능 illustration 삽화 precision 정밀도

해설 빈칸 뒤에 주어가 없으면 주격, 목적어가 없으면 목적격, 완성된 문장이 나오면 소유격 관계대명사가 정답이다. 빈칸 뒤에 5형식 문장이 완성되어 있으므로 소유격 관계대명사를 정답으로 골라야 한다.

126

Management was notified yesterday that the arrival of the shipment sent to the Seoul office ------- due to a customs issue.

(A) being delayed
(B) would be delayed
(C) has been delayed
(D) have delayed

경영진은 서울 사무소로 보낸 수송품의 도착이 통관 문제로 지연될 것이라고 어제 통보받았다.

어휘 management 경영진 notify 통보하다 shipment 수송품 customs 세관, 통관

해설 that절에 동사가 없으므로 빈칸에는 동사가 들어가야 하므로 준동사인 (A)는 제외하자. that절의 주어 the arrival이 단수 명사이므로 복수 동사 (D)도 제외해야 한다. "도착이 지연되었다고 통보받았다."라는 문장이 되려면 that절의 내용이 주절의 was notified보다 앞선 이야기가 되므로 빈칸에 과거완료 시제 동사가 들어가야 한다. 따라서 (C)도 오답이다. "도착이 지연될 것이라고 통보받았다."라는 문장인데, 주절이 과거 시제 동사를 사용하고 있으므로 종속절에서 시제를 일치시키기 위해 will의 과거형인 would를 사용해야 한다.

127

------- acknowledging their financial intentions, individuals should submit thorough documentation to their financial advisor.

(A) In addition to
(B) Provided that
(C) In order to
(D) So that

재정 자문가에게 재무 계획을 밝히는 것 뿐만 아니라, 꼼꼼하게 작성된 서류 제출도 해야 한다.

어휘 acknowledge 인정하다, 밝히다 intention 의도, 계획 thorough 철저한 documentation 문서, 서류

해설 Provided that과 So that 뒤에는 '주어 + 동사'가 있어야 하고, In order to 뒤에는 동사원형이 붙어야 한다. 빈칸에는 동명사를 목적어로 취하는 전치사가 들어가야 한다.

128

Most of the equipment in the storage room, along with several outdated monitors, ------- still in good condition despite years of use.

(A) is
(B) are
(C) being
(D) have been

창고에 있는 대부분의 장비는 몇 개의 구식 모니터와 함께 오랜 사용에도 불구하고 여전히 양호한 상태이다.

➡️ 어휘 equipment 장비 along with ~와 함께 outdated 오래된, 구식의

➡️ 해설 most[half / some / the rest / 분수 / percent] of 뒤에는 명사의 단수형과 복수형이 모두 올 수 있는데, 그 뒤에 오는 동사는 이 명사와 수가 일치되어야 한다. 빈칸에 문장의 동사가 들어가야 하므로 (A)와 (B) 중 정답을 선택해야 하는데, Most of 뒤에 단수 명사 the equipment가 있으므로 동사도 단수형이어야 한다.

129

Naomi Tanaka, a leading authority in sustainable land development, will serve as the ------- speaker at the Seventh Agroforestry Symposium.

(A) successive
(B) principal
(C) maximum
(D) immediate

지속 가능한 토지 개발 분야의 최고 권위자인 Naomi Tanaka는 제7회 혼농임업 심포지엄에서 주요 발표자로 나설 예정이다.

➡️ 어휘 leading 일류의, 뛰어난 authority 권위자 sustainable 지속 가능한 serve as ~의 역할을 하다 successive 연속적인 principal 주요한 maximum 최대의 agroforestry 혼농임업(임업을 겸한 농업) symposium 심포지엄, 학술 토론회

➡️ 해설 빈칸 앞뒤 will serve as the ------- speaker at the Seventh Agroforestry Symposium(심포지엄에서 [(A) 연속적인 (B) 주요한 (C) 최대의 (D) 즉각적인] 발표자로 나설 예정이다)의 의미를 자연스럽게 만들어 주는 형용사가 정답이다.

130

Recent studies show that a growing number of individuals are taking up video production and editing as an ------- for expressing their creativity.

(A) entry
(B) outcome
(C) outlet
(D) obstacle

최근 연구에 따르면 점점 더 많은 사람들이 창의력을 표현하기 위한 수단으로 영상 제작과 편집을 시작하고 있다.

➡️ 어휘 take up ~을 시작하다, 착수하다 production 제작 entry 참가, 입장 outcome 결과 outlet (감정 등의) 배출구, 표현 수단 obstacle 장애물

➡️ 해설 빈칸 앞뒤 are taking up video production and editing as an ------- for expressing their creativity(창의력을 표현하기 위한 [(A) 참가 (B) 결과 (C) 표현 수단 (D) 장애물](으)로 영상 제작과 편집을 시작하고 있다)의 의미를 자연스럽게 만들어 주는 명사가 정답이다.

PART 6

Questions 131 through 134 refer to the following product review.

131-134번 문제는 다음 상품 후기에 관한 것입니다.

I was ¹³¹hesitant to try powdered milk, as I doubted it would taste anything like fresh milk. However, when my neighborhood grocery store ran out of regular milk last week, I opted to give Lunara Milk a shot. I was ¹³²pleasantly surprised.

¹³³Achieving the ideal texture was tricky at first. Eventually, I used a high-speed blender and prepared a larger batch. This method requires additional time, but the result is a smooth and flavorful milk. I would absolutely recommend ¹³⁴it, even with the extra steps involved.

I will probably purchase fresh milk on my next shopping trip, but I will make sure to keep some Lunara Milk stocked at home. Unlike fresh milk, it can be stored for years without refrigeration.

분말 우유를 시도하는 것이 망설여졌습니다. 생우유 같은 맛이 날지 의심했기 때문이죠. 하지만 지난주에 저희 동네 식료품점에서 일반 우유가 다 떨어졌을 때 Lunara를 한 번 먹어 보기로 했습니다. 기쁘게도 놀라웠습니다.

처음에는 이상적인 질감을 내는 것이 까다로웠습니다. 결국 고속 믹서를 사용해서 많은 양을 한꺼번에 만들었습니다. 이 방식은 더 많은 시간이 걸리지만, 결과적으로 부드럽고 깊은 맛의 우유가 나옵니다. 추가적인 과정이 수반되기는 하지만 이 방식을 강력히 추천합니다.

다음에 장보러 갈 때는 아마 생우유를 사겠지만, Lunara 우유는 집에 꼭 비축해 놓아야겠어요. 생우유와 달리 냉장을 하지 않고도 수년 동안 보관할 수 있으니까요.

어휘 hesitant 주저하는 powdered 분말로 된 fresh milk 생우유 run out of ~이 다 떨어지다 regular 일반적인 opt to-V ~하기로 선택하다 give *sth* a shot ~을 시도해보다 texture 질감 tricky 까다로운 eventually 결국 blender (조리용) 믹서 batch 한 번에 만든 양 flavorful 맛이 깊은, 풍미가 강한 absolutely 절대적으로, 강력히 involve 수반하다 make sure to-V 반드시 ~하다 stock 비축하다 refrigeration 냉장 보관

131-134

131 (A) hesitated
  (B) hesitant
  (C) hesitates
  (D) hesitation

132 (A) rarely
  (B) remotely
  (C) probably
  (D) pleasantly

133 (A) I will not repeat that error in the future.
  (B) A bigger grocery store might have offered more choices.
  (C) Achieving the ideal texture was tricky at first.
  (D) Lunara Milk works well as a substitute in many dishes.

134 (A) it
  (B) several
  (C) them
  (D) some

131 **해설** be동사 뒤 주격 보어 자리에는 언제나 형용사가 정답이다. 선택지에 형용사가 없을 때는 분사가 정답이지만, 둘 다 있을 때는 대부분 형용사가 정답이다.

132 **어휘** rarely 거의 ~하지 않는 remotely 조금도, 원격으로, 멀리서

해설 생우유 같은 맛은 나지 않을 것 같다고 생각했던 사람이(I doubted it would taste anything like fresh milk.) 놀랐다고(surprised) 했으므로, 이 놀라움은 긍정적인 반응이다. 긍정적인 감정에 알맞은 부사를 정답으로 선택해야 한다.

133 (A) 앞으로는 그런 실수를 반복하지 않겠습니다.
  (B) 더 큰 식료품점이었다면 더 많은 선택권을 제공했을지도 모릅니다.
  (C) 처음에는 이상적인 질감을 내는 것이 까다로웠습니다.
  (D) Lunara 우유는 많은 요리에서 대용품으로 잘 쓰입니다.

어휘 work well 제대로 기능하다, 잘 쓰이다 substitute 대용품

해설 빈칸 뒤 문장이 Eventually로 시작하므로 앞 문장에는 at first가 들어 있는 것이 자연스럽다. 처음에 우유를 손으로 저어서 이상적인 맛을 내는 게 어려웠기 때문에, 결국 믹서를 사용했고, 믹서는 컵보다 용량이 크기 때문에 많은 양을 만들 수밖에 없었다는 내용이다.

134 **해설** 빈칸이 가리키는 것은 앞 문장에 들어 있는 This method이다. 시간도 오래 걸리고(requires additional time), 믹서를 사용하고 많은 양의 우유를 담을 용기를 준비하는 등 추가적인 과정이 필요하지만(even with the extra steps involved), 부드럽고 깊은 맛을 낼 수 있는(smooth and flavorful) 방식을 추천한다는 것이다.

A forthcoming analysis from the National Farming Outlook Council forecasts that soy output is expected to decline next year for the first time in two decades. **135**In contrast, grain yields are projected to rise. Industry specialists familiar with the findings say the primary drivers of these **136**changes are newly imposed regulations and recent breakthroughs in agricultural technology. **137**Shoppers may soon notice the impact at checkout counters. Soy prices could skyrocket, while abundant grain supplies help stabilize the cost of wheat, corn, and rice. Some market observers believe that an **138**anticipated shift toward soy alternatives will soon become evident.

135-138번 문제는 다음 기사에 관한 것입니다.

국립 농업 전망 위원회가 곧 발표할 분석 자료에서 내년에는 콩 생산량이 20년 만에 처음으로 감소할 것으로 예상된다는 관측이 나왔다. 그와 대조적으로 곡물 수확량은 증가할 것으로 보인다. 조사 결과에 정통한 업계 전문가들은 이러한 변화의 주요 동인이 새롭게 시행된 규정과 최근 농업 기술의 비약적인 발전이라고 말한다. 소비자들은 곧 계산대에서 그 영향을 보게 될 것 같다. 콩 가격은 치솟을 수 있는 반면 풍부한 곡물 공급 덕분에 밀과 옥수수, 쌀의 가격은 안정화될 것이다. 일부 시장 관측통들은 콩 대체제로의 예상되는 전환이 곧 뚜렷해질 것이라고 생각한다.

어휘 forthcoming 다가오는 outlook 전망 council 위원회 output 생산량 yield 수확량 be projected to-V ~할 것으로 예상되다 findings 조사 결과 driver 추진 요인, 동인 impose (법률 등을) 도입하다, 시행하다 breakthrough 비약적인 발전, 약진 checkout counter 계산대 skyrocket 치솟다, 급등하다 abundant 풍부한 supply 공급(량) stabilize 안정시키다 observer 관측통, 평론가 shift 변화, 전환 alternative 대안 evident 분명한, 뚜렷한

135-138

135 (A) To summarize
(B) For example
(C) In contrast
(D) Likewise

137 (A) **Shoppers may soon notice the impact at checkout counters.**
(B) The Council was financially supported by multiple eco-focused organizations.
(C) Agricultural machinery costs have surged significantly in recent years.
(D) Nutrition experts advocate for a varied eating pattern.

136 (A) purchases
(B) decisions
(C) tractors
(D) changes

138 (A) anticipation
(B) anticipating
(C) anticipated
(D) anticipate

---

135 **어휘** summarize 요약하다 likewise 마찬가지로

해설 빈칸 앞뒤 문장에 들어 있는 decline과 rise만 보면 정답을 알 수 있다.

136 **해설** 콩 생산량은 감소하고 다른 곡물들의 수확량은 증가하는 현상을 나타내기에 알맞은 명사는 changes이다. 또한 빈칸 앞에 있는 drivers가 '변화의 원인'이라는 뜻이다.

137 (A) 쇼핑객들은 곧 계산대에서 그 영향을 보게 될 것 같다.
(B) 위원회는 다수의 환경 관련 기관들로부터 재정적 지원을 받았다.
(C) 농기계류의 비용은 최근 몇 년 동안 크게 급증했다.
(D) 영양학 전문가들은 다양한 식습관을 지지한다.

어휘 eco-focused 환경 중심의 machinery 기계류 surge 급증하다 significantly 상당히 advocate 옹호하다, 지지하다 varied 다양한

해설 빈칸 앞에서는 콩 생산량의 감소와 다른 곡물 수확량 증가를 언급하고 있고(soy output is expected to decline next year for the first time in two decades. In contrast, grain yields are projected to rise.), 빈칸 뒤에서는 콩 가격의 급등과 다른 곡물 가격의 안정화를 예상하고 있다(Soy prices could skyrocket, while abundant grain supplies help stabilize the cost of wheat, corn, and rice). 가격 변화는 생산량 변화의 영향을 받는 것이라는 점을 생각하여 양쪽 내용을 이어주기에 알맞은 문장을 선택하면 된다.

138 **해설** 명사 앞 빈칸에는 형용사가 들어가야 하는데, 선택지에 형용사가 없으므로 (B)와 (C) 중 형용사를 대신할 분사를 선택해야 한다. 이동/변화(shift)가 '예상되는' 것이므로 수동의 의미가 있는 과거분사가 정답이다.

Questions 139 through 142 refer to the following e-mail.

To: Daniela Ruiz <druiz@solsticekitchen.com>
From: Julian Ortega <jortega@auroradininggroup.com>
Re: Assistant Chef Opportunity
Date: August 11

Dear Ms. Ruiz,

We appreciate your interest in and interview for the Assistant Chef role at Aurora Dining Group. We were surprised by the volume of applications we received. ¹³⁹As a result, we chose to meet with seven candidates in total. Ultimately, we selected an exceptionally experienced chef ¹⁴⁰who has received several prestigious culinary awards.

¹⁴¹That said, we were genuinely impressed by your qualifications. We are eager to reconnect with you about another opportunity in our kitchen team. If you are ¹⁴²interested, feel free to reach me at 646-555-7824, or simply reply to this message.

Thank you.

Julian Ortega

139–142번 문제는 다음 이메일에 관한 것입니다.

수신: Daniela Ruiz ⟨druiz@solsticekitchen.com⟩
발신: Julian Ortega
⟨jortega@auroradininggroup.com⟩
제목: 부주방장 채용 관련
날짜: 8월 11일

Ms. Ruiz께,

Aurora Dining Group 부주방장 자리에 관심을 보여 주시고 면접에 응해 주셔서 고맙습니다. 저희는 접수된 지원서의 양에 놀랐습니다. 결과적으로 총 7명의 지원자를 만나기로 했습니다. 그리고 최종적으로 요리 분야의 권위 있는 상을 여러번 받은 적이 있는 매우 경험이 풍부한 요리사를 선발했습니다.

그렇기는 하지만 저희는 귀하의 능력에 진심으로 깊은 인상을 받았습니다. 저희 주방 팀의 또 다른 기회에 대해 다시 연락 드리고 싶습니다. 관심이 있으시다면 646-555-7824로 언제든 저에게 연락 주시거나 이 메시지에 답장해 주시기 바랍니다.

고맙습니다.

Julian Ortega

어휘 application 지원서 ultimately 결국, 최종적으로 exceptionally 유난히, 매우 experienced 경험이 풍부한 prestigious 권위 있는, 명성이 높은 culinary 요리의 that said 그렇긴 하지만 genuinely 진정으로, 진심으로 impressed 깊은 인상을 받은 qualification 자격 요건, 능력

139-142

139 (A) Instead
(B) As a result
(C) On the contrary
(D) In the meantime

140 (A) that is receiving
(B) the reception of
(C) who has received
(D) whose reception is

141 (A) **That said, we were genuinely impressed by your qualifications.**
(B) Our culinary team had been excited to meet you.
(C) Additionally, we are planning updates to our dining space.
(D) We will soon be introducing new items to our food selection.

142 (A) worried
(B) occupied
(C) interested
(D) determined

---

139 어휘 on the contrary 반대로 in the meantime 그 동안에

해설 많은 사람들이 지원서를 냈는데(We were surprised by the volume of applications we received.), 심사 과정을 통해 추려 낸 결과 총 7명만 면접을 본다는(we chose to meet with seven candidates in total.) 내용에 알맞은 부사를 정답으로 선택해야 한다.

140 해설 select는 4형식 동사가 아니므로 목적어 an exceptionally experienced chef 뒤에 또 다른 목적어 the reception이 나올 수는 없으므로 (B)는 제외하자. (D)를 넣으면 복수 명사 several prestigious culinary awards가 앞에 있는 reception is와 수가 일치하지 않게 되므로 이것도 제외하자. (A)와 (C) 중 알맞은 시제의 동사를 선택해야 하는데, 선발된 요리사의 경력을 언급하는 내용이므로 현재완료 시제가 알맞다.

141 (A) 그렇기는 하지만 저희는 귀하의 능력에 진심으로 깊은 인상을 받았습니다.
(B) 저희 조리 팀은 당신을 만나는 것을 기대했습니다.
(C) 또한 저희는 식사 공간의 개조를 계획하고 있습니다.
(D) 곧 저희는 메뉴에 새로운 요리를 선보일 예정입니다.

어휘 update 새롭게 함, 개조 food selection 음식 구성, 메뉴

해설 빈칸 앞에서는 다른 요리사를 채용하기로 했다는 소식을 알리고 있는데(we selected an exceptionally experienced chef who has received several prestigious culinary awards.), 뒤에는 수신자에게 다른 자리를 제안하고 싶다는 말을 하고 있다(We are eager to reconnect with you about another opportunity in our kitchen team). "일단 다른 사람을 뽑기는 했지만 당신의 능력도 충분히 인정합니다."라고 말하는 것이 앞뒤를 이어 주기에 알맞은 내용이다.

142 **어휘** occupied 바쁜, 열중해 있는 determined 결심이 확고한, 단호한

해설 앞 문장이 다른 일자리를 제안하고 싶다는 내용이므로(We are eager to reconnect with you about another opportunity in our kitchen team.) 이어지는 문장으로는 "관심이 있으시다면 연락 주시기 바랍니다(If you are interested, feel free to reach me at 646-555-7824)."가 알맞다.

Questions 143 through 146 refer to the following e-mail.

To: All Staff <staff@lexfordglobal.com>
From: Fatima Elmasry <f.elmasry@lexfordglobal.com>
Date: October 3
Subject: Mandatory Training Session

To All Staff:

Ongoing developments in technology [143]present continuous challenges in handling our organization's information. At Lexford Global Counsel, we are committed to protecting [144]both our internal data and the sensitive information of our clients. That is why we have teamed up with SecureSphere, a top-rated data protection company based in Africa. They will be conducting this [145]security training, and all staff members have already been registered. The more informed we are, the more secure and, ultimately, more effective we become.

Please set aside 60 minutes to complete the training, which must be finished by November 15. [146]You will soon get an e-mail with a link to begin the training module.

Best regards,

Fatima Elmasry
Director of Information Technology

143-146번 문제는 다음 이메일에 관한 것입니다.

수신: 전 직원 〈staff@lexfordglobal.com〉
발신: Fatima Elmasry 〈f.elmasry@lexfordglobal.com〉
날짜: 10월 3일
제목: 의무 교육 시간

모든 직원 여러분께,

기술의 지속적인 발전은 우리 조직의 정보를 다루는 데 끊임없는 도전 과제를 제시합니다. Lexford Global Counsel은 내부 데이터와 고객들의 민감한 정보를 모두 보호하는 데 전념하고 있습니다. 이것이 저희가 아프리카에 본사를 두고 있는 최고 수준의 데이터 보호 회사 SecureSphere와 협력하는 이유입니다. 이 회사가 이번 보안 교육을 진행하며, 모든 직원들은 이미 등록이 되어 있습니다. 더 많은 지식을 갖출수록 더 안전하고, 궁극적으로 더 효과적으로 일할 수 있습니다.

교육을 이수하기 위해 60분을 할애해 주시기 바랍니다. 교육 이수는 11월 15일까지 완료해야 합니다. 교육 모듈을 시작하기 위한 링크가 담긴 이메일을 곧 받게 될 것입니다.

이만 줄입니다.

정보기술 책임자
Fatima Elmasry

어휘 mandatory 의무적인 ongoing 지속적인 present 제시하다 be committed to ~에 헌신하다, 전념하다 internal 내부의 team up with ~와 협력하다 top-rated 최고 수준[등급]의 based in ~에 본사를 둔 informed 정보력이 있는, 지식을 갖춘 secure 안전한 ultimately 궁극적으로 set aside 따로 떼어두다, 할애하다 training module 교육 모듈, 학습 단위

143-146

143 **(A) present**
(B) to present
(C) are presented
(D) presenting

144 (A) either
(B) both
(C) not only
(D) as though

145 (A) financial
(B) fitness
(C) security
(D) electrical

146 (A) Participation in this session is entirely voluntary for each team member.
(B) Your involvement will help our Web site appear more inviting to visitors.
(C) You will soon get an e-mail with a link to begin the training module.
(D) Our prosperity depends on how well we make use of the data we gather.

---

143 해설 문장에 동사가 없으므로 빈칸에는 동사인 (A)나 (C)가 들어가야 한다. 따라서 이 문제는 동사의 능동태와 수동태를 구분하는 문제이다. 빈칸 뒤에 목적어가 있으므로 능동태 동사가 정답이다.

144 해설 선택지를 미리 살펴보면 상관접속사 문제임을 알 수 있다. 빈칸 뒤의 and와 짝을 이루는 것을 정답으로 선택해야 한다. either는 or와, not only는 but (also)와 짝을 이루어 사용한다.

145 해설 앞 문장에서 SecureSphere라는 데이터 보호 서비스를 제공하는 회사를 소개하고 있다(SecureSphere, a top-rated data protection company based in Africa). 이들이 제공하는 교육이라면 데이터 보안이 주제인 것이 자연스럽다.

146 (A) 각 팀원이 이 세션에 참여하는 것은 전적으로 자율입니다.
(B) 여러분의 참여가 우리 홈페이지를 방문객들에게 더 매력적으로 보이도록 도와줄 것입니다.
(C) 교육 모듈을 시작하기 위한 링크가 담긴 이메일을 곧 받게 될 것입니다.
(D) 우리의 번영은 수집한 데이터를 얼마나 잘 활용하느냐에 달려 있습니다.

어휘 entirely 전적으로 voluntary 자발적인 involvement 참여 inviting 매력적인, 유혹하는 prosperity 번영 make use of ~을 활용하다

해설 시간을 내서 주어진 날짜까지 교육 이수를 완료하라는 지시(Please set aside 60 minutes to complete the training, which must be finished by November 15.)에 이어지는 문장이므로 관련되는 내용으로 교육을 시작할 수 있게 링크를 보내주겠다고 말하는 것이 자연스럽다.

Questions 147 through 148 refer to the following text message.

From: Omar Khan, 555-8239
To: Sofia Morales
Wednesday, October 12, 2:15 P.M.

Sofia, my laptop battery is nearly drained, and [148]I forgot my charger at headquarters. [147]Would you mind calling my upcoming client and letting her know I'll be delayed by around 45 minutes? [148]I'm heading back to pick it up now.

147-148번 문제는 다음 문자 메시지에 관한 것입니다.

발신: Omar Khan, 555-8239
수신: Sofia Morales
10월 12일 수요일 오후 2:15

Sofia, 내 노트북 배터리가 거의 다 닳았는데, 충전기를 본사에 두고 왔어요. 내 다음 고객에게 전화해서 내가 약 45분 정도 늦을 거라고 알려 줄래요? 지금 충전기 가지러 돌아가는 중이에요.

어휘 drained 방전된, 소모된 headquarters 본사 upcoming 다가오는 head back 돌아가다

147

Why did Mr. Khan send the text message to Ms. Morales?

(A) To check whether his charger was located
(B) To ask her to contact a customer
(C) To remind her to plug in a device
(D) To verify the location of a meeting

Mr. Khan은 왜 Ms. Morales에게 문자 메시지를 보냈는가?

(A) 자신의 충전기를 찾았는지 확인하기 위해
(B) 고객에게 연락해 달라고 요청하기 위해
(C) 장치의 플러그 꽂는 것을 상기시키기 위해
(D) 회의 장소를 확인하기 위해

어휘 locate 위치를 찾아내다 verify 확인하다

해설 Would you mind calling my upcoming client and letting her know I'll be delayed by around 45 minutes?에서 고객에게 연락해 달라고 부탁하는 것이 문자 메시지의 목적임을 알 수 있다.

148

What will Mr. Khan probably do next?

(A) Search for his computer
(B) Return to his workplace
(C) Purchase a new charger
(D) Contact technical support

Mr. Khan은 이후에 무엇을 하겠는가?

(A) 컴퓨터를 찾는다
(B) 직장으로 돌아간다
(C) 새 충전기를 구입한다
(D) 기술 지원 부서에 연락한다

해설 본사에 충전기를 두고 왔으므로(I forgot my charger at headquarters.) 그것을 가지러 돌아간다는 것은(I'm heading back to pick it up now.) 직장으로 돌아간다는 뜻이다.

Questions 149 through 150 refer to the following article.

City Highlights

[149]The owner of Golden Leaf Café, Lucia Delgado, has finalized a lease for a second dining location at 318 Maple Avenue. The site, adjacent to Orion Playhouse, previously housed a branch of Crescent Bank. Her new venture, named Soluna Bistro, is set to begin operations on September 12. Initially, the bistro will only be open in the evenings. [150]The goal is to build a customer base—particularly among theatergoers—before launching a lunch menu. Ms. Delgado's first successful eatery, Golden Leaf Café, is situated on Riverbend Road, near the Eastwood Farmers' Market bus stop. Head Chef Rafael Costa will manage both establishments.

149-150번 문제는 다음 기사에 관한 것입니다.

도시 소식

Golden Leaf Café의 소유주 Lucia Delgado가 Maple 대로 318번지에 두 번째 식당을 열기 위한 임대차 계약을 체결했다. 이곳은 Orion 극장에 인접해 있는데, 이전에 Crescent 은행의 지점이 있던 곳이다. Soluna Bistro라는 이름을 가진 그녀의 새 사업체는 9월 12일에 영업을 시작할 예정이다. 처음에는 저녁 시간에만 영업할 것이다. 목표는 점심 메뉴 출시 전, 특히 극장 관객을 중심으로 고객 기반을 다지는 것이다. 성공적으로 운영되고 있는 Ms. Delgado의 첫 식당 Golden Leaf Café는 Riverbend 길에 위치해 있으며 Eastwood Farmers' Market 버스 정류장에서 가깝다. 주방장 Rafael Costa가 두 식당을 모두 관리할 것이다.

어휘 highlight 흥미로운 부분, 주요 소식 lease 임대차 계약 adjacent 인접한 playhouse 극장 house 수용하다, 위치시키다 be set to-V ~할 예정이다 operation 운영 initially 처음에는 bistro 작은 식당 theatergoer 극장 관객 launch 시작하다, 출시하다 eatery 식당 situated ~에 위치한 establishment 시설, 기관

149

What is the purpose of the article?
(A) To highlight the achievements of a real estate agent
(B) To inform readers about the launch of a new business
(C) To explain the relocation of a dining establishment
(D) To share news about a business changing ownership

기사의 목적은 무엇인가?
(A) 부동산 중개업자의 성과를 강조하는 것
(B) 독자들에게 새 사업체의 개업을 알리는 것
(C) 식당의 이전에 대해 설명하는 것
(D) 소유권이 변경되는 사업체에 대한 소식을 전하는 것

어휘 highlight 강조하다 achievement 성과 real estate agent 부동산 중개업자 launch 개업, 개시 relocation 이전 ownership 소유권

해설 첫 문장 The owner of Golden Leaf Café, Lucia Delgado, has finalized a lease for a second dining location at 318 Maple Avenue.를 읽으면 기사의 목적이 새 사업체의 개업을 알리는 것임을 알 수 있다.

150

What is indicated about Soluna Bistro?
(A) It will begin offering lunch service on September 12.
(B) It is located close to a public transportation route.
(C) It is Ms. Delgado's first venture in the restaurant industry.
(D) It aims to attract customers who attend nearby theater shows.

Soluna Bistro에 관하여 무엇이 나타나 있는가?
(A) 9월 12일에 점심 서비스를 제공하기 시작할 것이다.
(B) 대중교통 노선 가까이에 위치해 있다.
(C) Ms. Delgado의 첫 번째 식당 사업 진출이다.
(D) 인근 극장 공연을 관람하는 고객의 유치를 목표로 한다.

어휘 route 노선 aim to-V ~하기를 목표로 하다 nearby 인근의, 가까운

해설 극장 관객들 사이에 고객 기반을 다지는 것을 목표로 하고 있다고 말하고 있다(The goal is to build a customer base—particularly among theatergoers—before launching a lunch menu).

Questions 151 through 153 refer to the following memo.

To: All staff at Strathmore Design Studio
From: Douglas Fairchild, Senior Partner
Re: Upcoming All-Staff Meeting
Date: 5 April

To All Staff,

On Thursday, 11 April, we will be welcoming a special guest to our all-staff meeting in room 407. [151]Anja Lindström, a senior architect at Vestergaard & Co. in Oslo, will be joining us. She has been with the firm for the past six years, and she led the design of Nordhavn Pavilion in Oslo as well as the Sundström Tower in Helsinki. Both structures have received international recognition for their sleek and innovative architecture. Before making a name for herself in Scandinavia, Ms. Lindström spent ten years working in Chicago at Morrison & Tate Architecture. [152]It was during her time at Morrison & Tate that I had the opportunity to collaborate with her on several notable projects. [153]Ms. Lindström will be visiting us here in York next week and has kindly agreed to speak at our meeting about some of her internationally acclaimed design work. We strongly urge all staff to attend.

151-153번 문제는 다음 공지문에 관한 것입니다.

수신: Strathmore Design Studio 전 직원
발신: 수석 파트너 Douglas Fairchild
제목: 다가오는 전 직원회의
날짜: 4월 5일

모든 직원 여러분께,

4월 11일 목요일에 우리는 407호에서 열리는 전 직원 회의에 특별 초대 손님을 모시게 되었습니다. Oslo에 있는 Vestergaard & Co.의 수석 건축가 Anja Lindström이 참석할 예정입니다. 그녀는 그 회사에서 지난 6년간 근무했으며 Oslo의 Nordhavn Pavilion과 Helsinki의 Sundström Tower까지 설계를 주도했습니다. 두 건축물 모두 세련되고 혁신적인 건축으로 국제적인 인정을 받았습니다. 스칸디나비아에서 이름을 알리기 전에 Ms. Lindström은 Chicago의 Morrison & Tate Architecture에서 10년간 근무했습니다. 제가 여러 주목할 만한 프로젝트에서 그녀와 협업할 기회를 가진 것도 그녀가 Morrison & Tate에서 근무한 시기였습니다. Ms. Lindström은 다음 주에 이곳 York에 방문할 것이며 감사하게도 우리 회의에서 그녀가 국제적으로 찬사를 받은 설계 작업 일부에 대해 이야기해 줄 것입니다. 모든 직원 여러분이 참석할 것을 강력히 권장합니다.

어휘 memo (사내) 공지문　architect 건축가　join us (회의에) 참석하다　A as well as B A 뿐만 아니라 B도, A 외에 B도　structure 구조물, 건축물　recognition 인정　sleek 매끈한, 세련된　innovative 혁신적인　architecture 건축　make a name for oneself 이름을 알리다　collaborate with ~와 협력하다　notable 주목할 만한　acclaimed 찬사를 받은　urge 촉구하다

151

What does the memo discuss? (A) Plans to launch a new office location (B) The hiring of a new employee (C) Recommendations for a design proposal **(D) An architect's professional accomplishments**	공지문이 무엇을 다루고 있는가? (A) 새 사무실 지점을 시작할 계획 (B) 신입 직원의 채용 (C) 설계 기획안 추천 (D) 한 건축가의 전문적 업적

어휘 discuss (문서가 ~을) 다루다　location 장소, 위치　accomplishment 업적

해설 Anja Lindström이라는 건축가가 북유럽에서 국제적인 인정(international recognition)을 받은 건축물들(Nordhavn Pavilion in Oslo, the Sundström Tower in Helsinki)을 설계한 일과 미국에서 주목할 만한 프로젝트들(several notable projects)을 수행한 것을 서술하고 있다.

152

What does Mr. Fairchild mention about Ms. Lindström? (A) She will contribute to one of his firm's upcoming projects. (B) She is preparing to establish her own company. **(C) She is a former colleague of his.** (D) She is in the process of relocating to a different city.	Mr. Fairchild가 Ms. Lindström에 관하여 무엇을 언급하는가? (A) Mr. Fairchild의 회사에서 곧 있을 프로젝트 중 하나에 기여할 것이다. (B) 자기 회사를 설립하려고 준비하고 있다. (C) Mr. Fairchild의 전 동료이다. (D) 다른 도시로 이주하는 중이다.

어휘 firm 회사　relocate 이주하다

해설 Ms. Lindström이 Morrison & Tate라는 회사에서 근무할 때 몇몇 프로젝트를 함께 맡아 협력할 기회가 있었다는 진술을 통해 정답을 알 수 있다(It was during her time at Morrison & Tate that I had the opportunity to collaborate with her on several notable projects).

<table>
<tr><td>

Where is Strathmore Design Studio based?

(A) In York
(B) In Chicago
(C) In Helsinki
(D) In Oslo

</td><td>

Strathmore Design Studio는 어디에 있는가?

(A) York에
(B) Chicago에
(C) Helsinki에
(D) Oslo에

</td></tr>
</table>

어휘 based ~에 위치한

해설 Ms. Lindström will be visiting us here in York next week에서 Strathmore Design Studio는 York에 있는 회사인 것을 알 수 있다.

Questions 154 through 155 refer to the following text-message chain.

Aidan Zhou 4:37 P.M.
[154]Leila forwarded you an e-mail containing the sales figures a little while ago. She's been curious about when she might receive your feedback.

Mateo Alvarez 4:38 P.M.
[154]I'm away from my workstation at the moment. Do you think she's uneasy because the figures came in below projections?

Aidan Zhou 4:38 P.M.
That's certainly a possibility.

Mateo Alvarez 4:39 P.M.
I got called away to inspect the bottling unit—it's been acting up.

Aidan Zhou 4:40 P.M.
Would you like me to contact a service technician?

Mateo Alvarez 4:42 P.M.
I'm hoping I can resolve it myself. [155]In the meantime, could you coordinate a conference call for Monday afternoon? The team will need to go over the report together.

Aidan Zhou 4:42 P.M.
Consider it done.

154-155번 문제는 다음 문자 메시지 대화에 관한 것입니다.

Aidan Zhou 오후 4:37
Leila가 조금 전에 당신에게 매출 수치를 포함한 이 메일을 전달했습니다. 언제쯤 피드백을 받게 될지 궁금해 하고 있고요.

Mateo Alvarez 오후 4:38
지금은 내가 자리에 없어요. 수치가 예상보다 낮게 나와서 불안해하는 것 같아요?

Aidan Zhou 오후 4:38
분명 그럴 가능성도 있죠.

Mateo Alvarez 오후 4:39
병입 장치를 점검해 달라고 호출 받았어요. 말썽을 부리고 있거든요.

Aidan Zhou 오후 4:40
서비스 기술자에게 연락해 드릴까요?

Mateo Alvarez 오후 4:42
내가 직접 해결해 보려고 해요. 그동안 월요일 오후로 화상 회의 일정을 잡아 줄래요? 팀 전체가 함께 보고서를 검토해야 할 거예요.

Aidan Zhou 오후 4:42
알겠습니다.

어휘 forward 전달하다 contain 포함하다 sales figures 매출액. 매출 수치 a little while ago 조금 전에 workstation 사무실 책상 at the moment 지금 당장은. 현재는 uneasy 불안한. 걱정스러운 figure 수치 projection 예상치 call *sb* away ~를 불러내다 inspect 점검하다 bottling 병에 담기. 병입 unit 기구, 장치 act up ~이 말을 듣지 않다. 말썽을 부리다 resolve 해결하다 in the meantime 그동안 coordinate 조율하다 conference call 원격 회의, 화상 회의 go over ~을 검토하다 Consider it done. (부탁 등을 흔쾌히 들어주며) 그러고 말고요, 걱정하지 마세요

154

At 4:38 P.M., what does Mr. Alvarez most likely mean when he writes, "I'm away from my workstation at the moment"?

(A) He has already left for the day.
(B) He will be unable to attend a scheduled meeting.
(C) He is currently in Mr. Zhou's office.
(D) He is not in a position to reply to Leila at the moment.

오후 4시 38분에 Mr. Alvarez가 "지금은 내가 자리에 없어요."라고 쓸 때, 이는 무엇을 의미하겠는가?

(A) 이미 퇴근했다.
(B) 예정된 회의에 참석할 수 없을 것이다.
(C) 현재 Mr. Zhou의 사무실에 있다.
(D) 지금은 Leila에게 답장할 수 있는 상황이 아니다.

어휘 leave for the day 퇴근하다 be in a position to–V ～할 수 있는 위치[상황, 처지]에 있다

해설 조금 전에 보낸 이메일에 대한 답장을 언제 해줄 수 있는지 알려 달라는 요청에 대해(Leila forwarded you an e-mail containing the sales figures a little while ago. She's been curious about when she might receive your feedback.) 지금은 자리에 있지 않다고 대답했으므로, 당장은 답장할 수 없다는 뜻이다.

155

What task is Mr. Zhou asked to do?

(A) Examine some documentation
(B) Organize a team meeting
(C) Finalize travel arrangements
(D) Troubleshoot a piece of machinery

Mr. Zhou는 어떤 업무를 하도록 요청받았는가?

(A) 문서를 검토한다
(B) 팀 회의를 준비한다
(C) 출장 준비를 마무리한다
(D) 기계의 결함을 찾아 수리한다

어휘 examine 검토하다 organize (행사, 활동 등을) 준비하다, 조직하다 arrangement 준비, 계획 troubleshoot 결함을 찾아 고치다, 수리하다 machinery 기계류

해설 오후 4시 42분에 Mr. Alvarez가 Mr. Zhou에게 팀원들과 함께 할 전화 회의 일정을 잡아 달라고 요청하고 있다(could you coordinate a conference call for Monday afternoon? The team will need to go over the report together).

Questions 156 through 158 refer to the following letter.

156–158번 문제는 다음 편지에 관한 것입니다.

Dear Mr. Bennett,

As a valued member of the Marisol Art Gallery, you will soon be able to enjoy the benefits of our Member Appreciation Month promotions. —[1]—. From 1 to 28 February, members will receive an additional 15 percent discount on all items in the gift shop. ¹⁵⁶Members will also be treated to a complimentary coffee or tea with any meal purchased in the café. Furthermore, those who register as first-time members by 28 February will receive a 10 percent reduction on their membership fee. —[2]—. We encourage you to invite your friends to visit our Web site and enroll.

—[3]—. ^{157 158}Each Saturday evening during the month, our third-floor galleries—normally closed to the public—will be open until 8:30 P.M. These galleries showcase sculptures and paintings by contemporary Jamaican artists. Selected pieces from these collections can also be viewed online.

—[4]—. We look forward to welcoming you soon.

Warm regards,

Tiana Morgan
Director of Member Services

Mr. Bennett께,

Marisol 미술관의 소중한 회원으로서 조만간 회원 감사의 달 프로모션 혜택을 받으실 수 있습니다. 회원은 2월 1일부터 28일까지 기념품 샵의 전 품목에 대한 15% 추가 할인을 받을 수 있습니다. 회원은 또한 카페에서 구입하시는 모든 식사와 함께 무료 커피나 차를 받게 됩니다. 아울러 2월 28일까지 회원으로 신규 가입하시는 분들은 10퍼센트의 회비 할인도 받게 됩니다. 친구분들께 저희 홈페이지를 방문하셔서 등록하시도록 권유해 주시기 바랍니다.

당월 토요일 저녁마다, 보통은 일반인에게 공개되지 않는 3층 전시관들이 저녁 8시 30분까지 개방됩니다. 이 전시관들에서는 현대 자메이카 미술가들의 조각과 회화 작품들을 선보입니다. 이 소장품들 중 선별된 작품들은 온라인으로도 보실 수 있습니다.

곧 당신을 맞이하게 되기를 기대합니다.

이만 줄입니다.

회원 서비스 책임자
Tiana Morgan

어휘 valued 소중한 treat A to B A에게 B를 대접하다 complimentary 무료의 reduction 할인 enroll 등록하다 showcase 전시하다 contemporary 현대의

156

What is true about the Marisol Art Gallery facility?	Marisol 미술관 시설에 관하여 무엇이 사실인가?
(A) It includes a restaurant. (B) It will be closed for a month. (C) It will feature photographic exhibits. (D) It offers studio space for art instruction.	(A) 식당이 있다. (B) 한 달 동안 문을 닫을 것이다. (C) 특별 사진 전시회가 있을 것이다. (D) 미술 강습을 위한 스튜디오를 제공한다.

어휘 feature 특별히 포함하다 exhibit 전시회 instruction 강습, 교육

해설 Members will also be treated to a complimentary coffee or tea with any meal purchased in the café.라는 문장을 통해 미술관에 식당이 있음을 알 수 있다.

157

According to the letter, what change will occur on Saturdays?	편지에 따르면 토요일마다 어떤 변화가 있을 것인가?
(A) Admission will be waived. **(B) Additional galleries will be accessible.** (C) Gift shop hours will be extended. (D) Jamaican artwork will be available for purchase.	(A) 입장료가 면제된다. (B) 추가 전시관들을 이용할 수 있게 된다. (C) 기념품 샵 영업시간이 연장된다. (D) 자메이카 미술 작품을 구입할 수 있게 된다.

어휘 admission 입장료 waive 면제하다 accessible 입장[이용] 가능한 extend 연장하다

해설 보통은 일반인에게 공개되지 않던 3층 전시관들을 개방할 것이다(Each Saturday evening during the month, our third-floor galleries—normally closed to the public—will be open until 8:30 P.M.).

158

| In which of the positions marked [1], [2], [3], and [4] does the following sentence best belong?

"February is an especially good time to explore the gallery for yet another reason."

(A) [1]
(B) [2]
(C) [3]
(D) [4] | 다음 문장은 [1], [2], [3], [4]로 표시된 자리 중 어느 곳에 가장 잘 어울리는가?

"2월은 또 다른 이유 때문에 미술관을 탐방하기에 특히 좋은 시기입니다." |

어휘 explore 탐방하다 yet another 또 하나의

해설 Each Saturday evening during the month, our third-floor galleries—normally closed to the public—will be open until 8:30 P.M.이 두 번째 문단의 첫 문장이라면 the month가 어느 달을 가리키는지 알 수 없게 된다. 이 문장 앞에 주어진 문장이 들어가면 2월이 미술관을 방문하기에 좋은 시기인 또 다른 이유를 설명하는 자연스러운 흐름이 된다.

To: Isabella Hartley <ihartley@novaterraentertainment.ca>
From: Mei-Ling Zhang <mzhang@novaterraentertainment.sg>
Subject: Novaterra's milestone celebration
Date: 14 July
Attachment: Opening Gala Invitation

Dear Executive Director Hartley,

[159]Preparations are well underway for Novaterra Entertainment's commemoration of forty years in Singapore, with a lineup of high-profile engagements and a diverse media campaign already in motion. The opening gala is scheduled to take place at the Celestia Regent Hotel in Singapore City on 5 September. We would be delighted to have you join us as our guest of honour. You'll find a formal invitation attached.

[159]In addition, we've just finalized promotional arrangements for a series of in-store anniversary campaigns that will roll out intermittently throughout the remainder of the calendar year. Each phase will be preceded by a press release to ensure optimal visibility. [160]I'll be sending you a comprehensive timeline once all details have been confirmed.

Sincerely,

Mei-Ling Zhang
Regional Communications Lead, Novaterra Entertainment

159-160번 문제는 다음 이메일에 관한 것입니다.

수신: Isabella Hartley
　　　〈ihartley@novaterraentertainment.ca〉
발신: Mei-Ling Zhang
　　　〈mzhang@novaterraentertainment.sg〉
제목: Novaterra 창립 40주년 기념행사
날짜: 7월 14일
첨부 파일: 개막 축제 초대장

Hartley 전무 이사님께,

세간의 이목을 끄는 행사들과 다양한 미디어 캠페인이 이미 진행 중인 가운데, Novaterra Entertainment의 싱가포르 진출 40주년 기념행사 준비가 순조롭게 이어지고 있습니다. 개막 축제가 9월 5일에 싱가포르 시내에 있는 Celestia Regent 호텔에서 열릴 예정입니다. 이사님께서 주빈으로 저희와 함께해 주신다면 더없이 기쁘겠습니다. 공식 초대장을 첨부했습니다.

아울러 올해 남은 기간 내내 간헐적으로 공개될 매장 내 기념 캠페인에 대한 홍보 준비도 방금 확정했습니다. 각 단계마다 최적의 노출도를 보장하기 위한 보도 자료가 먼저 배포될 것입니다. 모든 세부 사항이 확정되는 대로 종합 일정을 보내 드리겠습니다.

진심을 담아,

Novaterra Entertainment 지역 홍보 책임
Mei-Ling Zhang

어휘 milestone 중요한 사건, 중대 시점[단계] gala 축하 행사 underway 진행 중인 commemoration 기념(행사) lineup (행사의) 구성, 일정 high-profile 세간의 이목을 끄는 engagement 약속, 계약, 행사 diverse 다양한 in motion 진행 중인 take place 열리다 guest of honour 귀빈, 주빈 promotional 홍보의 roll out 출시되다, (활동이) 진행되다 intermittently 간헐적으로, 단계적으로 remainder 나머지 phase 단계 precede 앞서다 press release 보도 자료 optimal 최적의 visibility 가시성, 노출도 comprehensive 포괄적인, 종합적인

159

What is the purpose of the e-mail?

(A) To request information about promotional discounts
(B) To verify a hotel booking for an upcoming event
(C) To accept an invitation to a formal dinner
(D) To outline marketing initiatives related to an anniversary

이메일의 목적은 무엇인가?

(A) 판촉 할인에 대한 정보를 요청하는 것
(B) 다가오는 행사를 위한 호텔 예약을 확인하는 것
(C) 공식 만찬 초대를 수락하는 것
(D) 기념일과 관련된 마케팅 계획의 개요를 설명하는 것

어휘 outline 개요를 설명하다 initiative 계획, 프로젝트 related to ~과 관련된

해설 첫 문장에서 싱가포르 진출 40주년 기념행사를 준비하기 위해 여러 가지 행사와 미디어 홍보를 진행하고 있다고 말하고 있다(Preparations are well underway for Novaterra Entertainment's commemoration of forty years in Singapore, with a lineup of high-profile engagements and a diverse media campaign already in motion). 두 번째 문단에서도 매장 내에서 진행될 기념일 캠페인을 위한 홍보 준비를 마쳤다고 말한다(we've just finalized promotional arrangements for a series of in-store anniversary campaigns). 이런 내용을 통해 이메일의 목적을 알 수 있다.

160

What does Ms. Zhang promise to send later?

(A) An updated version of the invitation
(B) A detailed calendar of scheduled activities
(C) A finalized travel agenda
(D) A summary of recent retail performance

Ms. Zhang은 나중에 무엇을 보내겠다고 약속하는가?

(A) 초대장 수정본
(B) 예정된 활동의 자세한 일정
(C) 확정된 출장 일정
(D) 최근 소매 실적 요약

어휘 agenda 일정표 summary 요약 retail 소매 performance 실적

해설 행사의 모든 자세한 사항들이 확정되면 종합 일정을 보내겠다고 약속하는 마지막 문장에서 정답을 알 수 있다(I'll be sending you a comprehensive timeline once all details have been confirmed).

Questions 161 through 164 refer to the following article.

161–164번 문제는 다음 기사에 관한 것입니다.

Storm ZR Stalls Before the Storm

By Lucia Ramirez

Storm ZR, 폭풍 앞에 멈춰 서다

Lucia Ramirez 기자

[161]On Thursday, Kaito Engineering, the firm currently manufacturing Thunderline motorcycles, announced a postponement in the launch of its upcoming Storm ZR model. Industry competitors reacted with astonishment to the announcement. —[1]—. [164]Meanwhile, Thunderline enthusiasts took to social media en masse, voicing their disappointment over the cancellation of the highly anticipated April release.

The decision to incorporate a hybrid engine—combining gasoline and electric power—is to blame for the delay. According to Kaito Engineering, [162(A)(D)]the initial prototype was deemed unsuitable due to its excessive bulk and weight. [162(D)]The hybrid system's design would have necessitated a significantly larger motorcycle body than originally intended. [162(C)]Engineers also raised concerns over its insufficient power output. —[2]—.

[163]Beyond the technical setbacks, the Thunderline production facility, which had previously been optimized for earlier models, is currently ill-equipped to manufacture the Storm ZR hybrid. —[3]—. [163]The company will need to invest in new machinery, and the assembly floor must be reconfigured to accommodate the updated specifications.

[161][164]Just last year, Kaito Engineering was widely praised by motorcycle enthusiasts for rescuing Thunderline from financial collapse. What a contrast a single year can make. —[4]—.

현재 Thunderline 오토바이를 제조하고 있는 기업 Kaito Engineering은 목요일에 다가오는 Storm ZR 모델 출시의 연기를 발표했다. 업계 경쟁업체들은 이 소식에 놀라움으로 반응했다. 한편 Thunderline의 열성 팬들은 일제히 소셜 미디어로 몰려들어 큰 기대를 모았던 4월 출시의 취소에 대한 실망감을 표출했다. 가솔린과 전기 동력을 결합하는 하이브리드 엔진을 포함하기로 한 결정이 지연의 원인이다. Kaito Engineering에 따르면 첫 시제품이 과도한 부피와 무게로 인해 부적합하다고 판단되었다. 하이브리드 시스템 설계는 원래 의도했던 것보다 훨씬 더 큰 오토바이 차체를 요했을 것이다. 엔지니어들은 또한 불충분한 출력에 대한 우려도 제기했다.

기술적인 문제 외에도 Thunderline의 생산 시설이 이전 모델들에 최적화되어 있어서 현재는 하이브리드 Storm ZR을 만들 장비가 제대로 갖추어져 있지 않다. 회사가 새 기계에 투자해야 하며 조립 라인을 최신 사양에 맞게 재구성해야 한다.

작년만 하더라도 Kaito Engineering은 Thunderline을 재정 붕괴에서 구해낸 것으로 오토바이 애호가들로부터 널리 칭찬을 받았다. 단 1년 만에 생긴 큰 차이이다.

어휘 stall 멈추다, 멎다 manufacture 제조하다 postponement 연기 competitor 경쟁사 astonishment 놀라움 meanwhile 한편 enthusiast 열성 팬 take to ~로 가다 en masse 집단으로, 일제히 voice 표명하다 cancellation 취소 release 출시, 발매 incorporate 포함하여 넣다, 통합하다 be to blame for ~에 대한 책임이 있다, ~의 원인이다 initial 초기의 prototype 시제품 deem *sth* unsuitable ~을 부적합하다고 판단하다 excessive 과도한 bulk 부피 necessitate 필요로 하다 significantly 상당히, 훨씬 body 차체 raise 제기하다 insufficient 불충분한 power output 출력 setback 차질, 문제 optimize 최적화하다 ill-equipped 장비[기술]를 제대로 갖추지 않은 assembly 조립 floor 작업장 reconfigure (구조를) 변경하다, 재구성하다 accommodate 수용하다, 맞추다 updated 최신의, 갱신된 specification 사양 rescue 살리다, 구제하다 collapse 붕괴 contrast 차이, 대조

161

What is indicated about Kaito Engineering?

(A) It holds ownership of the Thunderline motorcycle brand.
(B) It intends to offer a model at a discounted rate.
(C) It is relocating its corporate headquarters.
(D) It will introduce a new motorcycle in April.

Kaito Engineering에 관하여 무엇이 나타나 있는가?

(A) Thunderline 오토바이 브랜드의 소유권을 보유하고 있다.
(B) 할인된 가격으로 모델을 제공할 계획이다.
(C) 본사를 이전하고 있다.
(D) 4월에 새 오토바이를 출시할 것이다.

해설 기사 첫 문장에 Kaito Engineering이 Thunderline 오토바이의 제조사라는 소개가 나오고 있고(Kaito Engineering, the firm currently manufacturing Thunderline motorcycles), 마지막 문단에도 Kaito Engineering이 Thunderline 브랜드를 인수함으로써 재무 위기에서 구해냈다는 언급이 있다(Kaito Engineering was widely praised by motorcycle enthusiasts for rescuing Thunderline from financial collapse).

162

What is NOT mentioned as a flaw with the power system? (A) It is excessively heavy. **(B) Its production cost is exorbitant.** (C) It fails to achieve optimal performance. (D) It demands structural expansion.	동력 시스템의 단점으로 언급되지 않는 것은 무엇인가? (A) 지나치게 무겁다. (B) 생산 비용이 지나치게 높다. (C) 최적의 성능을 달성하기 못한다. (D) 구조적 확장을 요한다.

해설 두 번째 문단을 보면 시제품이 과도한 부피와 무게 때문에 부적합 판정을 받았다고 말하고 있다(the initial prototype was deemed unsuitable due to its excessive bulk and weight). 여기서 (A)와 (D)를 제거해야 한다. 이어지는 문장에서도 하이브리드 시스템 설계 때문에 차체의 확장이 필요하다는 이야기를 하고 있으므로(The hybrid system's design would have necessitated a significantly larger motorcycle body than originally intended.) (D)를 제거할 수 있다. 그 다음 문장에서는 불충분한 출력(Engineers also raised concerns over its insufficient power output.), 즉 오토바이 성능의 문제를 언급하므로 여기서 (C)를 제거해야 한다.

163

Why will the factory undergo renovations? (A) It must comply with updated regulations. (B) It has not been modernized in over ten years. **(C) It had been set up for older models.** (D) It cannot produce multiple models simultaneously.	공장은 왜 보수 공사를 받게 될 것인가? (A) 개정된 규정을 준수해야 한다. (B) 10년이 넘도록 현대화되지 않았다. (C) 예전 모델들에 맞게 설치되어 있었다. (D) 다수의 모델을 동시에 생산할 수 없다.

해설 세 번째 문단을 보면, 공장에 새 기계를 들여 최신 사양의 제품을 생산하도록 구조를 변경해야 하는데(The company will need to invest in new machinery, and the assembly floor must be reconfigured to accommodate the updated specifications.) 이 생산 시설이 예전 모델들에 최적화되어 있기 때문이다(the Thunderline production facility, which had previously been optimized for earlier models).

164

In which of the positions marked [1], [2], [3], and [4] does the following sentence best belong? "Now they will need to regain the goodwill of these prospective buyers." (A) [1] (B) [2] (C) [3] **(D) [4]**	다음 문장은 [1], [2], [3], [4]로 표시된 자리 중 어느 곳에 가장 잘 어울리는가? "이제 그들은 이 잠재 구매자들의 신뢰를 되찾아야 한다."

해설 주어진 문장에서 앞뒤 문장과의 연결 고리가 될 키워드를 파악해야 한다. they가 누구를 가리키는지 앞에서 언급되어야 하며, 신뢰를 되찾아야 한다고(will need to regain the goodwill) 말하고 있으므로 앞에서는 신뢰를 잃어버렸다는 내용이 나와야 한다. 또한 these prospective buyers(이 잠재 구매자들)가 누구를 가리키는지 앞에서 찾아내야 한다. 첫 문단의 Thunderline enthusiasts took to social media en masse, voicing their disappointment over the cancellation of the highly anticipated April release.와 마지막 문단의 Kaito Engineering was widely praised by motorcycle enthusiasts for rescuing Thunderline from financial collapse. What a contrast a single year can make.를 통해 they는 Kaito Engineering이며, Thunderline 오토바이 브랜드를 인수함으로써 이 브랜드 열성 팬들의 호의를 샀던 이들이 이번에 실망을 안겨 주었기 때문에 다시 신뢰를 되찾기 위한 노력이 필요함을 알 수 있다. 잠재 구매자란 바로 이 열성 팬들(enthusiasts)이다. 그러므로 주어진 문장은 [4]에 들어가야 한다.

Questions 165 through 168 refer to the following text-message chain.

Marco Alvarez [7:42 A.M.] [165 167]Ms. Ito, tomorrow's weather report is calling for heavy rain, so the roofing job on your hotel's new wing will need to be put on hold.

Naoko Ito [7:43 A.M.] Does that mean no work at all tomorrow?

Marco Alvarez [7:43 A.M.] Not necessarily. My team can assist Jordan Kim's crew with reinforcing the support beams inside the older section of the building.

Naoko Ito [7:44 A.M.] How long do you think that will take?

Marco Alvarez [7:44 A.M.] Let me check in with him.

Marco Alvarez [7:45 A.M.] Jordan, any idea how close you are to wrapping up your current task?

Jordan Kim [7:47 A.M.] [166]We were on track until this morning, but the structural engineer came by and gave us some updates. We'll probably have to work late for the next few days.

Marco Alvarez [7:48 A.M.] How would you feel about my crew jumping in to help tomorrow?

Jordan Kim [7:49 A.M.] That'd be perfect! We might even be able to finish in a single day.

Naoko Ito [7:51 A.M.] So your team will only need access to the older building?

Marco Alvarez [7:52 A.M.] Yes, just for tomorrow. [167 168]Would it be okay if they parked their vehicles in front of that section?

Naoko Ito [7:54 A.M.] [167]No problem. There should be enough spots near the main entrance. Just remind them not to drive onto the lawn.

165-168번 문제는 다음 문자 메시지 대화에 관한 것입니다.

Marco Alvarez [오전 7:42] Ms. Ito, 내일 일기 예보에 따르면 폭우가 예상된다고 합니다. 그래서 호텔 새 별관의 지붕 공사 작업은 보류해야겠어요.

Naoko Ito [오전 7:43] 내일은 작업이 없을 거라는 말씀인가요?

Marco Alvarez [오전 7:43] 꼭 그렇지는 않습니다. Jordan Kim의 팀이 건물의 노후화된 부분에 지지 기둥 보강 작업을 하는데 저희 팀이 도와줄 수 있어요.

Naoko Ito [오전 7:44] 그게 얼마나 걸릴 것 같으세요?

Marco Alvarez [오전 7:44] 그에게 확인해 볼게요.

Marco Alvarez [오전 7:45] Jordan, 현재 진행 중인 작업을 마무리하기까지 얼마나 남았는지 알 수 있을까요?

Jordan Kim [오전 7:47] 오늘 오전까지는 순조로 왔는데, 구조 공학자가 들러서 몇 가지 업데이트를 해줬거든요. 아마 앞으로 며칠은 야근을 해야 할 것 같아요.

Marco Alvarez [오전 7:48] 내일 우리 팀이 참여해서 도와주는 거 어떻게 생각해요?

Jordan Kim [오전 7:49] 더할 나위 없이 좋죠! 하루 만에 끝낼 수도 있을 것 같은데요.

Naoko Ito [오전 7:51] 그러니까 기존 건물에만 들어갈 수 있게 해 드리면 되는 거죠?

Marco Alvarez [오전 7:52] 네, 내일은 그렇습니다. 팀원들이 그 구역 앞에 차를 세워 놓아도 괜찮을까요?

Naoko Ito [오전 7:54] 문제없어요. 정문 근처에 자리가 충분히 있을 거예요. 잔디 위로 올라가지만 않게 다시 한 번 말씀해 주세요.

어휘 call for ~을 예보하다 roofing 지붕 공사 wing 별관 put *sth* on hold ~을 보류하다 crew 작업팀 reinforce 보강하다 beam 기둥, 들보 check in with ~에게 확인하다 wrap up ~을 마무리하다 on track 순조롭게 진행 중인 structural engineer 구조 공학자 jump in ~에 뛰어들다. 끼어들다 access 접근 vehicle 차량

165

What does Mr. Alvarez say will cause an interruption in tomorrow's work?

(A) Equipment malfunction
(B) A shipment arriving late
(C) Unfavorable weather conditions
(D) Not enough crew members available

Mr. Alvarez는 무엇이 내일 작업 중단의 원인이라고 말하는가?

(A) 장비 고장
(B) 배송 지연
(C) 불리한 기상 조건
(D) 작업 인원 부족

어휘 interruption 중단 malfunction 고장. 오작동 shipment 배송. 운송 unfavorable 불리한

해설 첫 문장에서 내일 예보되고 있는 폭우 때문에 지붕 공사는 중단해야 한다고 말하고 있다(tomorrow's weather report is calling for heavy rain, so the roofing job on your hotel's new wing will need to be put on hold).

166

At 7:47 A.M., what does Mr. Kim most likely mean when he writes, "We'll probably have to work late for the next few days"?

(A) His crew has not been reporting to the site on time.
(B) His team plans to leave early on Wednesday.
(C) His workers are assigned to multiple locations.
(D) His project has become more complicated.

오전 7시 47분에 Mr. Kim이 "아마 앞으로 며칠은 야근을 해야할 것 같아요."라고 쓸 때, 이는 무엇을 의미하겠는가?

(A) 팀원들이 제 시간에 현장에 출근하지 않고 있다.
(B) 수요일에는 팀원들이 일찍 퇴근할 계획이다.
(C) 직원들이 여러 장소에 배정되어 있다.
(D) 프로젝트가 더 복잡해졌다.

어휘 report to (~에) 도착을 보고하다. 출근하다 site 현장. 부지 assign 배정하다

해설 아침까지만 하더라도 문제없이 작업이 진행되고 있었는데, 구조 공학자가 업데이트를 해준 후에(We were on track until this morning, but the structural engineer came by and gave us some updates.) 야근이 필요하게 되었다. 이것은 작업이 더 복잡해졌음을 의미한다.

167

Who most likely is Ms. Ito?

(A) A landscape architect
(B) A hotel manager
(C) A logistics supervisor
(D) A roofing contractor

Ms. Ito는 누구겠는가?

(A) 조경 건축가
(B) 호텔 매니저
(C) 물류 관리자
(D) 지붕 공사 하청업자

해설 첫 문장에 등장하는 키워드 your hotel만으로도 정답을 알 수 있다. 또한 대화 마지막에 Mr. Alvarez가 주차 허가를 구하자(Would it be okay if they parked their vehicles in front of that section?) 허가와 함께 잔디 위에 주차하지 않도록 주의를 주고 있다는 점도(No problem. ... Just remind them not to drive onto the lawn.) Ms. Ito가 호텔 관리자임을 알게 해주는 단서가 된다.

168

What is one topic Mr. Alvarez inquires about?

(A) Which entrance his team should use
(B) How to get to the older building
(C) The construction timeline for the new wing
(D) Whether parking will be available

Mr. Alvarez가 문의하는 한 가지 주제는 무엇인가?

(A) 팀원들이 어느 출입구를 사용해야 하는가
(B) 기존 건물까지 어떻게 가는가
(C) 새 별관의 공사 일정
(D) 주차가 가능한가

해설 7시 52분에 어떤 장소에 차를 세워 놓아도 괜찮은지 묻고 있다(Would it be okay if they parked their vehicles in front of that section?).

Questions 169 through 171 refer to the following advertisement.

InsightPilot
[169]*Discover the Data That Drives Your Business*

[169]**InsightPilot** is a robust, next-generation platform built to simplify the creation and administration of surveys. Our intuitive cloud-based interface helps you build surveys efficiently and monitor responses in real time.

[170]You asked—we delivered. InsightPilot includes the most requested features:

- [171(A)]A guided, step-by-step system for building surveys from start to finish
- A wide variety of question formats, including multiple choice, true/false, and open-ended, with expert tips on usage
- [171(B)]A curated collection of sample questions proven to capture meaningful insights
- [171(D)]Multiple fast and simple distribution options (e-mail, social media, and more)
- Real-time summaries and detailed analytics for instant reporting

Visit www.insightpilot.com to explore more.

169-171번 문제는 다음 광고에 관한 것입니다.

InsightPilot
비즈니스를 움직이는 데이터를 발견하세요

InsightPilot은 설문 조사 제작과 관리를 간소화하기 위해 구축된 강력한 차세대 플랫폼입니다. 직관적인 클라우드 기반의 인터페이스가 설문을 효율적으로 구축하고 응답을 실시간으로 모니터하도록 도와드립니다.

고객은 원했고 우리는 구현했습니다. InsightPilot은 요청이 가장 많았던 기능들을 포함합니다.

- 처음부터 끝까지 단계별 안내가 있는 설문 조사 제작 시스템
- 객관식, 참/거짓, 자유 형식 등 매우 다양한 질문 유형과 사용에 대한 전문적인 팁
- 의미 있는 통찰을 포착하는 것으로 입증된 선별된 견본 질문 모음
- 다수의 빠르고 간단한 배포 방식(이메일, 소셜 미디어, 기타 등등)
- 즉석 보고서 작성을 위한 실시간 요약 및 상세 분석

www.insightpilot.com에서 더 알아보세요.

어휘 drive 추진하다 robust 강력한, 튼튼한 simplify 간소화하다 administration 운영, 관리 intuitive 직관적인 feature 기능 from start to finish 처음부터 끝까지 open-ended 자유 형식의 curated 선별된 capture 포착하다 meaningful 의미 있는 insight 통찰 distribution 배포 real-time 실시간의 analytics 분석 instant 즉각적인 explore 탐색하다

169

How would a business most likely use InsightPilot?

(A) To conduct market research
(B) To build custom software applications
(C) To design promotional graphics
(D) To compile annual financial statements

사업체가 InsightPilot를 어떻게 사용하겠는가?

(A) 시장 조사를 실시하기 위해
(B) 맞춤 소프트웨어를 제작하기 위해
(C) 홍보용 그래픽을 디자인하기 위해
(D) 연간 재무제표를 작성하기 위해

어휘 custom 맞춤형의 compile (자료를 수집하여) 작성하다 financial statement 재무제표

해설 InsightPilot는 사업 운영에 필요한 데이터를 모으기 위해(Discover the Data That Drives Your Business) 설문 조사를 제작하여 시행하게 해주는 플랫폼이다(InsightPilot is a robust, next-generation platform built to simplify the creation and administration of surveys). 즉 InsightPilot의 용도는 시장 조사이다.

170

What is implied about the creators of InsightPilot?

(A) They were led by a software developer.
(B) They feature user testimonials on their Web site.
(C) They are known for manufacturing durable products.
(D) They incorporated customer input during development.

InsightPilot의 제작자들에 관하여 무엇이 암시되어 있는가?

(A) 소프트웨어 개발자의 지도를 받았다.
(B) 홈페이지에 사용자 추천의 글을 포함시켰다.
(C) 내구성 있는 상품을 제조하는 것으로 알려져 있다.
(D) 개발 과정에 고객의 의견을 반영했다.

어휘 testimonial 추천의 글 durable 내구성이 있는 incorporate 반영하다 input 조언, 의견

해설 You asked—we delivered. InsightPilot includes the most requested features:를 통해 개발자들이 고객의 요청 사항을 반영하여 제품의 기능을 구성했음을 알 수 있다.

171

What is NOT mentioned as a feature of InsightPilot?

(A) A guided setup process
(B) Prewritten survey questions
(C) Visual charts and graphs for results
(D) Tips for easy survey distribution

InsightPilot의 기능으로 언급되지 않는 것은 무엇인가?

(A) 안내가 있는 구성 과정
(B) 사전에 작성되어 있는 설문 조사 질문
(C) 결과를 보여주는 시각 차트와 그래프
(D) 쉬운 설문 조사 배포를 위한 팁

어휘 setup 구성, 설치, 설정 prewritten 미리 작성된

해설 우선 처음부터 끝까지 설문 조사 제작 과정을 단계별로 안내한다고 나와 있으므로(A guided, step-by-step system for building surveys from start to finish) (A)를 제거하자. 견본 질문을 볼 수 있다고 했으므로(A curated collection of sample questions) (B)를 제거한다. 설문 조사 배포를 위한 여러 방식을 제공하고 있으므로(Multiple fast and simple distribution options (e-mail, social media, and more)) (D)도 제거할 수 있다.

Questions 172 through 175 refer to the following notice.

172–175번 문제는 다음 공지문에 관한 것입니다.

Greenbay National Park Authority (GNPA)

Greenbay National Park encompasses both the coastal mainland and Greenbay Island. [172]Please be aware that new restrictions are now in force regarding access to the island during the upcoming summer season. [173]Visitors who are not part of an authorized tour group will be prohibited from making landfall on Greenbay Island. This policy also applies to individuals attempting to reach the island independently using private boats or other watercraft. While such individuals may anchor offshore and observe the island from the water, they must not step onto the island itself.

[173]The GNPA offers official guided boat tours to the island every day of the year. [174(C)] [175]Tours depart every two hours, beginning at 8:00 in the morning, with the final tour leaving at 4:00 in the afternoon. However, during the summer months—December through March—the last tour is extended to 6:00 P.M. To reserve a spot, call (08) 9456 3271. Each tour includes a short visit to the island, where guests can view bird-nesting areas under the supervision of a GNPA park ranger, who serves as an authorized escort.

Booking and Payment Details
- [174(A)]Each tour is capped at 20 participants. If your group includes fewer than 15 people, GNPA reserves the right to add other guests to your tour.
- Admission is $30 per adult (ages 12 and up) and $20 per child (under age 12).
- [174(B)]A nonrefundable deposit of $7 per person is required to secure group reservations. This deposit will be credited toward your total admission cost.
- [175]If your party fails to arrive at the scheduled time, GNPA reserves the right to shorten the tour as needed to avoid interfering with subsequent tours. Rescheduling is not available.

Greenbay 국립공원 관리청 (GNPA)

Greenbay 국립공원은 본토 해안과 Greenbay 섬을 모두 아우릅니다. 현재 다가오는 여름 기간 동안의 섬 출입에 관한 새로운 제한 사항이 시행 중임을 유의하시기 바랍니다. 승인받은 관광 단체의 일원이 아닌 방문객은 Greenbay 섬 상륙이 금지됩니다. 이 정책은 또한 개인 선박이나 기타 수상 교통수단을 이용하여 단독으로 섬에 접근하려는 개인에게도 적용됩니다. 해당 개인은 해상에 정박하고 수상에서 섬을 관찰할 수는 있지만, 섬 자체에 발을 들여놓을 수는 없습니다.

GNPA는 섬까지 가이드가 안내하는 공식 보트 투어를 연중 매일 제공합니다. 투어는 오전 8시부터 시작하여 두 시간마다 출발하며, 마지막 투어는 오후 4시에 출발합니다. 그러나 12월부터 3월까지의 여름 기간에는 마지막 투어가 오후 6시로 연장됩니다. 자리를 예약하려면 (08) 9456 3271로 전화하시면 됩니다. 각 투어는 짧은 섬 방문을 포함하며, 섬에서는 GNPA 공원 관리원의 감독 하에 새 둥지 구역을 관람할 수 있습니다. 관리원은 공식 안내원 역할을 수행합니다.

예약 및 결제 안내
- 각 투어는 최대 20명까지 참가할 수 있습니다. 귀하의 그룹이 15명 미만인 경우, GNPA는 다른 참가자를 투어에 추가할 권리를 보유합니다.
- 입장료는 성인(12세 이상) 30달러이며 어린이(12세 미만) 20달러입니다.
- 단체 예약을 확보하려면 환불 불가 보증금으로 1인당 7달러가 필요합니다. 이 보증금은 총 입장료에서 차감됩니다.
- 일행이 예정된 시간에 도착하지 않을 경우 GNPA는 이후에 있을 투어에 방해되는 것을 피하기 위해 필요에 따라 투어를 단축할 권리를 보유합니다. 일정 변경은 불가능합니다.

어휘 authority 관청, 국(局) encompass 포함하다, 아우르다 restriction 제한 in force 시행 중인 regarding ~에 관하여 authorize 승인하다 prohibit (공식적으로) 금지하다 make landfall 상륙하다 independently 단독으로 watercraft 수상 교통수단 anchor 닻을 내리다, 정박하다 offshore (해안에서 약간 떨어진) 앞바다에 step onto ~에 발을 들이다 depart 출발하다 extend 연장하다 nest 둥지를 틀다 supervision 관리, 감독 park ranger 공원 관리원 serve as ~의 역할을 하다 escort 안내자 cap 상한을 정하다 reserve the right to-V ~할 권리를 보유하다 nonrefundable 환불되지 않는 deposit 보증금 secure 확보하다 be credited toward ~에 충당하다 party 일행 shorten 단축하다 interfere with ~을 방해하다 subsequent 이후의

172

What is announced in the notice?	공지문에서 무엇을 발표하고 있는가?
(A) A newly introduced visitor service	(A) 새로 도입된 방문객 서비스
(B) A recently constructed tourist attraction	(B) 최근에 건설된 관광 명소
(C) A newly implemented rule	(C) 새로 시행되는 규칙
(D) A revised fee structure	(D) 수정된 요금 체계

어휘 tourist attraction 관광 명소 implement 시행하다 revise 수정하다 fee structure 요금 체계

해설 두 번째 문장에서 섬 출입에 대한 새 제한 규정을 시행한다고 밝히고 있다(Please be aware that new restrictions are now in force regarding access to the island during the upcoming summer season).

173

What is indicated about visiting Greenbay Island?	Greenbay 섬 방문에 관하여 무엇이 나타나 있는가?
(A) Guests are cautioned against disturbing nesting birds.	(A) 방문객들에게 둥지를 튼 새들을 방해하지 말라는 주의가 주어진다.
(B) Walking tours require a guide's presence.	(B) 도보 관광에는 가이드의 동행이 요구된다.
(C) Swimming near the island is not allowed.	(C) 섬 주변에서 수영은 허용되지 않는다.
(D) Viewing the island from a boat requires joining an official tour.	(D) 보트에서 섬을 관람하려면 공식 투어에 참여해야 한다.

어휘 caution sb against ~에게 ~하지 않도록 주의를 주다, 경고하다 disturb 방해하다 presence 동석, 입회

해설 첫 문단에 섬에 발을 들여놓으려면 공식 투어 그룹의 일원이 되어야 한다는 규정이 나와 있는데(Visitors who are not part of an authorized tour group will be prohibited from making landfall on Greenbay Island.), 두 번째 문단을 읽으면 이 투어에는 가이드의 안내가 제공된다는 것을 알 수 있다(The GNPA offers official guided boat tours to the island every day of the year). 즉 가이드의 안내를 받는 사람만 섬에 들어가서 관광을 할 수 있다.

174

What is NOT mentioned about the GNPA's tours?	GNPA 투어에 관하여 언급되지 않는 것은 무엇인가?
(A) There is a limit on the number of attendees.	(A) 참가자 수에 제한이 있다.
(B) Advance payment might be necessary.	(B) 사전 결제가 필요할 수 있다.
(C) Tour hours differ depending on the season.	(C) 투어 시간이 계절에 따라 다르다.
(D) Overnight excursions are available.	(D) 숙박 여행을 이용할 수 있다.

어휘 advance 사전의 overnight 하룻밤의 excursion 단체 관광[여행]

해설 두 번째 문단에 투어 시간에 대한 안내가 나오는데, 평소에는 마지막 출발 시간이 오후 4시이지만 여름에는 6시로 늦춰진다고 알려주고 있다(with the final tour leaving at 4:00 in the afternoon. However, during the summer months—December through March—the last tour is extended to 6:00 P.M.). 이 부분을 읽으면서 (C)를 제거하자. 예약 및 결제 안내의 첫 항목에 투어 참가 인원이 20명으로 제한된다는 내용이 나오므로(Each tour is capped at 20 participants.) 여기서 (A)를 제거하자. 세 번째 항목에서 단체 예약을 하려면 보증금을 내야 한다는 사실을 알 수 있으므로(A nonrefundable deposit of $7 per person is required to secure group reservations.) 여기서 (B)를 제거하자.

175

According to the notice, what might occur if a group arrives late for a scheduled tour?	공지문에 따르면 단체가 예정된 투어에 늦게 도착하면 무엇이 발생할 수 있는가?
(A) The tour could be canceled.	(A) 투어가 취소될 수 있다.
(B) The duration could be under two hours.	(B) 투어 시간이 두 시간이 안 될 수 있다.
(C) The cost could increase.	(C) 비용이 증가할 수 있다.
(D) The tour might be rescheduled.	(D) 투어 일정을 다시 잡을 수 있다.

■ **어휘** duration 지속 시간

■ **해설** 두 번째 문단에 따르면 투어는 원래 두 시간마다 출발한다(Tours depart every two hours). 그런데 예약 및 결제 정보의 마지막 항목에 따르면, 한 단체
가 예정된 출발 시간보다 늦게 도착하는 경우에는 다음 단체에 방해가 되지 않도록 GNPA가 투어 시간을 단축할 수 있다(If your party fails to arrive at
the scheduled time, GNPA reserves the right to shorten the tour as needed to avoid interfering with subsequent tours). 즉 늦게 도착하는 단체의
투어 시간은 두 시간 미만일 수 있다.

Questions 176 through 180 refer to the following Web page and customer review.

Event Forge — your trusted online partner for professional ticket printing!
We have produced tickets for thousands of occasions, from music festivals and athletic competitions to trade expos and more. Whatever your event, we will help you craft a ticket that reflects its unique character.

Step 1: Design Your Ticket
Browse our collection of elegant templates by choosing a category. You can easily adjust the text to reflect your event details. For those seeking greater control over the color scheme, typography, imagery, and layout, download our Event Forge Designer Suite. [176]This complimentary software empowers users to customize every visual element of their ticket beyond the default templates.

Step 2: Select Quantity
Whether you need just a few or several thousand, Event Forge accommodates orders of all sizes. Bulk discounts apply — the more you order, the less you pay per ticket.

Quantity	Price per ticket
100 – 500	45 cents
501 – 1,000	35 cents
[178]1,001 – 3,000	[178]25 cents
3,001 or more	20 cents

Step 3: Add an Invisible Verification Stamp
[177]For an additional 5 cents per ticket, you may opt to include a discreet invisible verification stamp printed in ultraviolet ink, visible only under black light. This feature enhances the authenticity of your tickets and helps prevent counterfeiting.

Step 4: Submit Your Order
Standard orders are processed within three business days, though larger requests may require additional time. We recommend placing your order well in advance of your event to ensure timely delivery.

176–180번 문제는 다음 웹 페이지와 고객 후기에
관한 것입니다.

**Event Forge — 신뢰할 수 있는 전문 티켓 온라인
인쇄 파트너!**
음악 축제와 스포츠 대회부터 무역 박람회 등 저희는
수천 건의 행사 티켓을 제작해 왔습니다. 어떤 행사
이든 고유한 특성을 반영하는 티켓을 제작하도록 도
와드립니다.

1단계: 티켓을 디자인하세요
카테고리를 선택하셔서 저희의 세련된 템플릿 컬렉
션을 둘러보세요. 문구는 쉽게 조정해서 행사 세부
사항을 반영할 수 있습니다. 색상 구성, 글꼴 디자인,
이미지 표현과 지면 배치를 더 조정하고 싶은 분들은
Event Forge Designer Suite를 다운로드하면 됩니다.
이 무료 소프트웨어는 사용자가 기본 템플릿을 넘어
티켓의 모든 시각적 요소를 원하는 대로 만들 수 있
는 권한을 줍니다.

2단계: 수량을 선택하세요
필요하신 수량이 몇 장이든 수천 장이든 Event
Forge는 모든 규모의 주문을 받습니다. 대량 주문에
는 할인이 적용됩니다. 더 많이 주문할수록 장당 가
격은 내려갑니다.

수량	장당 가격
100 – 500	45센트
501 – 1,000	35센트
1,001 – 3,000	25센트
3,001장 이상	20센트

3단계: 보이지 않는 보안 스탬프를 추가하세요
티켓당 5센트를 추가하면 자외선 잉크로 인쇄되어
블랙라이트 아래에서만 보이는, 잘 보이지 않는 보안
스탬프를 포함할 수 있습니다. 이 기능은 티켓의 진
품 신뢰성을 높이고 위조를 방지하는 데 도움이 됩
니다.

4단계: 주문서를 제출하세요.
일반 주문은 영업일 기준 3일 이내에 처리되지만, 주
문량이 많은 경우에는 시간이 더 필요할 수 있습니
다. 제때에 배송되도록 행사에 앞서 미리 주문하실
것을 권장합니다.

★★★★★ *I'm thrilled we chose Event Forge!*

I manage a small independent venue called Linden Hall, [178]and we recently ordered 3,000 tickets from Event Forge. We opted not to include the invisible verification stamp but did install the free design software to customize the layout and incorporate our venue's logo. The final product was outstanding! Several patrons complimented us on the new look, and we were especially impressed by the prompt delivery. Last year, [179][180]we ordered from a local vendor here in Fairhaven, and the tickets took six weeks to arrive. In contrast, Event Forge—despite being located across the country—delivered our order in just four business days!

— **Elliot Ramirez**

★★★★★ *Event Forge를 선택하기를 정말 잘 했어요!*

저는 Linden Hall이라는 작은 독립 행사장을 운영하고 있는데, 최근에 우리는 3,000장의 티켓을 Event Forge에 주문했습니다. 보이지 않는 보안 스탬프는 넣지 않는 걸로 선택했지만, 무료 디자인 소프트웨어를 설치해서 지면 배치를 맞춤으로 구성하고 행사장 로고를 포함시켰습니다. 최종 결과물은 훌륭했습니다! 여러 고객들이 새로워진 모양을 보고 우리를 칭찬했는데, 우리는 특히 신속한 배송에 깊은 인상을 받았습니다. 작년에는 이곳 Fairhaven에 있는 판매업체에 주문했는데, 티켓이 도착하는 데 6주나 걸렸습니다. 그에 반해 Event Forge는 전국 반대편에 있는데도 주문품을 불과 (영업일) 4일 만에 배송해 주었습니다!

— Elliot Ramirez

어휘1 occasion 행사 athletic 운동의 competition 대회 craft 공들여 제작하다 reflect 반영하다 browse 둘러보다 elegant 우아한, 세련된 template (그래픽) 템플릿, 견본 adjust 조정하다 seek 추구하다 color scheme 색상 구성 typography 글꼴 디자인 imagery 이미지 표현 layout 배치 suite 소프트웨어 묶음 empower 권한을 부여하다 customize 원하는 대로 만들다 default 초기 설정, 기본값 quantity 수량 bulk 대량의 apply 적용되다 invisible 보이지 않는 verification 검증, 보안 opt to-V ~하기로 선택하다 discreet 눈에 띄지 않는 ultraviolet 자외선의 visible 보이는 black light 비가시광선, 블랙라이트 enhance 높이다 authenticity 진품임, 진짜임 counterfeit 위조하다 process 처리하다 place an order 주문하다 in advance of ~에 앞서 timely 제때의

어휘2 thrilled 매우 기쁜 independent 독립적인 venue 행사장, 장소 install 설치하다 incorporate 포함하다 outstanding 뛰어난 patron 고객 compliment 칭찬하다 impressed 감명 받은 prompt 신속한 vendor 판매업체 in contrast 그에 반해, 대조적으로

176

According to the Web page, what does the free software enable users to do?

(A) Customize ticket visuals
(B) Confirm event attendees
(C) Maintain a company Web site
(D) Access customer databases

웹 페이지에 따르면 무료 소프트웨어는 사용자가 무엇을 할 수 있게 해주는가?

(A) 티켓의 시각 정보를 원하는 대로 만든다
(B) 행사 참가자들을 확인한다
(C) 회사 홈페이지를 유지 관리한다
(D) 고객의 데이터베이스에 접속한다

어휘 visuals 시각 정보 maintain 유지 관리하다 access 접속하다

해설 1단계에 대한 설명에 무료 소프트웨어가 사용자로 하여금 티켓의 모든 시각적 요소를 원하는 대로 만들 수 있게 해 준다고 나와 있다 (This complimentary software empowers users to customize every visual element of their ticket).

177

What is stated on the Web page about Event Forge?

(A) It provides multiple ticket dimensions.
(B) It offers an optional security feature.
(C) It uses a distinct numbering scheme.
(D) It operates several retail outlets.

웹 페이지에서 Event Forge에 대해 무엇이 언급되고 있는가?

(A) 다양한 크기의 티켓을 제공한다.
(B) 선택 사항인 보안 기능을 제공한다.
(C) 고유한 번호 체계를 사용한다.
(D) 여러 소매 판매점을 운영한다.

어휘 dimension 크기, 치수 security 보안 distinct 뚜렷한, 구별되는, 고유한 scheme 방식, 체계 operate 운영하다 retail outlet 소매 판매점

해설 3단계에 대한 설명을 읽어 보면, 장당 5센트를 추가하면 티켓에 보이지 않는 보안 스탬프를 찍어 위조를 방지할 수 있다(For an additional 5 cents per ticket, you may opt to include a discreet invisible verification stamp printed in ultraviolet ink, visible only under black light. This feature enhances the authenticity of your tickets and helps prevent counterfeiting). 즉 보안 기능이 선택적으로 제공된다.

What is indicated about Mr. Ramirez?	Mr. Ramirez에 관하여 무엇이 나타나 있는가?
(A) He paid twenty-five cents per ticket.	(A) 티켓 한 장당 25센트를 지불했다.
(B) He requested expedited processing.	(B) 더 신속한 처리를 요청했다.
(C) He used a default template.	(C) 기본적으로 제공되는 템플릿을 사용했다.
(D) He received more tickets than he ordered.	(D) 주문한 것보다 더 많은 티켓을 받았다.

어휘 expedite 더 신속하게 처리하다

해설 Mr. Ramirez는 평가에서 3,000장의 티켓을 주문했다고 진술하고 있는데(we recently ordered 3,000 tickets from Event Forge.), 웹 페이지에서 2단계 설명에 포함되어 있는 가격표를 보면 3,000장을 주문할 때는 제작비는 장당 25센트이다.

What is suggested about the Linden Hall?	Linden Hall에 관하여 무엇이 암시되어 있는가?
(A) It is located in Fairhaven.	(A) Fairhaven에 위치해 있다.
(B) It is planning a logo redesign.	(B) 로고 재디자인을 계획하고 있다.
(C) It recently lowered admission prices.	(C) 최근에 입장료를 인하했다.
(D) It distributes tickets via postal mail.	(D) 우편을 통해 티켓을 배포한다.

어휘 lower 낮추다 distribute 배포하다 via ~을 통해서

해설 we ordered from a local vendor here in Fairhaven에서 Mr. Ramirez가 운영하는 Linden Hall은 Fairhaven에 있음을 추론할 수 있다.

According to the review, why does Mr. Ramirez prefer Event Forge over previous vendor?	평가에 따르면 Mr. Ramirez가 이전 판매업체보다 Event Forge를 선호하는 이유는 무엇인가?
(A) It offers more competitive pricing.	(A) 더 경쟁력 있는 가격으로 책정한다.
(B) It ships internationally.	(B) 해외에도 배송한다.
(C) It uses superior printing technology.	(C) 우수한 인쇄 기술을 사용한다.
(D) It processes orders more efficiently.	(D) 주문을 더 효율적으로 처리한다.

어휘 competitive 경쟁력 있는 pricing 가격 책정 ship 운송하다 superior 더 우수한

해설 지역 업체에 주문했을 때는 티켓을 받는 데 6주나 걸린 반면, 나라 반대편의 훨씬 더 먼 곳에 있음에도 불구하고 Event Forge에 주문하면 4일밖에 걸리지 않는다(we ordered from a local vendor here in Fairhaven, and the tickets took six weeks to arrive. In contrast, Event Forge—despite being located across the country—delivered our order in just four business days!). 즉 Event Forge의 주문 처리 방식이 훨씬 더 효율적이라고 말할 수 있다.

Questions 181 through 185 refer to the following e-mail and business plan.

To: Claire Katsaros <ckatsaros@capitalhorizon.net>
From: Eleni Stavros <e.stavros@velvetstride.com>
Date: January 18
Re: Updated Business Plan
Attachment: Stavros_UpdatedPlan

Dear Ms. Katsaros,

[182]I truly appreciate your assistance in helping me secure financial support for my upcoming venture. [181]After reviewing your comments, I have revised my proposal accordingly. [183]Per your recommendation, I have included a section that identifies our expected customer population. [181]You will find the updated version attached. I believe this finalizes all the documentation required for my loan submission. Should you need any additional information, please feel free to reach out.

I'm eager to receive your formal confirmation regarding my application.

Regards,

Eleni Stavros

Revised Business Plan: Velvet Stride

Section 1. Objective
The Apollo Avenue area has evolved into a vibrant district filled with eateries, retail outlets, and entertainment venues. Velvet Stride aims to fill a noticeable gap among the existing apparel stores. [184]Our shop will specialize in women's footwear and fashion accessories. We are dedicated to delivering stylish, high-quality shoes at affordable prices in a welcoming, customer-focused setting.

[183]Section 2. Intended Customer Base
Velvet Stride will cater to professional women employed nearby. With numerous office buildings located within walking distance, we expect many customers to frequent during lunch breaks or after work. On weekends, we anticipate attracting shoppers and diners who come to the area for leisure and entertainment.

Section 3. Projected Schedule
Our grand opening is planned for June 15. Below are the estimated deadlines for each phase:

March 1 Finalize lease agreement and acquire business license
April 5   Renovate interior and set up product displays
May 10   Advertise job openings, conduct interviews, and hire team members
June 12 Stock inventory and prepare for launch

181-185번 문제는 다음 이메일과 사업 계획서에 관한 것입니다.

수신: Claire Katsaros 〈ckatsaros@capitalhorizon.net〉
발신: Eleni Stavros 〈e.stavros@velvetstride.com〉
날짜: 1월 18일
제목: 사업 계획서 업데이트
첨부 파일: Stavros_UpdatedPlan

Ms. Katsaros께,

곧 시작할 사업을 위해 재정 지원을 확보하는 데 도와주셔서 진심으로 감사합니다. 주신 의견을 검토해 보고 나서 그에 맞게 기획안을 수정했습니다. 권고에 따라 예상 고객층을 명시하는 부분을 포함했습니다. 수정된 버전은 첨부 파일로 확인하실 수 있습니다. 이로써 대출 신청에 필요한 모든 서류가 완비된 것 같습니다. 추가 정보가 필요하시면 언제든 연락 주시기 바랍니다.

신청에 대한 공식 승인을 기다리겠습니다.

이만 줄입니다.

Eleni Stavros

사업 계획서 수정본: Velvet Stride

1. 목표
Apollo 대로 주변 지역은 음식점과 소매점, 오락 시설이 밀집한 활기찬 구역으로 발전했습니다. Velvet Stride는 기존의 의류 판매점들 사이에서 눈에 띄는 틈새를 채우는 것을 목표로 합니다. 우리 가게는 여성용 신발과 패션 액세서리를 전문으로 할 것입니다. 우리는 고객 중심의 편안한 환경에서 세련된 고품질의 신발을 합리적인 가격에 제공하는 데 전념할 것입니다.

2. 대상 고객층
Velvet Stride는 인근 전문직 종사 여성들의 취향에 맞는 서비스를 제공할 것입니다. 수많은 사무실 건물들이 걸어서 갈 수 있는 거리에 위치해 있는 가운데, 우리는 많은 고객들이 점심시간이나 퇴근 후에 자주 방문할 것을 기대하고 있습니다. 주말에는 여가와 오락을 위해 이 지역을 찾는 쇼핑객들과 식당 손님들을 유치하게 될 것으로 예상합니다.

3. 예상 일정
개업은 6월 15일로 계획되어 있습니다. 각 단계는 아래 날짜 전에 완료될 것으로 예상됩니다.

3월 1일: 임대차 계약서 작성 및 사업 면허 취득
4월 5일: 내부 개조 및 상품 진열
5월 10일: 채용 공고 게시 및 면접 실시, 직원 채용
6월 12일: 재고 확보 및 개업 준비

Section 4. Financial Overview
[185]Please refer to the attached projection sheet for a breakdown of estimated expenditures and anticipated profits.

4. 재무 개관
예상 지출과 예상 수익의 세부 내역은 첨부된 전망 시트를 참조하시기 바랍니다.

어휘1 secure 확보하다　accordingly 그에 맞게　per ~에 따라　identify (문서, 계획에서) 명시하다　customer population 고객층　finalize 완료하다　documentation 문서, 서류　submission 제출　reach out ~에게 연락하다　confirmation 확인, 승인

어휘2 objective 목표, 목적　evolve 발전하다　vibrant 활기찬　entertainment 오락, 연예　noticeable 눈에 띄는　specialize in ~을 전문으로 하다　existing 기존의　footwear 신발류　be dedicated to ~에 전념하다　affordable 적당한 가격의　welcoming 아늑한, 편안함을 주는　intended 대상으로 삼은　cater to ~에(게) 맞춰 제공하다　within walking distance 걸어서 갈 수 있는 거리에　frequent 자주 방문하다　diner (식당의) 식사 손님　leisure 여가　project 예상하다　estimate 추정하다, 추산하다　stock 채워놓다, 넣어두다　inventory 재고, 상품 전체　overview 개요, 개관　refer to ~을 참조하다　projection 예상　breakdown 세부 내역　expenditure 지출

181

Why did Ms. Stavros send the e-mail?

(A) To congratulate someone on a recent promotion
(B) To provide steps for obtaining a business license
(C) To offer guidance to a new entrepreneur
(D) To address a specific recommendation

Ms. Stavros는 왜 이메일을 보냈는가?

(A) 어떤 사람이 최근에 승진한 것을 축하하기 위해
(B) 사업 면허를 취득하기 위한 절차를 설명하기 위해
(C) 새로 사업을 시작한 사람에게 조언하기 위해
(D) 특정 권고 사항을 다루기 위해

어휘 guidance 지도, 도움, 안내　entrepreneur 기업가, 사업가　address 다루다, 처리하다　recommendation 권고

해설 Ms. Stavros는 Ms. Katsaros의 의견에 따라 사업 계획서를 수정했고(After reviewing your comments, I have revised my proposal accordingly.), 수정된 계획서를 이메일에 첨부해서 Ms. Katsaros가 볼 수 있게 했다(You will find the updated version attached). 이메일을 보낸 것은 권고 사항에 대해 답신하기 위한 것이다.

182

In the e-mail, the word "secure" in paragraph 1, line 1, is closest in meaning to

(A) protect
(B) acquire
(C) assure
(D) affix

이메일에서 첫 문단 첫 번째 줄의 단어 "secure"와 의미상 가장 가까운 것은

(A) 보호하다
(B) 얻다, 획득하다
(C) 보장하다
(D) 붙이다, 부착하다

해설 선택지 네 개의 동사가 모두 secure의 동의어로 사용할 수 있지만, 본문에서 secure는 '재정 지원을 확보하다'라는 뜻으로 사용되었다.

183

Which part of the business plan was newly included?

(A) Section 1
(B) Section 2
(C) Section 3
(D) Section 4

사업 계획서의 어느 부분이 새로 포함되었는가?

(A) 1항
(B) 2항
(C) 3항
(D) 4항

해설 이메일을 보면 Ms. Katsaros의 조언을 받은 Ms. Stavros는 사업 계획서에 예상 고객층을 밝히는 부분을 추가했다(I have included a section that identifies our expected customer population). 사업 계획서를 읽어 보면 타깃으로 하는 고객층은 Section 2에서 설명하고 있다(Section 2. Intended Customer Base).

184

What type of business is Ms. Stavros planning to launch?

(A) A gourmet restaurant
(B) A staffing agency
(C) A beauty parlor
(D) A shoe boutique

Ms. Stavros는 어떤 유형의 사업을 시작할 계획인가?

(A) 고급 식당
(B) 채용 대행사
(C) 미용실
(D) 신발 가게

해설 사업 계획서의 Section 1에서 Ms. Stavros가 차릴 상점은 여성용 신발 및 패션 액세서리 전문점이라고 밝히고 있다(Our shop will specialize in women's footwear and fashion accessories).

185

According to the business plan, what information was submitted separately?

(A) Personal recommendation letters
(B) A list of contracted vendors
(C) Financial projections detailing expenditures
(D) An inventory catalog

사업 계획서에 따르면 어떤 정보가 별도로 제출되었는가?

(A) 개인 추천서
(B) 계약을 맺은 판매업체 명단
(C) 지출을 상술하는 재무 예상 보고서
(D) 상품 카탈로그

어휘 separately 별도로 detail 상세히 설명하다

해설 Section 4에서 예상 지출과 수입의 세부적인 내용을 별도의 문서로 첨부해 놓았다고 말하고 있다(Please refer to the attached projection sheet for a breakdown of estimated expenditures and anticipated profits).

📄 **Questions 186 through 190** refer to the following Web page, e-mail, and form.

186–190번 문제는 다음 웹 페이지와 이메일, 주문서에 관한 것입니다.

PHOTO GALLERY | **HOME** | BROWSE | ORDER FORM | CONTACT US

포토 갤러리 | **홈** | 둘러보기 | 주문서 | 문의하기

VistaForm Office Concepts

Welcome to our Web site! Browse our inventory to visualize office setups that are both modern and functional. We have proudly served the KwaZulu-Natal region for over 20 years, and you can count on our high quality furnishings to truly set your workspace apart.
We always offer the following deals:
• [187]Free shipping and handling for first-time customers
• [186]Special discounts for schools and nonprofit organizations (call for details)

VistaForm Office Concepts

저희 홈페이지에 오신 것을 환영합니다! 상품들을 둘러보시고 현대적이면서 실용적인 사무실 구성을 상상해 보세요. 저희는 20년이 넘도록 긍지를 가지고 KwaZulu-Natal 지역에 서비스를 제공해 왔으며, 저희의 고품질 가구가 귀사의 일터를 정말로 돋보이게 해 줄 것이라고 믿으셔도 좋습니다.
언제나 다음 혜택을 제공합니다:
• 첫 거래 고객을 위한 무료 배송 및 취급
• 학교들과 비영리 기관들을 위한 특별 할인 (자세한 내용은 전화 요망)

From: Daniel Mokoena [dmokoena@oakandledger.co.za]
To: Lerato Ndlovu [lndlovu@oakandledger.co.za]
Date: 14 June
Subject: Office furniture proposal

Hi, Lerato,

After doing some research, I'd like to recommend VistaForm Office Concepts for the desks and other items we'll need for our office upgrade. [187]Although we haven't ordered from them before, they provided references that included glowing feedback.

[189]For the main work zone, I suggest we go with a larger desk model—ten units—along with matching file cabinets and bookshelves. For the upstairs team and interns, a more compact desk style would be suitable.

[188]If you're on board with this plan, I'd like to place the order soon so that delivery happens while most of our staff are attending the conference in Richmond. Unfortunately, the workspace will look a bit chaotic as we clear out the old furniture and await the new pieces.

Let me know what you think of the proposal I've outlined above.

Best,

Daniel

발신: Daniel Mokoena
[dmokoena@oakandledger.co.za]
수신: Lerato Ndlovu
[lndlovu@oakandledger.co.za]
날짜: 6월 14일
제목: 사무실 가구 제안

안녕하세요, Lerato.

조금 조사를 해본 결과, 사무실 개선에 필요한 책상과 기타 가구를 위해 VistaForm Office Concepts를 추천하고 싶습니다. 우리는 전에 그곳에 주문한 적이 없지만, 그들이 매우 긍정적인 평가가 포함된 참고 자료를 제공했습니다.

주 업무 공간에는 큰 책상 모델(10대)과 그에 어울리는 파일 수납장 및 책장과 함께 선택할 것을 제안합니다. 위층에서 근무하는 팀과 인턴들에게는 더 작은 스타일의 책상이 알맞을 것 같습니다.

이 계획에 동의하신다면, 대부분의 직원들이 Richmond에서 열리는 학회에 참석하는 동안 배송이 이루어지도록 주문을 서두르고자 합니다. 안타깝게도 오래된 가구를 치우고 새것을 기다리는 동안에는 업무 공간이 다소 어수선해 보일 것입니다.

위에 대략 말씀드린 제안에 대해 어떻게 생각하시는지 알려주시기 바랍니다.

이만 줄입니다.

Daniel

Order code: R8427Z
Contact: Daniel Mokoena, (031) 774–2186
Delivery to: Oak & Ledger Associates, 88 Constitution Avenue, Pietermaritzburg 3201
Delivery window: 04–06 July, 08:30–16:30

Quantity	Product ID	Description
[189]10	VED4421	Vista Executive Desk
10	TFC2210	Trimline File Cabinet; brushed charcoal
3	BQ3095	Booknest Shelving Unit; brushed charcoal
[189]5	FD5127	Flexform Desk

Note: Due to high demand, Product BQ3095 is currently unavailable at our Howick location. [190]These units will be delivered to your office directly from our production facility, so they will be shipped into Pietermaritzburg from Durban rather than from Howick. This may result in a delay of one to three days. We will make every effort to deliver the full order on the same day.

주문 코드: R8427Z
연락처: Daniel Mokoena, (031) 774–2186
배송지: Oak & Ledger Associates, 88 Constitution Avenue, Pietermaritzburg 3201
배송 기간: 7월 4일–6일, 08:30–16:30

수량	제품 ID	품목
10	VED4421	Vista 고급 책상
10	TFC2210	Trimline 파일 수납장; 브러시 차콜
3	BQ3095	Booknest 선반; 브러시 차콜
5	FD5127	Flexform 책상

주의: BQ3095 제품은 높은 수요로 인해 현재 저희 Howick 지점에서 이용할 수 없습니다. 이 제품은 저희 생산 시설에서 고객님의 사무실로 직접 보내 드리겠습니다. 즉 Howick이 아니라 Durban에서 Pietermaritzburg로 배송됩니다. 이로 인해 1–3일의 지연이 생길 수 있습니다. 주문품 전체를 같은 날 배송해 드리도록 모든 노력을 다 하겠습니다.

어휘1 visualize 마음속에 그려보다 setup 구성, 배치 count on 기대하다, 믿다 furnishings 가구류 set apart ~을 차별화하다, 돋보이게 하다 deal 혜택 shipping 배송 handling 취급 nonprofit 비영리의

어휘2 reference 참고 자료 glowing 극찬하는 go with ~을 선택하다 unit (완성 제품의) 한 개 along with ~와 함께 compact 소형의 be on board with ~에 동의하다 chaotic 혼란스러운, 어수선한 clear out ~을 치우다 await 기다리다

어휘3 window 기간, 시간대 description 종류, 품목 executive 고급형의 brushed charcoal (브러시로 마감한 듯한 무광 질감의) 짙은 회색 shelving unit 선반 note 주의, 유의

186

What is indicated about VistaForm Office Concepts?

(A) It offers help with designing office layouts.
(B) It grants special deals to educational institutions.
(C) It has recently diversified its product line.
(D) It has recently launched a new store.

VistaForm Office Concepts에 관하여 무엇이 나타나 있는가?

(A) 사무실 배치 디자인에 도움을 제공한다.
(B) 교육 기관들에게 특별 혜택을 제공한다.
(C) 최근에 제품군을 다양화했다.
(D) 최근에 새 상점을 개업했다.

어휘 institution 기관 diversify 다양화하다 product line 제품군

해설 웹 페이지 마지막 문장에 학교들에게 주어지는 특별 할인 혜택이 언급되고 있다(Special discounts for schools).

187

What is probably true about Oak & Ledger Associates' furniture order?

(A) Its delivery expenses will be waived.
(B) It contains an item that has been discontinued.
(C) It missed the deadline for July delivery.
(D) It includes some furniture selected by interns.

Oak & Ledger Associates의 가구 주문에 관하여 무엇이 사실이겠는가?

(A) 배송비가 면제될 것이다.
(B) 단종된 제품이 포함되어 있다.
(C) 7월 배송을 위한 기한을 놓쳤다.
(D) 인턴사원들이 선택한 가구가 포함되어 있다.

어휘 waive 면제하다 contain 포함하다 discontinue 단종하다

해설 웹 페이지 마지막 부분에 첫 거래 고객에게는 배송과 취급이 무료라는 혜택을 언급하고 있는데(Free shipping and handling for first-time customers), 이메일을 읽어 보면 Oak & Ledger Associates는 VistaForm Office Concepts에 가구를 주문해 본 적이 없는 첫 거래 고객이다(Although we haven't ordered from them before). 그러므로 이번에 구매가 이루어진다면 Oak & Ledger Associates는 무료 배송을 받게 될 것이라고 추론할 수 있다.

188

Why does Mr. Mokoena probably prefer to schedule a delivery during a particular period of time?

(A) He expects to get an extra discount.
(B) He wants the furniture ready for an important meeting.
(C) He requires more time to discard outdated items.
(D) He strives to minimize disruption for his colleagues.

Mr. Mokoena는 왜 특정 기간 동안 배송 일정 잡는 것을 선호하겠는가?

(A) 추가 할인 받기를 기대한다.
(B) 중요한 회의를 위해 가구가 준비되기를 바란다.
(C) 오래된 물건을 버리기 위해 더 많은 시간이 필요하다.
(D) 동료들에 대한 방해를 최소화하기 위해 노력한다.

어휘 discard 버리다 outdated 오래된 strive to-V ~하려고 노력하다 minimize 최소화하다 disruption 방해

해설 이메일의 세 번째 문단을 읽어 보면, Mr. Mokoena는 가구 배송이 직원들이 대부분 학회에 가고 없는 기간에 이루어지기를 바라는데(I'd like to place the order soon so that delivery happens while most of our staff are attending the conference in Richmond.), 이유는 가구를 교체하는 동안 사무실이 어수선해질 것이기 때문이다(Unfortunately, the workspace will look a bit chaotic as we clear out the old furniture and await the new pieces). 즉 Mr. Mokoena는 가구 교체 과정이 되도록 직원들에게 방해가 되지 않기를 바라고 있다.

189

What furniture product will most likely be located on the upper story at Oak & Ledger Associates?

(A) Vista Executive Desk
(B) Trimline File Cabinets
(C) Booknest Shelving Unit
(D) Flexform Desks

Oak & Ledger Associates에서 위층에는 어떤 가구 상품이 설치되겠는가?

(A) Vista 고급 책상
(B) Trimline 파일 수납장
(C) Booknest 선반
(D) Flexform 책상

어휘 locate 두다, 설치하다 story (건물의) 층

해설 이메일의 두 번째 문단을 읽어 보면, 업무 공간으로 주 업무 공간(main work zone)과 위층(upstairs) 두 군데가 나온다. Mr. Mokoena이 주 업무 공간에 큰 책상 열 대를 놓고, 위층에는 작은 책상을 놓자고 제안하고 있다(For the main work zone, I suggest we go with a larger desk model—ten units—along with matching file cabinets and bookshelves. For the upstairs team and interns, a more compact desk style would be suitable). 주문서에 책상은 Vista Executive Desk와 Flexform Desks 두 가지이며, 주문된 Vista Executive Desk 10대는 주 업무 공간에 놓일 것이라고 추론할 수 있다. 따라서 위층에는 Flexform Desks가 설치될 것이다.

190

<table>
<tr><td>

According to the form, where is the furniture manufactured?

(A) Pietermaritzburg
(B) Durban
(C) Richmond
(D) Howick

</td><td>

주문서에 따르면 가구는 어디에서 제조되는가?

(A) Pietermaritzburg
(B) Durban
(C) Richmond
(D) Howick

</td></tr>
</table>

해설 주문서의 '주의' 부분을 보자. "이 제품은 저희 생산 시설에서 고객님의 사무실로 직접 보내 드리겠습니다(These units will be delivered to your office directly from our production facility). 즉 Howick이 아니라 Durban에서 Pietermaritzburg로 배송됩니다(so they will be shipped into Pietermaritzburg from Durban rather than from Howick)."라고 나와 있다. 이 문장의 내용을 종합해 보면 가구가 제조되는 곳은 Durban이라는 것을 알 수 있다.

Questions 191 through 195 refer to the following e-mail, menu, and comment card.

From: Matteo Ricci <mricci@villagusto.com>
To: Chiara Bianchi <cbianchi@villagusto.com>
Date: Tuesday, June 7
Subject: Preview Dinner Planning

Hi Chiara,

[191]Can you believe Mr. Martin will be arriving in less than three weeks? His column will be published in the *Liberty Gazette*, so we must ensure that our offerings reflect the very essence of Villa Gusto. To gather input on the dishes we'll present to him, I've decided we should host a preview dinner next Friday evening.

I've been thinking about the menu. [192]Let's include a hearty vegetarian entrée that can truly hold its own. That way, we can showcase our plant-based creativity. I also suggest featuring our steamed shellfish dish, which has been a customer favorite lately. [195]I'm adamant about including the new specialty pizzas we've been developing for the summer menu. That is, of course, assuming the brick oven installation is finalized by then. [193]And let's not forget our fruit-based desserts—they're always well received by critics. Naturally, I trust your judgment as our Executive Chef to finalize the selections.

One more thing—I'd love for our preview dinner guests to have the opportunity to tour the kitchen. Let me know your thoughts and how best to coordinate that.

Thanks,

Matteo

191–195번 문제는 다음 이메일과 메뉴, 의견 카드에 관한 것입니다.

발신: Matteo Ricci 〈mricci@villagusto.com〉
수신: Chiara Bianchi 〈cbianchi@villagusto.com〉
날짜: 6월 7일 화요일
제목: 시식 만찬 계획

안녕하세요, Chiara.

Mr. Martin이 방문할 날이 3주도 남지 않았다는 사실이 믿어지나요? 그의 칼럼이 *Liberty Gazette*에 실릴 예정이니 우리가 제공하는 음식이 반드시 Villa Gusto의 정수를 담아내도록 해야 합니다. 그에게 선보일 요리에 대한 의견을 모으기 위해 다음 주 금요일 저녁에 시식 만찬을 열기로 했습니다.

메뉴에 대해 생각해 봤어요. 정말 다른 무엇에도 뒤지지 않을 푸짐한 채식 주요리를 포함합시다. 그렇게 하면 우리의 채소에 기반한 창의성을 선보일 수 있죠. 또한 특별히 조개 찜요리를 넣으면 좋겠습니다. 최근 고객들이 가장 좋아한 것이었으니까요. 여름 메뉴를 위해 개발하고 있는 새 특선 피자는 꼭 포함해야 합니다. 물론 이것은 벽돌 오븐 설치가 그때까지 마무리된다는 것을 전제하는 것이지요. 그리고 과일로 만든 디저트를 잊지 맙시다. 언제나 비평가들의 호평을 받고 있잖아요. 물론 저는 메뉴 선정 확정에 대해 총괄 주방장인 당신의 판단을 신뢰합니다.

한 가지만 더요. 시식 만찬 손님들에게 주방을 둘러볼 기회를 드리고 싶어요. 당신의 생각과 어떻게 조율하면 가장 좋을지 알려주세요.

고맙습니다.

Matteo

<table>
<tr><td>

Villa Gusto Preview Dinner Menu
Saturday, June 17

Smoked salmon canapés with dill crème
Butter-roasted halibut with lemon zest
Grilled eggplant steak in tangy tomato-lemon glaze
Steamed mussels and prawns in coconut saffron broth
Tuscan-style roasted chicken with cannellini beans and wilted arugula
[193]Glazed almond peach tart

</td><td>

Villa Gusto 시식 만찬 메뉴
6월 17일 토요일

딜 크림을 얹은 훈제 연어 카나페
레몬 제스트를 곁들인 광어 버터구이
톡 쏘는 토마토 레몬 글레이즈를 입힌 가지 그릴 스테이크
코코넛 사프란 국물에 담긴 홍합 새우 찜
카넬리니 콩과 데친 아루굴라를 곁들인 토스카나식 로스트 치킨
글레이즈 아몬드 복숭아 타르트

</td></tr>
</table>

<table>
<tr><td>

Guest Feedback Card

Name: Isabella Moreau

Please share your thoughts on the preview dinner at Villa Gusto.

[194]The eggplant dish had a lovely sweetness, though the sauce was a bit too acidic for my taste. The halibut was absolutely divine—perfectly cooked and seasoned. The Tuscan chicken was tender, but lacked depth of flavor. As for the tart, it was pleasant, though slightly overbaked. I was impressed by the sleek layout of your kitchen. [195]I'm eager to try the new brick-oven pizzas once they're available. It's a shame they weren't ready for tonight's dinner.

</td><td>

고객 피드백 카드

이름: Isabella Moreau

Villa Gusto 시식 만찬에 대한 생각을 나누어 주세요.

가지 요리는 감미로웠지만, 소스는 제 입맛에 다소 신 맛이 강했습니다. 광어는 정말 끝내줬습니다. 완벽하게 익혀졌고 양념도 잘 되어 있었어요. 토스카나식 치킨은 부드러웠지만 맛의 깊이는 부족하더군요. 타르트에 관해서라면, 맛은 좋았지만 약간 지나치게 구워졌습니다. 주방의 세련된 배치는 인상 깊었습니다. 새로 나올 벽돌 오븐 피자는 출시되기만 하면 꼭 먹어 보고 싶네요. 오늘 저녁 만찬에서는 준비되지 않아 아쉽습니다.

</td></tr>
</table>

어휘1 preview 미리 보기, 사전 검토 Gazette ~ 신문 offering 제공된[내놓는] 것 essence 본질, 정수 input 의견 hearty 푸짐한 entrée (만찬의) 주요리 hold one's own 뒤지지 않다 that way 그렇게 하면 showcase 선보이다 I suggest (강하게) ~하면 좋겠다, ~을 권하다 steam 찌다 shellfish 조개류 adamant 요지부동의, 단호한 specialty 특선, 특제품 assume 가정하다, 전제하다 installation 설치 well received 호평을 받는 critic 비평가, 평론가 tour 둘러보다

어휘2 dill crème 딜 크림(딜 허브 향이 나는 크림) halibut 광어 zest 오렌지[레몬] 껍질 eggplant 가지 tangy 톡 쏘는 mussel 홍합 prawn 큰 새우 broth 수프, 맛국물 Tuscan 토스카나 지방의 wilted 데친

어휘3 acidic 신맛이 나는 divine (구어) 끝내주는 seasoned 양념된, 조미된 tender 부드러운 as for ~에 대해 말하자면 slightly 약간 a shame 안타까운 일, 아쉬운 일

191

<table>
<tr><td>

What is the purpose of the preview dinner?

(A) To prepare for a visit from a culinary journalist
(B) To choose dishes for a regional food festival
(C) To evaluate a new chef's performance
(D) To test items for the weekly specials

</td><td>

시식 만찬의 목적은 무엇인가?

(A) 요리 전문 기자의 방문을 준비하는 것
(B) 지역 음식 축제를 위한 요리를 고르는 것
(C) 새 요리사의 실력을 평가하는 것
(D) 주간 특별 메뉴에 올릴 품목을 테스트하는 것

</td></tr>
</table>

어휘 culinary 요리의 performance 실력

해설 Mr. Martin이 식당에 올 예정인데(Mr. Martin will be arriving), 이 사람이 쓰는 칼럼이 신문에 게재될 것이다(His column will be published in the *Liberty Gazette*). 여기서 Mr. Martin이 요리 전문 기자라는 사실을 알 수 있다. 시식 만찬을 여는 이유는 이 기자에게 선보일 요리에 대한 의견을 모으기 위해서(To gather input on the dishes we'll present to him, I've decided we should host a preview dinner), 즉 기자의 방문을 준비하기 위해서이다.

192

In the e-mail, the word "hearty" in paragraph 2, line 1, is closest in meaning to

(A) genuine
(B) abundant
(C) satisfying
(D) inventive

이메일에서 두 번째 문단 첫 번째 줄의 단어 "hearty"와 의미상 가장 가까운 것은

(A) 진심 어린
(B) 풍부한
(C) 만족감을 주는
(D) 독창적인

> **해설** hearty에는 '진심 어린'이라는 뜻이 있기 때문에 어떤 문맥에서는 (A)도 정답이 될 수 있겠지만, 이 지문에서 hearty는 그런 뜻이 아니다. hearty에는 '푸 짐한'이라는 뜻도 있어서, (B)를 정답으로 생각하기 쉽지만, 이것도 골라서는 안 된다. abundant는 단순히 많은 양으로 존재한다는 뜻인데, 푸짐하다는 것은 '넉넉하여 마음이 흐뭇한'이라는 뜻으로 감정의 측면도 들여다보는 단어이기 때문이다. hearty를 적절히 대체할 수 있는 단어는 (C) satisfying이다.

193

What is true about the preview dinner menu?

(A) It lists complimentary dishes for guests.
(B) It includes a dessert Mr. Ricci suggested.
(C) It was served inside the restaurant's kitchen.
(D) It is a recurring weekly event.

시식 만찬 메뉴에 관하여 무엇이 사실인가?

(A) 고객들을 위한 무료 요리가 포함되어 있다.
(B) Mr. Ricci가 제안한 디저트를 포함한다.
(C) 식당 주방 내부에서 제공되었다.
(D) 매주 반복되는 행사이다.

> **어휘** list 목록에 올리다 recurring 반복되는, 되풀이되는

> **해설** 이메일에서 Mr. Ricci가 과일을 기반으로 하는 디저트를 꼭 메뉴에 포함시키자고 제안하는데(And let's not forget our fruit-based desserts), 메뉴를 보 면 복숭아 타르트가 있다(Glazed almond peach tart). 즉 메뉴에는 Mr. Ricci가 제안한 디저트가 포함되어 있다.

194

Which menu item was most likely Ms. Moreau's favorite?

(A) The halibut
(B) The tart
(C) The eggplant
(D) The chicken

Ms. Moreau가 가장 좋아하는 메뉴 항목은 무엇이었 겠는가?

(A) 광어
(B) 타르트
(C) 가지
(D) 닭고기

> **해설** 피드백 카드에 Ms. Moreau의 평가가 적혀 있는데, 가지 스테이크는 너무 시고(the sauce was a bit too acidic) 닭 요리는 맛의 깊이가 부족하며(lacked depth of flavor), 타르트는 약간 많이 구웠다고 말한다(slightly overbaked). 너무 맛있었다는 평가만 하고 단점을 전혀 언급하지 않는 품목은 광어 요리 밖에 없다(The halibut was absolutely divine—perfectly cooked and seasoned). 이를 통해 가장 좋아한 것은 광어 요리라고 추론할 수 있다.

195

What is implied about the brick oven?

(A) It is too large for the kitchen space.
(B) It requires technical repairs.
(C) It did not pass a safety inspection.
(D) It has not been completed yet.

벽돌 오븐에 관하여 무엇이 암시되어 있는가?

(A) 주방 공간에 비해 너무 크다.
(B) 기술적 수리가 필요하다.
(C) 안전 점검을 통과하지 못했다.
(D) 아직 완성되지 않았다.

> **해설** 이메일에서 Mr. Ricci는 시식 만찬 행사 전에 벽돌 오븐이 설치된다면 특선 피자를 메뉴에 포함시켜야 한다고 주장한다(I'm adamant about including the new specialty pizzas we've been developing for the summer menu. That is, of course, assuming the brick oven installation is finalized by then). 그러나 Ms. Moreau는 피드백 카드에서 벽돌 오븐 피자를 먹어 보지 못해서 아쉽다고 말한다(I'm eager to try the new brick-oven pizzas once they're available. It's a shame they weren't ready for tonight's dinner). 양쪽 지문의 내용을 종합해서 생각하면 벽돌 오븐이 행사 전에 완성되지 않았 다는 것을 알 수 있다.

Questions 196 through 200 refer to the following e-mail, flyer, and text message.

To: Interns
From: Dr. Farah Almasi
Subject: Guest Lecture Series
Date: September 18

Dear team,

Exciting update! Ms. Hana Takeda has confirmed her participation in our Guest Lecture Series this fall. [200]As part of your student internship duties, please arrange her lodging here at the university for October 15–17 and ensure all necessary documentation is completed and approved so that she can receive her honorarium. Also, reserve a venue for her talk—[196]I suggest the Emerson Forum since it can accommodate the largest audience, but any room in the economics wing will suffice.

[200]Once Ms. Takeda sends her abstract, one of you should design a flyer and post it in the usual spots around the building. [197]I trust the five of you will coordinate without any issues. Much appreciated!

Dr. Almasi
Professor, Langford School of Economics

Langford School of Economics
Guest Lecture Series Presents:

Ms. Hana Takeda
Chief Strategy Officer, Sendai Capital Partners, Japan

Building Resilient Entrepreneurial Finance Models
October 16, 4:00 P.M.
[196]The Mirae Room

[198]In recent years, traditional banks have tightened lending policies to reduce exposure to risk. This practice has contributed to unfavorable market dynamics. How can financial institutions balance risk management with the need to support entrepreneurs? [198]One promising approach that is gaining in popularity is alternative finance. I will offer an overview of this practice, present compelling findings from a joint study by Sendai Capital Partners and Langford School of Economics, and explore how this innovation could revive the global financial sector.

196–200번 문제는 다음 이메일과 전단지, 문자 메시지에 관한 것입니다.

수신: 인턴
발신: Farah Almasi 박사
제목: 초청 강연 시리즈
날짜: 9월 18일

팀원 여러분,

신나는 소식입니다! Ms. Hana Takeda가 올 가을 초청 강연 시리즈 참가를 확정해 주었습니다. 여러분의 학생 인턴 업무의 일환으로, 10월 15일~17일에 이곳 대학교 내에 숙소를 준비해 주시고, 강연료를 받을 수 있도록 필요한 모든 서류가 작성되고 승인되도록 해주시기 바랍니다. 그리고 강연을 위한 장소를 예약해 주세요. 가장 많은 청중을 수용할 수 있어서 Emerson Forum을 추천하지만, 경제학 건물 내의 어느 강의실이든 괜찮습니다.

Ms. Takeda가 요약문을 보내 주면, 여러분 중 한 명이 전단지를 디자인하고 건물 주변 평소 위치에 게시해야 합니다. 여러분 다섯 명이 아무 문제없이 조율해 나갈 것이라고 믿습니다. 정말 고맙습니다!

Langford 경제학 대학 교수
Almasi 박사

Langford 경제학 대학
초청 강연 시리즈가 소개합니다.

Ms. Hana Takeda
일본 Sendai Capital Partners 전략기획실장

회복력 있는 기업 금융 모델 구축하기
10월 16일 오후 4시
The Mirae Room

최근 몇 년 동안 전통적인 은행들은 위험 노출을 줄이기 위해 대출 정책을 강화해 왔습니다. 이러한 관행은 시장의 바람직하지 못한 흐름의 요인이 되었습니다. 금융 기관들은 위험 관리와 기업가 지원 필요성 사이에서 어떻게 균형을 잡을 수 있을까요? 인기를 얻고 있는 유망한 접근법 중 하나가 대체 금융입니다. 이 방식에 대한 개관을 제공하고, Sendai Capital Partners와 Langford 경제학 대학의 공동 연구에서 나온 설득력 있는 결과를 발표하며, 이러한 혁신이 어떻게 세계 금융 분야를 되살릴 수 있을지 살펴보겠습니다.

From: Thomas Yoon
[200]To: Ava Patel
Received: October 2, 3:45 P.M.

[200]Ava, I'm in the print room reviewing the flyer you created, and I just noticed something—[199]Ms. Takeda's bio somehow got left out! Can you revise the flyer immediately and send it back to me? The print room closes in 15 minutes, and Dr. Almasi emphasized that the flyers must be posted this evening at the latest.

발신: Thomas Yoon
수신: Ava Psatel
수신 시간: 10월 2일 오후 3시 45분

Ava, 지금 인쇄실에서 네가 만든 전단지를 검토하고 있는데, 방금 발견한 게 있어. 어떻게 된 일인지 Ms. Takeda의 약력이 빠져 있어! 즉시 전단지를 수정해서 다시 보내줄 수 있겠어? 인쇄실은 15분 후에 문을 닫는데, Almasi 박사님은 전단지가 늦어도 오늘 저녁에는 게시되어야 한다고 강조하셨거든.

어휘1 participation 참석 arrange 준비하다, 미련하다 lodging 숙소, 숙박 approve 승인하다 honorarium 사례비 wing 부속 건물, 동 suffice 충분하다 abstract 초록, 요약문 flyer 전단지

어휘2 present 제시하다, 발표하다 resilient 회복력 있는 entrepreneurial 기업가의 tighten (규제 등을) 강화하다 lending 대출 exposure 노출 practice 관행 contribute to ~의 요인이 되다 unfavorable 바람직하지 않은, 불리한 dynamics 역학, 흐름 institution 기관 promising 유망한 gain in ~을 얻다 alternative 대안적인 overview 개요 compelling 설득력 있는 explore 탐구하다, 살펴보다 innovation 혁신 revive 되살리다

어휘3 bio(biography) 약력 somehow 어떻게 된 일인지 leave sth out ~을 빠뜨리다 immediately 즉시 emphasize 강조하다 at the latest 늦어도

196

What can be inferred about the Mirae Room?

(A) It is located outside the economics building.
(B) It houses all the events in the Guest Lecture Series.
(C) It has a smaller capacity than the Emerson Forum.
(D) It is available for use on October 17.

Mirae Room에 관하여 무엇을 추론할 수 있는가?

(A) 경제학 건물 바깥에 위치해 있다.
(B) 초청 강연 시리즈의 모든 행사를 수용한다.
(C) Emerson Forum보다 수용 인원이 더 적다.
(D) 10월 17일에 이용할 수 있다.

어휘 infer 추론하다 house 수용하다 capacity 수용 인원, 용량

해설 이메일 첫 문단에 나오는 I suggest the Emerson Forum since it can accommodate the largest audience를 통해 Emerson Forum이 건물 내에서 가장 큰 모임 장소라는 사실을 알 수 있으므로, 전단지에 강연 장소로 나오는 The Mirae Room은 당연히 Emerson Forum보다 작을 것이라고 추론할 수 있다.

197

In the e-mail, the word "issues" in paragraph 2, line 2, is closest in meaning to

(A) conflicts
(B) periodicals
(C) distributions
(D) offspring

이메일에서 두 번째 문단 두 번째 줄의 단어 "issues"와 의미상 가장 가까운 것은

(A) 충돌, 갈등
(B) 정기 간행물
(C) 배포
(D) 자녀, 자식

해설 issue는 여러 가지 의미가 있어서 선택지 네 개의 단어가 모두 동의어로 사용될 수 있다. I trust the five of you will coordinate without any issues.는 "여러분 다섯 명이 아무 문제 없이 일을 잘 조율해 나갈 것이라고 믿습니다."라는 뜻이므로, 이 문장에서 issues를 대신할 수 있는 단어는 conflicts이다.

198

What is Ms. Takeda's presentation about?

(A) A new trend in the banking industry
(B) A career opportunity in the finance field
(C) Unconventional methods of data collection
(D) Characteristics of successful entrepreneurs

Ms. Takeda의 발표는 무엇에 관한 것인가?

(A) 은행 업계의 새로운 경향
(B) 금융 분야의 취업 기회
(C) 참신한 데이터 수집의 방식
(D) 성공한 기업가들의 특징

어휘 trend 경향, 동향 unconventional 참신한, 판에 박히지 않은 characteristic 특징

해설 전단지를 읽어 보면, 대출 규제를 강화하는 최근 금융계의 동향을 언급하면서(In recent years, traditional banks have tightened lending policies to reduce exposure to risk), 자금 확보를 위한 대안으로 요즘 떠오르고 있는 대체 금융을 제시하고 있다(One promising approach that is gaining in popularity is alternative finance). 강연 주제는 금융계의 최신 동향이다.

199

What problem does Mr. Yoon mention?	Mr. Yoon은 어떤 문제점을 언급하는가?
(A) A name has been spelled incorrectly.	(A) 한 이름의 철자가 잘못 되었다.
(B) The flyer is missing some information.	(B) 전단지에서 정보가 빠져 있다.
(C) The flyer will not be posted by the deadline.	(C) 전단지가 기한 내에 게시되지 않을 것이다.
(D) The venue for the presentation is currently unavailable.	(D) 발표를 위한 장소가 현재 이용 불가능하다.

어휘 incorrectly 부정확하게, 틀리게 miss 빠뜨리다, 놓치다 post 게시하다

해설 Ms. Takeda의 약력이 전단지에서 빠져 있다고 말하고 있다(Ms. Takeda's bio somehow got left out!).

200

Who most likely is Ms. Patel?	Ms. Patel은 누구겠는가?
(A) A technician in the print room	(A) 인쇄실 기술자
(B) An executive assistant to Ms. Takeda	(B) Ms. Takeda의 비서
(C) A speaker from the Guest Lecture Series	(C) 초청 강연 시리즈의 강사
(D) A student at Langford School of Economics	(D) Langford 경제학 대학의 학생

해설 이메일에서 Almasi 박사는 학생 인턴들에게 지시를 내리고 있는데(As part of your student internship duties), 지시 사항 중 하나가 전단지를 디자인하는 것이다(one of you should design a flyer). 문자 메시지를 보면 수신자인 Ms. Patel이(To: Ava Patel) 전단지를 만들었음을 알 수 있다(the flyer you created). 두 지문의 내용을 종합해 보면 Ms. Patel은 인턴사원으로 일하고 있는 Langford 경제학 대학의 학생이다.

TEST 05

101	(C)	111	(B)	121	(A)	131	(D)	141	(A)	151	(B)	161	(A)	171	(C)	181	(C)	191	(D)
102	(D)	112	(A)	122	(D)	132	(A)	142	(D)	152	(A)	162	(B)	172	(B)	182	(A)	192	(C)
103	(B)	113	(A)	123	(A)	133	(C)	143	(B)	153	(C)	163	(D)	173	(C)	183	(D)	193	(B)
104	(C)	114	(A)	124	(C)	134	(D)	144	(C)	154	(A)	164	(D)	174	(A)	184	(B)	194	(B)
105	(C)	115	(C)	125	(B)	135	(A)	145	(D)	155	(A)	165	(B)	175	(D)	185	(B)	195	(A)
106	(D)	116	(B)	126	(D)	136	(D)	146	(D)	156	(D)	166	(D)	176	(B)	186	(C)	196	(B)
107	(D)	117	(D)	127	(A)	137	(D)	147	(B)	157	(B)	167	(B)	177	(C)	187	(D)	197	(C)
108	(A)	118	(B)	128	(D)	138	(B)	148	(C)	158	(B)	168	(D)	178	(C)	188	(C)	198	(A)
109	(D)	119	(D)	129	(B)	139	(B)	149	(C)	159	(B)	169	(B)	179	(A)	189	(D)	199	(B)
110	(B)	120	(B)	130	(C)	140	(C)	150	(D)	160	(A)	170	(A)	180	(C)	190	(A)	200	(D)

PART 5

101

Outgoing packages must be addressed ------- to avoid delivery issues.

(A) correct
(B) correcting
(C) **correctly**
(D) corrected

발송되는 소포는 배송 문제를 방지하기 위해 주소가 정확하게 적혀 있어야 한다.

어휘 outgoing 발송되는 address 주소를 쓰다 correct 올바른; 수정하다

해설 수동태 동사는 목적어를 취하지 않기 때문에 이것이 등장하면 문장이 완성되었음을 의미한다. 품사 문제에서 완성된 문장에 빈칸이 보이면 부사가 정답이다. '주어 + ------- + 동사', '타동사 + 목적어 + -------', 'be p.p. + -------', '1형식 자동사 + -------' 같은 구조가 보이면 문장이 완성된 것으로 알고 부사를 정답으로 선택하자.

102

Our team ------- in the policy meeting last Tuesday, but we had a scheduling conflict.

(A) can participate
(B) must have participated
(C) should participate
(D) **would have participated**

우리 팀은 지난주 화요일 정책 회의에 참석하기로 했으나, 일정이 겹쳤다.

어휘 conflict (약속, 계획 등의) 겹침

해설 과거완료 시제 가정법 문장의 if절을 but we had a scheduling conflict로 변형했다고 이해하면 된다. 원래는 if we had not had a scheduling conflict이었던 것이다. 과거완료 시제 가정법 문장은 주절에 would[could/should/might] have p.p. 형태의 동사를 사용한다.

103

Chef Zhang's culinary program is ------- to be broadcast on public television next month.

(A) given
(B) **scheduled**
(C) found
(D) considered

요리사 Zhang의 요리 프로그램이 다음 달에 공영 방송에서 방영될 예정이다.

어휘 culinary 요리의

해설 culinary program is ------- to be broadcast가 다음 달의 일정으로 해석되는 것이 자연스럽다.

104

Input from residents regarding the proposed Mapleview Market ------- by local officials.

(A) seeking   (B) sought
(C) was sought   (D) used to seek

제안된 Mapleview Market에 관한 주민들의 의견이 지역 관계자들에 의해 요청되었다.

어휘 input 의견, 정보 제공   regarding ~에 관하여   seek 요청하다, 구하다   official 공무원, 관계자

해설 [(A) 준동사 (B) 능동태 동사 (C) 수동태 동사 (D) 능동태 동사]이다. 문장에 동사가 보이지 않으므로 빈칸에는 동사가 들어가야 하며, 빈칸 뒤에 목적어가 없으므로 수동태가 정답이다.

105

The journalist for ------- the award was named had investigated several intriguing cases.

(A) when   (B) that
(C) whom   (D) whoever

그 상의 이름이 붙여진 기자는 여러 흥미로운 사건들을 조사해 왔다.

어휘 be named for ~의 이름을 따서 붙여지다   investigate 조사하다   intriguing 흥미로운   case 사건

해설 '선행사 + 전치사 + -------' 유형으로 출제되는 관계사 문제에서는 목적격 관계대명사가 정답이다. (B)와 (C)가 모두 목적격 관계대명사이지만, 전치사 뒤에는 관계대명사 that을 사용할 수 없다는 사실을 알아야 한다.

106

The warranty for Corvella cookware does not cover any damage caused by ------- use of the product.

(A) concise   (B) equivalent
(C) submissive   **(D) improper**

Corvella 조리 기구의 품질 보증은 제품의 부적절한 사용으로 인한 손상은 보장하지 않는다.

어휘 cookware 조리기구   cover 보장하다   concise 간결한   equivalent 동등한   submissive 순종적인   improper 부적절한

해설 빈칸 앞뒤 damage caused by ------- use of the product(제품의 [(A) 간결한 (B) 동등한 (C) 순종적인 (D) 부적절한] 사용으로 인한 손상)의 의미를 자연스럽게 만들어 주는 형용사가 정답이다.

107

To meet the high standards, the quality control team conducts ------- evaluations of each item.

(A) exhaust   (B) exhausted
(C) exhaustion   **(D) exhaustive**

품질 관리 팀은 높은 기준을 충족시키기 위해 각 제품에 대한 철저한 평가를 실시한다.

어휘 meet 충족시키다   exhaust 기진맥진하게 하다, 고갈시키다   exhaustive 철저한

해설 빈칸 앞뒤 conducts ------- evaluations만 잘 보면 정답을 알 수 있다. 품사 문제에서 명사 앞에 빈칸이 있으면 형용사가 정답이다. 선택지에 형용사가 없을 때는 분사가 정답이지만, 형용사와 분사가 모두 있을 때는 거의 대부분 형용사가 정답이다.

108

All straps ------- the equipment onto the platform need to be inspected thoroughly before use.

(A) securing   (B) secured
(C) secures   (D) secure

장비를 받침대에 고정시키는 모든 끈은 사용 전에 철저히 검사받아야 한다.

어휘 strap 끈, 줄   secure 단단히 매대[고정하다]   platform (작업용) 받침대   inspect 검사하다, 점검하다   thoroughly 철저하게

해설 문장에 need to be inspected라는 동사가 있기 때문에, 빈칸에 동사 (C)와 (D)는 들어갈 수 없다. 분사 (A)나 (B) 중 하나를 선택해서 ------- the equipment onto the platform이 앞에 있는 명사 All straps를 수식하게 해야 한다. 이런 유형의 분사를 선택하는 문제에서는 빈칸 뒤에 목적어가 있으면 현재분사가, 목적어가 없으면 과거분사가 정답이다.

109

The regulation ------- that all elevators be inspected annually does not apply to private residences.

(A) require
(B) requires
(C) required
(D) requirement

모든 승강기를 매년 검사해야 한다는 규정 요건이 개인 주택에는 적용되지 않는다.

▶**어휘** apply to ~에 적용되다　residence 주택, 거주지

▶**해설** 문장에 does not apply라는 동사가 있으므로 빈칸에 동사는 들어갈 수 없다. that all elevators be inspected annually와 'The regulation -------'이 동격으로서 문장의 주어이다. 즉 'The regulation -------'가 주어 역할을 하도록 복합명사로 만들어야 한다.

110

When Golden Hearth Bakery upgraded to larger delivery trucks, each one was ------- white and brown.

(A) changed
(B) painted
(C) alternated
(D) transferred

Golden Hearth Bakery가 더 큰 배송 트럭으로 업그레이드 하면서 모든 트럭을 흰색과 갈색으로 칠했다.

▶**어휘** upgrade to ~으로 업그레이드하다　alternate 번갈아 하다, 교대로 하다

▶**해설** 빈칸에 (A) changed를 넣으려면 전치사 to를 함께 사용해야 한다. (C) alternated는 사용하려면 능동태로 써야 하는데, 그렇게 해도 의미상 알맞지 않다. (D) transferred를 넣으려면 역시 뒤에 전치사 to가 있어야 하는데, to가 있다 하더라도 뒤에 색깔 이름이 나오는 것은 알맞지 않다.

111

Virell Research Center gains ------- from having staff scientists with strong interdisciplinary backgrounds.

(A) jointly
(B) immensely
(C) evenly
(D) impulsively

Virell 연구 센터는 탄탄한 학제간 배경을 갖춘 상근 연구원들을 보유함으로써 막대한 이점을 얻고 있다.

▶**어휘** gain from ~으로 이익을 얻다　jointly 공동으로　immensely 매우, 엄청나게　evenly 고르게, 균등하게　impulsively 충동적으로　interdisciplinary 학제간의, 여러 분야에 걸친　background 배경, 경력, 학력

▶**해설** (A) jointly는 함께 이득을 공유할 대상이 있어야 사용할 수 있고, (C) evenly는 이득이 발생하는 원천이 여러 개 언급되어야 정답이 될 수 있다. (D) impulsively는 의미상 동사 gains와 어울리지 않는다.

112

Morocco's two leading airlines have ------- to finalize the specifics of their joint initiative to boost tourism.

(A) yet
(B) up
(C) until
(D) else

모로코의 두 주요 항공사들은 관광업 증진을 위한 합동 프로젝트의 세부 사항들을 아직 확정하지 못했다.

▶**어휘** leading 주요한, 주도적인　have yet to-V 아직 ~하지 않았다　specifics 세부 사항　initiative 계획, 프로젝트　boost 촉진하다, 증진시키다

▶**해설** '아직 ~하지 못했다'라는 뜻으로 have yet to-V를 기억해 두자.

The series of workshops that ------- scheduled for next month focuses on sustainable business practices.

(A) is
(B) are
(C) has
(D) have

다음 달로 예정되어 있는 워크숍 시리즈는 지속 가능한 비즈니스 관행에 초점을 맞출 것이다.

▶**어휘** sustainable (환경 파괴 없이) 지속 가능한　practice 관행

▶**해설** 주격 관계대명사 앞에 있는 선행사와 뒤에 있는 동사는 서로 수가 일치되어야 한다. 전치사구는 수식어구이므로 of workshops 앞에 있는 The series의 수를 생각해야 하는데, 복수 명사인 것처럼 보이지만 단수이다. 따라서 빈칸에 들어갈 동사는 단수인 (A)와 (C) 중에서 선택해야 한다. scheduled 뒤에 목적어가 없으므로 수동태 동사가 되도록 be 동사를 선택하자.

114

Prices for electronics and home décor items ------- on our Web site are subject to updates without prior notice.

(A) listed
(B) have listed
(C) list
(D) will list

웹사이트에 게시된 전자 제품 및 홈 데코 제품의 가격은 사전 공지 없이 변경될 수 있습니다.

어휘 décor 실내 장식 list 기재하다, 게시하다 be subject to ~의 대상이다, ~이 될 수 있다 update 업데이트, 변경, 갱신 prior notice 사전 통지[공지]

해설 [(A) 동사/준동사 (B) 동사 (C) 동사/명사 (D) 동사]이다. 문장에 동사 are가 있으므로 동사는 빈칸에 들어갈 수 없다. 또한 빈칸에 단수 명사 list를 넣으면 뒤에 있는 동사 are와 수가 일치하지 않는다. 빈칸에는 준동사가 들어가야 한다.

115

Ms. Kapoor stands out among the applicants ------- she has an impressive track record of driving sales growth.

(A) while
(B) so
(C) because
(D) however

Ms. Kapoor는 매출 성장을 이끈 인상적인 실적이 있어서 지원자들 가운데 눈에 띈다.

어휘 stand out 두드러지다, 눈에 띄다 track record 실적, 업적 drive 추진하다, 이끌다

해설 빈칸 뒤에 있는 부사절이 앞에 있는 주절의 이유가 되며, 이 관계를 나타내기에 알맞은 접속사를 선택해야 한다.

116

Once the necessary protocols -------, the clinical trial is supposed to proceed to the next phase without delay.

(A) have implemented
(B) have been implemented
(C) being implemented
(D) will be implemented

일단 필요한 규정들이 시행되고 나면 임상 시험은 지체 없이 다음 단계로 진행되어야 한다.

어휘 protocol (실험·치료를 위한) 규정 implement 시행하다, 실행하다 clinical trial 임상 시험 proceeed to ~으로 넘어가다, 진행하다 phase 단계

해설 [(A) 능동태 동사 (B) 수동태 동사 (C) 준동사 (D) 수동태 동사]이다. 부사절에 동사가 없으므로 빈칸에 준동사 (C)가 들어갈 수는 없다. 빈칸 뒤에 목적어가 없으므로 수동태 동사인 (B)와 (D) 중 정답을 선택해야 한다. 해석상 부사절은 미래 사건을 진술하고 있지만, 시간/조건 부사절에서는 미래 시제 대신 현재나 현재완료 시제를 사용해야 한다는 사실을 기억하고 정답을 고르도록 하자.

117

Veltrix Automotive has not ------- any setbacks in manufacturing or shipments to retail partners this quarter.

(A) exerted
(B) submitted
(C) represented
(D) experienced

Veltrix Automotive는 이번 분기 제조 및 소매 협력 업체들에 대한 운송 과정에서 어떠한 차질도 겪지 않았다.

어휘 exert 발휘하다 represent 대표하다 setback 차질, 좌절 retail 소매

해설 빈칸 앞뒤 has not ------- any setbacks in manufacturing or shipment(생산이나 운송에 있어 어떠한 차질도 [(A) 발휘하지 (B) 제출하지 (C) 대표하지 (D) 겪지] 않았다)의 의미를 자연스럽게 만들어 주는 동사가 정답이다.

118

How ------- a company receives, documents, and reacts to complaints has an impact on customer satisfaction.

(A) efficient
(B) efficiently
(C) efficiency
(D) efficiencies

불만 사항을 얼마나 효율적으로 접수하고 기록하고 대응하는지가 고객 만족도에 영향을 미친다.

어휘 document 기록하다 have an impact on ~에 영향을 미치다

해설 의문사 how는 형용사나 부사와 짝을 이루어 사용하는데, 완성된 문장에 빈칸이 보이면 부사가 정답임을 기억하자. 명사절 How ------- a company receives, documents, and reacts to complaints가 완성된 3형식이므로 부사가 정답이다.

119

Atwell & Pierce CPAs provides a year-end financial overview as
------- of its standard bookkeeping package.

(A) piece (B) division
(C) section **(D) part**

Atwell & Pierce 공인 회계사 사무소는 표준 장부 관리 패키지의 일환으로 연말 재무 개관 보고서를 제공한다.

어휘 CPA (certified public accountant) 공인 회계사 bookkeeping 부기, 회계 기록

해설 (A)와 (C)는 보통 명사이기 때문에 사용하려면 앞에 관사가 있어야 한다. (B)는 셀 수 없는 명사로 사용하면 '분할, 분배'라는 뜻이 된다. '~의 일환[일부]로'라는 뜻으로 as part of를 기억하자.

120

The ------- of the newly developed inventory system has
notably affected our approach to resource management.

(A) habit **(B) adoption**
(C) trade (D) reservation

새로 개발된 재고 조사 시스템의 도입이 우리의 자원 관리 방식에 현저한 영향을 미쳤다.

어휘 adoption 채택, 도입 inventory 재고 조사 notably 눈에 띄게, 현저하게

해설 빈칸 앞뒤 The ------- of the newly developed inventory system(새로 개발된 재고 조사 시스템의 [(A) 습관 (B) 채택 (C) 거래 (D) 예약])의 의미를 자연스럽게 만들어 주는 명사가 정답이다.

121

At Fresh Basket, shoppers are encouraged to ask for help
rather than take items down from high shelves -------.

(A) themselves (B) their own
(C) them (D) their

Fresh Basket 고객 여러분은 높은 선반에서 직접 물건을 내리기보다는 도움을 요청하시기 바랍니다.

어휘 be encouraged to-V ~하도록 권장받다, ~하시기 바랍니다 rather than ~보다는 take *sth* down ~을 내리다

해설 'take items down from high shelves -------'에서 정답을 알 수 있다. '타동사 + 목적어 + -------'의 구조인 3형식 문장이다. 완성된 문장에 빈칸이 보이면 품사 문제에서는 부사가 정답이며, 인칭대명사 문제에서는 부사 자리에 재귀대명사를 넣어야 한다.

122

After extensive deliberation, the designers chose to abandon
the vivid orange gown ------- a more subdued alternative.

(A) favorable (B) out of favor
(C) favorite **(D) in favor of**

광범위한 검토 끝에 디자이너들은 더 은은한 색상의 대안을 선호하여 선명한 오렌지색 드레스는 포기하기로 선택했다.

어휘 extensive 광범위한, 포괄적인 deliberation 심사숙고, 신중한 검토 abandon 버리다, 포기하다 vivid 선명한 favorable 호의적인 out of favor 인기 없는 in favor of ~을 선호하여, ~을 지지하여 subdued 차분한, 은은한 alternative 대안

해설 a more subdued alternative를 목적어로 취할 전치사가 필요하다. 빈칸 앞뒤 abandon the vivid orange gown ------- a more subdued alternative 가 '더 은은한 색상의 대안을 선호하여 선명한 오렌지색 드레스는 포기하다'라는 뜻이 되도록 만드는 것이 의미상 자연스럽다.

------- preparing correspondence for clients, make sure to use
the updated letterhead provided by the association.

(A) When (B) During
(C) Meanwhile (D) Yet

고객에게 보내는 편지를 준비할 때는 반드시 협회에서 제공한 업데이트된 편지지를 사용하세요.

어휘 correspondence 서신 (왕래) make sure to-V 반드시 ~하다 letterhead 공식 서신용 머리글, 업무용 편지지 association 협회, 단체

해설 [(A) 접속사 (B) 전치사 (C) 부사 (D) 부사]이다. 접속사와 전치사를 구분하는 문제에서 부사는 항상 오답이므로 일단 지우고 시작하자. 빈칸 뒤에 분사 구문이 있을 때는 접속사가 정답이다. preparing이 전치사 during 다음에 동명사로 올 수 있다고 생각할 수 있지만, during 뒤에는 관용적으로 명사(구)만 쓰인다.

124

The initial agreements with Mariton Freight Services have just been shredded because they ------- exactly ten years ago today.

(A) submitted   (B) violated
(C) expired   (D) invalidated

Mariton Freight Services와의 초기 합의문은 정확히 10년 전 오늘 만료되었기 때문에 방금 파기되었다.

어휘 initial 초기의 freight 화물 shred (문서 분쇄기로) 파쇄하다, 파기하다 violate 위반하다 expire 만료되다 invalidate 무효화하다

해설 (A), (B), (D)는 모두 타동사로서 목적어가 필요하다. 빈칸 뒤에 목적어가 없으므로 자동사를 정답으로 골라야 한다.

125

While the instructions were somewhat confusing, the updated application ------- remained simple to navigate for novices.

(A) it   **(B) itself**
(C) themselves   (D) them

설명서는 다소 혼란스러웠지만, 업데이트된 애플리케이션 자체는 여전히 초보자도 간단하게 탐색할 수 있다.

어휘 instructions 사용 설명(서) somewhat 다소, 약간 navigate (디지털 장치를) 탐색하다 novice 초보자

해설 빈칸 앞뒤 the updated application ------- remained만 보고 정답을 알아내자. 품사 문제라면 주어와 동사 사이 빈칸에는 부사가 정답인데, 인칭대명사 문제라면 부사 자리에 재귀대명사가 정답이다. (B)와 (C) 중에서 골라야 하는데, 주어 the updated application이 단수 명사이므로 단수 대명사가 정답이다.

126

Following a strategic 15 percent price reduction, sales of Vireon television units surged ------- across key markets.

(A) accidentally   (B) expressively
(C) dramatically   (D) eagerly

전략적인 15퍼센트 가격 인하 이후 Vireon 텔레비전 제품의 판매량은 주요 시장 전반에 걸쳐 급격히 증가했다.

어휘 strategic 전략적인 unit (완성 제품의) 한 개 surge 급증하다 accidentally 우연히 expressively 표현력 있게, 감정을 담아 dramatically 극적으로 eagerly 열심히, 간절히

해설 항상 짝을 이루어 출제되는 어휘는 암기하고 있다가 재빨리 정답을 선택하자. 빈칸 앞뒤에 '증가, 감소'를 나타내는 동사가 보이면 항상 '많이'가 정답이다. increase, rise, expand, decrease, decline, reduce, drop, fall 등이 보이면 주저 없이 substantially, significantly, considerably, dramatically, markedly, sharply 같은 부사를 정답으로 선택하자.

127

The finance committee of the organization firmly opposes ------- any potentially high-risk investments during this fiscal year.

(A) making   (B) is making
(C) to make   (D) make

기관의 재무 위원회는 이번 회계 연도 동안 잠재적으로 위험성이 높은 투자를 하는 것에 단호히 반대한다.

어휘 firmly 단호하게 oppose 반대하다 high-risk 고위험의 fiscal year 회계 연도

해설 문장에 opposes라는 동사가 있으므로 동사인 (B)와 (D)는 제외하자. opposes의 목적어로 동명사와 to부정사 중에서 선택하는 문제이다. opposes는 목적어로 동명사를 선택해야 한다.

128

Although there was a ------- in the economy, the electronics sector managed to achieve a 20 percent increase in profits this year.

(A) protocol   (B) longevity
(C) drawback   **(D) downturn**

경기 침체가 있었음에도 불구하고 전자 제품 부문은 올해 20퍼센트의 수익 증가를 달성했다.

어휘 longevity 장수, 지속 기간 drawback 결점, 단점 downturn (경기) 침체, 하강 sector 분야, 부문 manage to-V (어려움에도) ~을 해내다

해설 빈칸 앞뒤 Although there was a ------- in the economy(경기 [(A) 규약 (B) 장수 (C) 단점 (D) 침체]이(가) 있었음에도 불구하고)의 의미를 자연스럽게 만들어 주는 명사가 정답이다.

129

The current ------- of seasonal decorations at Merriton Celebrations Co. suggests that the company is fully equipped for the holiday surge.

(A) proposal
(B) inventory
(C) consideration
(D) commitment

Merriton Celebrations Co.가 현재 보유한 계절 장식품 재고 목록은 회사가 휴일 수요 급증에 충분히 대비하고 있음을 보여준다.

어휘 inventory 재고, 목록 commitment 헌신, 약속 suggest ~임을 보여주다, 알 수 있다 fully 충분히, 완전히 be equipped for ~에 대비가 되어 있다 surge 급증

해설 휴가철 수요 급증에 대한 대비가 제대로 되어 있는지 알려면 재고를 보아야 한다.

130

The corporate legal department has ------- finished its assessment of company bylaws and anticipates submitting a proposal for improvements tomorrow.

(A) slightly
(B) frequently
(C) nearly
(D) continually

법무 팀은 회사 내규에 대한 평가를 거의 마쳤으며 개선을 위한 기획안을 내일 제출할 것으로 예상하고 있다.

어휘 corporate 기업의 frequently 자주, 빈번히 assessment 평가 bylaw 내규, 정관 anticipate 기대하다 proposal 기획안

해설 항상 짝을 이루어 출제되는 어휘는 암기하고 있다가 재빨리 정답을 선택하자. '------- + 숫자 / all / every / entire / finish(ed) / complete(d)'가 보이면 언제나 정답은 nearly나 almost이다.

Questions 131 through 134 refer to the following e-mail.

From: Pacific Horizon Airways
To: Margaret Brennan
Date: 12 July
Subject: Your flight reservation

Dear Ms. Brennan,

We appreciate your decision to fly with Pacific Horizon Airways and your utilizing our digital booking and check-in platform. [131]Your reservation has been successfully processed. To make your experience smoother when checking luggage and clearing the security checkpoints, we recommend printing your boarding pass at home. This will help guarantee your [132]timely arrival at the departure gate.

While you're at the airport, [133]take advantage of the secure wireless network available at our Horizon Retreat Lounge for a modest fee of just $12 NZD. You can easily arrange this [134]service using our booking system prior to your travel date.

131-134번 문제는 다음 이메일에 관한 것입니다.

발신: Pacific Horizon Airways
수신: Margaret Brennan
날짜: 7월 12일
제목: 비행편 예약

Ms. Brennan께,

Pacific Horizon Airways를 선택해 주시고 저희 디지털 예약 및 체크인 플랫폼을 이용해 주셔서 고맙습니다. 예약은 성공적으로 처리되었습니다. 수하물을 부치고 보안 검색대를 통과할 때 절차를 더 원활하게 하려면 집에서 탑승권을 출력해 오실 것을 권장합니다. 이것은 출발 게이트에 제시간에 도착하는 데 도움이 됩니다.

공항에 계시는 동안에는 Horizon Retreat 라운지에서 단 12달러(NZD)의 저렴한 요금으로 제공되는 보안 무선 네트워크를 이용해 보세요. 여행일 이전에 저희 예약 시스템으로 이 서비스를 간편하게 신청하실 수 있습니다.

어휘 utilize 활용하다 process 처리하다 check (수하물을) 부치다, 맡기다 clear 통과하다 checkpoint 보안 검색대 guarantee 보장하다 timely 제시간의, 시기 적절한 take advantage of ~을 이용하다 secure 안전한 modest 비싸지 않은, 저렴한 arrange 준비하다 prior to ~ 전에

131-134

131 (A) Kindly sign in to initiate the procedure.
(B) Our airline serves destinations across six continents.
(C) You'll have access to onboard wireless Internet.
(D) Your reservation has been successfully processed.

132 (A) timely
(B) quiet
(C) near
(D) together

133 (A) taking
(B) taken
(C) take
(D) took

134 (A) repair
(B) inspection
(C) journey
(D) service

131 (A) 로그인하여 절차를 시작해 주시기 바랍니다.
(B) 저희 항공사는 여섯 대륙에 걸쳐 취항지가 있습니다.
(C) 기내 무선 인터넷을 이용하실 수 있습니다.
(D) 예약은 성공적으로 처리되었습니다.

어휘 kindly 부디 sign in 로그인하다 initiate 시작하다 serve 제공하다 destination 행선지 have access to ~을 이용할 수 있다 onboard 기내의

해설 제목 Your flight reservation과 첫 문장 We appreciate your decision to fly with Pacific Horizon Airways and your utilizing our digital booking and check-in platform.을 통해 인터넷으로 항공권을 예약한 사람이 받는 예약 확인 이메일이라는 것을 알 수 있다. 여러 가지 안내가 나오기 전에 예약 확정 문구가 있어야 한다.

132 **해설** 명사 arrival 앞에 형용사가 들어가야 하므로 부사 (D)는 제외하자. 빈칸 앞뒤 guarantee your ------- arrival at the departure gate(출발 게이트에 [(A) 시간 맞춰 (B) 조용히 (C) 가까이] 도착하는 것을 보장한다)의 의미가 자연스러운 형용사가 정답이다.

133 **해설** 문장에 동사가 없으므로 빈칸에 동사가 들어가며, 명령문이므로 동사원형으로 시작한다.

134 **해설** 앞 문장에서 라운지에서 이용할 수 있는 무선 네트워크를 언급하고 있다(the secure wireless network available at our Horizon Retreat Lounge). 이것을 대신할 수 있는 말은 this service이다.

From: Rivera, Sofia
Sent: Thursday, December 11, 10:42 A.M.
To: Company Staff
Subject: Travel Reimbursement Guidelines and Receipt Requirements

Good morning, everyone.

Just a reminder: When submitting a travel reimbursement request, you must include itemized receipts for all purchases. This policy [135]applies to costs related to meals, lodging, airfare, local transportation, and other travel-related expenses. Credit card receipts by themselves do not offer complete [136]documentation of the specific products or services you paid for. We have recently received several reimbursement submissions from [137]employees who used their personal credit cards during business trips. [138]Sadly, they only turned in credit card receipts. Without detailed receipts, we are unable to process reimbursement payments. Please be sure to keep this in mind.

Sofia Rivera, Director of Accounting

135–138번 문제는 다음 이메일에 관한 것입니다.

발신: Rivera, Sofia
발송: 12월 11일 목요일 오전 10:42
수신: 회사 직원 전체
제목: 출장비 환급 지침 및 영수증 제출 요건

모두들 안녕하세요.

다시 한 번 알려 드립니다. 출장비 환급 신청서를 제출할 때는 모든 구매에 대해 항목별로 정리된 영수증을 포함해야 합니다. 이 정책은 식사와 숙박, 항공 요금, 현지 교통비에 관련된 비용과 기타 출장 관련 경비에 적용됩니다. 신용 카드 영수증만으로는 구매한 특정 상품이나 서비스에 대한 완전한 증빙 자료가 되지 않습니다. 최근에 출장 기간 동안 개인 신용 카드를 사용한 직원들로부터 제출된 몇몇 환급 신청서를 접수했습니다. 안타깝게도 그들은 신용 카드 영수증만 냈습니다. 상세 영수증 없이는 환급금을 처리해 드릴 수 없습니다. 이 점을 반드시 명심하시기 바랍니다.

회계부장 Sofia Rivera

어휘 reminder 상기시키는 것 reimbursement 환급 itemized 항목별로 나열된 apply to ~에 적용되다 lodging 숙박 airfare 항공료 documentation 증빙 자료 specific 특정한 submission 제출 sadly 안타깝게도 turn in ~을 제출하다 keep *sth* in mind ~을 명심하다

135-138

135 (A) applies (B) apply (C) is applying (D) had applied	**137** (A) visitors (B) suppliers (C) customers **(D) employees**
136 (A) document (B) documented (C) documenting **(D) documentation**	**138** (A) Regrettably, the company does not cover costs for leisure activities. **(B) Sadly, they only turned in credit card receipts.** (C) The majority of the charges pertained to office supplies. (D) It's common for staff to use personal credit cards while traveling.

135 해설 회사의 정책을 설명하는 문장이므로 현재 시제로 말하는 게 자연스럽다. 현재 시제인 (A)와 (B) 중에서 주어 This policy가 단수 명사이므로 단수 동사를 고른다.

136 해설 빈칸에 동사 do not offer의 목적어이면서 형용사 complete의 수식을 받는 명사가 들어가야 한다. (A)와 (D)가 명사인데, document는 보통 명사이므로 앞에 관사가 있어야 사용할 수 있다.

137 해설 출장을 다녀온 후 출장비 환급을 신청하는 사람은 당연히 회사 직원이다.

138 (A) 유감스럽게도 회사가 여가 활동 비용을 부담하지는 않습니다.
(B) 안타깝게도 그들은 신용 카드 영수증만 냈습니다.
(C) 대부분의 비용은 사무용품에 관련된 것이었습니다.
(D) 직원들이 출장 중에 개인 신용 카드를 사용하는 것은 흔한 일입니다.

어휘 regrettably 유감스럽게도 cover 부담하다, 지불하다 leisure 여가 pertain to ~과 관련되다 office supplies 사무용품

해설 앞부분에 출장비 환급을 신청하려면 항목별로 정리된 영수증을 제출해야 하며(when submitting a travel reimbursement request, you must include itemized receipts for all purchases.), 신용 카드 영수증만으로는 지출 비용에 대한 증빙이 되지 않는다는 설명이 나온다(Credit card receipts by themselves do not offer complete documentation of the specific products or services you paid for). 빈칸 뒤에 항목별로 정리된 영수증 없이는 환급이 불가능하다는 말이 나오는 것으로 보아(Without detailed receipts, we are unable to process reimbursement payments.) 빈칸에는 단순히 신용 카드 영수증만 제출한 사람이 있다는 문장이 들어가는 것이 문맥상 자연스럽다.

Questions 139 through 142 refer to the following article.

Martelli Named CEO at DentaraLink

DentaraLink Group, a nationwide alliance of dental service providers, has announced that industry veteran Giancarlo Martelli will serve as its incoming CEO. "Mr. Martelli shares our [139]commitment to excellence and growth, and we are so pleased to have him take us forward," said board member Luca Moretti.

Mr. Martelli brings 18 years of experience in expanding medical practices. He previously served as CEO of Solvia Surgery Centers and led its growth into 24 states. [140]Earnings rose by 12 percent during his leadership period. "I [141]am thrilled to move DentaraLink into new markets and grow the organization," said Mr. Martelli.

Headquartered in Tucson, DentaraLink collaborates with dentists [142]throughout the country to deliver management and operational support services.

139-142번 문제는 다음 기사에 관한 것입니다.

Martelli, DentaraLink CEO로 임명

치과 서비스 제공업체들의 전국 연합인 DentaraLink Group은 업계 베테랑 Giancarlo Martelli가 차기 CEO 자리를 맡을 것이라고 발표했다. 이사회 임원 Luca Moretti는 "Mr. Martelli는 탁월함과 성장에 대한 우리의 헌신을 공유하고, 우리를 이끌어 나가게 되어 기쁘게 생각합니다."라고 말했다.

Mr. Martelli는 의료 기관 확장 분야에서 18년 경력을 보유하고 있다. 이전에는 Solvia Surgery Centers의 CEO로 재직하며 회사의 24개 주로 진출하는 성장을 이끌었다. 그가 재임하는 동안 수익은 12퍼센트 올랐다. Mr. Martelli는 "DentaraLink를 새 시장에 진출시키고 조직을 성장시킬 생각에 매우 기쁩니다."라고 말했다.

Tucson에 본사를 두고 있는 DentaraLink는 전국의 치과 병원들과 협력하여 관리 및 운영 지원 서비스를 제공한다.

[어휘] name 임명하다　nationwide 전국적인　alliance 연합　commitment 헌신, 전념　take *sb* forward ~를 앞으로 이끌다　board 이사회　bring experience 경험을 보유하다　medical practice 병원, 의원　previously 이전에　surgery (외과) 수술　earnings 수입, 수익　thrilled 매우 기쁜　headquartered (~에) 본사가 있는　collaborate 협력하다　deliver (서비스, 가치를) 제공하다　operational 운영의

139-142

139 (A) committed
(B) **commitment**
(C) commit
(D) committee

141 (A) **am**
(B) was
(C) had been
(D) have been

140 (A) MedHire Solutions will be retained to oversee the recruitment process.
(B) That experience was accessible to all DentaraLink executives.
(C) **Earnings rose by 12 percent during his leadership period.**
(D) The consolidation came as a surprise to many in the dental industry.

142 (A) among
(B) along
(C) into
(D) **throughout**

139 **[해설]** 빈칸이 소유격 대명사 뒤에 있으므로 명사 (B)와 (D) 중 정답을 선택해야 하는데, "Mr. Martelli는 우리와 우수성과 성장에 전념하는 자세를 공유하고 있다."라고 말하는 것이 자연스러운 문장이다. commitment가 항상 전치사 to와 함께 사용된다는 사실도 기억해 두자.

140 (A) MedHire Solutions가 채용 절차를 감독하기 위해 고용될 것이다.
(B) 그러한 경력 정보는 모든 DentaraLink 임원들이 쉽게 입수할 수 있었다.
(C) 그가 재임하는 동안 수익은 12퍼센트 올랐다.
(D) 그 통합은 치과 업계의 많은 사람들에게 놀라움으로 다가왔다.

[어휘] retain 고용하다　oversee 감독하다　recruitment 채용　accessible to ~가 쉽게 이용할 수 있는　executive 임원, 간부　consolidation 통합, 합병

[해설] 앞선 두 문장이 Mr. Martelli의 경력과 업적에 관한 것이므로 이어지는 문장도 그에 관련된 것이어야 문맥이 자연스럽다.

141 **[해설]** DentaraLink에서 앞으로 이루고자 하는 일에 대해 Mr. Martelli가 현재 느끼는 감정을 말하는 문장이므로 현재 시제 동사를 정답으로 선택해야 한다.

142 **[해설]** 일단 among 뒤에는 복수 명사가 있어야 하므로 (A)는 제외하다. 빈칸 앞뒤 dentists ------- the country(나라 [(B) 을 따라서 (C) 안으로 (D) 곳곳에 있는] 치과 병원들)의 의미를 자연스럽게 만들어주는 전치사가 정답이다.

어휘 press release 보도 자료 release 발표, 공개 momentum 탄력, 가속도 interest 주식, 지분 offshore 앞바다의, 연안의 wind farm 풍력 발전 기지 critical 결정적인, 중대한 component (구성) 요소 financing 자금 조달[공급] pilot (본격 시행 전) 시험판, 실험판 erect 짓다, 세우다 unit (완성 제품의) 한 개 subsequent 그 다음의, 차후의 phase 단계 power 동력을 공급하다 urban 도시의 of consequence 중대한, 중요한 be on track to-V ~으로 착착 나아가다, 진행 중이다 involvement 관여, 참여 sponsor 후원자, 원조자 set a precedent 전례를 세우다 nature 성격, 종류, 유형 stimulate 활력을 불어넣다, 자극하다

143-146

143 (A) was acquired **(B) has acquired** (C) is acquiring (D) will acquire	**145** (A) as (B) or (C) so **(D) but**
144 (A) KHOM funds turbines on wind farms in other countries, too. (B) The wind farms will encounter some challenges in the foreseeable future. **(C) Fifty more units will be constructed in the subsequent phase of the project.** (D) Multiple companies chose not to finance supplemental turbines.	**146** (A) travel (B) events (C) regulations **(D) investment**

143 **해설** 빈칸 뒤에 목적어 a 30 percent interest가 있으므로 수동태 동사 (A)는 제외한다. 나머지에서 알맞은 시제의 동사를 선택해야 하는데, 이어지는 문장에서 KHMO의 지분 인수가 울산 프로젝트 자금 지원의 결정적인 요소였다고 과거 시제로 말하고 있으므로(This was a critical component in the financing of Ulsan), 빈칸에는 현재완료 시제 동사가 들어가야 한다.

144 (A) KHOM은 다른 국가들에서도 풍력 발전 기지의 터빈에 자금을 대고 있다.

(B) 풍력 발전 기지들은 가까운 장래에 어떤 시험대에 맞닥뜨리게 될 것이다.

(C) 프로젝트 다음 단계에서는 50기가 더 건설될 것이다.

(D) 다수의 기업이 추가 터빈에 대해서는 자금을 대지 않기로 했다.

어휘 fund(=finance) 자금[기금]을 대다 encounter 맞닥뜨리다 in the foreseeable future 가까운 장래에 supplemental 보충의, 추가의

해설 앞 문장에서 '시험 가동 기간(the pilot period)'과 '터빈의 개수(two turbines)'를 언급하고 있으므로 이어지는 문장으로 알맞은 것은 '다음 단계(the subsequent phase of the project)'와 추가로 건설되는 '터빈의 개수(Fifty more units)'를 언급하는 문장이다.

145 **해설** 상관접속사 문제는 짝만 찾아내면 된다. not only의 짝은 but also이다.

146 **해설** 앞 문장에서 국제적인 후원 업체들의 관여(the involvement of international sponsors), 즉 국제적인 규모로 이루어지는 자금 지원이 전례를 남길 것(will also set a new precedent for projects of this nature)이라고 했으므로, 이어지는 문장에서는 이 전례가 앞으로의 자금 지원, 즉 '투자'를 자극하게 되기를 바란다고 말하는 게 자연스럽다.

Questions 147 through 148 refer to the following instructions.

147-148번 문제는 다음 사용 설명서에 관한 것입니다.

[147]How to Execute a Global Reset

Initiating a global reset on your television's remote-control unit will erase all personalized configurations and reinstate the default operational parameters as defined by the manufacturer. To carry out this procedure, adhere to the following sequence:

Step 1
Depress and hold the POWER button for six seconds, then release it.

Step 2
Tap the left ARROW button. A brief auditory signal will confirm the action.

[148]Step 3
Press the CLEAR button. The red indicator light located at the top should be extinguished. Should it remain illuminated, press the button again prior to advancing to step 4.

Step 4
Enter your designated user code. A green light will blink, signifying that the global reset has successfully restored the standard settings.

If desired, you may now proceed to reconfigure the remote in order to customize its functionality to suit your preferences.

전체 초기화 실행 방법

텔레비전 리모컨의 전체 초기화를 시작하면 모든 개인 맞춤 설정은 삭제되고 제조업체가 정한 초기 작동 설정이 복원됩니다. 이 절차를 수행하려면 다음 순서를 따르시기 바랍니다.

1단계
전원 버튼을 6초 동안 누르고 있다가 놓아 주세요.

2단계
왼쪽 화살표 버튼을 눌러 주세요. 짧은 신호음이 동작을 확인해 줍니다.

3단계
CLEAR 버튼을 누르세요. 상단의 적색 표시등이 꺼집니다. 계속 켜져 있다면 4단계로 넘어가기 전에 버튼을 다시 눌러 주세요.

4단계
지정된 사용자 코드를 입력해 주세요. 녹색 표시등이 깜빡이며 전체 초기화로 표준 설정이 성공적으로 복원되었음을 나타냅니다.

원하신다면 이제 이어서 리모컨 재설정을 실시하여 선호도에 맞게 기능을 맞춤 설정할 수 있습니다.

어휘 instructions 사용 설명(서) execute 실행하다 global 전체적인, 전반적인 initiate 시작하다 remote-control unit 원격 조종 장치, 리모컨 personalize 개인의 요구[취향]에 맞추다 configuration 설정, 구성 reinstate 복원하다 default 초기 설정 operational 작동의 parameter 설정값, 매개 변수 define 정하다 carry out ~을 수행하다 adhere to ~을 준수하다 sequence 순서 depress (기계의 한 부분을) 누르다 release (잡고 있던 것을) 놓다 auditory 청각의 indicator light 표시등 extinguish 끄다 illuminate (전등을) 켜다 prior to ~하기 전에 advance 전진하다, 나아가다 designate 지정하다 blink 깜빡이다 signify 나타내다 reconfigure 재설정하다 remote 리모컨 customize 목적[취향]에 맞게 설정하다 functionality 기능

147

What do the instructions explain?
(A) How to remotely activate lighting features
(B) How to eliminate customized configurations from the device
(C) How to initiate subscription to additional television content
(D) How to enhance the visual resolution of the display

사용 설명서는 무엇을 알려주는가?
(A) 조명 기능을 원격으로 활성화하는 법
(B) 장치에서 맞춤 설정을 제거하는 법
(C) 추가 텔레비전 콘텐츠 구독을 시작하는 법
(D) 화면 해상도를 향상시키는 법

어휘 remotely 원격으로 feature 기능 activate 활성화하다 eliminate 제거하다 subscription 구독 enhance 향상시키다 resolution 해상도

해설 제목 How to Execute a Global Reset에서 완전 초기화를 통해 개인 맞춤 설정을 제거하는 법에 대한 설명이라는 것을 알 수 있다.

148

According to the instructions, which step might require repetition?

(A) Step 1
(B) Step 2
(C) Step 3
(D) Step 4

설명서에 따르면 어느 단계에서 반복이 필요할 수 있는가?

(A) 1단계
(B) 2단계
(C) 3단계
(D) 4단계

해설 3단계에서 CLEAR 버튼을 누른 후에(Press the CLEAR button.) 바람직한 결과가 나타나지 않으면 버튼을 다시 누르라고 지시하고 있다(press the button again).

Questions 149 through 150 refer to the following notice.

149–150번 문제는 다음 안내문에 관한 것입니다.

Notice to All Employees of Halston & Avery

[149]Please be advised that the staff kitchen will be inaccessible from November 3 through November 7. During this interval, the space will undergo repainting, and both a new dishwasher and refrigerator will be installed. Kindly refrain from entering the kitchen for any reason—including preparing beverages such as tea or coffee—while work is in progress. To accommodate your refreshment needs, [150]a temporary beverage station will be available in the foyer of the office. We appreciate your understanding and cooperation during this brief renovation period.

모든 Halston & Avery 직원 여러분께 알립니다.

11월 3일부터 11월 7일까지 탕비실에 출입할 수 없음을 알려 드립니다. 이 기간 동안 탕비실은 재도색 작업을 거치게 되며 새 식기세척기와 냉장고까지 모두 설치됩니다. 작업이 진행 중인 동안에는 커피나 차 같은 음료 준비 포함 어떤 사유로든 탕비실 출입을 삼가 주시기 바랍니다. 필요한 음료를 섭취할 수 있도록 사무실 로비에서 임시 음료 공간이 마련될 예정입니다. 이번 짧은 공사 기간 동안 여러분의 양해와 협조에 감사드립니다.

어휘 be advised that ~임을 알려주다 staff kitchen 탕비실 inaccessible 접근할 수 없는 interval (특정 목적의) 기간 undergo 경험하다, 거치다 kindly 부디, 죄송하지만 refrain from ~을 삼가다 in progress 진행 중인 accommodate 수용하다 refreshment 가벼운 식사, 음료 temporary 임시의 foyer 로비

149

What is one purpose of the notice?

(A) To promote the launch of a company-sponsored café
(B) To request that staff maintain cleanliness in the kitchen
(C) To inform employees of scheduled upgrades to kitchen facilities
(D) To declare a temporary closure of the office building

안내문의 목적 중 하나는 무엇인가?

(A) 회사가 후원하는 카페의 개업을 홍보하는 것
(B) 직원들이 탕비실을 청결하게 유지하도록 요청하는 것
(C) 직원들에게 예정되어 있는 탕비실 시설 개선을 알리는 것
(D) 사무실 건물의 임시 폐쇄를 발표하는 것

어휘 launch 개업, 개시 maintain 유지하다 declare 선언하다, 발표하다 closure 폐쇄

해설 첫 문장에서 탕비실 출입 제안을 예고하고 있는데(Please be advised that the staff kitchen will be inaccessible from November 3 through November 7.), 이 기간 동안 페인트칠과 새 장비 설치 등의 작업이 있을 것이라고 설명하고 있다(During this interval, the space will undergo repainting, and both a new dishwasher and refrigerator will be installed).

150

What will be provided in the foyer?

(A) A catered midday meal
(B) A registration list for kitchen access
(C) Packaged snacks available for purchase
(D) Tea and coffee for employee use

로비에서 무엇이 제공될 예정인가?

(A) 출장 요리로 제공되는 점심
(B) 탕비실 입장을 위한 등록 명단
(C) 구매할 수 있는 포장 간식
(D) 직원들이 이용할 수 있는 차와 커피

Questions 151 through 152 refer to the following text-message chain.

Claire O'Donnell (9:10 A.M.)
Hi Ingrid. You mentioned you'd be stopping by the office supply store today. Would you mind grabbing some binder clips for me?

Ingrid Voss (9:12 A.M.)
Sure thing. I'm currently at Supply Works. What kind are you looking for?

Claire O'Donnell (9:13 A.M.)
[151]I'm looking for a pack of assorted-size clips.

Ingrid Voss (9:20 A.M.)
[151]Looks like those are out of stock. Would you like me to pick up a different type? They have standard black clips available.

Claire O'Donnell (9:21 A.M.)
No worries—[I can wait.] Are we still on for lunch?

Ingrid Voss (9:22 A.M.)
Absolutely. [152]I'll meet you in the second-floor cafeteria at 1:00 P.M. Kenta Fujimoto from the finance team will be joining us as well.

151–152번 **문제**는 다음 문자 메시지 대화에 관한 것입니다.

Claire O'Donnell (오전 9:10)
안녕하세요, Ingrid. 오늘 사무용품 매장에 들를 거라고 했죠? 바인더 클립 좀 사다 주겠어요?

Ingrid Voss (오전 9:12)
물론이죠. 지금 Supply Works에 와 있어요. 어떤 종류를 찾고 있어요?

Claire O'Donnell (오전 9:13)
여러 크기의 클립 한 상자가 필요해요.

Ingrid Voss (오전 9:20)
그건 품절된 것 같아요. 다른 종류로 사다 줄까요? 표준형 검정 클립은 있어요.

Claire O'Donnell (오전 9:21)
괜찮아요. 기다릴래요. 점심 약속은 그대로인 거죠?

Ingrid Voss (오전 9:22)
당연하죠. 오후 1시에 2층 구내식당에서 만나요. 재무팀 Kenta Fujimoto도 함께 할 거예요.

151

At 9:21 A.M., what does Ms. O'Donnell most likely mean when she writes, "I can wait"?

(A) She is not feeling very hungry at the moment.
(B) She wants only assorted-size clips.
(C) She expects Ms. Voss to continue searching for the item.
(D) She plans to reschedule her meeting with Mr. Fujimoto.

Ms. O'Donnell이 오전 9시 21분에 "기다릴래요."라고 쓸 때, 이는 무엇을 의미하겠는가?
(A) 지금은 별로 배가 고프지 않다.
(B) 오직 여러 크기의 클립만 원한다.
(C) Ms. Voss가 계속해서 제품을 찾아 주기를 기대한다.
(D) Mr. Fujimoto와의 회의 일정을 다시 잡을 계획이다.

152

What is probably true about the writers?

(A) They work in the same office building.
(B) They typically commute to work together.
(C) They are employed at an office supply store.
(D) They are late for a business luncheon.

대화 당사자들에 관하여 맞는 말은 무엇이겠는가?

(A) 같은 사무실 건물에서 근무한다.
(B) 보통 함께 출근한다.
(C) 사무용품 매장에서 근무한다.
(D) 비즈니스 오찬에 늦었다.

어휘 typically 보통, 일반적으로 commute 통근하다 luncheon 오찬

해설 Ms. Voss가 9시 22분에 보낸 메시지에 오후 1시에 2층 구내식당에서 만나자고(I'll meet you in the second-floor cafeteria at 1:00 P.M.) 말하고 있는데, 구체적으로 어느 건물 2층인지 나와 있지 않다는 점을 통해 두 사람이 같은 건물에서 근무하고 있음을 알 수 있다.

Questions 153 through 155 refer to the following advertisement.

153-155번 문제는 다음 광고문에 관한 것입니다.

Lunaria Threads—Your Go-To Name in Style!

Lunaria Threads – 당신이 믿고 찾는 스타일 브랜드!

[153]For a limited period, enjoy savings of up to 40 percent off on all purchases!
[154]This special offer remains valid through October 31.

한정 기간 동안 모든 구입품에 대해 최대 40퍼센트까지 할인되는 혜택을 누리세요!
이번 특별 할인은 10월 31일까지 유효합니다.

[153]LunariaThreads.com is your trusted hub for fashion on the Web, featuring thousands of selections in women's and children's apparel. Browse our digital catalog to discover the latest trends in outerwear such as coats and jackets, as well as dresses, tops, skirts, swimwear, sleepwear, shoes, and accessories.

LunariaThreads.com은 신뢰할 수 있는 온라인 패션 중심지로서 수천 가지 여성복과 아동복을 제공하고 있습니다. 디지털 카탈로그를 살펴보시고 코트나 재킷 같은 외투를 비롯하여 드레스, 상의, 스커트, 수영복, 잠옷, 신발, 액세서리 등의 최신 트렌드를 알아보세요.

[155]And now, we are bringing fashion into your living space with a brand-new line of interior design products. Visit LunariaThreads.com today to explore our newest offerings in home décor.

또한 이제는 새로 나온 인테리어 디자인 제품군으로 여러분의 생활 공간에도 패션을 가져다 드립니다. 오늘 LunariaThreads.com을 방문하셔서 최신 가정용 실내 장식 제품들을 둘러보세요.

Take advantage of our long-standing free shipping policy on all orders exceeding $60.00.

60달러 초과 주문 시 오랜 기간 유지해 온 무료 배송 정책을 누리세요.

어휘 go-to 믿고 찾는, 가장 먼저 떠올리는 savings 절약, 혜택 off 할인하여 offer (한시적인) 할인 hub 중심지 feature (광고문에서) 제공하다, 갖추다 browse 둘러보다 discover 발견하다, 알아내다 outerwear 겉옷, 외투 top 상의 brand-new 완전히 새 것의 line 제품군 explore 살펴보다 offering 제품, 출시 상품 décor 실내 장식 take advantage of ~을 이용하다 long-standing 오래된, 장기간 계속되는 shipping 운송, 수송 exceed 초과하다

153

What is being advertised?

(A) A department store's rebranding initiative
(B) A recently enhanced fashion Web site
(C) A promotional discount for online shoppers
(D) A revision to the company's delivery terms

무엇이 광고되고 있는가?

(A) 백화점 리브랜딩 계획
(B) 최근에 개선된 패션 웹사이트
(C) 온라인 쇼핑객을 위한 프로모션 할인
(D) 회사 배송 조건의 개정

어휘 rebranding 브랜드 이미지 쇄신 initiative 계획, 프로젝트 revision 수정, 개정 terms 조건, 조항

해설 For a limited period, enjoy savings of up to 40 percent off on all purchases!를 통해 할인 행사가 진행되고 있다는 것을 알 수 있는데, 첫 문장 LunariaThreads.com is your trusted hub for fashion on the Web을 보면 할인을 제공하는 업체는 인터넷 패션 쇼핑몰이다. 광고 주제는 인터넷 쇼핑객들에게 제공되는 할인이다.

154

Based on the advertisement, what will happen on November 1?

(A) Customers will be charged regular prices.
(B) A new section for children's fashion will launch.
(C) Shoppers will become eligible for complimentary gifts.
(D) Shipping fees will be reduced across all orders.

광고에 따르면 11월 1일에 무엇이 발생할 것인가?

(A) 고객들에게 정가가 청구될 것이다.
(B) 새 아동 패션 코너가 개설될 것이다.
(C) 쇼핑객들이 무료 사은품을 받을 수 있게 될 것이다.
(D) 모든 주문에 대해 배송비가 할인될 것이다.

어휘 regular price 정가　launch 시작되다, 출시되다　eligible 자격이 있는　complimentary 무료의

해설 특별 할인 행사를 10월 31일까지 진행하므로(This special offer remains valid through October 31.), 11월 1일부터는 고객들이 정상가로 제품을 구입해야 한다.

155

What is being introduced for the first time?

(A) Home-decorating items
(B) Outerwear
(C) Children's clothing
(D) Footwear

최초로 무엇이 소개되고 있는가?

(A) 가정용 장식 용품
(B) 외투
(C) 아동복
(D) 신발류

해설 현재, 전에 없었던 완전히 새로운 인테리어 디자인 제품군을 판매하고 있다는 소식을 전하고 있다(And now, we are bringing fashion into your living space with a brand-new line of interior design products).

Questions 156 through 158 refer to the following article.

156-158번 문제는 다음 기사에 관한 것입니다.

Warm Welcome & Special Thanks

(March 12) — Readers of the *Selat Courier* may have noticed a new name added to the newspaper's masthead. [156]We are delighted to introduce Lina Hartono as our very first intern reporter.

Ms. Hartono recently relocated to Surabaya, having studied English and journalism in Australia. [157]For her initial assignment, she investigated the current difficulties facing our country's agriculture sector from a global perspective. Her debut article on this topic is featured in this issue.

The introduction of internships is another way we aim to fulfill our educational mission. Over the past 18 months, the *Selat Courier* has been sustained primarily through financial support from local academic institutions. Our publication now strives not only to keep the community informed, but also to serve career-development purposes.

One positive outcome of this new direction is the growing number of students who contribute to the paper in various capacities. [158]The editor would like to extend sincere gratitude to all the students who volunteer their time each month—including those who ensure the print edition reaches the doorsteps of our subscribers promptly every week.

따뜻한 환영과 특별한 감사

(3월 12일) – *Selat Courier* 독자 여러분은 발행인란에 추가된 새 이름을 알아차리셨을지도 모르겠습니다. 우리의 사상 첫 인턴 기자 Lina Hartono를 소개하게 되어 기쁩니다.

Ms. Hartono는 호주에서 영어와 언론학을 공부한 후 최근 Surabaya로 이주했습니다. 그녀는 첫 임무로 우리나라의 농업 분야가 직면한 현재의 어려움을 세계적 관점에서 조사했습니다. 이 주제에 관한 그녀의 첫 기사가 이번 호에 실려 있습니다.

인턴 제도의 도입은 우리가 교육적 사명을 완수하고자 하는 또 다른 방법입니다. 지난 18개월 동안 *Selat Courier*는 주로 지역 교육 기관들의 재정적 지원을 통해 유지되어 왔습니다. 이제는 우리 간행물로 지역 사회에 정보를 제공하는 것뿐만 아니라 경력 개발을 돕는 데에도 애쓰고자 합니다.

이 새로운 방향의 긍정적 결과의 하나는 다양한 역할로 신문에 기여하는 학생 수가 증가하고 있다는 점입니다. 편집자는 매달 자진하여 시간을 내는 모든 학생들, 특히 매주 구독자들의 문 앞까지 신문이 제때 배달되도록 힘써주는 학생들에게 진심 어린 감사를 전하고자 합니다.

어휘 Courier (신문 명칭) ~ 신문 masthead (신문, 잡지의) 발행인란 relocate 이주하다 journalism 언론학 initial 처음의 assignment 과제, 임무 investigate 조사하다 face (어려움 등에) 직면하다 perspective 관점 debut 첫선 be featured in ~에 실리다 issue (간행물의) 호(號) aim to-V ~을 목표로 하다 fulfill 달성하다, 수행하다 sustain 유지하다 academic 학업의, 학문의 institution 기관 publication 출판물, 간행물 strive to-V ~하려고 노력하다 keep *sb* informed ~에게 계속해서 정보를 제공하다 serve a purpose 도움이 되다, 기여하다 outcome 결과 capacity 지위, 역할 extend (환영, 감사 등을) 전하다 gratitude 감사 volunteer time 자진하여 시간을 내다 doorstep 현관 계단 subscriber 구독자 promptly 제때에

156

What is mentioned about the intern position?	인턴 직책에 대해 무엇이 언급되어 있는가?
(A) It is a new addition to the publication.	(A) 간행물에 새로 추가되었다.
(B) It involves travel abroad.	(B) 해외 출장을 포함한다.
(C) It is based in Australia.	(C) 호주에 본거지가 있다.
(D) It requires a degree in journalism.	(D) 언론학 학위가 필요하다.

어휘 position 직위, 직책 involve 수반하다, 포함하다 be based in ~에 본거지를 두다 degree 학위

해설 두 번째 문장에서 사상 첫 인턴 기자가 채용되었음을 알리고 있다(We are delighted to introduce Lina Hartono as our very first intern reporter). 인턴 제도는 최근에 신설된 것이다.

157

What is implied about Ms. Hartono?	Ms. Hartono에 관하여 무엇이 암시되어 있는가?
(A) She is an experienced interpreter.	(A) 경험 많은 통역사이다.
(B) She is contributing a series of articles.	(B) 시리즈 기사를 기고하고 있다.
(C) She will assist in recruiting future interns.	(C) 인턴 지원자 모집을 도울 것이다.
(D) She previously worked in the agriculture sector.	(D) 이전에 농업 분야에서 일했다.

어휘 experienced 경험이 많은, 노련한 interpreter 통역사 contribute 기고하다 recruit 모집하다 previously 이전에

해설 농업 분야가 겪고 있는 어려움(the current difficulties facing our country's agriculture sector)에 대해 Ms. Hartono가 쓴 첫 기사가 이번 호에 실린다고 했으므로(Her debut article on this topic is featured in this issue.), 앞으로 같은 주제에 대한 일련의 기사들이 계속 게재될 것이라고 추론할 수 있다.

158

What is indicated about the *Selat Courier*?	*Selat Courier*에 관하여 무엇이 나타나 있는가?
(A) It is provided free of charge to locals.	(A) 지역 주민들에게 무료로 제공된다.
(B) It is delivered by volunteers.	(B) 자원봉사자들에 의해 배달된다.
(C) It is published in several languages.	(C) 여러 언어로 발간된다.
(D) It receives funding from advertisements.	(D) 광고에서 자금 지원을 받는다.

어휘 free of charge 무료로 locals 지역 주민들

해설 편집자가 자원봉사자들에게 감사를 표하고 있는데(The editor would like to extend sincere gratitude to all the students who volunteer their time each month), 그중에는 종이 신문 배달 업무를 맡은 봉사자가 있다(including those who ensure the print edition reaches the doorsteps of our subscribers promptly every week).

📑 **Questions 159 through 160** refer to the following memo.

From: Naomi Sakamoto, Food Safety Supervisor
To: All Staff

[159]Maintaining proper hygiene is a year-round responsibility for all food handlers, but it becomes even more critical during the approaching cold and flu season. Viruses may linger on surfaces like countertops and cutting boards, travel via hands, and eventually find their way onto utensils and serving dishes. [159]To reduce the risk of spreading illness, every employee involved in food preparation or delivery must practice thorough handwashing before handling any food or related tools. [160]Guidelines on the proper handwashing technique have been posted at the kitchen entrance, inside the restrooms, and in the meeting room adjacent to the lobby. Please follow these instructions diligently to help ensure a safe and sanitary work environment.

159-160번 문제는 다음 공지문에 관한 것입니다.

발신: 식품 안전 관리자 Naomi Sakamoto
수신: 전 직원

알맞게 청결을 유지하는 것은 모든 식품 취급자에게 연중 내내 요구되는 책임이지만, 다가오는 감기와 독감 철에는 훨씬 더 중요해집니다. 바이러스가 주방 조리대나 도마와 같은 표면에 잔존하다가 손을 통해 이동하고 결국 각종 기구와 서빙용 접시에 이를 수 있습니다. 질병 확산의 위험을 줄이기 위해 음식 조리와 전달에 관여하는 모든 직원은 음식이나 관련 도구를 다루기 전에 철저한 손 씻기를 실천해야 합니다. 올바른 손 씻기 방법에 대한 지침이 주방 입구와 화장실 안, 로비에 인접한 회의실 안에 게시되어 있습니다. 안전하고 위생적인 근무 환경을 보장하는 데 도움이 되도록 이 지시 사항을 성실히 따라 주시기 바랍니다.

어휘 supervisor 관리자 hygiene 위생, 청결 year-round 연중 계속되는 critical 결정적인, 중대한 linger 잔존하다 countertop 주방 조리대 travel 이동하다 via ~을 통해 eventually 결국 find one's way 결국 ~에 이르다 utensil 도구, 기구 serving dish 서빙용 큰 접시 spread 확산시키다 involved 관련된 practice 실천하다 thorough 철저한 related 관련된 guidelines 지침 post 게시하다 adjacent to ~에 인접한 instructions 지시 (사항), 사용법 diligently 성실하게 sanitary 위생적인, 청결한

159

What is the primary focus of the memo?
(A) How to properly treat symptoms of a seasonal illness
(B) The importance of practicing a hygiene protocol
(C) A review of the company's sick-leave procedures
(D) Instructions for operating new kitchen appliances

공지문의 핵심 내용은 무엇인가?
(A) 계절 질병의 증상을 적절히 치료하는 법
(B) 위생 규정 실천의 중요성
(C) 회사 병가 절차의 검토
(D) 새 주방 기기 작동을 위한 사용법

어휘 treat 치료하다 symptom 증상 seasonal 계절의 protocol 규정 sick leave 병가 operate 작동시키다 appliance 기기, 전기 제품

해설 첫 문장에서 청결함을 유지하는 것이 매우 중요함을 강조하면서(Maintaining proper hygiene is a year-round responsibility for all food handlers, but it becomes even more critical during the approaching cold and flu season), 세 번째 문장에서 모든 직원들에게 철저한 손 씻기를 지시하고 있다(To reduce the risk of spreading illness, every employee involved in food preparation or delivery must practice thorough handwashing before handling any food or related tools).

160

What items are most likely mentioned in the posted guidelines?
(A) Hand cleanser and disposable towels
(B) Cooking oil and vinegar
(C) Napkins and tablecloths
(D) Mixing bowls and measuring cups

게시된 지침에서 어떤 물품이 언급되겠는가?
(A) 손 세척제와 일회용 수건
(B) 식용유와 식초
(C) 냅킨과 식탁보
(D) 믹싱 볼과 계량컵

어휘 disposable 일회용의 vinegar 식초 tablecloth 식탁보 measuring cup 계량컵

해설 게시된 지침은 올바른 손 씻기 방법에 대한 것이므로(Guidelines on the proper handwashing technique have been posted), 손 세척제나 일회용 수건 같은 물품들이 언급되는 것이 자연스럽다.

Questions 161 through 163 refer to the following e-mail.

To: Team@bradleyworks.com
From: Elliot Turner, Workplace Operations Lead
Date: 15 March
Subject: Desks Incoming

Dear team,

We're excited to announce that all staff desks will soon be upgraded to new hybrid models that support both sitting and standing work styles. These desks are scheduled to arrive on 22 March. —[1]—. I've arranged for the delivery to take place early in the morning before regular hours so it won't interrupt your workflow. —[2]—. [161]To help facilitate the transition, please ensure that all contents of your current desk—including any personal items—are transferred into a cardboard box on 21 March.

You can learn more about the desk model we selected by visiting www.hartleyfurnishings.co.uk/hybrid09. —[3]—. [162]Based on my research, this model stood out as the most intuitive and user-friendly. You can easily alter its height by flipping a latch and pressing a button.

[163]Many of you have expressed interest in hybrid desks for quite some time, so I'm thrilled we're making this happen. This upgrade is just one of several initiatives management plans to implement this year to make Bradley Works a more comfortable and health-conscious workplace. —[4]—.

Warm regards,
Elliot Turner

161-163번 문제는 다음 이메일에 관한 것입니다.

수신: Team@bradleyworks.com
발신: 업무 환경 운영 책임자 Elliot Turner
날짜: 3월 15일
제목: 책상 도착 예정

팀원 여러분께,

직원 여러분의 모든 책상들이 곧 좌식 및 입식 업무 스타일을 모두 지원하는 새 하이브리드 모델로 업그레이드될 것이라는 소식을 전하게 되어 기쁩니다. 책상들은 3월 22일에 도착할 예정입니다. 업무에 방해되지 않도록 하기 위해 배송은 정규 근무 시간 전 오전 일찍 이루어지도록 조처했습니다. 전환 작업을 원활하게 하는 데 도움이 되도록 3월 21일에는 현재 사용하시는 책상의 모든 내용물이(개인 물품을 포함) 반드시 종이 상자로 옮겨 주시기 바랍니다.

www.hartleyfurnishings.co.uk/hybrid09을 방문하시면 우리가 선택한 책상 모델에 관하여 더 알아보실 수 있습니다. 제가 조사했을 때 이 모델은 가장 직관적이고 사용하기 쉬운 것으로 눈에 띄었습니다. 걸쇠를 젖히고 버튼을 누름으로써 쉽게 높이를 바꿀 수 있습니다.

여러분 중 상당수가 꽤 오랫동안 하이브리드 책상에 관심을 보여 왔던 터라 이 일을 실현하게 되어 매우 기쁩니다. 이번 개선 작업은 Bradley Works를 더 편안하고 건강을 의식하는 직장으로 만들기 위해 경영진이 올해 시행할 계획인 여러 프로젝트들 중 하나일 뿐입니다.

이만 줄입니다.
Elliot Turner

어휘 operation 운영 lead 책임자 incoming 도착 예정인 hybrid 혼합형의 be scheduled to-V ~할 예정이다 arrange 조정하다, 조처하다 take place 일어나다 hours 근무 시간 interrupt 방해하다 workflow 업무의 흐름 facilitate 원활하게 하다 transition 전환, 변화 transfer 옮기다 cardboard 판지, 보드지 stand out 두드러지다, 눈에 띄다 intuitive 직관적인 user-friendly 사용자 친화적인, 사용하기 쉬운 alter 바꾸다, 수정하다 flip 젖히다 latch 걸쇠 quite some time 꽤 오랜 시간 thrilled 매우 기쁜 management 경영진 implement 시행하다 conscious ~을 의식하는

161

What should employees do to assist with the delivery process?

(A) Pack up their belongings
(B) Gather cardboard containers
(C) Finish their tasks before lunch
(D) Remove furniture from their workspaces

배송 과정을 돕기 위해 직원들은 무엇을 해야 하는가?

(A) 소지품을 챙긴다
(B) 종이 상자를 모은다
(C) 점심시간 전에 업무를 마친다
(D) 업무 공간에서 가구를 치운다

어휘 pack up 짐을 싸다 belongings 소지품 container 상자, 용기 remove 치우다, 옮기다

해설 가구 교체를 원활하게 진행하기 위해 책상에 있던 모든 물건을 상자에 넣어 달라는 지시를 하고 있다(To help facilitate the transition, please ensure that all contents of your current desk—including any personal items—are transferred into a cardboard box on 21 March).

What was the main reason the desk model was chosen?

(A) It offers ample storage space.
(B) It is simple to adjust.
(C) It can be shipped quickly.
(D) It is the most budget-friendly option.

그 책상 모델이 선택된 주된 이유는 무엇인가?

(A) 넉넉한 보관 공간을 제공한다.
(B) 조절이 간단하다.
(C) 빠르게 배송된다.
(D) 예산 부담이 가장 적은 옵션이다.

어휘 ample 넉넉한, 충분한 adjust 조정하다 ship 운송하다, 수송하다 budget-friendly 예산에 부담되지 않는

해설 두 번째 문단을 보면 이 모델은 사용이 쉽다는 소개에 이어, 걸쇠를 젖히고 버튼을 누르는 간단한 조작만으로 높이를 조절할 수 있는 부연 설명이 나오고 있다(this model stood out as the most intuitive and user-friendly. You can easily alter its height by flipping a latch and pressing a button).

In which of the positions marked [1], [2], [3], and [4] does the following sentence best belong?

"We're happy to hear any additional suggestions you might have."

(A) [1]
(B) [2]
(C) [3]
(D) [4]

다음 문장은 [1], [2], [3], [4]로 표시된 자리 중 어느 곳에 가장 잘 어울리는가?

"추가적인 제안이 있다면 기꺼이 듣겠습니다."

해설 주어진 문장에서 additional suggestions가 키워드이다. '추가적인 제안'이라고 말하고 있으므로 앞부분에 어떤 제안 사항이 언급되어야 한다. 마지막 문단에 많은 직원들이 하이브리드 책상을 제안했다는 말을 하고 있다(Many of you have expressed interest in hybrid desks for quite some time, so I'm thrilled we're making this happen). 또한 이어지는 문장에서 책상을 바꾸는 것 외에도 직원들의 업무 편의와 건강을 위한 여러 계획을 더 시행할 것이라고 말하고 있으므로(This upgrade is just one of several initiatives management plans to implement this year to make Bradley Works a more comfortable and health-conscious workplace.), 이 계획에 추가할 만한 어떤 제안이 있다면 기꺼이 듣겠다고 말하는 문장이 이어지는 것이 매우 자연스럽다.

Questions 164 through 167 refer to the following online chat discussion.

Emily Novak [10:02 A.M.]
Hi, everyone. [164]When we met last week, I asked you to come up with ideas to raise awareness about the community garden program. Has anyone made any progress?

Ryan Goodwin [10:03 A.M.]
[165]I got in touch with Daniel Chen from *Metro Pulse*, our local newspaper. [165] [166]You might be familiar with his column, "Urban Life."

Michael Landon [10:04 A.M.]
[166]The one that's published on Thursdays? [I never miss it!]

Ryan Goodwin [10:05 A.M.]
He has a strong online following as well. He's interested in interviewing me for an upcoming issue. That'll happen next week.

Emily Novak [10:05 A.M.]
That's great news. Will you be discussing the garden program as a whole?

Ryan Goodwin [10:06 A.M.]
I told Daniel that we're currently surveying garden members about water access concerns. So he wants to center the article around that topic.

Michael Landon [10:07 A.M.]
[167]Lena and I are compiling the survey findings. Emily, I'm about to send you a draft. Once you've approved it, I'll upload it to our Web site.

Emily Novak [10:08 A.M.]
Perfect. I'll review it later today.

164–167번 **문제**는 다음 온라인 채팅 대화에 관한 것입니다.

Emily Novak [오전 10:02]
모두들 안녕하세요. 지난주에 모였을 때 공동체 텃밭 프로그램에 대한 인식을 높이기 위한 아이디어를 내 달라고 부탁드렸습니다. 진전이 있는 분 있나요?

Ryan Goodwin [오전 10:03]
지역 신문 *Metro Pulse*의 Daniel Chen과 연락했습니다. 아마 그의 칼럼 'Urban Life'가 익숙하실 거예요.

Michael Landon [오전 10:04]
목요일에 게재되는 거요? 그건 절대 놓치지 않죠!

Ryan Goodwin [오전 10:05]
그는 열렬한 온라인 팬층도 있죠. 다음 호에 싣기 위해 저와 인터뷰하고 싶어 합니다. 다음 주에 할 거예요.

Emily Novak [오전 10:05]
정말 좋은 소식이군요. 텃밭 프로그램 전반에 대해 논할 건가요?

Ryan Goodwin [오전 10:06]
Daniel에게 우리가 물 사용 문제에 대해 현재 텃밭 회원을 대상으로 조사하고 있다고 말했어요. 그래서 기사의 초점을 그 주제에 두고 싶어합니다.

Michael Landon [오전 10:07]
Lena와 제가 설문 조사 결과를 작성하고 있어요. Emily, 지금 막 초안을 보내려고 합니다. 승인해 주시면, 홈페이지에 업로드하겠습니다.

Emily Novak [오전 10:08]
좋아요. 오늘 오후에 검토할게요.

어휘 come up with ~을 생각해내다 raise awareness 인식을 높이다 make progress 진전을 이루다 get in touch with ~와 연락하다 be familiar with ~에 익숙하다 publish 싣다, 게재하다 following 추종자, 팬층 be interested in ~하고 싶어하다 as a whole 전체적으로 survey ~를 대상으로 조사하다 access 접근, 이용 center A around B A의 초점을 B에 두다 compile (자료를 수집하여) 작성하다 findings (조사, 연구 등의) 결과 be about to-V 막 ~하려 하다 draft 초안 approve 승인하다

164

What is indicated about Ms. Novak?

(A) She was absent from last week's meeting.
(B) She recently came back from traveling.
(C) She disagrees with Ryan Goodwin's suggestion.
(D) She assigned a task to her colleagues.

Ms. Novak에 관하여 무엇이 나타나 있는가?

(A) 지난주 회의에 참석하지 않았다.
(B) 최근에 여행에서 돌아왔다.
(C) Ryan Goodwin의 제안에 동의하지 않는다.
(D) 동료들에게 과제를 부여했다.

어휘 disagree 반대하다 assign (책임, 업무 등을) 부여하다, 맡기다

해설 Ms. Novak은 지난주 회의에서 직원들에게 공동체 텃밭 프로그램에 대한 인식을 높이기 위한 아이디어를 내 달라는 과제를 부여했다(When we met last week, I asked you to come up with ideas to raise awareness about the community garden program).

165

Who is Mr. Chen?

(A) A municipal employee
(B) A journalist from the local press
(C) A potential hire
(D) A gardening specialist

Mr. Chen은 누구인가?

(A) 지자체 공무원
(B) 지역 언론사 기자
(C) 채용 후보자
(D) 원예 전문가

어휘 municipal 지방 자치(단체)의 press 신문, 언론 potential hire 채용 후보자

해설 Mr. Chen은 지역 신문사에서 근무하며(I got in touch with Daniel Chen from *Metro Pulse*, our local newspaper.), 칼럼 집필을 담당하는(You might be familiar with his column, "Urban Life".) 언론인이다.

166

At 10:04 A.M., what does Mr. Landon most likely mean when he writes, "I never miss it"?

(A) He enjoys joining in community events.
(B) He consistently finishes his work on time.
(C) He is a subscriber to *Metro Pulse*.
(D) He regularly reads a column.

오전 10시 4분에 Mr. Landon은 "그건 절대 놓치지 않죠!"라고 쓸 때 무엇을 의미하겠는가?

(A) 공동체 활동에 참여하는 것을 즐긴다.
(B) 언제나 제시간에 업무를 마친다.
(C) *Metro Pulse*의 구독자이다.
(D) 정기적으로 칼럼을 읽는다.

어휘 consistently 일관되게, 한결같이 on time 제시간에

해설 바로 앞에 나오는 문장들을 읽어 보면, Urban Life라는 칼럼이 매주 목요일에 신문에 게재된다고 말하고 있으므로(The one that's published on Thursdays?), I never miss it은 Mr. Landon이 이 칼럼을 절대 놓치지 않고 정기적으로 읽는다는 뜻이다.

What does Mr. Landon indicate he plans to do?

(A) Carry out a survey
(B) Post a document online
(C) Prepare questions for an interview
(D) Work on improving water access

Mr. Landon은 무엇을 할 계획이라고 알리는가?

(A) 설문 조사를 실시한다
(B) 문서를 온라인에 게시한다
(C) 인터뷰를 위한 질문을 준비한다
(D) 물 사용 개선을 위한 작업을 한다

어휘 indicate 밝히다, 알리다

해설 Mr. Landon은 설문 조사 결과 보고서를 작성하고 있는데(Lena and I are compiling the survey findings.), Ms. Novak이 초안을 검토한 후 승인해 주면(Emily, I'm about to send you a draft. Once you've approved it), 회사 홈페이지에 업로드하겠다고 말한다(I'll upload it to our Web site).

Questions 168 through 171 refer to the following notice.

[168]**Associate Publicist Opening
Silverpine Publishing House**

Silverpine Publishing House publishes a wide range of contemporary titles, including fiction, nonfiction, and poetry. [169]Among our fiction authors are Julian Mercer, Thomas Ellery, and Camila Ortega. —[1]—. Our nonfiction catalog primarily features books on personal finance, travel writing, wellness, and digital culture.

We are currently hiring an associate publicist to join our dynamic team. —[2]—. The successful candidate will assist senior staff and also take the lead on publicity campaigns for our authors. [170]Responsibilities include coordinating and managing author events such as book signings, festival appearances, and both domestic and international speaking engagements.

[171]Ideal applicants should have three to four years of experience in trade publishing, either in a publicity or editorial capacity. —[3]—. Candidates must demonstrate strong familiarity with social media platforms used in publishing, proficiency in word-processing tools, excellent written and verbal communication skills, and commendable attention to detail. —[4]—.

If this opportunity aligns with your background, please submit a cover letter and résumé no later than November 12 to careers@silverpinepublishing.com.

168-171번 문제는 다음 공고문에 관한 것입니다.

**홍보팀 대리직
Silverpine 출판사**

Silverpine 출판사는 소설, 비소설, 시를 망라하며 매우 다양한 현대 작품들을 출간하는 출판사입니다. 저희와 함께 소설을 펴낸 작가들 중에는 Julian Mercer와 Thomas Ellery, Camila Ortega가 있습니다. 비소설 목록에는 주로 개인 재무나 여행 에세이, 건강, 디지털 문화에 관한 책들이 포함됩니다.

현재 활발히 활동 중인 저희 팀에 합류할 홍보 담당 대리를 채용하려 합니다. 합격자는 선임 직원들을 보조하고, 작가들의 홍보 캠페인도 주도하게 될 것입니다. 업무에는 도서 사인회나 축제 출연, 국내외 강연 등 작가 행사들을 조율하고 관리하는 일이 포함됩니다.

이상적인 지원자는 일반 도서 출판 분야에서 홍보 또는 편집 역할로 3, 4년의 경력을 보유해야 합니다. 지원자는 출판 분야에서 사용되는 소셜 미디어 플랫폼에 대한 높은 이해도와 워드프로세싱 프로그램 숙련도, 탁월한 문서 및 구두 의사소통 능력, 세세한 부분에 대한 훌륭한 주의력을 입증해야 합니다.

이 기회가 본인의 경력과 부합한다면, 자기소개서와 이력서를 늦어도 11월 12일까지 careers@silverpinepublishing.com 으로 제출해 주시기 바랍니다.

어휘 associate (직함으로) 준[부] ~ publicist 홍보 담당자 publishing house 출판사 contemporary 현대의 title 출판물 dynamic 역동적인, 활발한 successful candidate 합격자 take the lead 주도하다 publicity 홍보 coordinate 조정하다, 조율하다 appearance 출연 domestic 국내의 engagement (공적인) 약속, 업무 applicant 지원자 trade publishing 일반 도서 출판 editorial 편집의 capacity 역할, 자격 demonstrate 입증하다 proficiency 능숙함 verbal 구두의, 말로 하는 commendable 칭찬할 만한, 훌륭한 align with ~과 일치하다, 부합하다 background 경력 cover letter 자기소개서 no later than 늦어도 ~까지

168

What is the purpose of the notice?

(A) To advertise an upcoming recruitment event
(B) To communicate changes in upper-level staffing to employees
(C) To motivate recent graduates to pursue internships
(D) To invite eligible candidates to apply for a position

공고문의 목적은 무엇인가?

(A) 곧 있을 채용 행사를 광고하는 것
(B) 고위직 인사 변동을 직원들에게 전달하는 것
(C) 최근 졸업생들이 인턴 과정에 도전하도록 독려하는 것
(D) 자격이 되는 지원자들이 지원하도록 권하는 것

어휘 upcoming 다가오는 recruitment 채용 communicate 전달하다 staffing 인력 배치 invite 권하다

해설 제목 Associate Publicist Opening만 읽어도 정답을 알 수 있다. 토익에서는 이렇게 본문 위아래의 자투리 부분에서도 정답을 알아낼 수 있는 경우가 종종 있다.

What do Mr. Mercer and Ms. Ortega have in common?

(A) They contribute to books on digital culture.
(B) They are signed to the same publisher.
(C) They organize literary events.
(D) They have participated in international speaking engagements.

Mr. Mercer와 Ms. Ortega은 어떤 공통점이 있는가?

(A) 디지털 문화에 대한 책을 집필한다.
(B) 같은 출판사와 계약했다.
(C) 문학 행사를 준비한다.
(D) 국제 강연 행사에 참여한 적이 있다.

어휘 have *sth* in common 공통의 ~을 가지다 sign 계약하다 organize 준비하다, 조직하다 literary 문학의

해설 Silverpine 출판사를 통해 소설을 출간하는 작가들 명단에 Mr. Mercer와 Ms. Ortega가 모두 포함되어 있다(Among our fiction authors are Julian Mercer, Thomas Ellery, and Camila Ortega). 두 작가는 같은 출판사와 계약을 맺었다.

170

What is listed as one of the responsibilities of an associate publicist?

(A) Scheduling author appearances
(B) Maintaining word processing software
(C) Interviewing prospective interns
(D) Attending industry conventions

홍보팀 대리직의 업무 중 하나로 무엇이 열거되어 있는가?

(A) 작가의 행사 출연 일정 잡기
(B) 워드프로세싱 소프트웨어 관리하기
(C) 인턴 지원자 면접 보기
(D) 업계 컨벤션 참석하기

어휘 prospective intern 인턴 지원자 convention (산업, 직종 관련) 대회, 회의

해설 홍보팀 대리직의 업무에는 작가들이 출연하는 각종 행사를 편성하고 관리하는 일이 포함된다(Responsibilities include coordinating and managing author events such as book signings, festival appearances, and both domestic and international speaking engagements).

In which of the positions marked [1], [2], [3], and [4] does the following sentence best belong?

"Two professional references from these positions are required."

(A) [1]
(B) [2]
(C) [3]
(D) [4]

다음 문장은 [1], [2], [3], [4]로 표시된 자리 중 어느 곳에 가장 잘 어울리는가?

"이 직책에 있는 전문가 두 명의 추천서가 필요합니다."

어휘 reference 추천서

해설 주어진 문장에서 these positions를 키워드로 볼 수 있다. '이 직책들'이 가리키는 대상이 보이는 문장은 Ideal applicants should have three to four years of experience in trade publishing, either in a publicity or editorial capacity.이다. 홍보나 편집 업무를 맡아 일한 경력 3, 4년이 필요하며, 이러한 자리에 있는 전문가가 써 준 추천서를 제출해야 한다는 내용이다.

Questions 172 through 175 refer to the following e-mail.

To: Eliza Morton <emorton@greenridgegroup.co.au>
From: Nolan Barrett <nbarrett@skyreachmedia.co.au>
Subject: New Service
Date: April 12

Dear Ms. Morton,

Regarding your recent order, before we process it, I wanted to inform you of an exciting opportunity. Skyreach Media is now offering an additional method for engaging with your customers: automated text messages. We are combining our distinctive lawn advertisements with the latest mobile technology to provide a swift, straightforward approach to expanding your client base. We've successfully aided numerous property rental agents in your vicinity and are currently providing free trials to new members.

Our automated text-messaging service starts with a few basic steps.

1. Navigate to our Web site, skyreachmedia.co.au, select the Registration page, and then New User. You will then be guided through our simple and efficient registration to set up an account.

2. Once your account is activated, you can begin entering the automated responses intended for interested renters. Be sure to include comprehensive details about each property. You also have the option to incorporate images, audio recordings, videos, and links to external Web sites.

3. Designate a unique keyword for each property. This keyword is what prospective renters will text to obtain more information about a rental unit. It should not be excessively long or challenging to spell, and it must be easy for clients to recall.

4. Afterwards, simply wait. Those searching for apartments will pass by the location, spot the keyword, and upon texting it, instantly access the message you have programmed!

Your complimentary trial includes us producing fresh rental signs for one of your properties so that your advertisements incorporate the keyword. Should you contact me before Wednesday, I will also extend the order to cover two additional properties. Thus, in addition to a month of our text-messaging service, you'll acquire updated signs for three rental units, all entirely free of charge. Once the trial period ends, you may choose from six reasonably priced packages, including the option of dispatching daily updates to preferred customers.

I eagerly await your reply!

Nolan Barrett

172–175번 문제는 다음 이메일에 관한 것입니다.

수신: Eliza Morton ⟨emorton@greenridgegroup.co.au⟩
발신: Nolan Barrett ⟨nbarrett@skyreachmedia.co.au⟩
제목: 신규 서비스
날짜: 4월 12일

Ms. Morton께,

최근 주문과 관련하여, 처리에 앞서 흥미로운 기회를 알려드리고자 합니다. Skyreach Media는 현재 고객과 소통하기 위한 추가 방식으로 자동 문자 메시지 서비스를 제공하고 있습니다. 저희는 독특한 잔디 광고와 최신 모바일 기술을 결합하여 고객 기반을 확대하는 신속하고 간단한 방식을 제공하고 있습니다. 인근 지역의 수많은 부동산 임대 중개업자들을 성공적으로 도와주었으며, 현재는 신규 회원에게 무료 체험을 제공하고 있습니다.

자동 문자 메시지 서비스는 몇 가지 기본적인 단계로 시작합니다.

1. 당사 홈페이지 skyreachmedia.co.au로 이동해서 등록 페이지에서 '신규 사용자'를 선택하세요. 이후 간단하고 효율적인 등록 절차를 안내받고 계정을 설정하게 됩니다.

2. 계정이 활성화되면 관심 있는 임차인 대상으로 자동 응답 메시지 입력을 시작할 수 있습니다. 반드시 각 부동산에 관한 포괄적인 상세 정보를 포함하세요. 이미지와 오디오 녹음 자료, 동영상, 외부 웹사이트로 연결되는 링크를 포함하는 옵션도 있습니다.

3. 각 부동산의 고유 키워드를 지정하세요. 이 키워드는 잠재 임차인이 임대 세대에 대한 추가 정보를 얻기 위해 문자로 보낼 내용입니다. 지나치게 길거나 철자가 어려워서는 안 되며 고객이 기억하기 쉬워야 합니다.

4. 이후에는 기다리기만 하면 됩니다. 아파트를 찾는 사람들이 해당 장소를 지나가다가 키워드를 발견하고 문자로 전송하면, 여러분이 설정해 놓은 메시지에 즉시 접속하게 됩니다.

무료 체험에는 부동산 중 한 곳에 대한 신규 임대 광고판을 제작해 드리는 서비스를 포함하고 있으며 광고에는 키워드가 반영되도록 합니다. 수요일 전에 연락 주시면, 추가로 부동산 두 곳이 포함하도록 주문을 확대해 드리겠습니다. 따라서 한 달간 문자 메시지 서비스에 더하여 세 곳의 임대 세대에 대한 업데이트된 표지판을 모두 무료로 얻게 될 것입니다. 체험 기간이 끝나면, 우대 고객에게 매일 업데이트를 발송하는 옵션을 포함해 적정한 가격의 여섯 가지 패키지 상품 중에 선택하실 수 있습니다.

답변을 기다리겠습니다!

Nolan Barrett

어휘 regarding ~에 관하여 engage with ~와 소통하다 distinctive 독특한, 특유의 swift 신속한 straightforward 간단한 expand 확대하다
base 기반 aid 돕다 property 부동산 rental 임대 vicinity 근처 trial (상품, 서비스 등의) 체험 (기간) automated 자동화된 navigate 이동하다
guide A through B A에게 B를 안내하다 set up ~을 설정하다 account 계정 be intended for ~을 대상으로 하다 renter 임차인
comprehensive 포괄적인 incorporate 포함하다, 반영하다 external 외부의 designate 지정하다 prospective 잠재적인 unit (건물의) 한 가구[호]
excessively 지나치게 challenging 어려운 recall 기억하다 afterwards 이후에 await 기다리다 spot 발견하다 upon V-ing ~하자마자
instantly 즉시 access 접속하다 extend 확대하다, 연장하다 in addition to ~에 더하여 reasonably priced 적당한 가격의 dispatch 발송하다
preferred customer 우대[우수] 고객

172

What can be inferred regarding Ms. Morton?

(A) She is interested in securing a property to rent.
(B) She works professionally as a property rental agent.
(C) She has recently purchased a new mobile telephone.
(D) She frequently dispatches text messages.

Ms. Morton에 관하여 무엇을 추론할 수 있는가?

(A) 임차할 부동산을 확보하고자 한다.
(B) 전문 부동산 임대 중개업자로 일한다.
(C) 최근에 새 휴대전화를 구입했다.
(D) 빈번하게 문자 메시지를 발송한다.

어휘 infer 추론하다 secure 확보하다, 확정하다 frequently 자주

해설 새로 출시된 서비스를 광고하는 이메일인데(Skyreach Media is now offering an additional method for engaging with your customers:), 이미 많은
다른 부동산 임대 중개업자들도 이 서비스를 이용하고 있다는 말로 서비스 가입을 유도하고 있는 것으로 보아(We've successfully aided numerous
property rental agents in your vicinity) Ms. Morton도 같은 직업을 갖고 있다고 추론할 수 있다.

173

What is indicated about Skyreach Media?

(A) It is a company that was recently founded.
(B) It fills orders with speed.
(C) It offers a novel service.
(D) It underwent a recent merger with another business.

Skyreach Media에 관하여 무엇이 나타나 있는가?

(A) 최근에 설립된 회사이다.
(B) 주문을 신속하게 처리한다.
(C) 새로운 서비스를 제공한다.
(D) 최근에 다른 기업과의 합병을 거쳤다.

어휘 found 설립하다 fill an order 주문을 이행하다 novel 새로운 undergo 거치다, 진행하다 merger 합병

해설 이메일 도입부에서 고객과의 소통을 위한 새로운 방식을 제공한다고 말하고 있다(Skyreach Media is now offering an additional method for engaging
with your customers:).

174

What is mentioned about the automated responses?

(A) They are not identical for all properties.
(B) They can be forwarded to an e-mail address.
(C) They incorporate images captured by Skyreach Media.
(D) They compel apartment seekers to establish a password.

자동 응답 메시지에 관하여 무엇이 언급되어 있는가?

(A) 모든 부동산에 대해 동일하지는 않다.
(B) 이메일 주소로 전달할 수 있다.
(C) Skyreach Media가 촬영한 이미지를 포함하고
있다.
(D) 아파트를 찾는 사람이 비밀번호를 설정하게 한다.

어휘 identical 동일한 forward 전달하다 capture 촬영하다 compel 강요하다 establish 설정하다

해설 자동 문자 메시지 서비스 시작에 대한 설명 두 번째 항목에서 각 부동산의 세부 사항을 자동 응답 메시지에 포함하라고 안내하고 있으며(Be sure to
include comprehensive details about each property.), 세 번째 항목에서는 각 부동산마다 고유의 키워드를 지정하라고 지시하고 있다(Designate a
unique keyword for each property). 이러한 내용을 통해 각 부동산마다 자동 응답 메시지의 내용이 다르다는 것을 알 수 있다.

175

According to the e-mail, why should Ms. Morton communicate with Mr. Barrett before Wednesday?

(A) To extend her current plan
(B) To discuss pricing details
(C) To arrange property tours
(D) To take advantage of complimentary services

이메일에 따르면 Ms. Morton은 왜 수요일 전에 Mr. Barrett과 연락해야 하는가?

(A) 현재 요금제를 연장하기 위해
(B) 가격 책정의 세부 사항을 의논하기 위해
(C) 부동산 투어 일정을 잡기 위해
(D) 무료 서비스를 이용하기 위해

Questions 176 through 180 refer to the following article and review.

This week's highlight

[176]Featured this week is the documentary series *Blueprints Uncovered*, which, following lengthy editing and multiple delays caused by production setbacks, is at last hitting television screens. This four-episode journey, directed by Karim Haddad and Eleanor Ashcroft, uncovers lesser-known facts behind some of the most celebrated architectural landmarks across the globe. [177]Viewers who admire actor and comedian Colin Radcliffe will be pleased to know he serves as the host, bringing both insight and humor to the narration. Produced by Erik Thorsen, the series is slated to appear on the Insight Sphere channel according to the schedule below.

EPISODE / AIRDATE

[179]**1. "Against All Odds" June 5**
This opening episode transports us to Ancient Egypt, where builders overcame formidable structural challenges to create enduring monuments.

2. "Hands That Built History" June 12
Without the benefit of modern machinery, medieval craftsmen in Europe constructed towering cathedrals that would dominate the cityscape for centuries.

[178]**3. "The Shape of Now" June 19**
Here, we explore the elegance of contemporary architecture and uncover gripping narratives behind the design and execution of today's most iconic buildings.

4. "Beyond the Skyline" June 26
The final installment looks ahead to concepts still in the making: revolutionary skyscraper designs, nature-inspired structures with reduced footprints, and other architectural marvels poised to grace future cities.

176–180번 문제는 다음 기사와 후기에 관한 것입니다.

이번 주 하이라이트

금주의 특집인 다큐멘터리 시리즈 *드러나는 청사진*이 오랜 편집 작업과 제작 차질로 인한 여러 번의 연기 끝에 마침내 텔레비전 스크린에 등장한다. 네 개의 에피소드로 구성된 이번 여정은 Karim Haddad와 Eleanor Ashcroft가 감독을 맡았으며, 전 세계적으로 가장 유명한 건축물들 뒤에 숨겨진 잘 알려지지 않은 사실들을 파헤친다. 배우이자 코미디언인 Colin Radcliffe를 좋아하는 시청자들은 그가 진행을 맡아 해설에 식견뿐만 아니라 유머까지 더해 줄 것이라는 사실을 알면 기쁠 것이다. Erik Thorsen가 제작을 맡은 이 시리즈는 Insight Sphere 채널에서 아래 일정에 따라 방영될 예정이다.

에피소드 / 방송 날짜

1. "모든 역경을 딛고" 6월 5일
첫 에피소드는 우리를 고대 이집트로 데려간다. 그곳에서 건축가들은 가공할 만한 구조적 난관을 극복하고 오래도록 남을 기념물을 창조해냈다.

2. "역사를 지은 손" 6월 12일
현대 기계의 혜택도 없이, 중세 유럽의 장인들은 수 세기 동안 도시 경관을 지배할 웅장한 대성당들을 건축했다.

3. "현재의 모양" 6월 19일
이 회차에서는 현대 건축의 우아함을 탐구하고 오늘날 가장 상징적인 건축물들의 설계와 제작 뒤의 눈을 뗄 수 없게 하는 이야기를 파헤친다.

4. "스카이라인 너머에" 6월 26일
마지막 회는 아직 구상 단계에 있는 개념들을 향한다: 혁신적인 초고층 건물 설계, 환경 영향을 줄인 자연에서 영감받은 건축물, 미래 도시들을 아름답게 꾸며줄 준비가 되어 있는 기타 건축 걸작들.

Freya Lindholm ★★★★★

[179]After watching the premiere of *Blueprints Uncovered*, I'm absolutely hooked! Radcliffe does a tremendous job recounting the story; he's informative but also entertaining. [180]The free companion booklet, available on Insight Sphere's Web site, should not be overlooked—it's packed with extra details about the buildings featured in the show and is indispensable for anyone eager to dive deeper into the subject.

Freya Lindholm ★★★★★

드라마는 청사진의 첫 회를 보고 나서 완전히 빠져버렸습니다! Radcliffe가 이야기를 전달해주는 역할을 너무나 잘 했습니다. 유용한 정보를 제공했을 뿐만 아니라 재미있기도 했죠. Insight Sphere 홈페이지에서 제공되는 무료 부록 소책자도 간과해서는 안 됩니다. 방송에서 다루는 건축물들에 대한 추가 정보로 가득 차 있어서 이 주제를 깊이 파고들기 원하는 사람이라면 없어서는 안 될 자료입니다.

어휘1 blueprint 청사진, 설계도 uncover 밝혀내다, 파헤치다 lengthy 오래 지속되는, 장시간의 setback 차질 hit (화면에) 등장하다 direct 감독하다 lesser-known 잘 알려지지 않은, 덜 알려진 celebrated 유명한 architectural 건축의 admire (유명인을) 매우 좋아하다 serve as ~의 역할을 하다 host 진행자 insight 통찰력, 식견 narration (영상의 음성) 해설 be slated to-V ~할 예정이다 airdate 방송 날짜 against all odds 모든 어려움을 무릅쓰고 transport 데려가다 formidable 가공할, 어마어마한 structural 구조적인 enduring 지속되는, 오래도록 남을 monument 기념물, 유적 benefit 혜택, 도움 machinery 기계(류) medieval 중세의 craftsman 장인 towering 우뚝 솟은, 웅장한 cathedral 대성당 dominate 지배하다 cityscape 도시 경관 explore 탐구하다 elegance 우아함, 세련됨 architecture 건축 uncover 밝혀내다, 파헤치다 gripping 손에 땀을 쥐게 하는, (시선을) 사로잡는 narrative 이야기 execution 실행, 제작 iconic 상징적인 skyline (고층 빌딩, 산 등이) 하늘과 맞닿은 윤곽선 installment 1회분, 1부 look ahead to ~을 내다보다 in the making 구상하고 있는 structure 구조물, 건축물 footprint 부지 면적, 환경 발자국 marvel 경이, 기적 be poised to-V ~할 준비가 되어 있다 grace 우아하게[아름답게] 꾸미다

어휘2 premiere (프로그램의) 첫 회 hooked 푹 빠진 tremendous 굉장한, 대단한 recount (자세히) 이야기하다 informative 유용한 정보를 제공하는 entertaining 재미있는 companion 부록, 보조, 참고 booklet 소책자 overlook 간과하다 packed with ~으로 가득 찬 indispensable 없어서는 안 될 dive into ~에 몰두하다

176

What is indicated about the making of the program?

(A) It was a very costly process.
(B) It was prolonged past the initial timeline.
(C) It was financed by multiple sponsors.
(D) It involved a considerable number of producers.

프로그램 제작에 관하여 무엇이 나타나 있는가?

(A) 비용이 매우 많이 드는 과정이었다.
(B) 처음의 일정을 넘어서 연장되었다.
(C) 다수의 후원 업체들이 자금을 지원했다.
(D) 상당수의 제작자들이 참여했다.

어휘 costly 비용이 많이 드는 prolong 연장하다 initial 초기의 finance 자금을 조달하다 considerable 상당한 involve 참여시키다, 관여시키다

해설 기사 첫 문장에서 제작이 여러 번 지연되었다는 사실을 알 수 있다(multiple delays caused by production setbacks).

177

Who appears in the documentary?

(A) Mr. Haddad
(B) Ms. Ashcroft
(C) Mr. Radcliffe
(D) Mr. Thorsen

다큐멘터리에 누가 출연하는가?

(A) Mr. Haddad
(B) Ms. Ashcroft
(C) Mr. Radcliffe
(D) Mr. Thorsen

해설 배우이자 코미디언인 Colin Radcliffe가 다큐멘터리의 진행자로 출연한다(Viewers who admire actor and comedian Colin Radcliffe will be pleased to know he serves as the host).

178

What episode highlights themes related to modern urban planning?

(A) Episode 1
(B) Episode 2
(C) Episode 3
(D) Episode 4

어느 에피소드가 현대 도시 계획에 관련된 주제를 집중 조명하는가?

(A) 에피소드 1
(B) 에피소드 2
(C) 에피소드 3
(D) 에피소드 4

해설 세 번째 에피소드에서 다루는 현대의 건축 양식과 현대를 대표하는 건물들의 설계 및 건설을 현대 도시 계획에 관련된 주제로 볼 수 있다(we explore the elegance of contemporary architecture and uncover gripping narratives behind the design and execution of today's most iconic buildings).

179

When did Ms. Lindholm most likely view the program?	Ms. Lindholm은 언제 프로그램을 시청했겠는가?
(A) On June 5	(A) 6월 5일에
(B) On June 12	(B) 6월 12일에
(C) On June 19	(C) 6월 19일에
(D) On June 26	(D) 6월 26일에

해설 Ms. Lindholm은 시리즈의 첫 회를 보았다고 말하고 있으므로(After watching the premiere of *Blueprints Uncovered*), 시청 날짜는 6월 5일이다 (1. "Against All Odds" June 5).

180

What does Ms. Lindholm recommend doing?	Ms. Lindholm는 무엇을 하기를 추천하는가?
(A) Purchasing movies starring a specific actor	(A) 특정 배우가 주연으로 출연하는 영화 구입하기
(B) Visiting the architectural sites shown in the series	(B) 시리즈에 등장하는 건축 유적지 방문하기
(C) Accessing supplementary content online	(C) 온라인으로 보충 자료 이용하기
(D) Watching other documentaries by the same director	(D) 같은 감독의 다른 다큐멘터리 시청하기

어휘 star ~를 주연으로 하다 site 유적지 access 접근하다, 이용하다 supplementary 보충의

해설 Insight Sphere 홈페이지에 있는 부록 소책자를 소개하면서 간과해서는 안 되며(The free companion booklet, available on Insight Sphere's Web site, should not be overlooked), 해당 주제에 대해 더 알고 싶은 사람에게는 필수라고 말하고 있다(and is indispensable for anyone eager to dive deeper into the subject). Ms. Lindholm은 온라인 보충 자료 이용을 추천하고 있다.

To: Daniel Solano <solano@selvaverdeeco.com>
From: Natalia Vetrova <nvetrova@pacificroutes.com>
Subject: New Booking Request
Date: July 18

Good afternoon, Mr. Solano,

[182]I thoroughly appreciated our collaboration again, alongside you and all the staff at Selva Verde Eco Lodge. My clients found the rain forest tour to be very enjoyable. [184]The couple who stayed in the Heliconia Bungalow commented that the view of the tropical garden from their room was breathtaking.

[181]At this time, I wish to secure a booking for a new client, Min-jae Park. Please make the following arrangements for Mr. Park and his companion:
[183]**Arrival:** August 14 (please arrange airport shuttle service)
[183]**Departure:** August 17 (shuttle service also requested)
Room type: Double occupancy
Tour type: Guided rain forest hike (5-hour tour)

Flight information:
Savannalink Airways Flight SL312 from Incheon, arriving at 4:10 P.M. August 14
Savannalink Airways Flight SL309 to Incheon, departing at 10:30 A.M. August 17

Thank you again for the exceptional care you provide to my clients.

Natalia Vetrova
Travel Consultant, Pacific Routes

To: Natalia Vetrova <nvetrova@pacificroutes.com>
From: Daniel Solano <solano@selvaverdeeco.com>
Subject: Park Reservation Confirmation
Date: July 19

Ms. Vetrova,

Thank you for your message and for passing along such positive remarks from your clients.

The information about Mr. Park's reservation is as follows. Kindly be aware of our limited room options. The room we booked for him is marginally more expensive, with single rooms being the sole other choices.

수신: Daniel Solano 〈solano@selvaverdeeco.com〉
발신: Natalia Vetrova 〈nvetrova@pacificroutes.com〉
제목: 신규 예약 요청
날짜: 7월 18일

안녕하세요, Mr. Solano.

Mr. Solano와 Selva Verde Eco Lodge의 모든 직원들과 다시 함께 협업할 수 있어서 정말 감사했습니다. 제 고객들이 열대 우림 투어를 매우 즐거워하셨습니다. Heliconia 방갈로에 묵은 부부는 방에서 보이는 열대 정원 경치가 숨이 멎을 정도로 아름다웠다고 말하더군요.

이번에는 새 고객 Min-jae Park의 예약을 확정하고자 합니다. Mr. Park과 동행자에 대해 다음 사항을 준비해 주시기 바랍니다.
도착: 8월 14일 (공항 셔틀 서비스 준비 부탁드립니다.)
출발: 8월 17일 (역시 셔틀 서비스 필요합니다.)
객실 유형: 2인용
투어 유형: 가이드 동반 열대 우림 하이킹 (5시간 투어)

비행 정보:
Savannalink Airways Flight SL312 인천발, 8월 14일 오후 4:10 도착
Savannalink Airways Flight SL309 인천행, 8월 17일 오전 10:30 출발

저희 고객들에게 보여 주신 세심한 배려 다시 한 번 고맙습니다.

Pacific Routes 여행 컨설턴트
Natalia Vetrova

수신: Natalia Vetrova 〈nvetrova@pacificroutes.com〉
발신: Daniel Solano 〈solano@selvaverdeeco.com〉
제목: Park 예약 확인
날짜: 7월 19일

Ms. Vetrova,

메시지를 보내 주시고 고객님들의 긍정적인 평가를 전해 주셔서 감사합니다.

Mr. Park의 예약에 대한 정보는 다음과 같습니다. 선택할 수 있는 객실이 제한되어 있음을 양해해 주시기 바랍니다. 그 분을 위해 예약한 방이 미미하게 더 비싼데, 선택할 수 있는 다른 객실은 1인실밖에 없습니다.

Check-in date: August 14
Check-out date: August 17
[184]**Room:** Heliconia Bungalow
Rate: $160 USD/night Total: $480 USD (excluding tax)
Tour type: Guided Rain Forest Hike; August 15, 7:30 A.M. to 12:30 P.M.
Tour fee: $85 USD

Please note that the transportation between the airport and the lodge has been arranged. [185]The bill must be settled in full no later than August 10.

We treasure the ongoing business we conduct with Pacific Routes. Should you have any questions or concerns, please don't hesitate to reach out to me.

Daniel Solano
Guest Services, Selva Verde Eco Lodge

체크인 날짜: 8월 14일
체크아웃 날짜: 8월 17일
객실: Heliconia 방갈로
요금: 1박 160달러(USD) / 총 480달러(USD) (세금 제외)
투어 유형: 가이드 동반 열대 우림 하이킹; 8월 15일 오전 7:30 – 오후 12:30
투어 요금: 85달러(USD)

공항에서 산장까지의 교통편이 마련되었음을 알려 드립니다. 청구액은 늦어도 8월 10일까지는 전액 결제가 되어 있어야 합니다.

저희는 Pacific Routes와 지속적으로 이어온 비즈니스를 소중하게 생각합니다. 질문이나 우려 사항이 있다면 주저 없이 저에게 연락 주시기 바랍니다.

Selva Verde Eco Lodge 고객 서비스
Daniel Solano

어휘1 confirmation 확인 thoroughly 완전히, 전적으로 collaboration 협업 alongside ~와 함께 lodge 산장 bungalow 방갈로 breathtaking 숨이 멎을 정도로 멋진 wish to–V ~하기를 원한다 make arrangements 준비하다 companion 동행 occupancy 수용 인원 exceptional 탁월한, 특출한

어휘2 pass along ~을 전달하다 remark 언급, 논평 as follows 다음과 같이 be aware of ~을 알다 marginally 미미하게, 근소하게 sole 유일한 excluding ~을 제외하고 settle a bill 청구액을 결제하다 in full 전부, 전액 no later than 늦어도 ~까지 treasure 소중히 여기다 ongoing 지속적인 hesitate 주저하다 reach out to ~에게 연락하다

181

Why did Ms. Vetrova write to Mr. Solano?

(A) To recommend a new tour destination
(B) To inquire about flight information
(C) To provide assistance to a client
(D) To make a revision to an itinerary

Ms. Vetrova는 왜 Mr. Solano에게 편지를 썼는가?

(A) 새 관광지를 추천하기 위해
(B) 비행 정보에 대해 문의하기 위해
(C) 고객에게 도움을 제공하기 위해
(D) 여행 일정을 수정하기 위해

어휘 destination 목적지 inquire about ~에 대해 문의하다 assistance 도움 make a revision to ~을 수정하다 itinerary 여행 일정

해설 Ms. Vetrova가 보낸 이메일 두 번째 문단을 보면 정답을 알 수 있다. 신규 고객 Min-jae Park이 묵을 객실을 마련해 주는 것이 목적이다(At this time, I wish to secure a booking for a new client, Min-jae Park).

182

What is suggested about Pacific Routes?

(A) It has a history of commercial activity with Selva Verde Eco Lodge.
(B) Its expertise lies in rain forest locales.
(C) It is situated in proximity to Selva Verde Eco Lodge.
(D) It is under Ms. Vetrova's ownership.

Pacific Routes에 관하여 무엇이 시사되어 있는가?

(A) Selva Verde Eco Lodge와 상업 활동을 한 적이 있다.
(B) 열대 우림 지역에 대한 전문성을 갖추고 있다.
(C) Selva Verde Eco Lodge에서 근접한 곳에 위치해 있다.
(D) Ms. Vetrova가 소유하고 있다.

어휘 commercial 상업의 expertise 전문성 locale 장소, 현장 in proximity to ~에 근접하여 under *sb*'s ownership ~가 소유하고 있는

해설 Ms. Vetrova가 보낸 이메일 첫 문장에서 Selva Verde Eco Lodge와 다시 협력했음을 언급하고 있으므로(I thoroughly appreciated our collaboration again, alongside you and all the staff at Selva Verde Eco Lodge.), 이것으로 두 사업체는 과거에 수차례 협업을 진행한 적이 있음을 추론할 수 있다.

What does Mr. Park request?	Mr. Park은 무엇을 요청하는가?
(A) A loyal customer discount	(A) 단골 고객 할인
(B) A booking confirmation	(B) 예약 확인
(C) A dining package	(C) 식사 패키지
(D) A conveyance solution	(D) 교통수단에 대한 해결책

어휘 loyal 충성스러운 conveyance 교통수단

해설 도착하는 날(Arrival)과 떠나는 날(Departure)에 공항과 산장 사이의 이동을 위한 셔틀 버스를 요구하고 있다(airport shuttle service).

184

What is indicated about Mr. Park?	Mr. Park에 관하여 무엇이 나타나 있는가?
(A) He has visited Selva Verde Eco Lodge on an earlier occasion.	(A) 과거에 Selva Verde Eco Lodge를 방문한 적이 있다.
(B) He will occupy a room that faces a garden.	(B) 정원에 면해 있는 방을 사용할 것이다.
(C) He has traveled in the company of Mr. Solano.	(C) Mr. Solano와 함께 여행한 적이 있다.
(D) He intends to travel by himself.	(D) 혼자 여행할 계획이다.

어휘 on an earlier occasion 이전에 occupy (방을) 사용하다 face 향하다, ~에 면하다 in the company of ~와 함께 intend to-V ~할 계획이다

해설 예약을 확인해 주는 답장에서 Mr. Park이 Heliconia Bungalow를 사용할 것임을 알 수 있는데(Room: Heliconia Bungalow), 첫 번째 이메일의 첫 문단을 보면 이 방갈로에 묵었던 사람들이 열대 정원의 경치를 마음에 들어 했다는 이야기가 있다(The couple who stayed in the Heliconia Bungalow commented that the view of the tropical garden from their room was breathtaking). 따라서 Mr. Park은 정원이 보이는 객실에 묵을 것이다.

185

By when does Mr. Solano anticipate the payment will be made?	Mr. Solano는 결제가 언제까지 이뤄질 것으로 예상하는가?
(A) July 19	(A) 7월 19일까지
(B) August 10	(B) 8월 10일까지
(C) August 14	(C) 8월 14일까지
(D) August 17	(D) 8월 17일까지

해설 답장에서 예약 사항을 확인해 준 후에 결제는 늦어도 8월 10일까지는 이루어져야 한다고 말하고 있다(The bill must be settled in full no later than August 10).

Questions 186 through 190 refer to the following Web page and e-mails.

About Us | **Home** | Testimonials | Rates | Contact Us

Clearhaven Cleaning delivers comprehensive cleaning solutions that cater to both domestic and commercial clientele. We have maintained exceptional service at competitive prices for more than 15 years.

[189]Beyond our standard offerings, we provide a premium cleaning option that utilizes all-natural, odor-free cleaning practices as well as products formulated to lessen allergens.

Clients may opt for weekly, biweekly, or monthly service plans, and we are happy to accommodate custom scheduling preferences. Our cleaning team is known for its punctuality in both arrival and completion. [190]We provide a money-back guarantee if you are not entirely content.

[186]Contact us to schedule a complimentary on-site assessment and quote. Call 1-303-555-0192 or head to our Web site at www. clearhavencleaning.com. Make sure to visit our testimonials page to read glowing reviews from our numerous satisfied clients.

186-190번 문제는 다음 웹 페이지와 두 이메일에 관한 것입니다.

회사 소개 | **홈** | 추천의 글 | 요금 | 문의하기

Clearhaven Cleaning은 가정 및 사업 고객 모두에 맞춘 종합 청소 솔루션을 제공합니다. 저희는 15년이 넘는 기간 동안 경쟁력 있는 가격에 탁월한 서비스를 유지해 왔습니다.

저희는 표준 제공 서비스를 넘어 천연, 무취 청소 방식과 알레르기 유발 물질을 줄이도록 제조된 제품을 활용하는 고급 청소 옵션도 제공합니다.

고객은 주간 및 격주, 월간 서비스 플랜 중 선택할 수 있으며, 선호하는 맞춤 일정으로 기꺼이 조정해 드립니다. 저희 청소 팀은 도착과 작업 완료 모두 시간을 엄수하는 것으로 알려져 있습니다. 완전히 만족하지 못하시는 경우 환불을 보장합니다.

연락 주시면 무료 현장 평가 및 견적 일정을 잡아 드립니다. 1-303-555-0192로 전화하거나 홈페이지 www.clearhavencleaning.com으로 오세요. 추천의 글 페이지를 꼭 방문하셔서 저희 서비스에 만족한 수많은 고객들의 칭찬 가득한 후기를 읽어 보세요.

To: support@clearhavencleaning.com
From: lharper@moduloformstudio.com
Re: Cleaning Service Concern
Date: November 9

To Whom It May Concern,

My company's premises were cleaned by Clearhaven Cleaning, whom I employed. [187]Your advertisement, coupled with the strong recommendations from clients on your site, led me to believe I would be entirely pleased with your performance. [188]Regrettably, that was not the case. [189]I had explicitly requested your premium treatment, but your cleaning personnel neglected to provide it. Evidently, an issue arose. I am contemplating discontinuing the next scheduled appointment.

Lydia Harper

수신: support@clearhavencleaning.com
발신: lharper@moduloformstudio.com
제목: 청소 서비스 문제
날짜: 11월 9일

담당자께,

제가 고용한 Clearhaven Cleaning이 저희 회사 구내를 청소했습니다. 귀사의 광고와 더불어 홈페이지에 나와 있는 고객들의 강력한 추천으로 저는 귀사의 업무 수행에 완전히 만족할 것이라 믿게 되었습니다. 유감스럽게도 실상은 그렇지 않았습니다. 저는 분명히 프리미엄 처리를 요청했는데, 청소 직원은 이를 제공하지 않았습니다. 분명히 문제가 발생한 것으로 보입니다. 다음 예약된 일정은 중단하려고 생각 중입니다.

Lydia Harper

To: lharper@moduloformstudio.com
From: rbennington@clearhavencleaning.com
Date: November 12
Subject: Cleaning on November 7

Dear Ms. Harper,

We sincerely regret that our service did not meet your expectations. We are currently training new cleaning personnel, who failed to adhere to the proper cleaning plan. We pledge to enhance our efforts to ensure their tasks are executed and inspected correctly going forward.

[190]On November 15, we would appreciate a chance to offer a cleaning session again, at no charge. If the results still fall short of your standards, we will gladly honor our satisfaction guarantee. Please indicate if this arrangement is acceptable.

Sincerely,

Ronan Bennington
Clearhaven Cleaning Customer Service Representative

수신: lharper@moduloformstudio.com
발신: rbennington@clearhavencleaning.com
날짜: 11월 12일
제목: 11월 7일 청소

Ms. Harper께,

저희 서비스가 고객님의 기대에 미치지 못해 진심으로 유감스럽게 생각합니다. 현재 신입 청소 직원을 교육 중인데, 이들이 적절한 청소 계획을 준수하지 못했습니다. 향후에는 업무가 제대로 수행되고 점검되도록 많은 노력을 하겠다고 약속드립니다.

11월 15일에 무료로 다시 청소 서비스를 제공할 기회를 주신다면 감사하겠습니다. 결과가 여전히 고객님의 기준에 부합되지 않는다면, 기꺼이 저희의 만족도 보장 방침을 이행하겠습니다. 이 제안이 수용 가능하신지 알려주시기 바랍니다.

진심을 담아,

Clearhaven Cleaning 고객 서비스 담당자
Ronan Bennington

어휘1 testimonial 추천의 글 rate 요금 comprehensive 포괄적인 cater to ~에 맞추다 domestic 가정의 clientele 고객층 competitive 경쟁력 있는 offering 제공 서비스 premium 고급의 utilize 활용하다 odor 냄새, 악취 practice (실행) 방식 A as well as B A 뿐만 아니라 B도, A 외에 B도 formulate 만들어내다 lessen 줄이다 allergen 알레르기 유발 물질 opt for ~을 선택하다 biweekly 격주의 accommodate 제조하다 custom 맞춤형의 punctuality 시간 엄수 money-back guarantee 환불 보장 content 만족하는 on-site 현장의 assessment 평가 quote 견적 head to ~로 향하다, 가다 make sure to-V 반드시 ~하다 glowing 칭찬으로 가득한

어휘2 to whom it may concern 담당자 귀하 premises 부지, 구내 couple A with B A를 B와 결합시키다 recommendation 추천 performance 수행, 이행 regrettably 유감스럽게도 case 실정, 사실 explicitly 명확하게 premium 고급의 treatment (청결, 보호의) 처리 personnel 직원 neglect to-V ~하지 않다, ~하는 것을 잊다 evidently 분명히 arise (문제가) 발생하다 contemplate 고려하다 discontinue 중단하다

어휘3 regret ~에 대해 유감으로 생각하다 expectation 기대 fail to-V ~하지 못하다 proper 적절한 pledge 약속하다 enhance 높이다 inspect 점검하다 correctly 정확히 going forward 앞으로 at no charge 무료로 fall short of ~에 미치지 못하다 honor (계약, 합의를) 이행하다 arrangement 합의, 제안 acceptable 수용 가능한 representative 담당자

186

What is indicated about Clearhaven Cleaning?

(A) It was recently established.
(B) It manufactures its own line of cleaning products.
(C) It delivers free in-person evaluations.
(D) It has just launched residential services.

Clearhaven Cleaning에 관하여 무엇이 나타나 있는가?

(A) 최근에 설립되었다.
(B) 자체 청소 제품군을 생산한다.
(C) 무료 직접 방문 평가를 제공한다.
(D) 최근에 주거지용 서비스를 개시했다.

어휘 in-person 직접 하는 residential 주거의

해설 웹 페이지 마지막 문단에서 업체에 연락하면 현장을 방문하여 평가를 실시한 후 견적을 내 준다고 말하고 있다(Contact us to schedule a complimentary on-site assessment and quote).

187

What is implied about Ms. Harper?

(A) She investigated other cleaners before contacting Clearhaven Cleaning.
(B) She was referred to Clearhaven Cleaning by a acquaintance.
(C) She is seeking employment at Clearhaven Cleaning.
(D) She read customer feedback online prior to hiring Clearhaven Cleaning.

Ms. Harper에 관하여 무엇이 암시되어 있는가?

(A) Clearhaven Cleaning에 연락하기 전에 다른 청소 업체들을 조사했다.
(B) 지인의 소개로 Clearhaven Cleaning을 추천받았다.
(C) Clearhaven Cleaning에 취업하기를 바란다.
(D) Clearhaven Cleaning을 고용하기 전에 온라인으로 고객들의 피드백을 읽었다.

어휘 investigate 조사하다 be referred to A by B B의 소개로 A를 추천받다 acquaintance 지인 employment 취업, 고용

해설 첫 번째 이메일에서 광고와 홈페이지에 실려 있는 고객들의 추천의 글을 읽고 나서 서비스에 대한 기대감이 생겼다고 말하고 있다(Your advertisement, coupled with the strong recommendations from clients on your site, led me to believe I would be entirely pleased with your performance). Ms. Harper는 청소 서비스를 신청하기 전에 온라인으로 고객들의 피드백을 읽었다.

188

In the first e-mail, the word "case" in paragraph 1, line 3, is closest in meaning to

(A) argument
(B) instance
(C) situation
(D) investigation

첫 번째 이메일 첫 문단 세 번째 줄의 단어 "case"와 의미상 가장 가까운 것은

(A) 주장, 논거
(B) 사례, 경우
(C) 상황
(D) 수사, 조사

해설 case는 '주장, 논거, 사례, 경우, 상황, 실정, (경찰이 조사 중인) 사건'이라는 뜻이 있기 때문에 선택지에 있는 네 개의 단어가 모두 동의어로 사용될 수 있다. 본문에서 that was not the case.는 "실상은 그렇지 않았다."라는 뜻이다.

189

Why did Ms. Harper express her dissatisfaction in writing?

(A) The office floors were not polished.
(B) The office kitchenette was not sterilized.
(C) The cleaners omitted shampooing the carpets.
(D) The cleaners did not employ eco-friendly products.

Ms. Harper는 왜 서면으로 불만을 표시했는가?

(A) 사무실 바닥에 광을 내지 않았다.
(B) 사무실 간이 주방을 살균 소독하지 않았다.
(C) 청소 인력이 카펫을 세제로 청소하지 않았다.
(D) 청소 인력이 친환경 제품을 사용하지 않았다.

어휘 dissatisfaction 불만 in writing 서면으로 polish 광을 내다 kitchenette 간이 주방 sterilize 살균하다 omit 빠뜨리다, ~하는 것을 잊다 shampoo (카펫 등을 세제로) 청소하다, 닦다 employ (특정 방법, 기술 등을) 동원하다, 이용하다

해설 첫 번째 이메일에 따르면 Ms. Harper는 분명히 고급 서비스를 요청했지만, 요청 사항이 이행되지 않았다(I had explicitly requested your premium treatment, but your cleaning personnel neglected to provide it). 웹 페이지 두 번째 문단을 보면 고급 서비스의 내용을 알 수 있는데, 완전 천연의 방식, 즉 친환경 제품을 사용하는 서비스이다(we provide a premium cleaning option that utilizes all-natural, odor-free cleaning practices).

190

What commitment does Mr. Bennington make if Ms. Harper remains unsatisfied after November 15?

(A) To reimburse her expenses
(B) To devise an updated cleaning strategy
(C) To assign different cleaning employees
(D) To offer a reduced rate on subsequent cleaning work

Ms. Harper가 11월 15일 이후에도 여전히 만족하지 못할 경우에 대하여 Mr. Bennington은 어떤 약속을 하는가?

(A) 비용을 상환해 준다
(B) 새로운 청소 방식을 고안한다
(C) 다른 청소 직원들을 배정한다
(D) 차후의 청소 작업에서 할인 요금을 제공한다

어휘 commitment 약속 reimburse 상환하다 assign 배정하다 subsequent 이후의, 차후의

해설 Ms. Harper에게 보낸 답장 두 번째 문단에서 Mr. Bennington은 11월 15일 청소도 그녀의 기준이 미치지 못한다면 만족도 보장 제도를 이행하겠다고 말하고 있다(On November 15, we would appreciate a chance to offer a cleaning session again, at no charge. If the results still fall short of your standards, we will gladly honor our satisfaction guarantee). 만족도 보장의 내용은 웹 페이지 세 번째 문단에 나오는데, 고객이 완전히 만족하지 못할 경우 환불을 보장하고 있다(We provide a money-back guarantee if you are not entirely content).

Waikiki Monarch Hotel	
Scheduled activities for guests in August Start time for all activities is 10:00 A.M. at the Guest Services desk in the lobby.	
Activity and instructor /guide	**Description**
Every Tuesday [195]Surfing lesson Conducted by Kalani Kealoha	Master the art of surfing in Waikiki. Should be an adept swimmer. $60 per person. All participants must be 12 years or older.
Every Wednesday [194]Hawaiian flower crafts Conducted by Elina Aquino	Your instructor will provide you with guidance in creating a lei: an ornamental Hawaiian flower garland or necklace. All supplies included. $12 per person.
Every Thursday History tour Conducted by Leilani Ogawa	This 2-hour walking tour will provide participants with an insight into Waikiki's history. No charge.
[191]*Every Friday* Hawaiian cookery class Conducted by head chef Jessica Chen	Learn how to prepare authentic Hawaiian cuisine. ([191]Lesson can be tailored to focus solely on vegetarian recipes.) All participants must be 12 years or older. $25 per person.
Visit the Guest Services desk for more information and to sign up.	

Waikiki Monarch 호텔	
예정된 8월 투숙객 활동 모든 활동의 시작 시간은 오전 10시이며, 장소는 로비의 고객 서비스 데스크입니다.	
활동 및 강사 /가이드	**설명**
매주 화요일 서핑 교습 진행 Kalani Kealoha	와이키키에서 파도 타는 기술을 익혀 보세요. 수영에 능숙해야 합니다. 인당 60달러. 모든 참가자는 12세 이상이어야 합니다.
매주 수요일 하와이식 꽃 공예 진행 Elina Aquino	강사가 레이(하와이식 장식용 화관 혹은 꽃목걸이) 만들기를 지도합니다. 모든 용품 포함. 인당 12달러.
매주 목요일 역사 탐방 진행 Leilani Ogawa	이 2시간짜리 도보 투어는 참가자에게 와이키키의 역사에 대한 식견을 제공합니다. 무료.
매주 금요일 하와이식 요리 강습 진행 주방장 Jessica Chen	정통 하와이식 요리 만드는 법을 배우세요. (수업은 채식 요리법에만 집중하도록 맞출 수 있습니다) 모든 참가자는 12세 이상이어야 합니다. 인당 25달러.
추가 정보나 신청을 위해 고객 서비스 데스크를 방문해주세요.	

To: Guest Services Staff <gsstaff@waikikimonarchhotel.com>
[194]From: Soo-Min Lee <smlee@waikikimonarchhotel.com>
Date: August 17
Subject: Update

Hi all,

[192]This month's program of guest activities needs to be revised. [192][194]Elina Aquino and Jessica Chen will be away August 20-26. I will lead Elina's activities and Astrid Geensen will lead Jessica's. Everything will return to normal on August 27, when Elina and Jessica both return.

Sincerely,

Soo-Min Lee
Guest Services Director, Waikiki Monarch Hotel

수신: 고객 서비스 직원들
　　　〈gsstaff@waikikimonarchhotel.com〉
발신: Soo-Min Lee
　　　〈smlee@waikikimonarchhotel.com〉
날짜: 8월 17일
제목: 업데이트

모두 안녕하세요.

이번 달 투숙객 활동 프로그램에 수정이 필요합니다. Elina Aquino와 Jessica Chen이 8월 20일부터 26일까지 자리를 비우게 됩니다. 제가 Elina의 활동을 맡고 Astrid Geensen이 Jessica의 활동을 맡습니다. 모든 것은 Elina와 Jessica가 모두 복귀하는 8월 27일에 정상으로 돌아옵니다.

그럼 이만 줄입니다.

Waikiki Monarch 호텔 고객 서비스 책임자
Soo-Min Lee

Comments:

My family and I thoroughly enjoyed our stay at your hotel. We really appreciated the activities that were planned and I would like to give all the instructors my compliments. [193]I had to skip the activity guided by Ms. Ogawa, but my family told me they learned a lot from her. [194]My daughter and I found it very entertaining to learn how to make flower garlands, and my husband has already cooked some of the dishes he was taught in Ms. Geensen's class. [195]Finally, my son and daughter both had a wonderful time with Mr. Kealoha. They are looking forward to putting his lessons to use when we travel on holiday to Costa Rica next year.

Name: Sarah Virtanen
Today's date: 13 September
Number of guests: 4
[194]Date of stay: 20-26 August

의견:

저희 가족과 저는 호텔에서의 투숙이 정말 즐거웠습니다. 준비한 활동들에 정말 감사드리며 모든 강사들에게 칭찬을 전하고 싶습니다. 저는 Ms. Ogawa가 지도한 활동을 참여하지 못했는데, 가족들이 그분에게 많이 배웠다고 말하더군요. 딸과 저는 화관 만드는 법을 배우는 게 참 재미있었고, 제 남편은 Ms. Geensen의 수업에서 배운 요리 몇 가지를 벌써 만들어 보았답니다. 끝으로 저희 아들, 딸은 모두 Mr. Kealoha와 멋진 시간을 보냈습니다. 아이들은 내년에 Costa Rica로 휴가 여행을 가면 배운 것을 써먹어 보기를 기대하고 있습니다.

이름: Sarah Virtanen
작성 날짜: 9월 13일
투숙객 수: 4
투숙 날짜: 8월 20 - 26일

어휘1 art 기술 adept 능숙한 participant 참가자 craft (수)공예 ornamental 장식용의 garland 화환, 화관 supplies 용품 insight 식견 cookery 요리(법) authentic 정통인 tailor (목적, 사람에) 맞추다, 조정하다 solely 오로지, 단지 sign up 신청하다, 등록하다

어휘2 revise 수정하다 away 자리에 없는

어휘3 comment 논평, 의견 thoroughly 대단히, 완전히 appreciate ~에 감사하다 compliment 칭찬 skip 거르다, 빼먹다 entertaining 재미있는, 즐거움을 주는 put *sth* to use ~을 활용하다

191

What activity can be customized?

(A) Tuesday's activity
(B) Wednesday's activity
(C) Thursday's activity
(D) Friday's activity

어느 활동을 원하는 대로 바꿀 수 있는가?

(A) 화요일 활동
(B) 수요일 활동
(C) 목요일 활동
(D) 금요일 활동

해설 안내문을 보면 금요일 활동인 요리 강습이 채식주의자를 위한 조리법에만 초점을 맞추도록 조정이 가능하다고 설명되어 있다(Hawaiian cookery class. Lesson can be tailored to focus solely on vegetarian recipes.).

192

What is the purpose of the e-mail?

(A) To welcome two new employees
(B) To address a guest inquiry
(C) To make changes to a schedule
(D) To arrange training sessions for staff

이메일의 목적은 무엇인가?

(A) 두 명의 신입 직원을 환영하는 것
(B) 투숙객의 문의를 다루는 것
(C) 일정을 변경하는 것
(D) 직원들을 위한 교육을 마련하는 것

어휘 address 다루다, 해결하려 하다 inquiry 질문, 문의

해설 8월 20일부터 26일까지 자리를 비우는 직원들이 있어서(Elina Aquino and Jessica Chen will be away August 20–26.), 원래 그들이 맡던 강습을 다른 사람들이 대신 진행한다는(I will lead Elina's activities and Astrid Geensen will lead Jessica's.) 내용이다. 이메일의 목적은 투숙객들을 위한 활동 일정의 변경을 알리는 것이다.

193

In the comment form, the word "skip" in paragraph 1, line 2, is closest in meaning to

(A) jump
(B) miss
(C) pay for
(D) look over

의견 서식에서 첫 문단 두 번째 줄의 단어 "skip"과 의미상 가장 가까운 것은

(A) 뛰어 넘다
(B) 거르다, ~을 하지 않다
(C) 대금을 내다
(D) ~을 대충 훑어보다

해설 skip을 '뛰어 넘다'라는 뜻으로 사용하면 (A)와, '어떤 일을 거르다'라는 뜻으로 사용하면 (B)와, '~을 건너뛰고 읽다'라는 뜻으로 사용하면 (D)와 동의어가 된다. 본문에서는 Ms. Ogawa가 진행한 활동에 참여하지 못했다고 했으므로(I had to skip the activity guided by Ms. Ogawa), skip은 miss로 바꿔 쓸 수 있다.

194

Who taught the course enjoyed by Ms. Virtanen and her daughter?

(A) Ms. Aquino
(B) Ms. Lee
(C) Ms. Ogawa
(D) Ms. Chen

Ms. Virtanen과 그녀의 딸이 즐긴 코스는 누가 지도했는가?

(A) Ms. Aquino
(B) Ms. Lee
(C) Ms. Ogawa
(D) Ms. Chen

해설 의견 서식을 보면 8월 20일부터 26일까지 이 호텔에 묵은(Date of stay: 20–26 August) Ms. Virtanen이 딸과 참여한 활동은 화관 만들기 강습이었는데(My daughter and I found it very entertaining to learn how to make flower garlands), 안내문을 보면 이 수업의 강사는 Elina Aquino이다(Hawaiian flower crafts Conducted by Elina Aquino). 그런데 이메일을 보면 이 가족이 투숙한 기간에 Elina Aquino가 자리를 비우기 때문에(Elina Aquino and Jessica Chen will be away August 20–26.), Ms. Aquino가 맡고 있던 활동은 Ms. Lee가 대신 진행한다고 말하고 있다(I will lead Elina's activities).

195

What are Ms. Virtanen's children planning to do in Costa Rica?

(A) Go surfing
(B) Learn traditional crafts
(C) Take a walking tour
(D) Try local food

Ms. Virtanen의 자녀들은 Costa Rica에서 무엇을 하려고 계획하고 있는가?

(A) 서핑을 한다
(B) 전통 공예를 배운다
(C) 도보 관광을 한다
(D) 지역의 음식을 먹어 본다

해설 의견 서식을 보면 Ms. Virtanen의 자녀들은 Mr. Kealoha의 강습을 재미있어 했으며(my son and daughter both had a wonderful time with Mr. Kealoha.), 내년에 Costa Rica로 휴가를 가면 Mr. Kealoha에게서 배운 것을 써먹어 보려고 기대하고 있다(They are looking forward to putting his lessons to use when we travel on holiday to Costa Rica next year). 안내문을 보면 Mr. Kealoha가 진행한 활동은 서핑 강습이므로(Surfing lesson Conducted by Kalani Kealoha), Ms. Virtanen의 자녀들은 Costa Rica에서 서핑을 할 것이라고 추론할 수 있다.

📘 **Questions 196 through 200** refer to the following brochure, e-mail, and notice.

Redwood National Park Trails

[198]**Friendship Ridge Loop** - *8.5 Kilometers*
[198]Enjoy views of the Klamath River from the summit of Friendship Ridge. This path, of moderate difficulty, entails a steady incline to the summit of the ridge, followed by a well-defined trail that loops back and descends to the north parking lot.

[196]**Ossagon Slope** - *6 Kilometers*
[196]Trek up the side of Ossagon Ridge. This challenging trail features rocky terrain and intermittent steep climbs, providing scenic views of Orick Palisades Valley. The trailhead is located 100 meters to the south of the ranger station.

[198]**River's Edge** - *6.7 Kilometers*
[198]This trail stretches along the bank of the Klamath River. Starting at the north parking lot, the level trail leads to Orick Palisades Park.

Trillium Falls Trail - *3 Kilometers*
This leisurely trail commences at the rear of the main pavilion and extends through the Redwood Forest before culminating at Trillium Falls. Picnic and barbeque areas are scattered along the route.

To: Nature Explorers Club
From: Anne Zelnikova
Subject: Nature hike on Saturday
Date: September 12
Attachment: Map

Hi, everyone

The nature hike this month is set for Saturday at 6:00 A.M.
[197][198]Since a number of people during our last trip to Fern Canyon expressly mentioned their desire to view the Klamath River, we decided to meet up at Redwood National Park this month. [200]Please arrive in the north parking lot by 5:45 A.M. I have attached a park map for your reference. Don't forget to pack a lunch and plenty of water. Our hike will last approximately 5–6 hours.

See you on Saturday!

Anne

196–200번 문제는 다음 안내 책자와 이메일, 안내문에 관한 것입니다.

Redwood 국립공원 등산로

Friendship 능선 순환로 - *8.5 킬로미터*
Friendship 능선 정상에서 Klamath 강의 경치를 즐기세요. 중간 난이도의 이 길은 능선의 정상까지 이어지는 꾸준한 경사로이며, 잘 정비된 순환하는 등산로가 이어지며, 북쪽 주차장으로 내려오게 됩니다.

Ossagon 경사로 - *6 킬로미터*
Ossagon 능선의 측면을 올라가 보세요. 이 어려운 등산로는 바위가 많은 지형과 간헐적으로 나타나는 가파른 오르막이 특징이지만, Orick Palisades 계곡의 훌륭한 경치를 제공합니다. 등산로 입구는 관리 사무소 남쪽 100미터 지점에 있습니다.

강변로 - *6.7 킬로미터*
이 등산로는 Klamath 강둑을 따라 뻗어 있습니다. 북쪽 주차장에서 시작하여 평탄한 등산로가 Orick Palisades 공원으로 이어집니다.

Trillium 폭포 등산로 - *3 킬로미터*
이 여유로운 등산로는 메인 파빌리온 뒤편에서 시작되어 Redwood 숲을 통과하여 이어지다가 Trillium 폭포에서 끝납니다. 경로를 따라 피크닉 및 바비큐 구역이 간간이 있습니다.

발신: 자연 탐사 클럽
수신: Anne Zelnikova
제목: 토요일 자연 탐사 하이킹
날짜: 9월 12일
첨부 파일: 지도

모두 안녕하세요.

이번 달 자연 탐사 하이킹이 토요일 오전 6시로 정해졌습니다. 지난번 Fern Canyon 여행 때 많은 사람이 특별히 Klamath 강을 보고 싶다는 바람을 말씀하셨기 때문에 이번 달에는 Redwood 국립공원에서 만나기로 했습니다. 북쪽 주차장으로 오전 5시 45분까지 와 주세요. 참고로 공원 지도를 첨부했습니다. 잊지 말고 점심과 충분한 물을 챙기시기 바랍니다. 하이킹은 대략 5–6시간 계속될 것입니다.

토요일에 만납시다!

Anne

NOTICE

Posted September 14

198The River's Edge trail has been closed due to flooding caused by recent rain storms and will not reopen until further notice. Please refrain from traveling on this trail and locations adjacent to the Klamath River bank until the floodwaters recede. 199 200The north parking lot was also affected by the floodwaters, and is currently under construction. Kindly leave your automobile in the east parking lot and follow the Ranger Path to reach the trailheads.

안내문

9월 14일 게시

최근의 폭우로 인한 범람으로 강변 등산로가 폐쇄되었으며 추후 공지가 있을 때까지 재개방하지 않습니다. 범람한 물이 빠질 때까지 이 등산로와 Klamath 강둑에 인접한 장소에서는 통행을 삼가시기 바랍니다. 북쪽 주차장 또한 범람한 물의 영향을 받았으며 현재 공사 중입니다. 자동차는 동쪽 주차장에 세워 놓으시고 공원 관리 직원용 통행로를 따라 등산로 입구로 가시기 바랍니다.

어휘1 brochure 안내 책자 trail 등산로 ridge 산등성이, 능선 loop 순환로; 고리 모양으로 이동하다 summit 정상, 산꼭대기 moderate 보통의, 중간의 entail 수반하다 incline 경사(면) well-defined 윤곽이 뚜렷한, 잘 정비된 descend 내려가다 trek (힘들게 오래) 걷다 terrain 지형, 지역 intermittent 간헐적인 steep 가파른 climb 등산 구역 scenic 경치가 좋은 palisades (강가나 해안의) 깎아지른 절벽 trailhead 등산로 입구 ranger station (공원) 관리 사무소 stretch 뻗어 있다 bank 둑, 제방 level 평평한, 반반한 lead (도로가 특정 방향, 장소로) 이어지다 falls 폭포 leisurely 여유로운, 느긋한 commence 시작되다 at the rear of ~ 뒤편에서 pavilion 파빌리온(공원의 쉼터나 공연장) extend 펼쳐지다, 이어지다 culminate 끝이 나다, 막을 내리다 scattered 드문드문 있는, 산재한

어휘2 hike 하이킹, 도보 여행 expressly 특별히 meet up (약속해서) 만나다 reference 참고 approximately 대략

어휘3 flooding 범람, 홍수 until further notice 추후 공지가 있을 때까지 refrain from ~을 삼가다 floodwaters 홍수로 불어난 물 recede (서서히) 물러나다 under construction 공사 중 ranger 공원[삼림] 관리원

196

How long is the trail that goes up Ossagon Ridge? (A) 3 kilometers **(B) 6 kilometers** (C) 6.7 kilometers (D) 8.5 kilometers	Ossagon 산등성이를 따라 올라가는 등산로는 길이가 얼마나 되는가? (A) 3킬로미터 (B) 6킬로미터 (C) 6.7킬로미터 (D) 8.5킬로미터

해설 안내 책자를 읽어 보면 Ossagon 산등성이를 따라 올라가는 등산로는(Trek up the side of Ossagon Ridge.) Ossagon 경사로인데, 길이는 6킬로미터다(Ossagon Slope − 6 Kilometers).

197

In the e-mail, the phrase "expressly" in paragraph 1, line 2, is closest in meaning to (A) affectionately (B) correctly **(C) specifically** (D) totally	이메일 첫 문단 두 번째 줄의 단어 "expressly"와 의미상 가장 가까운 것은 (A) 애정을 담아, 다정하게 (B) 올바르게, 정확히 (C) 특별히 (D) 완전히, 전적으로

해설 expressly를 '분명히, 명확히'라는 뜻으로 사용하면 (B)가, '특별히'라는 뜻으로 쓰면 (C)가 동의어인데, 본문에서는 Klamath 강을 보고 싶은 바람을 '특별히' 언급한 회원들에 대해 말하고 있으므로(Since a number of people during our last trip to Fern Canyon expressly mentioned their desire to view the Klamath River), 바꿔 쓸 수 있는 부사는 specifically이다.

198

Where will Nature Explorers Club members likely hike?

(A) On Friendship Ridge Loop
(B) On Ossagon Slope
(C) On River's Edge
(D) On Trillium Falls Trail

자연 탐사 클럽은 어디에서 하이킹을 하겠는가?

(A) Friendship 산등성이 순환로
(B) Ossagon 경사로
(C) 강변로
(D) Trillium 폭포 등산로

해설 이메일을 보면 Klamath 강을 보고 싶어 하는 회원들을 위해 Redwood 국립공원을 찾는다고 했다(Since a number of people during our last trip to Fern Canyon expressly mentioned their desire to view the Klamath River, we decided to meet up at Redwood National Park this month). 안내 책자를 보면, Klamath 강을 볼 수 있는 등산로는 Friendship 산등성이 순환로(Enjoy views of the Klamath River from the summit of Friendship Ridge.)와 강변로다(This trail stretches along the bank of the Klamath River). 그런데 공원 안내문을 보면 강변로는 강물의 범람으로 인해 폐쇄되었다(The River's Edge trail has been closed due to flooding). 그렇다면 자연 탐사 클럽이 오를 등산로는 Friendship 산등성이 순환로일 수밖에 없다.

199

What is indicated about Redwood National Park?

(A) It offers guided nature walks.
(B) It has multiple parking areas.
(C) It provides food for purchase.
(D) It opens at 6:00 A.M.

Redwood 국립공원에 관하여 무엇이 나타나 있는가?

(A) 가이드 동반 자연 산책 프로그램을 제공한다.
(B) 여러 개의 주차 공간이 있다.
(C) 구매 가능한 음식을 제공한다.
(D) 오전 6시에 문을 연다.

해설 북쪽 주차장이 강물 범람으로 인해 피해를 입어 공사 중이므로 동쪽 주차장을 이용하라고 권장하고 있다(The north parking lot was also affected by the floodwaters, and is currently under construction. Kindly leave your automobile in the east parking lot). Redwood 국립공원에는 주차장이 최소 2개 있다.

200

What will Nature Explorers Club members likely do upon arriving at the park?

(A) See Trillium Falls
(B) Eat at the pavilion
(C) Purchase a trail map
(D) Walk along Ranger Path

자연 탐사 클럽 회원들은 공원에 도착하자마자 무엇을 할 것 같은가?

(A) Trillium 폭포를 본다
(B) 파빌리온에서 식사한다
(C) 등산로 지도를 구매한다
(D) 공원 관리 직원용 통행로를 따라 걷는다

해설 이메일 지시에 따라 북쪽 주차장에 도착한 회원들은(Please arrive in the north parking lot by 5:45 A.M.) 안내문을 보고 동쪽 주차장으로 이동하여 차를 세우고 관리 직원용 통행로를 따라 등산로 시작점으로 걸어갈 것이다(The north parking lot was also affected by the floodwaters, and is currently under construction. Kindly leave your automobile in the east parking lot and follow the Ranger Path to reach the trailheads).

당신이 찾던 토익책
토익마법
2주의 기적
실전편1
RC